Welcome to

McGraw-Hill Education
LSAT

*C*ongratulations! You've chosen the LSAT guide from America's leading educational publisher. You probably know us from many of the textbooks you used in school and college. Now we're ready to help you take the next step—and get into the law school of your choice.

This book gives you everything you need to succeed on the test. You'll get in-depth instruction and review of every topic tested, tips and strategies for every question type, and plenty of practice exams to boost your test-taking confidence. To get started, go to the following pages where you'll find:

- ◢ How to Use This Book: Step-by-step instructions to help you get the most out of your test-prep program.

- ◢ Your LSAT Action Plan: Use the interactive Test Planner app or the book's study plan to make the best use of your preparation time.

- ◢ Getting the Most from the Practice Tests: Download the Premium Practice Test App to your tablet or smartphone or visit the companion website for additional test-taking practice.

- ◢ Problem-Solving Videos: View videos demonstrating the use of problem-solving strategies on the practice test app or companion website.

ABOUT McGRAW-HILL EDUCATION

This book has been created by McGraw-Hill Education. McGraw-Hill Education is a leading global provider of instructional, assessment, and reference materials in both print and digital form. McGraw-Hill Education has offices in 33 countries and publishes in more than 65 languages. With a broad range of products and services—from traditional textbooks to the latest in online and multimedia learning—we engage, stimulate, and empower students and professionals of all ages, helping them meet the increasing challenges of the 21st century knowledge economy.

Learn more. Do more.

How to Use This Book

This book provides all the material you need to score well on the LSAT. It will teach you the knowledge that is required for this difficult exam, including information about each type of question the test includes. It also provides practice for you to refine the skills you are learning. It is important that you also test yourself with full-length practice tests.

1 Learn about the LSAT

Chapter 1 will familiarize you with the format of the LSAT and briefly introduce its four different sections. You will also find valuable tips on how to approach test day and information about how the test is scored. The Diagnostic Test in Chapter 2 will help you get a sense of your strengths and weaknesses and how much you need to improve. The diagnostic test is also available on the Premium Practice Test App and on the companion website.

2 Prepare for the Logic Games section

LSAT Logic Games do not "come naturally" to most test takers. They require a particular set of skills—classifying the games by type, diagramming the games, symbolizing the clues, and making deductions—that are unfamiliar to many people. Fortunately, these skills are readily learnable and improvable. Chapter 3 introduces these skills with step-by-step demonstrations. You can learn more about how to solve logic games and other LSAT questions by viewing the videos on this book's companion website.

3 Prepare for the Arguments sections

Because there are two Arguments sections on each test, half of your LSAT score will be derived from your performance on Arguments questions. Chapter 4 introduces you to the ten different types of questions you'll encounter in the Arguments section. It also contains guidelines on how to identify right answers and common types of wrong answers for each of these question types.

4 Prepare for the Reading Comprehension section

Chapter 5 lays out annotative reading, the style of reading that is best-suited to the requirements of the Reading Comprehension section of the LSAT. Chapter 5 also provides techniques for tackling each of the six different question types you will encounter in Reading Comprehension and provides strategies for approaching the comparative reading passage.

5 Prepare for the Writing Sample section

Because the Writing Sample section is not scored, it is the least important of the test's four sections. Chapter 6 details a five-paragraph format you can use to write a response to the Writing Sample that is sure to be satisfactory in the event an admissions officer reads your essay.

6 Take the Practice Tests

Get ready for the actual exam by taking the practice tests. You have a number of options on how to take them. You will find two practice tests at the end of the book. These tests are also available on the Premium Practice Test App and on the companion website. Both the app and the companion website include four additional practice tests.

Your LSAT Action Plan

To make the best use of your LSAT preparation time, you'll need a personalized action plan that's based on your needs and the time you have available. *McGraw-Hill Education: LSAT* provides two options. Use the **interactive Test Planner app** to create your study schedule on your smartphone or tablet.

> To download the interactive Test Planner app, search "McGraw-Hill Education Test Planner app" in the iTunes app store or Google Play for Android devices.

Or follow these steps to create an LSAT action plan to meet your goals:

Step 1: Identify Your Needs

The LSAT is a unique test. While parts of it are likely to be familiar, it also contains some question types that you probably have never encountered before. Thus, it's important to begin your action plan by taking a diagnostic exam. Doing so will help you both familiarize yourself with the LSAT and also determine which areas of the test you'll need to focus on during your preparation.

Step 2: Build Your Skills

Each section of the LSAT tests a different skill set. The process of improving your LSAT score starts with learning and refining the skills and techniques you'll use to approach each section of the test.
The cases in chapters 3 through 6 introduce these techniques and help you build your skills in applying them.

Step 3: Practice under Test-Like Conditions

Improving your performance on the LSAT is like learning to ride a bike; the only way to do it is with consistent, repeated practice. Once you've learned how to approach each section of the LSAT, the final step is to practice applying your new skills under test-like conditions. You can practice using the two sample tests that appear at the back of this book or on the app or companion website. Four more practice tests are available on the app and website.

Sample LSAT Action Plans

On the following pages are two sample action plans. The first is a plan you can follow if you have two months to prepare; the second assumes you have one month to prepare. In general, the more time you can spend studying and practicing, the more likely you are to significantly improve your score.
So if you're still trying to decide when you need to get started, remember: the earlier the better. You can tweak these plans to suit your own individual needs, or you can modify them to fit a two-week, six-week, or ten-week schedule.

Sample Action Plan 1—If You Have Two Months to Prepare

Two months is an adequate time for most people to prepare for the LSAT, but the time you'll need depends on how busy you are with school, work, or personal commitments and on how much of an effort you'll need to reach your target score.

Week 1

- Take the LSAT Diagnostic Test in Chapter 2 of this book. It will help you get a sense of your starting point in preparing for the test and which problem-solving skills you need to work on.

- Using the LSAC's online law-school database, review the admissions criteria of the law schools you're most interested in. Based on your undergraduate GPA, calculate the LSAT score you need to get to make yourself competitive for admission to these law schools. For more on how to use this database, see Chapter 7.

- Read the introduction and Cases 1 through 3 in Chapter 4, LSAT Arguments.

- Work all of the Conclusion, Deduction, and Principle questions in the Arguments sections in the Practice Tests at the back of this book. Work them at your own pace, not under timed conditions. Focus on implementing the techniques correctly. Study the answer explanations to understand why you missed any questions you missed.

- Read the introduction, Case 1, and Case 2 in Chapter 5, LSAT Reading Comprehension.

Week 2

- Read the introduction and Cases 1 through 3 in Chapter 3, LSAT Logic Games.

- Work all of the one-tiered ordering games and all of the grouping games in the Logic Games sections in the Practice Tests at the back of this book. Work them at your own pace, not under timed conditions. Focus on implementing the techniques correctly. Study the answer explanations to understand why you missed any questions you missed.

- Read Cases 3 through 9 in Chapter 5, LSAT Reading Comprehension.

- Work the four passages in the Reading Comprehension section in Practice Test 1 at the back of this book. Work them at your own pace, not under timed conditions. Focus on implementing the techniques correctly. Study the answer explanations to understand why you missed any questions you missed.

Week 3

- Work the four passages in the Reading Comprehension section in Practice Test 2 at the back of this book. Continue to work at your own pace with a focus on correctly implementing the techniques and studying the answer explanations.

- Read Case 4 in Chapter 3, LSAT Logic Games.

- Work all of the two-tiered ordering games in the Logic Games sections in the Practice Tests at the back of this book. Continue to work at your own pace with a focus on correctly implementing the techniques and studying the answer explanations.

- Read Cases 4 through 7 in Chapter 4, LSAT Arguments.

- Work all of the Assumption, Strengthen, Paradox, and Weaken questions in the Arguments sections in the Practice Tests at the back of this book. Continue to work at your own pace with a focus on correctly implementing the techniques and studying the answer explanations.

- Read Case 5 in Chapter 3, LSAT Logic Games
- Work all of the "1-2-2 or 1-1-3?" games in the Logic Games sections in the Practice Tests at the back of this book. Continue to work at your own pace with a focus on correctly implementing the techniques and studying the answer explanations.
- Read Cases 8 through 10 in Chapter 4, LSAT Arguments.
- Work all of the Describe and Flaw questions in the Arguments sections in the Practice Tests at the back of this book. Continue to work at your own pace with a focus on correctly implementing the techniques and studying the answer explanations. Based on your score on the diagnostic exam and the success you've had in working the practice Arguments questions, make a preliminary decision about whether it makes sense for you to attempt to work any Parallel questions. If it does, work all of the Parallel questions from the sample tests in the same manner.

- Catch up on any work you've fallen behind on.
- Read Case 6 in Chapter 3, LSAT Logic Games.
- Read Case 11 in Chapter 4, LSAT Arguments.
- With your practice sections, analyze the questions that you answered incorrectly. Try to identify what made you select the answer you did and why you overlooked the correct answer. If you find that you are consistently missing the same kinds of questions, re-read the cases that address those questions.

- Read Case 10 in Chapter 5, LSAT Reading Comprehension.
- With your practice sections, analyze the questions that you answered incorrectly. Try to identify what made you select the answer you did and why you overlooked the correct answer. If you find that you are consistently missing the same kinds of questions, re-read the cases that address those questions.

- Read Chapter 6, The LSAT Writing Sample.
- Write one or two practice Writing Sample essays.

- Work timed practice sections out of the tests that are available online. (See p. 7A.)
- With your practice tests, analyze the questions that you answered incorrectly. Try to identify what made you select the answer you did and why you overlooked the correct answer. If you find that you are consistently missing the same kinds of questions, re-read the case that addresses those questions.

Sample Action Plan 2—If You Have One Month to Prepare

If you plan to master the LSAT in only four weeks, you'll have to prioritize; focus on your weaknesses and take as many practice tests as possible. The more time and energy you can carve out for preparation, the better.

Week 1

- Take the LSAT Diagnostic Test in Chapter 2 of this book. It will help you get a sense of your starting point in preparing for the test and which problem-solving skills you need to work on.
- Using the LSAC's online law-school database, review the admissions criteria of the law schools you're most interested in. Based on your undergraduate GPA, calculate what LSAT score you need to obtain to make yourself competitive for admission to these law schools. For more on how to use this database, see Chapter 7.
- Read the introduction and Cases 1 through 5 in Chapter 3, LSAT Logic Games.
- Work each of the games in the Logic Games section in Practice Test 1 at the back of this book. Classify each game by type before you work it. Work the games at your own pace, not under timed conditions. Focus on implementing the techniques correctly. Study the answer explanations to understand why you missed any questions you missed.

Week 2

- Read the introduction and Cases 1 through 10 in Chapter 4, LSAT Arguments.
- Work all of the arguments in the two Arguments sections in Practice Test 1 at the back of this book. Classify each argument by type before you work it. Work the questions at your own pace, not under timed conditions. Focus on implementing the techniques correctly. Study the answer explanations to understand why you missed any questions you missed.
- Read the introduction and Cases 1 through 9 in Chapter 5, LSAT Reading Comprehension.
- Work all of the passages in the Reading Comprehension section in Practice Test 1 at the back of this book. Work the questions at your own pace, not under timed conditions. Focus on implementing the techniques correctly. Study the answer explanations to understand why you missed any questions you missed.

Week 3

- Read Case 6 in Chapter 3, LSAT Logic Games.
- Read Case 11 in Chapter 4, LSAT Arguments.
- Read Case 10 in Chapter 5, LSAT Reading Comprehension.
- Work each of the sections in Practice Test 2 at the back of this book as timed practice sections. After you work each section, analyze the questions that you answered incorrectly. Try to identify what made you select the answer you did and why you overlooked the correct answer. If you find that you are consistently missing the same kinds of questions, re-read the case that addresses those questions.
- Read Chapter 6, The LSAT Writing Sample.
- Write one or two practice Writing Sample essays.

Week 4

- Work timed practice sections out of the tests that are available online. (See p. 7A.)
- With your practice tests, analyze the questions that you answered incorrectly. Try to identify what made you select the answer you did and why you overlooked the correct answer. If you find that you are consistently missing the same kinds of questions, re-read the case that addresses those questions.

Getting the Most from the Interactive Practice Tests

McGraw-Hill Education: LSAT gives you a number of options to practice for the exam. You can practice using this book, your tablet or smartphone, or your laptop or home computer. Whether you use a PC or Mac or a tablet or smartphone with the Apple, Android, or Windows platform, you'll be able to practice on the device of your choosing.

The diagnostic test and two practice tests in this book are also available as digital versions as part of the **Premium Practice Test App** and on the companion website, **MHE Practice Plus**. In addition to these tests, you will find **three more practice tests** on both the app and companion website.

Features of the Interactive Practice Tests

The interactive practice tests found on the mobile app and the companion website offer a number of features that will help you meet your study goals:

● The app and the companion website include the diagnostic test and two practice tests from the book, allowing you to take advantage of the digital versions of these tests.

● The app and website include three additional practice tests that will enhance your preparation for the exam.

● You can choose whether to take a test section timed or open-ended, depending on your practice goals.

● When you finish a section of the test, you'll immediately receive a score that shows the percentage of correct answers.

● Your scores will be saved so you can refer back to them and follow your progress.

● Review mode allows you to see your answer and the correct answer together. (We hope they're the same!) Here you'll find a concise and clear explanation for the answer. Moreover, you'll still be able to see the original question for reference.

● If you exit a test section before finishing it you can simply return to where you left off at a later time.

Accessing the Premium Practice Test App

If you take the diagnostic test and five additional practice tests on your tablet or smartphone, you will find the Premium Practice Test App to be the ideal companion to your study plans. Depending on the device you have, go to one of the following websites:

Apple → iTunes

Android → Google Play

Windows → Apps for Windows

Once you're at the appropriate app store, search "McGraw-Hill Education LSAT Premium Practice Test App" and download.

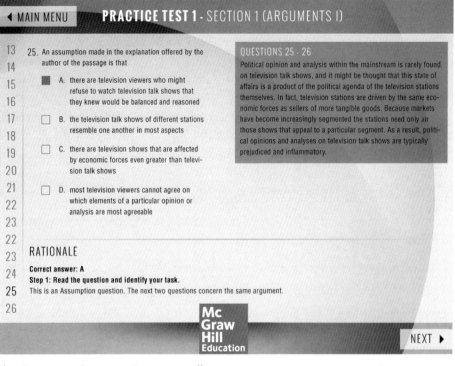

The Premium Practice Test App allows you to see a given question, its related passage, your answer, and the correct answer and its rationale all at once. By scrolling further, you can read the entire rationale behind an answer.

Accessing the Practice Tests Online

Visit **www.mhpracticeplus.com/lsat.php** to access the online version of the practice tests. Click on "Begin practice tests" and you'll have access to the diagnostic test and six additional practice tests to use on your laptop or home computer.

Problem-Solving Videos

You will find 20 instructional videos on both the Premium Practice Test App and on the companion website, MHE Practice Plus. These videos will show you how to solve key problems found on the LSAT, covering the Logic Games, Arguments, and Reading Comprehension sections. After watching these videos, you should be able to understand how to use the problem-solving strategies and apply them to the questions you encounter on the exam.

McGraw-Hill Education

LSAT
2O17

McGraw-Hill Education

LSAT 2017

Russ Falconer, JD • Drew D. Johnson

Mc
Graw
Hill
Education

New York   Chicago   San Francisco   Athens   London   Madrid
Mexico City   Milan   New Dehli   Singapore   Sydney   Toronto

1 2 3 4 5 6 7 8 9 10   RHR   21 20 19 18 17 16 (book for cross-platform prep course)
1 2 3 4 5 6 7 8 9 10   RHR   21 20 19 18 17 16 (book alone)

ISBN   978-1-259-64211-1 (cross-platform prep course)
MHID   1-259-64211-9

e-ISBN   978-1-259-64212-8 (e-book cross-platform prep course)
e-MHID   1-259-64212-7

ISBN   978-1-259-64209-8 (book alone)
MHID   1 -259-64209-7

e-ISBN   978-1-259-64210-4 (e-book)
e-MHID   1-259-64210-0

33614057603481

LSAT is a registered trademark of the Law School Admission Council, which was not involved in the production of, and does not endorse, this product.

McGraw-Hill Education books are available at special quantity discounts to use as premiums and sales promotions or for use in corporate training programs. To contact a representative, please visit the Contact Us pages at www.mhprofessional.com.

CONTENTS

PART II   **LSAT Practice Tests**

McGraw-Hill Education

LSAT
2017

PART I

All About the LSAT

CHAPTER 1

Introducing the LSAT

- Why you should use this book to prepare for the LSAT

- How to register for the LSAT

- The format of the LSAT and how it is scored

- Basic information about each of the four sections on the LSAT

- How to approach test day

Welcome to *McGraw-Hill's LSAT.* If you've already purchased this book, congratulations! You've made the right choice. Success on the Law School Admission Test is a critical component of a strong law school application. The LSAT is a prerequisite for admission to all law schools that are accredited by the American Bar Association and to many law schools that are not ABA-accredited but are accredited by a state bar association (most notably the California Bar Association). The tools, techniques, and strategies you'll learn in this book will enable you to maximize your LSAT score, including:

- **Proven tactics from veteran teachers.** The authors have more than a decade of combined LSAT experience as classroom teachers, private tutors, curriculum developers, and prep-book authors. These techniques have been honed through years of practice in the field.

- **A curriculum based on exhaustive research and analysis.** Four different LSATs are administered every year. Three of those four exams are released to the public. As a result, more than 60 LSATs are now available to the general public for practice and review. The content and techniques in this book were developed based on a comprehensive review of thousands of the questions that have appeared on these real tests.

- **Updated techniques to reflect a changing test.** The LSAT is a dynamic test that evolves over time. Each year, new question types crop up while old question types fall by the wayside. The curriculum in this book has been written with a particular emphasis on capturing the newly emergent trends in the 15 publicly available tests that were administered between 2006 and 2010. We've developed techniques that will help you stay ahead of the curve on these new question types.

- **A unique, casebook-style instructional approach.** Casebooks and the case-based model of instruction are the backbone of the law school curriculum. This book is the only LSAT-prep book on the market that is written as a casebook. Major question types and key strategies and techniques are presented as separate cases for study. This model will help you organize your studying and make important material easier to digest and remember.

- **The best practice tests on the market.** Practice—and then more practice—is the key to success on the LSAT. But practice only helps if you're practicing on questions that are similar to the ones you'll encounter on the day of the test. The practice tests at the back of this book have been carefully designed to simulate actual LSATs as closely as possible. In addition, each practice test comes with a complete set of answer explanations that do more than simply tell you what the correct answer is and why the other four answers are wrong. They walk you through the process of arriving at the correct answer.

This chapter is dedicated to the nuts and bolts of the LSAT. It will explain how to register for the test, introduce you to the structure and format of the test, briefly preview the types of questions you'll encounter on each of the four sections, explain how you should approach test day, and help you develop a study plan. Chapter 2 offers a diagnostic test to show you where you are now in your preparation and help you determine which question types need the most attention. Techniques for tackling each section of the test are covered in detail in Chapters 3, 4, 5, and 6, while chapter 7 provides an overview of the law school application process, including a discussion of the factors you should consider when deciding on where to apply and the logistics of submitting your applications.

Test Dates and Registration Information

The LSAT is written and administered by the Law School Admission Council (LSAC), a nonprofit corporation that provides a variety of admissions-related services to its more than 200 members. In addition to overseeing the LSAT, the LSAC also runs the Credential Assembly Service (CAS). The CAS is a centralized law school admissions clearinghouse that allows you to apply to as many law schools as you'd like simply by filling out a standardized package of forms that are somewhat akin to the Common Application you may have filled out when you were applying to college.

The LSAT is administered four times a year, in February, June, October, and December. The June exam is administered at 12:30 p.m. on a Monday afternoon. The February, October, and December exams are administered at 8:30 a.m. on Saturday mornings. For test takers whose religious observances prevent them from taking the exam on Saturdays, the LSAC offers a Saturday Sabbath observers administration, which typically takes place on the Monday following the Saturday administration. To be eligible for a Saturday Sabbath observers administration, a test taker must submit a letter from his or her minister or rabbi on official stationery.

The best way to register for the LSAT is online. Go to http://www.lsac.org/jd/LSAT/about-the-LSAT.asp and click on the purple button at the top of the page that says "Register Now." To register online, you will have to create an LSAC.org account. There is no charge to create an account, and it is the same account you'll use to register for the CAS and submit online applications for admission. You can also register for the LSAT over the phone by calling 215-968-1001 on weekdays during East Coast business hours. But since you'll inevitably need to create an LSAC account at some point during the application process, it makes better sense to go ahead and get set up online now.

Once you know when you'd like to start law school, select a test date that's well in advance of your enrollment date. December is the last test administration date that most law schools will look at for fall admissions. For example, if you want to begin law school in the fall of 2014, the latest possible date you could take the LSAT would be December 2013. But you'll help your chances for admission by taking the test earlier—preferably no later than June of 2013. Chapter 7 will explain in greater detail why taking an earlier test will improve your chances for admission.

Once you've selected a test date, register for it as early as possible. When you register, you will have to pay a $165 fee and you'll be asked to select a testing site. The seats at each testing site are given on a first come, first served basis. Wait too long and you run the risk of being forced to take the test at an inconvenient location. Make sure you've thought over where you want to take the test before you register. If you decide later that you want to take the test at a different location, you'll have to pay a $36 change fee.

The registration deadline is typically about five weeks before the day of the test. The late-registration deadline is 7 to 10 days after the first deadline, and you'll have to pay an additional $70 fee. You can find more information about the registration deadline for a particular test date by visiting http://www.lsac.org/JD/LSAT/test-dates-deadlines.asp.

The Format of the LSAT

The LSAT is not a content-based test. Rather, it is a skills test made up of six 35-minute sections. It is designed to measure your acquired abilities in the areas of reading, verbal reasoning, and spatial reasoning. The score you receive on the LSAT will be based entirely on your performance on the following four sections.

- One section of analytical reasoning, more commonly known as the Logic Games section
- One section of Reading Comprehension
- Two sections of logical reasoning, more commonly known as the Arguments sections

These sections contain somewhere between 99 and 103 multiple-choice questions, each of which includes five answer choices.

The fifth multiple-choice section you take will be an experimental section. This section does not count toward your score; the LSAC uses these sections to design future LSATs (that's right, you get to pay for the privilege of being a research guinea pig). Your experimental section could be Logic Games, Reading Comprehension, or Arguments, and you won't necessarily get the same experimental section as the person sitting next to you. The LSAC uses multiple experimental sections during each test administration. You won't know which particular section was experimental. If you have three Arguments sections, for example, all you'll know is that one of the three won't count toward your score.

These five sections can be presented in any order. After you've taken the first three sections, you'll get a short break of about 10 or 15 minutes so that you can go to the restroom, stretch your legs, or have a quick snack. After the break, you'll take the final two multiple-choice sections. The administrators will collect your test booklet and your answer sheet. Then they will administer the sixth section—the Writing Sample.

The Writing Sample section always comes last. It is the only section of the LSAT that isn't multiple choice. And like the experimental section, it also is not scored. The LSAC simply scans your answer and sends a copy of it along with the rest of your application materials to every law school you apply to.

Sample LSAT

SECTION TYPE	LENGTH
(instructions and set up)	≈ 30 minutes
(1) Reading Comprehension	35 minutes
(2) Arguments	35 minutes
(3) Experimental section	35 minutes
(break)	≈ 10–15 minutes
(4) Logic Games	35 minutes
(5) Arguments	35 minutes
(collect Scantrons; distribute Writing Sample)	≈ 20 minutes
(6) Writing Sample	35 minutes
(collect Writing Samples)	≈ 15 minutes
Total	**≈ 4 hours, 50 minutes**

How the LSAT Is Scored

The LSAT is scored on a 120-to-180 scale. Your scaled score is based on your raw score. Your raw score is the number of multiple-choice questions you answered correctly in the four scored sections. Each question counts for one point, and there is no penalty for wrong answers. For each administration of the LSAT, each raw score (ranging from 0 to 103) is assigned a particular scaled score.

Your scaled score is essentially a percentile ranking. The LSAT is designed so that scaled scores mean the same thing from test to test. For example, no matter what test you take, if you get a 158, you answered more questions correctly than 75 percent of the people who took the same test you took, and you answered fewer questions correctly than 25 percent of the people who took the same test you took. The chart below summarizes the estimated percentile rankings of various LSAT scores.

SCORE	PERCENTILE
180	99.9%
175	99.7%
170	97.7%
165	93.2%
160	81.9%
155	64.7%
152	52.0%
150	44.9%
145	26.6%
140	13.5%

The raw score that is assigned to a particular scaled score varies from test to test. For example, a 163 is the scaled score that puts you in the 90th percentile of all test takers. On some tests you need a raw score of 83 to get a scaled score of 163. On other tests, it takes a raw score of just 77. These variations result from the fact that some tests are harder than others, but since the LSAT is scored this way, you don't have to worry about that. You're scored relative to the people who took the same test as you.

Since no points are subtracted for wrong answers, you should not leave any questions blank. If you have no idea what the answer is (or if you don't have time to attempt all of the questions in a section), bubble in a random letter; do that five times and odds are you'll get one question right. It doesn't matter whether you bubble in different letters or choose one letter and bubble it in every time you guess. Just make sure you've bubbled something in for every question.

One final note about the scoring scale that's important to keep in mind as you study. As you can see from the chart above, a person who gets a 178 only did 0.9 percent better than a person who got a 173, but a person who gets a 158 did nearly 20 percent better than a person who got a 153. Law schools care about those percentile differences. So don't get discouraged if, after a few weeks of studying and working practice problems, your score has only gone up three or four points. Every point makes a difference to your admissions prospects.

A Brief Introduction to the LSAT's Four Sections

Below is a brief introduction to what you can expect from the Logic Games, Arguments, Reading Comprehension, and Writing Sample sections, each of which is covered in greater detail in a subsequent chapter.

Logic Games (Chapter 3)

Each Logic Games section contains four "games." You will be asked to answer between five and seven questions about each game. Most Logic Games sections have 23 questions. Below are the actual directions that appear at the top of the Logic Games section. These directions are the same on every test. Read and learn them now so that you don't have to spend any time reading them on the day of your test.

> Directions: Each group of questions in this section is based on a set of conditions. In answering some of the questions, it may be useful to draw a rough diagram. Choose the response that most accurately and completely answers each question and blacken the corresponding space on your answer sheet.

So what is a logic game? A logic game consists of two parts: the setup and the clues. The setup is the fact pattern; it provides you with the basic information that you'll be working with as you work the game. That basic information consists of a list of elements and a task to perform with those elements.

The clues are rules, conditions, and constraints that organize the elements and define and limit the ways in which you can use the elements to perform the task you've been assigned. The clues appear in a list underneath the setup.

There are only two basic tasks that you will have to perform on the Logic Games section: ordering (putting the elements of the game in sequential or chronological order) and grouping (assigning the elements of the game to one or more groups or teams). That's it. Some games will involve both ordering and grouping, but those are the only two things you have to learn how to do to successfully navigate the Logic Games section. The best way to perform these tasks is to draw a simple diagram and use it to keep track of all the information in the setup and the clues. Chapter 3 will teach you how to identify the task that a particular game requires you to perform, create a diagram that keeps track of the information, and systematically work your way through the questions.

For most test takers, the Logic Games section is both bad news and good news. The bad news is that it's probably the section of the LSAT that is the most foreign to you. While we all have at least some experience with reading academic essays and analyzing short arguments, the task you're asked to perform on the Logic Games section—understand and visually represent the logical relationships between a set of variables—is likely an unfamiliar one. The good news is that your inexperience and unfamiliarity won't hurt you. Not only are all of your fellow test takers in the same boat, but Logic Games is the most teachable section of the LSAT. With a smart approach and consistent practice, most LSAT students can dramatically improve their performance on this section of the test.

Arguments (Chapter 4)

Half of your score on the LSAT will be determined by your performance on the Arguments sections. You'll have to work two Arguments sections, each of which will contain between 24 and 26 questions. The questions are arranged roughly in order of difficulty. Although there are some exceptions, the first 10 questions as a group will be easier than the last 10 questions. The official directions for the Arguments section are as follows:

> Directions: The questions in this section are based on the reasoning contained in brief statements or passages. For some questions, more than one of the choices could conceivably answer the question. However, you are to choose the *best* answer; that is, the response that most accurately and completely answers the question. You should not make assumptions that are by commonsense standards implausible, superfluous, or incompatible with the passage. After you have chosen the best answer, blacken the corresponding space on your answer sheet.

Each argument is relatively short: three or four sentences or about 100 words. You'll be asked to answer one question about each of the arguments. Although older LSATs sometimes asked two questions about a single argument, more recent exams have consistently stuck with a one-to-one ratio. The arguments are drawn from a variety of sources and address a wide range of topics. Typically the content is academic in nature, with a heavy emphasis on the natural sciences, psychology, economics, and ecology. No preexisting knowledge of these topics is required to answer the questions. The questions pertain solely to the information presented in the arguments.

The question types in the Arguments section test one or more of the following three skills: (1) understanding the content of an argument; (2) identifying a gap where information is missing from an argument; and (3) analyzing the reasoning of an argument. In Chapter 4 you'll learn how to identify each of the major question types that you'll encounter in the Arguments section. You'll take a slightly different approach to reading and analyzing the argument depending on which skill the question is testing. The arguments themselves and the right and wrong answers exhibit consistent, predictable patterns. Familiarizing yourself with those patterns will help you answer the questions faster and with a higher rate of accuracy.

Reading Comprehension (Chapter 5)

The Reading Comprehension section will probably be the section of the LSAT that looks the most familiar to you. The format is virtually identical to the format of the reading comprehension sections on other standardized tests. Each Reading Comprehension section contains four passages. You will be asked to answer between 5 and 8 questions about each passage for a total of about 27 questions. These are the official directions for the Reading Comprehension section:

> Directions: Each set of questions in this section is based on a single passage or pair of passages. The questions are to be answered on the basis of what is *stated* or *implied* in the passage or pair of passages. For some of the questions, more than one of the choices could conceivably answer the question. However, you are to choose the *best* answer; that is, the response that most accurately and completely answers the question, and blacken the corresponding space on your answer sheet.

Every Reading Comprehension section contains one passage from each of the four following general topic areas: (1) law, (2) hard science, (3) fine arts, and (4) social sciences or the humanities. The level of difficulty depends less on the topic of the passage and more on the density of its language and the complexity of its structure. Three passages will be a single piece of writing between 420 and 550 words long. The fourth passage will be a pair of shorter excerpts between 200 and 275 words each. This pair of shorter excerpts is known as the comparative-reading passage.

The Reading Comprehension section is fundamentally a test of information retrieval. It doesn't require you to go beyond the text of the passage by thinking critically about it, analyzing it, or pondering its broader implications. The questions test your ability to understand what you've read. In Chapter 5 you'll learn that you should not rely on your memory or recall of the passage when answering the questions. Instead, you should go back to the passage, reread the relevant portion, and find the answer to the question in the passage's text. With practice, this simple but powerful technique will yield a dramatic improvement in your performance on the Reading Comprehension section.

The Writing Sample (Chapter 6)

The final section of the LSAT is the writing sample. After you've finished all five multiple-choice sections, you'll have to write a two-page, handwritten essay in response to a brief factual prompt. The prompt will describe a factual scenario in which a person is presented with some kind of decisional problem. The prompt will describe two goals that the person hopes to accomplish. The prompt will also present two possible options for how the person might attempt to accomplish those goals. Using the facts that are included in the prompt, your task is to write an essay that selects and defends one of the options as a superior choice in light of its ability to better accomplish the two enumerated goals.

The official directions are as follows:

> Directions: The scenario presented below describes two choices, either one of which can be supported on the basis of the information given. Your essay should consider both choices and argue for one over the other, based on the two specified criteria and the facts provided. There is no "right" or "wrong" choice: a reasonable argument can be made for either.

Although the writing sample does not contribute to your LSAT score, it is read by law school admissions officers. You don't want an officer who is on the fence about your application to read a poorly written essay. Start thinking about the writing sample about a week or two before you take the LSAT. Chapter 6 introduces a five-paragraph structure you can use to write an effective essay.

How to Approach Test Day

As the date of your LSAT draws closer, there are a few practical things you should do to prepare. First, visit the location where you'll be taking the test. Figure out how you'll get there, how long it will take, and where you'll park (or which public transportation stop you'll use). Having this all nailed down in advance will reduce your stress level on the day of the main event.

Two nights before the test, be sure you get a good night's sleep. You should try to get a good night's sleep the night before the test, too, but sometimes nervous energy makes that impossible. That's OK—you can overcome one bad night of sleep and still be alert and focused. But if you've had two nights of bad sleep in a row, your test-day performance will suffer. So make it a point to turn in early on Thursday night (or Saturday night if you're taking the test in June).

The night before the test, take it easy. Don't stay up late working practice tests, trying to learn new material, or intensively reviewing material you've already learned. By this point, you know what you're going to know. One last cram session is more likely to make you feel tired and discouraged than help your performance.

Take a moment the night before the test to assemble everything you're going to bring with you to the test. There are only three things that you absolutely have to bring: (1) your admissions ticket; (2) a photo ID; and (3) number 2 pencils. When you register for the LSAT, the LSAC will send you an admissions ticket. It will be e-mailed to you if you register online and mailed to you if you register by phone or mail. They won't let you into the testing room if you don't have this admissions ticket. For the photo ID, a driver's license or a passport will work. And yes, you do have to use number 2 pencils; mechanical pencils are prohibited. Bring a handful with you, and make sure they are sharpened.

There are a few additional things that, while not absolutely necessary, it would be wise of you to bring. These include:

- **A small, nonelectric pencil sharpener.**
- **A white eraser stick.** White erasers work much better than the pink erasers that are attached to the ends of number 2 pencils. If you need to change an answer on your Scantron, clean and complete erasure will make sure that the scoring machine reads your answer sheet correctly.
- **Pain relievers.** Grab a few ibuprofen, aspirin, or acetaminophen, just in case.
- **A snack.** You'll want something to eat during the 10- to 15-minute break.
- **A bottle of water.** You won't be allowed to leave the test room to get a drink while the test is being administered.

- **A jacket, sweater, or fleece.** The test proctors typically will not be able to control the temperature in the test room. Dress in layers so that you won't be hot if the room is a little stuffy or cold if the air-conditioning is cranked up too high.
- **An analog wristwatch.** Digital timers are prohibited. So are analog stopwatches. If you want to keep track of time for yourself, you'll have to use an analog wristwatch. And it's a good idea to plan to do this: you won't necessarily be able to see a clock in the testing room, and you'll want to keep an eye on your time as you're working.
- **A large Ziploc bag to put all this stuff in.** That's the only kind of container you're allowed to bring into the testing center.

Finally, note that all of the following items are prohibited from the test room:

- Backpacks, messenger bags, briefcases, handbags, and the like
- Electronic timers of any kind, including digital watches
- Any electronic equipment, including cell phones, tablets, and PDAs
- Pens
- Earplugs
- Scratch paper
- Books, notes, or other LSAT test-prep materials

For a complete list of items that are prohibited from the test room, visit http://www.lsac.org/JD/LSAT/day-of-test.asp.

On the morning of your test, stick to your normal routine. Eat the same kind of breakfast you normally eat, and drink the same amount of coffee or soda or whatever it is that you normally drink. Studies show that test takers perform better if they've had a healthy breakfast, but if you never, ever eat breakfast, today's not the day to start.

Before you go to the test center, take 10 or 15 minutes to review some test materials. Look over one Logic Game, one Reading Comprehension passage, and one two-page set of Arguments questions. Do not work new practice problems. Instead, review problems that you've already worked (preferably ones that you did well on). The purpose of this review is to get your brain awake and warmed up. And reviewing problems that you answered correctly will help you put yourself into a positive, confident state of mind.

Be on time. The start time will be printed on your admissions ticket. The test proctors will close the doors precisely at that time. If you're late, they won't let you in, and you'll forfeit your opportunity to take the LSAT that day.

Obtaining or Cancelling Your Score

You can expect to receive your score by e-mail about three weeks after the test. If you've registered with the LSAC, the score will be e-mailed to you free of charge. If you don't have an LSAC account, or if you would prefer to have a hard copy mailed to you, you'll have to pay a fee of $25. Hard-copy score reports are usually mailed about a month after you take the test. For specific information on the score release date for the test you're taking, visit http://www.lsac.org/JD/LSAT/test-dates -deadlines.asp and click on the link for your test date.

If you feel that the test has gone poorly, you'll have two opportunities to cancel your score. First, you can cancel your score on the day you take the test. Your LSAT answer sheet will contain a section allowing you to cancel your score. Instructions on how to do so will be provided. Second, you can cancel your score by mailing or faxing in a score-cancellation sheet within six days after you take the test.

It never makes sense to cancel your score on the day of the test. Plenty of people get freaked out and have a crisis of confidence while they're taking the LSAT (especially if they have the misfortune of drawing an experimental section in which the LSAC is road-testing a batch of its most difficult questions). If you finish your test and feel like it's gone poorly, do not cancel your score that day. Go home, blow off some steam, get a couple days' distance from the test, and then revisit the issue Monday morning (or Wednesday morning if you take the test in June). Once you've gotten some perspective, you may remember other sections of the test that you felt really good about. Or you may talk to a friend who took the test the same day, hear that she didn't have the same brutally hard Games section that you had, and realize that the section you struggled with was the unscored experimental section. By waiting to make the keep-or-cancel decision, you'll prevent yourself from doing anything rash.

And there's no risk associated with waiting. All you have to do to cancel your score after the fact is fill out a one-page form and either mail or fax it to the LSAC. You have six days to do this. Since you can fax the form in, you can guarantee that it arrives on time. If you do decide to cancel your score, more information on how to go about doing so is available at http://www.lsac.org/jd/lsat/score-cancellations.

If you get a score you're unhappy with, you're free to take the LSAT again (up to a maximum of three times in any two-year period). If you take the LSAT multiple times, the LSAC will report all of your scores to each law school you apply to. The LSAC will also provide an average of all your scores. The decision on which score to consider varies on a school-by-school basis. Some schools will only consider your highest score; others consider the average of all your scores.

If you're thinking about taking the LSAT for a second time, it's worth it to call the admissions offices at the law schools you're most interested in and ask them what their policy is on reviewing applications with multiple LSAT scores. You'll get a lot more bang for your buck as a second-time taker if you're applying to schools that are willing to look only at your highest score. It's much harder to make a big upward jump at a school that averages scores.

CHAPTER 2

LSAT Diagnostic Test

This diagnostic test is designed to closely resemble the real LSAT in types and numbers of questions, in time limits, and in degree of difficulty. Use it to assess your test readiness as you begin your LSAT preparation.

For best results, try to simulate exam conditions as you take this test. Complete the test in a single sitting and follow directions and time limits. At the end of the test, you will find an Answer Key as well as answers and explanations for every question. Score yourself using the Answer Key, then read the explanations, paying particular attention to those for questions that you missed or that were difficult for you to answer. Don't skip the explanations for questions you answered correctly; you may learn simpler or easier ways to reach the right answer.

Your score on this test will indicate your current level of readiness to take the LSAT. Use it as a starting point to help you plan your preparation program. Which types of questions were easiest for you? Which ones were the most difficult? Were there any that you found confusing or that you could not answer at all? Instructional material on each LSAT question type is presented in the following chapters. As you read through the chapters, focus on the question types that you found most difficult. Pay careful attention to the examples and solution strategies presented. Then sharpen your problem-solving skills by tackling the practice tests at the end of this book. Additional LSAT practice is available on the companion website at MHPracticePlus.com.

You can also take the diagnostic test on your tablet or smartphone as well as your laptop or home computer. See page 7A of the Welcome insert for more information.

Answer Sheet

Directions: Before beginning the test, photocopy this answer sheet or remove it from the book. Mark your answer to each question by filling in the corresponding answer oval in the columns below. If a section has fewer questions than answer spaces, leave the extra spaces blank.

Section I	Section II	Section III	Section IV
1. Ⓐ Ⓑ Ⓒ Ⓓ Ⓔ	1. Ⓐ Ⓑ Ⓒ Ⓓ Ⓔ	1. Ⓐ Ⓑ Ⓒ Ⓓ Ⓔ	1. Ⓐ Ⓑ Ⓒ Ⓓ Ⓔ
2. Ⓐ Ⓑ Ⓒ Ⓓ Ⓔ	2. Ⓐ Ⓑ Ⓒ Ⓓ Ⓔ	2. Ⓐ Ⓑ Ⓒ Ⓓ Ⓔ	2. Ⓐ Ⓑ Ⓒ Ⓓ Ⓔ
3. Ⓐ Ⓑ Ⓒ Ⓓ Ⓔ	3. Ⓐ Ⓑ Ⓒ Ⓓ Ⓔ	3. Ⓐ Ⓑ Ⓒ Ⓓ Ⓔ	3. Ⓐ Ⓑ Ⓒ Ⓓ Ⓔ
4. Ⓐ Ⓑ Ⓒ Ⓓ Ⓔ	4. Ⓐ Ⓑ Ⓒ Ⓓ Ⓔ	4. Ⓐ Ⓑ Ⓒ Ⓓ Ⓔ	4. Ⓐ Ⓑ Ⓒ Ⓓ Ⓔ
5. Ⓐ Ⓑ Ⓒ Ⓓ Ⓔ	5. Ⓐ Ⓑ Ⓒ Ⓓ Ⓔ	5. Ⓐ Ⓑ Ⓒ Ⓓ Ⓔ	5. Ⓐ Ⓑ Ⓒ Ⓓ Ⓔ
6. Ⓐ Ⓑ Ⓒ Ⓓ Ⓔ	6. Ⓐ Ⓑ Ⓒ Ⓓ Ⓔ	6. Ⓐ Ⓑ Ⓒ Ⓓ Ⓔ	6. Ⓐ Ⓑ Ⓒ Ⓓ Ⓔ
7. Ⓐ Ⓑ Ⓒ Ⓓ Ⓔ	7. Ⓐ Ⓑ Ⓒ Ⓓ Ⓔ	7. Ⓐ Ⓑ Ⓒ Ⓓ Ⓔ	7. Ⓐ Ⓑ Ⓒ Ⓓ Ⓔ
8. Ⓐ Ⓑ Ⓒ Ⓓ Ⓔ	8. Ⓐ Ⓑ Ⓒ Ⓓ Ⓔ	8. Ⓐ Ⓑ Ⓒ Ⓓ Ⓔ	8. Ⓐ Ⓑ Ⓒ Ⓓ Ⓔ
9. Ⓐ Ⓑ Ⓒ Ⓓ Ⓔ	9. Ⓐ Ⓑ Ⓒ Ⓓ Ⓔ	9. Ⓐ Ⓑ Ⓒ Ⓓ Ⓔ	9. Ⓐ Ⓑ Ⓒ Ⓓ Ⓔ
10. Ⓐ Ⓑ Ⓒ Ⓓ Ⓔ	10. Ⓐ Ⓑ Ⓒ Ⓓ Ⓔ	10. Ⓐ Ⓑ Ⓒ Ⓓ Ⓔ	10. Ⓐ Ⓑ Ⓒ Ⓓ Ⓔ
11. Ⓐ Ⓑ Ⓒ Ⓓ Ⓔ	11. Ⓐ Ⓑ Ⓒ Ⓓ Ⓔ	11. Ⓐ Ⓑ Ⓒ Ⓓ Ⓔ	11. Ⓐ Ⓑ Ⓒ Ⓓ Ⓔ
12. Ⓐ Ⓑ Ⓒ Ⓓ Ⓔ	12. Ⓐ Ⓑ Ⓒ Ⓓ Ⓔ	12. Ⓐ Ⓑ Ⓒ Ⓓ Ⓔ	12. Ⓐ Ⓑ Ⓒ Ⓓ Ⓔ
13. Ⓐ Ⓑ Ⓒ Ⓓ Ⓔ	13. Ⓐ Ⓑ Ⓒ Ⓓ Ⓔ	13. Ⓐ Ⓑ Ⓒ Ⓓ Ⓔ	13. Ⓐ Ⓑ Ⓒ Ⓓ Ⓔ
14. Ⓐ Ⓑ Ⓒ Ⓓ Ⓔ	14. Ⓐ Ⓑ Ⓒ Ⓓ Ⓔ	14. Ⓐ Ⓑ Ⓒ Ⓓ Ⓔ	14. Ⓐ Ⓑ Ⓒ Ⓓ Ⓔ
15. Ⓐ Ⓑ Ⓒ Ⓓ Ⓔ	15. Ⓐ Ⓑ Ⓒ Ⓓ Ⓔ	15. Ⓐ Ⓑ Ⓒ Ⓓ Ⓔ	15. Ⓐ Ⓑ Ⓒ Ⓓ Ⓔ
16. Ⓐ Ⓑ Ⓒ Ⓓ Ⓔ	16. Ⓐ Ⓑ Ⓒ Ⓓ Ⓔ	16. Ⓐ Ⓑ Ⓒ Ⓓ Ⓔ	16. Ⓐ Ⓑ Ⓒ Ⓓ Ⓔ
17. Ⓐ Ⓑ Ⓒ Ⓓ Ⓔ	17. Ⓐ Ⓑ Ⓒ Ⓓ Ⓔ	17. Ⓐ Ⓑ Ⓒ Ⓓ Ⓔ	17. Ⓐ Ⓑ Ⓒ Ⓓ Ⓔ
18. Ⓐ Ⓑ Ⓒ Ⓓ Ⓔ	18. Ⓐ Ⓑ Ⓒ Ⓓ Ⓔ	18. Ⓐ Ⓑ Ⓒ Ⓓ Ⓔ	18. Ⓐ Ⓑ Ⓒ Ⓓ Ⓔ
19. Ⓐ Ⓑ Ⓒ Ⓓ Ⓔ	19. Ⓐ Ⓑ Ⓒ Ⓓ Ⓔ	19. Ⓐ Ⓑ Ⓒ Ⓓ Ⓔ	19. Ⓐ Ⓑ Ⓒ Ⓓ Ⓔ
20. Ⓐ Ⓑ Ⓒ Ⓓ Ⓔ	20. Ⓐ Ⓑ Ⓒ Ⓓ Ⓔ	20. Ⓐ Ⓑ Ⓒ Ⓓ Ⓔ	20. Ⓐ Ⓑ Ⓒ Ⓓ Ⓔ
21. Ⓐ Ⓑ Ⓒ Ⓓ Ⓔ	21. Ⓐ Ⓑ Ⓒ Ⓓ Ⓔ	21. Ⓐ Ⓑ Ⓒ Ⓓ Ⓔ	21. Ⓐ Ⓑ Ⓒ Ⓓ Ⓔ
22. Ⓐ Ⓑ Ⓒ Ⓓ Ⓔ	22. Ⓐ Ⓑ Ⓒ Ⓓ Ⓔ	22. Ⓐ Ⓑ Ⓒ Ⓓ Ⓔ	22. Ⓐ Ⓑ Ⓒ Ⓓ Ⓔ
23. Ⓐ Ⓑ Ⓒ Ⓓ Ⓔ	23. Ⓐ Ⓑ Ⓒ Ⓓ Ⓔ	23. Ⓐ Ⓑ Ⓒ Ⓓ Ⓔ	23. Ⓐ Ⓑ Ⓒ Ⓓ Ⓔ
24. Ⓐ Ⓑ Ⓒ Ⓓ Ⓔ	24. Ⓐ Ⓑ Ⓒ Ⓓ Ⓔ	24. Ⓐ Ⓑ Ⓒ Ⓓ Ⓔ	24. Ⓐ Ⓑ Ⓒ Ⓓ Ⓔ
25. Ⓐ Ⓑ Ⓒ Ⓓ Ⓔ	25. Ⓐ Ⓑ Ⓒ Ⓓ Ⓔ	25. Ⓐ Ⓑ Ⓒ Ⓓ Ⓔ	25. Ⓐ Ⓑ Ⓒ Ⓓ Ⓔ
26. Ⓐ Ⓑ Ⓒ Ⓓ Ⓔ	26. Ⓐ Ⓑ Ⓒ Ⓓ Ⓔ	26. Ⓐ Ⓑ Ⓒ Ⓓ Ⓔ	26. Ⓐ Ⓑ Ⓒ Ⓓ Ⓔ
27. Ⓐ Ⓑ Ⓒ Ⓓ Ⓔ	27. Ⓐ Ⓑ Ⓒ Ⓓ Ⓔ	27. Ⓐ Ⓑ Ⓒ Ⓓ Ⓔ	27. Ⓐ Ⓑ Ⓒ Ⓓ Ⓔ
28. Ⓐ Ⓑ Ⓒ Ⓓ Ⓔ	28. Ⓐ Ⓑ Ⓒ Ⓓ Ⓔ	28. Ⓐ Ⓑ Ⓒ Ⓓ Ⓔ	28. Ⓐ Ⓑ Ⓒ Ⓓ Ⓔ
29. Ⓐ Ⓑ Ⓒ Ⓓ Ⓔ	29. Ⓐ Ⓑ Ⓒ Ⓓ Ⓔ	29. Ⓐ Ⓑ Ⓒ Ⓓ Ⓔ	29. Ⓐ Ⓑ Ⓒ Ⓓ Ⓔ
30. Ⓐ Ⓑ Ⓒ Ⓓ Ⓔ	30. Ⓐ Ⓑ Ⓒ Ⓓ Ⓔ	30. Ⓐ Ⓑ Ⓒ Ⓓ Ⓔ	30. Ⓐ Ⓑ Ⓒ Ⓓ Ⓔ

SECTION I

Time—35 minutes
26 Questions

Directions: The questions in this section are based on the reasoning contained in brief statements or passages. For some questions, more than one of the choices could conceivably answer the question. However, you are to choose the *best* answer; that is, the response that most accurately and completely answers the question. You should not make assumptions that are by commonsense standards implausible, superfluous, or incompatible with the passage. After you have chosen the best answer, blacken the corresponding space on your answer sheet.

1. Since David Ellington became chief of police, several of the most decorated officers have resigned, the number of recruits has decreased, the department has instituted fewer community outreach programs, crime is on the rise, and polls show our police force is less popular than ever before. It's obvious the city council appointed Ellington to undermine our civic order.

   The reasoning in the argument is flawed because the argument

   (A) confuses quantitative results with qualitative results
   (B) leaps to a general conclusion based on a few anomalous instances
   (C) ignores that someone can be perceived as incompetent without actually being incompetent
   (D) assumes that because an action is followed by a result that the action was taken to bring about that result
   (E) restates something that has already been proven

2. An apartment complex is installing alarm systems in every apartment due to an increase in crime in the area. The manager reasons that he does not need to install an alarm system in apartment 3B because the tenant is a police officer and can protect himself.

   Which one of the following decisions is based on a flawed reasoning that is most similar to the apartment manager's reasoning?

   (A) A deliveryman has limited time to deliver all his packages before returning to his office. The deliveryman reasons that they should be delivered in order of largest to smallest because there might not be enough time to deliver all of them.
   (B) A candidate for mayor must prioritize the areas of the city where she must focus campaigning efforts. The candidate reasons that she spend all her resources in these areas where voters are less likely to vote for her because the other voters do not need to be convinced to vote for her.
   (C) Members of a jury are given four hours to reach their verdict or the judge will dismiss them and declare a mistrial. The jury reasons they should have the foreman review the evidence and determine a verdict because the foreman is a lawyer.
   (D) The captain of a yacht requires that all his passengers go through a safety training session. He reasons that one passenger did not have to attend because he was a former US naval officer.
   (E) A manager discovers an employee has stolen food from the break room. He reasons that he should force all his employees to go through ethics training to make sure the guilty party never steals food again.

GO ON TO THE NEXT PAGE

3. Larry: Some laws passed by Congress are considered to be bad by our nation's citizens even though they deliver positive results. A law is good only if it delivers positive results. So, some laws considered to be bad by our nation's citizens are actually good laws.

   Carrie: Although I agree with your conclusion I disagree with your reasons for it. Some good laws actually do not deliver positive results. But no laws that are considered to be bad by our nation's citizens deliver positive results, so your conclusion, that some laws that are considered bad by our nation's citizens are actually good, still holds.

   Which one of the following correctly describes an error in both Larry's and Carrie's reasoning?

   (A) Assuming that if a law's having a certain quality is necessary for its being a particular type of law, then having that quality is sufficient for being that type of law.
   (B) Assuming that if a particular quality is shared by two types of laws, then that quality is the only quality distinguishing the two types of law from laws of other types.
   (C) Assuming that if most laws of a particular type share a particular quality, then all laws share that quality.
   (D) Assuming that if a particular quality is shared by laws of a particular type among a particular nation, then that quality is shared by laws of that type among all nations.
   (E) Assuming that if a certain quality distinguishes one type of law from another type of law, then that quality is one of many qualities distinguishing the two types of laws.

4. Based on new evidence, anthropologists now believe that during the Neolithic Age there was a "white revolution," when Middle Eastern milk-drinking farmers conquered the hunter-gatherer tribes of Europe, and set up permanent settlements where the hunter-gatherer communities used to exist. Previously, experts thought that representatives of the Middle Easterners only traveled through Europe and brought their ideas like evangelists, converting the indigenous people to a new way of life. This new evidence finally proves that the transition of Europe to a farming and milk-drinking society was much more violent and transformative than thought before.

   Which one of the following, if true, most weakens the argument?

   (A) a discovery of several Middle Eastern villages in northern Europe with tools that show its members ate only vegetables and fruits and never raised cows
   (B) evidence that several hunter-gatherer societies drank milk long before the Middle Eastern farming communities migrated into the region
   (C) the discovery of land scarred from battle of that period as well as mass graves of the Middle Eastern farmers and hunter-gatherers
   (D) evidence that villages of Middle Easterners were established near the hunter-gatherer communities and trade existed between the two types of communities
   (E) the discovery of children with genetic markers from both hunter-gatherer and farming peoples, proving that there was sexual intermingling

GO ON TO THE NEXT PAGE

5. A rise in the number of young people entering the workforce in a small country between 2000 and 2006 correlates with a rise in the percentage of young people who graduate from high school in that country. Since young people in that small country are generally either high school graduates or high school dropouts, the correlation leads to the conclusion that the country's ability to employ young people in the workforce depends substantially on the number of people it can graduate from high school.

Which of the following statements can most properly be inferred from the argument?

(A) The percentage of young people who had completed at least two years of college was greater in 2006 than in 2000.

(B) Between 2000 and 2006 the percentage of high school dropouts hired into the workforce rose.

(C) Most of the available jobs require using technology and performing tasks that are too complicated for high school dropouts.

(D) A larger number of high school dropouts in the small country were hired into the workforce in 2006 than in 2000.

(E) Many of the young people who entered the workforce between 2000 and 2006 were high school graduates.

6. Speaker: The government must recognize that contemporary business firms are able to behave as irresponsibly as they want without fear of losing power. In a modern society, Davis and Blomstrom's Iron Law of Responsibility, which says that "in the long run, those who do not use power in a manner which society considers responsible will tend to lose it," no longer applies and never did. History shows that in the long run firms are able to obscure their bad acts with effective public relations or just wait out the short attention span of the public. Thus, a business that wants to act irresponsibly can do so without fear of losing power in society.

Which one of the following statements, if true, most strengthens the speaker's argument?

(A) Some institutions reach a critical mass at which they are too big to fail and will, in a sense, live forever.

(B) Some businesses that have used power in socially irresponsible ways have lost power.

(C) The power of some institutions grows faster than the power of others, whether they are socially irresponsible or not.

(D) Government institutions are as immune to the Iron Law of Responsibility as business institutions.

(E) Public relations often are transparent and fail to mask a corporation's truly irresponsible actions.

GO ON TO THE NEXT PAGE

Questions 7–8

A number of serious amateur photographers have tested the new Apheron digital camera. With it, they observed that the camera took photographs with much finer detail both in bright and low light situations than with the 10-megapixel Norwich, even though the Norwich cameras offer a higher resolution at 10 megapixels than the 8-megapixel Apheron cameras. Given these amateur photographers' observational findings, any serious photographer ought to choose the Apheron if she or he is buying a digital camera for both bright and low light situations.

7. The argument proceeds by

   (A) describing how a testing situation approximates the real-life conditions of ordinary use
   (B) using the claims of a subset of a group to make a recommendation to the larger group
   (C) evaluating the credibility of a recommendation made by a particular group
   (D) distinguishing between the actual reasons why a certain group did a particular thing and the best reasons for doing that thing
   (E) placing an experience in a wider context in order to explain it

8. The reasoning in the argument is flawed because it

   (A) assumes that the lens of the Apheron is made of the same materials as that of the Norwich
   (B) bases the conclusion on the size of the sensor rather than the number of pixels
   (C) does not acknowledge that the quality of detail in photographs is only one of several factors that, when taken together, should determine whether the camera is worth purchasing
   (D) assumes that the amateur photographers made their observations and comparisons during several sessions and at different times of the day
   (E) fails to consider that many serious amateur photographers have no intention of buying a digital camera to take photographs under such extreme conditions

9. Fifty years ago, the percentage of the nation's tax revenues spent on the maintenance of the national parks was twice what it is today. Given that tax revenues have risen over the past 50 years, we can conclude that tax revenues have risen at a greater rate than the cost of maintaining the nation's national parks.

   Which one of the following is the assumption upon which the argument's conclusion relies?

   (A) In general, the national parks are in better condition today and less costly than they were 50 years ago.
   (B) The national parks today have the same maintenance requirements as they did 50 years ago.
   (C) Unlike the national parks, expenditures to maintain the federal buildings are the same percentage of tax revenues as they were 50 years ago.
   (D) The amount spent per square mile of national park space is identical to the amount spent per square mile of national park space 50 years ago.
   (E) The costs related to maintenance of other federal properties have risen faster than the price of maintaining the national parks over the past 50 years.

GO ON TO THE NEXT PAGE

10. The amount of water consumed in Anderville on any given day in the summer is directly proportional to the heat index on that day. Since the average heat index this July was four points higher than the average heat index last August, it follows that more water was consumed in Anderville this July than last August.

Which one of the following arguments has a pattern of reasoning most similar to the one in the argument above?

(A) The number of doctors working in the emergency room on any day is directly proportional to the number of services delivered by the emergency room that day and also directly proportional to the number of patients that visit the emergency room. Thus, the number of services offered by the emergency room on any given day is directly proportional to the number of patients that visit the emergency room on that day.

(B) The number of doctors working in the emergency room on any given day is directly proportional to the number of nurses working in the emergency room on that day. But the emergency room employs the same number of orderlies every day. Hence, there are usually more doctors than orderlies working in the emergency room.

(C) The bill paid by a patient at the emergency room is directly proportional to the number of medical professionals the patient sees during his or her visit. Since the number of patients going through the emergency room is increasing, it follows that the emergency room is collecting a greater amount in fees paid by patients than it used to.

(D) The increase in patients at the emergency room is directly proportional to the amount of advertising the hospital has done the previous year. The hospital seeks to attract more patients to its emergency room by increasing the amount the hospital spends on advertising.

(E) The amount of analgesics prescribed in an emergency room is directly proportional to the number of patients that go through the emergency room on a given day. Since the emergency room handled 15 percent more patients in the last year than in the previous year, more analgesics were prescribed in the emergency room last year than in the previous year.

11. Isabella: The bestselling cooker in the country has to be the new solar cooker. It harnesses the free energy from the sun for cooking and baking, and it can even create clean water. Since it does not use fire, the people who use it do not inhale any smoke and are safe from fire hazards.

Noah: It does sound good, but the facts speak for themselves. Sales for the solar cooker are far below sales for conventional cookers.

Which of the following, if true, best resolves the apparent paradox?

(A) Solar cookers cost roughly the same as conventional cookers.

(B) Infrared cookers also prevent many of the hazards caused by conventional cookers.

(C) It takes a long time for solar cookers to bring water to a boil, and they require ample sunlight, which is not always available.

(D) The money saved by using the free energy of a solar cooker can be used to pay for food, education, health care, and so on.

(E) Solar cookers are a great solution to a host of problems in the developing world.

GO ON TO THE NEXT PAGE

12. Joe's Lumber stocks only two types of 2 × 4 planks, pine and oak. Roberto never uses pine to build his tables because he likes the heavier feel of oak and believes it is more durable. When he built Marion a dining room table, he used only 2 x 4 wood planks from Joe's Lumber.

Which of the following can be most properly inferred?

(A) Roberto made an exception to his no-pine rule because Marion preferred the look of pine.
(B) Marion's dining room table is made of oak.
(C) Marion wants her dining table to be durable and last a long time.
(D) Roberto always buys his wood from Joe's Lumber.
(E) Roberto also bought all the hardware for the table at Joe's Lumber.

13. A building inspector has been accused of ignoring serious structural defects on a building. Although the records have been lost and the building has since been demolished, his inspections of more recent buildings have been reviewed and found to be flawless. Therefore, the accusation should be dismissed.

Which of the following describes an error in the reasoning used in the argument above?

(A) The argument assumes that past performance is the same as current performance.
(B) The argument bases its conclusion on the character of the person making the accusation.
(C) The argument uses ambiguous terms in its premises.
(D) The argument assumes that the absence of evidence constitutes evidence of absence.
(E) The argument overlooks the possibility that recent inspections had problems that were not noticed in the review.

GO ON TO THE NEXT PAGE

Video solution ■ available on the Practice Test App. (See pp. 7A–8A.)

14. Every employee who takes public transportation to and from work eats lunch in the company break room. It follows that some employees who have their own office do not take public transportation to work.

The conclusion of the argument follows logically if which of the following is assumed?

(A) Some employees who do not have offices eat lunch in the company break room.
(B) Some employees who eat lunch in the company break room have an office.
(C) Every employee who eats lunch in the break room has an office.
(D) Some employees who do not have an office do not eat lunch in the company break room.
(E) Every employee who eats lunch in the company break room takes public transportation to and from work.

15. Archaeologists have found underwater etchings near the jungle city of Manaus, following a drought in the Brazilian Amazon. Previously, archaeologists studying the Amazon believed that the rainforest was too inhospitable to host a major civilization and that the only civilizations in the area were nomadic. The new discovery proves this theory incorrect and that thousands of years ago the Amazon was home to large civilizations.

Which of the following statements, if true, would most weaken the above argument?

(A) Remnants of large established villages with well-trodden roads going by or through them were unearthed near the location of the drawings.
(B) The etchings exhibited an unexpected sophistication for that period, yet they still showed the telltale signs of being of that period.
(C) Archaeologists proved that a nomadic artist created the etchings and very similar etchings almost 100 miles away.
(D) The drought that exposed the submerged etchings was the first in that area in more than 2,000 years.
(E) The etchings included a representation of hunters walking across a plain and people building small domiciles.

16. A new study observed people who watch television and their happiness level. The study indicated that people who have more channels and thus more choices of what to watch are not necessarily happier than those with fewer choices of what to watch. Thus, people in highly industrialized nations who have more choices in all aspects of their daily lives are not happier than those in less developed nations with fewer choices in their daily lives.

The above argument depends on the presupposition that

(A) it is equally likely that people in less developed nations have as many television channels as people in highly industrialized nations
(B) the inverse relationship between happiness and the number of television channels is the same among other categories of goods and services regardless of other factors related to where people live in the world
(C) people in less developed nations are unfamiliar with the number and quality of choices available to those in highly industrialized nations
(D) people in highly industrialized nations have visited less developed nations and determined that their choices are of lesser quality and less likely to make them happier
(E) the relationship between the number of television channels and happiness is directly related to the stage of a society's industrialization and thus an industrialized nation will feel the effects of such disparities more significantly

GO ON TO THE NEXT PAGE

17. A high school cheerleading squad held its annual bake sale on the first day of school to raise money for the coming year. In order to increase sales this year the squad decided to lower the prices on everything. Despite their strategy, the cheerleaders had lower sales than in any previous year.

Each of the following, if true, contributes to reconciling the apparent discrepancy indicated above EXCEPT:

(A) Student enrollment at the high school dropped significantly from the previous year to this year.

(B) Other school groups planned their fund-raisers for the same day, which had not been done in previous years.

(C) Because of the increase in prices for sugar and flour, the cost of making the baked goods increased this year.

(D) The faculty handed out gift baskets on the first day of school that included cupcakes and other sweet items.

(E) Due to construction on a new auditorium the cheerleading squad was not able to locate their bake sale tables in the same well-known location as in previous years.

18. The Redville Community Center, a nonprofit organization, was facing a budgetary crisis due to rising utility costs and expensive building repairs that were necessary to keep the center open. The board of directors decided to raise the membership fees and assess a building fee to raise the necessary funds. Toward the end of the year the board discovered that the costs were less than they thought and the fee changes actually gave the center a budget surplus. The board decided to use the surplus funds to buy a new van to shuttle people from the nearby nursing home to the center even though the old van was still serviceable. But before doing so, the board should obtain permission from the members who paid the additional fees.

Which one of the following policies, if put into effect, would most justify the position advocated above and yet place the least restriction on the use of funds by community centers?

(A) Beneficiaries of a nonprofit organization with a vested fee-based interest should be considered to be placing their trust in the directors of those organizations to use the money wisely according to whatever circumstance might arise.

(B) Beneficiaries of a nonprofit organization with a vested fee-based interest cannot delegate to the directors of those organizations the responsibility of allocating the funds received for various purposes consonant with the purposes of the organization as the directors of the organization see fit.

(C) Directors of nonprofit organizations cannot allocate assessments to any purposes for which the directors had not specifically earmarked the funds in advance.

(D) Fees assessed by a nonprofit organization for a specific purpose should only be used for that purpose, or if that is unable to happen then should only be used according to the express wishes of those who pay the assessments.

(E) Directors of nonprofit organizations who assess additional fees for specific purposes must return funds received from such assessments if more money is received than can practicably be used for the specified purpose of the assessment.

 Video solution available on the Practice Test App. (See pp. 7A–8A.)

GO ON TO THE NEXT PAGE

19. Scientist: My peers have said that my theory regarding molecular cohesion in glass is based on sheer conjecture and has no experimental basis. This is simply not true. I've based my theory on several findings that have been published recently by reputable research organizations. Even though I have not reviewed every detail of their experiments, I am confident in their work. Besides, you may recall that I was asked to develop theories on molecular cohesion in wood fibers five years ago and I used findings from the same labs then as well.

The scientist's argument is LEAST vulnerable to which one of the following criticisms?

(A) It bases a conclusion about the scientific findings of the research organizations on uncertain recollections.
(B) It assumes that the experiments done by the research organizations are unaffected by bias or human error.
(C) It assumes that the experiments done by the research organizations are the only work necessary to develop a scientific theory.
(D) It hastily concludes that the experiments done by the research organizations are accurate, without having studied them in detail.
(E) It assumes that having in the past used the experiments done by the research organizations as a basis to develop a scientific theory justifies using them to develop the current theory.

Questions 20–21
The city performed its annual testing of lead levels in the drinking water and discovered that about 14 percent of the samples taken exceeded federal standards for allowable lead levels. Regardless of these findings, the lead levels, even in the ones that exceeded federal standards, were still too low to pose any immediate health threat. So, it's perfectly safe for the city's residents to drink all the tap water they want.

20. Which one of the following is an assumption on which the argument depends?

(A) The city's residents often disregard federal guidelines when it comes to public health issues because the standards are overly stringent.
(B) The most dangerous contaminant in drinking water is lead.
(C) Statistical sampling is not the most accurate basis for determining health threats even though the federal government and the city must depend on them.
(D) Lead levels even slightly above federal standards do not have long-term effects on people's health.
(E) People feel safer when they heed warnings from the federal government even if they are not entirely accurate.

21. Which of the following, if true, most strengthens the argument?

(A) Most lead in city drinking water is absorbed by the lining of the pipes.
(B) Due to budgetary cuts the city had to test water sourced from one central location instead of sampling randomly throughout the city as in past years.
(C) Studies show that children who absorb levels of lead above federal standards experience adverse long-term effects.
(D) The local hospital has had an increase in lead-poisoning cases among people who drink large quantities of water on a regular basis.
(E) Several medical associations have lobbied for higher standards and harsher punishments on cities that do not take actions to reduce lead contamination in their drinking water.

Questions 22–23

Jaime: The life span for both African and Asian
elephants is much shorter in zoos than in the
national reserve parks. Studies have proven
this by comparing the life spans of elephants
in zoos to the life spans of elephants in nature
reserves in both Kenya and Myanmar. Thus,
our government should take a serious look at
how zoos treat their elephants and possibly
implement a temporary ban on the acquisition
of new elephants until this issue is resolved.

Eleanor: But both the reserves you mention are
protected areas where the animals do not face
the threat of poaching and other unnatural
dangers. Also, the data in those studies go back
more than 40 years and do not take into account
more recent advances in captive animal care
that will most definitely extend the life spans of
elephants currently in zoos.

22. Which one of the following is an assumption on
which Eleanor's argument depends?

(A) There are genetic differences between
African and Asian elephants that effect
variance of life spans between those
particular species.

(B) Predators and diseases within the confines
of a nature reserve affect the life span of an
elephant to a lesser extent than threats an
elephant faces outside the parks.

(C) The training of zookeepers and those
who manage nature reserves is exactly
the same; thus, the care of the elephants
should be exactly the same.

(D) A zookeeper in 1970 was unable to help
extend the lives of elephants in captivity
due to budgetary restraints that plagued
zoos at that time.

(E) The professionals that manage nature
reserves are more aware of the threat of
poachers than zookeepers; thus, they do a
better job of protecting their elephants
from them.

23. Eleanor's rejection of Jaime's conclusion
employs which one of the following techniques
of argumentation?

(A) Producing a single contradicting example
that establishes that a stated generalization
is false

(B) Questioning the validity of a conclusion
because the supporting statements cannot
be experimentally verified

(C) Pointing out that potentially more favorable
evidence exists that has been neglected

(D) Rejecting a problematic correlation and a
potential variance shift with relation to the
supporting statements that underlie the
conclusion

(E) Reanalyzing the underlying assumptions
and pursuing a wider data sampling that
underlie the conclusion

24. A teacher decided to challenge 10 of
her students to do their mathematics
work without a calculator or computer
for three months, while the rest of her
class was able to use whatever tools they had
at their disposal. She discovered that the 10
students' scores improved on their homework
assignments and their exams. On the basis
of this experiment the teacher determined
that students perform better when forced to
complete their work manually rather than
depending on machines.

Which of the following would, if valid, most
weaken the reasoning above?

(A) The 10 students were performing poorly in
the teacher's course before the experiment.

(B) The 10 students were being tutored by other
students who did have the advantage of a
calculator or computer.

(C) The 10 students happened to be the best
students at mathematics in the class.

(D) During the three months of the
experiment, the class studied mathematics
that only the 10 students had studied
previously.

(E) The teacher coached the students on how
to do their homework without the help of a
calculator or computer.

GO ON TO THE NEXT PAGE

25. A recent survey showed that 60 percent of employers polled believe that an employee should be fired from the job if the employee has been charged with a crime, whereas 40 percent believe that an employee should be fired only if the employee has been convicted of a crime. Therefore, more employers believe that an employee should be fired if charged of a crime than believe they should be fired if convicted.

The reasoning above is flawed because it

(A) uses a sample of the population to draw a conclusion about the general population
(B) bases a conclusion on an ambiguous term in the supporting statements
(C) uses two different beliefs to draws a conclusion about a different belief altogether
(D) is based on premises that cannot all be true
(E) confuses a sufficient condition with a required condition

26. Editorial: History has shown that even though politicians promise that the profits from a lottery will be devoted to educational purposes, the funds are inevitably redirected to other purposes that have nothing to do with education. Therefore, our representatives in the state legislature should not support the proposed lottery because they will inevitably break their promise to use the profits to fund education and direct the funds elsewhere.

The reasoning above is flawed because it

(A) draws a conclusion about a specific population based on a study of a larger population
(B) uses historical data to draw incorrect conclusions about a similar situation in the future
(C) presupposes that a pattern of behavior under one set of conditions will recur under a completely different set of conditions
(D) rejects a proposed solution based on the track record of an altogether different solution
(E) assails a proposed lottery by attacking those who support it rather than the merits of the proposed lottery

STOP

IF YOU FINISH BEFORE TIME RUNS OUT, CHECK YOUR WORK ON THIS SECTION ONLY. DO NOT GO ON TO ANY OTHER TEST SECTION.

SECTION II

Time—35 minutes
24 Questions

Directions: The questions in this section are based on the reasoning contained in brief statements or passages. For some questions, more than one of the choices could conceivably answer the question. However, you are to choose the *best* answer; that is, the response that most accurately and completely answers the question. You should not make assumptions that are by commonsense standards implausible, superfluous, or incompatible with the passage. After you have chosen the best answer, blacken the corresponding space on your answer sheet.

1. Chancellor of Mayfield Academy: Mayfield Academy must grow if it is to survive, so as we have agreed, efforts should be made to attract students in all grades K–12. The best strategy for attracting students is to build new facilities for athletics, computer science, and the arts, including a new auditorium. Parents demand that their children receive the very best facilities to explore their interests to the fullest. Also, as other schools are investing in similar facilities, we must keep up with the competition. Therefore, parents will move their kids to our school as our facilities match or surpass other institutions.

   The argument leads to the conclusion that

   (A) the Mayfield Academy should attract more students
   (B) parents who want the best facilities for their children's interests should choose Mayfield Academy
   (C) parents should consider public as well as private institutions
   (D) the Mayfield Academy should invest in new facilities
   (E) parents who have children in public school should transfer them to Mayfield Academy

2. Business executive: Attempting to create an ethical company by teaching ethics to our employees is a waste of time and money because the corporate structure at its foundation is inherently neither ethical nor unethical. No matter what we do, people will inevitably act in an unethical manner. All we can do is create monitoring systems to prevent problems from occurring and to protect the company when they do.

   Ethicist: To claim that we should not train employees in ethics because they will inevitably act unethically makes about as much sense as arguing that we should not spend money on driver's education because all drivers will inevitably cause an accident.

   The method the ethicist uses to object to the business executive's argument is to

   (A) argue that there are problems that time and money, no matter how judiciously spent, cannot solve
   (B) attack the character of the business executive rather than the position the business executive is taking
   (C) show that the executive's line of reasoning would lead to an unacceptable conclusion if applied to a different situation
   (D) show that the executive must present more evidence to substantiate the business executive's position
   (E) explicate a dilemma that is central to the business executive's argument

GO ON TO THE NEXT PAGE

Video solution available on the Practice Test App. (See pp. 7A–8A.)

3. Renfield should not be promoted to the management position. His performance as a member of our staff, while exemplary, has shown little of his management ability. Everything he has said and done up to this point has been directed toward obtaining this promotion rather than showing us that he has the ability to manage other people. Therefore, we cannot trust that he will be an effective manager once in the position.

Which one of the following is an assumption on which the argument relies?

(A) The duties of a staff member do not in and of themselves prove that the person is capable of managing people.

(B) Renfield cannot be trusted even with his current duties as a member of the staff.

(C) When Renfield obtains the promotion, he does not intend to act in the best interest of the staff under his management.

(D) The staff will not follow Renfield's lead as a manager once he receives the promotion.

(E) Managers rarely are promoted from the staff because they are unable to handle the higher level of responsibility.

4. Real progress in society is not something that can happen without significant and transformative action. It only comes when those who are in power have the courage to overcome significant opposition and overturn previously accepted norms that are detrimental to society.

The reasoning in the argument is fallacious because the argument

(A) undermines its own premise that a particular attribute is present in all instances of a particular phenomenon

(B) concludes that, because an influence is the paramount influence on a particular phenomenon, that influence is the only influence on that phenomenon

(C) denies that the observation that a particular pattern is common to phenomena within society might contribute to observing a causal explanation of the phenomenon

(D) concludes that the characteristic of a type of phenomena in society occurring at one time is characteristic of similar phenomena at all times

(E) selects one influence on a particular phenomenon in society as indicating that its influence outweighs any other influence on those phenomena

5. Enrollment in online college courses is growing each year. Students rank these courses among the highest in terms of student satisfaction. Despite these facts, professors have not embraced the idea of teaching virtually.

The apparent discrepancy above can best be explained by which of the following?

(A) While students report that they enjoy these classes, their grades in online courses are lower than their grades in traditional classes.

(B) Some students are not able to take an online course because they do not have the equipment needed.

(C) Professors prefer in-person interaction because they can see and hear their students' responses to lectures, something that is difficult to assess online.

(D) The number of students enrolled in college courses has grown dramatically over the past five years.

(E) Students find online courses more convenient because some parts of the course can be accessed at any time of the day.

GO ON TO THE NEXT PAGE

6. Until recently it was believed that weight training did not help children but in fact did harm and possibly stunted their growth. A new study has determined that weight training among children between ages 6 and 18 helped them grow stronger even though they did not gain muscle mass like adults. Therefore, our government should require weight training for all children in public schools who are between the ages of 6 and 18.

Which one of the following statements, if true, most seriously weakens the argument?

(A) The school year is only nine months of the year, and with children, weight training must be done on a consistent basis all year round. A home-based program is required for success.

(B) Since the children do not gain muscle mass, measuring their progress will be difficult without the specialized instruments used in the study.

(C) The study was performed with subjects from only one geographic location where weight training is more culturally acceptable.

(D) The gain in strength over a nine-month school year will be minimal. It takes at least a year for the children to show significant results from weight training.

(E) Children do not respond positively to government requirements and low morale may adversely affect results of any government-instituted weight training requirements.

7. Vicki: My dentist charges me $1,500 for a crown when I see her at her office in my neighborhood. When she works at the city clinic in Bristow, she only charges the people who go there $250 for a crown.

Bruce: That does seem unfair. I know that the city clinic feels it has a responsibility to provide care to those who need it most, even if they cannot pay what the service is worth. I suppose that since most of the people in your neighborhood have higher incomes than the people in Bristow, the dentist charges more than what the service is worth in order to balance out the discounted services she provides at the city clinic. Still, this is really unfair because some of the people in Bristow make plenty of money, and some of the people in your neighborhood are unemployed or work low-paying jobs.

Which one of the following principles, if valid, most helps justify Bruce's reasoning?

(A) Professionals should charge everyone the same fees, regardless of their ability to afford them.

(B) Basic services, such as health and dental care, should be provided by the government, at no charge to the patients.

(C) Professionals have an obligation to forgo some of their profit to assist those who do not have enough money to pay their fees.

(D) Professionals should evaluate each individual's needs in determining fees for services rather than charging all the people in a certain area the same fees.

(E) The people in wealthy neighborhoods should not have more dental care available than do people in poorer neighborhoods.

GO ON TO THE NEXT PAGE

8. During the first 140 million years of existence on earth, mammals were relatively small, ranging from 2 to 22 pounds, but once the dinosaurs became extinct, mammals grew in size up to 1,000 times bigger and as large as 17 tons. Once the herbivorous dinosaurs were gone the mammals no longer needed to compete for space to roam and vegetation for food. They could eat all the food they wanted, and the larger mammals were better able to fend off predators. This is why we have our hippopotamuses and giraffes of today.

If the statements above are true, which one of the following must also be true on the basis of them?

(A) If the dinosaurs had lived longer, mammals today would be much smaller yet still herbivorous.

(B) If the hippopotamus we know today was a 1,000 times smaller, other mammals would also be significantly smaller.

(C) If other larger nonmammals had survived the event that made the dinosaurs extinct, modern mammals may have been much smaller due to competition for resources.

(D) If mammals had been larger during the time of the dinosaurs, the resulting competition would have made both extinct.

(E) If hippopotamuses and giraffes had evolved as carnivores and not herbivores, large mammals most likely would not have competed with the dinosaurs for space and food.

9. At an auction, nobody wants to buy the statue by Alberto Giacometti more than Jody, but Jody will not be participating in the bidding, so no matter how much the auctioneers lower the minimum bid not one person will bid on the statue.

The flawed reasoning in the argument above most closely parallels that in which of the following?

(A) The jockey who most wants to ride the horse Black Lightning in the next race is Cornwall, but he suddenly told the owner he could not ride in the next race. This means the other jockeys who had given up hope of riding Black Lightning will double their efforts.

(B) Better than anyone, Larry can spot a forgery of a Renaissance painting, but he has yet to find any flaws in Renny's painting. So there must be a forgery among the other paintings in his collection.

(C) If anyone can translate this ancient text it is Professor Ricardo, but he is currently engaged in a project to translate a much more significant text and will probably not be interested in doing this smaller project. So we will have to hope that we can find someone of equal stature to take on the translation.

(D) Even though Emilio is the most intent of anyone to obtain the sales position, he is not applying for the position. It follows that nobody else will apply for the sales position no matter how high a salary is being offered.

(E) Sherry wanted to join an extra-credit group project for her science class, but each time they called a meeting she was too busy with cheerleading practice to join them. So, the closer she gets to becoming head cheerleader, the less time she can devote to her studies.

GO ON TO THE NEXT PAGE

Video solution available on the Practice Test App. (See pp. 7A–8A.)

10. If the conductor does not want to participate in the New York competition, then we should consider other competitions. If the orchestra does not want to participate in the New York competition, then we should skip the competitions altogether. And, it is bound to be the case that either the conductor or the orchestra does not want to participate in the New York competition.

If the statements above are true, which one of the following must also be true?

(A) If the orchestra agrees to participate in the New York competition, then we should skip the competitions altogether.

(B) We should consider other competitions only if it makes it more likely that both the conductor and the orchestra will participate.

(C) We should attempt to convince both the conductor and the orchestra to participate in the New York competition.

(D) If the conductor agrees to participate in the New York competition, then we should skip the competitions altogether.

(E) We should consider other competitions only if the conductor is more likely to participate.

11. The concept of proportionality is used as a criterion of fairness and justice in statutory interpretation processes, especially in constitutional law, as a logical method intended to assist in discerning the correct balance between the restriction imposed by a corrective measure and the severity of the nature of the prohibited act.

Which of the following situations would violate the principle established above?

(A) In a civil lawsuit over property boundaries, both parties agreed to arbitration rather than going to trial.

(B) Two students cheated on an economics exam. One of the students was caught cheating and was given a zero on the exam.

(C) A state senator was accused of accepting bribes. After a lengthy investigation, she was exonerated.

(D) Two workers clock in late for their shift. For both, it is the first incidence. One is reprimanded by his manager, and the other is fired by the same manager.

(E) A mechanic does not have the same brand of part he needs to repair a customer's car engine, so he uses a similar brand and does not inform the owner of the car of the substitution.

GO ON TO THE NEXT PAGE

12. Press release: A committee of physicians analyzed nearly 1,000 publications and determined that the high level of vitamin D and calcium recommended by physicians and testing labs to sustain bone health is unnecessary. Food producers are adding vitamin D and calcium to foods people eat every day, not to mention that people get vitamin D from exposure to sunlight. Therefore, everyone should stop taking high levels of vitamin D and calcium immediately.

Which one of the following describes the primary flaw in the conclusion drawn above?

(A) It precludes the possibility that vitamin D and calcium work together better than they do when taken separately.

(B) It ignores the possibility that high levels of vitamin D and calcium have benefits other than sustaining bone health.

(C) It inappropriately assumes a correlation between vitamins and bone health.

(D) It assumes that physicians recommend high levels of vitamin D and calcium only to those patients who have poor bone health.

(E) It fails to define what amount is considered high levels of vitamin D and calcium.

13. Philosopher: Pragmatism is the view that meaning or worth is determined by practical consequences. If a course of action has the desired effect, then it is good. So if a theory works in practice, it is right. If it does not work, then it must be wrong. Pragmatism, however, is a dangerous philosophy because it is impossible to develop a general truth that applies to everyone or gives guidance for making moral or ethical decisions. What is "good" for one person may not be for someone else.

Which one of the following is the best example of the principle of pragmatism?

(A) A high school teacher in an urban school in a densely populated city teaches a course on agricultural science.

(B) In order to rid his garden of squirrels, the owner erected a wire fence around the entire garden perimeter, but the squirrels found a way over it.

(C) A politician refuses to change her position on an issue, even when confronted with evidence that her position will harm her constituents.

(D) A doctor prescribes a new medication for a patient after a previous one did not achieve the desired effect.

(E) A company opened a cafeteria so that its employees would not need to leave for lunch, but most of the employees did not like the food and returned to their practice of eating out.

GO ON TO THE NEXT PAGE

Questions 14–15

The board of directors of Company X has decided to sell its underperforming divisions that have been dragging down the stock price. To some analysts this seems like a drastic move, but the president of Company X has long maintained that among the troubled divisions are some with antiquated systems and low-quality products. He has argued that it would be too costly to improve their operations. Hence, the board's action would not hurt but would actually help Company X's stock price.

14. The conclusion drawn depends on which one of the following assumptions?

    (A) All the companies being considered for sale are 100 percent owned by Company X.
    (B) Only a very savvy buyer will be willing to buy such underperforming divisions from Company X.
    (C) Company X will be able to sell its underperforming units only after it has improved their operations.
    (D) All the companies the board decides to sell will include those recommended by the president for sale.
    (E) Buyers of companies are unable to recognize an underperforming division.

15. Which one of the following, if true, most weakens the argument?

    (A) The stock price is determined not just by the company's highest-performing divisions but by the interaction among all its divisions.
    (B) The better-performing divisions command a much higher price than the underperforming units.
    (C) The underperforming divisions have always been thought to be poor investments by Company X.
    (D) Buyers who buy underperforming divisions in order to sell them later at a higher price care little about the resulting inflation in the marketplace, but large companies like Company X are highly concerned about the resulting inflation.
    (E) The directors are currently conducting research to find a means other than selling off its underperforming divisions that would improve the company's stock price.

16. A new restaurant that survives beyond six months is popular either among its local patrons or among the food critics. Last year, all the new restaurants that were popular with the food critics were also very popular with its local patrons. Therefore, every new restaurant that survived beyond six months last year was popular among the food critics.

The pattern of reasoning in which one of the following arguments is most similar to that in the argument above?

(A) All auto service garages in the Caedmon Township will do maintenance on both foreign and domestic automobiles. Larry's Auto Shop is an auto service garage that will not perform maintenance on foreign automobiles. Hence, Larry's Auto Shop is not in the Caedmon Township.
(B) In their second year, all apprentices at the Willow Construction Company study dry wall or cabinetry. This year, all the apprentices who are studying dry wall are also studying cabinetry. Therefore, every apprentice at Willow is studying dry wall.
(C) Former members of Congress either go on to teach at their hometown university or write a book about their years in politics. Mary Seldon is a former congresswoman who is teaching at Riverside University in her hometown of Riverside. Therefore, Seldon is not writing a book about her years in politics.
(D) Every bestselling novel published last year is both well written and has a suspenseful plot. The novel Jacob Rain published last year is well written and has a suspenseful plot. Therefore, Jacob Rain's novel is a bestseller.
(E) In order to succeed, most new movies require either a big advertising campaign or a cast with big stars. But most movies with a cast of big stars automatically get a big advertising campaign. Hence, a movie that has a cast of big stars is guaranteed to succeed.

GO ON TO THE NEXT PAGE

17. It has been discovered that a rice plant has protein molecules that recognize and bind to specific molecules on invading organisms, signaling the plant to mount an immune response and fend off microbial infection and disease. This immune response is not at all dissimilar to a human immune system's method of warding off diseases. It will not be long before we can discover how plants fight off the common cold.

Which one of the following is an assumption on which the argument depends?

(A) The same diseases that attack humans also attack plants.
(B) The common cold is a disease that the human immune system fails to ward off.
(C) Because the immune system of plants and humans is similar, diseases attack both in the same manner.
(D) The immune system of a rice plant is the same as the immune system of other plants.
(E) Protein molecules bind to the invading molecules in plants in the same configuration that they do in humans.

18. Joseph: Evening customer service representatives at a computer company handle complaints 20 percent faster than day customer service representatives on average, yet they offer similar quality service when handling complaints. So, the evening representatives work more efficiently.

Davis: Your conclusion is unfair. Different times of the day bring different demands on the customer service representatives. Since the evening calls are more often about home computer problems, they are less complex problems than those during the day when more business-oriented calls come into the customer service center.

The issue in dispute between Joseph and Davis is

(A) why the evening customer service representatives are able to remain on the late shift as opposed to the day shift
(B) the relationship between the time of day and the time it takes for a customer service representative to handle a customer complaint
(C) how the company may decide to move customer service representatives back and forth between the evening and day shift to increase efficiency at handling complaints
(D) the accuracy of the figure of 20 percent with regard to the difference in speed of handling complaints between evening and day customer representatives
(E) the reason why evening customer service representatives are able to offer equal quality service as day customer representatives while spending less time with each customer on average

GO ON TO THE NEXT PAGE

19. In a legislature much of the legislation is written by industry experts who also serve as lobbyists on behalf of their respective industries that will ultimately be affected by the legislation they draw up. Since these experts know the industry much better than the legislators, they can better design legislation that will do what the legislators require without harming the companies or entities that must abide by the resulting regulations. But clearly this strategy is based on poor reasoning. After all, as lobbyists, industry experts are paid to represent the interests of their employer and any legislation they write will most likely be weakened in the favor of their employer's self-interest and not in the best interest of the legislature's constituents.

The point made by the author is that the most common way of creating legislation might not be in the best interest of the legislature's constituents because

(A) many industry experts might let their self-interest as industry lobbyists affect their role, as writers of legislation, in acting on behalf of elected officials

(B) most industry experts, thanks to outside lobbying contracts, are heavily influenced financially to write unfair legislation

(C) most legislators would be less corrupt in writing legislation than industry experts would be

(D) many industry experts create weakened legislation in order to obtain lucrative jobs in their respective industries some day

(E) many industry experts are paid generously and want to keep the lobbying jobs by creating weak legislation that favors their respective industries

20. All diamonds cut by Richman are over three carats, and all its rubies are less than three carats. Most of the precious stones cut by Richman have a clarity rating below SI2. All the diamonds and rubies cut by Allister have a clarity rating above SI2 and are less than three carats. Ellington Jewelry, which only buys its diamonds and rubies from these two companies, only purchases stones that are less than 3 carats. Ellington is currently purchasing a large diamond shipment.

If the statements above are true, which of the following must be true on the basis of them?

(A) Ellington buys only diamonds.

(B) All the stones from Allister have a lower clarity than those from Richman.

(C) The diamond shipment being purchased has a clarity rating above SI2.

(D) The diamond shipment being purchased belongs to Richman.

(E) Ellington does not purchase stones from Allister.

GO ON TO THE NEXT PAGE

Questions 21–22

Coal plant manager: No matter what technical advances come over the next 30 years, coal will remain the most cost effective source of energy. Despite what some people claim, the cost of alternative sources of power like solar and wind technologies will never drop to a level that will compete with coal. Coal is here to stay.

Environmentalist: I disagree. There have been significant improvements in solar cells and wind turbine technologies over the last 10 years. They are more efficient than ever. These new technologies continue to advance while the coal industry has been slow to adopt the latest clean coal technologies. Eventually, coal will face obsolescence.

21. The reasoning in the environmentalist's argument is flawed because the argument

   (A) ignores the length of time that it will take for alternative sources of energy to become competitive with coal
   (B) fails to acknowledge the cost advantage of coal over alternative sources of energy like solar and wind technologies
   (C) mistakes the coal plant manager's discussion of technical advances as a statement that the coal industry intends to adopt clean coal technologies
   (D) overlooks the possibility that coal and alternative technologies might collaborate to create a cleaner energy future
   (E) assumes that costs of alternatives to coal will drop with the introduction of more efficient solar and wind technologies

22. Which one of the following, if true, most strongly supports the environmentalist's counterargument?

   (A) Engineers have discovered limitations to technological advancement in the coal industry that do not exist in the solar and wind power industries.
   (B) Thirty years is too small a time window to judge whether one energy technology will win out over another.
   (C) A direct relationship has been determined between technological advancements in the energy sector and the cost-adoption factors.
   (D) A coal company in one state is currently converting its facilities over to clean coal technology.
   (E) Improvements in solar and wind technologies have accelerated but costs have only slightly improved over the last 10 years.

GO ON TO THE NEXT PAGE

23. Randy's boss asked him to write a management report concerning the training of new financial advisors coming into the company, but because of other projects assigned to him he put it off until the day before he is supposed to make a presentation based on the report to his boss. Randy could still complete the report by the deadline, but only if he works on it all evening without interruption. However, one of his clients invited him to a dinner party and requested that Randy remain afterward to discuss the client's portfolio in detail. Thus, Randy will be forced to choose between satisfying his boss and his client obligations.

The argument proceeds by

(A) providing one version of events and an alternative version of events where both exhibit an incompatibility among the factors involved

(B) explaining the inherent difficulties in a situation by using another situation with equivalent difficulties

(C) showing how one set of responsibilities with its own conditions that need satisfying is incompatible with another set of responsibilities and creates for the individual a conundrum

(D) exhibiting the struggles involved as one set of events creates another set of events that leaves the subject in a quandary

(E) delving into how one person's failure to act in a situation leads to a difficult conundrum and how the person's choices in that situation can lead to inevitable harm to the other parties involved

24. Bumblebees have been discovered to visit and pollinate red or striped snapdragons more often than white or pink flowers. Bumblebees are the most important pollinator of the snapdragon because the pollen carried by the bumblebee is necessary for the flower to open its petals. Thus, in order to increase the population of bumblebees, nurseries are being encouraged to grow more of the striped and darkly pigmented varieties of snapdragons.

Which of the following can be properly inferred from the passage?

(A) The bumblebee population is in danger from a lack of striped or darkly pigmented varieties of snapdragons.

(B) If there are not enough striped or darkly pigmented snapdragons, then all snapdragons will fail to open their petals.

(C) If there are more striped and darkly pigmented snapdragons, then other insects will be forced to open the petals of the white and pink varieties.

(D) The bumblebee population is smaller than desired, and more striped and darkly pigmented snapdragons will help increase their numbers.

(E) The red and striped varieties of snapdragons are endangered, and more bumblebees are needed to increase their numbers.

STOP

IF YOU FINISH BEFORE TIME RUNS OUT, CHECK YOUR WORK ON THIS SECTION ONLY. DO NOT GO ON TO ANY OTHER TEST SECTION.

Video solution available on the Practice Test App. (See pp. 7A–8A.)

SECTION III

Time—35 minutes
26 Questions

Directions: Each group of questions in this section is based on a set of conditions. In answering some of the questions, it may be useful to draw a rough diagram. Choose the response that most accurately and completely answers each question and blacken the corresponding space on your answer sheet.

Questions 1–6

A mechanic is considering using coils D, E, G, H, I, J, and K to replace old ones in a machine. The mechanic has devised a test to determine their quality, but the mechanic has only so much time to test the coils. Only those coils that are tested can be used in the machine. The selection process must meet the following requirements:

> If G is tested, I is tested.
> If E is tested, G is tested.
> D is tested.
> H is not used unless J is tested.
> D is not used unless H is tested.
> If J is used and I is tested, K is used.

1. Which of the following could be a complete and accurate list of the coils that are tested?

    (A) D, E, G
    (B) D, E, I
    (C) D, E
    (D) D, I
    (E) D, G

2. Which one of the following could be true?

    (A) E and three other coils are the only coils tested.
    (B) E and two other coils are the only coils tested.
    (C) E and one other coil are the only coils tested.
    (D) D, G, and H are the only coils tested.
    (E) I and J are the only coils tested.

3. If J is not tested, which one of the following must be true?

    (A) D is not used.
    (B) H is not tested.
    (C) D is tested but H is not used.
    (D) D is used but H is not used.
    (E) H is tested but not used.

4. If E and five other coils are the only coils tested, and if exactly three coils are used in the machine, then which one of the following could be an accurate list of the coils used?

    (A) D, I, J
    (B) D, H, J
    (C) E, G, I
    (D) H, I, K
    (E) E, G, J

5. If every coil that is tested is used, and if I is used, then each of the following coils must be tested EXCEPT:

    (A) K
    (B) H
    (C) J
    (D) D
    (E) G

6. If K is not used, and if exactly four coils are used, then which one of the following must be false?

    (A) I is used.
    (B) J is used.
    (C) G is tested.
    (D) H is tested.
    (E) E is tested.

 Video solution available on the Practice Test App. (See pp. 7A–8A.)

GO ON TO THE NEXT PAGE

Questions 7–13

Exactly seven children—Barry, Ezra, Jaime, Karly, Pakhi, Sharon, and Usef—go to a craft class at the same time. During class, they have a choice of three activities: ceramics, drawing, and origami. Each child participates in exactly one of the activities. The activities occur only once and one activity at a time. The following restrictions must apply:

> Exactly twice as many of the children choose drawing as choose ceramics.
> Sharon and Usef participate in the same activity as each other.
> Ezra and Karly do not participate in the same activity as each other.
> Barry and Pakhi do not participate in the same activity as each other.
> Barry participates in either ceramics or origami.
> Jaime participates in drawing.

7. Which of the following could be a correct matching of children to activities?

    (A) Karly-drawing; Pakhi-drawing; Usef-origami
    (B) Karly-origami; Pakhi-origami; Sharon-origami
    (C) Ezra-drawing; Pakhi-drawing; Sharon-ceramics
    (D) Barry-origami; Ezra-ceramics; Sharon-ceramics
    (E) Barry-drawing; Ezra-origami; Karly-drawing

8. Which one of the following could be a complete and accurate list of the children who do not choose drawing?

    (A) Barry, Ezra, Pakhi
    (B) Barry, Sharon, Usef
    (C) Barry, Karly, Usef
    (D) Barry, Karly
    (E) Barry, Pakhi

9. Each of the following must be false EXCEPT:

    (A) Exactly two children choose origami.
    (B) Usef is the only child to choose origami.
    (C) Exactly three children choose drawing.
    (D) Pakhi is the only child to choose drawing.
    (E) Pakhi is the only child to choose ceramics.

10. If exactly one of the children chooses origami, then which one of the following must be true?

    (A) Karly chooses ceramics.
    (B) Sharon chooses drawing.
    (C) Barry chooses ceramics.
    (D) Pakhi chooses drawing.
    (E) Ezra chooses ceramics.

11. If Sharon chooses the same activity as Barry does, then which of the following could be true?

    (A) Ezra chooses drawing.
    (B) Pakhi chooses origami.
    (C) Barry chooses ceramics.
    (D) Usef chooses ceramics.
    (E) Sharon chooses drawing.

12. Each of the following could be a complete and accurate list of the children who choose ceramics EXCEPT:

    (A) Barry, Karly
    (B) Karly, Pakhi
    (C) Ezra, Pakhi
    (D) Barry, Ezra
    (E) Sharon, Usef

13. Which one of the following must be true?

    (A) Ezra chooses a different activity than Sharon does.
    (B) Ezra, Jaime, and Sharon do not all choose the same activity.
    (C) Ezra chooses a different activity than Jaime does.
    (D) Barry, Jaime, and Karly do not all choose the same activity.
    (E) Barry chooses a different activity than Ezra does.

GO ON TO THE NEXT PAGE

Questions 14–20

Exactly seven cargo trucks—P, Q, R, T, U, W, and Z—are to be unloaded at seven warehouse docks, exactly one cargo truck to a dock. The seven docks are side by side and numbered consecutively 1 through 7. Assignment of cargo trucks to docks must meet the following conditions:

P is unloaded at a lower numbered dock than T.
W is unloaded at the dock numbered one lower than the dock at which Q is unloaded.
R is unloaded at dock 1 or else dock 7.
Z is unloaded at dock 4.

14. Which one of the following is an acceptable assignment of cargo trucks to warehouse docks, in order from dock 1 through dock 7?

(A) R, W, Q, Z, T, P, U
(B) R, U, Z, W, Q, P, T
(C) P, U, T, Z, W, Q, R
(D) P, W, U, Z, Q, T, R
(E) P, T, U, Z, R, W, Q

15. It must be true that the lowest numbered dock on which

(A) P can be unloaded is dock 2
(B) Q can be unloaded is dock 3
(C) T can be unloaded is dock 2
(D) U can be unloaded is dock 3
(E) W can be unloaded is dock 2

16. If U is unloaded on dock 5, which one of the following is a pair of trucks that could be unloaded, not necessarily in the order given, at docks whose numbers are consecutive to each other?

(A) R, T
(B) T, W
(C) W, Z
(D) Q, R
(E) Q, T

17. There can be at most how many docks between the dock at which P is unloaded and the dock at which T is unloaded?

(A) five
(B) four
(C) three
(D) two
(E) one

18. If U is unloaded at dock 2, which one of the following must be true?

(A) Z is unloaded at a lower numbered dock than T.
(B) W is unloaded at a lower numbered dock than T.
(C) T is unloaded at a lower numbered dock than R.
(D) P is unloaded at a lower numbered dock than Z.
(E) R is unloaded at a lower numbered dock than Q.

19. If Q is unloaded at a dock numbered one less than the dock at which P is unloaded, then which one of the following must be true?

(A) W is unloaded at dock 6.
(B) U is unloaded at dock 5.
(C) R is unloaded at dock 1.
(D) Q is unloaded at dock 5.
(E) P is unloaded at dock 3.

20. If W is unloaded at dock 1, which one of the following could be true?

(A) U is unloaded at a dock numbered one lower than the dock at which Q is unloaded.
(B) Q is unloaded at a dock numbered one lower than the dock at which U is unloaded.
(C) Q is unloaded at a dock numbered one lower than the dock at which T is unloaded.
(D) P is unloaded at a dock numbered one lower than the dock at which U is unloaded.
(E) P is unloaded at a dock numbered one lower than the dock at which R is unloaded.

GO ON TO THE NEXT PAGE

Questions 21–26

Of eight cargoes—L, N, O, P, R, S, T, and W—only six can be loaded on the three available trucks—Truck 1, Truck 2, and Truck 3. Each cargo must be loaded into one of two holds—front and back. The loads must be loaded in order, front first, then back, under the following conditions:

L can only go in Truck 2.
T and W cannot go in the back hold of a truck.
If S is loaded on a truck, then N and O go on the next truck, unless S is loaded on Truck 3.

21. Which one of the following could be the loading register for the cargo?

(A) Truck 1: Front, S; Back, N
    Truck 2: Front, W; Back, R
    Truck 3: Front, T; Back, R
(B) Truck 1: Front, N; Back, W
    Truck 2: Front, T; Back, O
    Truck 3: Front, R; Back, P
(C) Truck 1: Front, T; Back, S
    Truck 2: Front, O; Back, N
    Truck 3: Front, P; Back, L
(D) Truck 1: Front, R; Back, N
    Truck 2: Front, L; Back, P
    Truck 3: Front, W; Back, O
(E) Truck 1: Front, O; Back, T
    Truck 2: Front, N; Back, P
    Truck 3: Front, S; Back, R

22. If P and R are not loaded, then the front sections of Truck 1, Truck 2, and Truck 3 could carry the following cargo:

(A) T, W, and O
(B) O, W, and N
(C) W, L, and N
(D) N, L, and S
(E) S, N, and T

23. Which one of the following is a pair of cargoes, if loaded on the same truck, that must go on Truck 3?

(A) O and W
(B) L and R
(C) N and S
(D) T and P
(E) P and S

24. If L, S, and W are loaded in different trucks from each other, which one of the following could be true?

(A) T is on Truck 1.
(B) S is on Truck 2.
(C) N is on Truck 3.
(D) W is on Truck 3.
(E) S is on Truck 1.

25. If N, P, and R, not necessarily in that order, are loaded in the fronts of the three trucks, which of the following must be true.

(A) P is on Truck 3.
(B) O is on Truck 3.
(C) P is on Truck 2.
(D) N is on Truck 1.
(E) O is on Truck 1.

26. If P is on the back of Truck 2, and N is on the back of Truck 3, which one of the following could be the list of cargoes in the fronts of Truck 1, Truck 2, and Truck 3, respectively?

(A) W, O, and R
(B) W, L, and O
(C) R, L, and O
(D) O, R, and S
(E) S, O, and R

STOP

IF YOU FINISH BEFORE TIME RUNS OUT, CHECK YOUR WORK ON THIS SECTION ONLY. DO NOT GO ON TO ANY OTHER TEST SECTION.

SECTION IV

Time—35 minutes
25 Questions

Directions: Each passage in this section is followed by a group of questions to be answered on the basis of what is *stated* or *implied* in the passage. For some of the questions, more than one of the choices could conceivably answer the question. However, you are to choose the *best* answer; that is, the response that most accurately and completely answers the question, and blacken the corresponding space on your answer sheet.

American astronomer Edwin Hubble proved in the mid-twentieth century that galaxies were moving farther apart from each other and the form and function of that phenomenon has eluded scientists
(5) as they try to discover what forces are at work in an expanding universe. As recent as the 1990s, scientists believed gravity would prove stronger than whatever force was counteracting its influence and the expansion of the universe would eventually
(10) slow down and begin contracting. Only recently have scientists come to believe the universe is ever expanding, thanks to observations delivered by the Hubble telescope. The scientific community needed an explanation for such unfettered expan-
(15) sion and the prevailing hypothesis is the mysterious "dark energy," a force whose existence has yet to be observed. Scientists have established how much energy was necessary to bring about the rate of expansion both in the past and currently, but every-
(20) thing else about dark energy remains theoretical. According to their estimates, dark energy constitutes roughly 70 percent of the universe, for the first time putting matter and dark matter as minority players in the cosmological makeup of the universe.

(25) Several theories have emerged concerning the nature of dark energy in the universe. Albert Einstein's rejected theory of gravitation with the troublesome cosmological constant has led scientists to the theory that this constant constitutes
(30) the energy density of the vacuum of space. As the universe fills with more and more space, dark energy forces the universe to expand at an ever-increasing pace. Quantum theorists incorporated this theory into their models and hit a wall. Their

(35) calculations predicted a space with energy 10^{120} times what it should be, which led some scientists to suggest that a new theory of gravity was necessary. Such an undertaking would entail much more than explaining an expanding universe. The very
(40) basic things thought explained by previous theories would need to be revisited. However, many still think Einstein's theory holds promise once more observational evidence is brought to bear.

An approach being advanced is that of quintes-
(45) sence. The term *quintessence* derives from an ancient word referring to the "fifth element." Medieval scientists believed the universe consisted of four elements (earth, air, fire, and water) and a fifth one that caused the motion of the moon and planets.
(50) Those advancing the quintessence theory put forward that dark energy is a spatially inhomogeneous energy fluid or field with negative pressure. This fluid or field evolves with the growing universe and exerts increasingly expansionary forces. They
(55) envision dark energy flowing through space like a network of large rivers or seas of energy fields that fill space and exert the opposite effect of matter and normal energy.

Regardless of the theory, the previous conception
(60) of the universe as consisting mostly of matter like planets and stars is gone and the notion that gravity is the dominant force in the universe is no longer sustainable. Its replacement, dark energy, is still theoretical, but several space exploration vehicles
(65) have been proposed to measure and test it. They are expensive propositions, costing several billions of dollars, and recent budgetary issues may preclude such efforts.

GO ON TO THE NEXT PAGE

1. Which of the following best states the main idea of the passage?

    (A) The theoretical nature of dark energy and the exorbitant cost of space exploration mean that scientists will never understand what is causing an ever-expanding universe.

    (B) The disagreement between two opposing factions with irreconcilable theories on dark energy are hindering progress on understanding the ever-expanding universe.

    (C) While the universe's future, contraction or infinite expansion, remains unresolved, several theories concerning the force causing its expansion are fueling the current scientific discussion.

    (D) Since Einstein's theory of gravity has failed to deliver an explanation for dark energy, scientists have turned to the theory of quintessence because it lacks the burden of the cosmological constant.

    (E) Until scientists obtain observational evidence through experiments in space they are left with the theoretical concept of dark energy, which has fueled several hypotheses as to how it works.

2. The author of the passage mentions in the first paragraph that it was known how much energy was necessary to cause the past and current rate of expansion of the universe in order to

    (A) show that scientist do have some understanding of the larger universe even if they lack the specific understanding of what is causing it to expand

    (B) show that scientists remain in a theoretical quandary with regard to the nature of dark energy

    (C) prove that the universe is ever-expanding and will not contract as thought previously

    (D) explain the high level of uncertainty with scientists' theoretical models for explaining dark energy

    (E) give credence to the theory that dark energy constitutes the vast majority of the makeup of the universe

3. It can be inferred from the passage that which one of the following is true of quintessence?

    (A) It proves that Einstein's theory of gravity is flawed and needs to be replaced with a new one.

    (B) Observational evidence is unnecessary because its equations do not include the troublesome cosmological constant that burdened Einstein's theory of gravity.

    (C) Dark energy is not inherent in space itself and not consistently present throughout the universe.

    (D) Quantum theorists do not have the same problem of finding too much energy as they did with Einstein's equations.

    (E) Dark energy replaces gravity and explains all forces, both attractive and expansionary.

4. The attitude of the author towards proposals to measure dark energy can best be described as

    (A) unbiased consideration
    (B) repressed incredulity
    (C) guarded pessimism
    (D) grounded optimism
    (E) uncommitted ambivalence

5. According to the passage, all of the following are theoretically possible characteristics of dark energy EXCEPT:

    (A) It is a naturally occurring phenomenon of space itself.
    (B) It is increasing with the expansion of the universe.
    (C) It supplants gravity as the dominant force in the universe.
    (D) Evolving rivers of it flow through space.
    (E) It will eventually give way to gravity and the universe will contract.

GO ON TO THE NEXT PAGE

6. Which of the following, if true, would lend the greatest support to the theory of quintessence?

(A) A previously unobserved type of subatomic particle that exerts positive pressure on matter is discovered.

(B) Through high-precision measurements of the expansion of the universe, a scalar field is observed whose energy density has varied over time.

(C) Scientists reveal that some of the most distant Type 1a supernovae appear to be accelerating because of the way intervening dust scatters their light, but they are actually closer than previously believed.

(D) A respected astronomer confirms the existence of a cosmological constant.

(E) A newer telescope, with farther range than the Hubble telescope, confirms that the universe is expanding and that its expansion is accelerating.

PASSAGE A

During the Great Depression, a host of theater groups sprouted up with the desire to bring "serious theater" to Broadway and beyond. Some believed their plays should bring real life into the theater
(5) and portray all of human existence, including the suffering and angst. One of the best examples of this school of thought was the Group Theatre, founded in 1931 by Harold Clurman, Lee Strasburg, and Cheryl Crawford.
(10)   While many of these new theater groups radically departed from theatrical norms, including the hiring of nonprofessional actors and staging plays in untraditional venues, the Group Theatre's productions tended to be more conventional. Performances
(15) were restricted to the traditional theater houses, and characters in the plays had working-class names like "Joe," "Edna," and "Frank." One of the Group Theatre's guiding principles was a devotion to Strasburg's unique version of Stanislavski's "The
(20) Method," more commonly known as method acting. Cast members of the Group Theatre presented themselves as a collection of serious professional actors interested in the best possible performance.
    Despite this adherence to theatrical convention,
(25) one of the Group Theatre's hallmark productions, *Waiting for Lefty* by Clifford Odets, exhibited much of the strident political language of what would come to be known as agit-prop theater. While the Group Theatre did not adhere to all the principles
(30) of agit-prop, this particular production concluded with many of the actors standing in the audience, yelling "Strike! Strike! Strike!" in a not-so-subtle call to action. While agit-prop theater would fade with the Depression, the Group Theatre's devotion to the
(35) principles of method acting transformed Broadway's theatrical landscape, creating a template that serious actors still adhere to today.

PASSAGE B

The Great Depression of the 1930s not only brought about significant social and economic upheaval in the United States, it also helped transform the American theater from mere entertainment to a
(5) form of social activism. Many theatrical groups, including the Group Theatre and the Worker's Theater, set about creating realistic depictions of this economic turmoil. But other theater groups wanted to move beyond merely presenting soci-
(10) etal ills. They wanted to bring about actual social change. One example of this type, sometimes called agit-prop theater, was the Shock Troupe.
    The Shock Troupe tended to perform plays with generically named characters, thus allowing the
(15) characters to become symbolic representations of a particular segment of society. In its most popular play, *Newsboy*, some of the characters' names were "Black Man," "Unemployed Man," and "Kindly

Old Lady." The actors themselves were, for the
(20) most part, untrained amateurs, and the plays were
performed in whatever way best instigated people to
take action. As with most agit-prop theater groups,
the Shock Troupe even performed its works outside
the environment of an actual theatre, for instance,
(25) performing *Newsboy* in front of the picket lines of
striking workers to inspire them to continue their
efforts to organize and fight for better working
conditions.

Eventually, the Shock Troupe discovered that in
(30) order to present their ideas more effectively to audiences, it needed a stronger artistic sensibility and
better actors, turning to acting teacher and Group
Theatre founder Lee Strasburg to provide this
training. Despite this movement towards increased
(35) professionalism, however, the Shock Troupe
remained a potent force for social change through
much of the Great Depression.

7. Which of the following best describes
the relationship between passage A
and passage B?

(A) Passage A and passage B both
present similar solutions to the same
problem.
(B) Passage A presents a problem and passage
B presents a solution to that problem.
(C) Passage B explicitly contradicts a set of implicit
assumptions made by the author of passage A.
(D) Passage A and passage B both describe
similar movements arising from the same
circumstances.
(E) Passage B discusses a refinement of an idea
that passage A presents as a broad outline.

8. According to Passage A, which of the
following is true of theater after the
end of the Depression?

(A) The advent of agit-prop theatre
was a wholly new concept of political
theatre intended to provoke its audience to
take action.
(B) The political ideas advocated by plays such
as the push for organized labor was the
result of people like Lee Strasburg importing
ideas from Russians like Stanislavski.
(C) The technique of method acting continued
beyond the use of agit-prop theater.
(D) Audiences lost interest in "serious drama"
after the end of the Depression.
(E) Playwrights and actors resented the
political nature of the plays and, when
the Depression ended, forced the theater
managers to go back to the pre-Depression
types of theater.

9. Each of the following is mentioned as being a
point of difference between the Group Theatre
and the Shock Troupe EXCEPT

(A) the use of untrained actors
(B) the depiction of societal ills
(C) the physical location in which the play is
staged
(D) the names of the characters in the plays
(E) the avocation of societal change

10. According to passage B, the Shock
Troupe would least likely perform a
play that includes which the following:

(A) a staged argument between
"Freed-Slave Man" and "White Slave
Owner" about the lingering effects of
slavery and racism in America
(B) a public re-enactment of the workers
walking off the production line at a local
car manufacturing plant in protest of poor
working conditions
(C) a dramatic argument between Jack, an
unemployed ironworker, and his wife,
Mary, about her long hours working as an
assistant to a corporate executive, who Jack
believes has romantic intentions toward
her
(D) an unemployed man sells his last
belongings to a bartender in exchange for
a place to sleep in a storeroom and then
giving a speech about how the American
free market system stripped him of his
dignity
(E) an impromptu performance before a
miners' union meeting that through
dramatic effect calls on workers to rise
up and speak out about low wages and
dangerous working conditions

GO ON TO THE NEXT PAGE

Video solution available on the Practice Test App. (See pp. 7A–8A.)

11. Which of the following would the author of passage B most likely believe about the Group Theatre as it is described in passage A?

   (A) The Group Theatre's use of trained professional actors allowed it to better to connect with audiences.
   (B) The Group Theatre was better known than the Shock Troupe with theater audiences of the 1930s.
   (C) Actors working with the Shock Troupe were less idealistic than the actors associated with the Group Theatre.
   (D) The Group Theatre's production of *Waiting for Lefty* was ultimately more popular with contemporary audiences than the Shock Troupe's production of *Newsboy*.
   (E) "The Method," as employed by actors in the Group Theatre, is the most effective means of teaching acting.

12. Which of the following is the meaning of the term "agit-prop" as implied by the context of both passages?

   (A) Agriculture-Proposition
   (B) Agitation-Proposal
   (C) Agitation-Propaganda
   (D) Agitation-Propagation
   (E) Agitation-Proper

Politicians, social scientists, and economists are constantly arguing about the merits of the welfare state and its role in a democratic society. In the United States, programs such as public education,
(5) social security, and welfare have all come under fire. Critics say these programs create a culture of dependency. Others say that they are too costly and the taxation required to fund them slows economic growth. Then there are those who say that such
(10) programs are too intrusive by the government or that the welfare state is a wealth transfer mechanism that reduces the dynamism of a competitive society. On the other side of the issue are those who say that an advanced society should have compas-
(15) sion for its less fortunate citizens and that welfare programs elevate the poor to a level where they can still participate in democracy, thus preventing a plutocracy. Very few of these critics or advocates address a simpler concept—whether the participants
(20) are happier under a welfare state or a state that institutes aspects of a welfare state.

One may quibble over whether happiness is truly measurable or even whether it should be the goal of any government or political system. Bo Rothstein, a
(25) prominent Swedish political scientist and professor, in his essay *Happiness and the Welfare State*, argues that happiness is just as valid as any other basis to judge a government's success or failure. He uses a measurement called "subjective well-being" (SWB)
(30) as the basis for his assessments and applies it to northern European nations, including his own. Of course, Rothstein cannot help but reveal his bias in favor of the welfare state. He says that data reveal that people have a higher SWB under a welfare state,
(35) more specifically a universal welfare state, especially one that has a well-established program with a high level of social trust and a low degree of corruption. He even goes as far as to say that the data prove that the more comprehensive the welfare state, the
(40) happier its citizens are.

Rothstein bases his essay on several studies, including Alexander Pacek and Benjamin Radcliff's *Assessing the Welfare State: The Politics of Happiness*, which he says uses "high quality data" in analyzing
(45) eighteen OECD countries. These studies also base their work on the SWB as well as other data, but the SWB is the most controversial basis of these studies. Rothstein writes that happiness is a way to judge a society since it uses a more widespread arbiter as
(50) opposed to a more elitist arbiter such as political scientists or public policy experts, who might judge using more conceptual criteria. But even Rothstein admits there are other aspects of a society than its political system that determine happiness, such as
(55) culture and even geographical features. Rothstein argues that the quality of the analysis in studies that take into account these factors crowds out those concerns.

GO ON TO THE NEXT PAGE

So, where do Rothstein's arguments leave the
(60) discussion with regard to the welfare programs
in the United States? The United States is a more
diverse and thus more complex society than the
northern European nations that Rothstein holds
up as the hallmark of welfare state happiness. Still,
reviewing his conclusions as well as the studies he
(65) bases his arguments on can have pedagogical value
as politicians take on budgetary issues relating to
welfare programs in the future.

13. Which one of the following best states the main
point of the passage?

(A) People are happier under a universal
welfare state than under a partial welfare
state and thus the United States as a partial
welfare state will have difficulty making its
people happy.

(B) People are happier under a universal
welfare state but happiness is a poor basis
for judging a society and thus the recent
studies on the relationship between the
welfare state and happiness are flawed.

(C) While the United States is engaged in a
battle between those for or against welfare
programs, the rest of the world has forged
ahead at establishing welfare states that
have achieved a high level of societal
happiness.

(D) While politicians, social scientists, and
economists argue about the welfare
state using arguments unsupported by
data, Rothstein, Pacek, and Radcliff offer
unique support for it through analysis of
well-researched data.

(E) Happiness as a basis for analyzing the
success of a political state is valid but the
SWB measurement is flawed. Only through
improved data collection and a more
accurate happiness index can study of the
welfare state be accepted by the thinkers of
today.

14. Which of the following best describes the
organization of the passage?

(A) A social issue is discussed. An alternative
method of viewing that issue is discussed.
The alternative method is assessed. The
social issue is discussed in relation to the
alternative method.

(B) A social problem is presented. An approach
to solving the problem is discussed. The
approach is evaluated. The approach is
discussed in relation to one specific nation
that is experiencing the social problem.

(C) Alternative views of a social problem
are presented. An approach to resolving
the problem is presented. A critique is
presented that discredits that approach. A
particular case study is given to show that
the approach is not feasible.

(D) A social problem is analyzed. A solution to
the problem is proposed. The strengths and
weaknesses of the solution are discussed.
The practical difficulties of delivering the
solution are presented.

(E) A social problem is discussed. A unique
approach to the problem is discussed.
The validity of the approach's underlying
assumption is discussed. A particular case
is discussed in relation to the approach.

15. The author of the passage refers to Rothstein's
bias in line 32 because

(A) Rothstein is a well-known and outspoken
advocate for social welfare programs

(B) Rothstein was an unnamed author of the
study with Pacek and Radcliff and thus has
a vested interest in bringing attention to
their ideas

(C) Rothstein lives in a northern European
country that happens to be a long-standing
universal welfare state

(D) Rothstein invented the SWB measurement
and wants it to be used in future studies

(E) Rothstein is currently running for political
office in his country and retaining the
welfare state is his central reason for
running

GO ON TO THE NEXT PAGE

16. Which of the following statements most undermines Rothstein's argument regarding the "arbiter" in lines 48 to 52?

(A) Political scientists and public policy experts experience happiness and unhappiness due to social welfare programs just as much as anyone, so their criteria are not much different from those of the widespread public.

(B) Happiness or unhappiness is influenced by factors outside the political spectrum such as the availability of companionship, community support, and social opportunities, while the experts filter out those issues and focus on the specific problems.

(C) Political scientists and public policy experts tend to see problems from a more theoretical perspective and don't see the very basic elements that might affect whether a social welfare state is successful or not.

(D) The widespread public tends to be swayed by waves of economic ups and downs that affect happiness while the political scientists and public policy experts are all wealthy individuals who are unaffected by economic changes.

(E) The SWB measurement has been found to be very accurate in predicting the success of welfare programs, while simulation models created by political scientists and public policy experts have rarely been successful at making such predictions.

17. Based on the first paragraph of the passage, which of the following, if true, would support an argument made by advocates for a more universal welfare program in the United States?

(A) The results of a study show that unemployment benefits reduce the number of applicants for jobs.

(B) A survey of welfare recipients shows that a large majority save the money and do not spend it.

(C) Research determines that the number of registered voters increased significantly during the 10 years after certain welfare programs were instituted.

(D) A survey of welfare program participants revealed that a large percentage expressed substantial resentment toward the government.

(E) The results of a study show that a large portion of the population is happier due to the existence of welfare programs.

18. Which of the following best describes the author's attitude toward Rothstein's approach to happiness and the welfare state?

(A) cautious neutrality
(B) strong condemnation
(C) moderate advocacy
(D) moderate skepticism
(E) grudging acceptance

19. Which of these claims would Rothstein be least likely to accept?

(A) The ability of its people to retain family ties and establish new ones is a factor that might cloud the relationship between SWB and the establishment of a universal welfare state.

(B) The addition of a program to protect children from the effects of poverty will make a nation's people happier.

(C) Northern European states have a higher SWB than the United States and other states with nonuniversal welfare programs.

(D) A long-standing program that all people of the nation have come to depend on and know will be there when they need it will increase the SWB for that nation.

(E) The discovery that a large portion of welfare program funds was misappropriated to a politician's pet project proves that the welfare state is a failure.

GO ON TO THE NEXT PAGE

Corporations spend billions of dollars on philanthropic causes and participate in philanthropic activities. It is well known that corporations give large donations to charities, but recently there has
(5) been an increase in a different kind of philanthropic effort, one that is less obvious and where the lines between philanthropic and profit-making activities are less clear. Corporations integrate their philanthropic activities into their supply, production, and
(10) sales operations such that they become part and parcel with their corporate and product identity, but the financial equation is no different from that of simple donations.

Many companies are actively engaged in
(15) sourcing all their raw materials using fair trade principles. The most active companies pursuing fair trade suppliers are those in the coffee and cocoa industries, but other industries such as clothing and cosmetics have moved in this direction as well. Some
(20) companies are pursuing production processes that have a low impact on the environment. A company may develop processes that reduce the amount of energy and material utilized in production and also take the waste and reuse it in its other products, or
(25) it may sell the waste products to others to be made part of a home's insulation or for other products. Finally, there are ways that marketing and sales integrate philanthropy, whether the company uses environmentally friendly packaging or a portion of
(30) sales flows through to a particular charity.

These philanthropic practices are not much different from a company simply cutting a check to a charity and publicizing it. All corporate philanthropic activities, direct or indirect, decrease
(35) profitability and shareholder value. Usually, the companies most actively involved in the above-mentioned practices are ones that can handle the higher cost and, of course, pass that cost on to their customers through premium prices, thus transfer-
(40) ring the "good deed" to someone else. In effect, the customer is extorted into paying at least part of a philanthropic contribution. If the customer could get that money back he or she might choose to donate it to a charity and use that contribution as
(45) a deduction on his or her taxes. With the corporate philanthropy model, such choice and benefits are not possible.

There is also the question of why these companies are involved in philanthropy in the first place.
(50) Many suspect that corporations are philanthropic as a marketing tactic to make the company look good to the customers, shareholders, and employees of the company. Another objection has been that the managers of corporations are possibly
(55) using other people's money to fund their own pet charity projects and marketing them as a benefit of the company. Whether or not these motives are true, the company is still doing good things. Then, there is the moral argument. Since business
(60) school academics and other scholars argue that a corporation is considered the equivalent of an individual in society, a corporation's behavior should be judged as an individual's would. Thus, a corporation may be obligated as a member of a compassionate
(65) society to at least consider participating in philanthropy in whatever forms it chooses to take.

20. Which one of the following most accurately expresses the main idea of the passage?

(A) Corporations have found a way to integrate philanthropy into their operations and sales to avoid the stigma associated with cash donations, which are seen as cheap marketing tactics. Why they participate in philanthropy is a more complicated question.

(B) Corporations are increasingly integrating philanthropy into their operations, but the financial effect on customers, shareholders, and employees is no different from a corporation making a cash donation to a charity. Why corporations do it is a more complicated question.

(C) Regardless of how corporations' actions are perceived, as an integral part of society corporations have a moral obligation to not only make charitable donations but also to integrate philanthropic values into their operations.

(D) Integrating philanthropic activities into the company's operations is the equivalent of extortion, forcing customers to participate in an unwanted philanthropic effort. Companies would do better to just make a charitable donation. Why they participate in philanthropy is a more complicated question.

(E) Corporations are increasing their commitment to philanthropy. As a result, they find themselves in more complicated relationships with their customers, shareholders, and employees. Why corporations participate in philanthropy in the first place is a more complicated question.

GO ON TO THE NEXT PAGE

21. Which one of the following most accurately describes the author's attitude toward the corporate philanthropy model discussed in lines 8–13?

    (A) confident that it offers corporations a new and better way to be philanthropic without negatively affecting profits and shareholder value

    (B) certain that it will give customers more power over their relationship to the philanthropic transaction implied by the purchase of the company's products

    (C) convinced that it offers little new in the way of a financial equation or explanation for corporate philanthropic efforts

    (D) satisfied that it comes up short at doing much better than individuals could if they had control of the funds directed to philanthropic causes

    (E) pleased that corporations have found a more creative way to commit financial resources to philanthropic causes than just cutting a check

22. Which one of the following sentences would most logically begin a paragraph immediately following the end of the passage?

    (A) Logically, we must move on to discuss how a company that is committed to philanthropy can truly know that its suppliers are abiding by the fair trade rules and whether its production processes actually create more waste rather than eliminate it.

    (B) Thus, the question becomes, are the billions of dollars sent from companies toward public good worth it, and if so, which philanthropic model is more effective at allowing a company to maximize the benefit from that contribution?

    (C) It is impossible to know why a corporation engages in philanthropy because corporations are more complex than individuals. Instead, the question to ask is whether the government should stop corporations from participating in this unprofitable activity and leave philanthropy to individuals.

    (D) Therefore, corporations should be limited to the philanthropic model that involves donating cash and not the one that hides the donation within the cost of goods sold and results in inflating the price the consumer pays.

    (E) In an effort to understand why corporations engage in philanthropy, we must survey the guidelines for morals and ethics established by corporations as guiding principles for employees. After all, a corporation is just the sum of its employees.

GO ON TO THE NEXT PAGE

23. The relationship between the descriptions of how corporations integrate philanthropic contributions in the first and third paragraphs can most accurately be described as

    (A) no significant relationship because they represent two unrelated factual statements
    (B) the author's opinion agreeing with another opinion reported by the author in the earlier lines
    (C) a hypothetical situation clarifying a statement reported by the author in the earlier lines
    (D) agreement in general with the earlier position but disagreement over the particulars
    (E) essentially equivalent assertions with the latter being an explicit clarification of the earlier lines

24. It can be inferred from the passage that the author holds that a corporation that engages in philanthropy should

    (A) inform the customer that all funds are tax deductible
    (B) allow customers to opt out of paying the portion of the price that goes toward philanthropic causes
    (C) inform its customers, employees, and shareholders that price, profit, and shareholder value will be affected by its philanthropy
    (D) educate the public on the corporate misuse of philanthropic funds
    (E) establish a moral code and publish it for its customers, employees, and shareholders to see

25. According to the passage, which of the following is NOT a way in which companies are reducing their impact on the environment?

    (A) They may sell waste to other companies for alternative uses.
    (B) They may implement strategies to lessen energy expenditures.
    (C) They may utilize their wasted material in other products made by the company.
    (D) They may employ alternative work schedules to maximize efficiency.
    (E) They may decrease the quantity of certain components used in production.

STOP

IF YOU FINISH BEFORE TIME RUNS OUT, CHECK YOUR WORK ON THIS SECTION ONLY. DO NOT WORK ON ANY OTHER TEST SECTION.

LSAT Diagnostic Test Answer Key

Section I	Section II	Section III	Section IV
1. D	1. D	1. D	1. E
2. D	2. C	2. A	2. A
3. A	3. A	3. C	3. C
4. D	4. E	4. C	4. B
5. E	5. C	5. E	5. E
6. A	6. A	6. B	6. B
7. B	7. D	7. B	7. D
8. C	8. C	8. A	8. C
9. B	9. D	9. E	9. B
10. E	10. D	10. B	10. C
11. C	11. D	11. A	11. A
12. B	12. B	12. E	12. C
13. A	13. D	13. D	13. B
14. B	14. D	14. C	14. E
15. C	15. A	15. C	15. C
16. B	16. B	16. A	16. B
17. C	17. A	17. B	17. C
18. D	18. E	18. D	18. D
19. A	19. A	19. E	19. E
20. D	20. C	20. B	20. B
21. A	21. B	21. D	21. C
22. B	22. C	22. A	22. B
23. D	23. C	23. C	23. E
24. D	24. D	24. C	24. C
25. E		25. E	25. D
26. A		26. B	

Calculate Your Score

Complete the following table.

Your Raw Score

SECTION	TYPE	NUMBER OF QUESTIONS	NUMBER CORRECT
1	Arguments	26	_____
2	Arguments	24	_____
3	Logic Games	26	_____
4	Reading Comprehension	25	_____

Total Raw Score _____

Your Approximate Scaled Score

It is impossible to say with complete precision what raw score will translate to what scaled score on future LSATs, but here is a rough estimation.

NUMBER OF QUESTIONS MISSED	APPROXIMATE SCALED SCORE
3	~180
8	~175
15	~170
20	~165
25	~160
25–35	between 155–160
35–45	between 150–155
45–55	between 145–150
55–60	between 140–145
60–70	between 135–140
70–80	between 125–135
More than 80	120–125

LSAT Diagnostic Test Answers and Explanations

SECTION I

1. Answer: D

STEP 1: **Read the question and identify your task.**

This is a Flaw question. You are looking for a flaw in the argument or something illogical in the argument that calls into question its conclusion.

STEP 2: **Read the argument with your task in mind.**

The argument makes an unqualified leap in logic. Instead of attributing the civic disorder to David Ellington, it says that the city council intended to undermine civic order by hiring the incompetent Ellington.

STEP 3: **Know what you're looking for.**

The correct answer will point out that flawed logic.

STEP 4: **Read every word of every answer choice.**

When you read each answer closely, certain words help you eliminate answers. Answer A does not resemble what you are looking for at all. It focuses on "quantitative" results versus "qualitative" results, but the argument does not include any quantitative results, so it cannot be the correct answer. Answer B also does not work. Yes, the conclusion is fairly general, but the descriptor "anomalous" is inaccurate. Answer C describes Ellington's incompetence as "perceived," but specific results are discussed, and it does not address the argument's conclusion. Answer D says the flaw is the assumption that an action leads to a result (hiring of Ellington leads to civic disorder), and that the action was taken to bring about that result (hiring Ellington was intended to bring about the civic disorder). This fits your understanding of the flaw perfectly and would seem to be the right answer. Before you make a decision, you must finish reviewing all the answers. Answer E says the flaw is a "restatement," but no part of the argument serves as a restatement, so this cannot be the correct answer. **The correct choice is answer D.**

2. Answer: D

STEP 1: **Read the question and identify your task.**

This is a Parallel question. The question asks that you match the reasoning in the answer to the one in the statement, so you are looking for a similar pattern of thinking between the two.

STEP 2: **Read the argument with your task in mind.**

The argument tells of a maintenance man who makes an exception based on a judgment that a police officer, due to his special skills, can protect himself.

STEP 3: **Know what you're looking for.**

The correct answer will include a judgment and an exception to that judgment that matches the kind made in the argument.

STEP 4: **Read every word of every answer choice.**

In answer A the deliveryman makes a judgment to organize his deliveries, but he makes no exceptions, so this does not resemble your pattern of thinking and is not the correct answer. Answers B and C both fail your test because both the candidate and jury make a judgment regarding certain areas or one person to the exclusion of all others, not the other way around as your maintenance man does. In answer D the captain of the yacht judges that the US naval officer has special skills that enable him or her to handle an emergency situation, so the captain excludes the officer from the training. This resembles your required pattern of thinking and is most likely the correct answer, but you must complete your review of the answers. Answer E says the manager makes no exceptions at all, forcing everyone to participate, and this does not fit your pattern, so **the correct choice is answer D.**

3. Answer: A

STEP 1: **Read the question and identify your task.**

This is a Describe question. It asks you to describe the error in both Larry and Carrie's reasoning.

STEP 2: Read the argument with your task in mind.

Larry and Carrie discuss the relationship between positive results and how this quality determines whether the law is bad or good. Larry and Carrie incorrectly assume that because a law has positive results it is a good law, and therefore, because a law shows positive results, such evidence is sufficient to consider it a good law.

STEP 3: Know what you're looking for.

The correct answer will identify the shared weakness in the exchange between Larry and Carrie. Pay close attention to the words in the argument—what is *considered* good or bad by the citizenry versus what *is* good or bad. In order for both their arguments to hold up, they have to presuppose that a law is good if it has positive results and vice versa.

STEP 4: Read every word of every answer choice.

Answer A describes Larry and Carrie's assumption almost exactly, that a law having a certain quality (positive results) is necessary for it to be a particular type (good or bad) of law and that having that quality is sufficient for being that type of law. But, let's review the remainder of the answers to make sure, paying close attention to specific words. The quality is a determinant of the type of law, not a "shared" attribute and they never say the quality is the "only" quality distinguishing between the two types of laws, so answer B is incorrect. Their reasoning includes no extrapolation from "most" laws to "all" laws, so answer C is incorrect. Answer D is incorrect because Larry and Carrie make no comparison between a "particular nation" and "all nations." Finally, answer E is incorrect because they do not extrapolate one distinguishing quality to mean anything with regard to other qualities of the laws. **The correct choice is answer A.**

4. Answer: **D**

STEP 1: Read the question and identify your task.

This is a Weaken question. It tells you that you must pay close attention to the bases for the argument and discover how a counterargument might weaken it.

STEP 2: Read the argument with your task in mind.

This is an anthropological argument saying that there is a new belief that the "white revolution" occurred due to one society conquering another in a "violent and transformative" manner, while it was previously thought to be a more peaceful process.

STEP 3: Know what you're looking for.

A weakening statement would contradict or discredit this argument, proving that in fact it was as previously thought, not violent but a peaceful transition to a milk-based society.

STEP 4: Read every word of every answer choice.

Answer A talks specifically of northern Europe and not the wider continent. Also, milk may have still been part of the Middle Eastern diet even if someone else raised the cows. But more importantly, the transition in Europe still could have been violent. For answer B, just because the Europeans drank milk before the Middle Easterners arrived does not mean that their society did not go through the later violent conversion mentioned in the argument, so this answer fails to weaken the argument. Answer C actually strengthens the argument, proving that violence occurred at the time, and you are looking for a statement that weakens the argument. Answer D says that the Middle Easterners had settlements next to the hunter-gatherers, and they engaged in peaceful trade. Such coexistence and peaceful trade definitely weakens the argument that the transition was violent and transformative. And finally, the evidence of "sexual intermingling" mentioned in answer E does not rule out the possibility that the hunter-gatherer society went through the cataclysmic conversion, so **the correct choice is answer D.**

5. Answer: **E**

STEP 1: Read the question and identify your task.

This is a Deduction question. You are looking for a statement that must be true based on the statements in the argument.

STEP 2: Read the argument with your task in mind.

The argument bases its conclusion on a trend over six years during which there was a rise in young people entering the workforce at the same time there was a rise in percentage of young people graduating from high school. It uses this basis to state that increasing graduates will increase employment of young people.

<u>STEP 3:</u> **Know what you're looking for.**
Keep these statements in mind when you read through the answers.

<u>STEP 4:</u> **Read every word of every answer choice.**
Answer A discusses only completion of years in college, while the argument discusses graduation and dropout rates. Since it is dealing with different terms altogether, it cannot be the right answer. Answer B says there was also a rise in percentage of high school dropouts hired between 2000 and 2006, indicating that the rise in employment benefited all young people, graduates and nongraduates. This weakens the correlation between graduation and employment and thus weakens the reverse correlation between employment and graduation. Answer C speaks to the jobs and their difficulty, but says nothing about the relationship between graduate or nongraduate status and employment. Also, it is possible that the jobs are too complicated for graduates as well. You would not know because the statement doesn't say anything about that. Answer D tries to confuse you by using the term "number" versus "percentage," and even though a larger number of dropouts were hired, this cannot be concluded. Answer E is entirely consistent with the argument and must be true. **The correct choice is answer E.**

6. Answer: **A**

<u>STEP 1:</u> **Read the question and identify your task.**
This is a Strengthen question. You need to find a statement that strengthens the speaker's statement.

<u>STEP 2:</u> **Read the argument with your task in mind.**
The speaker talks about how corporations can use public relations to gloss over any malfeasance on their part and ultimately get away with anything as long as they wait out the "short attention span of the public."

<u>STEP 3:</u> **Know what you're looking for.**
The correct answer will provide a statement that supports this idea.

<u>STEP 4:</u> **Read every word of every answer choice.**
Answer A strengthens the argument, saying that a company can become too big to fail despite any socially irresponsible actions. Answer B essentially

undermines the argument, and it speaks in past tense and does not address what the case might be in the future. Answer C also restates the argument, but with the caveat of faster and slower growth among the corporations. Answer D adds government institutions to the argument, which does not weaken it. Answer E says that public relations are often seen through by the public and fail to mask a corporation's irresponsible actions. This weakens the argument. **The correct choice is answer A.**

7. Answer: **B**

<u>STEP 1:</u> **Read the question and identify your task.**
This is a variation of a Describe question—a Describe How the Argument Proceeds question. It asks you to find the answer that describes how the argument "proceeds," that is, how it comes to its conclusion.

<u>STEP 2:</u> **Read the argument with your task in mind.**
Based on the experience of "a number" of amateur photographers with a particular camera, the argument urges "any" (= all) such photographers to choose that camera.

<u>STEP 3:</u> **Know what you're looking for.**
The correct answer will describe how the argument applied the assertions of a small group (the amateur photographers with the Apheron camera) to make a suggestion to a larger group (all amateur photographers).

<u>STEP 4:</u> **Read every word of every answer choice.**
Answer A talks about testing conditions, while the argument makes no mention of testing conditions, so it is off the mark. Answer B says that the argument uses a subset to make a recommendation for a larger group, and this meets your criteria. The amateur photographers are the subset and the "any" photographers are your larger group. With answer C the credibility of the amateur photographers is accepted as a given and is not part of the argument. For answer D, the motivations for buying the camera are never discussed in the argument. The experience of the smaller group of photographers is not given any wider context. It is only used to recommend the camera to a larger group, so answer E is incorrect. **The correct choice is answer B.**

8. Answer: **C**

STEP 1: **Read the question and identify your task.**
This is a Flaw question. You are asked to find the main error in the author's reasoning.

STEP 2: **Read the argument with your task in mind.**
Look back at the basis for the camera recommendation, in this case that the camera offers finer detail despite its having a lower resolution than the other competing Norwich cameras.

STEP 3: **Know what you're looking for.**
The correct answer will identify the flaw the author made when drawing his or her conclusion.

STEP 4: **Read every word of every answer choice.**
With answer A the makeup of the lens does not change the results discussed in the argument, so this is not relevant. Answer B is not much different from answer A, except with regard to sensor size instead of lens substance. For answer C, the criterion under which the argument makes its recommendation is the finer detail the camera is able to achieve in both bright and low light situations. If other criteria exist for amateur photographers when considering a camera, then the argument is most definitely flawed and this would seem to be your correct answer. Answer D describes conditions under which the testing results seem more credible, which would strengthen the argument. Answer E is not relevant. **The correct choice is answer C.**

9. Answer: **B**

STEP 1: **Read the question and identify your task.**
This is an Assumption question. The question asks that you identify an assumption that justifies the conclusion of the argument.

STEP 2: **Read the argument with your task in mind.**
The argument states that as a percentage of tax revenues, the cost of maintaining the national parks is half today what it was 50 years ago. It tells you that tax revenues rose after the last 50 years and then concludes that tax revenues rose at a greater rate than the cost of maintaining the parks. The argument moves from rate of growth to actual growth and back to rate of growth. If actual tax revenues grew, the only way that the rate of growth of tax revenues could be higher than the rate of growth of maintenance costs would be if

the actual costs of park maintenance increased very little or not at all.

STEP 3: **Know what you're looking for.**
You would expect the correct answer to be along this line of thinking.

STEP 4: **Read every word of every answer choice.**
Answer A states that the parks are in better condition and less costly to maintain today than they were 50 years ago. Nothing in the argument suggests that the costs of maintenance have decreased. It says only that the percentage of revenues has decreased. Also, the conclusion suggests an increasing growth rate of both maintenance cost and tax revenues, so your assumption should suggest something to do with growth, not reduction. Answer B is similar to your expected answer. It suggests that the parks require the same maintenance today as 50 years ago. This might very well be your answer, but you must review the remaining options. Answer C is completely irrelevant since the maintenance of federal buildings is not even part of the argument. Answer D tries to confuse you by focusing on another type of rate, breaking down the cost to "per square mile" of the national parks, but the argument is concerned only with the total national expenditures on national parks. It is possible that the cost per square mile remained identical while the total area of national parks decreased or increased (no telling by how much). Answer E is similar to answer C, focusing on an irrelevant fact, the cost of maintaining "other federal properties." **The correct choice is answer B.**

10. Answer: **E**

STEP 1: **Read the question and identify your task.**
This is a Parallel question. It asks you to find an argument that follows the same logical pattern.

STEP 2: **Read the argument with your task in mind.**
The given argument says that because there is a directly proportional relationship between a higher use of water and a higher heat index (increase leads to increase), then because the average heat index is four points higher, more water will be used.

STEP 3: **Know what you're looking for.**
You must look for a similar relationship in the answers.

STEP 4: **Read every word of every answer choice.**

Answer A creates two proportionalities (doctors to services, doctors to patients) in relation to the first statement (doctors). Then it tries to create a relationship between the two conditionals (services to patients). This is a much more complicated relationship than you are looking for and thus not your answer. Answer B starts out with the right kind of proportionality between two terms (doctors and nurses), but then it adds an unrelated statement about orderlies and draws an unsupportable relationship between the doctors and orderlies, so it is also not your answer. Answer C starts out well with a directly proportional relationship, higher bill to higher number of medical professionals seen, but the conclusion is based on the number of patients and not the number of medical professionals the patients see during their visit, which is a break from the premise. Thus answer C cannot be your answer. Answer D makes a recommendation based on the premise but does not draw a conclusion. Answer E describes a directly proportional relationship. More analgesics are prescribed when there are more patients, and since the number of patients this year is up 15 percent, then the number of analgesics must be up as well. Thus, **the correct choice is answer E.**

11. Answer: **C**

STEP 1: **Read the question and identify your task.**
This is a Paradox question. You are asked to find an answer that explains the paradox.

STEP 2: **Read the argument with your task in mind.**
In Isabella's argument you learn about the many benefits of solar cookers with the conclusion that they must be the bestselling cookers in the country. Noah says that their sales are actually far below those of conventional cookers.

STEP 3: **Know what you're looking for.**
You need an answer that explains why these seemingly great cookers are not selling well.

STEP 4: **Read every word of every answer choice.**
Answer A removes price as a factor, but it does not solve the paradox. Answer B is beyond the scope of the argument. Answer C gives some weaknesses of the solar cooker, which would explain the low sales. Answer D makes the paradox even worse by making solar cookers sound

better. Choice E might make the paradox worse, but you don't know if the speakers are talking about a developing country. **The correct choice is answer C.**

12. Answer: **B**

STEP 1: **Read the question and identify your task.**
This is a Deduction question. You are asked to find an answer that must be true based on the argument.

STEP 2: **Read the argument with your task in mind.**
The argument tells you that Joe's Lumber sells only two types of lumber, pine and oak, and that Roberto never uses pine to build tables. He bought wood to make Marion a table from Joe's Lumber.

STEP 3: **Know what you're looking for.**
Keep these statements in mind when you read through the answers.

STEP 4: **Read every word of every answer choice.**
Answer A cannot be deduced from the statements. Answer B makes sense. If Joe's only sells oak and pine and Roberto bought his wood there and never uses pine, he must have used oak. Answer C seems logical, but the statements do not assert that. Answers D and E are irrelevant. The only thing the argument covers is the wood used for Marion's table. **The correct choice is answer B.**

13. Answer: **A**

STEP 1: **Read the question and identify your task.**
This is a Flaw question. You are asked to find an answer that describes a flaw in the argument's reasoning.

STEP 2: **Read the argument with your task in mind.**
The argument says that a building inspector is accused of ignoring problems in a building that has since been demolished and no records exist. The author says this accusation should be dismissed because the inspector's recent inspections have been flawless. The author seems to be assuming that the quality of the inspector's work is the same now as it was then.

STEP 3: **Know what you're looking for.**
You need an answer that talks about previous inspections having nothing to do with current ones.

STEP 4: **Read every word of every answer choice.**

Answer A says what you are looking for, but remember to read every choice. Answer B is not correct because the argument does not even say who made the accusation. Answer C is not correct because none of the terms used have double meanings. Answer D may seem possible since there is no evidence of faulty inspections, and the conclusion is that there were no faulty inspections, but the flaw of this argument is assuming that past equals present. Answer E is certainly possible, but you cannot know this from the argument. **The correct choice is answer A.**

14. Answer: **B**

STEP 1: **Read the question and identify your task.**

This is an Assumption question. The question asks which answer makes the logic of the argument successful.

STEP 2: **Read the argument with your task in mind.**

In the argument, despite the claim that the second statement "follows" from the first, it does not actually do so.

STEP 3: **Know what you're looking for.**

Therefore, you must find the assumption that, when inserted between the first and second statements, will make the conclusion work.

STEP 4: **Read every word of every answer choice.**

Answer A ignores the condition of having or not having an office and thus does not help the conclusion. Answer B seems to meet your needs. Since every employee who takes public transportation eats lunch in the company break room, it follows that if some employees who eat in the company break room have an office (as stated in answer B), then there are some employees with an office who do not eat in the break room and thus do not take public transportation. Answer C results in every employee with an office taking public transportation, which contradicts the conclusion. Answer D does not lead to any conclusion involving those who have an office or whether they take or do not take public transportation. Answer E tells you something about those who eat in the break room but nothing about those who have an office or whether they might or might not take public transportation. Thus, **the correct choice is answer B.**

15. Answer: **C**

STEP 1: **Read the question and identify your task.**

This is a Weaken question. The question prompts you to find the statement among the answers that most weakens the argument.

STEP 2: **Read the argument with your task in mind.**

You need to read the argument and discover the central basis for its conclusion, then formulate what kind of answer will weaken that basis. In this case, the argument reveals a discovery that leads archaeologists to believe that a larger, more permanent civilization existed in the Brazilian Amazon.

STEP 3: **Know what you're looking for.**

A weakening statement may indicate that a smaller, less permanent civilization was responsible for the etchings.

STEP 4: **Read every word of every answer choice.**

Answer A uses words like *large* and *established* to strengthen the conclusion that there was a well-developed civilization in the Amazon, so this cannot be the correct answer. Answer B offers irrelevant facts and no insight into the nomadic or permanent nature of the civilization. It only relates to the sophistication of either form. Answer C reveals a discovery of similar etchings 100 miles away by a "nomadic" artist. You can infer that the artist was a member of a nomadic civilization as was originally thought before the discovery. This weakens the argument and would seem to be your answer. Regarding answer D, the argument does not say the civilizations in question did not exist before the 2,000-year flood window, and this answer also does not address the nomadic or permanent nature of the civilization. Answer E is interesting but does not weaken the argument as well as Answer C. While the content of the etchings is relevant, they do not necessarily prove the nature of the civilization since they could be depictions of previous civilizations or other civilizations. **The correct choice is answer C.**

16. Answer: **B**

STEP 1: **Read the question and identify your task.**

This is an Assumption question. It is asking you to find a statement upon which the logic of the passage depends.

STEP 2: Read the argument with your task in mind.

The conclusion is that people in industrialized nations with more choices "in all aspects of their life" are not happier than people in less developed nations with fewer choices.

STEP 3: Know what you're looking for.

The conclusion extrapolates from television to all aspects of people's lives, so you expect that the correct answer will support the conclusion and most likely the extrapolation.

STEP 4: Read every word of every answer choice.

Answer A focuses only on the television aspect of daily life and not other aspects of their lives. It also somewhat weakens the comparison of nations. Answer B states an inverse relationship—that more channels equals less happiness—also exists among "other categories." If the same relationship exists among other goods and services regardless of other factors related to where people live in the world, then people in nations with more choices are less happy than people in nations with fewer choices. Thus answer B would seem to give strong support to the argument and to be your answer. For answer C, the argument says nothing about awareness between nations, only that the number of choices determines happiness. For answer D, how each nation judges each other's choices is irrelevant to their own experience. Like answer A, answer E discusses only the television aspect of daily life. **The correct choice is answer B.**

17. Answer: **C**

STEP 1: Read the question and identify your task.

This is a Paradox question. Reading the question, you discover that it wants you to find the one answer that does *not* explain the phenomenon described in the argument.

STEP 2: Read the argument with your task in mind.

In the argument you learn that the cheerleading squad experienced lower sales than usual for its bake sale after it decided to lower prices.

STEP 3: Know what you're looking for.

Therefore, you must find the one answer that does nothing to explain the lower sales.

STEP 4: Read every word of every answer choice.

For answer A, a lower population of potential buyers would very likely hurt sales. For answer B, competing fund-raisers would most likely decrease funds students have to spend on baked goods. In answer C, the cost of sugar and flour may affect profitability but has nothing to do with sales. Since answer C does not contribute to reconciling the apparent discrepancy, it would seem to be your answer, but you should continue to review the rest of your answers to make sure. For answer D, students probably would not buy more baked goods if they already had free cupcakes from the teachers, so that would definitely hurt sales. Finally, for answer E, location could very likely affect sales, especially if students had come to expect their sale table to be located in a traditional location. **The correct choice is answer C.**

18. Answer: **D**

STEP 1: Read the question and identify your task.

This is a Strengthen question. It asks you to find the policy that fits the situation.

STEP 2: Read the argument with your task in mind.

In this case, you need a policy that allows the community center to use the additional funds as it desires but also satisfies the interests of those who donated the money.

STEP 3: Know what you're looking for.

You will look for something similar in your answer options.

STEP 4: Read every word of every answer choice.

Answer A gives the center complete freedom to do what it wants with all the funds but ignores the interests of those who donated the money. Answer B states that the center can do nothing with the money except what the donors approve, which ties the hands of the center while giving too much power to the donors. Answer C hamstrings the center by saying the directors must approve the purpose for all spending in advance, but it does not address funding overages and thus is not helpful in the situation described in the argument. Answer D states that the center should use the money for the intended purpose unless those funds cannot be used for that purpose, in which case the donors should be consulted. This policy fits the situation perfectly. It allows the center to use the money as it sees fit until the allocations are fulfilled. Then, they must consult the donors. Answer E requires that the center return the money, which is in complete contradiction to the situation. Therefore, **the correct choice is answer D.**

19. Answer: **A**

    <u>STEP 1:</u> **Read the question and identify your task.**

    This is a Strengthen question. It asks you to find the answer that weakens the argument least, or in other words, most strengthens the argument.

    <u>STEP 2:</u> **Read the argument with your task in mind.**

    The scientist argues that his peers' statements that his theories are "based on sheer conjecture and have no experimental basis" are wrong because his theories are based on recent, reputable data. Although the scientist admits that he hasn't read "every detail" of the information, he trusts the sources.

    <u>STEP 3:</u> **Know what you're looking for.**

    The correct answer is a criticism that has little or no effect on discrediting the argument. As you review your answer choices, a process of elimination works best in this situation.

    <u>STEP 4:</u> **Read every word of every answer choice.**

    Answer A describes the basis of the conclusion as "uncertain recollections" even though the recollection does not seem uncertain at all. He refers to a specific study and use of the same research organizations. There is nothing uncertain about those recollections. Answer A seems like a good option. Considering answer B, if the experiments are affected by human error, then such a criticism would definitely weaken the scientist's argument that the research supported the theory. Since the scientist argues that the experiments done by the research organizations are all that are necessary to support his theory, answer C would seriously weaken the argument by saying more support is necessary. Answer D calls into question the quality of the research, and since the scientist uses these studies as the sole support for the theory, this criticism most definitely weakens the scientist's argument. Finally, if the logical pattern of using the lab's results to support a theory does not work for the current theory, then the scientist's argument is again weakened. Since answers B, C, D, and E all render the scientist's argument vulnerable to further scrutiny, they can be eliminated, which means **answer A is the correct choice.**

20. Answer: **D**

    <u>STEP 1:</u> **Read the question and identify your task.**

    This is an Assumption question. For this first question you must find the assumption that the argument depends on in order to hold true.

    <u>STEP 2:</u> **Read the argument with your task in mind.**

    The argument is about annual tests of the lead levels in drinking water. The conclusion is that the water is safe to drink, even though some samples exceeded federal standards, because the levels were still too low to pose any risks.

    <u>STEP 3:</u> **Know what you're looking for.**

    The correct answer will address the relationship between the federal standards and the amount of lead that causes health problems.

    <u>STEP 4:</u> **Read every word of every answer choice.**

    Answer A says the standards are too stringent, but the lead levels still may be harmful to people's health, and whether they disregard the guidelines or not, they take a risk by drinking the water. Answer B seems to weaken rather than support the argument, and that is not what the question is asking. Answer C calls into question the method of testing and leaves open the option that the situation might be worse than stated, possibly leading to the opposite recommendation, that people should not drink the water. For answer D, if lead levels slightly above federal standards are still not harmful to people's health, then it is valid to say that drinking the water is still safe for the city's residents. This very much supports the argument and is critical for the argument's conclusion. Answer E has nothing to do with the lead levels or drinking the water. Rather, it gives an irrelevant observation about human behavior. Therefore, **answer D is the correct choice.**

21. Answer: **A**

    <u>STEP 1:</u> **Read the question and identify your task.**

    This is a Strengthen question. This question is asking you to find the answer that actually bolsters the claim in the argument.

    <u>STEP 2:</u> **Read the argument with your task in mind.**

    The argument is about annual tests of the lead levels in drinking water. The conclusion is that the water is safe to drink, even though some samples exceeded federal standards, because the levels were still too low to pose any risks.

STEP 3:   Know what you're looking for.
The correct answer will best support the conclusion that the water is safe to drink.

STEP 4:   Read every word of every answer choice.
Answer A says that most lead never makes it to the faucet as it is absorbed by the lining of the pipes, thereby lowering the threat of people being exposed to the lead and being harmed. This seems to give great strength to the argument and is most likely the correct answer. Answer B creates doubts about the testing methods, but it does not address the actual results. Answer C says children exposed to lead levels above the federal standards will be harmed, the opposite of what you are looking for. Answer D is anecdotal at best since the hospital was dealing with people who happened to drink large quantities of water, not the normal amount. Answer E does indicate a problem with the current federal standards, but it does not say on what basis the medical associations make their argument, and it is still not as strong an answer as A. **Answer A is the correct choice.**

22. Answer: **B**

STEP 1:   Read the question and identify your task.
This is an Assumption question. The first question asks that you find the one answer upon which Eleanor's argument is based. The word *depends* requires that the statement be central to holding up the argument to scrutiny.

STEP 2:   Read the argument with your task in mind.
The subject of this conversation between Jaime and Eleanor is the life span of elephants in captivity. Jaime's conclusion is based on studies that show that elephants living in two protected reserve parks in Kenya and Myanmar live longer than those that live in zoos. Eleanor's argument is that zoos are painted in a bad light because the elephants in parks don't face the same dangers as elephants in the wild and that the studies that Jaime cites on zoos are outdated.

STEP 3:   Know what you're looking for.
Eleanor assumes that poaching and unnatural dangers are the more dominant threat to animals outside protected reserve parks. The correct answer will address this issue.

STEP 4:   Read every word of every answer choice.
Answer A may be true concerning the genetic differences between African and Asian elephants, but says nothing about what happens when either type is kept in a zoo versus an unprotected reserve. Answer B states that predators and diseases affect the life span of an elephant to a lesser extent than other threats beyond the protected parks. This would seem to be central to Eleanor's argument since she indicates that the threat of poaching and unnatural dangers affect the life span of elephants much more than any other threats inside protected parks. Answer C contradicts the second part of Eleanor's argument and is thus incorrect. Answer D says why an elephant's life span in a zoo was shortened in 1970 but nothing to support Eleanor's claim that care is better today. Also, it says that the poorer care then was due to budgetary reasons. Eleanor indicates that the science of care advanced, not funding. Answer E actually contradicts Eleanor's argument by saying that elephants are safer in reserves from poachers and unnatural threats. **The correct choice is answer B.**

23. Answer: **D**

STEP 1:   Read the question and identify your task.
This is a Describe question. It asks you to find the answer that accurately describes the argumentation technique that Eleanor uses to make her case.

STEP 2:   Read the argument with your task in mind.
The subject of this conversation between Jaime and Eleanor is the life span of elephants in captivity. Jaime's conclusion is based on studies that show that elephants living in two protected reserve parks in Kenya and Myanmar live longer than those that live in zoos. Eleanor's argument is (1) that zoos are painted in a bad light because the elephants in parks don't face the same dangers as elephants in the wild and (2) that the studies that Jaime cites on zoos are outdated.

STEP 3:   Know what you're looking for.
Eleanor discards the premises that Jaime uses to reach his conclusion—namely, the link between living in a reserve park and a longer life, as well as the studies he cites, which she says are obsolete.

STEP 4:   Read every word of every answer choice.
Regarding answer A, Eleanor does not offer such an example, so it cannot be your answer. For

answer B, Eleanor does not question the conclusion, only how Jaime reached it. Also, she does not question the verity of his data, only his choice of data population. Answer C says that Eleanor is trying to bolster Jaime's argument, which is definitely not the case. Answer D states that Eleanor rejects the correlation between the zoos and nature reserves that Jaime chose to make his argument and that changing his data pool will affect Jaime's supporting statements that led to his conclusion. These both seem to be exactly what Eleanor is doing with her argument. Answer E is partially correct in that she is questioning his assumptions, but she is not pursuing a wider data sampling but a different data sample altogether. Therefore, **answer D is the correct choice.**

24. Answer: **D**

   STEP 1:   **Read the question and identify your task.**
   This is a Weaken question. You need to find the answer that most weakens the argument.

   STEP 2:   **Read the argument with your task in mind.**
   What is the basis on which the teacher makes the argument? In this case, based on an experiment with 10 of her students, the teacher concludes that all her students would be better off doing mathematics manually than with machines.

   STEP 3:   **Know what you're looking for.**
   Most likely, the weakening statement will undermine the experiment in some fashion.

   STEP 4:   **Read every word of every answer choice.**
   Answer A actually strengthens the teacher's reasoning by making the students' achievement even more impressive, so this option does not qualify. Answer B seems to indicate that the 10 students were receiving help that might have improved their performance. This could weaken the argument, but it does not indicate whether the other students were receiving help as well, so this option may not be as strong as another answer. Answer C only indicates how the 10 students compared to the other students but does not affect the judgment that they showed improvement from their own past performance. Thus, it does not weaken the argument. Answer D says that the students undergoing the experiment had seen the material before while the other students had not. This indicates that they had an advantage that improved their performance, and the lack of

a calculator may have had nothing to do with it. This very much undermines the teacher's reasoning and may be your strongest candidate. Answer E indicates only that the teacher gave them a methodology for working without a calculator, but this does not mean that such training enhanced their performance and does not necessarily affect the teacher's reasoning. **Answer D is the correct choice.**

25. Answer: **E**

   STEP 1:   **Read the question and identify your task.**
   This is a Flaw question. The question is looking for a description of the logical flaw, rather than the flaw itself.

   STEP 2:   **Read the argument with your task in mind.**
   The argument concludes that there are more employers who believe one idea (people charged with a crime should be fired) over another (only people convicted of a crime should be fired), using the result of a recent survey.

   STEP 3:   **Know what you're looking for.**
   The correct answer will describe why the statistics are misleading, specifically why one or both of the survey statistics may be double counting or undercounting the number who believe a person should be fired in either case.

   STEP 4:   **Read every word of every answer choice.**
   Answer A is a true description of what the statement does but does not necessarily describe a flaw. Most polls extrapolate from a sample to draw a conclusion about the general population. For answer B, there is no ambiguous term used in the supporting statements, nor is any such term used as a basis for the conclusion, so this one cannot be correct. Regarding answer C, the conclusion compares the two beliefs mentioned in the supporting statements and makes no mention of a third belief. For answer D, there is no doubt that all the premises can be true. Finally, regarding answer E, in order to be convicted, one must be charged, so it is very likely that more employers believe that an employee should be fired if convicted of a crime than those who believe the employee should be fired if just charged with a crime. A sufficient condition is being confused with a required condition. Thus the poll and the reasoning are flawed. **The correct choice is answer E.**

26. Answer: **A**

STEP 1:   Read the question and identify your task.

This is a Flaw question. It is asking for the flaw in a complete-the-sentence form.

STEP 2:   Read the argument with your task in mind.

Find the logical flaw that leads the editorialist to believe that the politicians will redirect the funds away from education.

STEP 3:   Know what you're looking for.

The statement asserts that because politicians in general have betrayed the purpose of the lottery that the current legislature will do the same. You will look for something similar in your answer options.

STEP 4:   Read every word of every answer choice.

Answer A states that the argument draws a conclusion about a specific population ("our representatives in the state legislature") based on a study of a larger population ("politicians"). This would seem to describe the editorialist's mistake perfectly, but you should read through the rest of the answers to make sure. Answer B might look good, but the statements do not mention any historical data. It only makes general historical statements. Answer A remains the stronger answer. Answer C is incorrect because you do not know the conditions, historical or current, but even so, the current option on the table, a public lottery to support education, is the same. Both the historical politicians and the current legislature are considering the same solution, so answer D cannot be correct. None of the statements attacks the supporters or the merits of the lottery, only the resulting malfeasance once it is approved, so answer E cannot be the correct choice. **The correct choice is answer A.**

SECTION II

1. Answer: D

STEP 1:   **Read the question and identify your task.**

This is a Conclusion question. It is asking you to find among the answers a logical conclusion that can be reached as a result of the chancellor's argument.

STEP 2:   **Read the argument with your task in mind.**

Thus, you read the chancellor's statement with the expectation that it will lead you to an inevitable conclusion or assumption. Put simply, the chancellor argues that the school needs to invest in new facilities in order to attract new students and beat out the competition.

STEP 3:   **Know what you're looking for.**

The correct answer will sum up the argument. In this case, the chancellor argues that Mayfield Academy must grow to survive, and building new facilities is a way to generate that growth, so you must look for a conclusion that the Mayfield Academy must invest in new facilities in order to grow.

STEP 4:   **Read every word of every answer choice.**

Answer A seems like it might work, but it only mentions attracting more students and not how that should be achieved. Answer B seems like something parents might say when or if the school actually agrees and executes the specifics of the chancellor's recommendation, but this is not exactly a conclusion you can take from the argument. Answer C discusses a consideration of the parents and something unrelated to the school's need to attract more students. Answer D states that the academy should invest in new facilities, a conclusion that the school might very well come to based on the chancellor's argument. This seems like your answer, but you should review the final answer to be sure. Similar to answer A, answer E states what the school would like to be the inevitable decision parents make, to move their children to Mayfield, but it does not discuss how the Mayfield Academy can achieve that result, which is the subject of the argument. **The correct choice is answer D.**

2. Answer: C

STEP 1:   **Read the question and identify your task.**

This is a Describe question. The question asks you to describe the method the ethicist uses to respond to the business executive's argument

STEP 2:   **Read the argument with your task in mind.**

In essence, the business executive argues that teaching ethics to employees is a waste of time because they will inevitably act unethically.

STEP 3:   **Know what you're looking for.**

First you notice by the tone that the ethicist indicates disagreement with the executive ("makes as much sense as . . . ") and that the ethicist uses an analogous situation ("spending money on driver's education") and that the analogous situation has what the ethicist considers an absurd justification ("all drivers will inevitably cause an accident"), indicating that such thinking will have an equally bad result. You will look for something similar in your answer options.

STEP 4:   **Read every word of every answer choice.**

Answer A seems closer to a description of the business executive's thinking than the ethicist's. Your question asks for the ethicist's method, not the executive's. With answer B, the ethicist makes no attack on the executive's character, only on his argument, so this is not the correct answer. For answer C, the ethicist does use another (analogous) situation to show the executive's reasoning is flawed and would lead to a bad result, so this answer seems like your best option, but let's continue to review the rest of the options. Answer D does not seem right because the ethicist makes no demands for further evidence. For answer E, the ethicist does not think there is any dilemma to explicate. For the ethicist, there is no dilemma at all, as you see by his use of an analogous situation that is fairly black-and-white. **The correct choice is answer C.**

3. Answer: A

STEP 1:   **Read the question and identify your task.**

This is an Assumption question. You must describe the assumption upon which the argument depends.

STEP 2: Read the argument with your task in mind.

In this case, the argument makes a case that Renfield is not qualified for a management position despite his qualifications and based on certain disqualifications.

STEP 3: Know what you're looking for.

The correct answer will most likely discuss either the qualifications or disqualifications, since they are the basis for the conclusion that Renfield should be a manager.

STEP 4: Read every word of every answer choice.

Answer A describes the argument's assumption with regard to Renfield's one qualification, that "his performance as a member of your staff, while exemplary" does not in and of itself prove that the person can be a manager. This is definitely an assumption upon which the arguer makes the case, and it is very likely your answer, but you should read the rest of the answers to make sure. Answer B says Renfield cannot be trusted even with his regular duties, something the argument actually contradicts by saying that his performance has been "exemplary." With regard to answer C, nothing in the statement is based on whose interest Renfield will represent once he is a manager. Rather, it is based on his management abilities. Answer D deals with the staff's behavior and not Renfield's, so this does not qualify for your answer. Finally, answer E is a very general statement regarding the general practices of the organization. It says nothing of the specifics of Renfield's case and thus cannot be your answer. **The correct choice is answer A.**

4. Answer: **E**

   STEP 1: Read the question and identify your task.

   This is a Flaw question. You need to figure out why the argument is false, but it structures the question in complete-the-sentence form, so the answer will most likely be a description of the logical flaw rather than the flaw itself.

   STEP 2: Read the argument with your task in mind.

   In this case, the statement makes a simple argument—overturning accepted norms is the only way to make real progress.

   STEP 3: Know what you're looking for.

   The argument singles out one specific influence on the issue of real progress—overturning

accepted norms—and it doesn't allow for the possibility that another factor could have an impact. You will look for something similar in your answer options.

STEP 4: Read every word of every answer choice.

Answer A seems to be describing another argument altogether since the argument does not undermine its own premise and the term *attribute* seems to be a fairly inaccurate description of what is discussed. Answer B might seem like the correct answer to the question, but the problematic word is *because* since there is no causal relationship being offered between the first statement and the second statement. Answer C is problematic with the first word, *denies*, because the argument is actually affirming such a contribution, not denying it. Answer D does not work because the argument does not isolate its observation to a particular time. It is more general than that. Answer E is your last remaining possibility. The argument makes the mistake of saying that one influence outweighs all other influences on progress. **The correct choice is answer E.**

5. Answer: **C**

   STEP 1: Read the question and identify your task.

   This is a Paradox question. You are asked to find an answer that explains the paradox.

   STEP 2: Read the argument with your task in mind.

   The argument says that online classes are popular with students but not with professors.

   STEP 3: Know what you're looking for.

   You need an answer that explains why online classes can be popular with students but not with professors.

   STEP 4: Read every word of every answer choice.

   Answer A does not explain why professors do not like online courses and makes it seem odd that students would. Answers B and C are beyond the scope of this argument and do not address professors at all. Answer D explains why professors might not like online classes and does not discount that students do like them. Answer E shows that students like online courses but does not address why professors don't. **The correct choice is answer C.**

6. Answer: **A**

    STEP 1: **Read the question and identify your task.**

    This is a Weaken question. You must find among the answers the statement that "most seriously" weakens the argument.

    STEP 2: **Read the argument with your task in mind.**

    The statement argues that the government should require weight training in public schools for all children between ages 6 and 18 based on a new study.

    STEP 3: **Know what you're looking for.**

    You expect that the correct answer will be a statement that seriously undermines some aspect of this recommendation to the government.

    STEP 4: **Read every word of every answer choice.**

    Answer A looks very likely to be your answer since it says that a school-based program will be ineffective and that a home-based program is what is required for real success. You need to read through the remainder of the answers to be sure. Answer B puts a damper on the ability to measure progress, but it does not undermine the benefits of the program or the recommendation. Answer C adds facts about the study, but the particulars are not the kind that would undermine the results of the study. Answer D only speaks to the time it takes to notice measurable results, which does not change the fact that such weight training is beneficial and thus does not weaken the argument. Finally, answer E might give you pause. Yes, there might be some health risks to weight training at such a young age and adding those tests to the study might have been helpful, but the results might have been positive as well. You do not have enough information to know and thus, this answer does not weaken the argument more than answer A. **Answer A is the correct choice.**

7. Answer: **D**

    STEP 1: **Read the question and identify your task.**

    This is a Principle question. You are asked to find a general principle that Bruce is adhering to in his argument.

    STEP 2: **Read the argument with your task in mind.**

    Bruce says that the practice of charging different fees in different areas of town is unfair because

not everyone in a particular part of town has the same ability to pay.

    STEP 3: **Know what you're looking for.**
    You need an answer that states the principle that fees should be determined by income.

    STEP 4: **Read every word of every answer choice.**
    Answer A would make it difficult for poorer people to get care or difficult for the dentist to make any profit. Bruce does not argue for this idea. Answer B is out of scope. The issue of whether the government should pay is not relevant here. Answer C is not what Bruce is arguing either. He acknowledges the dentist's need to make a profit. Answer D is much more in line with Bruce's argument. He wants a system that is fair and based on income. Answer E is out of scope. Availability of care is not discussed. **The correct choice is answer D.**

8. Answer: **C**

    STEP 1: **Read the question and identify your task.**
    This is a Deduction question. It asks you to find a statement that must be true on the basis of the given statements.

    STEP 2: **Read the argument with your task in mind.**
    The argument gives you a paleontological discussion concerning the survival of large mammals like the hippopotamuses and giraffes after the extinction of the dinosaurs.

    STEP 3: **Know what you're looking for.**
    The correct answer will most likely be a conclusion you can come to based on how such survival occurred, mainly the competition for living space and food.

    STEP 4: **Read every word of every answer choice.**
    Answer A tries to relate a later timing of extinction to the smaller size of the surviving mammals, but nothing in the argument leads you to believe there is a relationship between the two, only that when it happened their size changed. The only thing you can assume is that the increase in size would have been delayed. With regard to answer B, the statements give no size relationship between the large mammals like the hippopotamus and other mammals. It tells only of large mammals and how they grew in size. Answer C is a very good option for your question. The statements discuss how the large mammals grew in size because they no

longer had to compete for space and food with dinosaurs. Thus, you can assume that if larger nonmammals had survived the extinction event, they would have been competitors for space and food and the larger mammals would have been smaller. Answer D may be true, but nothing in the statements leads you to believe that the size of the dinosaurs had anything to do with their extinction. Answer E states something that cannot be verified by the statements. It is possible they would have competed with carnivorous dinosaurs and the same evolutionary process would have occurred. **Answer C is the correct choice**.

9. Answer: **D**

STEP 1: **Read the question and identify your task.**
This is a Parallel question. It asks that you find among the answers a situation that "parallels" the one given.

STEP 2: **Read the argument with your task in mind.**
The given situation is that of an auction that Jody is not participating in; because nobody wants to buy the Giacometti statue more than she does, then "not one person" will bid on the statue no matter how low the bidding starts.

STEP 3: **Know what you're looking for.**
Most likely the correct answer will use similar extreme or all-or-nothing terms like "most," "nobody," or "not one person" and will create an equally absurd notion. The correct answer will have a similar flawed logic.

STEP 4: **Read every word of every answer choice.**
Answer A starts out well, saying that one jockey wants something the "most," but it breaks down later in the statement because it says the other jockeys will just double their efforts. This is not the all-or-nothing statement you need. Answer B starts off with Larry being the most qualified to spot a forgery, but the rest of the statement is wrong because it says that since one item has no flaws, others must be forgeries. This is not an all-or-nothing result of the first statement. Answer C does not say Professor Ricardo is the only one who can translate the text. It leaves open the possibility that there are others, definitely not an all-or-nothing result. In answer D, Emilio is the "most" intent to get the sales position, and because he is not applying, nobody else will apply no matter how high the salary goes. You have your extreme

("most") and all-or-nothing result ("nobody else") words and the statement is equally flawed in logic. This would seem to be your answer, but you must read your last option. In answer E, Sherry is not the most motivated to join the group, and her timing conflicts result in only a gradually worsening situation, not an all-or-nothing situation. **The correct choice is answer D**.

10. Answer: **D**

STEP 1: **Read the question and identify your task.**
This is a Deduction question. It asks you to find among the answers the one statement that must be true assuming the statements in the passage are true.

STEP 2: **Read the argument with your task in mind.**
The argument gives a set of conditionals, one for the conductor, one for the orchestra, and one that binds them together. Use shorthand to note these conditions: if C not NY, then other competitions. If O not NY, then no competitions. Lastly, C or O not NY. You can infer from the last statement that if C yes NY, then O not NY, or if O yes NY, then C not NY.

STEP 3: **Know what you're looking for.**
The correct answer will most likely test that you understand how these conditionals work together. As you begin to read the answers, you notice that they are a series of "if . . . then" statements. You should attempt the same shorthand with each to evaluate them.

STEP 4: **Read every word of every answer choice.**
Answer A says O yes NY, then no competitions. This contradicts your second conditional altogether, so this is not your answer. Answer B cannot be done in shorthand because it discusses a probability ("more likely"), and your given conditionals are not based on likelihoods. They are certainties, so this cannot be your answer. Answer C also cannot be done in shorthand because it is a recommendation, not a statement. The word *should* is key to recognizing the problem with this option. Answer D says C yes NY, then no competitions. You know that if C yes NY, then O not NY. Thus, if O not NY, then no competitions. This would seem to be your answer. Answer E, similar to answer B, deals in probabilities ("likely") and disqualifies this option. **The correct choice is answer D**.

11. Answer: **D**

STEP 1: Read the question and identify your task.

This is a Principle question. You are asked to find a situation that would violate the general principle in the argument.

STEP 2: Read the argument with your task in mind.

The argument says that there should be a balance between the punishment for an infraction and the severity of the infraction. In other words, the punishment for major infractions should be serious and the punishment for minor infractions should be minor.

STEP 3: Know what you're looking for.

You need an answer that presents a situation in which the punishment does not fit the crime.

STEP 4: Read every word of every answer choice.

Answer A does not involve punishment at all. Answer B certainly seems unfair, but the student who was not caught is irrelevant. Only known infractions can be evaluated, and in this case the punishment does fit the crime that was known. Answer C perhaps describes an unfair accusation, but there was no punishment. Answer D violates the proportionality principle because the same crime resulted in a harsh punishment for one (firing) while the other punishment was reasonable (a reprimand for a first-time minor offense). Answer E is out of scope. It is unclear whether this is an infraction and, in any case, it was not punished. **The correct choice is answer D**.

12. Answer: **B**

STEP 1: Read the question and identify your task.

This is a Flaw question. You are asked to find a flaw in the reasoning of the argument.

STEP 2: Read the argument with your task in mind.

The argument says that researchers found that high levels of vitamin D and calcium are not necessary to maintain bone health. The author concludes that everyone should stop taking high levels of vitamin D and calcium.

STEP 3: Know what you're looking for.

You need an answer that describes the main flaw in this argument. The researchers said high levels were not necessary to *maintain bone health*. What if they are necessary, or helpful, for other reasons?

STEP 4: Read every word of every answer choice.

Answer A is not relevant to the issue. Answer B is close to what you are looking for. The argument assumes that they are taken for no other reason. Answer C is incorrect because the argument establishes that bone health and vitamin D and calcium are correlated. Answer D is not established by the argument and it is not a necessary assumption, so it cannot be a flaw in the argument. Answer E, while true, is not the main flaw in this argument. **The correct choice is answer B**.

13. Answer: **D**

STEP 1: Read the question and identify your task.

This is a Principle question. You are asked to find an example of pragmatism.

STEP 2: Read the argument with your task in mind.

The philosopher explains the principle of pragmatism: that what works in practice is right and what does not is wrong. He then criticizes the principle by stating that what works for some may not work for all.

STEP 3: Know what you're looking for.

Since you are asked to find an example of pragmatism, look for a choice in which something is tried and works.

STEP 4: Read every word of every answer choice.

Answer A is incorrect because while the outcome of the course is unknown, farming does not seem like practical knowledge to teach urban students. Answer B may seem like a practical solution to the problem, but it did not work. Answer C does not seem pragmatic because if the mayor harms her constituents, she will probably not be reelected. Answer D is similar to answer A in that the outcome of the experiment is unknown, but changing a medicine that does not work for one that might is pragmatic. Keep this choice. Answer E is similar to answer B in that what seemed to be a solution did not work. **The correct choice is answer D**.

14. Answer: **D**

STEP 1: Read the question and identify your task.

This is an Assumption question. It asks you to find a statement upon which the conclusion depends, so you are looking for something that must be true for the conclusion to work.

<u>STEP 2</u>: **Read the argument with your task in mind.**

In this case, the argument says that Company X is going to sell underperforming divisions that are dragging down the stock price. The analysts are concerned. As evidence that this is a good move, you are told that the president has long recommended that some divisions are outdated and are too expensive to bring up to date. The conclusion is that the board's move will help the stock price.

<u>STEP 3</u>: **Know what you're looking for.**

The correct answer will be something that allows you to believe that, given the facts, the sale will actually benefit the stock price.

<u>STEP 4</u>: **Read every word of every answer choice.**

Answer A is an interesting fact but is not necessarily critical to the conclusion. Answer B relates to the chances of success or failure of the sale but not the conclusion that once they are sold, that will help the stock value. Answer C may mean a delay in the sale, but whether the sale helps the stock price does not depend on when the sale goes through, rather that it goes through at all. Answer D seems rather important. The argument bases its conclusion on the statement that the president has long maintained that certain companies should be sold. Thus, those companies must be part of the sale or the stock price improvement may not happen. This seems to be a promising option. Answer E is about the buyers, and whether the buyers recognize an underperforming division or not would seem irrelevant to the sale and its effect on the stock price. **The correct choice is answer D.**

15. Answer: **A**

<u>STEP 1</u>: **Read the question and identify your task.**

This is a Weaken question. It asks that you find among the answers a statement that weakens the argument.

<u>STEP 2</u>: **Read the argument with your task in mind.**

In this case, the argument says that Company X is going to sell underperforming divisions that are dragging down the stock price. The analysts are concerned. As evidence that this is a good move, you are told that the president has long recommended that some divisions are outdated and are too expensive to bring up to date. The conclusion is that the board's move will help the stock price.

<u>STEP 3</u>: **Know what you're looking for.**

You are looking for an answer that undermines the recommendation to sell the underperforming divisions.

<u>STEP 4</u>: **Read every word of every answer choice.**

Answer A suggests that all divisions are integral to maintaining the stock price. If all divisions must stay together, then the sale of some of the divisions might hurt the "interaction" between all of the divisions and, therefore, the stock price. This is a strong candidate for your selection since it indicates that selling some divisions might actually drag the stock price down further rather than bolstering it. You must read through the other answers to make sure it is the strongest among them. Answer B tells you an interesting fact about selling different types of divisions, but since the monies received for the underperforming divisions is of little consequence to the conclusion, this cannot be your selection. Answer C tells you something of the history of the company, but again, the past "thought" concerning the divisions is of little consequence to the conclusion. Answer D is about inflation, and inflation is not even discussed in the argument. Answer E says the company is looking for alternative ways Company X can bolster its stock price. Some alternate way may exist, but we don't know if they work. And either way, it does not say that the sale of the divisions is not still a good option or even a preferable option. Thus, **the best choice is answer A.**

16. Answer: **B**

<u>STEP 1</u>: **Read the question and identify your task.**

This is a Parallel question. It asks you to find among the answers a statement that follows the same pattern of reasoning as the argument.

<u>STEP 2</u>: **Read the argument with your task in mind.**

As you read the argument, pay close attention to the structure of the argument. The argument structure can be simplified as follows: IF restaurants over six months, THEN popular with patrons OR food critics. Last year, IF restaurants popular with food critics, THEN popular with patrons. THEREFORE, last year, IF a restaurant was over six months, THEN it was popular with food critics.

<u>STEP 3:</u> **Know what you're looking for.**
This is a fairly complicated pattern of logic but it should be repeated in the answer.

<u>STEP 4:</u> **Read every word of every answer choice.**
Answer A is IF garages are in Caedmon, THEN they do maintenance on both foreign AND domestic automobiles. You can stop right there since the first sentence does not include the "or" construction. This cannot be your selection. Answer B is IF apprentices are at Willow, THEN apprentices study dry wall OR cabinetry. This year, IF apprentices study dry wall, THEN they study cabinetry. THEREFORE, this year, IF an apprentice is at Willow, THEN the apprentice is studying dry wall. This is exactly the pattern and is probably your answer. Check the rest of the answers to be sure. Answer C starts out well with IF a congressperson is no longer in Congress, THEN the congressperson teaches OR writes a book. This answer then gives a specific example of Mary Seldon, and this is not in the pattern of your argument that stays general in its terms. Thus this cannot be your selection. Answer D makes the same mistake as answer C in that in the second part it goes into a specific example. Answer E is problematic from the start because it speaks in terms of "most" new movies when your argument talks in absolutes ("all" or "every"). Thus, **the correct choice is answer B**.

17. Answer: **A**

<u>STEP 1:</u> **Read the question and identify your task.**
This is an Assumption question. It asks you to find the assumption upon which the argument depends.

<u>STEP 2:</u> **Read the argument with your task in mind.**
In this case, the argument makes a claim that a plant's immune system behaves similarly to the human immune system and then makes an outlandish claim that you can discover how plants fight off the common cold.

<u>STEP 3:</u> **Know what you're looking for.**
You read through the answers for the one statement that seems to uphold this comparison.

<u>STEP 4:</u> **Read every word of every answer choice.**
Answer A says the same diseases that attack humans also attack plants. This is deceptively simple, and you might think it too simple to be the correct answer. Nevertheless, this may be your best option, since the outlandish conclusion is based on the very idea that the common cold attacks plants as well as humans. You must review the rest of the options to be sure. Answer B is definitely true, but it is not a claim upon which the comparison between plants and humans depends. It also says nothing about plants at all. Answer C is close to saying the same thing as answer A, but it creates a causal relationship ("because") that does not necessarily serve as a foundation to the argument. It also creates unnecessary complications by discussing how the disease attacks either one. Still, if answer A was not so effective, you might consider this option. Answer D is definitely important to the conclusion of the argument that makes the generalization about all plants based on the rice plant, but this option says nothing about the common cold or disease and is still not as strong as answer A. Answer E enhances the comparison between the immune systems of plants and humans, but this does not support the entire argument concerning the common cold and disease. Therefore, **the best choice is answer A**.

18. Answer: **E**

<u>STEP 1:</u> **Read the question and identify your task.**
This is a variation of a Describe question—an Identify a Point of Disagreement question. You need to figure out the central disagreement between two people.

<u>STEP 2:</u> **Read the argument with your task in mind.**
Joseph makes a value judgment that the evening customer service representatives are more efficient than the morning representatives based on certain performance statistics. Davis disagrees, arguing that each shift has different demands and the representatives face different kinds of problems.

<u>STEP 3:</u> **Know what you're looking for.**
You can expect that the issue in dispute will describe how Joseph and Davis differ on their definition of efficiency.

<u>STEP 4:</u> **Read every word of every answer choice.**
Answer A says they disagree about why the evening shift is able to remain on that shift and not on the day shift. This is totally unrelated to the efficiency issue and cannot be the correct answer. Answer B says the disagreement is about the

relationship between the time of day and the amount of time it takes to handle a complaint. This is close to being a good description, but it seems somewhat inadequate. You should read the rest of your answers to see if there is a better option. Answer C cannot be your answer because neither of them discusses whether the company will move representatives back and forth between shifts. Answer D is incorrect because they do not disagree on the accuracy statistic itself. Rather, they disagree about why the statistical discrepancy exists at all and whether that should be used to judge their efficiency. Answer E says the disagreement is about why the two shifts can offer quality service but one shift is faster than the other. This seems to be a perfect description of the disagreement and much better than answer B, your second best answer, which focuses only on one aspect, how the time of day relates to the time it takes to handle a complaint. **The correct choice is answer E**.

19. Answer: **A**

   STEP 1: Read the question and identify your task.
   This is a Conclusion question. In essence, the question is asking you to identify an answer that states the reason legislation is not working in the best interest of constituents.

   STEP 2: Read the argument with your task in mind.
   The first part of the argument is a description of the current way legislation is drawn up. Starting with "But clearly this strategy . . . ," you learn what the problem is, which is that the industry experts, as lobbyists, are paid by the industry they represent and thus act in the industry's interest, not the constituents'.

   STEP 3: Know what you're looking for.
   You are looking for something similar among the answers.

   STEP 4: Read every word of every answer choice.
   Answer A says that the industry experts will let their self-interest as industry lobbyists affect their writing of legislation. This is almost exactly your expected answer, but you should read through the remaining options to be sure. In answer B, several words work against it, especially "heavily influenced financially" and "unfair." The argument says they are paid, but you have no idea how much their compensation influences them. Also, the argument says only that the legislation

is weakened, but there is no indication of how unfair it is. These terms make it difficult to choose this option. Answer C discusses the legislators being less corrupt in writing legislation. Although this is a corollary of the argument, this is not the reason the current method is not in the best interest of constituents. Answer D may be true, but it is constructing new information and attributing a motive to the industry experts that is not even mentioned in the argument. You have no idea whether they expect to obtain lucrative jobs in their respective industries at a later date. This cannot be your answer. Similar to answer B, answer E contains words that disqualify it as your choice. The words "generously" and "want to keep" give information not evident in the argument. There is no mention of how much they are paid or that their jobs are at risk in this relationship. Thus, **the correct choice is answer A.**

20. Answer: **C**

   STEP 1: Read the question and identify your task.
   This is a Deduction question. The question asks that you find which answer must be true based on the statements in the argument.

   STEP 2: Read the argument with your task in mind.
   The argument gives a set of conditionals, so you can simplify them into basic logical statements. The first sentence says Diamonds(R) > 3 carats and Rubies(R) < 3 carats. The second sentence: Most Diamonds(R) and most Rubies(R) < SI2. The third sentence: Diamonds(A) and Rubies(A) > SI2. Also, Diamonds(A) and Rubies(A) < 3 carats. Because Ellington only buys stones < 3 carats, you can figure out that E can buy Rubies(R), Rubies(A), and Diamonds(A). In the final sentence you learn that Ellington is buying only a diamond shipment. Thus, Diamonds(A) is the only option. Allister is the only source for that shipment.

   STEP 3: Know what you're looking for.
   You read through the answers with this in mind.

   STEP 4: Read every word of every answer choice.
   Answer A is too absolute and cannot be true. Ellington may be buying only diamonds currently, but there is nothing telling us that the company never buys rubies and only buys diamonds. Answer B says the opposite of what is given in the statements. In fact, Allister sells higher clarity stones than Richman. Answer C says the diamond shipment has a clarity rating above SI2.

This works. Since Ellington must buy this shipment from Allister and Allister only sells stones with a clarity rating above SI2, then the diamond shipment must be rated above SI2. As for the other answers, answer D cannot be true since Ellington only buys stones < 3 carats and you know that Diamonds(R) > 3 carats. Answer E cannot be true because Allister is the only source that Ellington can buy the diamond shipment from. **The correct choice is answer C.**

21. Answer: **B**

    <u>STEP 1:</u> **Read the question and identify your task.**
    This is a Flaw question. The first question asks that you find the flaw in the environmentalist's response to the coal plant manager.

    <u>STEP 2:</u> **Read the argument with your task in mind.**
    The coal plant manager claims that because of its cost effectiveness, coal will remain a dominant source of energy. The environmentalist argues that technology will improve the efficiency of alternative energy sources and this will enable them to beat out coal.

    <u>STEP 3:</u> **Know what you're looking for.**
    You can see that the environmentalist discusses technology and its efficiency benefits, but does not address directly the manager's discussion of the cost benefits of coal over alternatives. You will look for something similar in your answer options.

    <u>STEP 4:</u> **Read every word of every answer choice.**
    With answer A, the environmentalist does fail to address the length of time it would take to become competitive, but time is not central to the discussion in the first place and this is a weaker option. Answer B says the environmentalist fails to acknowledge the cost advantage of coal over alternatives. This matches what you noticed about the environmentalist's statement and is most likely your answer. You should review the remaining options to be sure. Answer C is incorrect because the environmentalist makes no such statement. In fact, the environmentalist says that the coal industry has been slow to make such an adoption of clean coal. Answer D discusses a scenario that neither the coal manager nor the environmentalist discusses and thus cannot be your answer. You might be able to infer answer E from the environmentalist's statements, but because the environmentalist makes no mention

of an eventual cost advantage, you cannot choose this one. **The correct choice is answer B.**

22. Answer: **C**

    <u>STEP 1:</u> **Read the question and identify your task.**
    This is a Strengthen question. This question asks you to find among the answers a statement that supports the environmentalist's argument.

    <u>STEP 2:</u> **Read the argument with your task in mind.**
    The environmentalist's argument is based on technology and efficiency and the coal industries' slow adoption of new technologies

    <u>STEP 3:</u> **Know what you're looking for.**
    The correct answer will be along those terms, and you should expect that it helps the environmentalist overcome the weakness discovered in the previous question, addressing the cost effectiveness issue.

    <u>STEP 4:</u> **Read every word of every answer choice.**
    Answer A seems to contradict the environmentalist's statement with regard to clean coal, and it does not help the environmentalist overcome the cost effectiveness issue. Answer B weakens the coal plant manager's argument but does not strengthen the environmentalist's argument. Answer C says there is a direct relationship between technological advancement and cost-adoption factors. This matches your requirements by saying that the environmentalist's focus, technological advancement, affects cost effectiveness. You should review the remainder of the answers. Answer D discusses only one company, and the experience of one company does not necessarily weaken or bolster either argument. Lastly, answer E actually seems to weaken the environmentalist's argument, saying that cost benefits have been minimal despite technological advances. Therefore, **the correct choice is answer C.**

23. Answer: **C**

    <u>STEP 1:</u> **Read the question and identify your task.**
    This is a Describe question. The question is asking you to find the answer that describes the method by which the argument is made.

    <u>STEP 2:</u> **Read the argument with your task in mind.**
    In this case, the argument gives a scenario. In essence, Randy must work on a report all evening

for his boss, but a client has asked him to dinner and a discussion afterward that same evening. The final statement says that he has a difficult choice between satisfying his boss and satisfying his client, but he cannot do both.

<u>STEP 3:</u>   Know what you're looking for.
You must look for a similar pattern in the answers.

<u>STEP 4:</u>   Read every word of every answer choice.
Answer A cannot be correct because the argument does not give alternative versions of Randy's evening. It speaks of choices. Answer B cannot be correct because the argument does not give another situation for comparison. There is just the one situation that Randy faces. Answer C looks like it is your answer. The argument does talk about one set of responsibilities (the boss) and shows how it is incompatible with another set of responsibilities (the client), which results in a conundrum (cannot do both). This would seem to be your answer, but you should read through the remaining options to be sure. Answer D cannot be correct because the boss's requirements do not lead to the client's requirements. They are concurrent circumstances. Answer E starts off well. Randy did fail to work on the report in a timely manner, which led to the conundrum, but nothing in the arguments indicates that harm will inevitably come to any of the parties involved. **The correct choice is answer C.**

24. Answer: **D**

<u>STEP 1:</u>   Read the question and identify your task.
This is a Deduction question. Reading the question, you learn that you must choose an answer that can be inferred or derived from the content of the argument.

<u>STEP 2:</u>   Read the argument with your task in mind.
The argument tells you that bumblebees prefer red or striped snapdragons. Then, you are told that the bumblebee is critical to the survival of the snapdragon. Lastly, the nursery grows more striped and darkly pigmented snapdragons to encourage growth in the bumblebee population.

<u>STEP 3:</u>   Know what you're looking for.
You expect your correct answer to discuss the relationship between snapdragons and the bumblebee population.

<u>STEP 4:</u>   Read every word of every answer choice.
Answer A cannot be inferred because nothing in the argument indicates that the bumblebee population is in danger from a lack of a particular snapdragon. The argument just suggests that growing the snapdragons will help increase the population. Answer B cannot be inferred because the argument says that the bumblebee visits the striped or darkly pigmented snapdragons more often, but it does not say that without that type it will stop pollinating snapdragons altogether. Answer C cannot be inferred because the argument gives no relationship between the bumblebee's behavior and that of other insects. Answer D seems promising. It is evident from the argument that the bumblebee population needs to grow, so it is not much of a reach to infer that the population is smaller than desired. Also, you can infer that more striped and darkly pigmented snapdragons will help increase their numbers because the nurseries would not execute such a strategy if they did not believe it would do so. Read the last option just to be sure it is not better. Answer E says the opposite of what the argument is stating, that the bumblebees are necessary to save the snapdragons, which is not the case. **Answer D is the correct choice.**

SECTION III

Questions 1–6

As with all logic games you follow the six-step process.

STEP 1: Identify the Game Type.

The wording of this logic game is tricky. It asks that you maintain an order: a coil cannot be used unless it is tested first. It also asks that you group the coils into untested, tested, and used. The game also does not tell you how many of the coils are in each group, and a coil can be in both the tested and used groups. This is one of the rare hybrid games that cannot be easily classified. As part of your test-taking strategy, you might choose to leave this game to last when taking the exam. Proceed to step 2 under that assumption.

STEP 2: Begin Your Diagram.

You visualize a process of coils moving from left to right, from untested to tested to unused to used. Here is your diagram.

D E G H I J K

UNTESTED (UT)	TESTED (T)	USED (U)

STEP 3: Symbolize the Clues.

In symbolizing the clues, you will pair the coil with its status. Techniques for symbolizing are explained in Chapter 3

The first clue says "If G is tested, I is tested." This is a simple "if . . . then" statement. You will use the equals sign to say that a coil is in a particular stage of the process. This clue can be symbolized as follows:

$$G = T \rightarrow I = T$$

The second clue is "If E is tested, G is tested," which is another simple "if . . . then" statement. You use the same format as the previous clue:

$$E = T \rightarrow G = T$$

The third clue is a straight definition and can be symbolized simply as:

$$D = T$$

The next two clues are worded as complex conditional statements that need to be translated into "if . . . then" language. They are:

> H is not used (~H), unless J is tested (J)
> D is not used (~D), unless H is tested (H)

You negate the first terms (~H and ~D) and put the later terms (J and H) after the arrows. The end results are as follows:

$$H = U \rightarrow J = T$$
$$D = U \rightarrow H = T$$

Finally, you are given the clue "If J is used, and I is tested, K is used." This is a compound "if . . . then" statement that can be symbolized as follows:

$$J = U \, \& \, I = T \rightarrow K = U$$

This completes your symbolization, and you move on to step 4.

STEP 4: Double-check your symbolizations.

To double-check your symbolizations, translate your symbolized clues back into normal English and see whether they match the original language of each clue.

Your page should look like the following:

D E G H I J K

UNTESTED (UT)	TESTED (T)	USED (U)

$$G = T \rightarrow I = T$$
$$E = T \rightarrow G = T$$
$$D = T$$
$$H = U \rightarrow J = T$$
$$D = U \rightarrow H = T$$
$$J = U \, \& \, I = T \rightarrow K = U$$

STEP 5: Make deductions.

Finally, before you tackle the questions, see if you can make any deductions based on the setup of the game and the clues. Go through each type of deductions.

1. Can't-be-first-or-last deductions

   This is not an ordering game, but it has some ordering elements in it. Based on what you know, you can make the following deductions:

   If G is tested, then I is tested, so G can never be tested without I also being tested.

If E is tested, then G is tested, so E can never be tested without G also being tested.

If H is used, then J is tested, so H can never be used without J also being tested (J will always precede H).

If D is used, then H is tested, so D can never be used without H also being tested (H will always precede D).

If J is used and I is tested, then K is used, so you can deduce that when J is used and I is tested then J and K will both be used together.

2. Repeated-element deductions

You see immediately that the first two "if . . . then" statements share the term G = T (G is tested). You see that E = T → G = T and G = T → I = T. Thus, using the reflexive law (if a = b and b = c, then a = c), you see that E = T → I = T.

Thus, you deduce that if E is tested, then G and I are tested. You can also add the "if . . . then" statement:

$$E = T \rightarrow G = T \ \& \ I = T$$

There are no other repeated elements that can be used to make further deductions.

3. Down-to-two deductions

There are no limitations on the number that can be in each stage, and the deductions do not put any limiting factors with words like "only" or "must have." Therefore, you have no down-to-two deductions.

4. Block-splitting deductions

Notice that a coil can appear in the tested and the used column.

STEP 6: **Answer the questions in the smartest order.**

On test day, answer the questions in this order:

1. Answer the Complete and Accurate List question.

2. Answer questions that give you more information to work with.

3. Answer the remaining questions.

In this example, questions 1 and 4 are Complete and Accurate List questions and should be done first. Questions that give you more information include:

Question 3 ("J is not tested")

Question 4 ("E and five other coils are the only coils tested, and if exactly three coils are used in the machine . . . ")

Question 5 ("Every coil that is tested is used, and if I is used . . . ")

Question 6 ("K is not used, and if exactly four coils are used . . . ")

Once you have answered these questions, that leaves just question 2 to answer.

THE ANSWERS

1. Answer: **D**

This question asks which of the answers could be a complete and accurate list of the coils that are tested. You are concerned only with the tested coils. Since you are dealing with only one group, you can solve this question without your visual. It is best in this case to look through the answers one by one and check whether they follow the rules. You know that D is tested. Every answer includes D, so disqualification will have to come from the other clues. In answer A, E is tested and you know that if E is tested, then G must be tested. So far so good, since G is the next one listed. But, thanks to your deductions, you also know that if E is tested, I must also be tested. Since this answer does not include I in the list, it can be eliminated. Answer B has a similar problem. It has D and E and I, but it excludes G. Answer C is even worse. It includes E, but both G and I are missing. Answer D says that the mechanic tests D and I. There is no clue that requires that D or I be tested with any other coil, so this could very well be your complete and accurate list. Answer E has D and G, but you know that if G is tested, I must also be tested, and I is not listed in answer E, so you can eliminate it as your choice. **The correct choice is answer D.**

2. Answer: **A**

This question is asking which statement could be true. The key is the word *could*, which tells you that the answer must be "possible" given the game setup and clues. The other answers will be impossible given the same facts. The way to answer this question is to review the answers and test them against your clues and deductions. Scanning all the answers, you can quickly see that all the answers are about which coils are tested, so you are not concerned about the ones that are used. You know that D is tested no matter what, so this will figure into your considerations. Answer A says that E and three other coils are used. You use the one certainty, that coil E is tested, to figure out whether this answer could be true. You run through the clues related to coil E. You know that if E is tested, then G is tested. That leaves one last coil to figure out. Through your deduction you know that if E is tested, I is also tested. That gives you three other coils (D, G, and I). This scenario is not only possible but also necessary when given that E is tested. You look through the other clues and see that none of them makes it necessary that another coil be tested. You could stop right there, but let's review the other answer choices. Answer B is not possible because you have already proved that with E there must be three other coils tested. Answer C has the same problem; with E there must be three other coils tested, so it cannot be possible that E and one other coil are tested. Answer D says that D, G, and H are the only coils tested. The key word is *only*, which means only these three coils are tested and no others. This cannot be true because your rules say that if G is tested, then I must be tested. Since I is not in the list, this answer can be eliminated. Finally, answer E says that I and J are the only coils tested. Again the key word is *only*. This cannot be the case since your rules say that D is tested and this answer does not include D in its list. **The correct choice is answer A**.

3. Answer: **C**

This question gives you new information to work with. It says J is not tested. The question asks you to figure out which answer must be true. The key word is *must*, which means that because J is not tested, a certain requirement is created for other coils. You look at your clues and deductions and see what that condition might be. The J coil appears in the first clue as follows:

$$H = U \rightarrow J = T$$

Because your given fact is the negative of the term on the right side of the arrow, it might be useful to develop the contrapositive of this clue. You flip sides:

$$J = T \rightarrow H = U$$

Then, you negate both sides:

$$J \neq T \rightarrow H \neq U$$

And now you have a new version of your clue that fits this question. It says that if J is not tested, then H is not used. You can add this to your list of clues in case it helps you with later questions. The last clue also involves J and can be symbolized this way:

$$J = U \, \& \, I = T \rightarrow K = U$$

This clue is based on J being used, but your question asks about J not being tested, so this clue cannot help you.

With your new information you evaluate your options. Answer A says D is not used. In your given situation, J not being tested only tells you about other coils being tested or not being tested. It tells you nothing about what coils are used. You cannot know whether D is used or not, so this cannot be your answer. Answer B says H is not tested. The only thing you can derive from your clues is that because J is not tested, H is not used. H may or may not be tested. You cannot be sure given your clues, so answer B is not your choice. Answer C says that D is tested, but H is not used. The first part is given by your clues. D is tested regardless of the scenario. The second part is confirmed by the second part of your contrapositive above. This appears to be your answer, but you should go through the final two answers just to be sure. Answer D states that D is used, but that does not have to be true, and the question asks what must be true. Answer E says H is tested but not used. The second part of this answer is confirmed by your contrapositive, but the first part is not. You do not know whether H is tested or not, given the clues. **The correct choice is answer C**.

4. Answer: **C**

The question tells you that coil E and five other coils are the only coils tested and exactly three coils are used in the machine. The key words are *only* and *exactly*. These words create a constraint that will most likely help you determine your answer. Since this question requires an accounting of both tested and used coils, you will use your visual tools to represent the various scenarios. You also notice that it asks what "could be" an accurate list. This means you need to determine only what is possible, not what must be true. You know that D is tested, and you are given that E is tested by the question. Put both in the tested column of your diagram. The question says that there are five other coils that are tested in addition to E. D counts as one, so you need to figure out four more.

~~D E G~~ H I J K

UNTESTED (UT)	TESTED (T)	USED (U)	
	D	—	G = T → I = T
	E	—	E = T → G = T
	—		D = T
	—		H = U → J = T
	—		D = U → H = T
	—		J = U & I = T → K = U
			J ≠ T → H ≠ U

Using the clues to the right of your diagram, you know that if E is tested, then G is tested as well. You can also use your deduction to derive that if E is tested, then I is tested. You add G and I to your tested column. As represented below, this leaves H, J, and K as options to fill out the remaining two tested slots. One of the three will remain untested and also remain unused, since only those tested can be used.

~~D E G~~ H I J K

UNTESTED (UT)	TESTED (T)	USED (U)	
	D	—	G = T → I = T
	E	—	E = T → G = T
	G	—	D = T
	I		H = U → J = T
	—		D = U → H = T
	—		J = U & I = T → K = U
			J ≠ T → H ≠ U

There is nothing more you can do to fill out the grid, so you look at your answers and see whether any of them work under the scenario you have built. Answer A says D, I, and J are used. You test this scenario. If D is used, then H is tested, which leaves you one more test slot for J or K. Then, you have I and J to contend with. Coil I works since it's already tested. J must be tested in order for it to be used, so the last two test slots are taken by H and J, leaving K untested and unused. You have a problem, though. If J is used and I is tested, then your last clue tells you that K must be used. K cannot be used because only three coils can be used, and including K would make it four. That is enough to disqualify this answer, but you can also say that if K is used then it must be tested, and you have run out of test slots for K, which is a double disqualification. This scenario is represented like this:

~~D E G~~ H I J K

UNTESTED (UT)	TESTED (T)	USED (U)	
	D	D	G = T → I = T
	E	I	E = T → G = T
	G	J	D = T
	I	~~K~~	H = U → J = T
	H		D = U → H = T
	J		J = U & I = T → K = U
	K		J ≠ T → H ≠ U

Answer B says that D, H, and J are the three coils used. As before, if D is used, then H gets one of your two remaining test slots. Another clue says that if H is used, then J is tested, so J takes the last remaining test slot. Again, you have a problem, because if J is used and I is tested, then K is used and K would make it four coils used, which is impossible under the conditions of the question. Answer C says that E, G, and I are the three coils used. You already know that E, G, and I are tested, so they can be used. None of these triggers any conditions that break your limitations, so this is very likely your answer. You will review the rest of the answers to be sure. Answer D says that H, I, and K are the coils used. First, if H is used, then it must have been tested, so it takes one of your two remaining available test slots. From the clues, you know that if H is used, then J is tested and it takes the last of your test slots. You have no more test slots available, which is a problem. If K is used, it must be tested as well and there is no test slot available for it. This cannot be your answer. Answer E says that E, G, and J are the three coils used. You know that E and G are tested, so they can be used. If J is used, then it triggers your last clue and K must be used, but that is not possible because only three coils can be used, and once again, K would make four. **The correct choice is answer C.**

5. Answer: **E**
This question says that every coil that is tested is used and coil I is used. It also asks which coil does not have to be tested. In other words, four out of the five options must be tested and one does not. You must find the one exception. You use your visual again. Since every coil that is tested is used, and you know that a coil must be tested in order to be used, both D and I occupy your tested and used columns.

UNTESTED (UT)	TESTED (T)	USED (U)	D E G H I J K
	D	D	$G = T \rightarrow I = T$
	I	I	$E = T \rightarrow G = T$
			$D = T$
			$H = U \rightarrow J = T$
			$D = U \rightarrow H = T$
			$J = U \,\&\, I = T \rightarrow K = U$
			$J \neq T \rightarrow H \neq U$

Based on what you know already, you review your clues to see whether they tell you anything more. According to your fifth clue, if D is used, then H must be tested. So, answer B is eliminated. Since H is tested, it will be used because, according to the question, all coils tested are used. From clue 4, if H is used, then J must be tested. Thus, answer C is eliminated. Accordingly, since J is tested, it will be used. From clue 6 you know that if J is used and I is tested, then K is used and therefore must be tested. This eliminates answer A. You are left with answers D and E. Thanks to your clues you know that coil D must be tested, so answer D is eliminated. This leaves answer E and it must be your answer. Of course, you can go through the clues and see that G does not necessarily have to be tested or used. The second clue is never invoked. E is never tested, so G does not need to be tested. **The correct choice is answer E.**

6. Answer: **B**

This question tells you that K is not used and exactly four coils are used. The word *exactly* is important for it will be a constraining factor that will help you eliminate possibilities and determine the correct answer. Also, the question asks you to find the answer that is false. You must eliminate the true answers to find your choice. You use your visual to help you.

UNTESTED (UT)	TESTED (T)	USED (U)	D E G H I J K
	D	—	$G = T \rightarrow I = T$
		—	$E = T \rightarrow G = T$
		—	$D = T$
		—	$H = U \rightarrow J = T$
			$D = U \rightarrow H = T$
			$J = U \,\&\, I = T \rightarrow K = U$
			$J \neq T \rightarrow H \neq U$

The term "K is not used" is the negative of the last term in the sixth clue, so you should create the contrapositive of that statement to help you with this question. First you flip sides:

$$K = U \rightarrow J = U \,\&\, I = T$$

Then you flip signs:

$$K \neq U \rightarrow J \neq U \,\&\, I \neq T$$

Finally, you flip connectors:

$$K \neq U \rightarrow J \neq U \,/\, I \neq T$$

You add this new contrapositive to your list of clues alongside your visual.

UNTESTED (UT)	TESTED (T)	USED (U)	D E G H I J K
	D	—	$G = T \rightarrow I = T$
		—	$E = T \rightarrow G = T$
		—	$D = T$
		—	$H = U \rightarrow J = T$
			$D = U \rightarrow H = T$
			$J = U \,\&\, I = T \rightarrow K = U$
			$J \neq T \rightarrow H \neq U$
			$K \neq U \rightarrow J \neq U \,/\, I \neq T$

Thanks to your new clue you know that because K is not used, either J is not used *or* I is not tested. You evaluate your answers based on the given situation. Answer A says I is used. If I is used, it must have been tested. According to your new contrapositive clue either I is not tested *or* J is not used. Therefore, if I is tested, then it must be the case that J is not used. That leaves D, E, G, and H to fill the remaining three slots (I takes the first). There is nothing in your clues that keeps you from using any of those coils to fill the remaining three slots. Answer A is not false and cannot be your selection. Answer B says J is used. According to your new contrapositive clue, if J is used, then it must be the case that I is not tested. This is the negative of a term in the first clue, and creating another contrapositive might be helpful. We will not go through all the steps here, but this is the result:

$$I \neq T \rightarrow G \neq T$$

This contrapositive leads to another contrapositive based on the second clue:

$$G \neq T \rightarrow E \neq T$$

These tell you that if I is not tested, then G cannot be tested, and if G cannot be tested, then E cannot be tested. This leads also to the conclusion that if I, G, and E cannot be tested, they also cannot be used. That leaves only D and H, only two coils, to fill the final three slots, and that is not enough. Answer B has to be false and therefore is your answer to this question. The last three answers are about certain coils being tested. With regard to testing, the only coil affected by K not being used is I, which is not in answer C, D, or E. Also, just because a coil is tested does not mean that coil is used and your constraint exists only in the used column. Thus, none of these answers must be false. **The correct choice is answer B**.

Questions 7–13

As with all logic games you follow the six-step process.

STEP 1: Identify the game type.

This is a grouping game. You know it is a grouping game because it is asking you to sort the seven children into the three activities. It also says that a child can participate in only one of the activities and the activities occur only once.

STEP 2: Begin your diagram.

Create a grid with three areas for each group—ceramics, drawing, and origami. Then shorten the names of the children to their first initials (B, E, J, K, P, S, and U) and put them in the upper right corner. The groups can also be shorthanded to C, D, and O.

B E J K P S U

CERAMICS (C)	DRAWING (D)	ORIGAMI (O)

STEP 3: Symbolize the clues.

The game description does not give you any information to work on, except that each child must participate in one of the activities and cannot participate in more than one at a time. Also, it tells you that the activity occurs only once. You go clue by clue.

Clue 1: Exactly twice as many children choose drawing as choose ceramics.

You can use the abbreviated letter for each activity to represent the number of children in each group. Therefore, this clue can be represented as follows:

$$D = 2C$$

Clue 2: Sharon and Usef participate in the same activity as each other.

You use the children's initials as symbols for the children. The words "participate in the same activity" is in effect saying that if Sharon, then Usef and if Usef, then Sharon, so you symbolize this clue with two representations as follows:

$$S \rightarrow U$$
$$U \rightarrow S$$

Clue 3: Ezra and Karly do not participate in the same activity as each other.

The phrase "do not participate" is the same as "if Ezra then not Karly" and vice versa.

$$E \rightarrow \sim K$$
$$K \rightarrow \sim E$$

Clue 4: Barry and Pakhi do not participate in the same activity as each other.

This is similar to the third clue and looks like this:

$$B \rightarrow \sim P$$
$$P \rightarrow \sim B$$

Clue 5: Barry participates in either ceramics or origami.

This clue can be represented directly in the diagram with B appearing above ceramics and origami with a "/" after or before it to indicate that it can be in either column.

Clue 6: Jaime participates in drawing.

You can represent this clue directly in the diagram and do not need to symbolize it.

STEP 4: Double-check your symbolizations.

To double-check your symbolizations, translate your symbolized clues back into normal English and see whether they match the original language of each clue.

Here is your visual again, now with your symbolized clues alongside it:

B/		/B	B E J K P S U
CERAMICS (C)	DRAWING (D)	ORIGAMI (O)	
	J		D = 2C
			S → U
			U → S
			E → ~K
			K → ~E
			B → ~P
			P → ~B

STEP 5:   Make deductions.

Finally, before you tackle the questions, see if you can make any deductions based on the setup of the game and the clues. Go through each type of deduction.

1. Can't-be-first-or-last deductions

    This is not an ordering game, so you will not find this kind of deduction in this game.

2. Repeated-element deductions

    There are two clues affecting Barry. The only thing you can deduce from these rules is that if Barry is in ceramics, then Pakhi will be in origami or drawing, and if Barry is in origami, Pakhi will be in drawing or ceramics. There are no other repeated elements that help you come to any deductions.

3. Down-to-two deductions

    Since there is no constraint put on the size of each group, this sort of deduction does not come into play. The first rule, D = 2C, may cause some sort of constraint on the size of those two groups, but that constraint cannot be calculated at this time.

4. Block-splitting deductions

    Clues 2, 3, and 4 create situations where blocks might cause constraints, but since you do not know the size of the groups yet, you cannot deduce anything yet. These constraints will become apparent as the questions add information to the game.

In this case, your attempt at finding deductions has not resulted in any additional clues, but you might come to further deductions as you work through your questions. You move on to answering the questions.

STEP 6:   Answer the questions in the smartest order.

Approach the questions in this order:

1. Answer the Complete and Accurate List question.

2. Answer questions that give you more information to work with.

3. Answer the remaining questions

Questions 8 and 12 are Complete and Accurate List questions and should be done first. The questions that offer more information are the following:

> Question 10 ("exactly one of the children chooses origami")
> Question 11 ("Sharon chooses the same activity as Barry . . . ")

The remaining questions are 7, 9, and 13 and can be answered in that order.

THE ANSWERS

7. Answer: **B**

    This question asks you to judge which answer *could* be a correct matching of children to activities. The answers are about particular children and do not ask you for a complete assignment of children to activities. So, you should go through the answers and use your grid to test each one.

    (A) Karly-drawing; Pakhi-drawing; Usef-origami

    See the diagram that follows. Place each child in the appropriate group. You are left with B and E to assign to an activity. You know that E cannot be in the same group as K, and you know that B cannot be in the same group as P. Thus, you are left with an uneven number of children in the drawing group. This arrangement cannot be possible because of your first clue, D = 2C, which could be reformulated as C = 1/2D. The drawing group must be divisible by 2. Thus, this answer cannot be correct and you can later add your deduction to your list of clues.

B/ /B B E J̶ K̶ P̶ S̶ U̶

CERAMICS (C)	DRAWING (D)	ORIGAMI (O)
	J	U
	K	S
	P	

D = 2C
S → U
U → S
E → ~K
K → ~E
B → ~P
P → ~B

(B) Karly-origami; Pakhi-origami; Sharon-origami

This scenario leaves B, E, and U to be assigned. Because B cannot be assigned with P to origami, then B must be in ceramics. U is assigned to origami because of clue 2. Therefore, E must be assigned to drawing. This scenario is in accordance with your clues and the game, so it is a possible matching of children to activities. This is your answer. You can stop here, but let's explore the other answers, for learning purposes.

B/ /B B E J̶ K̶ P̶ S̶ U

CERAMICS (C)	DRAWING (D)	ORIGAMI (O)
B	J	K
	E	P
		S
		U

D = 2C
S → U
U → S
E → ~K
K → ~E
B → ~P
P → ~B
C = ½D

(C) Ezra-drawing; Pakhi-drawing; Sharon-ceramics

This scenario leaves B and K to be assigned. Neither B nor K can be assigned to drawing and you need one more in drawing for clue 1 to work, so this cannot be your answer.

B/ /B B E J̶ K P S̶ U̶

CERAMICS (C)	DRAWING (D)	ORIGAMI (O)
B/	J	/B
S	E	
U	P	

D = 2C
S → U
U → S
E → ~K
K → ~E
B → ~P
P → ~B
C = ½D

(D) Barry-origami; Ezra-ceramics; Sharon-ceramics

This scenario leaves K and P to be assigned. Your drawing group must include at least six children to satisfy the first clue because you already have three children in the ceramics group. Since you only have two children to assign to the drawing group, you cannot reach that number and this cannot be your answer.

B/ /B B̶ E̶ J̶ K P S̶ U̶

CERAMICS (C)	DRAWING (D)	ORIGAMI (O)
E	J	B
S		
U		

D = 2C
S → U
U → S
E → ~K
K → ~E
B → ~P
P → ~B
C = ½D

(E) Barry-drawing; Ezra-origami; Karly-drawing

You do not need to use your diagram for this one, since Barry cannot be assigned to the drawing group. According to clue 5 he must be assigned to the ceramics or origami group. This cannot be your answer.

The correct choice is answer B.

8. Answer: **A**

This question is asking for a complete and accurate list of the children who *do not* choose drawing. Again, look at each scenario. This means that all the other children choose drawing, so you must find the answer that allows everyone but those listed to take drawing together and still follow your clues.

(A) Barry, Ezra, Pakhi

To test this scenario, use your diagram. You only need one scenario to work, so for argument's sake, you say that B chooses ceramics. P cannot be in the same group but also cannot choose drawing, so she chooses origami. E can go in either ceramics or origami, so you choose one, in this case ceramics. You have S and U remaining and they can go into any group, but they have to go together because according to your clues they choose the same group. Since you need to make your first rule work, you put them in drawing. This scenario works and this is your answer. Let's explore the other options for learning purposes.

B/   /B   ~~B E J K P~~ S U

CERAMICS (C)	DRAWING (D)	ORIGAMI (O)	
B	J	P	D = 2C
E	K		S → U
	S		U → S
	U		E → ~K
			K → ~E
			B → ~P
			P → ~B
			C = ½D

(B) Barry, Sharon, Usef

This answer does not work because E and K cannot be in the drawing group together.

B/   /B   ~~B E J K P S U~~

CERAMICS (C)	DRAWING (D)	ORIGAMI (O)	
B	J	S	D = 2C
	P	U	S → U
			U → S
			E → ~K
			K → ~E
			B → ~P
			P → ~B
			C = ½D

(C) Barry, Karly, Usef

You do not even need your diagram for this one. Usef and Sharon must be in the same group. Sharon cannot be in drawing and she is not included in this answer, so this answer breaks the rule in the second clue.

(D) Barry, Karly

You do not need your diagram for this one either. Because only two choose not to draw, five children are left to the drawing group. This means the ratio of drawing to ceramics is 5 to 2 (assuming B and K both choose ceramics), which is greater than 2 to 1 and breaks with your first clue.

(E) Barry, Pakhi

This one has the same problem as answer B. E and K are forced to take drawing together and that breaks the rule in clue 3. Even if you were to ignore that clue (which you can't), it also breaks the ratio in clue 1. This cannot be your answer.

The correct choice is answer A.

9. Answer: **E**

The question asks you to find the one *true* statement among the answers. You can evaluate these without the use of a diagram. Answer A cannot be true because it leaves five children to choose between drawing and ceramics. The ratio between these groups is 2 to 1, and there is no configuration of five children that will give you an exact ratio of 2 to 1. Answer B cannot be true because you know that S and U must be in the same group. Usef cannot be the only child in any group. Answers C and D cannot be true for the same reason as answer A: the number of children in drawing must be an even number and able to give you a 2-to-1 ratio to those in ceramics. By process of elimination, answer E becomes your choice, but you can test it to be sure. See the diagram that follows. All the other children can be arranged to match your clues and leave P in ceramics alone. **The correct choice is answer E.**

B/		/B	B E J K P S U
CERAMICS (C)	DRAWING (D)	ORIGAMI (O)	
P	J	B	D = 2C
	E	S	S → U
		U	U → S
		K	E → ~K
			K → ~E
			B → ~P
			P → ~B
			C = ½D

10. Answer: **B**

This question tells you that *exactly* one child chooses origami and asks you which among the answers *must* be true. You have already created a scenario similar to this in an earlier question, and in a test situation you will want to use that knowledge to quickly answer any later questions that create the same scenarios. Of course, you know that with only one child in origami, that leaves six children for the two remaining groups. To make clue 1 work there must be two children in ceramics and four in drawing, which gives you the 2-to-1 ratio you need. You must look at what groups of children, going left to right, of 2-4-1 will work. The next diagram is the same as the one you created in question 8. You can use this example as a guide. Look at the possible answers and see which one must be true. Answer A says K chooses ceramics. You see in the diagram that K could take drawing, but you could also make K the child who is alone in origami and move P to drawing without upsetting the game. Answer B says that S chooses drawing. S and U must choose the same group, so S cannot be the lone origami child. Also, you cannot switch S and U with B and E because E and K cannot be in the same group. You can switch B, P, E, and K around in all kinds of configurations, but it remains true that S must choose drawing. This is your correct answer, but let's review the remaining answers for learning purposes. Answer C says that B chooses ceramics, but this cannot be your answer because B could

easily switch with P and be your lone origami participant. Answer D says P chooses drawing, but P could easily switch with B and take ceramics, so this cannot be your answer. Answer E says that Ezra chooses ceramics. You see in the diagram that is possible, but it is also possible to switch E with K in drawing, so this is not necessarily true.

B/		/B	~~B E J K P S U~~
CERAMICS (C)	DRAWING (D)	ORIGAMI (O)	
B	J	P	D = 2C
E	K		S → U
	S		U → S
	U		E → ~K
			K → ~E
			B → ~P
			P → ~B
			C = ½D

The correct choice is answer B.

11. Answer: **A**

This question tells you that S chooses the same activity as B. This fact leads you to some new deductions that are pertinent to this question and only this question. Your clues tell you that S and U choose the same activity. Therefore, you know that B, S, and U all choose the same activity. You also know that B, S, and U do not choose the same activity as P. In addition, according to clue 5, S and U participate in either ceramics or origami. Lastly, all three cannot choose ceramics because clue 1 would require that six children choose drawing, but there are only four other children, so all three must choose origami. This new deduction actually negates the previous deduction. So you now have these added clues:

$$S \rightarrow B \text{ and } B \rightarrow S$$
$$B \rightarrow U \text{ and } U \rightarrow B$$
$$B \& S \& U \rightarrow \sim P$$
$$\sim\sim\text{S \& U = C or O}\sim\sim$$
$$B \& S \& U = O$$

These rules apply only to this one question; keep your new clues separated from your previous clues so that you do not accidentally use them for future questions. The question asks you which among the answers *could* be true (not *must*). Using your new information you look to your diagram to evaluate the options. You see that there are only three children left to allocate—E, K, and P. Clue 1 says the drawing group must be twice the size of the ceramics group K or P, so the most you can add to the drawing group is one. In fact, you can only allocate one to each group. Answer A says Ezra chooses drawing, which could be true. Ezra could choose ceramics or drawing, so this is your likely answer. You know that P cannot share the same group with B, so P cannot be in origami. This eliminates answer B. Answers C, D, and E cannot be true because your deductions made all three impossible. **The correct choice is answer A.**

B/   /B   B̶ E J̶ K P S̶—U̶

CERAMICS (C)	DRAWING (D)	ORIGAMI (O)	
	J	B	D = 2C
		S	S → U
		U	U → S
			E → ~K
			K → ~E
			B → ~P
			P → ~B
			C = ½D

12. Answer: **E**

The question asks you to find among the answers the one that does not work as a complete and accurate list of children in the ceramics group. Each answer has two names, so according to clue 1 you need four children in the drawing group. You already have J in the drawing group, so you need only to ask yourself whether there are three children who can be together in the drawing group with J and remain consistent with your clues. The one that fails this test is your answer. You evaluate each answer choice.

(A) Barry, Karly

This leaves E, P, S, and U. You can group E, S, U and P, S, U together in drawing. Therefore, this cannot be your answer.

(B) Karly, Pakhi

This leaves B, E, S, and U. You can group B, S, U and E, S, U together in drawing. Therefore, this cannot be your answer.

(C) Ezra, Pakhi

This leaves B, K, S, and U. You can group B, S, U and K, S, U together in drawing. Therefore, this cannot be your answer.

(D) Barry, Ezra

This leaves K, P, S, and U. You can group K, S, U and P, S, U together in drawing. Therefore, this cannot be your answer.

(E) Sharon, Usef

This leaves B, E, K, and P. There is no group of three that works, mainly because B → ~P and E → ~K. There are too many conflicts. Besides, you are out of options. This must be your answer. **The correct choice is answer E.**

13. Answer: **D**

Your last question in this game asks which among the answers *must* be true. You do not need your diagram to solve this question. You just need to test each statement against your clues, and you can also use your experience with the previous questions. Of course, you could use your diagram to devise situations that test each one.

(A) E chooses a different activity than S does.

There is nothing among the rules that indicates E and S have to choose a different activity from each other. For example, the scenario below shows them sharing origami, so this cannot be your answer.

B/   /B   B E J K P S U

CERAMICS (C)	DRAWING (D)	ORIGAMI (O)	
B	J	E	D = 2C
	K	S	S → U
		U	U → S
		P	E → ~K
			K → ~E
			B → ~P
			P → ~B
			C = ½D

(B) E, J, and S do not choose the same activity.

You can create the following scenario to disprove this one. Since E, J, and S can choose the same activity, this cannot be your answer.

B/		/B
CERAMICS (C)	DRAWING (D)	ORIGAMI (O)
B	J	P
K	E	
	S	
	U	

B E J K P S U

$D = 2C$
$S \rightarrow U$
$U \rightarrow S$
$E \rightarrow \sim K$
$K \rightarrow \sim E$
$B \rightarrow \sim P$
$P \rightarrow \sim B$
$C = \frac{1}{2}D$

(C) E chooses a different activity than J.

The above scenario shows that E and J can choose the same activity, so this cannot be your answer.

(D) B, J, and K do not all choose the same activity.

This means that B and K must be with J in drawing because of clue 6. This is impossible, because it conflicts with clue 5, which requires that B choose ceramics or origami, so it must be true that B, J, and K cannot all choose the same activity. This is your answer, but let's review the last answer for learning purposes.

(E) B chooses a different activity than E does.

You can create the following scenario to disprove this one. Since B and E can share the same activity, this option does not have to be true.

B/		/B
CERAMICS (C)	DRAWING (D)	ORIGAMI (O)
B	J	P
E	S	
	U	
	K	

B E J K P S U

$D = 2C$
$S \rightarrow U$
$U \rightarrow S$
$E \rightarrow \sim K$
$K \rightarrow \sim E$
$B \rightarrow \sim P$
$P \rightarrow \sim B$
$C = \frac{1}{2}D$

The correct choice is answer D.

Questions 14–20

As with all logic games you follow the six-step process.

STEP 1:   Identify the game type.
This is an ordering game. You know it is an ordering game because you are asked to arrange the trucks in sequential order at docks 1 through 7; and because you are asked to assign each truck to only one dock, it is a one-tiered ordering game.

STEP 2:   Begin your diagram.
The diagram for this game will be a simple grid with seven columns into which you will place your trucks. You can put the truck names in the upper right corner for easy reference.

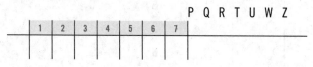

P Q R T U W Z

1	2	3	4	5	6	7

STEP 3:   Symbolize the clues.
You symbolize the clues as follows:

Clue 1: P is unloaded at a lower numbered dock than T.

Using your visualization of the docks, the clue says that P must be to the left of T. This can be symbolized using the line notation, as follows:

$$P - T$$

Clue 2: W is unloaded at the dock numbered one lower than the dock at which Q is unloaded.

This clue gives you the exact order of two trucks, but it does not say specifically where in the order they appear together. You use your box notation to show that they must be next to each other, with the W truck to the left of the Q truck.

W	Q

Clue 3: R is unloaded at dock 1 or else dock 7.

The clue says that R is located at 1 or 7. It also says that R cannot be unloaded at docks 2 through 6. You can represent this clue by writing ~R above columns 2 through 6.

Clue 4: Z is unloaded at dock 4.

The clue says truck Z is unloaded at dock 4, and you can represent this clue by simply putting Z in column 4 of your diagram.

STEP 4: Double-check your symbolizations.
To double-check your symbolizations, you translate your symbolized clues back into normal English and see whether they match the original language of each clue. Once you have verified that your symbolizations work, you can add them to your diagram. Your diagram should look as follows:

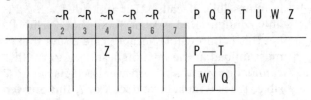

STEP 5: Make deductions.
Finally, before you tackle the questions, you see if you can make any deductions based on the setup of the game and the clues. You go through each type of deduction.

1. Can't-be-first-or-last deductions

   Clue 1 tells you that P must come before T. Therefore, you can deduce that P cannot be last in the order. Also, T cannot be first since P must come before it. You can write ~T above column 1 and ~P above column 7.

   Clue 2 tells you that W must come before Q. Therefore, you can deduce that W cannot be last in the order. Also, Q cannot be first since W must come before it. You can write ~Q above column 1 and ~W above column 7.

2. Repeated-element deductions

   No deductions of this type are possible in this game.

3. Down-to-two deductions

   Clue 3 already tells you that column 1 or 7 must unload truck R, but the second truck could be any of the other trucks, except those the other clues exclude. No further deductions of this kind are possible.

4. Block-splitting deductions

   Clue 2 creates a block of W and Q. Also, truck Z must be at dock 4, so your diagram is split into two groups of three docks. Truck W cannot be unloaded at dock 3 because Q would have to be unloaded at dock 4, which is already occupied by Z. You can write ~W above column 3.

You add the deductions and your complete diagram should look as follows:

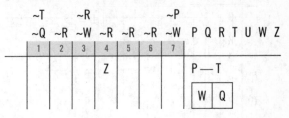

STEP 6: Answer the questions in the smartest order.
As you take the test, approach the questions in this order:

1. Answer the Complete and Accurate List question.

2. Answer questions that give you more information to work with.

3. Answer the remaining questions.

   Question 14 is the only Complete and Accurate List question for this game. It should be answered first. Questions that give more information are as follows:

   Question 16 ("U is unloaded on dock 5 . . .")
   Question 18 ("U is unloaded at dock 2 . . .")
   Question 19 ("Q is unloaded at a dock numbered one less than the dock at which P is unloaded . . .")
   Question 20 ("W is unloaded at dock 1 . . .")

The remaining questions are 15 and 17, and they can be answered in that order.

THE ANSWERS

14. Answer: **C**

    The question asks you to identify an acceptable loading assignment for the trucks among the possible answers. The following diagram depicts each answer choice. Answer A is unacceptable because P is loaded in a higher dock than truck T and this is inconsistent with clue 1. Answer B is unacceptable because Z is not unloaded at dock 4, which is inconsistent with clue 4. Answer C is consistent with all your clues and is your answer. Answer D is unacceptable because truck W and truck Q are not unloaded next to each other, which is inconsistent with clue 2. Answer E is unacceptable because R is not loaded at dock 1 or 7, which is inconsistent with clue 3. **The correct choice is answer C.**

	~T		~R				~P
	~Q	~R	~W	~R	~R	~R	~W	P Q R T U W Z
	1	2	3	4	5	6	7
(A)	R	W	Q	Z	T̶	P	U	P—T
(B)	R	U	Z̶	W̶	Q	P	T	W | Q
(C)	P	U	T	Z	W	Q	R
(D)	P	W̶	U	Z	Q̶	T	R
(E)	P	T	U	Z	R̶	W	Q

15. Answer: **C**

The question asks which answer gives the correct lowest numbered dock at which a specified truck can be unloaded. The trick is to test each answer and see whether the truck can be unloaded at a lower dock. Looking at your diagram you see that if R is unloaded at dock 7, then that makes room for P to be unloaded at dock 1, which is lower than dock 2. Therefore, answer A cannot be the correct choice. Again, if R is unloaded at dock 7, then W can be unloaded at dock 1 and Q can be unloaded at dock 2, which is lower than dock 3. Therefore, answer B cannot be correct. Considering answer C, your deductions allowed you to determine that T cannot be unloaded at dock 1. The lowest T can be unloaded is dock 2. Therefore, answer C must be the answer. Truck U is unrestrained by any of your clues. If R is unloaded at dock 7, U can be unloaded at dock 1 or dock 2, both of which are lower than dock 3. Therefore, answer D cannot be your choice. In considering answer B, you determined that W could be unloaded at dock 1, which is lower than dock 2. Therefore, answer E cannot be your choice. **The correct choice is answer C.**

16. Answer: **A**

The question tells you that truck U is unloaded at dock 5, then asks which of the pairs could be unloaded at consecutive docks, but not necessarily in the order given in the answer. This means that all but one of the pairs could not possibly be unloaded at consecutive docks. It also means that each answer creates a new block with which you must contend in each scenario. You add the new information to your diagram and assess each pair. With answer A, R can be unloaded at dock 7 and T could be unloaded at dock 6. See the following diagram for this configuration. This must be your answer, but let's review the remaining options for learning purposes. The pair given by answer B, TW, is not possible. The pair cannot be at the higher docks because there would not be a

dock to accommodate Q, which must be after W. They also cannot be located in the lower docks because they must accommodate P, which must come before T. If you unload P, T, and W at docks 1, 2, and 3, then again you do not have room for truck Q, which must be unloaded right after W. This answer cannot be correct. Answer C, WZ, is impossible. Because U is unloaded at 5, the only configuration is W at 3 and Z at 4 (clue 4), but this is impossible because clue 2 says that Q must unload at the next highest dock to W. This cannot be your answer. Answer D, QR, is not possible. Truck R must be at dock 1 or 7. This answer asks whether Q could be unloaded at dock 2 or 6. Neither is possible. If Q is at dock 6, then W must be at 5, but the question requires that U be unloaded at 5. If Q is at dock 2, then W must be at 1, which is impossible because R is unloaded at that dock. This cannot be your answer. Finally, answer E, QT, is not possible. Truck T must be loaded after P. If Q and T are unloaded at docks 2 and 3 (in whatever order), then P must be unloaded at dock 1, but this configuration leaves no room for Q to come after W. The same is true for docks 6 and 7. **The correct choice is answer A.**

	~T		~R				~P
	~Q	~R	~W	~R	~R	~R	~W	P Q R T U W Z
	1	2	3	4	5	6	7
				Z	U			P—T
(A)	P	W	Q	Z	U	T	R	W | Q

17. Answer: **B**

The question asks what is the most number of docks that can come between the docks at which P is unloaded and T is unloaded. You can test this by putting T at the highest dock (since it must come after P) and moving P around to see how far up you can move it. You unload T at dock 7, so R must be unloaded at dock 1. If you put W and Q at 5 and 6, you can put P and U at 2 and 3 respectively. This order is acceptable given the clues of your game. This is the farthest you can place P and T from each other. There are four docks between them. Therefore, **the correct choice is answer B.**

	~T		~R				~P
	~Q	~R	~W	~R	~R	~R	~W	P Q R T U W Z
	1	2	3	4	5	6	7
	R	P	U	Z	W	Q	T	P—T
								W | Q

18. Answer: **D**

The question tells you that U is unloaded at dock 2 and asks you to identify the statement among the possible answers that must be true. This means that all but one of the answers may or may not be true. You put the new information into your diagram and assess the answers based on what you see. Before you even look at the answers, you recognize that W and Q must be unloaded either at 5 and 6 or 6 and 7 to be consistent with clue 2, because those are the only consecutive loading docks available. Of course, this makes it impossible for both P and T to be to the right of Z. Actually, regardless of where T is unloaded, P must be to the left of Z, because there is only one remaining open dock to the right of Z. Answer A may or may not be true. Truck T can be unloaded at dock 3 as long as P is unloaded at dock 1 and R is unloaded at dock 7, so Z could be unloaded at a higher dock (4) than T (3). That means answer A cannot be correct. For the same reason, W could be unloaded at a higher dock (5 or 6) than T (3), so answer B cannot be your answer. If you unload truck R at dock 1, P at dock 3, and T at dock 7 (W and Q are at 5 and 6 respectively), then T could be unloaded at a higher dock than R. Therefore, answer C cannot be the correct choice. Answer D must be true. As you deduced, no matter where T is unloaded, P must be to the left of Z, so it must be unloaded at a lower dock. This is your answer. Answer E cannot be correct because no matter where W and Q are situated, you still have the option of unloading R at 1 or 7. If R is at 7, then it is being unloaded at a higher dock than Q. **The correct choice is answer D.**

~T   ~R   ~P
~Q ~R ~W ~R ~R ~R ~W P Q R T U W Z

1	2	3	4	5	6	7
	U		Z			

P—T
W Q

19. Answer: **E**

The question tells you that Q is unloaded at a dock numbered one less than the one that unloads P and then asks you to pick the answer that must be true. Because Q is part of the WQ block, the new fact creates an even larger block, WQP. In order for three trucks to be together, they must be at docks 1 through 3 or docks 5 through 7. But you also know that T must come after P. Therefore,

the block cannot be unloaded at docks 5 through 7. They must be unloaded at docks 1 through 3. You can write these deductions into your diagram. Answer A cannot be true because W must be unloaded at dock 1. Answer B may or may not be true. U could be unloaded at 5 or 6. It is interchangeable with T. Answer C cannot be true because W is unloaded at dock 1. Answer D cannot be true because Q must be unloaded at dock 2. Finally, answer E must be true. Truck P must be unloaded at dock 3 for the order to be consistent with the new fact and your clues. **The correct choice is answer E.**

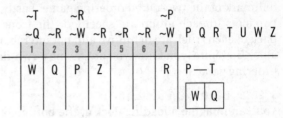

~T   ~R   ~P
~Q ~R ~W ~R ~R ~R ~W P Q R T U W Z

1	2	3	4	5	6	7
W	Q	P	Z			R

P—T
W Q

20. Answer: **B**

The question tells you that W is unloaded at dock 1, then asks you which of the answers could be true. This means that all but one of the answers must be false. Since W is unloaded at dock 1, clue 2 tells you that Q must be unloaded at dock 2. Also, clue 3 tells you that because W is at dock 1, truck R must be at dock 7. You put the new information as well as your deductions into your diagram. There are still three docks unassigned. You now assess each answer. Answer A must be false. Truck U cannot be unloaded at a dock one lower than Q because that is reserved for W in order for the configuration to be consistent with clue 2. Answer B could be true because you can assign U to dock 3, P to dock 5, and T to dock 6. This order is consistent with your clues and the facts given by the question, so this must be the correct answer. For learning purposes, let's review the remaining options. Answer C must be false because if T is assigned to dock 3, then P must be assigned to a higher dock than T and this is inconsistent with clue 1. Answer D cannot be true. Trucks P and U would have to be assigned to docks 5 and 6 respectively and T would have to be assigned to dock 3. This order is inconsistent with clue 1 because T would be assigned a lower dock than P. Answer E must be false. Since R is assigned to dock 7 and P to dock 6, T would be assigned a lower dock than P and this is also inconsistent with clue 1. **The correct choice is answer B.**

Questions 21–26

As with all logic games you follow the six-step process.

STEP 1: **Identify the game type.**

Paying close attention to the language of the game, you can see that this is a two-tiered ordering game. It includes both grouping and ordering language. For example, it requires that you group six of the eight cargoes into three trucks. This is definitely a grouping requirement. Then, it says that the cargo must be loaded in a particular order—front first, then back—and this is definitely ordering language. Each truck has two elements—front and back—which is another hallmark of the two-tiered ordering game. Lastly, the two slots in each group are specified. The front and back of each truck are definitive and not interchangeable. Therefore, you know you are facing a two-tiered ordering game.

STEP 2: **Begin your diagram.**

You can imagine a loading dock at the bottom of the diagram with the trucks lined up from left to right. (This may seem confusing, but remember that dock loaders must go through the back to load the front, thus the loading dock is at the bottom.)

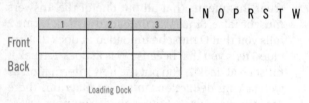

STEP 3: **Symbolize the clues.**

In this game there are only three clues. Go through them one at a time.

Clue 1: L can only go in Truck 2.

This can be represented in the diagram. The clue does not tell you whether L has to be in the front hold or back hold, so you put the letter L above the column for Truck 2.

Clue 2: T and W cannot go in the back hold of a truck.

This is really two different clues. You can represent both using the box method of representation:

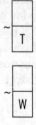

Clue 3: If S is loaded on a truck, then N and O go on the next truck, unless S is loaded on Truck 3.

This clue is a complex conditional statement. In essence it says that if S is on Truck 1, then N and O are loaded on Truck 2. Also, if S is loaded on Truck 2, then N and O are loaded on Truck 3. But, if S is loaded on Truck 3, N and O can be loaded on any truck. You can set this up as two separate conditionals to represent the first part of the statement:

$$S_1 \rightarrow N_2 \ \& \ O_2$$
$$S_2 \rightarrow N_3 \ \& \ O_3$$

The contrapositives are as follows:

$$\sim N_2/\sim O_2 \rightarrow \sim S_1$$
$$\sim N_3/\sim O_3 \rightarrow \sim S_2$$

The last part of the statement is implied; if S is on Truck 3, no restriction has been placed on N and O.

STEP 4: **Double-check your symbolizations.**

To double-check your symbolizations, translate your symbolized clues back into normal English and see whether they match the original language of each clue. When you are through, your page should look like this:

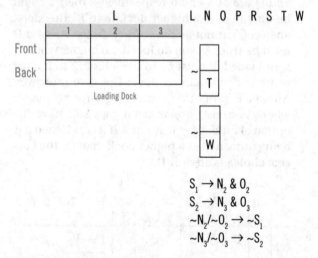

$$S_1 \rightarrow N_2 \ \& \ O_2$$
$$S_2 \rightarrow N_3 \ \& \ O_3$$
$$\sim N_2/\sim O_2 \rightarrow \sim S_1$$
$$\sim N_3/\sim O_3 \rightarrow \sim S_2$$

STEP 5: **Make deductions.**

1. Can't-be-first-or-last deductions

   At first you might think that your third clue gives you the opportunity to make this deduction. After all, if N and O must be loaded on the next truck after S, then S cannot be last, but this is not the case. The "unless" clause on that clue takes this opportunity away. S can be loaded on Truck 3 because the clue says that if it is, N and O can be loaded anywhere. Only if S is loaded on Truck 1 or 2 do N and O have to be loaded on the next truck. Therefore, you cannot make this sort of deduction for this game.

2. Repeated-element deductions

   You do not have an opportunity to make this sort of deduction since there are no repeated elements among the clues.

3. Down-to-two deductions

   You cannot definitively place any cargo in a particular hold. You need more information to make this sort of deduction.

4. Block-splitting deductions

   If S is located in either Truck 1 or Truck 2, then the next truck will become fully loaded with N and O. This creates a block that cannot be split and will most likely restrict the loading of cargo. Also, since T and W both cannot be loaded in the back hold of a truck, they obviously cannot be loaded on the same truck. You can add these clues to your list:

$$T \rightarrow {\sim}W$$
$$W \rightarrow {\sim}T$$

   Finally, before you tackle the questions, see if you can make any deductions based on the setup of the game and the clues. Unfortunately, there are not many clues in this particular two-tiered ordering game and none of the clues, when taken together, lead to any further deductions.

STEP 6: **Answer the questions in the smartest order.** Answer the questions in this order:

1. Answer the Complete and Accurate List question.

2. Answer questions that give you more information to work with.

3. Answer the remaining questions.

   Question 21 is the Complete and Accurate List question for this game and should be answered first. Questions with more information include the following:

   Question 22 ("P and R are not loaded . . . ")
   Question 24 ("L, S, and W are loaded in different trucks . . . ")
   Question 25 ("N, P, and R . . . loaded in the fronts . . . ")
   Question 26 ("P is on the back of Truck 2, and N is on the back of Truck 3 . . . ")

   That leaves question 23 to be answered last.

THE ANSWERS

21. Answer: **D**

   The question is asking you to determine which answer gives a valid loading register. You do not need your diagram to help you answer this one. You can use your clues to test each answer. Thankfully, you only need the first clue to find the correct answer on this question, as the only answer with L in the second truck is D. You do not have to look further and there is no reason to check the answer against the other clues. **The correct choice is answer D**.

22. Answer: **A**

   The question tells you that P and R are not loaded, then asks for a possible listing of those cargoes that are loaded into the front holds of the three trucks. The facts given tell us that L, N, O, S, T, and W are left as possible cargoes, and you must have six filled holds. Thus, all these items must be loaded. Clue 1 tells you that T and W must be loaded in the front, so the only answer that will work will include T and W. Luckily, answer A is the only option that includes both T and W. **The correct choice is answer A**.

23. Answer: **C**

   This question asks that you determine which pair of cargoes, if loaded together, must go on Truck 3. Notice that the question does not say the pairs are in any particular order, front and back, so order is not the issue, only pairing. This question also does not require your diagram. You know from your third clue that if S is paired with either N or O, then they must be on Truck 3. Answer C pairs S and N, and they can only be on Truck 3. Thus, **the correct choice must be answer C**.

24. Answer: **C**

   The question tells you that L, S, and W are each loaded on a different truck, then asks you to choose which among the answers *could* be true. This means that four out of the five answers have to be false. Use your diagram to check each scenario. You know that L is on Truck 2, so S and W must be on Trucks 1 and 2, but you don't know which is on which truck. You must test each answer and see what happens.

(A) T is on Truck 1

Clue 2 tells you that T must be loaded in the front of Truck 1. Therefore, W cannot be on Truck 1. W cannot be on Truck 2 because according to clue 1,

L must be on that truck, so W must be on Truck 3. That leaves Truck 1 for S. According to clue 3, N and O must be loaded on Truck 2, but there is not enough room and you cannot split that block. Therefore, this cannot be your answer.

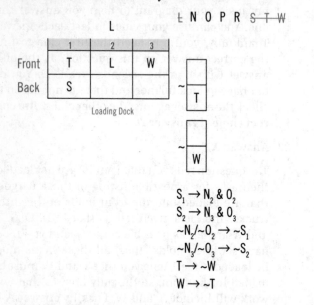

$S_1 \rightarrow N_2 \& O_2$
$S_2 \rightarrow N_3 \& O_3$
$\sim N_2/\sim O_2 \rightarrow \sim S_1$
$\sim N_3/\sim O_3 \rightarrow \sim S_2$
$T \rightarrow \sim W$
$W \rightarrow \sim T$

(B) S is on Truck 2.

The question says that L, S, and W are loaded on different trucks, but clue 1 tells you that L must be loaded on Truck 2, so if S is on Truck 2 the conditions given by the question cannot be met and this cannot be your answer.

(C) N is on Truck 3.

This situation does not trigger any conditions set out by your clues, and as you can see in the diagram, you can create a viable loading scenario, so this is your answer. But let's go through the remainder of the answers for learning purposes.

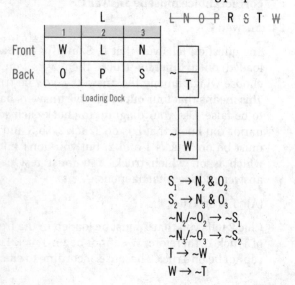

$S_1 \rightarrow N_2 \& O_2$
$S_2 \rightarrow N_3 \& O_3$
$\sim N_2/\sim O_2 \rightarrow \sim S_1$
$\sim N_3/\sim O_3 \rightarrow \sim S_2$
$T \rightarrow \sim W$
$W \rightarrow \sim T$

(D) W is on Truck 3.

Again, L must be on Truck 2 and S must be on Truck 1, which leaves no room on Truck 2 for N and O. Since you cannot satisfy clue 3 this cannot be your answer.

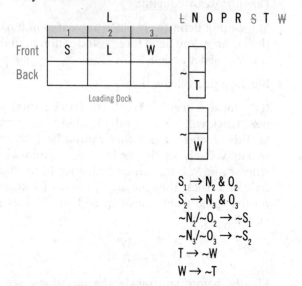

$S_1 \rightarrow N_2 \& O_2$
$S_2 \rightarrow N_3 \& O_3$
$\sim N_2/\sim O_2 \rightarrow \sim S_1$
$\sim N_3/\sim O_3 \rightarrow \sim S_2$
$T \rightarrow \sim W$
$W \rightarrow \sim T$

(E) S is on Truck 1.

As with the previous answers you know that L must be on Truck 2. If S is on Truck 1, then N and O must be on Truck 2, but L makes it impossible for N and O to be loaded together. This cannot be your answer.

The correct choice is answer C.

25. **Answer: E**

This question tells you that N, P, and R are loaded into the fronts of the three trucks, but the order is indeterminate. You must find the answer that *must* be true no matter what order they are in. You know immediately that T and W cannot be loaded since there are no more front holds available. Therefore, only L, O, and S are left to load in the three remaining holds. Clue 1 tells you that L must be in the back hold of Truck 2. You look at your diagram to figure out which answer must be true under the conditions. To test the answers, you put N, P, and R in no particular order to see what might happen. You quickly see that S cannot be in Truck 1 because there is no room for N and O together in Truck 2. There is no room for S in Truck 2 either, so it must be in Truck 3. Thus, O must be on Truck 1. You can quickly see answer E must be the correct choice. You can rearrange N, P, and R, but O must be on Truck 1 regardless of the order, because Truck 2 and Truck 3 become filled by L and S respectively. **The correct choice is answer E.**

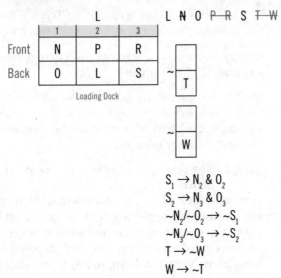

$$S_1 \rightarrow N_2 \,\&\, O_2$$
$$S_2 \rightarrow N_3 \,\&\, O_3$$
$$\sim N_2 / \sim O_2 \rightarrow \sim S_1$$
$$\sim N_3 / \sim O_3 \rightarrow \sim S_2$$
$$T \rightarrow \sim W$$
$$W \rightarrow \sim T$$

26. Answer: **B**

You are given that P is in the back hold of Truck 2 and N is in the back hold of Truck 3. You are to choose the answer that includes a possible list of cargoes in the fronts of Trucks 1, 2, and 3. This means that four out of the five options are impossible given the conditions of the question. The list of cargoes in each answer is in order (1, 2, 3). You look at your diagram and test each scenario.

(A) W, O, and R

This scenario leaves L, S, and T to load and only one hold, the back of Truck 1. None of these cargoes can go into that hold. Clue 1 says L must be on Truck 2. Loading S requires that N and O be loaded together on Truck 2 and that is not possible. Finally, clue 2 tells you that T cannot be loaded in the back of any truck.

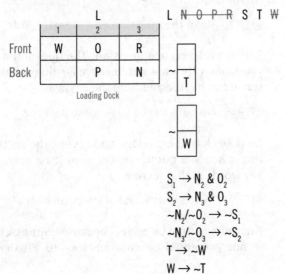

$$S_1 \rightarrow N_2 \,\&\, O_2$$
$$S_2 \rightarrow N_3 \,\&\, O_3$$
$$\sim N_2 / \sim O_2 \rightarrow \sim S_1$$
$$\sim N_3 / \sim O_3 \rightarrow \sim S_2$$
$$T \rightarrow \sim W$$
$$W \rightarrow \sim T$$

(B) W, L, and O

This scenario works. All the cargoes in the front holds are consistent with your clues and you are left with R, which can be loaded in the back of Truck 1 without conflicting with your clues. This is your answer, but let's go through the remaining answers for learning purposes.

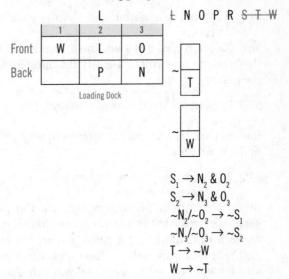

$$S_1 \rightarrow N_2 \,\&\, O_2$$
$$S_2 \rightarrow N_3 \,\&\, O_3$$
$$\sim N_2 / \sim O_2 \rightarrow \sim S_1$$
$$\sim N_3 / \sim O_3 \rightarrow \sim S_2$$
$$T \rightarrow \sim W$$
$$W \rightarrow \sim T$$

(C) R, L, and O

This option leaves S, T, and W as possible cargoes to be loaded in the one remaining hold on the back of Truck 1. All three fail your tests. S requires N and O to be loaded on Truck 2, but there is no room for them. According to clue 2, neither T nor W can be loaded in the back hold of any truck. Note that just because N and O are together on Truck 3 does not necessarily mean that S must be on Truck 2. The "if . . . then" conditional goes from left to right but not the reverse. Either way, this cannot be your answer.

(D) O, R, and S

This scenario leaves L, T, and W as possible cargoes to be loaded in the one remaining hold on the back of Truck 1. All three fail your tests. Clue 1 tells you that L must be on Truck 2. Clue 2 tells you that both T and W cannot be loaded on the back hold of any truck, so this cannot be your answer.

(E) S, O, and R

This is merely a reordering of answer D and the same conditions apply. This is not your answer.

The correct choice is answer B.

SECTION IV

PASSAGE 1

1. Answer: **E**

   STEP 1:   **Read the question and identify your task.**
   This is a Main Idea question. The first question for this passage asks you to identify the main idea of the passage.

   STEP 2:   **Go back to the passage to find the answer.**
   Review the first and last paragraphs to get a sense of the main idea.

   STEP 3:   **Read every word of every answer choice.**
   Answer A cannot be correct because the passage suggests that budgetary conditions may make it difficult, but the passage does not suggest that it is impossible. When an answer uses such categorical terms as *never*, you can almost always eliminate that answer. Answer B cannot be correct because the passage never discusses a disagreement between the two different theories. It merely presents the different theories and posits that future research could reconcile them. Nor does the passage suggest that any of the theories are hindering progress. Only the lack of money is hindering progress, according to the passage. Answer C cannot be correct because the universe's future is not unresolved. The passage states for certainty that it is expanding and not contracting. Answer D cannot be correct because Einstein's theory did not necessarily fail to deliver an explanation. The passage makes it clear that one of his failed theorems offers a possible explanation, so this cannot be your choice for the answer. Finally, answer E seems to give a good explanation of the main idea. The passage is suggesting that until tests are done, scientists are left with a theoretical concept (dark energy) and several hypotheses about how it works within the universe. **The correct choice is answer E.**

2. Answer: **A**

   STEP 1:   **Read the question and identify your task.**
   This is an Information Retrieval question. The question asks you to identify the reason that the author mentions the known quantity of the energy necessary to sustain the current rate of expansion in the universe.

   STEP 2:   **Go back to the passage to find the answer.**
   Reread those particular lines in the passage (at the end of paragraph one).

   STEP 3:   **Read every word of every answer choice.**
   Answer A seems like a good answer. It is true that the passage is suggesting that scientists understand the overall universe and what is necessary to sustain its expansion, but they hardly know what is enabling it to do so, so this is probably the correct choice. Still, you must review the remaining options to be certain. Answer B is true but limited in scope. It focuses on what is not known, not on why the passage mentions what is known about the universe. Therefore, this cannot be your answer. Answer C cannot be correct because at that point in the passage the expansion of the universe is considered a given. The author is not still trying to prove that point. Answer D is incorrect because the author has not yet gotten to the discussion of the theoretical models that explain dark matter. Finally, answer E is also a bit premature since at this point you do not know the estimated magnitude of dark energy's makeup of the universe. Knowing the total energy needed to expand the universe gives no indication of what makes up that energy. **The correct choice is answer A.**

3. Answer: **C**

   STEP 1:   **Read the question and identify your task.**
   This is an Inference question. The question asks you to identify what statement regarding quintessence can be inferred from the passage.

   STEP 2:   **Go back to the passage to find the answer.**
   Look back at the passage and review the section that discusses quintessence, or at least scan for key words in that section.

   STEP 3:   **Read every word of every answer choice.**
   Answer A cannot be correct because quintessence is not presented as contradictory to Einstein's

theory. The passage presents quintessence as one hypothesis that might explain the behavior of dark energy within Einstein's cosmological constant. Answer B cannot be true because the conclusion of the entire passage is that quintessence and other ideas are just theoretical, and until observational evidence is obtained, we will never know the nature of the universe. Answer C says that dark energy is not inherent in space and is not consistent throughout the universe. The passage implies both of these ideas. It says that quintessence conceptualizes dark matter as a force that evolves with the growing universe. Also, quintessence conceptualizes dark matter as an "inhomogeneous energy fluid or field" that is not consistently present. This is most likely your answer, but you should review your remaining options. Answer D cannot be correct because the scientists have used Einstein's cosmological constant to explain the excess energy. The excess energy is not a problem with Einstein's equations as the answer suggests. Finally, answer E is too certain about what dark energy or quintessence has replaced or explained. Since it is still theoretical, you cannot yet accept such certainty even if the results seem likely. **The correct choice is answer C.**

4. Answer: **C**

STEP 1:   Read the question and identify your task.

This is a Tone question that asks you to identify the author's attitude towards proposals to measure dark energy.

STEP 2:   Go back to the passage to find the answer.

Refer to the last paragraph of the passage where this is discussed. The author says that the proposals are expensive and that *budgetary issues may preclude such efforts.*

STEP 3:   Read every word of every answer choice.

Answer A is not correct, because while the author does consider the proposals, he or she is quite restrained and concludes that they are not fiscally practical. Answer B is far too extreme for the tone of this passage. Keep answer C because the author certainly seems pessimistic. Answer D is incorrect because the author is not optimistic about the proposals. Answer E is not the best choice, because the author is not ambivalent, but instead feels that the experiments proposed may not be possible. **The correct choice is answer C.**

5. Answer: **E**

STEP 1:   Read the question and identify your task.

This is an Information Retrieval question. The question asks that you identify the answer that is *not* a theoretically possible characteristic of dark energy.

STEP 2:   Go back to the passage to find the answer.

You refer to the passage and review the characteristics of dark energy.

STEP 3:   Read every word of every answer choice.

Answer A is what Einstein's cosmological constant argues is the nature of dark energy when it says that dark energy constitutes the "energy density of the vacuum of space." Answer B is mentioned in paragraph three, which says that quintessence theorizes that dark energy "evolves with the growing universe and exerts increasingly expansionary forces." Answer C is mentioned in the first and last paragraphs, when the passage discusses dark energy as making up more of the universe and turning dark matter and matter into "minority players." Also, the paragraph says that "the notion that gravity is the dominant force in the universe is no longer sustainable." Answer D is a characteristic of the quintessence theory. Lastly, consider answer E. The passage says in the first few sentences that this characteristic of dark energy is no longer held to be true, so **the correct choice is answer E.**

6. Answer: **B**

STEP 1:   Read the question and identify your task.

This is an Arguments-style question that asks you to find an answer that would support the theory of quintessence.

STEP 2:   Go back to the passage to find the answer.

Refer to the third paragraph of the passage where quintessence is discussed. The author says that this theory involves dark energy that is inhomogeneous, has negative pressure, exerts expansionary force, and flows like large rivers or seas.

STEP 3:   Read every word of every answer choice.

Answer A is incorrect because quintessence proposes dark energy with negative pressure. Answer B mentions that the energy density observed has varied over time. This would be evidence of inhomogeneity. Keep answer B for now. Answers C and D would both weaken the argument for quintessence. Answer E neither strengthens nor weakens, since this is already known and quintessence is a method for explaining the phenomenon. **The correct choice is answer B.**

PASSAGE 2

7. Answer: **D**

STEP 1: Read the question and identify your task.
This is a Main Idea question. However, in the case of paired passages, look for answer choices that articulate the main ideas of both passages, as they relate to each other.

STEP 2: Go back to the passage to find the answer.
Refer to your passage summary.

STEP 3: Read every word of every answer choice.
Answer A discusses solutions to problems, which is never addressed in either passage. Although the two theater movements discussed here both arose in response to societal ills, there is no sense from the passages that these were "solutions" to the problem of the Great Depression. For similar reasons, answer choice B can be eliminated. Passages A and B both deal with the same circumstance: the Great Depression. And both discuss theater movements arising from these social and economic circumstances. But passage B is not a solution to a problem in passage A. There is also no contradiction between the passages, so eliminate answer choice C. Answer choice D, however, in its broad strokes, gets the relationship correct. The passages are very similar, with both describing theater groups that came about as a response to the circumstances of the Great Depression. This is very likely the correct answer. Answer choice E cannot be correct. There is no suggestion that the Shock Troupe is a refinement of Group Theatre. If anything, passage B suggests that the opposite is true, due to the Shock Troupe's later adoption of some of the Group Theatre's methods. **The correct answer must be D.**

8. Answer: **C**

STEP 1: Read the question and identify your task.
This is an Information Retrieval question. The question is asking about a specific part of the passage and what is true.

STEP 2: Go back to the passage to find the answer.
Refer back to the part of Passage A that talks about theater after the Depression, specifically the last part of the passage. It says that agit-prop theater faded, but that method acting continued.

STEP 3: Read every word of every answer choice.
Looking back at the passage you can see that Answer A cannot be correct since it says that agit-prop theatre was an evolution from an earlier form of theater. Thus agit-prop was not a wholly new concept. Answer B makes an unwarranted connection between a political movement and Strasburg's efforts, which were artistically motivated, not politically motivated. Answer C is an excellent candidate for your choice. Refer back to the part of Passage A that talks about theater after the Depression, specifically the last part of the passage. It says that agit-prop theater faded, but method acting continued. This is most likely your answer, but you should review the remaining options. Answers D and E cannot be inferred from the passage. **The correct answer is C.**

9. Answer: **B**

STEP 1: Read the question and identify your task.
This is a Line ID question. The answer choices will contain four points that are explicitly mentioned as being points of difference in the passage. The correct answer will not be mentioned at all or will be a point of similarity.

STEP 2: Go back to the passage to find the answer.
In this case, go back to passages A and B, and look for discussion about the differences between these theater groups and others.

STEP 3: Read every word of every answer choice.
Passages A and B both explicitly mention that fact that the Group Theatre used trained actors while the Shock Troupe did not, so eliminate answer choice A. Answer choice B, however,

immediately looks promising. Both groups were concerned with presenting plays that depicted societal ills. This will most likely be your correct answer. Answer choice C is another point of difference between the two. The passages mention that the Group Theatre used conventional theatrical staging, whereas the Shock Troupe sometimes performed in the street. The names of the characters are another point of difference, explicitly mentioned in both passages, so eliminate answer choice D. Finally, answer E may be tempting, but passage B states that the Group Theatre merely wanted to depict societal ills whereas the Shock Troupe wanted to move further and actually advocate societal change. **The correct answer is B.**

10. Answer: **C**

   STEP 1: **Read the question and identify your task.**

   This is an Inference question. This question is asking you to use the information about the Shock Troup as the basis for a judgment, mainly which play the theater would least likely perform.

   STEP 2: **Go back to the passage to find the answer.**

   You go back to the part of passage B that describes the theatrical philosophy of the Shock Troup.

   STEP 3: **Read every word of every answer choice.**

   The Shock Troup was a politically oriented theater group, so the answer that is least political will be the correct choice. Answer A, B, D, and E are all very politically or socially strident plays. The play described in answer C seems rooted in the drama of everyday life. There is little social or political content in it. **The correct answer is C.**

11. Answer: **A**

   STEP 1: **Read the question and identify your task.**

   This is an Inference question. The correct answer will correctly identify the attitude of the author of passage B toward the Group Theatre as that attitude is presented in the passages.

   STEP 2: **Go back to the passage to find the answer.**

   Passage B only mentioned the Group Theatre in passing, noting at the beginning of the passage that the Group Theater was concerned only with societal ills whereas the Shock Troupe wanted to also advocate change. At the end, the author also

mentions that the Shock Troupe wanted to train its actors using the Group Theatre's method, that it might better connect with audiences.

   STEP 3: **Read every word of every answer choice.**

   Answer A is promising right away. The Group Theatre was brought in to train the Shock Troupe's actors to allow those actors to better connect with audiences. Answer choice A is most likely correct. Answer choice B discusses which theater group was better known, which is never discussed. Eliminate answer choice B. Answer choice C discusses comparative idealism, which is not discussed here. Additionally, the information in the passage would seem to support the opposite contention, since the Shock Troupe thought theater could change society, not merely present the ills of society. Much like answer choice B, you have no way of knowing which play was more popular. Finally, although you know that the Shock Troupe believed that "The Method" was an effective means of teaching acting, you cannot know that they believed it to be the most effective means of teaching acting. **The correct answer must be A.**

12. Answer: **C**

   STEP 1: **Read the question and identify your task.**

   This is a Line ID question. This question takes a technical term and asks you to choose the answer that most closely represents what it means.

   STEP 2: **Go back to the passage to find the answer.**

   You look back at the passage and derive that agitprop theaters were politically motivated, and that those theaters took extreme measures to put their political ideas in front of the masses. Thus, the answer will be oriented toward this sort of description. All the answers extend the shortened words on each side of the hyphen so you must assess both words.

   STEP 3: **Read every word of every answer choice.**

   For answer A, both words are inadequate. Agitprop theater was not concerned with agriculture and it did not make propositions through its performances. Answer B does well with the first part of the term. Agit-prop theater definitely used its performances to agitate, especially when they performed at picket lines or in front of workers as they went to work. But, the second term, "proposal," seems too weak a description of what they did. Answer C is much better. The first term, as discussed, fits well. The second term works as well, because they definitely used their performances to spread propaganda or politically charged ideas. This is most likely your answer, but you must assess the remaining choices as well. The second term in answer D is problematic. Propagation is a term that could be used to describe the dissemination of ideas, but it also has a more common meaning related to breeding. Such ambiguity hurts this option's chances. Answer E is way off the mark since the word "proper" does not fit agit-prop theater at all. They were not interested in being a proper theater, especially since they performed their plays outside the theater. **The correct answer is C.**

PASSAGE 3

13. Answer: **B**

    STEP 1: **Read the question and identify your task.**

    This is a Main Idea question, which in essence is asking you to find among the answers the one statement that sums up the author's argument or thesis.

    STEP 2: **Go back to the passage to find the answer.**

    Refer to your passage summary.

    STEP 3: **Read every word of every answer choice.**

    Answer A focuses on Bo Rothstein's essay but ignores the rest of the passage, which puts Rothstein's claims in context of a wider discussion of the merits of a welfare state. Answer B starts with Rothstein's essay, then adds the context, the evaluation of happiness as a measure of success and perspective on whether the studies help you with the larger argument afoot. Even though this answer is not perfect, it is your best candidate so far. You must evaluate the remaining options. Answer C gives a good description of the political part of the passage but ignores the essays and studies discussed, so this is most likely not your choice. Answer D is problematic because the passage does not say the politicians, social scientists, and economists are unsupported by data, just that they are not focused on the happiness factor. Most likely they do have their own data, just not Rothstein, Pacek, and Radcliff's data that takes happiness into account. Answer E starts out well. The passage does note some flaws in the SWB measurement, but the passage makes

no claim that an improvement in the data fueling this measurement would make it more acceptable to the "thinkers of today." You are left with the only answer that works, answer B, flawed though it may be. **The correct choice is answer B.**

14. Answer: **E**

    STEP 1: **Read the question and identify your task.**

    This is an Arguments-style question. It asks that you choose the answer that best describes the structure used in the passage's argument.

    STEP 2: **Go back to the passage to find the answer.**

    To do this, you look back at the passage and read the first sentence or two of each paragraph to get a sense of how the passage moves from one subject to the next. You notice that the first paragraph starts with a very general discussion of the current conflict over the welfare state. The second paragraph moves to a discussion of measuring happiness. The third paragraph goes deeper into the basis of Rothstein's work on happiness. Finally, the concluding paragraph brings the discussion back to the United States. Now, you assess your choices.

    STEP 3: **Read every word of every answer choice.**

    Answer A is a very good description of the passage, and you might stop here, but the description does not seem to do justice to paragraph three. Paragraph three does not simply "assess" the happiness measurement. Still, you will hold on to this option as a possibility and read through the remaining options to see if there is a better one. In answer B the word "solution" in the second sentence is inappropriate for this passage. The author of the passage offers no solutions since the existence of the welfare state is not a social problem (such as crime) that must be "solved." Instead, the passage discusses the merits of the universal welfare state and how to evaluate its success or failure. Answer C is incorrect because its organization does not match the passage. The third paragraph actually goes on to provide more information on the basis of Rothstein's work on happiness. It does not "discredit" that work. Answer D also says that a solution to the problem is proposed and there is no solution offered, so this cannot be your choice. Finally, answer E offers answer A some competition. In this case, the answer seems more descriptive, especially with regard to paragraph three, saying that it discusses the validity of the happiness measurement, something answer A ignores. Between answers A and E, answer E is the better description, so **the correct choice is answer E.**

15. Answer: **C**

   <u>STEP 1:</u>   **Read the question and identify your task.**

   This is a Line ID question. This question asks that you look at a specific sentence or comment within the passage and explain the author's purpose for using it.

   <u>STEP 2:</u>   **Go back to the passage to find the answer.**

   Look back at the identified line and read the sentence and possibly its context to understand the author's reasons for including it. Your options will most likely be related to how that comment fits within that context.

   <u>STEP 3:</u>   **Read every word of every answer choice.**

   Answer A restates the author's comment in more explicit terms, but it does not explain why this comment appears where it does in the passage. Answer B may be true, but this relates to the next paragraph about Pacek and Radcliff and not to the paragraph in which the comment appears. Answer C is very promising. The sentence before the bias comment discusses how Rothstein focused his study on northern European countries, which you learn have long-standing welfare states, and you have already learned that he is Swedish, that is, from a northern European country. This explanation fits within your context and explains the comment very well. You should evaluate the remaining options just in case there is a better answer. Answer D may be true, but this explanation refers to a very different bias from the one the author is referring to in this context. Finally, answer E gives a totally unrelated fact and again refers to a different type of bias that does not fit into the context of where the comment appears in the passage. **The correct choice is answer C.**

16. Answer: **B**

   <u>STEP 1:</u>   **Read the question and identify your task.**

   This is a Weaken question. This question is very similar to a question you might find in the Arguments section of the LSAT. It asks which answer would most undermine or weaken a particular argument Rothstein is advancing.

   <u>STEP 2:</u>   **Go back to the passage to find the answer.**

   Rothstein feels that the SWB measurement is a better measurement of society because it is a "widespread" arbiter rather than an elitist one that the experts create.

   <u>STEP 3:</u>   **Read every word of every answer choice.**

   Answer A makes a case that the experts, due to their own biases, make judgments that are not much different from the happiness measurement. This weakens Rothstein's statement somewhat, but it is not a very strong attempt. You should expect that there might be a stronger effort in the other options. Answer B actually makes a case that the experts are superior because they filter out cultural factors that cloud one's ability to focus on the political problem at hand. This is stronger than answer A because it makes a case that the experts are better, but you should continue to review the remaining options. Answer C restates Rothstein's argument to a certain extent and does nothing to weaken it. Answer D may be true, but this also supports Rothstein's argument that his measurement is superior at assessing the success of the welfare state. If the experts are, in fact, unaffected by economic changes, they might remain an elitist arbiter and continue to make poor assessments of political progress. Finally, answer E also supports rather than weakens Rothstein's argument. If the SWB measurement is truly more accurate at making such predictions than the models created by the experts, then it is also a better arbiter. **The correct choice is answer B.**

17. Answer: **C**

   <u>STEP 1:</u>   **Read the question and identify your task.**

   This is a Strengthen question. This question is very similar to one you might find in the Arguments section of the LSAT.

   <u>STEP 2:</u>   **Go back to the passage to find the answer.**

   You must find a statement that supports the arguments presented in the first paragraph, advanced by those who support universal welfare programs in the United States.

   <u>STEP 3:</u>   **Read every word of every answer choice.**

   Answer A actually supports those in the opposing camp who believe that social welfare is harmful to the nation, so this cannot be your answer. Answer B also gives support to the opposition to welfare programs, saying that welfare recipients do not use the funds the federal government gives them. Answer C says that new welfare programs increase political participation. This very much supports the argument advanced in the passage that welfare programs are important to maintaining an active democracy. Therefore, this is most likely the correct answer. You should review the remaining answers to be sure. Answer D may be true, but whether recipients like or dislike the government does not seem relevant to either the supporters or the critics of social welfare programs. Answer E would definitely be helpful to the supporters of welfare programs, but it discusses an argument advanced by Rothstein later in the passage. The question asks that you base the answer just on paragraph one. Since this is not really addressing the specific arguments in the first paragraph, it is not as strong as answer C. **The correct choice is answer C.**

18. Answer: **D**

    STEP 1: **Read the question and identify your task.**
    This is a Tone question. For this question you are to use your own judgment at assessing the author's tone or attitude toward Rothstein's approach.

    STEP 2: **Go back to the passage to find the answer.**
    Specific words in the passage give you clues to this attitude. For example, the comment regarding Rothstein's bias in the second paragraph indicates that the author might have some doubts about Rothstein's conclusions. Consider the phrases "He even goes as far as to say" and "the SWB is the most controversial basis of these studies." These and other phrases, though tepid, attest to the author's doubts regarding Rothstein. You assess your options with this in mind.

    STEP 3: **Read every word of every answer choice.**
    These observations regarding the author's language make it impossible to think "cautious neutrality" can be correct, so answer A cannot be your choice. The author does not use strong enough language for you to consider answer B. Regarding answer C, the author acknowledges that Rothstein's work might be helpful to the discourse regarding the welfare state, but "moderate

advocacy" would mean the author is recommending it and this is not the case. Answer D is very likely your choice for the author does show a fair amount of skepticism with regard to Rothstein's work. Finally, in answer E, nothing in the language shows a grudging acceptance of Rothstein's ideas. This would require the author to ultimately admit an error in judgment and words of contrition as Rothstein's ideas won over. You see none of that in the passage. Thus, **the correct choice is answer D.**

19. Answer: **E**

    STEP 1: **Read the question and identify your task.**
    This is an Information Retrieval question. You must find among the answers the one statement Rothstein would disagree with.

    STEP 2: **Go back to the passage to find the answer.**
    You refer to the passage and read the sections that give Rothstein's views. Paragraphs two, three, and four all discuss his views. The one answer that is not consistent with those views concerning social happiness will be the correct answer.

    STEP 3: **Read every word of every answer choice.**
    In paragraph three you learn that Rothstein admits that cultural factors like the one in answer A could affect happiness. Even though he dismisses such concerns, he might agree that the abilities listed in answer A would cloud the relationship between the SWB and the establishment of a universal welfare state. For answer B, Rothstein would surely agree that a program protecting children would increase national happiness. Answer C relates to Rothstein's bias, which you have already seen favors the northern European states, so he would most likely agree with this statement. Next look at answer D. As the passage states, Rothstein believes that people need a long-standing trust in their institutions to achieve happiness, so he would definitely agree that such a long-standing program will increase their SWB. Finally, in answer E, Rothstein would never agree that a misappropriation proved the failure of a welfare state in general. He would say only that the particular welfare state had failed one of the key elements necessary to bring happiness to its recipients. **The correct choice is answer E.**

PASSAGE 4

20. Answer: **B**

STEP 1: Read the question and identify your task.

This is a Main Idea question, which asks you to find among the answers the one statement that encapsulates the passage.

STEP 2: Go back to the passage to find the answer.

Refer to your passage summary.

STEP 3: Read every word of every answer choice.

Read through the answers paying close attention to the language. Answer A attributes a motive to the corporations not supported by the passage. The passage says nothing about a "stigma" associated with cash donations or that they are seen as cheap marketing tactics. Actually, the passage states that they are no different from each other. Answer B is promising. The passage does argue that whether corporations integrate philanthropic activities into their operations or they just cut a check, the effect to all parties is the same, and the passage does explore the reasons for corporate philanthropy without coming to any particular conclusion. This is most likely your answer, but you need to review the remaining options to be sure. Answer C is too strong an opinion to be summarizing the main idea of this passage, which retains a certain amount of objectivity. The passage does not make such a strong recommendation to do both or either one. For answer D, extortion is one idea explored in the passage, but it is not the entire idea of the passage. This answer makes it too central, and the passage definitely does not make an outright recommendation that corporations just make a charitable donation. Finally, answer E is not bad, but it is fairly general in its discussion. There is no mention of the integration of philanthropy into operations and sales versus just cutting a check, which is central to the passage's argument. Thus, **the correct choice is answer B.**

21. Answer: **C**

STEP 1: Read the question and identify your task.

This is a Line ID question. You need to look at the lines specified in this question and assess the author's attitude or tone with regard to the philanthropy model discussed.

STEP 2: Go back to the passage to find the answer.

In this case, the lines discuss the philanthropic model in which corporations integrate philanthropy into their "supply, production, and sales operations such that they become part and parcel with their corporate and product identity." Reading the lines you discover that the author feels that this model is "no different than that of simple donations."

STEP 3: Read every word of every answer choice.

With this in mind you read through your answers. You learn later in the passage that answer A is not true, but you do not need the rest of the passage to know that nothing in the lines specified indicates such a positive perspective on the philanthropic mode. Answer B also discusses elements later in the passage that are contradictory to what they say. Still, the lines under consideration give no indication that the author views this model as empowering to the customers. Answer C is most likely your answer. The author definitely does not seem to believe that the new model is really anything new at all and also offers no insights into why corporations engage in philanthropy. You should review the remaining options to be sure. Answer D ventures into areas that are explored later in the passage and are out of the scope of this questions. And regarding answer E, the author does not seem very pleased with the new way of being philanthropic since the language indicates that the author does not see a difference between it and cutting a check. Therefore, **the correct choice is answer C.**

22. Answer: **B**

STEP 1: Read the question and identify your task.

This is an Inference question. This question is one of the rare ones that ask you to imagine the passage continuing into another paragraph, and you must select the answer that fills that role best. In essence, it is asking you to infer what will come after the last paragraph.

STEP 2: Go back to the passage to find the answer.

Return to the passage and scan the last paragraph. The last few sentences give you a clue as to where the author might continue with his or her thoughts. The last paragraph discusses the justifications for corporate philanthropy, and the last few sentences compare a corporation to an individual in society and how that view affects the analysis.

Read every word of every answer choice.

Answer A might be a good paragraph to be inserted after the second paragraph, which discusses integration of philanthropy into supply lines, but not at the end of the passage, which has moved on to other considerations. Answer B might very well be the next topic, moving on from corporate philanthropy to address whether the dollars they devote to charity do any good and which method works best. This is not a perfect option, but it might work. You will need to read through the other options to see if there is a better one. Answer C starts out well, but the second sentence veers off to make an odd logical leap into government intervention. Nothing in the passage mentions government involvement, so this is most likely not the correct choice. If the passage had ended with paragraph three, answer D might be correct, but the fourth paragraph makes this one impossible to choose, since it has moved on to address the larger question of whether corporations should be engaged in philanthropy at all. Finally, answer E is tempting, but it actually belongs as another point within the last paragraph rather than a new paragraph, which should move on to a new topic altogether but one that follows the previous paragraph logically. **Answer B is the correct choice.**

23. Answer: **E**

STEP 1: **Read the question and identify your task.**

This is an Information Retrieval question. You are asked to compare two different sections of the passage and choose the answer that most accurately describes the relationship between them.

STEP 2: **Go back to the passage to find the answer.**

You look at the specified sections of the passage and discover that the latter passage is almost a restatement of the earlier passage, except that the later passage seems more explicit and thus could be considered a clarification.

STEP 3: **Read every word of every answer choice.**

You can quickly eliminate answer A because you can see that both sections discuss the lack of difference between the two options and they both discuss the financial equation involved in the integration of philanthropy into operations and

sales. It cannot be true that there is no relationship. There is no other opinion than what the author has revealed in either section, so answer B can be eliminated. There also is no hypothetical situation offered in either section. No particular examples are discussed at all, so answer C cannot be the correct choice. Regarding answer D, there is agreement with the position but no disagreement over particulars. You have eliminated all the other answers, so answer E must be correct, but you must read it to be sure. The sections are equivalent assertions that integration versus just donating are not much different, and the latter section gives clarification to the financial aspect of why they are not different, specifically how both decrease profitability and shareholder value. **The correct choice is answer E.**

24. Answer: **C**

STEP 1: **Read the question and identify your task.**

This is an Inference question. This question asks that you make an inference based on the author's views on corporate philanthropy.

STEP 2: **Go back to the passage to find the answer.**

This question is asking for an inference based on your impression of the content of the entire passage and the author's opinion regarding corporate philanthropy. You must have read the entire passage to answer this question, but if you need to you can skim the passage for clues that might help you as you review the answers.

STEP 3: **Read every word of every answer choice.**

Regarding answer A, informing the customer that the corporation is getting a tax deduction is not exactly useful to the customer or the corporation. It is unlikely the author would agree with such an idea. For answer B, such a proposition might discourage the corporation from engaging in the philanthropic activity altogether, and it is unlikely the author wants that to happen since there are indications that the author supports corporate philanthropy even if some practices are questionable. Answer C seems like a valid idea that the author might agree with. The author implies that the customer is not informed that the increase in purchase price is a result of philanthropic efforts, so the author might support informing the customer about the effects of integrating philanthropy into operations and sales. This is probably your answer, but you should review the remaining options to be sure. Answer D is a nice idea, but this seems out of the scope of the passage. The author is not concerned about misuse of funds but in philanthropic efforts in general. Answer E is an interesting possibility as well, but the author is not really concerned about morality or ethics within corporations or that customers know about the company's morals. **The correct choice is answer C.**

25. Answer: **D**

   STEP 1: **Read the question and identify your task.**

   This is an Information Retrieval question. You are asked about a specific part of the passage and what is true based on what you read.

   STEP 2: **Go back to the passage to find the answer.**

   This question asks how companies reduce their effect on the environment. Look for those keywords.

   STEP 3: **Read every word of every answer choice.**

   Remember, you are looking for the answer that is NOT mentioned in the passage. Answers A, B, C, and E are all described in lines 19–26. Alternative work schedules are not discussed. **The correct choice is answer D.**

LSAT Logic Games

- How to work each of the four types of games you might encounter on the Logic Games section

- How to diagram and symbolize the information presented to you in each game

- How to draw deductions from the information presented to you in each game

- The best techniques and methods for working each kind of question

- How to approach the Logic Games section as a whole

- Diagram and symbolize the setup and the clues
- Make deductions from that information
- Answer each of the different kinds of questions you'll come across

We'll also discuss the best strategy for tackling the Logic Games section as a whole.

Accordingly, this chapter contains six cases. Four of them—Case 1, Case 3, Case 4, and Case 5—introduce a particular type of game. Those four cases include a sample game and a detailed explanation of how to work the sample game. Case 2 introduces you to conditional statements, which are a particularly important type of clue and can appear on any type of game. Finally, Case 6 discusses section-wide strategy.

Two important notes before you turn to the first case:

- As you'll soon see firsthand, an effective Logic Games strategy involves a good bit of writing: you'll draw a diagram, symbolize clues, and map out your answers to each question. Unfortunately, you're not allowed to bring scratch paper into the LSAT. You have to do all your work in the blank space in your test booklet. As you practice, get in the habit of working in the small space you'll have available to you.
- The sample games used in these cases are not representative of the average difficulty of the games you'll see on test day. The games are teaching tools; they are designed to demonstrate the fundamentals of a sound approach to working games. Each case concludes with setup drills that reflect the difficulty of real games.

This chapter focuses on the Logic Games section (formally known as the Analytical Reasoning section). The cases in this chapter will teach you a six-step approach you can use to work every game you encounter. The Logic Games section can seem daunting at first, so we'll break it down into parts. As noted in Chapter 1, the Logic Games section requires you to perform only two tasks: ordering and grouping. The test writers use some combination of those two tasks to create four different types of games.

This chapter introduces you to each of the four major game types that appear on the LSAT. You will learn the best way to:

- Determine what kind of game you're working based on the information in the setup and the clues

Practicing is the only way to truly get a sense of how hard logic games really are. The Logic Games sections in the practice tests included at the back of this book contain a mix of games that is representative of what you're likely to encounter on the actual LSAT.

Case 1

One-Tiered Ordering Games: Emily Walks the Dogs

This case serves two primary functions. First, it introduces the general approach you should use to work every logic game. That approach involves the following six steps:

1. Identify the game type
2. Begin your diagram
3. Symbolize the clues
4. Double-check your symbolizations
5. Make deductions
6. Answer the questions in the smartest order

Because you'll use this same six-step approach on every game you encounter, this case is the longest case of this chapter. As you work different kinds of games and more difficult games, you'll want to return to this case to review the fundamentals.

Second, this case introduces you to a particular type of logic game: one-tiered ordering games. One-tiered ordering games have been by far the most common type of game on recent LSATs. As noted in Chapter 1, the LSAC has released to the public 15 of the 20 LSATs that it administered between 2006 and 2010. Of the 60 games that appear on those LSATs, 24—or 40 percent—were one-tiered ordering games. That's an average of just under two per test. Mastering one-tiered ordering games is therefore an indispensable component of success on test day.

We'll introduce ordering games using a sample game, which we'll walk through together step by step. If you want to take a shot at working it on your own beforehand, feel free. You might find the explanation of how to set up and work the game easier to understand if you've spent some time trying to work it yourself. But you don't need to do so; after all, the purpose of this chapter is to introduce you to a new, more effective method of solving logic games.

A dog walker named Emily has been hired to walk six dogs: a Labrador, a Mutt, a Poodle, a Retriever, a Schnauzer, and a Terrier. She walks each dog exactly once, and she walks them one at a time. The order in which Emily walks the dogs must be consistent with the following:

She walks the Labrador some time before the Terrier.
She walks the Poodle immediately after the Mutt.

She walks the Retriever either immediately before or immediately after the Terrier.
She walks the Schnauzer fourth.

1. Which of the following could be the order, from first to last, in which Emily walks the dogs?

   (A) L, T, R, S, M, P
   (B) M, L, P, S, T, R
   (C) T, R, L, S, M, P
   (D) L, M, P, R, T, S
   (E) R, L, T, S, M, P

2. Which of the following must be false?

   (A) Emily walks the Terrier second.
   (B) Emily walks the Labrador third.
   (C) Emily walks the Mutt third.
   (D) Emily walks the Retriever sixth.
   (E) Emily walks the Poodle sixth.

3. If Emily walks the Retriever third, which of the following must be true?

   (A) Emily walks the Terrier fourth.
   (B) Emily walks the Poodle sixth.
   (C) Emily walks the Poodle fifth.
   (D) Emily walks the Labrador second.
   (E) Emily walks the Mutt first.

4. Which of the following must be false?

   (A) Emily walks the Mutt first.
   (B) Emily walks the Labrador second.
   (C) Emily walks the Terrier fifth.
   (D) Emily walks the Labrador first.
   (E) Emily walks the Retriever third.

5. Which one of the following is a complete and accurate list of the positions in which Emily could walk the Retriever?

   (A) 5, 6
   (B) 3, 5
   (C) 3, 5, 6
   (D) 2, 3, 5, 6
   (E) 1, 2, 3, 5, 6

6. If Emily walks the Mutt second, which of the following could be false?

    (A) She walks the Labrador before she walks the Mutt.

    (B) She walks the Terrier after she walks the Schnauzer.

    (C) She walks the Retriever after she walks the Terrier.

    (D) She walks the Schnauzer before she walks the Retriever.

    (E) She walks the Poodle after she walks the Labrador.

STEP 1: Identify the Game Type

To determine what kind of game you're dealing with, look to *language in the setup* and *language in the clues.* It's important that you read both the setup and the clues before you begin your diagram. Sometimes the information you need appears in the clues and sometimes there are clues in the setup.

Because you're being asked to arrange the elements (the dogs) in sequential order (which one was walked first, second, etc., down to sixth), this is an ordering game. Because you're assigning exactly one element to each slot in the game, this is a one-tiered ordering game (we'll discuss a different kind of ordering game—two-tiered ordering games—in Case 4).

What's the language in the setup that marks this as an ordering game? Here, the setup explicitly says "the *order* in which Emily walks the dogs." The other language in this setup that is the hallmark of an ordering game is, "She walks each dog *exactly once*, and she walks them *one at a time*." You're putting things in order, one at a time. Here are some other examples of language the LSAT could use to set up an ordering game:

- Five basketball players are ranked by height from tallest to shortest. There are no ties.
- The new children's book series has exactly eight chapters.
- A real-estate agent must show seven houses. She does not show any of the houses more than once, and no two houses are shown at the same time.

When you see "exactly once" and "one at a time" language in the setup and comparative language in the clues, you're dealing with an ordering game.

Similarly, comparative language in the clues is a strong indicator that this is an ordering game: Emily walks some dogs "before" and "after" other dogs. Clues that assign a particular element a numbered

rank ("She walks the Schnauzer fourth") are also an ordering-game staple. Here is some other language you might see in the clues of ordering games:

- Before and after
- Earlier and later
- Higher and lower
- More expensive and less expensive
- Taller and shorter
- Younger (or newer) and older
- Numbering language: "cannot be third," "must be either first or last," and so on

STEP 2: Begin Your Diagram

Once you've classified the game as a one-tiered ordering game, you can begin drawing your diagram. Your goal is to draw a diagram that is a visually accurate representation of the logical relationship between the elements. In other words, when you're trying to figure out what kind of diagram to draw, just ask yourself, "What does this game look like?"

To determine what kind of diagram to use, ask yourself, "What does this game look like?"

This game asks you to create a list numbered 1 through 6 of the order in which Emily walks the dogs. So, your diagram will look like this:

1	2	3	4	5	6

Next, you'll symbolize the game's elements and each of the clues. First, abbreviate each element using a letter. Then list the letters off to the side of the diagram so you can keep track of them as you work.

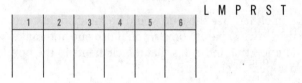

STEP 3: Symbolize the Clues

Symbolize the clues in a vertical line off to the side of your diagram. Keep the space underneath your diagram clear because you'll need to expand the diagram as you work the questions. The same principle that determined how you drew your diagram will now dictate how you symbolize each clue: What does it look like?

Clue 1: "She walks the Labrador some time before the Terrier."

You don't know exactly how far apart L and T have to be. It would be consistent with this clue for Emily to walk L first and T sixth, or she could walk L third and T fourth. All you know is that L will be somewhere to the left of T in the diagram. So you'll symbolize this clue accordingly:

$$L - T$$

Then check off "L" and "T" on your list of elements. It's important to get in the habit of doing this as you work. Once you've symbolized all the clues, if one of the elements is not checked off, you know it is a "free agent"; there are no restrictions on where it can go. This can be a powerful aid in working a game.

Clue 2: "She walks the Poodle *immediately* after the Mutt."

Here, you know exactly how far apart these two elements have to be: wherever they are plugged into the diagram, M will immediately precede P. What will that look like?

$$MP$$

Clue 3: "She walks the Retriever either immediately before or immediately after the Terrier."

Here again you know that wherever these two elements are plugged into the diagram, they'll be right next to each other. While these two elements have to be adjacent, the order in which they must appear is not yet determined. In other words, your diagram could look like this:

$$RT$$

or it could look like this:

$$TR$$

and in either case the clue would be satisfied. Instead of using two separate boxes, you'll use one and make a notation that indicates that the elements in the box can appear in either order.

$$R \leftrightarrow T$$

Clue 4: "She walks the Schnauzer fourth."

The purpose of symbolizing clues is to help you figure out where to place the elements in your diagram. This clue skips straight to the punch line and places an element for you. Accordingly, you should symbolize this clue directly into your diagram:

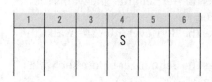

STEP 4: Double-Check Your Symbolizations
The single most costly mistake you can make on the Logic Games section is to incorrectly symbolize a clue. You can easily wind up working through most of the questions before realizing your mistake. You can't afford to lose that time. It is absolutely vital that you double-check your symbolizations before proceeding any further.

The most effective way to double-check your symbolizations is to translate them back into English. For example, you symbolized the first clue in this game like this:

$$L - T$$

Translated into English, that says, "Emily walks L before she walks T." After making that translation, compare it to the language of the clue. Since your translation matches the language of the clue, you know you've symbolized that clue correctly. You'll repeat this process for every clue before beginning to Make deductions.

It's better to double-check this way than by re-symbolizing each clue. Why? If you misunderstood the clue the first time you read it, you're likely to make the same mistake the second time and you'll end up with the wrong symbolization again. Plus, when you translate your symbolization into English, the double-checking process is as simple as comparing your translation to the clue. If the two don't match, you'll spot it right away.

After double-checking your clues, you should have a diagram and clue list that looks like this:

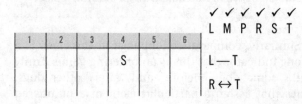

STEP 5: Make Deductions

The final step before you begin working the questions is to investigate the clues to see if you can make any deductions about the placement of the elements in the game. It can be tempting to skip this step and dive straight into the questions—making deductions takes time, and time is of the essence. But these deductions will drastically reduce the time it takes you to answer the questions.

Many LSAT students initially find the process of making deductions to be a mysterious one. Fortunately, there are a few categories of deductions that show up repeatedly on the Logic Games section. And there is a consistent set of steps you can follow that will allow you to make those deductions.

Look for opportunities to make the following kinds of deductions:

1. Can't-be-first-or-last deductions
2. Repeated-element deductions
3. Down-to-two deductions
4. Block-splitting deductions

The first deduction is relevant to those "before or after" clues. Think about it this way. If someone must stand in line after you, you can't be the last in line. And if someone must come before you, you can't be first.

For example, take the first clue in this game:

$$L - T$$

You can deduce from this clue that Emily cannot walk T first. If she did, it would be impossible for her to satisfy the condition that she walk L before she walks T. For similar reasons, you can deduce that she cannot walk L sixth.

If someone must come after you, you can't be last. If someone must come before you, you can't be first.

The best way to symbolize that deduction is with a notation above your diagram:

~T   ~L

1	2	3	4	5	6
			S		

(Note: This book uses the "~" sign to mean "not." Many test takers choose to represent "not" with a strikethrough, so that "not T" would be symbolized "T̶.")

Either method is fine; pick the one that you feel more comfortable with and use it consistently.)

The second clue (MP) is amenable to the same deduction: Emily cannot walk M last, and she cannot walk P first:

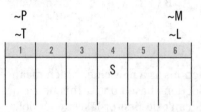

There is another, similar deduction you can make from this clue. M cannot be placed in any slot where it is impossible to place P in the slot immediately to the right. Since S must be fourth, you know that M cannot be third:

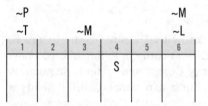

The third clue will not support this kind of deduction, as Emily can walk R and T in any order so long as she walks them consecutively.

Once you've completed the process of making can't-be-first-or-last deductions, turn next to repeated-element deductions. Use a two-step process to make repeated-element deductions:

1. Identify any element that appears in more than one clue.
2. See if you can combine those clues to produce new information.

Identify any element that appears in more than one clue and attempt to combine those clues.

In this game, the only element that shows up in more than one clue is T, which appears in both the first (L — T) and third clues. And it's possible to combine those clues to produce new information.

In plain English, the third clue tells you that R and T appear consecutively. As a consequence, it's impossible for L to appear in between R and T. Since R and T are right next to each other and the first clue tells you that L must come before T, it follows that L also must come before R.

Symbolically,

$$L — T$$

plus

$$R \leftrightarrow T$$

equals

$$L — R \leftrightarrow T$$

This deduction functions as a new clue, which means you can make deductions based on it. This new clue will support two can't-be-first-or-last deductions. Take a moment to see if you can make them.

Deductions are like clues: you can make deductions based on your deductions.

First, you now know that L must come before R, so it follows that R can't come first. Second, you now know that *both* R *and* T must come after L. So not only can L not be sixth, but it also can't be fifth. It needs at least two available spaces after it to house both R and T. You can symbolize these new deductions directly into your diagram:

~R
~P   ~M
~T   ~M   ~L   ~L

1	2	3	4	5	6
			S		

Next up, look for what we'll call down-to-two deductions. In the Logic Games section, being able to limit a slot to only two elements is almost as valuable as being able to definitively place one element in that slot. While it's rare to be able to definitively place an element, you'll frequently be able to make a down-to-two deduction that limits a slot to two possibilities.

The question to ask is, "Is there any slot in this game that is so restricted that it can be occupied by only one of two elements?" Here, you know from your prior deductions that neither R nor P nor T can occupy the first slot. And since S must be fourth, you also know that S cannot occupy the first slot. Four of the six elements are thus barred from being first: only L and M remain. You can note that deduction directly into your diagram using a slash as an either/or symbol:

~R
~P   ~M
~T   ~M   ~L   ~L

1	2	3	4	5	6
L/M			S		

No other down-to-two deductions are available, so let's turn to the final type of deduction, which is to look for possibilities of block-splitting. Block-splitting is one of the most commonly recurring concepts on the Logic Games section, showing up in all four types of games. The test writers frequently use it to generate correct and incorrect answers.

What is block-splitting? In this game, clues 2 and 3 require M and P and R and T to always appear right next to each other. Those clues create two-element "blocks." The basic concept of block-splitting is that in a game that involves blocks of elements, you can't place the nonblocked, single elements in a way that makes it impossible to place all of the blocks.

Here's a simple example. Suppose Emily only had to walk three dogs—S, R, and T—but she still had to walk R and T consecutively. If Emily walked S second, there would be no way for her to legally walk all three dogs. Walking S second would split the R—T block.

Making a block-splitting deduction is the process of taking a moment at the beginning of the game to think about where you can place any multi-element blocks. Sometimes the need to preserve room to place the block will make it impossible to place a single, unblocked element in a particular slot in the game. To make a block-splitting deduction, follow these steps:

1. Identify all of the blocked elements.
2. Determine the various places within the game where the block(s) can be placed.
3. Look for any slots where placing a single, unblocked element would split the block (i.e., make it impossible to place the blocked elements anywhere).

In this game, you have two two-element blocks: MP and RT, and your diagram looks like this:

~R
~P   ~M
~T   ~M   ~L   ~L

1	2	3	4	5	6
L/M			S		

The blocks take up four slots, and there are only three slots to the left of S. So you know that one of the blocks must be in 5 and 6, and the other block must be somewhere in the first three slots.

That enables you to make the following deduction: if you place one of the nonblocked elements in slot 2, you won't have room to place both of the blocks. L is the only nonblocked element that you haven't placed yet, so you can deduce that L can never go in slot 2:

~R					
~P				~M	
~T	~L	~M		~L	~L
1	**2**	**3**	**4**	**5**	**6**
L/M			S		

If you found it difficult to follow the reasoning that led to that deduction, don't worry. Block-splitting deductions are the most difficult kind of deduction to make. It also gets easier to make them the more you practice working games.

STEP 6: **Answer the Questions in the Smartest Order**
The order in which the questions associated with a game appear is *not* the order in which you should work those questions. You want to work the questions in the way that is most helpful to you. That means you want to work easier questions before harder questions. You also want to work the questions in such a way that you can use the work you do on the first few questions to help you answer the last few questions. The most strategically advantageous order in which to work the questions is as follows:

1. Answer the Complete and Accurate List question.
2. Answer questions that give you more information to work with.
3. Answer the remaining questions.

Complete and Accurate List Questions. The first question associated with your game about Emily walking the dogs is a Complete and Accurate List question. Complete and Accurate List questions ask, "Which of the following answer choices is an acceptable way to fill in every slot in this game?" These are by far the easiest kind of question you'll see on the Logic Games section. If a game has one (and most games do), you should always work it first. How can you identify a Complete and Accurate List question? It will ask you to pick an arrangement that complies with all the clues, and it will always be the first question associated with the game.

If a game has a Complete and Accurate List question, it will always be the first question.

---

1. Which of the following could be the order, from first to last, in which Emily walks the dogs?

   (A) L, T, R, S, M, P
   (B) M, L, P, S, T, R
   (C) T, R, L, S, M, P
   (D) L, M, P, R, T, S
   (E) R, L, T, S, M, P

To answer a Complete and Accurate List question, take each clue and scan the answer choices looking for one that violates the rule that clue establishes.

Your first clue tells you that L must come before T. Scanning the answer choices, T is listed before L in answer choice C, so you can eliminate that choice. Answer B violates clue 2, answer E violates clue 3, and answer D violates clue 4, so the correct choice for question 1 is answer A.

Questions That Give You More Information. Information is the coin of the realm in the Logic Games section. The more you know about where the elements must, can, or cannot go, the easier it is to work with the game. For that reason, questions that contain new information are generally easier and less time-consuming to work than questions that require you to work only with the information given in the setup.

Questions that begin with if typically give you additional information to work with.

In this game, questions 3 and 6 are examples of this kind of question: each of them instructs you to assume an additional fact that further limits the ways in which Emily can walk the dogs.

3. If Emily walks the Retriever third, which of the following must be true?

   (A) Emily walks the Terrier fourth.
   (B) Emily walks the Poodle sixth.
   (C) Emily walks the Poodle fifth.
   (D) Emily walks the Labrador second.
   (E) Emily walks the Mutt first.

The first step in working this kind of question is to plug the new information directly into your diagram:

```
 ~R
 ~P                      ~M
 ~T   ~L   ~M        ~L   ~L
  1    2    3    4    5    6
                S
3.             R    S
```

Next, you'll combine that information with your clues and deductions. Start with any clue that applies to the same element(s) about which the question has given you new information. Here, the third clue tells you that T and R must appear consecutively. Since S must appear right after R, you know that T must appear right before R in slot 2:

```
 ~R
 ~P                      ~M
 ~T   ~L   ~M        ~L   ~L
  1    2    3    4    5    6
L/M             S
3.        T    R    S
```

Since Emily must walk T second, you'll immediately look down to the answer choices to see if that's listed as one of the answer choices. As it turns out, it's not, but if it had been, you could have selected it and moved on without doing any more work. Your goal on the Logic Games section is to do exactly as much work as you have to to get the right answer, and no more. Each time you place an element, check the answer choices to see if you've got the answer.

Your next step will be to combine the new information you have about T with any clues you have about T. From the first clue, you know that L must come before T. Since you know that T must be second, L must be first:

```
 ~R
 ~P                      ~M
 ~T   ~L   ~M        ~L   ~L
  1    2    3    4    5    6
L/M             S
3.   L    T    R    S
```

Once again, scan the answer choices to see if "L must be first" is among them. It's not, so you'll keep going. Only two slots remain open, and from the second clue you can determine that M and P must be fifth and sixth, respectively:

```
 ~R
 ~P                      ~M
 ~T   ~L   ~M        ~L   ~L
  1    2    3    4    5    6
L/M             S
3.   L    T    R    S    M    P
```

Just by virtue of knowing that R comes third, you're able to completely fill in the game. As the diagram illustrates, the correct choice for question 3 is answer B: Emily must walk the Poodle sixth.

6. If Emily walks the Mutt second, which of the following could be false?

(A) She walks the Labrador before she walks the Mutt.

(B) She walks the Terrier after she walks the Schnauzer.

(C) She walks the Retriever after she walks the Terrier.

(D) She walks the Schnauzer before she walks the Retriever.

(E) She walks the Poodle after she walks the Labrador.

Pay close attention to language. What exactly is the question asking you to determine? Question 3 asks what *must* be *true*; question 6 asks what *could* be *false*. Another question may ask you what *must* be *false* or what *could* be *true*. It is crucial that you carefully note what the question is asking, and to keep it at the forefront of your mind as you work.

Both must-be-true and could-be-false questions require you to determine what must be true.

As it turns out, questions 3 and 6 are mirror images of each other: anything that *must* be true *cannot* be false. On a must-be-true question, you diagram the new information, definitively place as many other elements as possible, and pick an answer choice that matches what you've diagrammed. On a could-be-false question, the first two steps are the same, but instead of *selecting* the answer that matches your diagram, you *eliminate* it as an incorrect choice. It cannot be false (or in other words, it must be true).

Question 6 tells you that M comes second. First, you'll plug that into the diagram:

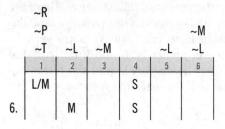

If M comes second, the second clue tells you P must come third:

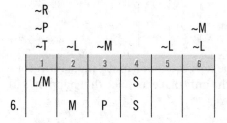

Scanning the answer choices reveals that you can't cross anything out yet. Next, your down-to-two deduction tells you that if M is second, L must come first:

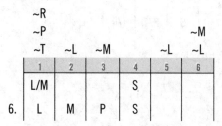

That tells you that L must come before both P and S, so you can eliminate answer choices A and E.

Finally, the third clue tells you that R and T must appear consecutively, so they go in slots 5 and 6. You don't know what order R and T appear in, so you'll place them using the "either/or" notation.

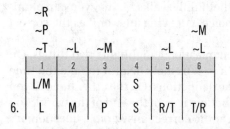

That tells you that S must come before both T and R, which eliminates answers B and D. That leaves you with answer C: "Emily walks the Retriever after she walks the Terrier." Not necessarily! Emily could walk the Terrier after the Retriever, as your diagram clearly shows. Therefore, answer C could be false, so it is the right answer.

Again, carefully read the language of the question and always keep in mind what the question is asking you to determine. For question 6, if you thought you were looking for an answer that *must* be false instead of one that *could* be false, you would definitely waste a lot of time on a wild goose chase.

Questions That Do Not Give You New Information. Having worked all of the questions that give you new information, you'll finally turn to the questions that don't. Use a three-step process to tackle such questions:

1. Can you answer this question using the clues and your deductions?
2. Can you answer this question using work you did on previous questions?
3. Can you answer this question using the process of elimination?

Each of the three remaining questions illustrates one step in that process.

2. Which of the following must be false?

   (A) Emily walks the Terrier second.
   (B) Emily walks the Labrador third.
   (C) Emily walks the Mutt third.
   (D) Emily walks the Retriever sixth.
   (E) Emily walks the Poodle sixth.

Question 2 simply asks you to pick an answer choice that must be false based only on the information in the setup and the clues.

The first step on a question that does not give you any new information is to look for the answer in your deductions.

The correct answer to a question like this one is never merely a restatement of one of the clues. You might be able to use the clues to eliminate some incorrect answer choices, but arriving at the correct answer will always require you to make some kind of deduction.

The best place to start is with the deductions you already made. Here, that's all it takes. You already deduced that M can never be in slot 3. That deduction makes answer C the correct choice.

4. Which of the following must be false?

    (A) Emily walks the Mutt first.
    (B) Emily walks the Labrador second.
    (C) Emily walks the Terrier fifth.
    (D) Emily walks the Labrador first.
    (E) Emily walks the Retriever third.

Question 4 asks which of its answer choices *must be false*. On must-be-false questions, you can eliminate any answer choice that *could be true*.

Therefore, your first step is to check to see if any of the answer choices match up with any of your deductions to create a legal arrangement of the elements. Once again, you're in luck. Your block-splitting deduction tells you that L can't be second, so it must be false. Therefore, answer B is the correct choice.

But you noted above that block-splitting deductions are the most difficult kind of deduction to make. What would you do if you hadn't made the block-splitting deduction? In that case, you would use the second tactic for approaching questions that don't give you any new information: rely on the work you've done in answering previous questions.

The second step on a question that does not give you any new information is to use your work on previous questions to select or eliminate answer choices.

If you hadn't made the block-splitting deduction, at this point your diagram would look like this:

~R
~P   ~M
~T   ~L   ~M   ~L   ~L

1	2	3	4	5	6
L/M			S		

	1	2	3	4	5	6
3.	L	T	R	S	M	P
6.	L	M	P	S	R/T	T/R

In the course of diagramming your answers to questions 3 and 6, you've already generated several examples of ways in which all six of the elements in the game could legally be placed. Accordingly, if your answers to those questions demonstrate that one or more of the answer choices to question 4 could be true, you can eliminate those choices. Using this tactic, you can eliminate answer choices D and E based on your answer to question 3 and answer choice C based on your answer to question 6.

All that's left is to pick between answer A and answer B. Your work on previous questions does not enable you to eliminate either choice, so you'll have to turn to your third and final tactic for these kinds of questions: using the process of elimination. There are only two choices left, so you can just pick one and diagram it. If it must be false, you've got your answer.

Start with answer choice A. Could it be true that Emily walks M first? If you plug M into slot 1, the second clue tells you that P must come second:

~R
~P   ~M
~T   ~L   ~M   ~L   ~L

	1	2	3	4	5	6
	L/M			S		
4.	M	P		S		

The third clue tells you that R and T must be in consecutive slots; the only place to make that happen is in slots 5 and 6:

~R
~P   ~M
~T   ~L   ~M   ~L   ~L

	1	2	3	4	5	6
	L/M			S		
4.	M	P		S	R/T	T/R

That forces L into slot 3:

~R
~P   ~M
~T   ~L   ~M   ~L   ~L

	1	2	3	4	5	6
	L/M			S		
4.	M	P	L	S	R/T	T/R

Having L in slot 3 and T in slot 5 or slot 6 satisfies the first clue, so this is a legal arrangement. Since it could be true that Emily walks M first, you can eliminate answer choice A, leaving answer B as the correct answer to question 4.

Your work on question 4 highlights two things. On the one hand, it is extremely helpful to take the time up front to Make deductions. On the other hand, if you overlook a deduction, it's not the end of the world. You can still arrive at the correct answer to a question; it's just going to take you longer.

Finally, turn to question 5.

5. Which one of the following is a complete and accurate list of the positions in which Emily could walk the Retriever?

(A) 5, 6
(B) 3, 5
(C) 3, 5, 6
(D) 2, 3, 5, 6
(E) 1, 2, 3, 5, 6

Don't let the wording of the question confuse you; this is not the kind of question you should always work first. Not only is it not the first question associated with the game, but it asks you only about one element instead of every element in the game.

Here, you're looking for a list of the slots where R could appear that is both accurate (no wrong answers included) and complete (no right answers excluded). The steps to working this question are the same. First you turn to your deductions. You know that R can't go first, so you can eliminate choice E as inaccurate.

Next, you'll use your work on previous questions:

~R
~P   ~M
~T   ~L   ~M   ~L   ~L

1	2	3	4	5	6
L/M			S		
L	T	R	S	M	P
L	M	P	S	R/T	T/R
M	P	L	S	R/T	T/R

(rows labeled 3., 6., 4.)

Your work on question 3 tells you that R can go third, so answer A is an incomplete list. Your work on questions 4 and 6 tells you that R can go sixth, so you can also eliminate answer B as incomplete.

The only choices left are answers C and D, and you can't eliminate either one based on your answers to other questions, so you'll have to use the process of elimination. Since the only difference between those two answers is whether R can go second, you'll plug that into your diagram and see if you can make it work.

~R
~P   ~M
~T   ~L   ~M   ~L   ~L

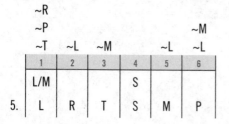

1	2	3	4	5	6
L/M			S		
L	R	T	S	M	P

(row labeled 5.)

And you can: the third clue places T in slot 3; the second clue places M and P in 5 and 6; and the first clue places L in slot 1.

Since R can appear in slot 2, answer C is an incomplete list. Accordingly, choice D is the correct answer to question 5.

Clue Symbolization Drills

The game that you've just worked through is a relatively straightforward example of a one-tiered ordering game. There are many different ways the test writers can increase the difficulty level of one-tiered ordering games. By far the most common technique they use is giving you clues that are difficult to understand, difficult to symbolize, and difficult to work with. These symbolization drills are designed to introduce some of those more difficult clue types.

Instructions: Below are examples of clues applied to the setup of the sample game that might appear in one-tiered ordering games. Use the "what does it look like?" principle to symbolize each of these clues (remember you can input some clues directly into your diagram). Also make a note of any can't-be-first-or-last deductions. Answers appear on the following page.

1. Emily cannot walk the Terrier second.
2. Emily must walk the Labrador before she walks both the Mutt and the Retriever.
3. Emily must walk either the Schnauzer or the Poodle immediately before she walks the Mutt.
4. Emily must walk the Labrador before she walks the Terrier but after she walks the Poodle.
5. The Poodle must be one of the last three dogs Emily walks.
6. Emily must walk exactly two dogs in between the Mutt and the Retriever.
7. Emily must walk at least two dogs in between the Mutt and the Retriever.
8. Emily walks the Terrier either at some time before she walks the Labrador or at some time after she walks the Poodle, but not both.
9. Either Emily walks the Poodle before both the Retriever and the Mutt, or she walks both the Retriever and the Mutt before the Poodle.
10. Emily walks the Terrier before the Mutt, or else she walks the Terrier before the Labrador, but not both.

Clue Symbolization Answers

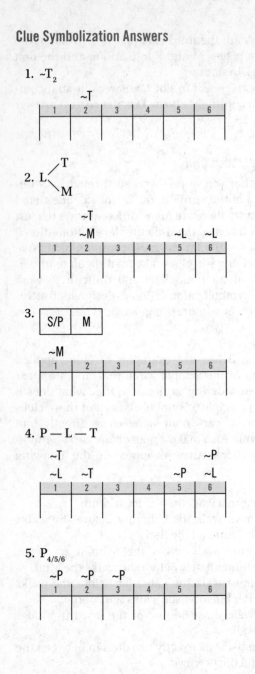

1. $\sim T_2$

       ~T
1	2	3	4	5	6

2. L ⟨ T
       M

           ~T
       ~M   ~L   ~L
1	2	3	4	5	6

3. | S/P | M |
   |-----|---|

       ~M
1	2	3	4	5	6

4. P — L — T

       ~T   ~P
   ~L   ~T   ~P   ~L
1	2	3	4	5	6

5. $P_{4/5/6}$

   ~P   ~P   ~P
1	2	3	4	5	6

6. | M/T | | | T/M |
   |-----|--|--|-----|

7. $\sim M \leftrightarrow R$

   ~ | M/R | | R/M |

   +

   | M/R | | R/M |

8. T — L/P — T

   ~(P — T — L)

   Note that this clue does not support any can't-be-first-or-last deductions.

9. P ⟨ M   M ⟩ P
       R / R

   ~(M/R — P — R/M)

   Note that this clue does not support any can't-be-first-or-last deductions.

10. T — M / T — L

    ~T ⟨ M
         L

    M/L — T — L/M

    ~T   ~T
1	2	3	4	5	6

Case 2

Working with Conditional Statements

As noted at the beginning of the chapter, there are only two tasks the Logic Games section will ask you to perform: ordering and grouping. Case 1 introduced you to ordering games. Before you can turn to grouping games, however, you need to take a moment to learn how to identify and work with a particular type of clue.

The purpose of this case is to introduce you to conditional statements. Working with conditional statements is essential to success on the Logic Games section. It is *guaranteed* that on test day you will have to symbolize and work with multiple clues that are conditional statements. In recent years, every single grouping game on the LSAT has had at least one conditional-statement clue. Many ordering games employ them as well.

This case will proceed in three parts. First, we'll discuss what a conditional statement is, how to symbolize a basic conditional statement, and how to make the deduction that every conditional statement supports. Next, we'll deal with translating and symbolizing more complex conditional statements. Last, you'll have a chance to practice these skills with a series of drills.

Basic Conditional Statements

A conditional statement is an "if-then" statement. For example, "If something is an apple, then it is a fruit" is a conditional statement. We'll call the portion of the statement that follows the "if" the *condition*, and the portion that follows the "then" we'll label the *consequence*.

A conditional statement is a statement that says, "If (condition), then (consequence)."

Each time you see a conditional statement on the Logic Games section, you'll take the same three steps:

1. Abbreviate the elements that make up the statement.
2. Symbolize the statement using an arrow.
3. Symbolize the statement's contrapositive.

For step 1, abbreviate "apple" as "A" and "fruit" as "F."

Next, symbolize the conditional statement using an arrow. The condition—that's the statement that follows "if"—goes in front of the arrow. The consequence—the statement that follows "then"—goes behind the arrow. So, "If something is an apple, then it is a fruit" becomes "A → F."

Third, you'll make the standard deduction that follows from every conditional statement. That deduction is known as the *contrapositive*. If something is an apple, then it must be a fruit. Therefore, if something is not a fruit, then it cannot be an apple. A conditional statement and its contrapositive are logically equivalent to one another: when you know a conditional statement is true, you can be certain that its contrapositive is also true.

Symbolically, to take the contrapositive of "A → F," follow these two steps:

1. **Flip sides.** Take the element before the arrow and move it after the arrow. Take the element after the arrow and move it before the arrow.
2. **Flip signs.** Take any element that is positive and negate it. Take any element that is negative and make it positive.

Thus, the contrapositive of "A → F" is "~F → ~A."

Working with Conditional Statements

You now know that two things are true:

$$A \rightarrow F$$
$$\sim F \rightarrow \sim A$$

Based on those two conditional statements, what do you know if:

1. Something is an apple?
2. Something is not an apple?
3. Something is a fruit?
4. Something is not a fruit?

Again, start in plain English.

1. If something is an apple, then it must be a fruit.
2. If something is not an apple, does it follow that it is not a fruit? No. The thing could be an orange or a pear.
3. If you know that something is a fruit, does it follow that it must be an apple? No. Again, it could be another type of fruit.
4. If something is not a fruit, you can be sure that it is not an apple.

Conditional statements are based on their conditions. The statement only tells you something if the condition is satisfied. If the condition is not satisfied, the statement tells you nothing.

Always follow the arrow when working with conditional statements.

Understanding this distinction is critical to success on the Logic Games section. The first half of a conditional statement can be false, and the second half can still be true. Here's an easy way to remember this rule: Follow the arrow.

$$A \rightarrow F$$
$$\sim F \rightarrow \sim A$$

If you know A, the arrow points you to F. If you know ~F, the arrow points you to ~A. But if you know F or ~A, the conditional statement tells you nothing; you're on the wrong side of the arrow. As long as you never go against the arrow, you won't misinterpret a conditional statement.

Complex Conditional Statements: Multiple Elements

Statements in the form of "If A, then B" are the simplest kind of conditional statement. But the Logic Games section also employs conditional statements in more complicated forms. Fortunately, you can use a standard set of steps to symbolize these more complicated conditionals and accurately state their contrapositives.

As an example, start with the statement, "If not A or B, then C and not D." You can symbolize that statement using your standard "~" as a negative and the "&" and "/" signs for "and" and "or," respectively:

$$\sim A / B \rightarrow C \& \sim D$$

The tricky part is correctly writing out that statement's contrapositive. To do so, follow these three steps:

1. **Flip sides.** This is the same as before: take the elements before the arrow and move them after the arrow, and vice versa.
2. **Flip signs.** This is also the same as before. Flip all negatives into positives, and negate anything that is positive.
3. **Flip connectors.** "And" becomes "or," and "or" becomes "and." Take any "&" and make it a "/." Take any "/" and make it an "&."

When symbolizing a contrapositive, everything flips: sides, signs, and connectors.

Here's what those steps look like when applied to a conditional statement in the form of ~A / B → C & ~D:

1. C D → A B
2. ~C D → A ~B
3. ~C / D → A & ~B

That's all there is to it. "If not C or D, then A and not B" is the contrapositive of the statement "If not A or B, then C and not D."

Complex Conditional Statements: Ordering Clues

One type of complex conditional statement is particularly relevant. To illustrate it, return to the game you worked in Case 1. Suppose that game had included the following clue: "If Emily walks the Retriever before she walks the Terrier, then she must walk the Mutt before she walks the Schnauzer."

You would symbolize such a clue like this:

$$R — T \rightarrow M — S$$

Clues like this—conditional statements that dictate the order in which certain elements appear—have been very common on recent LSATs. To take its contrapositive, all you have to do is flip sides and flip signs:

1. M — S → R — T
2. ~(M — S) → ~(R — T)

In the context of the sample game, there's a more useful way to flip signs. Recall that Emily must walk the dogs one at a time. If M is not before S, that means that M is after S. Thus, when you're flipping signs on a clue like this, "before" becomes "after," and "after" becomes "before." That rule will allow you to diagram the contrapositive the same way you would diagram the other clues:

$$S — M \rightarrow T — R$$

Complex Conditional Statements: Translating Phrases Other Than If–Then

The final skill you'll need to work effectively with conditional statements is the ability to translate and symbolize conditional statements that use nonstandard language. For example, each of the following is a conditional statement:

1. B only if A
2. Not B unless A
3. All A are B
4. No A are B
5. B if, but only if, A

The following list offers ways each of these statements can be symbolized using the standard $\rightarrow$ sign for conditionals.

$$B \text{ only if } A = B \rightarrow A$$

Symbolizing "only if" statements can be tricky. In a standard "if-then" statement, whatever comes after "if" is placed in front of the arrow. By contrast, when the clue uses "only if" language, whatever comes after the "only if" is placed *behind* the arrow.

$$\text{"Not B unless A"} = B \rightarrow A$$

Translating an "unless" statement into a conditional involves two steps:

1. Take what follows "unless" and make it the back half of your symbolization.
2. Take what comes before the "unless," negate it, and make it the front half of your symbolization.

$$\text{"All A are B"} = A \rightarrow B$$
$$\text{"No A are B"} = A \rightarrow \sim B$$

These two are fairly straightforward. The trick is recognizing that all-or-nothing statements like these are actually conditional statements.

$$\text{"B if, but only if, A"} = A \rightarrow B \text{ and } B \rightarrow A$$

This is probably the trickiest type of conditional statement you might run across on test day. The reason it's tricky is that it's actually two conditional statements—(1) "B if A"; and (2) "B only if A"—disguised as one. That's why it takes two separate symbolizations to diagram it correctly.

Conditional Statement Drills

You'll practice working with conditional statements in grouping games in the next case. Below are examples of conditional-statement clues that might appear in one-tiered ordering games. The clues refer back to the game you worked in Case 1 in which Emily walked the dogs. For each of these questions, symbolize the clue and symbolize the contrapositive. Answers follow.

QUESTIONS

1. Emily must walk the Mutt fifth if she does not walk the Terrier second.

2. Emily walks the Schnauzer second if, but only if, she walks the Retriever sixth.
3. If Emily walks the Mutt before the Poodle, then she walks the Terrier after the Labrador.
4. Emily walks the Retriever first, unless she walks the Schnauzer fifth.
5. Emily does not walk the Retriever first unless she walks the Schnauzer fifth.
6. If Emily walks the Mutt third, then she walks the Retriever immediately before she walks the Schnauzer.
7. If Emily walks the Terrier third, then she walks the Terrier before both the Labrador and the Schnauzer.
8. If Emily walks the Retriever before she walks the Mutt, then she walks the Schnauzer before both the Terrier and the Labrador.

ANSWERS

1. $\sim T_2 \rightarrow M_5$

$$\sim M_5 \rightarrow T_2$$

2. Emily walks the Schnauzer second if she walks the Retriever sixth.

$$R_6 \rightarrow S_2$$
$$\sim S_2 \rightarrow \sim R_6$$

Emily walks the Schnauzer second only if she walks the Retriever sixth.

$$S_2 \rightarrow R_6$$
$$\sim R_6 \rightarrow \sim S_2$$

3. $M - P \rightarrow L - T$

$$T - L \rightarrow P - M$$

4. $\sim R_1 \rightarrow S_5$

$$\sim S_5 \rightarrow R_1$$

5. $R_1 \rightarrow S_5$

$$\sim S_5 \rightarrow \sim R_1$$

6. $M_3 \rightarrow \boxed{R\,S}$

$$\sim \boxed{R\,S} \rightarrow \sim M_3$$

7. $T_3 \rightarrow T \Big\langle \begin{smallmatrix} L \\ S \end{smallmatrix}$

$$L/S - T \rightarrow \sim T_3$$

8. $R - M \rightarrow S \Big\langle \begin{smallmatrix} T \\ L \end{smallmatrix}$

$$T/L - S \rightarrow M - R$$

Case 3

Grouping Games: Ralph Hosts a Dinner Party

The purpose of this case is to introduce grouping games. Of the 60 games that appeared on the 15 publicly available LSATs from 2006 to 2010, 16—about 27 percent—were grouping games. That means that, on average, one of the four games in a Logic Games section is a grouping game.

Recall from Case 1 the six-step method that you learned for tackling one-tiered ordering games:

1. Identify the game type
2. Begin your diagram
3. Symbolize the clues
4. Double-check your symbolizations
5. Make deductions
6. Answer the questions in the smartest order

This case will show you how to use this same method to work grouping games. The primary difference will be in how the game is set up—and, correspondingly, what your diagram looks like. Take a moment to attempt this game before you turn to the discussion and explanation that follows.

Ralph is hosting a dinner party. Because his table has limited seating, he must invite exactly four guests. He will select his guests from the following list of eight of his friends: Angelica, Brunson, Cathy, Daisuka, Finley, Grant, Helen, and Isaiah. Based on what he knows about his friends, Ralph will choose whom to invite to the party consistent with the following:

He does not invite both Angelica and Brunson.
He does not invite Grant if he invites Finley.
If he invites Angelica, he does not invite Isaiah.
If he invites Daisuka, then he also invites Angelica.
He invites either Helen or Isaiah, but he does not invite them both.
If he does not invite Cathy, he invites Grant.

1. Which of the following could be the four guests whom Ralph invites to dinner?

   (A) Angelica, Brunson, Cathy, and Helen
   (B) Angelica, Cathy, Daisuka, and Helen
   (C) Angelica, Daisuka, Finley, and Helen
   (D) Cathy, Finley, Grant, and Helen
   (E) Cathy, Daisuka, Grant, and Helen

2. If Ralph invites Daisuka, then which of the following could be true?

   (A) He also invites Brunson.
   (B) He does not invite Helen.
   (C) He also invites Cathy.
   (D) He does not invite Angelica.
   (E) He also invites Finley.

3. If Ralph invites Brunson and Helen, then which of the following guests must he also invite?

   (A) Cathy
   (B) Finley
   (C) Isaiah
   (D) Grant
   (E) Daisuka

4. Ralph could invite either Angelica or Brunson if he also invites which of the following pairs of guests?

   (A) Cathy and Daisuka
   (B) Cathy and Isaiah
   (C) Grant and Isaiah
   (D) Daisuka and Helen
   (E) Grant and Helen

5. If Ralph invites Cathy, which of the following guests, if invited, would result in the guest list for the party being completely determined?

   (A) Isaiah
   (B) Finley
   (C) Daisuka
   (D) Brunson
   (E) Grant

STEP 1: Identify the Game Type

Again, to determine what type of game you're dealing with, you look to the language in the setup and the language in the clues. This game asks you to sort the elements into two lists: those who are invited to the dinner party, and those who are not. That makes this a grouping game.

The setup of a grouping game will contain language that instructs you to "select," "choose," or "assign" certain elements "from" or "among" a list to a particular group, bin, or team. The setup may introduce the clues with language telling you that the clues limit the composition of each group, the formation of each team, or the assignment or selection of the elements.

In the clues, look for language that keeps elements together or forces them apart by assigning them to the same or a different group or team. Similarly, the clue might tell you that a certain team or group cannot have a particular element, must have a particular element, must have both of two elements, or must have one or the other but not both of two elements. In addition, most grouping games utilize conditional clues that tell you what happens if a certain element is included, excluded, selected, omitted, on, off, in, or out.

> Grouping games contain language in the setup telling you to select, choose, or assign elements to teams, groups, or bins.

This game, with Ralph hosting a dinner party, is the most typical type of LSAT grouping game in two respects. First, it has only two groups. You'll also encounter grouping games with more groups, but two-group games are much more common.

Second, the "people who are not invited" is a second, equally important group. That's typical of two-group grouping games on the LSAT: the game tells you only that certain elements must be invited, selected, chosen, assigned, or taken. It's left to you to create a second group.

STEP 2: Begin Your Diagram
Create a diagram that captures the logical relationship between the game's elements. What does this game look like?

Imagine Ralph drawing up his guest list. On one side of the list are the people he's inviting, and on the other side are the folks who didn't make the cut. As to each element, the game asks, "Are you invited? Yes or no?" That points the way to the beginning of a diagram:

A B C D F G H I

YES	NO

This game provides one additional piece of information that is critical to a proper diagram: "he must invite exactly four guests." A more difficult grouping game might leave the number of elements in each group undefined, limited only by the information in the clues. But here, we know we have two groups of equal size: four yeses, four nos; we'll draw that fact directly into our diagram:

A B C D F G H I

YES	NO
_ _ _ _	_ _ _ _

STEP 3: Symbolize the Clues
Recall the general principles of symbolization discussed in Case 1. You should symbolize the clues so that they look on the page as they'll look in the diagram. And whenever possible, symbolize clues directly into the diagram.

Clue 1: "He does not invite both Angelica and Brunson."

This clue tells you that A and B cannot both be in the "yes" group; that means one slot in the "no" group will always be reserved for either A or B. You should symbolize this clue directly into your diagram using a *placeholder* in the "no" group:

A B C D F G H I

YES	NO
_ _ _ _	A/B _ _ _

That placeholder tells you that one slot in the "no" is always spoken for by either A or B.

Two-group grouping games like this one are where you'll really reap the benefits of mastering Case 2's discussion of conditional statements. This clue also tells you that if Ralph invites Angelica, he cannot invite Brunson:

$$A \rightarrow \sim B$$

and that if he invites Brunson, he cannot invite Angelica:

$$B \rightarrow \sim A$$

List those clues out to the side of your diagram.

A B C D F G H I

YES	NO	
_ _ _ _	A/B _ _ _	$A \rightarrow \sim B$
		$B \rightarrow \sim A$

Recall from Case 2 that there is a standard deduction that follows automatically from every conditional statement: its contrapositive. Any time you symbolize a conditional statement, you should immediately also symbolize its contrapositive. It's important to get in the habit of doing this automatically. Here, that means you should also write the following out to the side of your diagram:

$$\sim A \rightarrow B$$
$$\sim B \rightarrow A$$

Clue 2: "He does not invite Grant if he invites Finley."

This is a common wrinkle: a conditional clue that lists the consequence before the condition. As long as you remember that the condition is the statement that follows "if," you'll diagram these clues correctly:

$$F \rightarrow \sim G$$
$$G \rightarrow \sim F$$

Any time you symbolize a conditional clue, you should also immediately symbolize its contrapositive.

Clue 3: "If he invites Angelica, he does not invite Isaiah."

Clue 4: "If he invites Daisuka, then he also invites Angelica."

These two clues are more of the same:

$$A \rightarrow \sim I, \text{ and its contrapositive:}$$
$$I \rightarrow \sim A$$

$$D \rightarrow A, \text{ and its contrapositive:}$$
$$\sim A \rightarrow \sim D$$

Clue 5: "He invites either Helen or Isaiah, but he does not invite them both."

This is a very useful clue because it's actually two clues. First, it tells you that one spot in your "yes" group is always occupied by either H or I, as is one spot in your "no" group. You can use placeholders to symbolize that information directly into your diagram:

A B C D F G H I

YES	NO
H/I _ _ _	A/B I/H _ _

Second, this clue tells you both that if Ralph invites H, he can't invite I, and also that if he doesn't invite H, then he must invite I. You should also symbolize each of those conditional statements along with its contrapositive.

$$H \rightarrow \sim I, \text{ and its contrapositive:}$$
$$I \rightarrow \sim H$$

$$\sim H \rightarrow I, \text{ and its contrapositive:}$$
$$\sim I \rightarrow H$$

Clue 6: "If he does not invite Cathy, he invites Grant."

By now the proper symbolization of this clue should be familiar:

$$\sim C \rightarrow G, \text{ and}$$
$$\sim G \rightarrow C$$

STEP 4: Double-Check Your Symbolizations
Translate your symbolizations into English, then verify what you come up with against the language of the clue. Once you've done that, you should have a setup and a list of clues that look like this:

✓ ✓ ✓ ✓ ✓ ✓ ✓ ✓
A B C D F G H I

YES	NO	
H/I _ _ _	A/B I/H _ _	$A \rightarrow \sim B$
		$B \rightarrow \sim A$
		$F \rightarrow \sim G$
		$G \rightarrow \sim F$
		$A \rightarrow \sim I$
		$I \rightarrow \sim A$
		$D \rightarrow A$
		$\sim A \rightarrow \sim D$
		$H \rightarrow \sim I$
		$I \rightarrow \sim H$
		$\sim H \rightarrow I$
		$\sim I \rightarrow H$
		$\sim C \rightarrow G$
		$\sim G \rightarrow C$

STEP 5: Make Deductions
Recall the three types of deductions you looked for in Case 1's ordering game in which Emily walked the dogs:

1. Can't-be-first-or-last deductions
2. Repeated-element deductions
3. Down-to-two deductions

Since the elements don't appear in any order, you won't be able to make the first type of deduction.

That takes you to repeated-element deductions. This game presents an opportunity to make a particular kind of repeated-element deduction, which we'll call *conditional-combination deductions.*

To make a conditional-combination deduction:

1. Look for an element that appears in the front half of one conditional clue and in the back half of another. In other words, the same element needs to be on the left side of one arrow and the right side of a different arrow.
2. Combine the statements.

To make conditional-combination deductions,
look for an element that is on the left side of
one arrow and the right side of another.

For example, your list of clues for this game looks like this (the clues are numbered on this list for ease of reference):

1. A → ~B
   B → ~A
2. F → ~G
   G → ~F
3. A → ~I
   I → ~A
4. D → A
   ~A → ~D
5. H → ~I
   I → ~H
   ~H → I
   ~I → H
6. ~C → G
   ~G → C

Look at clues 6 and 2. G appears on the right side of the arrow in clue 6 (~C → G), and it appears on the left side of the arrow in the contrapositive of clue 2 (G → ~F). Therefore, you can combine those two statements to make the following deduction: ~C → G & ~F. You can add that deduction to the bottom of your list of clues.

You can make a similar deduction by combining clues 1 and 4. Take a moment to make it yourself.

The net result of B → ~A and ~A → ~D is B → ~A & ~D.

This game will support one final conditional-combination deduction, and it's a big one: four separate clues are involved. See if you can identify which ones they are. Remember, find an element that appears on the right side of one arrow and the left side of another. Continue to repeat the process until no more combinations are available.

Here, your big deduction starts with clue 4: D → A. Clue 1 gives you A → ~B, clue 3 gives you A → ~I, and the last part of clue 5 gives you ~I → H. Put them together and you've got:

$$D → A, ~B, ~I, \& H$$

In a two-group grouping game like this, this is an immensely valuable deduction. If D is in the "yes" group, it dramatically constrains the game; you automatically know what happens with five out of the eight elements.

At this point, the list of clues and deductions running down the side of your diagram should look like this:

CLUES

A → ~B
B → ~A
F → ~G
G → ~F
A → ~I
I → ~A
D → A
~A → ~D
H → ~I
I → ~H
~H → I
~I → H
~C → G
~G → C

DEDUCTIONS

~C → G & ~F
B → ~A & ~D
D → A, ~B, ~I, & H

That's a lot of information to keep track of; this is one of the ways the LSAT's writers can increase the difficulty level of a game.

No other conditional-combination deductions are available, so look now for down-to-two deductions. Two-group grouping games like this one frequently support a particular type of down-to-two deduction.

Recall clue 2: "He does not invite Grant if he invites Finley." You symbolized that clue as:

F → ~G
G → ~F

This is a one-or-the-other clue. If Ralph invites Finley, he can't invite Grant. If he invites Grant, he can't invite Finley. There's no scenario in which both F and G are in your "yes" group. That means that at least one or the other of F and G will always be in the "no" group. Make note of that fact using a placeholder:

A B C D F G H I

YES	NO
H/I G/C _ _	A/B I/H F/G _

Importantly, there's no placeholder in the "yes" group. It would be perfectly consistent with clue 2 for both F and G to be in the "no" group.

So how do you identify a one-or-the-other clue that will support this particular kind of down-to-two deduction? To make down-to-two deductions in two-group grouping games with conditional clues, look for clues that tell you that one element must be a "yes" if the other is a "no." In other order words, the language of the clue will track the names of the groups. You have two groups in this game: "yes" and "no." And clue 2 tells you that if one element (F) is in "yes," then another element (G) must be in "no."

There is one other clue in this game that will support the same kind of deduction. Take a moment to see if you can identify it.

Clue 6 tells you that there is no scenario under which Ralph invites neither Grant nor Cathy. If Grant is a "no," Cathy is a "yes." If Cathy is a "no," Grant must be a "yes." One or the other of them must be in your "yes" group, so represent that fact with a placeholder:

	YES		NO	
H/I	G/C _ _	A/B	I/H	F/G _

A B C D F G H I

There are no other down-to-two deductions available, and there are no block clues in this game, so you won't be able to make any block-splitting deductions. That means you're ready to turn to the questions.

STEP 6: Answer the Questions in the Smartest Order
The way to approach the questions in a grouping game is the same as the way to approach them in an ordering game:

1. Answer the Complete and Accurate List question.
2. Answer questions that give you more information to work with.
3. Answer the remaining questions.

The Complete-and-Accurate-List Question. Question 1 is a Complete and Accurate List question, although it might not look like one at first.

1. Which of the following could be the four guests whom Ralph invites to dinner?

   (A) Angelica, Brunson, Cathy, and Helen
   (B) Angelica, Cathy, Daisuka, and Helen
   (C) Angelica, Daisuka, Finley, and Helen
   (D) Cathy, Finley, Grant, and Helen
   (E) Cathy, Daisuka, Grant, and Helen

Each answer choice is a complete list of the members of a "yes" group; correspondingly, each "no" group is made up of the four elements not listed. To answer this question, work with each of the clues one at a time. Pick a clue, then scan the answers looking for a choice that violates the rule that clue establishes. Repeat this process with all of the clues.

Here, answer A violates clue 1, answer D violates clue 2, none of the answers violates clue 3, answer E violates clue 4, none of the answers violates clue 5, and answer C violates clue 6. The down-to-two deduction you made based on clue 6 is helpful here; it makes it much easier to recognize that answer C must be eliminated because it contains neither Grant nor Cathy. As a result, the correct choice is answer B.

Questions That Give You More Information. Next up is question 2, which instructs you to plug D into the "yes" group and asks what *could be true* a result.

2. If Ralph invites Daisuka, then which of the following could be true?

   (A) He also invites Brunson.
   (B) He does not invite Helen.
   (C) He also invites Cathy.
   (D) He does not invite Angelica.
   (E) He also invites Finley.

Reviewing your list of clues and deductions, you see that putting D in the "yes" group is the triggering condition for your biggest deduction:

$$D \rightarrow A, \sim B, \sim I, \& H$$

A and H also go in "yes," while B and I must go to "no":

		YES			NO	
	H/I	G/C _ _	A/B	F/G	I/H _
2.	H _	D A	B _	I _

A B C D F G H I

Just by plugging in that deduction, you learn that answer choices A, B, and D can be eliminated; they all must be false.

You have only one spot open in the "yes" group, which clue 6 tells you must be filled by either G or C. None of the rest of the clues requires that last spot to be filled by G in particular or C in particular, so you know it can be either one. With your "yes" group filled, you know that F must be a "no," along with the other of G or C:

		YES			NO	
	H/I	G/C _ _	A/B	F/G	I/H _
2.	H	G/C D A	B F	I C/G

A B C D F G H I

Since F must be a "no," answer E must be false. As the diagram illustrates, the correct answer to question 2 is answer C: it could be true that Ralph invites Cathy.

Question 3 asks who must also be invited if Brunson and Helen are invited.

3. If Ralph invites Brunson and Helen, then which of the following guests must he also invite?

(A) Cathy
(B) Finley
(C) Isaiah
(D) Grant
(E) Daisuka

The question gives you concrete new information to work with: B and H are both in the "yes" group. The first step is to plug that new information into the diagram and then combine it with the clues and deductions that also give you information about B and H. Here, clue 1 tells you that if B is a "yes," A must be a "no," and clue 5 tells you that if H is a "yes," then I must be a "no."

ABCDFGHI

	YES	NO
	H/I G/C _ _	A/B F/G I/H _
3.	H _ B _	A _ I _

Scanning the answer choices, you see that you can already eliminate answer choice C. Because A is not invited, the fourth clue tells you that D must also be in the "no," group:

ABCDFGHI

	YES	NO
	H/I G/C _ _	A/B F/G I/H _
3.	H _ B _	A _ I D

That allows you to eliminate answer choice E, but that's as far as you can go, and you don't yet have enough information to answer the question. What next?

Unable to fill in the rest of your diagram, you have to turn to the process of elimination. But that doesn't mean you should just grab the first answer choice you see and plug it into your diagram. That approach is time-consuming; you could end up having to diagram three or four possibilities. There's a smarter way to eliminate answer choices. It's based on the down-to-two concept you're familiar with from making deductions.

When you have to use the process of elimination, look for a slot in your diagram that is restricted to two possibilities.

The down-to-two strategy for the process of elimination works like this: If there's any slot in your diagram that you know is restricted to two possibilities, diagram both of them. Once you do, you'll know

you've exhausted all of the game's possible arrangements. That will allow you to determine what must be or what could be true.

Here, you know that the last slot in the "no" group must be occupied by either F or G. So you can draw two scenarios—one where F is a "no," and one where G is a "no"—and be certain you've covered the full universe of possibilities.

If F is a "no," that forces both G and C into the "yes" group:

ABCDFGHI

	YES	NO
	H/I G/C _ _	A/B F/G I/H _
3.	H C B G	A F I D

Scanning through your clues, you can verify that this arrangement doesn't violate any of the rules. Next, if G is a "no," that forces F and C into the "yes" group:

ABCDFGHI

	YES	NO
	H/I G/C _ _	A/B F/G I/H _
3.	H C B G	A F I D
3.	H C B F	A G I D

This arrangement, too, is consistent with all the clues. This allows you to arrive at answer A as the correct answer to question 3: Ralph *could* invite either Finley or Grant, but he only *must* invite Cathy.

The last question that gives you new information is question 5.

5. If Ralph invites Cathy, which of the following guests, if invited, would result in the guest list for the party being completely determined?

(A) Isaiah
(B) Finley
(C) Daisuka
(D) Brunson
(E) Grant

This is one of the more difficult question types you'll encounter on the Logic Games section. You want to look for answer choices that contain elements that are heavily restricted. The more information you have about an element, the more likely it is that placing that element will completely determine the game.

On questions that ask which element must be placed to completely determine the game, start with the elements about which you have the most information.

In this game the choice is easy. The last conditional-combination deduction you made showed you that if D is in the "yes" group, you automatically know what happens with four other elements:

$$D \rightarrow A, \sim B, \sim I, \& H.$$

In other words, if D is a "yes," A and H must also be "yeses." The question tells you that C also must be a "yes"—that makes four elements in the "yes" group, which completely determines the game. Consequently, the correct answer to question 5 is answer C.

If you hadn't been able to zero in on D based on your deductions, you would have worked through the answer choices one at a time. If, after plugging in the answer, any slot in the game is not definitively filled, you would eliminate that choice and move on. There's no faster or smarter way to tackle these kinds of questions.

The Remaining Questions. That brings you to question 4, the only question associated with this game that does not give you any new information.

4. Ralph could invite either Angelica or Brunson if he also invites which of the following pairs of guests?

(A) Cathy and Daisuka
(B) Cathy and Isaiah
(C) Grant and Isaiah
(D) Daisuka and Helen
(E) Grant and Helen

You'll approach this question by applying the three techniques introduced in Case 1 in sequential order:

1. Can you answer this question using the clues and your deductions?
2. Can you answer this question using work you did on previous questions?
3. Can you answer this question by plugging the answer choices into your diagram?

Question 4 asks which two guests can be invited so that Ralph would still be free to invite either Angelica or Brunson. In other words, what pair of invitees makes A and B interchangeable?

First, work with the clues and your deductions. The correct answer will not contain any element that, when placed in the "yes" group, requires either A or B to be invited. Similarly, the correct answer will not contain any element that, when placed in the "yes" group, prohibits either A or B from being invited.

1. Find either A, ~A, B, or ~B as a consequence, behind the arrow.
2. Eliminate the element that is the condition.

1. A → ~B   3. A → ~I   5. H → ~I   6. ~C → G
   B → ~A   I → ~A   I → ~H   ~G → C
2. F → ~G   4. D → A   ~H → I
   G → ~F   ~A → ~D   ~I → H

Looking over your clues, you first come across the contrapositive of clue 3: I → ~A. If I is invited, Ralph is prohibited from inviting A. That allows you to eliminate answer choices B and C. Next up is clue 4: D → A. Since inviting D obligates Ralph to also invite A, you can eliminate answer choices A and D. By the process of elimination, you know that the correct answer must be answer choice E.

Grouping Game Setup Drills

The grouping game you just finished was not particularly easy. The fact that every single clue was a conditional statement added a substantial measure of difficulty. On the other hand, the fact that the game specified that each group had exactly four members made working it a lot easier.

There are a variety of ways that grouping games can be made more difficult. The following page contains two setup drills that are designed to introduce you to some of the variants on grouping games you might encounter on test day. Each drill contains the setup and the clues of a grouping game, but no questions. For each drill, symbolize the clues, begin your diagram, and make deductions. Answers and comments follow the games.

Drill 1

A doctor will make rounds on which she visits her patients three times today: in the morning, afternoon, and evening. She visits exactly five patients: A, B, C, D, and E. On each round she visits at least two patients, and she must visit each patient at least once. The doctor visits her patients in accordance with the following restrictions:

On each round, she visits either C or D.
She visits both C and E on exactly one of her rounds.
She visits B on exactly two of her rounds.
She does not visit A on a round unless she is not visiting either E or D.

Drill 2

A car dealer has received 10 new cars: three sedans—A, B, and C—four trucks—F, G, H, and I—and three economy models—X, Y, and Z. The dealer only has room in his showroom to display six of the cars. He must display the cars consistent with the following conditions:

He must display at least one of X or Y.
He displays exactly two trucks.
He does not display B if he displays C.
If he displays I, he also displays G.
If he displays A, he also displays Z.

DRILL 1

| | | | ✓ ✓ ✓ ✓ ✓ |
MORNING	AFTERNOON	EVENING	A B C D E
C/D _	C/D _	C/D _	each patient 1+
			each group 2+
			ex. 1 [CE]
			ex. B B
			A → ~E & ~D
			E/D → ~A

Comments. Four aspects of this game add to its difficulty:

1. **Identifying the game type.** At first glance, you might mistakenly identify this as an ordering game, since the doctor is visiting patients on three sequential rounds. It's not until you read the clues (which have no "before/after" or "earlier/later" language) that it becomes clear this is a grouping game.
2. **Repeated elements.** Clue 3 specifies that B appears exactly twice, and the setup and the other clues leave open the possibility that the other elements also could appear two or maybe three times. That adds a degree of difficulty to the game.
3. **Variable number of elements per group.** The setup tells you that each group must have at least two elements, but it gives you no guidance on what the upper limit to the groups' size is. Based on clue 4, you know that no group will have all five elements, but that's all you know. The lack of a fixed number of elements per group also makes this game more difficult.
4. **Clues that are hard to symbolize.** Clues 1 and 4 are pretty standard, but clues 2 and 3 are not. You just have to find a way to notate the information they present in a way that makes sense to you (here, "exactly" has been abbreviated as "ex.").

DRILL 2

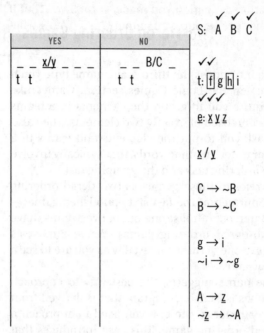

Comments. Three features of this game add to its difficulty:

1. **Multiple element types.** This is a common way the LSAT makes grouping games more difficult: creating multiple types, kinds, or categories of elements. When the game does that, your symbolizations should visually distinguish between the different kinds of elements: here, the diagram shows upper-case, lower-case, and underlined letters to distinguish the three kinds of automobile.
2. **Sheer size.** Increasing the number of elements involved in the game makes the game more difficult. It's harder to keep track of 10 elements than it is to keep track of 6.
3. **Identical elements.** Two elements in this game—f and h—are free agents. Other than the fact that they are trucks, the game places no restrictions on them. They are functionally identical to each other; anything one can do, the other can do, and vice versa. That's an easy thing to lose sight of while working a game; here, those two elements are circled as a reminder.

Case 4

Two-Tiered Ordering Games: Trudy Picks Her Course Schedule

This case introduces the third major game type you'll encounter on the Logic Games section. Games like these require you to group the elements into teams that are composed of exactly two elements. They also usually ask you to put the elements and teams in a particular order. In other words, they typically involve both the ordering task and the grouping task.

We'll refer to these games as two-tiered ordering games. Fourteen of the last sixty published games—that's 23 percent, almost one out of every four—have been two-tiered ordering games. You're almost as likely to see one of these on test day as you are to see a grouping game.

As the name suggests, the best way to approach these games is to use a diagram that is derived from and very similar to the one you used to approach a one-tiered ordering game. This case introduces that setup and some of the distinctive kinds of clues two-tiered ordering games frequently utilize.

A sample two-tiered ordering game appears follows. This game has an abbreviated set of questions because you'll use the same approach to working questions on two-tiered ordering games that you use on other types of games. The few included here are designed to help familiarize you with working with this kind of diagram. Take a moment to try to work this game on your own using the familiar six-step approach before you turn to the explanation.

Trudy is a college student who is planning her course schedule for the upcoming semester. To satisfy the requirements for graduation, she must take the following six classes: Linguistics, Macroeconomics, Oceanography, Philosophy, Rhetoric, and Sociology. She takes classes only on Mondays, Tuesdays, and Wednesdays. She takes exactly two classes per day, one at 11:00 a.m. and one at 3:00 p.m. Trudy must schedule her classes consistent with the following:

> She cannot take Macroeconomics and Rhetoric on the same day.
> She must take Macroeconomics and Sociology on consecutive days.
> She must take Philosophy on a later day than Oceanography.
> She must take Linguistics sometime after she takes Sociology.
> She must take Oceanography at 11:00 a.m.

1. If Trudy takes Sociology at 11:00 a.m. on Wednesday, which one of the following must be true?

   (A) She takes Macroeconomics at 11:00 a.m. on Tuesday.
   (B) She takes Oceanography at 11:00 a.m. on Tuesday.
   (C) She takes Philosophy at 3:00 p.m. on Tuesday.
   (D) She takes Linguistics at 3:00 p.m. on Monday.
   (E) She takes Rhetoric at 3:00 p.m. on Monday.

2. Which of the following cannot be the pair of classes Trudy takes at 11:00 a.m. and 3:00 p.m. Tuesday, respectively?

   (A) Philosophy and Sociology
   (B) Sociology and Rhetoric
   (C) Rhetoric and Linguistics
   (D) Linguistics and Macroeconomics
   (E) Macroeconomics and Philosophy

3. If Trudy takes both Macroeconomics and Philosophy at 11:00 a.m., which of the following must be true?

   (A) She takes Philosophy on Tuesday.
   (B) She takes Macroeconomics on Tuesday.
   (C) She takes Linguistics on Wednesday.
   (D) She takes Rhetoric on Monday.
   (E) She takes Oceanography on Monday.

STEP 1: Identify the Game Type
As always, you'll identify what type of game you're dealing with by looking to the language in the setup and the language in the clues. Two-tiered ordering games have three linguistic hallmarks:

1. The setup and the clues will use both grouping language and ordering language.
2. The game will have you assign exactly two elements to each group.
3. The two slots in each group will be specified.

For example, the setup of this game has a clear ordering component. Trudy is taking classes in sequential order: first Monday, then Tuesday, then Wednesday, and each day her 11:00 a.m. class comes before her 3:00 p.m. class. And the clues are rife with ordering language: some classes must be taken on a later day than, consecutive days with, or sometime before other classes.

At the same time, the setup of this game tells you that you're assigning elements (from a list of classes) to a particular group (a day of the week). And the first clue tells you that M and R can't be assigned to the same day. Both of those instructions utilize grouping language.

The second hallmark is also clearly present: Trudy "takes exactly two classes per day." That type of instruction is a strong indicator that this is a two-tiered ordering game.

Finally, not only does each group (day of the week) have two members, but the slots into which those members will be placed are specified: one slot is "11:00 a.m." and the other is "3:00 p.m." And the slots are not interchangeable, as the fifth clue makes abundantly clear. This feature of the game—two-member groups in which each member is assigned a specified slot—is also a telltale sign of a two-tiered ordering game.

Not all two-tiered ordering games will have all three of these hallmarks. Whenever you see a game that has two of the three, you should use the two-tiered ordering setup.

One final point about identifying two-tiered ordering games. Not all two-tiered ordering games will exhibit all three of these telltale features. But as long as a game exhibits two of these three features, you should still use the two-tiered ordering setup.

For example, some games might have you assign elements into two-member groups, but the slots in the group will be interchangeable. Others will have you assign exactly two elements to each group, and the slots in the group will be specified, but there will be no ordering component to the game. You should still use the diagram introduced in this case to set up those kinds of games.

Yes, you read that right: there are situations in which you should use the two-tiered ordering setup *even when the game does not involve ordering.* If the game tells you that each group has two slots, and each slot is specified, the approach you're learning in this game is the best one to use.

STEP 2: Begin Your Diagram

What does it look like? Visualize Trudy's calendar. The days of the week run left to right. The hours in the day proceed from top to bottom. We'll use that image to guide the structure of our diagram:

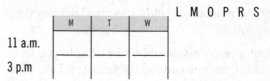

As we'll see when we turn to symbolizing the clues, this diagram allows you to accurately capture several different kinds of logical relationships between the elements.

STEP 3: Symbolize the Clues

Clue 1: "She cannot take Macroeconomics and Rhetoric on the same day."

What would this clue look like? If Trudy took M and R on the same day, they would appear on top of each other in the diagram. This clue tells you that can't happen, so you'll add the "not" sign. And finally, you'll use the switching arrow to convey that the clue means M and R can't be on the same day.

Note that this does not mean that M can't be at 11:00 and R at 3:00 (or vice versa) on any given day.

Clue 2: "She must take Macroeconomics and Sociology on consecutive days."

You saw a clue very similar to this one in Case 1, where Emily walked the Retriever either immediately before or immediately after the Terrier. Your first inclination might be to symbolize this clue the same way:

$$M \leftrightarrow S$$

But that symbolization could be misleading. It would be consistent with this clue for Trudy to take Macroeconomics on Tuesday afternoon and Sociology on Wednesday morning. In other words, this clue permits M and S to appear in consecutive slots, but in different tiers within those slots. You should diagram it accordingly:

Clue 3: "She must take Philosophy on a later day than Oceanography."

This type of clue also should be familiar to you from Case 1. This time, you can use the same symbolization here that you used there, because it is an accurate representation of how this clue will look in the diagram.

$$O - P$$

Clue 4: "She must take Linguistics sometime after she takes Sociology."

Careful—this clue is something of a trap. Take a moment to compare it to clue 3. Clue 4 permits an arrangement between L and S that clue 3 forbids between P and O. Do you see it? This clue would allow Trudy to take Sociology at 11:00 a.m. on Wednesday and Linguistics at 3:00 p.m. the same day. But clue 3 would prohibit her from taking O and P in those same time slots.

This type of clue—one that tells you only that one element must come "sometime" after the other, preserving the possibility that they could appear in the same group—is a common feature of two-tiered ordering games. And it's not easy to diagram because there's no single symbolization that accurately represents all the possibilities this clue allows. Both

$$S - L$$

and

$$\boxed{\begin{array}{c} S \\ L \end{array}}$$

are legitimate options. You can add those two options, separated by a slash (/) to indicate that either is acceptable, to your list of clues:

$$S - L / \boxed{\begin{array}{c} S \\ L \end{array}}$$

What you know definitively is that clue 4 bars both of the following two arrangements:

$$\sim (L - S)$$

and

$$\sim \boxed{\begin{array}{c} L \\ S \end{array}}$$

You can add both of those to your list.

Clue 5: "She must take Oceanography at 11:00 a.m."

This clue takes you back to first principles: whenever possible, symbolize a clue directly into your diagram:

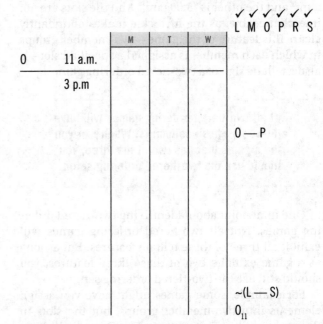

                                        L M O P R S

		M	T	W
O	11 a.m.			
	3 p.m			

STEP 4: Double-Check Your Symbolizations
This step is the same from game to game: translate your symbolizations into English, then make sure that your translations match up with the language of each clue. Do this fully and carefully; there is no more valuable investment of time on the Logic Games section.

                                   ✓ ✓ ✓ ✓ ✓ ✓
                                        L M O P R S

		M	T	W
O	11 a.m.			
	3 p.m			

                                        O — P

                                        ~(L — S)

                                        O₁₁

STEP 5: Make Deductions
Two-tiered ordering games give you an opportunity to make each of the four major types of deductions:

1. Can't-be-first-or-last deductions
2. Repeated-element deductions
3. Down-to-two deductions
4. Block-splitting deductions

   In the first category, clue 2 tells you that P must come on a later day than O. That means that P can't be on Monday, and O can't be Wednesday:

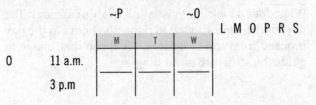

     ~P   ~O
                                        L M O P R S

		M	T	W
O	11 a.m.			
	3 p.m			

Clue 4 tells you that S must come sometime earlier than L, so you know that S can't be Monday at 11, and L can't be Wednesday at 3:

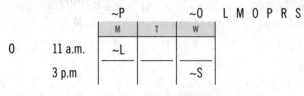

You don't have any other before-and-after type clues, so turn to repeated-element deductions. Both M and S appear in multiple clues. But there's no way to combine the clues. Why not? Because in each case one clue tells you what the element must do, while the other tells you what the element must not do.

Next, look for down-to-two deductions. You know from clue 5 that O must be in one of the 11:00 a.m. slots, and your deduction from clue 2 tells you that O can't be at 11:00 a.m. on Wednesday. You can combine those two clues to determine that O must appear either at 11:00 a.m. Monday or at 11:00 a.m. Tuesday:

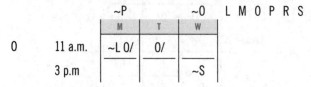

Finally, look for any block-splitting deductions:

1. Identify the blocked elements.
2. Determine where the block(s) can be placed.
3. Look for any slots where placing a single, unblocked element would split the block.

Your only block clue here is clue 3: M and S must appear on consecutive days. How could you satisfy that clue? You could place one on Monday and one on Tuesday, or one on Tuesday and one on Wednesday. And that points the way to a block-splitting deduction: no matter what, one of either M or S must be on Tuesday: if, for example, you put both O and R on Tuesday, there would no way to fill in the rest of the game that was consistent with clue 3.

Note that fact above your diagram:

		~P	M/S	~O	L M O P R S
		M	T	W	
O	11 a.m.	~L O/	O/		
	3 p.m			~S	

And now you're ready to tackle the questions.

STEP 6: Answer the Questions in the Smartest Order

As noted above, this game has an abbreviated set of questions. Since there is no Complete and Accurate List question, turn directly to the questions that give you new information. We start with question 1.

1. If Trudy takes Sociology at 11:00 a.m. on Wednesday, which one of the following must be true?

   (A) She takes Macroeconomics at 11:00 a.m. on Tuesday.
   (B) She takes Oceanography at 11:00 a.m. on Tuesday.
   (C) She takes Philosophy at 3:00 p.m. on Tuesday.
   (D) She takes Linguistics at 3:00 p.m. on Monday.
   (E) She takes Rhetoric at 3:00 p.m. on Monday.

First you'll utilize any clues that also give you information about S. Clue 4 tells you that L must come after S; there's only one slot in the game that satisfies that requirement:

		~P	M/S	~O	L M O P R S
		M	T	W	
O	11 a.m.	~L O/	O/		
	3 p.m			~S	
	1.			S	
				L	

That allows you to eliminate answer choice D. Clue 3 tells you that if S is on Wednesday, then M must be sometime on Tuesday:

		~P	M/S	~O	L M O P R S
		M	T	W	
O	11 a.m.	~L O/	O/		
	3 p.m			~S	
	1.		M/	S	
			/M	L	

Now that you know that M must be on Tuesday, clue 1 tells you that R must be on Monday, as M and R can't be on the same day:

		~P	M/S	~0	L M O P R S
		M	T	W	
0	11 a.m.	~L 0/	0/		
	3 p.m			~S	
1.		R/	M/	S	
		/R	/M	L	

A scan of the answers reveals that you can't select or eliminate any more choices, so you'll keep working. All that's left is to place P and O, and clues 2 and 5 make that relatively easy. From clue 2, you know that P must be on Tuesday and O on Monday. Clue 5 tells you that O must be Monday at 11:00 a.m., which means R must be in the afternoon. You don't have any further information on M and P, however, so either of those elements could occupy either Tuesday slot:

		~P	M/S	~0	L M O P R S
		M	T	W	
0	11 a.m.	~L 0/	0/		
	3 p.m			~S	
1.		0	M/P	S	
		R	P/M	L	

As the diagram illustrates, the correct answer to question 1 is answer E. Answers B and D must be false, while answers A and C could be, but need not, be true.

Now we'll look at question 3.

3. If Trudy takes both Macroeconomics and Philosophy at 11:00 a.m., which of the following must be true?

(A) She takes Philosophy on Tuesday.
(B) She takes Macroeconomics on Tuesday.
(C) She takes Linguistics on Wednesday.
(D) She takes Rhetoric on Monday.
(E) She takes Oceanography on Monday.

Clue 5 tells you that O also must be at 11:00 a.m., so you now know that M, P, and O must occupy the three morning slots, while S, L, and R must be in the afternoon. What next? Although this question gives you new information, it may not be immediately apparent how to plug this new information into the diagram.

In this situation, turn to the down-to-two principle and look for an element or slot in the diagram that has only two possibilities. Once you diagram them both, you'll know you've covered everything.

You know that O can go in only one of two slots, thanks to clue 2. That gives you a good place to start on this question: if you plug O into Monday and Tuesday at 11:00 a.m., you'll have covered all your bases.

First, try O at 11:00 a.m. Tuesday. Clue 2 also tells you that P must be on Wednesday, and the question narrows that down to Wednesday at 11:00 a.m. Since the question also requires M to be in an 11:00 a.m. slot, M must be on Monday:

		~P	M/S	~0	L M O P R S
		M	T	W	
0	11 a.m.	~L 0/	0/		
	3 p.m			~S	
3.		M	O	P	

Turning to the afternoon slots, since M and S must appear on consecutive days, S must be on Tuesday afternoon. In turn, clue 4 tells you that L must be on Wednesday, which forces R into the Monday at 3:00 p.m. slot:

		~P	M/S	~0	L M O P R S
		M	T	W	
0	11 a.m.	~L 0/	0/		
	3 p.m			~S	
3.		M	O	P	
		R	S	L	

Do you see the problem with this arrangement? Clue 1 prohibits M and R from being on the same day. Therefore, O can't be on Tuesday.

Ordinarily the next step would be to plug O into the Monday slot and continue diagramming possibilities. Fortunately, however, placing O on Tuesday allows you to identify answer choice E as the correct answer, so there's no need to work any further. It must be true that O is in the 11:00 a.m. Monday slot.

One final note on this question: Since you'll sometimes use prior work to eliminate answer choices on questions that don't give you any new information, it's important that you prominently note to yourself that this arrangement (with O on Tuesday morning) is *not* valid. You don't want to inadvertently look back at it and use it to select a wrong answer on a later question. The best way to do that is to lightly cross it out:

		~P	M/S	~0	L M O P R S
		M	T	W	
0	11 a.m.	~L 0/	0/		
	3 p.m			~S	
3.		M	O	P	
		R	S	L	

Now turn to question 2.

2. Which of the following cannot be the pair of classes Trudy takes at 11:00 a.m. and 3:00 p.m. Tuesday, respectively?

(A) Philosophy and Sociology
(B) Sociology and Rhetoric
(C) Rhetoric and Linguistics
(D) Linguistics and Macroeconomics
(E) Macroeconomics and Philosophy

On questions that give you no new information, your first step is to attempt to use your clues and deductions to eliminate or select answer choices. Here, that's as far as you have to go. Your block-splitting deduction tells you that Trudy must take either M or S on Tuesday. Answers A and B contain S, while answers D and E contain M. Since putting both R and L on Tuesday would split the M–S block, the correct answer to question 2 is choice C.

Two-Tiered Ordering Game Setup Drills

Recall from our discussion of step 1 that two-tiered ordering games have three hallmarks, the presence of any two of which is enough to signal that you should set up the game using the diagram you learned in this case. One of the main challenges that two-tiered ordering games present is the fact that they can sometimes be difficult to identify.

Following are two setup drills of games that are harder to identify as two-tiered ordering games. Each drill contains the setup and the clues of a two-tiered ordering game, but no questions. for each drill, symbolize the clues, begin your diagram, and make deductions. Answers and comments appear after the games. Pay close attention to the language in the setup and the clues; see if you can pinpoint exactly what makes each game a two-tiered ordering game.

Drill 1

Six volleyball teammates—Maria, Nancy, Rebecca, Priscilla, Tanya, and Yvonne—are to practice on three courts: court one, court two, and court three. Each team member is assigned to a position as either a setter or a hitter. Exactly two teammates—one setter and one hitter—practice on each court. They are assigned to the courts consistent with the following:

> Yvonne is a hitter.
> Priscilla does not practice on court three.
> Tanya and Nancy play the same position.
> Priscilla practices on the same court as either Maria or Rebecca.

Drill 2

A law firm's file clerk is placing six case files in a file cabinet: B, D, G, H, J, and K. The files will be placed in order from front to back. Each file is from a case whose status is either active or closed. The clerk organizes the files in accordance with these conditions:

> Each file from an active case has a file from a closed case directly behind it.
> B is an active case.
> K is somewhere in front of H.
> G is the fourth file in the cabinet.
> The second file in the cabinet is from an active case

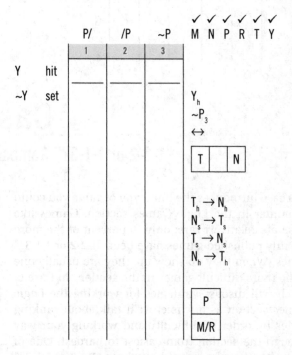

Comment. This game has two of the three hallmarks of a two-tiered ordering game—you are assigning exactly two elements to each group, and the slots in the groups are specified—despite the fact that there is no ordering component to this game. The benefit of using this setup for a game like this is that it allows you to use blocks in diagramming both clues 3 and 4.

DRILL 2

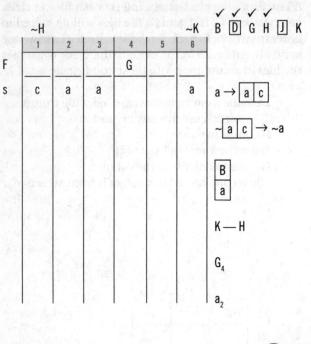

Comments. Two points will help you solve this game.

1. **Correctly identifying the game type:** This is a fairly common type of two-tiered ordering game: you're assigning elements to slots, and each of those elements has one of two particular characteristics. When you see a game like this, this is the best setup: the element in the top tier, and the characteristic in the bottom tier.

2. **Making deductions based on clue 1:** Two-tiered ordering games like this one almost always have a clue similar clue 1, from which you can deduce a lot of information about the second tier of the game. It's important that you identify that this kind of clue (1) should be diagrammed as a conditional statement, *and* (2) will support an "if someone must be after you, you can't be last" deduction.

Case 5

"1-2-2 or 1-1-3?" Games: A Bellman Carries Bags

This case introduces the final type of game you could encounter in the Logic Games section. Games like these are relatively rare: only 10 percent of the more recently published games have been "1-2-2 or 1-1-3?" games. When they do show up, they are usually one of the more difficult games in the section. In Case 6, which will discuss strategies for working the Logic Games section as a whole, we'll talk about ranking games by order of difficulty and working your way through the section from easiest to hardest. One of the best reasons to learn about these "1-2-2 or 1-1-3?" games is to learn how to identify them and postpone working on them until you've already completed the easier games.

So what exactly is a "1-2-2 or 1-1-3?" game? Like two-tiered ordering games, these games are hybrid games that involve both the ordering task and the grouping task. Unlike two-tiered ordering games, they do not assign a fixed number of slots to each group. The defining feature of a "1-2-2 or 1-1-3?" game is that instead of dictating the number of elements assigned to each group in the setup, it requires you to determine this as part of the game.

The bad news about these games is that the number of elements assigned to each group can vary from question to question. That variability adds difficulty to these games. The good news is that there is always a very small number of possibilities for how many elements there might be in each group. Typically, there are only two possible ways to distribute the elements among the groups. Hence the name we're using to describe these games. For example, a game might list five elements, create three groups, and tell you nothing more than that each group contains at least one element. In this hypothetical game, there are only two ways to distribute the elements among the groups: 1, 2, and 2; or 1, 1, and 3. Taking the time up front to identify the different possible distributions of elements among the groups is the key to conquering these games.

A sample game of this type follows. Like the game in Case 4, this game contains only a few sample questions. Try to work this game on your own before you turn to the explanation. As you work it on your own, focus on trying to identify how many ways the elements can be distributed among the groups.

A bellman at a hotel must deliver bags to six guests of the hotel. Each bag belongs to exactly one guest: Anand, Blake, Carmina, Deanna, Eun, or Francisco. The bellman makes exactly three trips to deliver the six bags. Each bag is delivered in exactly one trip. The bellman delivers at least one and no more than three bags per trip. The bellman delivers the bags in accordance with the following conditions:

> He delivers Eun's bag at the same time he delivers either Anand's bag or Blake's bag, but not both.
> He delivers Francisco's bag before he delivers Eun's bag.
> He delivers Deanna's bag before he delivers Blake's bag.
> He does not deliver Carmina's bag before he delivers Eun's bag.

1. If the bellman delivers Anand's and Carmina's bags and no others on his third trip, then which of the following must be true?

   (A) He delivers exactly one bag on his first trip.
   (B) He delivers exactly one bag on his second trip.
   (C) He delivers exactly two bags on his second trip.
   (D) He delivers exactly three bags on his first trip.
   (E) He delivers exactly three bags on his second trip.

2. If the bellman delivers Anand's bag on his first trip, which of the following must be true?

   (A) He delivers Deanna's bag on his first trip.
   (B) He delivers Deanna's bag on his second trip.
   (C) He delivers Carmina's bag on his third trip.
   (D) He delivers Eun's bag on his third trip.
   (E) He delivers Francisco's bag on his second trip.

3. If Blake's is the only bag the bellman delivers on one of his trips, which of the following could be true?

   (A) He delivers Deanna's bag on his third trip.
   (B) He delivers Carmina's bag on his second trip.
   (C) He delivers Blake's bag on his first trip.
   (D) He delivers Anand's bag on his first trip.
   (E) He delivers Francisco's bag on his second trip.

STEP 1: Identify the Game Type

Like a two-tiered ordering game, the setup and clues of a "1-2-2 or 1-1-3?" game will contain both ordering language and grouping language. The key difference between the two is in the number of elements that are assigned to each group, bin, or team. Instead of being fixed at exactly two, the number will vary from a required minimum of one up to a maximum of three (or—on very rare occasions—four). That combination—language that is a hybrid of ordering and grouping plus a variable number of elements per group—is the hallmark of a "1-2-2 or 1-1-3?" game.

The language the game uses to convey that combination will vary. In some games—including this one—the setup will expressly instruct that "each [group] must have at least one [element], and each [group] can hold up to three [elements]." When you see that kind of language—each group contains a minimum of one and a specified maximum of three or more—you know you're dealing with a "1-2-2 or 1-1-3?" game.

Other times, however, these games are harder to identify. The setup might only specify that each group contains at least one element, leaving the maximum number of elements per group undefined. That, too, is a hallmark of a "1-2-2 or 1-1-3?" game, although it's not always easy to spot. In fact, when a game involves both ordering and grouping, it's very easy to make the mistake of assuming that it's a two-tiered ordering game. Be mindful of this possibility.

In sum, once you recognize that a game involves both ordering and grouping, your next step should be to look at the number of elements assigned to each group. If it's specified that each group must have exactly two elements, you're dealing with a two-tiered ordering game. If the number of elements in each group can vary, you're dealing with a "1-2-2 or 1-1-3?" game. Sometimes you'll know the number of elements can vary because the game tells you that the maximum per group is more than two. Other times the game will not specify any maximum.

When a game has both ordering and grouping components and the setup does not explicitly state that each group must have exactly two elements, you're dealing with a "1-2-2 or 1-1-3?" game.

STEP 2: Begin Your Diagram

A "1-2-2 or 1-1-3?" game asks you to assign elements to groups, so you'll use the same basic diagram structure here that you used on grouping games. Here, the bellman is making three trips, so your diagram will look like this:

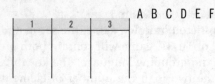

This game also involves ordering, though, so you might be wondering why you wouldn't use a tiered ordering diagram similar to the one you used in Case 4 when Trudy picked her course schedule. The reason is that a tiered ordering setup can quickly become unwieldy and difficult to work with on a "1-2-2 or 1-1-3?" game. You don't know how many tiers to put in each group, and not every group will have the same number of tiers. The traditional grouping setup can better accommodate the flexible, variable group size in "1-2-2 or 1-1-3?" games.

STEP 3: **Symbolize the Clues**

Clue 1: "He delivers Eun's bag at the same time he delivers either Anand's bag or Blake's bag, but not both."

This clue is actually two clues wrapped into one. It tells you that E must be with one of two other elements, and it also tells you that E cannot be with both of those other two elements. Diagram each piece of information separately:

$$\boxed{E \quad A/B}$$

and also

Clue 2: "He delivers Francisco's bag before he delivers Eun's bag."

Clue 3: "He delivers Deanna's bag before he delivers Blake's bag."

These two clues should be familiar from your work with one-tiered and two-tiered ordering games. Diagram them the same way here that you did in those games:

$$F — E$$
$$D — B$$

These clues tell you how the elements must be ordered *between* the groups, not *within* the groups. Visually, the representation of the clue is accurate, but it is slightly more susceptible to misinterpretation. Unfortunately, there's no better way to draw the diagram and/or symbolize the clue. This is another reason why "1-2-2 or 1-1-3?" games tend to be some of the hardest games you'll encounter in the Logic Games section.

Clue 4: "He does not deliver Carmina's bag before he deliver's Eun's bag."

This clue is similar to one you saw in Case 4 in that it tells you only that one arrangement of the elements is impermissible:

$$\sim(C — E)$$

This clue creates two possibilities for how those elements can legally be arranged: C and E can be delivered at the same time, or C can be delivered after E. Again, you'll note that using the either/or symbol:

$$E — C / \boxed{EC}$$

STEP 4: **Double-Check Your Symbolizations**
This step should be very familiar by now: translate your symbolizations back into English, then compare the language of your translation with the language of each clue. The result should be that your page looks like this:

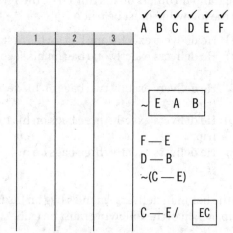

STEP 5: **Make Deductions**
"1-2-2 or 1-1-3?" games require you to make a new kind of deduction in addition to the three standard deductions that you've already learned. On games like these, one of your core tasks is to determine how many different ways there are to distribute the elements among the groups. The first deduction you should make on a "1-2-2 or 1-1-3?" game—and these games will *always* support this kind of deduction—is to list out the different possible group-size combinations. You can call these *group-size deductions*.

Group-size deductions are a combination of the process of elimination and counting. The most systematic way to make group-size deductions is to start small and work your way up. Try to make as many groups as possible that have only one element in them. Gradually work your way down so that only one group has only one element. Then, try to have as many as you can with only two elements in them, and then three.

For example, in this game, there are three groups and six elements. Each group must contain at least one and at most three elements. So start by asking if you could possibly have two groups with exactly one element. That would force four elements into the third group, so the answer is no. What about one group with exactly one element? If you put two elements in the second group and three in the third, that works. So you know one possible arrangement: 1-2-3.

If the smallest group has two elements, the distribution is even: 2-2-2. Could the smallest group have three elements? If so, two groups would each have three elements, while the third group would have none. Since the setup tells you that each group must have at least one element, there is no legal arrangement where the smallest group has three elements.

That leaves only two possibilities for how the elements can be distributed among the groups: 1-2-3, or 2-2-2. That's typical: most games of this type only allow two legal arrangements (on rare occasions there will be three possibilities).

Make sure you make a note of the possible arrangements somewhere on the page. Limitations on how the elements can be distributed among the groups invariably play a large role in determining the correct answers to questions on "1-2-2 or 1-1-3?" games.

Now let's turn to the more familiar deductions.

Clues 2 and 3 both support can't-be-first-or-last deductions:

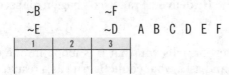

Next, both B and E appear in multiple clues, so look for repeated-element deductions. Clues 1 and 2 will support a very straightforward deduction:

$$F \;-\; \boxed{E \;\; A/B}$$

Clues 2 and 4 can also be combined. Since F must come before E, and C cannot come before E, it follows that C must come after F:

$$F - C$$

and thus also that C cannot appear in group 1:

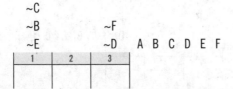

Finally, look for down-to-two deductions. With this game, this process is quick. You can see that only three of the elements can ever end up in group 1, but you can't narrow it down any further, so turn to the questions.

STEP 6: Answer the Questions in the Smartest Order
This game also has an abbreviated set of questions that does not include a Complete and Accurate List question, so turn directly to the questions that give you new information.

1. If the bellman delivers Anand's and Carmina's bags and no others on his third trip, then which of the following must be true?

    (A) He delivers exactly one bag on his first trip.
    (B) He delivers exactly one bag on his second trip.
    (C) He delivers exactly two bags on his second trip.
    (D) He delivers exactly three bags on his first trip.
    (E) He delivers exactly three bags on his second trip.

This question tells you that A and C (and no other bags) are delivered in group 3, and asks you what *must be true* as a result. Plug that new information into the diagram and then combine it with the clues that give you information about those two elements:

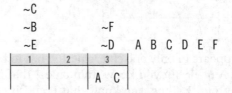

Clue 1 tells you that either A or B must be with E. Since A and C are the only elements in group 3, you know that B and E must be together in one of the first two groups. Since C is in the last group, you know that clue 4 will be satisfied no matter what you do with E.

Having exhausted the clues that give you information about the elements in the question, turn next to the remaining clues. Clue 2 tells you that F must be in an earlier group than E. Given that no additional elements can be placed in group 3, there's only one way to satisfy clue 2:

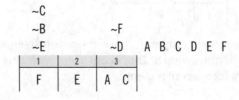

The same logic applies to clue 3, which allows you to place D and B:

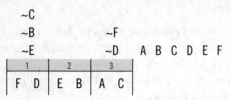

That definitively places all six elements; all six can only go in one particular group. That allows you to identify choice C as the correct answer.

2. If the bellman delivers Anand's bag on his first trip, which of the following must be true?

   (A) He delivers Deanna's bag on his first trip.
   (B) He delivers Deanna's bag on his second trip.
   (C) He delivers Carmina's bag on his third trip.
   (D) He delivers Eun's bag on his third trip.
   (E) He delivers Francisco's bag on his second trip.

This question tells you that A is in group 1, and asks what *must be true* as a result.

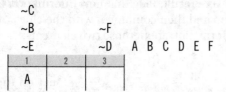

A appears in only one clue, clue 1: E has to be with either A or B. But you know from clue 2 that E can't be in group 1. Thus, you know that E and B have to be together in one of the two later groups. Nothing in the question, the clues, or your deductions tells you which group E and B will be in, but that's okay. You'll use your down-to-two tactic and diagram both possibilities.

If E and B are in group 2, clues 2 and 3 require F and D to be in group 1:

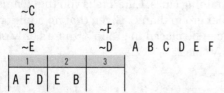

Since each group must have at least one element, C is forced into group 3. That's consistent with clue 4, so this is a legal arrangement:

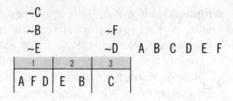

That allows you to eliminate choices B, D, and E.

If E and B are in group 3, clue 4 tells you that C must also be in group 3:

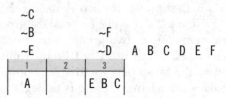

And that's as far as you need to go to answer this question: under both scenarios, C is in group 3, and that makes choice C the correct answer to question 2.

Finally, turn to question 3.

3. If Blake's is the only bag the bellman delivers on one of his trips, which of the following could be true?

   (A) He delivers Deanna's bag on his third trip.
   (B) He delivers Carmina's bag on his second trip.
   (C) He delivers Blake's bag on his first trip.
   (D) He delivers Anand's bag on his first trip.
   (E) He delivers Francisco's bag on his second trip.

This question tells you that B is alone in one of the groups and asks what could be true as a result. If B is alone, clue 1 tells you that E and A must be together. The question doesn't specify which group B is alone in, but your deduction from clue 3 tells you that B can never be in group 1. Not only does that allow you to eliminate answer choice C, but you also once again find yourself down to two possibilities, so you can start diagramming.

Start by plugging B into group 2 (if you want to, you can draw a line through the rest of the space in the group as a way to remind yourself that no other elements can be there):

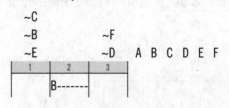

Clue 3 immediately tells you that D must be in group 1:

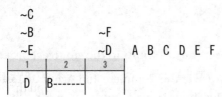

Clue 2 tells you that F must be in an earlier group than E. Since B is the only element in group 2, there is only one way to satisfy clue 2: E must be in group 3, and F must be in group 1 (your deductions above each group indicated this, too):

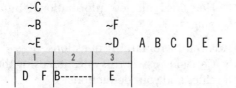

Since either A or B must be with E (clue 1), you know that A will also be in group 3:

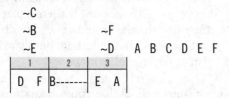

And since C cannot be delivered before E (clue 4), it too must go in group 3:

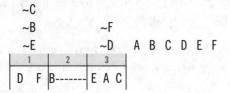

Unfortunately, this arrangement doesn't get you a correct answer, so try the second of your down-to-two possibilities:

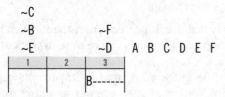

Based on clue 2, you know that F must be in group 1 and E must be in group 2:

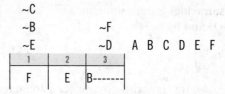

Clue 1 tells you that E and A must be together, and clue 4 tells you that C also has to be in group 2:

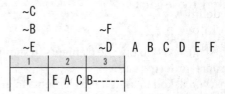

Since group 2 now has the maximum number of elements, D must be in group 1, and that's consistent with clue 3, which is the only restriction on D's location:

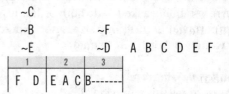

This arrangement allows you to identify choice B as the correct answer.

Conclusion

Because "1-2-2 or 1-1-3?" games appear on the LSAT so infrequently, this case does not include any setup drills with additional examples of these games. The key things to remember are the following:

1. If you see a game that (1) involves ordering and grouping, and (2) does not specify that there are two elements in each group, you're dealing with a "1-2-2 or 1-1-3?" game.
2. Every "1-2-2 or 1-1-3?" game will support a group-size deduction.
3. If you see one of these games, it's likely to be one of the more difficult games in the section.

Case 6

Section-Wide Strategy

You're now familiar with all four types of games that you're likely to encounter in the Logic Games section. Below is a summary of the six-step approach you'll use to work those games:

1. **Identify the game type.**
   - Are you asked to put the elements in sequential order? (ordering game)
   - Are you asked to assign the elements to groups? (grouping game)
   - Are two of the following true: (1) You are asked to do both ordering and grouping; (2) there are exactly two slots per group; (3) the slots in the group are specified? (two-tiered ordering game)
   - Are you being asked to do both ordering and grouping, but the group size is not limited to two? ("1-2-2 or 1-1-3?" game)

2. **Begin your diagram.**
   - What does this game look like?
   - Have you listed out all the elements in the game?

3. **Symbolize the clues.**
   - Visually, what will this clue look like when it's placed in the diagram?

4. **Double-check your symbolizations.**
   - When you translate your symbolization back into English, does it match the language of the clue?

5. **Make deductions.**
   - Can you make a group-size deduction? ("1-2-2 or 1-1-3?" games only)
   - Can you make any can't-be-first-or-last deductions? (not applicable in grouping games)
   - Can you make any repeated-element deductions using elements that appear in more than one clue? If there are multiple conditional clues, can you make any conditional-combination deductions?
   - Can you make any down-to-two deductions? Are there any one-or-the-other clues that will allow you to use placeholders?
   - Can you make any block-splitting deductions?

6. **Answer the questions in the smartest order.**

   (A) Answer the Complete and Accurate List question.
   - Is this the first question associated with the game?
   - Which clue does each answer choice violate?

   (B) Answer questions that give you more information.
   - How does this new information fit into your diagram?

   (C) Answer the remaining questions.
   - Can you answer this question using the clues and your deductions?
   - Can you answer this question using work you did on previous questions?
   - Can you answer this question using the process of elimination? Is there a place in the game that is limited to two possibilities, so that if you diagram them both you know you've covered all your bases?

Those six steps will enable you to work any game you encounter. The final piece of the puzzle is a strategy for tackling the Logic Games section as a whole.

There are two components to an effective section-wide Logic Games approach:

1. **Work the games in the right order.** You should work the easier games before you work the harder games.
2. **Work the games at the right speed.** You should work at the pace that maximizes your accuracy.

Accuracy Over Speed

Accuracy is more important than speed, even if being accurate means you don't have time to work all of the questions.

Put differently, your goal is not to answer every question. Your goal is to answer as many questions *correctly* as you can. And the best strategy for answering questions correctly is not to hurriedly work every single question on all four games, racing to beat the 35-minute buzzer. On the contrary, most LSAT takers are better served by slowing down and concentrating their effort on fewer questions.

Consider: every Logic Games section contains four games and is 35 minutes long; most have 23 questions. Let's say you take 32 minutes to answer the 18 questions associated with the three easiest games. Because you're able to work carefully, you answer those questions at a 90 percent rate of accuracy. With the remaining time, you work the complete-and-accurate-list question on the final game (which, with practice, you'll be able to answer correctly every time). You guess on the other four questions; since each question has five choices, on each question you have a 20 percent chance that your guess will be right.

On average, that strategy will net you 18 correct answers: $(18 \times 0.9) + 1 + (4 \times 0.2) = 18$. Eighteen out of twenty-three is 78 percent, which will earn you a score of around 163. That's high enough to make you competitive for admission to virtually any law school in the country.

Work smarter, not faster. If you answer most of the questions you work correctly, you'll get a score you'll be happy with. With that in mind, here is the three-step approach you should use to tackle the Logic Games section as a whole:

1. Rank the games by difficulty.
2. Work the easiest game first.
3. Work the easiest questions first.

Ranking Games by Difficulty

Your goal is to work the easier games before the harder games. So what is it about a game that makes it easier or harder? As you're scanning through the games, you should pay attention to three things:

1. What type of game is it?
2. What do the clues and the setup look like?
3. What do the questions look like?

What Type of Game Is It? The first thing you have to figure out is what kind of game you're dealing with. As discussed in Case 5, if you see a "1-2-2 or 1-1-3?" game, it's almost certainly one of the harder games in the section. Leave it for last.

As for the other games, keep in mind that everyone has individual strengths and weaknesses. After you've practiced working Logic Games for a while, you may find that grouping games give you more trouble than ordering games, or that you tend to do well on two-tiered ordering games. Incorporate that kind of personal knowledge into your decision about which games to work first.

What Do the Clues and the Setup Look Like? The test writers have a standard set of tricks they use to make each type of game more or less difficult. As you're scanning the setup and the clues, keep an eye out for the following elements.

ONE-TIERED AND TWO-TIERED ORDERING GAMES

- **Are the clues hard to understand, symbolize, and work with?** You saw some examples of complex clues like these in the drills following Case 1 and Case 2. This is by far the most important thing to focus on when you're assessing the difficulty of any kind of ordering game.
- **How does the number of elements compare to the number of slots?** Ideally, the numbers should be the same—that is, you're putting six elements in order from one to six. Therefore, the easiest ordering games will say that each element is used "exactly once." If the elements must be used "at least once" (e.g., you have to use five elements to fill eight slots) that means you're going to be repeating elements, so the game will be a little bit trickier. If the game doesn't specify, some elements may not be used at all (e.g., you have to fill seven slots from a group of ten elements).

GROUPING GAMES

- **Is the number of elements in each group variable or fixed?** Games where the number of elements within each group is fixed tend to be easier. Games that say you can have "up to three" elements or "at least two" elements will be harder.
- **Are there multiple types of elements, or are all the elements the same?** It's typically easier to work games that involve only one kind of element. Games where the elements are divided into sub-categories are more difficult, such as drill 2 of the grouping games, the one with the 10 cars that were divided into three types (sedans, trucks, economy models), which then had to be grouped into six slots.
- **How big is the game?** It tends to be easier to sort 6 elements into groups than it is to sort 12 elements into groups.
- **How many conditional clues are there?** Having all conditional clues or multiple conditional clues tends to make a game more difficult.
- **Do all of the elements have to be used?** On this factor, grouping games and ordering games are similar. The easiest grouping games use each element exactly once. More difficult games allow elements to be repeated or don't require all the elements to be used.

What Do the Questions Look Like? There are three things to look for in the questions that might influence your decision about which games to work first.

1. First, how many questions give you new information? Those questions tend to be among the easiest to work. So, for example, a game with a Complete and Accurate List question, three questions that give you new information, and one other question is preferable to a game with a Complete and Accurate List question, one question that gives you new information, and three other question types, such as those that require you to rely solely on your deductions and your answers to previous questions.

2. Are there any questions associated with the game that are notoriously difficult or time-consuming? There are two question types in particular to look out for:
   - Which of the following, if substituted for clue 4, would have the same effect on the composition of the game?
   - Which of the following, if known, allows the order of the elements (or the composition of the groups) to be completely determined?

Each of these types of questions is difficult and time-consuming. However, that doesn't mean that you should skip the game entirely. If the game otherwise looks good, you might work all the other questions, guess on this question, and use the time you save to work the easier questions on another game.

3. If all else fails and two games appear to be equally difficult, look to how many questions there are associated with the game. Other things being equal, a game with six questions is preferable to a game with only five.

All in all, the process of ranking the games in order of difficulty should only take you 90 seconds to two minutes. That's not a lot of time, so you'll necessarily be making some snap judgments. It doesn't matter if you're slightly off and work the second easiest game before the easiest one. The most important thing is to identify the game that is likely to give you the most trouble and work it last (if at all).

CHAPTER 4

LSAT Arguments

This chapter focuses on the Arguments section (officially known as the Logical Reasoning section) with cases designed to familiarize you with a four-step method you can use to answer every question. There are 11 cases in all. The first 10 introduce you to the 10 types of questions that appear in the Arguments section. The final case discusses how you should approach the section as a whole.

The Arguments section tests three basic skills:

1. **Understanding the content of the argument.** This skill turns your attention to the information that's already on the page. These are essentially reading-comprehension questions:

   - Identify the conclusion (Conclusion questions)
   - Make a deduction (Deduction questions)
   - Apply a principle (Principle questions)

2. **Figuring out what's missing from the argument.** This skill requires you to read the argument with a critical eye, identifying gaps and potential weak points in the argument's reasoning that you'll either fortify or exploit. These questions ask you to find a new piece of information that interacts with the argument in a designated way:

   - Identify an assumption (Assumption questions)
   - Strengthen the argument (Strengthen questions)
   - Resolve a paradox (Paradox questions)
   - Weaken the argument (Weaken questions)

3. **Analyzing the reasoning of the argument.** This skill shifts you away from focusing on the substantive content of the argument and toward understanding its argumentative strategy, method, pattern, and structure.

   - Describe the reasoning (Describe questions)
   - Criticize the reasoning (Flaw questions)
   - Parallel the reasoning (Parallel questions)

Variations in how you are asked to apply those skills produce a total of 10 different question types.

To every Arguments question you work you'll apply the same four-step method. The cases focus on how to adapt that method to each particular question type. In general terms, the four steps of that method are:

1. Read the question and identify your task.
2. Read the argument with your task in mind.
3. Know what you're looking for.
4. Read every word of every answer choice.

Two final notes: First, the Arguments section requires you to take a comparative approach to the answer choices. In the Logic Games section, there was one answer choice that was objectively, demonstrably right, and four choices that were objectively, demonstrably wrong. You won't have the same luxury of certainty in the Arguments section. Here it's all relative. Sometimes the right answer will jump off the page. Other times you'll read all five choices and think that none can be the correct answer. Identifying the correct answer to an Arguments question is a comparative process.

Second, the same advice that the introduction to the Logic Games chapter concluded with—practice, practice, practice—is equally applicable here. The best way to improve your performance on the Arguments section is to work a large number of practice questions; the practice tests in the back of this book are a good place to start.

The cases in this chapter are designed to equip you with a set of conceptual categories you can use to describe and understand the ideas you'll be working with in the Arguments section. Those conceptual categories will become more useful as you fill them in with examples that define the contours of their meaning. To do that, you have to apply them repeatedly. In the absence of practice, they'll be little more than empty labels. Working practice questions will help you develop a capacity for judgment that will serve you well on test day.

Case 1

What's the Point? Identify the Conclusion

This case will teach you how to approach Arguments questions in which your task is to identify the argument's conclusion. Conclusion questions make up just 6 percent of the test on average. That means you're only likely to see about three of these questions on your two Arguments sections.

Even so, mastering Conclusion questions is a critical component of your Arguments-section strategy. Why? For one, these questions tend to be some of the easiest in the Arguments sections. With a sound approach, you should be able to answer almost all of them correctly. More important, your approach to almost every other question on the Arguments section will begin with your identifying the premises and conclusion of the argument. The tools and techniques you'll learn in this case are the fundamental building blocks of a successful approach to the entire Arguments section.

Background: The Parts of an Argument

An argument is an attempt to convince the reader of the correctness of an opinion by presenting facts and evidence in support of that opinion. Every argument is made up of two basic types of statements: premises and a conclusion.

A *premise* is a reason, fact, or piece of evidence offered to support the truth of the conclusion. The *conclusion* is the main point. It is the opinion, point of view, or explanation that the argument is trying to convince you is true. For example, below is a very well known argument:

All men are mortal.
Socrates is a man.
Therefore, Socrates is mortal.

In this argument, the first two statements are the premises, and the last statement is the conclusion.

This is not to say that every single statement you encounter on the Arguments section will be either a premise or a conclusion. Some arguments will include general background information to help you better understand the content of the argument. But the work of every argument is done by its premises and conclusion.

STEP 1:   **Read the Question and Identify Your Task**
The single most valuable piece of advice you can get about the Arguments section is this: always read the question before you read the argument. Each question asks you to perform a specific task. Fortunately, the LSAT uses stock, predictable language to identify the task you need to perform, which each case will teach you to recognize.

Conclusion questions task you with identifying the argument's conclusion. Such questions invariably use wording along the lines of this:

■ Which one of the following best or most accurately states, expresses, or renders . . .
■ the main conclusion drawn in the argument above?
■ the conclusion of the argument as a whole?
■ the main point of the office manager's reasoning?
■ the argument's overall conclusion?

STEP 2: **Read the Argument with Your Task in Mind**
The nature of your task will have a dramatic impact on how you read the argument. Sometimes you will focus exclusively on the material in the argument. Other times you will be looking for a point in the argument where you can supply a piece of missing information. The wording of the question will help to identify the task you need to perform; you'll read each passage with a clear focus on what's most important. You should be an engaged reader, circling key terms and jotting notes that identify the different parts of the argument.

- Conclusion questions ask you to find something that's already on the page. The argument has a conclusion; your job is to locate it. There are two primary tools you can use to help you distinguish between what you're looking for (the conclusion) and the rest of what makes up the argument (premises and background information).
- First, you're looking for an opinion. The conclusion is likely to be phrased so that it expresses some kind of point of view, solution, proposal, explanation, or prediction. By contrast, the premises (as well as any background statements) are statements of fact, objective expressions of information and details about the situation.

Premises are facts. Conclusions are opinions.

- Second, keep an eye out for *indicator words*. Indicator words appear at the beginnings of sentences. Their presence is a sign that the sentence serves a particular logical function. Certain words serve to introduce premises. Others words signal to the reader that the writer is introducing a conclusion. When you see an indicator word, you're well on your way to identifying the role that sentence plays in the argument:

PREMISE INDICATORS	CONCLUSION INDICATORS
Because	Therefore
Since	Thus
As	As a result
Plus	Accordingly
In view of	It follows that
In light of	Hence
Given that	Consequently
In addition	Clearly
Seeing as	In view of these facts
Considering the fact that proves	This shows/suggests/
For . . . and	Based on this

STEP 3: **Know What You're Looking For**
After you've read the argument, you will know what the correct answer should look like and what function it needs to serve, even if you won't know exactly what the phrasing will be. Being aware of what you're looking for before you begin reading the answer choices will help you sort through them more quickly and more accurately.

Once you've read the argument, determine which of the sentences states the conclusion of the argument. Remember to be an active reader: once you've made your selection, indicate in writing that you believe this to be the conclusion. Put brackets around it, put an asterisk next to it in the margin, do something. Marking up the argument will help ensure (1) that you know what answer you're looking for when you turn to the answer choices; and (2) that you don't lose your train of thought while you're working through the choices.

What if you've read the argument once and you're not certain you've correctly identified the conclusion? Try this technique:

1. Read the section of the argument that you believe presents the background information and premises.
2. As the last sentence, insert "Therefore," then follow it with the sentence that you think is the conclusion.

If the argument makes sense as rewritten, you've correctly identified the conclusion. Here's an example:

> The mayoral election is approaching. I plan to vote for the incumbent mayor, since her record on fighting crime is strong and nothing is more important to our city than public safety.

Rewritten using this technique, this argument reads as follows:

> The mayoral election is approaching. The incumbent mayor's record on fighting crime is strong. Nothing is more important to our city than public safety. Therefore, I plan to vote for the incumbent mayor.

The reason this technique works is that arguments are easiest to follow when the premises are presented before the conclusion. One of the ways the LSAT writers make Conclusion questions more difficult is by burying the conclusion in the middle of several premises. Another way is to include no premise indicators or conclusion indicators. This technique addresses both of those sources of difficulty.

STEP 4: Read Every Word of Every Answer Choice
There is a substantial reading comprehension component to the Arguments section. The difference between a right or wrong answer can turn on the presence or absence of a single word. Because you're working under time constraints, it can be tempting to begin reading a choice, assume you know where it's going, and not read all the way through to the end. This is a costly mistake. Read every word of every answer choice every time.

The right answer to a Conclusion question will be the choice that most closely matches the argument's conclusion. The test writers will use paraphrasing and synonyms to make the correct answer more difficult to spot. They'll also sometimes change the sentence structure, so that if there are two clauses in the conclusion sentence, the correct answer will reverse their order.

COMMON TYPES OF WRONG ANSWER CHOICES

1. **Introduces new information.** This is the easiest type of wrong answer choice to identify. If you read a statement in the answer choice that you didn't see in the argument, it can't be the correct answer to a question that asks you to indentify the conclusion. The right answer must be somewhere in the argument.
2. **Restates a premise.** By far the most common type of incorrect answer to a Conclusion question is a restatement of one of the premises or a piece of background information from the argument. The test writers also know you are more likely to select an answer choice if it contains a statement you've already seen.
3. **Inaccurately summarizes the conclusion.** You'll also frequently see answer choices that reference the argument's conclusion but do not accurately restate it. Such choices might add information to the conclusion, change the scope of the conclusion (make it too broad or too narrow), or change the effect of the conclusion by using language that is too powerful (words such as "always" or "never") or too weak.

Practice Question

Office Manager: The new building that our firm is moving into has enough square footage that we could install additional conference rooms. With the extra conference rooms, the new building would have exactly enough offices and cubicles for the firm's current staff. Therefore, in light of the fact that our firm is growing so quickly that we expect to double our staff within the next 18 months, we will probably use the extra square footage for additional offices and cubicles.

Which one of the following most accurately expresses the conclusion of the office manager's argument?

(A) The firm is growing so quickly that it expects the size of its staff will double within the next 18 months.
(B) Most of the firm's new staff will require offices instead of cubicles.
(C) The new building the firm is moving into has enough square footage that the firm could install conference rooms.
(D) The extra square footage in the new building is more likely to be used for offices and cubicles than for conference rooms.
(E) With conference rooms, the new building would have enough office and cubicle space for all of the firm's current employees.

Answer and Analysis. The correct answer is choice D. Note that this answer choice is the only statement of opinion in the argument. You also have a conclusion indicator, "Therefore," pointing you to this statement, although this argument illustrates a common way in which Conclusion questions will try to throw you off track. The conclusion is separated from its indicator word by another premise, which makes it harder to identify.

Choice C restates the first sentence, which is background information. Choices A and E restate the argument's premises. And choice B introduces new information that appears nowhere in the argument.

Variation: Logically Completes the Argument Question

Take a look at the following argument:

The new office space that our firm is moving into has enough square footage that we could install conference rooms alongside the offices and cubicles. With conference rooms, the new office space would have exactly enough offices and cubicles for the firm's current staff. But our firm is growing so quickly that we expect to double the size of our staff within the next 18 months. Therefore, _____.

Which one of the following most logically completes the argument?

This is just a slightly more difficult version of a Conclusion question. You're asked to pick an answer choice that most accurately states the argument's conclusion. (Another way of phrasing this that you might come across is "Which one of the following most reasonably completes the last sentence of the passage?") So instead of identifying the conclusion, you're supplying it. These questions aren't particularly common (they average less than one per LSAT), but they show up often enough to merit a brief discussion.

You should approach these Logically Completes the Argument questions using techniques similar to the ones you use to answer standard Conclusion questions. Everything you see is either background information or a premise. The argument will build toward a conclusion but stop short of stating it. Before you turn to the answer choices, jot down on the page what you think the conclusion will be.

The correct answer will express an opinion that is the result of combining one or more of the ideas or facts presented in the argument's premises. Typically this opinion will repeat specific words and phrases that appeared in the premises. By contrast, many incorrect answers to this type of question will present an opinion that combines the information from the premises with a new fact or consideration not previously discussed. The other most common type of wrong answer is a simple restatement of one of the premises.

Case 2

What Do I Know for Sure? Make a Deduction

This case focuses on questions that ask you to make a deduction based on the content of the argument. Deduction questions are historically the third most common type of Arguments question, making up 12 percent of the questions (an average of about six per test).

Like Conclusion questions, Deduction questions focus your attention on what's already on the page. But where Conclusion questions ask you to identify a single statement in the argument, Deduction questions ask you to combine. Deduction questions instruct you to assume that every statement in the argument is true. The correct answer takes two statements from the argument and combines them to produce a new statement that, based on the facts contained in the argument, you can be sure is also true.

Before turning to the details of how to apply the four-step method to Deduction questions, this case begins with a discussion of the two most common ways that Deduction questions combine statements.

Background, Part 1: Words of Quantity, Frequency, and Probability

Frequently the argument associated with a Deduction question will contain several statements describing the argument's subject matter in terms of quantity, frequency, or probability, and the correct answer will be a deduction that results from the combination of two of those statements. Deduction questions repeatedly use a handful of descriptive terms to make those descriptions. These terms carry very precise meanings. It's important to understand exactly what those meanings are so you won't mistakenly assume that an argument has told you any more than it actually has.

WORDS OF QUANTITY

- *All/Each/Every/Any*: 100%
- *Most*: more than 50%, less than 100%
- *Many*: more than one, less than 100%
- *Some*: one or more, less than 100%
- *Few*: one or more, less than 50%
- *Only*: exactly one, no more and no less
- *None/No*: 0%

Yes, you read that correctly: on Deduction questions, the only difference between *many* and *some* is that if there are *many* things, you can safely assume there is more than one. The word *some* could imply just one thing. Otherwise the two terms are interchangeable.

WORDS OF FREQUENCY

- *Always/Every time/Invariably*: 100% of the time
- *Usually*: more than 50% of the time, less than 100% of the time
- *Often/Frequently*: more than one time, less than 100% of the time
- *Sometimes*: at least one time, less than 100% of the time
- *Rarely*: at least one time, less than 50% of the time
- *At least once*: one or more times
- *Once*: 1 time
- *Never*: 0 times

Again, the same (somewhat counterintuitive) rule is true here: the only difference between *sometimes* and *often* is the assurance that *often* means "more than once."

WORDS OF PROBABILITY

- *Must/Definite/Certain*: guaranteed, 100% chance
- *Probable/Likely*: More than a 50% chance
- *Possible/Can/May/Could*: Not impossible, not certain
- *Unlikely/Improbable*: Not impossible, less than a 50% chance
- *Impossible/cannot*: foreclosed, 0% chance

Background, Part 2: Reviewing Conditional Statements

Deduction questions also require you to revisit a topic covered in Case 2 of the Logic Games chapter: conditional statements. Many Deduction questions present information in the form of conditional statements. To identify the correct answer to these questions, you have to know how such statements can and cannot be combined. Three aspects of conditional statements are particularly important to Deduction questions: (1) making the deduction that is the contrapositive; (2) figuring out what you know and what you don't know; and (3) translating nonstandard conditional statements.

First, a conditional statement is any statement that takes the form "If A, then B." Symbolically, such a statement is represented as "A → B." A conditional statement is logically equivalent to its contrapositive. Whenever you know "If A, then B," you also know that statement's contrapositive, "If not B, then not A," which is symbolized as "~B → ~A."

Understanding contraposition is essential to success on Deduction questions. A recurring pattern in Deduction questions is the presentation of an argument that contains two statements in the following form: "If A, then B" and "Not B." The correct answer to such a question—by operation of the statement's contrapositive—is almost always in the form "Not A." This is the most common type of conditional statement–based deduction that you'll make on Deduction questions.

Second, when you have a conditional statement, it's important to keep track of what you know and what you don't. Remember: follow the arrow. Always start on the left side of the statement. For example, suppose one statement in the argument tells you "A → B." The contrapositive means you automatically also know "~B → ~A." How might that statement interact with a later statement in the argument?

IF YOU KNOW	YOU ALSO KNOW
A	B
B	Nothing
~A	Nothing
~B	~A

Third, unlike the Logic Games section, where conditional statements typically took the standard "if, then" form, the Arguments section frequently uses conditional statements in nonstandard form.

Below is a table summarizing how to symbolize such statements:

STATEMENT	SYMBOLIZATION	CONTRAPOSITIVE
If A, then B or C	A → B / C	~B & ~C → ~A
If A and B, then not C	A & B → ~C	C → ~A / ~B
B only if A	B → A	~A → ~B
A unless B	~A → B	~B → A
Not A unless B	A → B	~B → ~A
All A are B	A → B	~B → ~A
No A are B	A → ~B	B → ~A
B if, but only if, A	A → B and B → A	~A → ~B and ~B → ~A

You would do well to memorize this chart. On test day, you are virtually certain to encounter a Deduction question that requires you to translate and manipulate a nonstandard conditional statement. In particular, "Unless," "All," None," and "Only if" statements are Deduction-question hallmarks.

STEP 1: Read the Question and Identify Your Task
Deduction questions always tell you to assume that everything in the argument is true and ask you, based on that assumption, what else you know to be true. Within that general framework, however, there are two subtypes of Deduction questions.

One subtype of question asks you to pick an answer choice that is conclusively established. The other subtype asks you to pick the answer choice that is most strongly supported by the argument. The differences between these two subtypes won't affect how you read the argument, but they will affect what kind of answer choice you're looking for. Common phrasings of each include the following:

CONCLUSIVELY ESTABLISHED

- If all of the statements above are true, which one of the following must be true?
- Which one of the following follows logically from the statements above?
- Which one of the following can be properly inferred from the information above?

STRONGLY SUPPORTED

- The statements above, if true, most strongly support which one of the following?

■ Which one of the following is most strongly supported by the statements above?

■ Which one of the following can most reasonably be concluded on the basis of the information above?

<u>STEP 2:</u>   **Read the Argument with Your Task in Mind**
There is a very important difference between Deduction questions and Conclusion questions. The "arguments" associated with Deduction questions typically do not contain a set of premises and a conclusion. Rather, they are simply collections of factual statements. Consequently, as you read the argument you don't have to worry about identifying its constitutive parts. Rather, your focus should be on identifying and understanding each factual statement the argument contains.

Be an active, engaged reader. As to each sentence of the argument, ask yourself what factual information it contains. Be on the lookout for logically operative trigger words, circling them as you go, including the following:

■ Terms of quantity, probability, and frequency (as previously discussed)
■ Terms that signal a conditional statement
■ Terms of comparison (*more, less, like, unlike, also,* etc.)

<u>STEP 3:</u>   **Know What You're Looking For**
You're looking for facts: concrete, specific statements that are squarely supported by the content of the argument. When the question is worded such that you're looking for an answer choice that is conclusively established, you need something that is absolutely, positively, 100 percent guaranteed to be true based on the argument. When you're looking for the answer choice that is most strongly supported by the argument, the correct answer doesn't have to be logically compelled by the argument, but it should require only the tiniest of inferential leaps from the information in the argument to the statement in the answer choice.

If you see that the argument uses conditional statements, you should quickly symbolize those statements (and their contrapositives) in the margin of your test booklet. When an argument contains multiple conditional statements, the correct answer is almost always a combination of those statements. Symbolizing them will enable you to combine them quickly and accurately.

<u>STEP 4:</u>   **Read Every Word of Every Answer Choice**
Identifying the right answer to a Deduction question is like trying to pick out a faint radio signal against a wall of background noise. The right answer never involves every statement contained in the argument. Indeed, the primary way the test writers make

Deduction questions more difficult is by providing you with information that you don't need. If the argument only contained two statements, it wouldn't be hard to find the answer choice that combined them. But when the argument contains six statements, finding an answer choice that appropriately combines two of them is much more difficult.

The right answer will be a factual statement that, depending on the wording of the question, either is guaranteed to be true or is very, very likely to be true based on the content of the argument.

COMMON TYPES OF WRONG ANSWER CHOICES

1. **Deductions not supported by conditional statements.** Errors in contraposition, deductions that go against the arrow, and mistakes in translating "unless" and "only if" conditionals are common wrong answers on Deduction questions whose arguments include conditional statements.

2. **Answers that discuss new or outside information.** Deduction questions ask you what must be true based on the content of the argument. Not surprisingly, then, answers that discuss topics and information that are not discussed in the argument cannot be correct. That might sound straightforward, but there are two ways the test writers will try to tempt you to select one of these choices. The first way is by playing on your outside knowledge of related topics. For example, if the argument gave you information about the calorie content of a hamburger, wrong answer choices might discuss the levels of vitamins, fiber, salt, or protein in a hamburger. The second way is by using the word *only.* That one word quietly makes a comparison between what's listed in the answer choice and everything else in the entire world; *only* is a giant red flag in an answer choice to a Deduction question.

3. **Implying an inference based on context.** If someone told you, "My friend Calvin is tall. My friend Gus is tall and thin," you might reasonably infer that Calvin is not thin. But on a Deduction question, that kind of inference is impermissible. You can't assume that a fact is true based on only context. Deduction questions are about explicit information; you need to be able to point to the portion of the argument that expressly tells you the fact you're relying on.

4. **Mismatched quantity, probability, or frequency.** Be on the lookout for subtle shifts and slip-ups in the use of these terms. An argument that tells you that something "may" be true won't support an answer choice that says something "must" be true. If "some" things have a quality, you don't know that

"all," "most," or even "many" of them have that quality, too.

5. **Answers involving normative language.** Like the word *only*, normative words of quality and judgment—*should, ought to, bad, good, better, worse,* etc.—are red flags in Deduction question answer choices. Unless the argument contains these same kinds of judgment-passing words—and the arguments associated with Deduction questions rarely do—they disqualify any answer choice in which they appear. A set of descriptive, factual statements cannot guarantee the truth of a normative, value-laden conclusion.

Practice Question 1

The world is home to more than a dozen species of wolves. Some of them are not threatened by habitat destruction, but the Great Plains wolf is. The enactment of a federal habitat-restoration program would increase the number of Great Plains wolves in the wild without causing overpopulation. If the Great Plains wolf population increased in size without becoming overpopulated, the wolves would hunt Northern pocket gophers, which would benefit many farming communities throughout the Midwest.

If the above statements are true, which one of the following must be also be true?

(A) At least some Midwest farming communities would benefit if a federal habitat-restoration program were enacted.

(B) If a federal habitat-restoration program is not enacted, the size of the Great Plains wolf population will not increase in size.

Answer and Analysis. On a Deduction question, always check for statements that you can symbolize as conditionals, like the fourth sentence of this argument. Whereas in the Logic Games section you used single letters to symbolize conditionals, in the Arguments section you should use shorthand notations so you can better keep track of the contents of the statements. Here, you might symbolize that sentence as:

increase in size → hunt gophers and benefit communities

Although it may not be immediately apparent, the third sentence of this argument is also a conditional statement: If a federal habitat-restoration program is enacted, then the Great Plains wolf population would increase in size without becoming overpopulated:

federal program → increase in size

This question thus introduces the second most common type of conditional statement–based deduction you'll make on Deduction questions. An argument that contains two statements in the form of "If A, then B" and "If B, then C" will support the deduction "If A, then C." Here, that means the conditional statements

federal program → increase in size
increase in size → hunt gophers and benefit
                       communities

can be combined to form the deduction:

federal program → hunt gophers and benefit
                      communities

Choice A is a version of that deduction (federal program → benefit communities) and thus would be the correct answer to this question. Compare it to choice B. If you represent choice B symbolically, it becomes:

no federal program → no increase in size

You can't draw that conclusion based on either of the conditional statements contained in the argument; it's an erroneous attempt to state the contrapositive of the third sentence.

Practice Question 2

Electronics manufacturer: Developing a line of smartphones would require a research-and-development push that would directly trade off with our R&D efforts on five other products. Plus, a line of MP3 players—another product we have discussed developing—has an inherently higher profit potential than a line of smartphones and would be cheaper to manufacture.

The electronics manufacturer's statements, if true, most strongly support which one of the following?

(A) Developing a line of MP3 players would not trade off with the R&D efforts on any other products.

(B) The manufacturer is more likely to make money by developing a line of MP3 players than it is by developing a line of smartphones.

(C) Developing a line of smartphones would be a bad business decision for the manufacturer.

(D) The manufacturer will make money if it develops a line of MP3 players.

(E) The only new product that would be profitable for the manufacturer is a line of MP3 players.

Answer and Analysis. The correct answer here, choice B, illustrates the difference between a "conclusively establish" Deduction question and a "strongly support" Deduction question. The argument does not come right out and say that a line of MP3 players would be "more likely to make money" than a line of smartphones. But the argument does say that a line of MP3 players "has an inherently higher profit potential." It takes an inference to go from the latter to the former, but that inference is not a very big one, and it's even easier to make in light of the fact that MP3 players are cheaper to manufacture.

Meanwhile, choice A makes an implied inference; the argument is silent on the question of whether developing MP3 players would entail any R&D trade-offs. You might reasonably assume that it would not—why criticize smartphones on that ground if MP3 players are not immune from the same criticism?—but the argument never comes right out and says so. A reasonable assumption is not a deduction. Choice C introduces normative language—a "bad" business decision—not taken from the argument. Choice D is a mismatch of probability: although the MP3 has a higher profit *potential*, it is not *guaranteed* to be profitable. And choice E has the watchword *only*, which implicitly discusses a wealth of outside information. Nothing in the argument states that the electronics manufacturer could not profitably develop, for example, earphones, car stereos, or tablet computers.

Case 3

From General to Specific One Step at a Time: Apply a Principle

This case discusses Arguments questions that ask you to apply a general principle to a specific situation. Over the past five years, Principle questions have been one of the least common types of Arguments question, making up a little more than 7 percent of the questions (an average of just three per test). Still, it is one you should be familiar with.

This is the third question type that focuses your attention exclusively on the content of the argument. Conclusion questions ask you to identify a particular statement in the argument. Deduction questions ask you to combine two statements in the argument. And Principle questions ask you to pick an answer choice that accurately describes the content of the argument in more general terms.

STEP 1: Read the Question and Identify Your Task

Principle questions require you to select an answer choice (or "principle") that is an accurate, more general description of the argument. Typical wordings of such questions include:

- Which one of the following principles is best illustrated by the argument above?
- The reasoning above most closely conforms to which one of the following principles?
- Which one of the following most accurately expresses the principle underlying the argument above?

Sometimes the question will use the term *proposition* or *generalization* in place of *principle*.

STEP 2: Read the Argument with Your Task in Mind

Since your ultimate task is to identify a principle that accurately restates the argument in more general terms, your first step is to understand the specific terms of the argument. Sometimes the argument associated with a Principle question will be a true argument, offering one or more premises in support of a conclusion. When you see an argument like this, use the techniques you learned in Case 1 to identify the argument's parts.

Other times the argument will simply be a collection of factual statements. In that case, you should draw on the techniques you learned in Case 2. Identify each separate factual claim the argument makes. Check to see if the argument establishes any kind of relationship between those factual claims or makes any comparison or connection between them.

STEP 3: Know What You're Looking For

The right answer to a Principle question will preserve the logical relationship between the various statements in the argument while summarizing or recasting the argument at a higher level of generality. How much more general will the principle be? It depends. Some principles sweep very broadly. Others are so specific that they can feel like the right answer to a Deduction question. But the level of generality at which the principle is stated will not affect how you tackle the question: you'll break the principle down into parts and work with the parts one at a time.

STEP 4: **Read Every Word of Every Answer Choice**
Finding the right answer to a Principle question is a step-by-step process of parsing and matching. Each answer choice will list a different principle. Parsing requires you to break each of those principles down into its component parts so that you can work with the parts one at a time.

The principle usually has two parts: (1) a statement of a rule to guide behavior or decisions; (2) a caveat that limits the contexts or circumstances in which the rule applies. You'll work with each part individually, looking to see whether there is a portion of the argument that corresponds to that part of the principle. You'll repeat this process with each part of each principle in each answer choice.

The right answer will state a principle that accounts for each factual component of the argument and the logical relationship between those components

Common Types of Wrong Answer Choices. There's only one kind of wrong answer to a Principle question: an answer choice that contains one or more component parts that do not correspond to any portion of the argument. Most wrong answers will conform to some parts of the argument but not all of them.

Practice Question

> Horticulturalist: Amateur gardeners often spray their gardens with a particular type of pesticide known as fungicides in an attempt to rid their gardens of stinging nettle. They should not do so. Stinging nettle is a flowering herb. Fungicides do not stunt the growth of flowering herbs. Spraying a fungicide on stinging nettle thus will not stunt its growth. Plus, fungicides have the potential to severely damage the topsoil in most gardens.

Which one of the following most accurately expresses the principle underlying the horticulturalist's reasoning?

(A) An amateur gardener should not use a pesticide to rid a garden of a particular weed if the pesticide will not stunt the growth of that weed and may have other harmful effects on the garden.

(B) An amateur gardener should use every pesticide that is likely to stunt the growth of any weed.

(C) An amateur gardener should not use a pesticide if the pesticide will stunt the growth of a weed without killing it.

(D) An amateur gardener should not use a pesticide to rid a garden of a particular weed if it is unclear whether the pesticide will stunt the growth of that weed.

(E) An amateur gardener should not use a pesticide that might have negative consequences for the garden, even if that pesticide would stunt the growth of some weeds.

Answer and Analysis. This argument offers a conclusion—amateur gardeners should not attempt to rid their gardens of stinging nettle by spraying their gardens with fungicides—and two premises in support of that conclusion: (1) fungicide does not stunt the growth of stinging nettles; (2) fungicides have the potential to severely damage most gardens' topsoil. You're looking for an answer that tracks the content of the argument and reinforces the logical relationships between the various statements.

To assess the principles in the answer choices, break each one of them down into parts and look for a part of the argument that corresponds to each part of the principle. Start with choice A. Its conclusion is "An amateur gardener should not use a pesticide to rid a garden of a particular weed." That part of the principle is consistent with the argument: "a pesticide" is a more general description of "fungicides," and "a weed" is a more general description of "stinging nettle." Next, the principle conditions its conclusion on the presence of two facts. The first fact is that "the pesticide will not stunt the growth of that weed"; that part of the principle tracks premise (1) of the argument. The second fact, that the pesticide "may have other harmful effects on the garden," tracks premise (2), which states severe topsoil damage is a harmful effect. Therefore, choice A is the correct answer to this question. All three parts of the principle it states correspond to different parts of the argument.

Compare choice B. Its conclusion—"An amateur gardener should use every pesticide"—does not match the conclusion of the argument. And the second part of choice B also does not match any part of the argument. The argument tells you nothing about pesticides that are effective in stunting weed growth.

The conclusion of choice C matches the conclusion of the argument, but the second part of its principle has the same problem that choice B had: it discusses pesticides that do stunt weed growth. It also introduces a new consideration—killing weeds instead of merely stunting their growth—that has no counterpart in the argument.

The conclusion of choice D matches that of the argument, but the second part of its principle does not. The argument says fungicide should not be used because it absolutely will not stunt the growth of stinging nettle, while the corresponding part of this principle would prohibit pesticide use even when a pesticide's effectiveness is only uncertain.

In choice E, two of its three parts correspond to the argument. But its statement that the rule against using a pesticide should be followed "even if that pesticide would stunt the growth of some weeds" has no counterpart in the argument.

As this example illustrates, working a Principle question can be a meticulous process. Breaking the choices down into smaller, more manageable parts is the best way to identify subtle differences between wrong answers and the argument.

Variation: Finding a Fact Pattern That Fits Within a Principle

Sometimes the argument itself states a principle, the answer choices contain various collections of factual statements, and you must select the answer choice that falls within the range of situations covered by the principle. Principle questions of this type are typically worded like this:

- Which one of the following is consistent with the principle expressed by the argument?
- Which one of the following most closely conforms to the principle stated above?

This variation is not a substantive one. You'll still parse the principle by breaking it down into parts, and you'll attempt to match each of those parts to a part of each of the factual scenarios or "arguments" contained in the answer choices. Instead of working with multiple general principles, you're working with multiple factual scenarios. Both your task—finding an answer choice that accurately restates the argument at a different level of generality—and the process by which you perform that task will remain the same.

Case 4

Bridging the Gap: Identify an Assumption

This case focuses on Arguments questions that ask you to identify an assumption of the argument. Over the past several years, Assumption questions have been the single most common question type. About 16 percent—that's eight questions across the two sections—are likely to be Assumption questions.

Unlike question types discussed in the first three cases, which focused on material that was part of the argument, Assumption questions focus on what's missing—what's not on the page but should be. Your task is to provide the missing link that bridges the gap between the argument's premises and its conclusion. This case will teach you how to do so by focusing on differences between the wording of the premises and the wording of the conclusion.

Background: What Is an Assumption?

An *assumption* is an unstated premise. It is a fact or piece of evidence that is not part of the argument's support, but the argument nonetheless relies on it. When an assumption is identified and stated explicitly, the logic of the argument becomes clearer. If the assumption is true, the argument becomes more persuasive. If the assumption is false or questionable, the argument's persuasive force is diminished. Consider the following example:

Anyone who is an American is not a Canadian. Therefore, Tanya is not a Canadian.

This simple argument proceeds on the assumption that Tanya is an American.

<u>STEP 1:</u>   **Read the Question and Identify Your Task**
Assumption questions ask you to identify an assumption made by the argument. The following are the most common ways in which Assumption questions are phrased:

- The argument depends on the assumption that:
- Which one of the following is an assumption required by the argument?
- The argument relies on assuming which one of the following?
- The conclusion follows logically from the premises if which one of the following is assumed?
- Which one of the following, if assumed, enables the conclusion of the argument to be properly drawn?

<u>STEP 2:</u> **Read the Argument with Your Task in Mind**
Unlike a Conclusion question, where the answer is already written on the page, an Assumption question asks you to find something that should be there but isn't. That affects how you should read the argument. Instead of looking for the answer, you'll be looking for the place in the argument where the answer fits in.

> **Assumption questions require you to identify differences between the wording of the premises and the wording of the conclusion.**

An assumption is an unstated premise that bridges the gap between the conclusion and the premises offered in support of that conclusion. On the LSAT, assumptions lurk in shifts in language and changes in wording between the premises and the conclusion. Accordingly, you need to focus on three things as you read the argument:

1. **Identify the argument's conclusion and premises.** Use the tools and techniques you learned in Case 1 to perform this step (keeping in mind that some statements may just be background information).
2. **Identify new language in the conclusion.** Look carefully for terms, words, or phrases in the conclusion that you don't see anywhere else in the argument. Draw circles around any new language that shows up for the first time in the conclusion.
3. **Identify the gap between the premises and the conclusion.** Look for language that appears in the premises but does not appear in the conclusion. The conclusion substitutes the new language you found in step 2 for the language you're finding here at step 3.

Consider the following argument:

> Consumer psychologist: Car manufacturers will soon begin to include side airbags as a standard feature on most cars they manufacture. This makes sense, for these manufacturers want to maximize the number of cars they sell, and most parents will not purchase a new car unless it is safe and will reduce the risk of injury in case of an accident.

The first sentence of this argument is its conclusion. It is supported by two premises in the next sentence, which are introduced using the "For ... and ... " premise indicator.

In the conclusion, we see that car manufacturers "will soon begin to include side airbags as a standard feature." That's the first time in the argument that we see language about airbags.

Look at the second premise: most parents will purchase a new car only if "it is safe and will reduce the risk of injury in case of an accident." That language does not appear in the conclusion. That's the gap we're looking for: the conclusion has replaced "is safe and will reduce the risk of injury in case of an accident" with "include side airbags as a standard feature."

Identifying a language gap is a mechanical process that you can apply to even the most difficult Assumption questions. Once you've identified the conclusion, circle the words you don't see anywhere else in the argument. Then review the premises one by one and look for words used in the premises that have dropped out of the conclusion. With practice, you'll be able to pick out these shifts in wording even in arguments that you have a hard time understanding.

<u>STEP 3:</u> **Know What You're Looking For**
Before you turn to the answer choices, articulate to yourself the words or phrases you want to connect. With the practice question argument you might say, "I'm looking for an answer that connects the inclusion of side airbags as a standard feature with safety and the ability to prevent injuries in an accident." Don't worry about the specifics of how those phrases will be connected. There's no way you can anticipate the exact phrasing that the correct answer will use.

<u>STEP 4:</u> **Read Every Word of Every Answer Choice**
The correct answer to an Assumption question will bridge the gap between the premises and the conclusions, not just linguistically but logically. Once you've identified what you think is the correct answer choice, double-check yourself by using the "plug it in as a premise" technique. Reread the argument (premises first, then conclusion, the same way you reread it on Conclusion questions), but plug in your answer choice as the final premise right before the conclusion. This new premise should contain the new language from the conclusion that's missing from the rest of the argument and also cause the argument to make better sense.

COMMON TYPES OF WRONG ANSWER CHOICES

---

1. **Introduces irrelevant new information.** This is the most common type of wrong answer choice to an Assumption question. These answer choices will discuss a fact or idea that is superficially related to but logically distinct from the topic of the argument. These choices tend to be worded very generally and offer very little concrete information.

2. **Makes an irrelevant comparison.** This is a subcategory of choices that introduce irrelevant new information. An answer choice that makes an irrelevant comparison might state that the topic of the argument has some quality or characteristic in common with a different topic. Or, it might make some kind of comparative claim about the topic of the argument that is the "best" or "only" of a particular category. These choices go astray because they broaden the argument's scope instead of strengthening the connection between its premises and its conclusion.

3. **Bolsters or provides more detail about a premise.** These choices can be intuitively appealing because they can make the argument seem more credible. But knowing more about the premises doesn't help bridge the gap between those premises and the conclusion.

4. **Weakens the argument.** This is another frequent type of wrong answer. It can be appealing because many of the arguments in the Arguments section are questionable or even wrong, and these choices point out something that the argument overlooks. But remember, your job is always to find the assumption that makes the argument work.

Practice Question

Let's take another look at the argument from earlier, this time with answer choices as well:

> Consumer psychologist: Car manufacturers will soon begin to include side airbags as a standard feature on most cars they manufacture. This makes sense, for these manufacturers want to maximize the number of cars they sell, and most parents will not purchase a new car unless it is safe and will reduce the risk of injury in case of an accident.

> Which one of the following is an assumption required by the argument?

> (A)   Parents are also concerned with safety and reducing the risk of injury in case of an accident when they purchase a used car.

(B)   Safety is more important to parents who are purchasing new cars than aesthetics and price.

(C)   Cars that include side airbags as a standard feature are safe and will prevent many injuries in case of an accident.

(D)   Car manufacturers study their customers' preferences and buying habits in great detail.

(E)   People who are not parents purchase new cars on a far more frequent basis than parents do.

Answer and Analysis. Only choice C attempts to bridge the gap between airbags and safety. And it does so in a way that makes sense in the context of the argument.

The argument is concerned only with parents who are purchasing new cars. Choice A gives you *irrelevant new information* about the parents who are purchasing used cars, which does not bridge the gap between airbags and safety. Choice B compares the importance of safety to the importance of aesthetics and price. A choice like this one goes outside the scope of the argument to introduce new, tangential considerations. Choice D simply *provides more detail about a premise.* And choice E *weakens the argument,* which is the opposite of what you're being asked to do. This choice actually demonstrates why the argument should be rejected.

The "plug it in as a premise" technique introduced earlier in the chapter makes it clear that choice C is the correct answer. Consider:

> Consumer psychologist: Car manufacturers want to maximize the number of cars they sell, and most parents will not purchase a new car unless it is safe and will reduce the risk of injury in case of an accident. Cars that include side airbags as a standard feature are safe and will prevent many injuries in case of an accident. Therefore, car manufacturers have begun to include side airbags as a standard feature on most cars they manufacture.

Read like that, this argument is airtight, so you can be confident that choice C is the correct response.

Case 5

Causes, Explanations, and Predictions: Strengthen the Argument

This case addresses questions that ask you to select the answer choice that strengthens the argument's conclusion. You're likely to encounter about five Strengthen questions on test day.

Strengthen questions follow a consistent pattern. The argument's premises present a set of facts, usually based on some kind of research, study, or survey. The argument draws a conclusion based on the data presented in the premises. That conclusion might be a prediction, an explanation of past events, or a claim about causation. The correct answer provides additional, concrete information that lends further support to the argument's conclusion. The test writers repeatedly utilize the same small handful of argumentative strategies to generate right answers to Strengthen questions. This case will teach you what those strategies are.

STEP 1:   Read the Question and Identify Your Task

Strengthen questions ask you to identify an answer choice that presents a concrete fact that bolsters the argument. They use some variation of the following wording:

■ Which one of the following, if true, . . .
■ most strengthens the argument?
■ provides (or "lends" or "adds") the most support for the speaker's position?
■ would most strengthen the reasoning above?
■ most helps to support [a particular claim] made in the argument?

STEP 2:   Read the Argument with Your Task in Mind

Your priority here is the same as it was on Conclusion and Assumption questions: identify the conclusion and the premises offered in support of it. Use indicator words to guide you. The premises of the argument will introduce some kind of data: the results of historical research, a scientific study, or simple observation. The conclusion will then state an opinion about or based on that data.

Consider the following argument:

> Stockbroker: My firm classifies all of its brokers as either risk-averse or risk-tolerant. We recently undertook a comprehensive study of our brokers' investment philosophies and found that over the past year the portfolios managed by risk-tolerant brokers were performing 16 percent better than those managed by risk-averse brokers. It is thus clear that success in investing in the stock market is a consequence of risk tolerance.

The argument's conclusion appears in the last sentence, introduced by the conclusion indicator *thus*. The first sentence provides background on the study. The second sentence offers direct evidentiary support for the conclusion.

STEP 3:   Know What You're Looking For

Before you turn to the answer choices, determine what kind of conclusion the argument has drawn. The conclusion of a Strengthen argument will take one of the following three forms:

1. A claim about *causation* (A causes B)
2. An *explanation* (A is the reason B happened in the past)
3. A *prediction* (A suggests B will happen in the future)

Being aware of what type of conclusion the argument has drawn will make it easier to identify the correct answer.

In this example, the conclusion is a claim about causation. The stockbroker claims that risk tolerance is the cause of successful investing in the stock market.

STEP 4:   Read Every Word of Every Answer Choice

Right answers to Strengthen questions are concrete, factual, and specific. In fact, the test writers repeatedly use a few basic types of right answers to Strengthen questions. The correct answer to a Strengthen question will:

1. **Provide data or evidence that is consistent with the conclusion.** This is the most common type of right answer to a Strengthen question. Where the argument's conclusion is some kind of theory, the right answer provides new information that makes the theory look more credible.

   Example: "A separate study showed that stockbrokers who became more conservative and risk-averse over time saw a steady decrease in the profitability of their investments."

2. **Rule out an alternative causation or explanation.** If the argument concludes that A causes B, the correct answer might rule out C causing B. If the conclusion is an explanation or a prediction, the right answer might rule out alternative predictions or explanations.

   Example: "Risk-tolerant stockbrokers are not more likely to receive training, advice, and hands-on management than risk-averse stockbrokers."

3. **Bolster the reliability of the data.** Strengthen arguments base their conclusions on the results of a study, a survey, or some other kind of research. The correct answer to some questions will firm up the study's credibility.

   Example: "The study undertaken by the stockbroker's firm has been repeated, with similar results, by every major investment firm in the city."

4. **Rule out reverse causation.** While the first three types of right answers could show up regardless of whether the argument's conclusion makes a claim about causation, explanation, or prediction, this last category is specific to causation questions (which are the most common subtype of Strengthen questions). If the conclusion claims A causes B, the correct answer might rule out B causing A.

   Example: "Experiencing success as an investor does not cause a stockbroker to become more risk-tolerant."

COMMON TYPES OF WRONG ANSWER CHOICES

1. **Weakens the argument.** These choices can be tempting for the same reason they're tempting on Assumption questions: if you find the argument's conclusion to be questionable or problematic, these choices can play to your instincts, even though they do the opposite of what the question asks. There's at least one wrong answer that weakens the argument on virtually every Strengthen question. Circling the words in the question that identify your task can help prevent you from selecting these choices.
2. **Provides additional, irrelevant data about the evidence.** Strengthen questions are normative: you're looking for a choice that makes the conclusion better, more persuasive. A purely descriptive choice doesn't perform that task.
3. **Makes a general statement about the topic of the argument.** Correct answers to Strengthen questions are usually concrete and precise. Generalizations that paint in broad strokes can be tempting because they're uncontroversial; they don't seem wrong when you read them.
4. **Offers support for a different conclusion.** These choices can make the argument seem stronger in some undefined way. This is why it's important to have a precise understanding of what the argument concludes: you're looking for a choice that shares the same narrow focus.

Practice Question

Let's take another look at the argument from earlier, this time with answer choices as well:

> Stockbroker: My firm classifies all of its brokers as either risk-averse or risk-tolerant. We recently undertook a comprehensive study of our brokers' investment philosophies and found that over the past year the portfolios managed by risk-tolerant brokers were performing 16 percent better than those managed by risk-averse brokers. It is thus clear that success in investing in the stock market is a consequence of risk tolerance.

Which one of the following, if true, most strengthens the argument?

(A) The performance of the brokers' investment portfolios over the past year has not been representative of how those portfolios typically perform.
(B) The firm's study utilized a combination of self-reporting and empirical data analysis to classify its brokers as risk-tolerant or risk-averse.
(C) Some stockbrokers will not be able to earn a profit no matter what their level of risk tolerance is.
(D) Risk-tolerant stockbrokers also exhibit more of the traits associated with being a good manager than do risk-averse stockbrokers.
(E) All the stockbrokers in the study received an equal amount of training and were supervised by the same management team.

Answer and Analysis. Choice E is the correct answer, as it *eliminates an alternative causation or explanation.* Choice A weakens the argument. It undermines the conclusion that risk-tolerant brokers are more successful. Choice B is a purely descriptive choice; it does nothing more than give you additional, descriptive details about something you already know. Choice C is a general statement. It lacks any hard facts that specifically connect it to the claim made by the argument's conclusion. And finally, you might think of choice D as strengthening the argument in an irrelevant way. Knowing that risk-tolerant brokers also make good managers doesn't tell you anything about profitable investing, and profitable investing is the only thing the conclusion concerns itself with.

Variation: Using a General Principle to Strengthen the Argument

There is an additional type of Strengthen question that you might come across in the Arguments section. These questions ask you to select a principle that strengthens the line of reasoning contained in the argument.

A question like this is different from a typical Strengthen question. These questions require you to combine the tools and techniques you've learned in this case with the ones you learned in Case 3's discussion of Principle questions.

Step 1: Read the Question and Identify Your Task. Each of the following is a typical phrasing of a question that asks you to strengthen an argument using a general principle:

- Which one of the following principles, if valid, most helps to justify the reasoning of the argument above?
- Which one of the following principles most helps to justify drawing the conclusion in the argument?
- Which one of the following principles, if valid, provides the most support for the argument above?
- Which one of the following, if true, most justifies the above application of the principle?

Step 2: Read the argument with your task in mind. A standard Strengthen question is like a snapshot from a science class. The argument gives you empirical data (the facts, evidence, or study results in the premises) and a theory (an explanation, prediction, or claim about causation) that is based on that data. The right answer, in some form or fashion, reinforces the connection between the data and the theory.

By contrast, a Strengthen with a General Principle question is more like a snapshot from a philosophy class. The conclusion of the argument associated with these questions will be a normative statement: a claim that someone should or should not do something; an assessment that a proposed course of action should or should not be taken; or an evaluation that endorses or criticizes a proposal, practice, or idea. The premises will explain the factual background and context in which the conclusion applies. The right answer will be a general principle that justifies the conclusion's normative stance.

As you're reading the argument, your focus should remain on identifying the conclusion and any premises offered in support of it. In addition to using the standard indicators to help you identify the conclusion, the conclusion to a Strengthen with a General Principle question will feature some kind of normative language: *should, should not, appropriate, unethical, responsible for,* and so on.

Step 3: Know what you're looking for. The right answer to a Strengthen with a General Principle question will provide additional justification for the argument's normative stance. Before you turn to the answer choices, you should articulate to yourself what that stance is: that entails identifying both the conclusion and the reasons offered in support of it. The arguments associated with these questions typically contain a lot of background information that you'll need to sort out. Restating the argument to yourself in the form of "X because Y" will help you zero in on those portions of the argument that directly support the conclusion. Once you can do so, you're ready to move on to the answer choices.

Step 4: Read every word of every answer choice. Your approach to the answer choices will be virtually identical to the approach you use on Principle questions, discussed in Case 3. Two aspects of that approach bear special emphasis here. First, the key to success is parsing and matching. Break each answer choice down into its component parts. Typically there will be two parts to the principle: a rule to govern decisions or behavior, and a condition or context that triggers the rule. After you've broken the principle down into parts, see if you can match each part of the principle to a corresponding part of the argument. This bite-sized, back-and-forth approach builds in analytical precision. The right answer will match 100 percent; wrong answers will have one or more mismatched components.

Second, the right answers to Strengthen with a General Principle questions vary tremendously in their level of generality. Some of them are very concrete, utilizing the same terms as the argument. Others speak at a very high level of abstraction, pronouncing general ethical and decisional principles that would make a philosophy professor proud.

Practice Question

Oil-rig operator: The government should not fine me for negligently operating the rig, even though it is possible I could have prevented the drill pipe from rupturing if I had been monitoring the pressure gauge more carefully. At the time the pipe ruptured, I was operating the rig in compliance with all relevant federal regulations. If the hydraulic-release valve had been correctly installed on the rig, pressure would not have built up inside the drill pipe, and the pipe would not have ruptured.

Which one of the following principles, if valid, provides the most support for the operator's argument?

(A) When the drill pipe on an oil rig ruptures, the government should not fine the rig operator if the sole, exclusive cause of the rupture was the incorrect installation of a hydraulic-release valve.

(B) The government should fine oil-rig operators after accidents only when an operator should have anticipated the accident.

(C) The government should fine an oil-rig operator whenever the operator's failure to comply with relevant federal regulations causes a drill pipe to rupture.

(D) When the drill pipe on an oil rig ruptures, the government should not fine the rig operator if the cause of the rupture was anything other than the operator's failure to comply with a relevant federal regulation.

(E) When a drill pipe on an oil rig ruptures, the party whose negligence most proximately causes the rupture must bear all cleanup costs associated with the rupture.

Answer and Analysis. The term *should not* in the opening sentence of the argument indicates that the first clause of this sentence is the argument's conclusion. Using the "X because Y" technique, this argument contends that the government should not fine the oil-rig operator because he or she was operating the rig in compliance with all relevant federal regulations at the time the drill pipe ruptured. The rest of the argument functions as background information.

That means you're looking for an answer that (1) announces the same rule of decision (no fine after a drill-pipe rupture); (2) for the same reason (regulatory compliance). The correct answer is thus choice D.

Note the low level of generality of this answer choice: it's less a general principle and more a restatement of various parts of the argument. This isn't uncommon on Strengthen with a General Principle questions.

Choice A is a match on rule of decision, but it gets the reason wrong. According to the argument, the operator might have been able to prevent the rupture by more closely monitoring the gauge, so the faulty valve was not the sole, exclusive cause of the rupture. Choices B and C both misstate the rule of decision (each proposes a scenario when a fine is appropriate; you're looking to justify a decision not to impose a fine). Both are also a mismatch on the reason: there's nothing in the argument about reasonable anticipation, and the argument expressly belies the claim that the operator failed to comply with the relevant federal regulations. Finally, choice E is simply off topic: the argument is concerned with whether the government should fine the operator, not the broader question of who will be responsible for cleanup costs.

Case 6

Now, Why Would That Be? Resolve a Paradox

This case explains the best approach for answering Arguments questions that ask you to resolve an apparent paradox. Paradox questions have made up only 7 percent of the questions over the past few years, which is an average of three or four questions per LSAT.

Paradox arguments are made up of two statements. There will appear to be some kind of tension, inconsistency, discrepancy, or conflict between them. Each of the answer choices will introduce some new information that pertains to the topic of the two statements. The correct answer will help dissolve or explain away the apparent inconsistency between the argument's two statements.

Paradox questions are most similar to Assumption and Strengthen questions. Each asks you to identify a piece of new information that can be added to the argument so that all of the argument's parts fit together in a logically coherent way.

STEP 1:   **Read the Question and Identify Your Task**
You'll know you're facing a Paradox question when you see any of the following language:

■ Which one of the following, if true, most helps to . . .
■ resolve the apparent paradox described above?

■ contribute to an explanation of the apparent discrepancy between the results of the two studies?
■ explain the conflict between [part one of the argument] and [part two]?
■ account for the findings of the study described in the argument?

STEP 2:   **Read the Argument with Your Task in Mind**
On each of the previous question types we've discussed, your focus has been on identifying the argument's conclusion and premises. But a Paradox question has neither. It has a pair of observations (sometimes accompanied by a sentence of background information to help orient you to the conflict presented). Accordingly, as you read, your focus should be on identifying the two conflicting statements. The conflict itself usually appears near the end of the argument.

Because the nature of these questions requires the argument to introduce two divergent facts, findings, or points of view, Paradox arguments usually—although not always—include some kind of *transition indicator*, a word or phrase that signals to the reader that the passage is changing course. The two conflicting statements will appear on either side of the transition indicator. The list below offers some of the more common transition indicators:

TRANSITION INDICATORS

But	Surprisingly
However	Instead
Yet	On the other hand
While	In contrast
Nonetheless	Nevertheless
Even so	Whereas

Consider the following argument:

> Cuisine from the south of Italy is one of the most popular kinds of food in the United States. But this is not the case for northern Italian cuisine. In fact, in a recent survey, northern Italian cuisine was voted one of the least popular styles of cooking in the country.

The use of *but* as a transition indicator helps you to locate the conflicting or contradictory statements in the argument. You have two seemingly similar types of food—one of them is popular while the other is not.

STEP 3: Know What You're Looking For

The correct answer to a Paradox question will introduce a new fact, consideration, or interpretation. But it can do so in any number of ways. Therefore, do not turn to the answer choices until you can accurately state to yourself what the paradox is that needs resolution. You can do so by framing the paradox as a question that the answer choice needs to address. That question should take one of these two forms:

1. Why would statement 1 be true while statement 2 is also true?
2. Why would statement 1 be true if statement 2 is not also true?

Continuing with this example, before turning to the answer choices you could ask yourself: "Why would southern Italian cuisine be so popular while northern Italian cuisine is so unpopular?"

STEP 4: Read Every Word of Every Answer Choice

You're looking for the answer choice that provides the best answer to the question you asked yourself at step 3. The correct answer to a Paradox question will address both sides of the conflict and explain away the difference between them.

COMMON TYPES OF WRONG ANSWER CHOICES

1. **Offers a generic background statement.** This is the most common type of wrong answer on Paradox questions—all fluff and no substance. These answers read like something you might say in response to a professor's question when you haven't done the reading for class.
2. **Makes the conflict worse.** This second most common type of wrong answer exacerbates the conflict instead of helping to dispel it. On test day, when you're working under time pressure, selecting a choice that addresses both sides of the paradox without reading it carefully is an easy mistake to make.
3. **Has the same effect on both sides of the conflict.** Another common varietal of wrong answer is a choice that introduces a factor or consideration that applies to both sides of the conflict with equal force or in the same manner. A Paradox question presents two statements that are diverging where you wouldn't expect them to. The correct answer will affect the two sides of the conflict differently.
4. **Makes an irrelevant comparison.** This common type of answer choice introduces a third statement or category of information over and above the two in the argument.
5. **Draws a distinction within one side.** Answer choices like these ignores half of the question. Subdividing one half of a paradox into smaller parts and distinguishing among those parts doesn't shed light on the reasons for the discrepancy between the two halves of the conflict.

Practice Question

Let's take another look at the argument from earlier, this time with answer choices as well:

> Cuisine from the south of Italy is one of the most popular kinds of food in the United States. But this is not the case for northern Italian cuisine. In fact, in a recent survey, northern Italian cuisine was voted one of the least popular styles of cooking in the country.
>
> Which one of the following, if true, most helps to resolve the apparent paradox described above?
>
> (A) The variety, quality, and affordability of international cuisine available in the United States have skyrocketed in recent years.
> (B) Northern Italian cuisine frequently incorporates obscure ingredients that are difficult to locate, while the ingredients necessary to prepare southern Italian cuisine are easily found in most American grocery stores.

(C) Southern Italian cuisine is more time-consuming and labor-intensive to prepare than northern Italian cuisine is.

(D) Immigrants from all parts of Italy brought their local cuisines with them when they came to the United States in great numbers in the nineteenth and twentieth centuries.

(E) Southern Italian cuisine has recently become more popular in the United States than French cuisine, which for many years was this country's favorite international food.

Answer and Analysis. The correct answer is choice B. To help you determine whether you've identified the right answer, ask yourself the question you formulated in step 3, then say, "Because ..." and read the answer choice. The question and answer should make sense next to each other. Applying this technique here yields this result:

Why would southern Italian cuisine be so popular while northern Italian cuisine is so unpopular? Because northern Italian cuisine frequently incorporates obscure ingredients that are difficult to locate, while the ingredients necessary to prepare southern Italian cuisine are easily found in most American grocery stores.

We can see why southern Italian cuisine is popular (it incorporates ingredients that are easy to find), and we know why its northern counterpart is less so (the necessary ingredients are more difficult to locate). This technique will also help you confirm that the choice you've selected addresses both halves of the paradox.

Choice A is a generic background statement that is loosely connected to the topic of the argument but engages in generalization or pontification. Choice C addresses both sides of the question you formulated in step 3, but it tells you that the southern cuisine is more troublesome and yet it is more popular, making the argument even more of a paradox. In choice D, knowing that Italian immigrants from all regions of Italy brought their native cuisines with them to the United States does not provide an explanation for why two subtypes of Italian cuisine have fared so differently. It therefore has the same effect on both sides of

the conflict, and is the wrong choice. Choice E makes an irrelevant comparison. The right answer needs to reconcile the popularity of two different kinds of Italian cuisine. Learning about French cuisine doesn't aid that effort.

Discrediting a Study: A Particularly Common Type of Right Answer

We'll conclude this case by describing a trend that's emerged among Paradox questions on recent tests. The single most frequent way a correct answer resolves an apparent paradox is by discrediting a study, survey, interview, poll, or piece of research.

For example, consider the following argument:

Mayor: Last week my staff took to the streets of downtown and polled thousands of pedestrians about their views on the city's proposed bond package. More than 55 percent of the people we polled said they planned to vote in favor of having the city issue bonds. Yet the bond proposal was defeated on Election Day.

Which one of the following, if true, most helps to account for the discrepancy between the poll results and the defeat of the bond proposal?

This question asks, "Why did the bond package fail even though a majority of people polled said they supported it?" The correct answer might say something like, "Persons who live and work in the downtown area have historically been much more likely to vote in favor of bond packages than residents of other parts of the city."

Highlighting a mismatch between measurement and reality is a common ploy of correct answers to Paradox questions. The basic assumption that underlies studies, research, surveys, interviews, and polls is the idea that they can accurately describe the outside world. Paradox questions frequently feature right answers that interrupt the connection between the study and its object, giving you a reason to say, "There is no paradox here. The reason there's a discrepancy between the study and reality is that the study was flawed."

Case 7

Reading with a Skeptic's Eye: Weaken the Argument

This case introduces the strategy for working Arguments questions that ask you to pick an answer choice that weakens the conclusion of the argument.

Weaken questions typically account for about 9 percent of the questions on the Arguments section, an average of four or five per test.

Weaken questions are the fourth variety of question that asks you to find something that's missing from the argument. Whereas the question types just covered asked you to be the argument's ally, Weaken questions make you the argument's enemy. Your orientation shifts from aiding the argument to undermining it.

Weaken questions follow a predictable pattern similar to the one described in Case 5. The argument associated with a Weaken question invariably starts out with premises that present specific facts, data, information, or evidence. The conclusion then formulates a theory, explanation, prediction, or solution based on that data. The correct answer to a Weaken question will somehow show that the data do not support the conclusion.

<u>STEP 1:</u> **Read the Question and Identify Your Task**
Weaken questions require you to pick the answer choice that does the most damage to the argument's ability to support its conclusion. The question will have a structure like those that follow:

- Which one of the following, if true, . . .
- most seriously weakens [the speaker's] argument?
- most undermines the argument?
- most calls into question the claim above?
- most strongly counters [the speaker's] claim?
- most seriously calls into question the evidence offered in support of the conclusion above?

<u>STEP 2:</u> **Read the Argument with Your Task in Mind**
You will approach a Weaken question in virtually the same way as a Strengthen question. Your first priority is to identify the conclusion and the premises used to support it.

Case 1 introduced the idea that conclusions are statements of opinion, while premises are statements of fact. A version of that idea holds true on Weaken questions. The opinion expressed by the conclusion to such a question will be a theory, explanation, prediction, or solution. Accordingly, the conclusion will use words that express probability, likelihood, or normativity. Examples include *probable, improbable, likely, unlikely, should, ought to, need to, never, rarely, always, frequently, will, would,* and *cause.*

Consider the following argument:

> Political consultant: Most of the candidates in the upcoming election believe that the economy is the single most important issue to voters. However, in the latest poll conducted by my firm, a majority of voters did not select "strong record on job creation" as the quality they thought was most important in a candidate.

This is evidence that the candidates are overestimating the likelihood that most voters will base their voting decision on economic issues.

Here, a conclusion indicator ("This is evidence that. . .") introduces the last sentence. That sentence also uses the term *likelihood*, which is typical of the kinds of opinions that the conclusions of arguments associated with Weaken questions will express. The argument's first sentence provides background information, and the second sentence contains the data or evidence on which the argument's conclusion is based.

<u>STEP 3:</u> **Know What You're Looking For**
Weaken questions are all about the relationship between a specific fact or piece of data and a conclusion that, while based on that data, speaks in broader, more general terms. The answer choices will test the relationship between the data and the conclusion. There are two techniques you may be able to use to help you home in on that relationship.

First, before you turn to the answer choices, answer the following three questions:

1. What theory, explanation, prediction, or solution does the conclusion advance?
2. What evidence or data do the premises offer in support of that conclusion?
3. How do the data support the conclusion?

The correct answer to a Weaken question will cast doubt on the relationship between the premises and the conclusion. Articulating the precise nature of that relationship will make it easier to spot the correct answer.

Continuing with this example, the conclusion's theory is that candidates are overestimating the importance of economic issues to voters. The evidence offered in support of that theory is that most voters surveyed did not list job creation as an issue that was important to them. That data support the conclusion because job creation is an example of an economic issue.

Second, think back to Case 4 on Assumption questions, which discussed the importance of language gaps and being on the lookout for terms in the conclusion that do not appear anywhere in the premises. You will sometimes be able to use that language-gap concept on Weaken questions, too. Here, the conclusion substitutes in a broad new term—"economic issues"—in the place of a more specific one from the premises: "strong record on job creation."

Not every Weaken question has a language gap like this, but many do. When you see one, take note; it's likely the key to finding the correct answer. Whereas on Assumption questions you would have been looking for an answer that bridged the language gap between these two terms, on a Weaken question you should be on the lookout for an answer choice that points out this gap or somehow emphasizes its significance.

STEP 4: Read Every Word of Every Answer Choice
The right answer to a Weaken question will show that the facts, data, or evidence contained in the premises do not actually support the theory, explanation, prediction, or solution offered by the conclusion. It will do so in one of two ways:

1. **Undermine the connection between the data and the conclusion.** This is by far the most common type of right answer to a Weaken question: an answer choice that undermines the connection between the data in the premises and the theory in the conclusion. Such an answer choice typically provides new details or information that reveals a flaw or shortcoming in the data. Put differently, the answer choice will make explicit an assumption built into the data and demonstrate that the assumption is faulty.

   Example: "Nearly 45 percent of voters selected 'strong record on job creation' as the most important quality in a candidate, while no other choice was selected by even 15 percent of voters."

2. **Introduce new data that are inconsistent with the conclusion.** Another common type of right answer on Weaken questions is one that introduces new facts, data, evidence, or information that is inconsistent with the conclusion. Whereas the previous type of right answer would provide additional details about the evidence contained in the premises, this type of answer will introduce entirely new evidence, facts, and information wholly outside the scope of the premises. Where the argument is one, such as this example, that has a language gap between the premises and the conclusion, the correct answer will frequently introduce new data that highlight that gap.

   Example: "The two qualities that voters were most likely to select as most important in a candidate were 'committed to reducing the trade deficit' and 'favors tax breaks for small businesses.'"

COMMON TYPES OF WRONG ANSWER CHOICES

1. **Strengthens the argument.** You'll find this type of wrong answer on almost every Weaken question you encounter. These choices can be tempting because so many of the questions on the Arguments section ask you to select an answer choice that bolsters, or is at least consistent with, the information in the argument.

2. **Weakens a straw man.** A straw man is a misrepresentation or a mischaracterization of an argument. Many wrong answers to Weaken questions employ this argumentative tactic, undermining a conclusion that, upon close inspection, is not the conclusion advocated by the argument. Straw-man answer choices usually misrepresent the argument's conclusion by restating it in more extreme, categorical, black-and-white terms.

3. **Offers a generic background statement.** This type of wrong answer should look familiar to you by now; it also shows up on Assumption, Strengthen, and Weaken questions. The choice might provide additional information about the topic of the argument or clarify a premise. A choice like this illustrates why it's important to answer the three questions listed in step 3 before you turn to the answer choices.

4. **Invites you to make an inference.** This final category of wrong answer choice can be a vexing one. A correct answer to a Weaken question will directly undermine the soundness of the argument's conclusion without requiring you to import any outside knowledge or information. If you find yourself going beyond the information on the page to postulate ways that the choice might weaken the argument, you're likely in the process of talking yourself into an incorrect answer.

Practice Question

Take another look at the argument from earlier, this time with answer choices as well:

> Political consultant: Most of the candidates in the upcoming election believe that the economy is the single most important issue to voters. However, in the latest poll conducted by my firm, a majority of voters did not select "strong record on job creation" as the quality they thought was most important in a candidate. This is evidence that the candidates are overestimating the likelihood that most voters will base their voting decision on economic issues.

Which one of the following, if true, most undermines the argument?

(A) The voters polled by the consultant's firm were a representative sample of all voters likely to participate in the upcoming election.

(B) The polling conducted by the consultant's firm did not establish that there is no likelihood that any voter will base his or her voting decision on economic issues.

(C) The consultant's firm conducted its polling of voters using methods developed in the quantitative political-science literature.

(D) Polls whose questions are followed by a list of answers from which the poll respondents must choose have been shown to produce markedly different results from polls that allow respondents to generate their own answers to the poll questions.

(E) A recent poll by the same firm revealed that more than 50 percent of voters selected "supports overhaul of the US tax system" as the most important quality in a candidate

Answers and Analysis. The correct answer is choice E, as it undermines the connection between the data in the premises and the theory in the conclusion. Choice A strengthens the argument, which is the opposite of what the question asks you to do. A wrong answer choice like this will certainly trip up the test taker who did not read the question carefully. Choice B weakens a straw man. The consultant does not claim to have proven that there will not be a single voter who bases his or her vote on economic issues. Rather, the conclusion says the *likelihood* that a *majority* of voters will do so is low. Choice C cannot be the correct answer; it says nothing about whether voters are concerned with economic issues. Finally, it can be easy to talk yourself into a choice such as choice D by speculating about the consequences of the information it contains: "Oh yeah, that could weaken the argument. If a different kind of poll might have produced a different result, then maybe this poll wasn't accurate and if they'd used the other method it would have shown that job creation is a high priority for voters." That kind of thinking is a red flag.

Case 8

Taking a Step Back: Describe the Reasoning

This case discusses questions in the Arguments section that ask you to describe the argument's reasoning. In the recent past, Describe questions represented a little more than 9 percent of all the questions in the Arguments section, for an average of about four or five per test.

Describe questions are the first of three question types that require you to understand and analyze the method, pattern, and structure of the reasoning employed by the argument. In one sense, Describe questions are a change of pace from Strengthen, Weaken, and Paradox questions.

Describe questions pertain entirely to what's already written on the page; you won't have to look for gaps or figure out what's missing. Even so, Describe questions build heavily on the skills you've developed while working the previous cases. The ability to identify an argument's conclusion, premises, and background statements is the backbone of a sound approach to Describe questions.

This case uses the heading "Describe the Reasoning" to encompass three different kinds of Arguments questions:

1. Questions that ask you to explain the role that a particular statement plays in an argument
2. Questions that ask you to describe how the argument proceeds

3. Questions that ask you to identify the point over which two speakers disagree

The common thread between these questions is the importance of identifying the different parts of an argument and describing how they fit together.

The most common type of Describe question asks you to explain what role a particular statement plays in the argument, so this case focuses on such questions and concludes with a brief discussion of the other two types of Describe questions.

STEP 1: **Read the Question and Identify Your Task**
Below are the most common phrasings of questions that focus your attention on defining the role a particular statement plays in an argument (where you see an ellipsis, the question would reproduce verbatim the relevant portion of the argument).

■ Which one of the following most accurately describes the role played in the argument by the statement that [. . .]?
■ The observation that [. . .] plays which one of the following roles in the argument?
■ The claim that [. . .] figures in the argument in which one of the following ways?

STEP 2: Read the Argument with Your Task in Mind
The question tasks you with determining the role played by a particular statement in the argument. The first thing you should do when reading the argument is to circle the statement in the argument that you're concerned with.

Next, read the argument and identify its parts. Start out by using the techniques you learned in Case 1 of this chapter to identify the argument's conclusion, the premises, and any background information. In addition, be aware that the answer choices to these Role of the Statement questions make frequent use of a few additional classifications that you should become familiar with and be attentive to as you read the argument:

1. **An intermediate or subsidiary conclusion.** Consider this simple argument: "All men are mortal. Socrates is a man. Therefore, Socrates is mortal. No one who is mortal lives forever. Therefore, Socrates will not live forever." In this argument, the statement "Socrates is mortal" is an intermediate or subsidiary conclusion. It is a conclusion because it is supported by the first two premises of the argument. But it is subsidiary because it, in turn, supports the argument's main or ultimate conclusion that Socrates will not live forever. Identifying that a particular statement is an intermediate conclusion is the most common classification that a Role of the Statement question will ask you to make.

2. **The statement to be refuted.** "Some people contend that Socrates is immortal. This is false. Socrates is a man, and all men are mortal. Therefore, Socrates is mortal." In this example, the argument's ultimate conclusion is that Socrates is mortal. What role does the first sentence of the argument play vis-à-vis that conclusion? It is the claim the argument sets out to disprove. The statement is not the argument's conclusion; indeed, it states the opposite of the conclusion. Nor is it a premise, because it doesn't lend any support to the conclusion. Even so, it plays an important role in the argument by framing the discussion as one that criticizes a particular idea or viewpoint. Identifying a statement as one that the argument sets out to disprove is the second most common classification that Role of the Statement questions ask you to make.

3. **The difference between an analogy and evidence.** Being the basis for an analogy is a different role for a statement than being a piece of evidence. Evidence is a fact that directly supports a conclusion. An analogy is a comparison of one situation to another similar situation. For example, "Teachers should make use of visual aids in the classroom.

Doing so would help students retain the material they were being taught, just as sales presentations that use visual aids are more effective at winning customers." The statement about sales presentations is not direct evidence for the conclusion about teaching, but as an analogy it offers an indirect reason to accept the argument's conclusion.

STEP 3: Know What You're Looking For
Once you've read the argument, take a moment to attach a label to the statement that's the subject of the question. You should be able to articulate to yourself what role the statement plays before you turn to the answer choices. Be precise.

For example, if an argument has both an intermediary conclusion and an ultimate conclusion and the statement at issue is a premise, make sure you know which of the two conclusions that premise supports.

STEP 4: Read Every Word of Every Answer Choice
The right answer will correctly describe the role the statement plays in the argument. There are no telltale signs of right answers or categories of wrong answers here. You'll see the same few descriptive terms repeated across these questions: ultimate conclusion, intermediate conclusion, premise, the statement to be refuted; an example that illustrates the conclusion; evidence in support of the conclusion; an analogy that strengthens the conclusion; a response to an objection; and so on. Whether one of those labels is right or wrong depends entirely on the context of the question.

Practice Question

Athletic trainer: A severe case of plantar fasciitis is unlikely to be ameliorated by a traditional program of physical therapy, since plantar fasciitis is an inflammation of the ligaments that run along the bottom of the foot. Because traditional physical-therapy programs feature stretching and exercise, which cause blood flow to the muscles and connective tissue in the patient's feet to increase, such programs result in inflammation of the ligaments along the bottom of the foot.

Which one of the following most accurately describes the role played in the argument by the athletic trainer's statement that traditional physical-therapy programs feature stretching and exercise?

(A) It is a premise that directly supports the argument's main conclusion.

(B) It is the argument's intermediary conclusion.

(C) It expresses a viewpoint with which the argument expresses disagreement.

(D) It is a premise that supports the argument's intermediate conclusion.

(E) It is the argument's ultimate conclusion.

Answer and Analysis. This argument illustrates several of the concepts that this case introduces. Rewritten using the techniques from Case 1, the argument reads like this:

> Athletic trainer: (1) Traditional physical-therapy programs feature stretching and exercise. (2) Stretching and exercise cause blood flow to the muscles and connective tissue in the patient's feet to increase. (3) Therefore, traditional physical-therapy programs cause inflammation of the ligaments along the bottom of the foot. (4) Plantar fasciitis is an inflammation of the ligaments that run along the bottom of the foot. (5) Therefore, a severe case of plantar fasciitis is unlikely to be ameliorated by a traditional program of physical therapy.

As the rewrite illustrates, this argument has both an intermediate conclusion (sentence 3) and an ultimate conclusion (sentence 5). Since the argument asks you what role statement 1 plays, you can eliminate choices B and E. Statement 1 is a premise; it helps the argument build toward its conclusions. Since it is a simple, descriptive statement of fact that expresses no viewpoint, you can also eliminate choice C. As a premise, it directly supports the intermediate conclusion. Sentences 1 and 2 enable the argument to draw the conclusion stated in sentence 3, which then combines with sentence 4 to directly support the ultimate conclusion in sentence 5. Therefore, the correct answer to this question is choice D.

One final note: suppose the question instead had asked what role was played in the argument by the claim or notion that "a traditional program of physical therapy can ameliorate a severe case of plantar fasciitis." That statement would fall within the "foil of the argument" classification—the claim or viewpoint to be refuted.

Two More Variations

As previously noted, there are two additional varieties of Describe questions. One will ask you to identify the point of disagreement in an argument between two speakers; the other will ask you to describe how the argument proceeds.

Identify a Point of Disagreement. In the "identify a point of disagreement" question type, the argument will contain two short passages spoken by two participants in a conversation. The question will be worded as follows:

> [Speaker A]'s and [Speaker B]'s statements provide the strongest support for concluding that they disagree with each other over [. . .]:

Your basic approach to reading these arguments is the same as it is to a "Role of the Statement" question. You should read each speaker's argument and identify its conclusion and premises.

Once you've done so, you should articulate the specific point over which they disagree. Do so by formulating a statement in this form: "The first speaker thinks X, while the second speaker thinks Y."

Typically, the speakers disagree by reaching a different conclusion on a particular topic. Sometimes, however, they agree on the conclusion but disagree over the reason that conclusion is true. The answer choices to these questions will be concrete and tied to the subject matter of the argument.

For example, consider the following argument:

> Clarence: All students should take art classes, as they derive many benefits from doing so. Students find painting, drawing, and other forms of artistic expression to be relaxing, and these artistic forms foster creativity and an appreciation for aesthetics. Plus, students who study art have been shown to be less impulsive and more empathetic. Art classes promote healthy, well-rounded development.

> Ruth: My objection to students' taking art classes is that such classes reduce the total instruction time spent on math and science. These subjects help prepare students for the modern workforce. Art classes do not.

Clarence's and Ruth's statements provide the strongest support for holding that they disagree with each other over whether:

(A) art classes are the only way in which schools can promote healthy, well-rounded development

(B) students should take art classes

(C) students who take music classes are less impulsive and more empathetic

(D) art classes promote healthy, well-rounded development

(E) art classes or math and science classes do more to prepare students for the modern workforce

Answer and Analysis. The correct answer is choice B. The conclusion of Clarence's argument is the first half of its first sentence: "All students should take art classes." The rest of his argument offers six or seven premises in support of that conclusion. Ruth, on the other hand, has an "objection to students taking art classes." That's the basic point about which they disagree. Clarence thinks all students should take art classes, while Ruth thinks they should not. Choice B encapsulates this dispute.

Choice A is incorrect because it introduces an irrelevant comparison. Ruth does not object to Clarence's proposal because she thinks there are better ways to promote healthy, well-rounded development; she is focused on a different issue entirely (namely, preparing students to join the modern workforce). Choice C is incorrect because it is not tied to the subject matter of the argument; it introduces a new topic (music classes) that was not discussed by either speaker. Choice D is incorrect because Ruth does not take issue with the truth of Clarence's premises; instead, she argues that he is focusing on the wrong considerations. Choice E is wrong for a similar reason; Clarence does not attempt to defend art classes on the ground that they prepare students to join the workforce.

Describe How the Argument Proceeds. The final variety of Describe questions is a question that asks you, in very general terms, to explain how an argument proceeds. Such questions are worded like this:

- [Speaker A] responds to [Speaker B] by:
- The argument proceeds by:

Again, you should start out by identifying the argument's premises and conclusion. But you should also go one step further. Once you've labeled each part of the argument, attach a sublabel to it. Is the conclusion a prediction, an opinion, a solution, a theory, a principle, or a policy judgment? Are the premises anecdotes, observations, examples, data, or the results of a study?

As you work through the answer choices to these questions, make use of the parse-and-match method you learned in Case 3. Each choice will have several different components. Take one part of the choice and see if it corresponds to one part of the argument. If it does, repeat the process with the next part of the description; if it doesn't, move on to the next answer choice. The correct answer will accurately describe the argument's reasoning without any omissions or additions.

Let's take a look at a sample argument:

Doctor: It is highly likely that my patient is suffering from either mononucleosis or a penicillin-resistant bacterial infection. Blood work confirms that the patient is not suffering from a penicillin-resistant bacterial infection. As a result, I am virtually certain that my patient has contracted mononucleosis.

The argument proceeds by:

(A) evaluating the correctness of a particular diagnosis in light of an ongoing epidemiological trend
(B) refuting a claim that a particular diagnosis is correct by offering evidence that an alternative diagnosis is likely correct
(C) hypothesizing that a particular diagnosis must be correct based on the particular set of symptoms presented
(D) concluding that a particular diagnosis is very likely correct by ruling out the only probable alternative
(E) inferring, from a claim that one of two possible diagnoses must be correct, that the other diagnosis is incorrect

Answer and Analysis. The correct answer is choice D. The doctor's conclusion appears in the last sentence of the argument: she is virtually certain that the patient has contracted mononucleosis. She draws this conclusion based on two premises: (1) it is highly like that her patient has either mono or a bacterial infection, and (2) blood work has ruled out the possibility of a bacterial infection. Thus, the premises present two possible diagnoses and then rule out one of them. The conclusion endorses the correctness of the other diagnosis. Each part of choice D corresponds to one portion of the argument.

The parse-and-match method eliminates each of the remaining answer choices. Choice A is incorrect because the argument does not discuss an ongoing epidemiological trend. Choice B is incorrect because the argument does not refute a claim. The doctor is advancing her own theory about the patient's diagnosis, not rebutting a theory offered by someone else. Choice C is incorrect because the doctor does not discuss the particular symptoms that led her to her diagnosis. And choice E gets the argument's structure backwards: from the premise that one of two possible diagnoses must be *incorrect*, the argument concludes that the other diagnosis must be *correct*.

Case 9

Finding a Flaw: Criticize the Reasoning

This case addresses Arguments questions that ask you to criticize or find a flaw in the reasoning of an argument. Flaw questions have been the second most common question type on recent LSATs, accounting for about 16 percent of the test (an average of eight questions).

Flaw questions are like Describe questions with an editorial bent. The arguments associated with Flaw questions typically commit one of a handful of common errors of reasoning. Once again you'll start out by breaking the argument down into parts and understanding what role each part plays. You'll then go one step further and find the "flaw" in the argument. This case will introduce you to those errors of reasoning and teach you how to identify them.

STEP 1: Read the Question and Identify Your Task
Flaw questions ask you to select an answer choice that identifies a flaw or error in the argument's reasoning. These questions use some variation of the following wording:

- The argument above is most vulnerable to criticism on the grounds that it:
- The argument above is flawed in that it:
- The argument's reasoning is questionable in that it fails to consider the possibility that (or, "in that it takes for granted that"):
- Which one of the following most accurately describes a reasoning flaw in the argument above?
- Which one of the following most accurately describes the error in [the speaker]'s reasoning?

STEP 2: Read the Argument with Your Task in Mind
You should take the same approach to reading the argument associated with a Flaw question that you take on Describe questions. Start out by breaking the argument down into background information, premises, and conclusions. Pay attention to the relationship between the premises and the conclusion. Does the argument offer a theory to explain some data? A prediction based on a survey or a poll? An opinion based on experience?

Many Flaw questions use arguments that attempt to undermine or discredit an opposing viewpoint. These arguments go something like, "Some people say X. But they're wrong for Y reason." In the previous case, you learned how to identify when part of an argument is playing the role of the statement to be refuted. If you see such a statement on a Flaw

question, pay close to attention to how the argument attempts to discredit it.

STEP 3: Know What You're Looking For
Since this is a Flaw question, you know the argument somehow fails to establish its conclusion. There is an almost infinite number of ways that an argument can commit an error of reasoning, but on the LSAT, a small handful of errors show up over and over. Below is a brief summary of the nine most common errors of reasoning committed in the arguments associated with Flaw questions:

Necessary Versus Sufficient Conditions. Sometimes a particular outcome depends in some way on a condition. A condition can be either necessary or sufficient. A necessary condition is a deal-breaker. The absence of a necessary condition forecloses the outcome from being obtained. For example, being a fruit is a necessary condition of being an apple. A sufficient condition is a deal-maker. Satisfying a necessary condition isn't always enough to guarantee that an outcome will be obtained, and sometimes an outcome can be obtained even if a sufficient condition is not satisfied. For example, being an apple is a sufficient condition for being a fruit.

Confusing Parts and Wholes. When a whole is composed of multiple parts, it frequently takes on qualities that are not shared by any of its parts standing alone. For example, if a paragraph is very long, it does not follow that each of the sentences in that paragraph is also very long. The paragraph could be composed of numerous short sentences. Conversely, each individual component of a bicycle might be able to fit in the trunk of your car, but it does not follow that the bicycle itself will also fit in the trunk.

Inadequate or Unrepresentative Sample. Flaw questions often use arguments that base generalizations, predictions, or theories on a limited set of data or experiences. Those conclusions often sweep much more broadly than the data will support. For instance:

> Tourist: I've seen three people walking down the street today drinking Red Bull. Red Bull must be very popular in New York.

The fact that three people have been seen drinking a particular beverage is not an adequate basis on which to conclude that the beverage is very popular in a city with millions of residents.

Confusing Correlation with Causation. Causation is a frequently recurring topic in Flaw questions. Do not confuse correlation with causation. Correlation is a simple observation that two things or events appear together, often frequently. Causation, however, is the claim that those two things or events are associated because one causes the other. Consider this argument:

> Paleontologist: My research into the fossil record reveals a high concentration of volcanic ash in the atmosphere during periods with high rates of species extinction. Therefore, volcanoes cause mass extinction.

The mere fact of correlation (the fossil record and volcanic ash), without any additional facts or evidence, is not enough to support an inference of causation.

Ignoring a Third Cause or Reversing Causality. This is another error of reasoning related to causation. Many Flaw questions will observe that A and B are correlated and conclude that A causes B, without considering the possibility that C—some third, unnamed factor—is the cause of both A and B. For instance:

> Market analyst: The Nikkei Index dropped by more than 7 percent today, while the Hong Kong Stock Exchange was down nearly 5 percent. Clearly the market in Hong Kong was responding to the slow trading in Tokyo.

This argument overlooks the possibility that the drop in both markets was caused by some third factor—such as a dip on the New York Stock Exchange, increased oil prices, a natural disaster, the release of poor earnings reports, or any number of other reasons. Similarly, an argument might erroneously assume that A causes B when in actuality B causes A ("Whenever it rains, people carry umbrellas. Therefore, carrying an umbrella makes it more likely to rain").

Shifts in Meaning and Ambiguous Language. Another common error is using the same term twice in the course of an argument, but assigning it a different meaning each time. For instance:

> Boy: I deposited my money in a bank. There are two banks along every river. Therefore, I probably deposited my money somewhere along a river.

This is a silly and obvious example. It's far more common for a shift in meaning to be more subtle.

Ad Hominem Attack. *Ad hominem* is Latin for "to the man." An ad hominem attack is an attempt to discredit an argument by making personal attacks against the person advancing the argument instead of making logical attacks against the content of the argument. On the LSAT, these unreliable arguments often look something like this:

> Researcher: My colleague suggests that the results of my study are not reliable because I used a faulty research method. But she herself used the same method in her last study.

This kind of argument inappropriately criticizes the speaker instead of what is spoken.

Straw Man. A straw-man argument is one that attempts to respond to or discredit an opposing position by misrepresenting the content of that position. (This kind of argument is called a "straw man" because the position it attacks is not the real point at issue, just as a scarecrow made of straw is not a real person.) For example:

> It is foolish to suggest that handgun ownership should be banned. How could people feel safe in their homes without any firearms to defend themselves against intruders?

Suggesting that a total ban on all forms of firearms (handguns, shotguns, rifles, etc.) would make people feel unsafe is not responsive to the more limited proposal to ban handguns.

Appeal to Popularity. On the LSAT, an argument stands or falls on the soundness of the logical relationship between its premises and its conclusion. The wisdom of the crowd has no place in the Arguments section. Flaw questions often present arguments in which the fact that many people agree with or advocate a proposition is presented as evidence of the proposition's truth. For example,

> Patient: Dr. Hernandez is an excellent doctor. She has the longest waiting list of any doctor in the city.

Popularity is not evidence of reliability or accuracy.

<u>STEP 4:</u> **Read Every Word of Every Answer Choice**
The right answer will correctly describe the error in reasoning committed by the argument. It might do so using very general language, such as, "The analyst erroneously infers that something is true of a whole based on the fact that something is true of each of the parts." Or the answer might be phrased in concrete terms that are tied to the subject matter of the argument: "The choreographer errs by inferring that the dance is easy based on the fact that each step is simple to execute in isolation."

COMMON TYPES OF WRONG ANSWER CHOICES

1. **Inapplicable flaws.** You can expect to see more than one of the common fallacies and errors of reasoning listed above as answer choices for each Arguments question. Only one flaw can be the right answer. When you're picking between flaws, you should be able to pinpoint where the flaw occurs using the work you did in steps 2 and 3.

2. **Circular reasoning.** An argument engages in circular reasoning when it assumes the truth of the point that it sets out to prove. For example: "Jane and Lila played a game of tennis. Jane lost. Therefore, Lila won." This argument is circular. By stating "Jane lost" as a premise, the argument takes it for granted that Lila won. The odds of your seeing a Flaw question in which the argument displays circular reasoning are less than 5 percent. But "the argument engages in circular reasoning," "the argument assumes the truth of what it sets out to prove," and "the argument begs the question" are some of the most common wrong answer choices on Flaw questions. When you see circular reasoning as one of the answer choices, you should indulge a superstrong presumption against picking that choice.

3. **A feature of the argument that is not a flaw.** For example, an answer choice might accuse an argument of "rejecting a view merely on the ground that an inadequate argument has been made in support of it." That might be an accurate description of the argument, but that's not a flaw! Rejecting a view because it has been inadequately supported is the essence of logical reasoning. This type of answer choice can be very tempting because it is an accurate description of the argument. Don't select a choice unless you agree that the pattern of reasoning it describes is questionable, unreliable, or faulty.

Practice Question

Pet-store owner: When you purchase a coral trout, you can be assured that you are purchasing one of the most beautiful fish in the world. The wide array of fish, sea snakes, turtles, and mollusks that inhabit the waters around the Great Barrier Reef make up the world's most beautiful collection of marine fauna. And the coral trout's natural habitat is the waters around the Greater Barrier Reef.

The pet-store owner's argument is most vulnerable to criticism on the grounds that it:

(A) takes a mere correlation to be evidence of a causal relationship
(B) bases a generalization on a sample that is unlikely to be representative
(C) uses the term *beautiful* in two different senses
(D) provides an inadequate definition of the term *habitat*
(E) takes for granted a characteristic of a group is shared by all members of that group

Answer and Analysis. The correct answer to this question is choice E. The conclusion of this argument is its first sentence: the coral trout is one of the most beautiful fish in the world. But the only evidence for that conclusion is that the coral trout can be found in the Great Barrier Reef. The beauty of the Great Barrier Reef's sea life, as a group, does not guarantee that every species that lives near the reef is also, individually, beautiful.

Choice A is incorrect because the argument does not assert the existence of any causal relationship. Choice B is incorrect because the argument does not rest on a sample (i.e., the problem with the argument is not that most coral trout are dissimilar to the coral trout discussed by the pet-store owner). Choice C is incorrect because there is no indication in the argument that the term *beautiful* has shifted in meaning. And choice D is incorrect because the argument does not turn on the precise meaning of the term *habitat*; the focus of the argument is the beauty of the fish.

Case 10

Mapping for Similarity: Parallel the Reasoning

It can be hard to generalize about the level of difficulty of most of the question types you'll encounter in the Arguments section. The exception to that rule is a question that asks you to identify the answer choice that most closely parallels the argument's reasoning. None of these questions is easy. Many of them are among the hardest questions you'll encounter in the Arguments section. All of them are inordinately time-consuming. Fortunately, over the past few years they've made up a little less than 8 percent of the questions in the Arguments sections.

STEP 1:   Read the Question and Identify Your Task

You know you're dealing with a Parallel question when you see any of the following:

- The reasoning in which one of the following is most similar to the reasoning in the argument above?
- Which one of the following arguments is most similar in its reasoning to the argument above?
- The pattern of reasoning in which one of the following is most similar to that in the argument above?

A Parallel question might also be worded like this:

- The flawed pattern of reasoning in which one of the following is most closely parallel to that in the argument above?
- Which one of the following arguments exhibits a pattern of flawed reasoning most similar to that in the argument above?
- The questionable reasoning in the argument above is most similar in its reasoning to which one of the following?

These latter questions tell you that the argument is flawed, questionable, or unsound; the former questions imply that the argument is valid. That distinction doesn't make a difference to how you should approach these questions, but it can sometimes help you ensure you're on track to finding the right answer.

STEP 2:   Read the Argument with Your Task in Mind

When you read the argument associated with a Parallel question, your focus should be not on its substantive content but rather on the structure of the reasoning it employs. Most arguments are nothing more than a series of conditional statements. You should use symbolizations to map out the reasoning employed by such arguments.

Parallel questions do not require you to substantively manipulate conditional statements or make deductions based on them. Instead, they require you to keep track of the ways in which the argument and the five answer choices use conditional statements. Rare indeed is the Parallel question whose argument employs nothing but standard-form "If A, then B" conditional statements.

STATEMENT	SYMBOLIZATION	CONTRAPOSITIVE
If A, then B or C	A → B / C	~B & ~C → ~A
If A and B, then not C	A & B → ~C	C → ~A / ~B
B only if A	B → A	~A → ~B
A unless B	A → ~B	B → ~A
Not A unless B	A → B	~B → ~A
All A are B	A → B	~B → ~A
No A are B	A → ~B	B → ~A
B if, but only if, A	A → B *and* B → A	~A → ~B *and* ~B → ~A

Even beyond these complicated but familiar translations, Parallel questions will test your ability to recognize when a natural-language statement can be translated into a conditional symbolization. For example, a sentence that begins "every" or "any" is usually an "All A are B" conditional statement.

STEP 3:   Know What You're Looking For

The correct answer to a Parallel question will utilize a pattern, structure, method, or strategy of reasoning that is identical to the one employed by the argument. So before you turn to the answer choices, you should use your symbolization tools to map out the pattern of reasoning the argument employs.

For example, consider the following argument and question:

> Strategist: Politicians who are not firmly committed to a core set of beliefs will formulate new campaign strategies and talking points before each upcoming election. Politicians are elected to serve multiple terms in office only if they formulate new campaign strategies and talking points before each upcoming election. Therefore, politicians who are not firmly committed to a core set of beliefs are elected to serve multiple terms in office.
>
> Which one of the following displays a flawed pattern of reasoning most closely parallel to that in the strategist's argument?

It may not be obvious at first, but every statement in that argument is—or at least can be made into—a conditional statement. Before you turned to the answer choices on this question, you would need to symbolize the entire argument in conditional-statement form. You can do so at the bottom of the test-booklet page.

Instead of using single capital letters to symbolize these sentences, symbolize them in a way that reminds you of what they actually say. You might choose shorthand (as we did in Case 2), so that:

"firmly committed to a core set of beliefs" thus might become "firmly committed"

"formulate new campaign strategies and talking points before each upcoming election" becomes "formulate new"

"elected to serve multiple terms in office" becomes "multiple terms"

Alternatively, you might choose to use a longer symbolization:

"firmly committed to a core set of beliefs" becomes "FCCSB"

"formulate new campaign strategies and talking points before each upcoming election" as "FNCS&TP"

"elected to serve multiple terms in office" become "ESMTO"

Anything that makes sense to you is fine; we'll use shorthand here. Recast as conditional symbolizations, this argument looks like this:

not firmly committed → formulate new

multiple terms → formulate new

Therefore, not firmly committed → multiple terms

Remember the rule from the Logic Games chapter and this chapter's discussion of Deduction questions that the only way to a make a valid deduction using conditional statements is to follow the arrow. This symbolization illustrates why the question tells you that this argument "displays a flawed pattern of reasoning." It makes an invalid deduction by going against the arrow in its combination of the two conditional-statement premises.

That's how the difference between a question that asks you to parallel the reasoning and a question that asks you to parallel the flawed reasoning can help you double-check that you're on track to find the right answer. On a Parallel the Flaw question, your symbolization should show that the argument's conclusion is a deduction that goes against the arrow. On a regular Parallel question, the conclusion should be a valid, arrow-following deduction.

STEP 4: Read Every Word of Every Answer Choice

You can already begin to see why Parallel questions are so time-consuming; translating each sentence in the argument into a conditional statement and then symbolizing each conditional statement is no easy task. But that's not even the half of it. To identify the correct answer on a Parallel question, you have to repeat that process for each answer choice until you find a choice

that employs the same pattern of reasoning as the argument. The only silver lining within this great cloud is that it's the one argument type with one answer that is objectively correct. Once you find an answer whose structure matches the argument, pick it and move on. There's no need to diagram the remaining choices.

Practice Question

Take another look at the argument from earlier, this time with answer choices as well:

Strategist: Politicians who are not firmly committed to a core set of beliefs will formulate new campaign strategies and talking points before each upcoming election. Politicians are elected to serve multiple terms in office only if they formulate new campaign strategies and talking points before each upcoming election. Therefore, politicians who are not firmly committed to a core set of beliefs are elected to serve multiple terms in office.

Which one of the following displays a flawed pattern of reasoning most closely parallel to that in the strategist's argument?

(A) Music that is pleasing to the ear is melodic. Music that is melodic involves chords and harmony. Thus, music is pleasing to the ear only if it involves chords and harmony.

(B) A loyal person is a likeable person, for a loyal person always stands by her friends and a likeable person also always stands by her friends.

(C) A well-constructed house includes code-compliant framing, wiring, and insulation. A house is marketable only if it is well constructed. Therefore, a marketable house includes code-compliant framing, wiring, and insulation.

(D) Nuclear proliferation will accelerate only if there is widespread access to fissile material. Widespread access to fissile material goes hand in glove with increased regional instability. Therefore, nuclear proliferation will not accelerate unless there is an increase in regional instability.

(E) If health-care costs continue to rise, foreign currency markets will devalue the dollar. But health-care costs will not continue to rise. Therefore, foreign currency markets will not devalue the dollar.

Answer and Analysis. Symbolically, these choices look like this:

(A) pleasing → melodic
melodic → chords and harmony
therefore, pleasing → chords and harmony

(B) loyal → stand by friends
likeable → stand by friends
therefore, loyal → likeable

(C) well constructed → code-compliant
marketable → well constructed
therefore, marketable → code-compliant

(D) nuclear prolif → fissile-material access
fissile-material access → regional instability
therefore, nuclear prolif → regional instability

(E) continued rising costs → devalued dollar
no continued rising costs
therefore, no devalued dollar

As these symbolizations illustrate, the correct answer to this question is choice B. One trick the test writers will use to make it more difficult to identify the correct answer is to switch the order in which the statements appear. You see this in choice B, where the conclusion is listed before the two premises, while the argument lists the premises before the conclusion. The order in which statements appear has no bearing on the logical relationship between them, but changing that order can make the passages appear superficially dissimilar.

Most of the previous cases discussed the common types of wrong answer choices that are associated with a particular question type. With two exceptions, it's not possible to undertake such a generalized discussion about Parallel questions because whether an answer is right or wrong depends entirely on the structure of the argument. In short, Parallel questions, like Principle questions, require you to play a matching game. All you can do is symbolize each choice one by one until you find one that matches.

As for those two exceptions, here are two generally applicable pieces of advice about wrong answer choices on Parallel questions. First, on questions that ask you to find a parallel pattern of flawed reasoning, one or more of the answer choices will present you with a valid, nonflawed argument. You see that here with choices A, C, and D. Second, it's also common for two or more answer choices to employ an identical pattern of reasoning. Again, choices A, C, and D illustrate this. You don't even have to read the argument to know that such choices cannot be correct; if one were right, necessarily the other(s) would be too.

Case 11

Section-Wide Strategy

You're now familiar with all 10 types of questions you'll encounter on the Arguments section and the frequency with which you'll encounter them. The table below summarizes that information:

	QUESTION TYPE	PERCENTAGE	AVERAGE PER TEST
1	Assumption	16%	8
2	Flaw	16%	8
3	Deduction	12%	6
4	Strengthen	10%	5
5	Weaken	9%	4–5
6	Describe	9%	4–5
7	Parallel	8%	4
8	Paradox	7%	3–4
9	Principle	7%	3
10	Conclusion	6%	3
	Total	**100%**	**48–51**

This case discusses the strategy you should use to approach the Arguments section as a whole. Section-wide strategy for the Arguments section is less complicated than it is for the Logic Games and Reading Comprehension sections. An effective approach to the Arguments section is one that abides by the following five guidelines.

Accuracy Trumps Speed . . .

This principle is a constant across all three sections of the test. Rushing your way through the Arguments section in a desperate bid to work every single question is a bad strategy. Your goal is not to answer as many questions as possible. Your goal is to *correctly* answer as many questions as possible. Again, as discussed in the Logic Games chapter, if you answer 75 percent of the questions (that's 19 or 20 of the 25 or 26 questions in an Arguments section) at a 90 percent rate of accuracy and then bubble in blind guesses for the remaining 5 questions, you'll be on track for an excellent score.

. . . But Speed Is Not Unimportant

If your aim is to work 20 Arguments questions in 35 minutes, you have about 1 minute, 45 seconds per question. That's not a ton of time to read the question, read the argument, work through all five answer choices, and bubble in your selected answer. Accuracy requires you to be careful, precise, and thorough in your approach to the questions. But you also must be efficient and decisive. Time is always a factor.

With Two Exceptions, Decide Which Questions to Skip on a Case-by-Case Basis

Conclusion questions tend to be among the easiest, most straightforward questions in the Arguments section. You should plan to work every one that you see. Skip all Parallel questions until you've already worked every other question in the section. Should you have time left over, come back and try your hand at a Parallel question. Those two exceptions aside, it's not possible to speak in general terms about the difficulty of each question type. There is tremendous variation within each category.

What's more, you can't reliably predict how many of each question type will appear in a given Arguments section. The table at the beginning of this case summarizes the average number of questions of each type that appear on the LSAT as a whole. But there is variation from test to test and from section to section. One recent test had a total of two Strengthen questions (the fourth most common question type); another had seven Principle questions (the second least common question type). You need to be comfortable working all non-Parallel question types.

So how do you decide which questions to skip? Skip a question if, after the first time you read the argument, you do not understand what you've read. If you're having a hard time making sense of the content of the argument, your chances of correctly answering the question are very low. Don't let stubbornness get the best of you here. You don't have time to read the argument two or three times and then decide that you're going to skip the question; you need to save that time for questions you'll actually answer. By all means, put a star in the margin, circle the question number, or make some other note to yourself that you've skipped the question. That way, once you've worked through all the easier questions, you can come back and give it a second look. But if the first read leaves you scratching your head, move on.

Always Work the Very Last Question in the Section

This is the exception to the general rule that the questions get harder as the section goes on. The last question in the section is almost always an easy or medium-difficulty question. It's usually preceded by three or four of the very hardest questions in the section, so if you get bogged down on those, it's easy to run out of time. Develop a rule for yourself about when you'll always work the last question in the section. It could be after you've worked sequentially up to a particular question number; it could be when you see there are only 10 minutes left in the section. Whatever your rule, stick to it, and make sure you take advantage of this opportunity to pick up an easy point.

LSAT Reading Comprehension

- The importance of retrieval, not recall, in the Reading Comprehension section

- How to apply annotative-reading techniques to the passages

- The six different types of questions you will encounter and techniques for working each one

- How to approach the comparative reading passage

- How to approach the Reading Comprehension section as a whole

A s noted in Chapter 1, each Reading Comprehension section contains four passages (one of which, the comparative reading passage, is actually a pair of two shorter passages). There will be one passage from each of the following general content areas: law, science, the arts, and social science/humanities. Examples of specific topics that you might encounter include:

- **Law:** international law, intellectual property, legal theory, legal history, courtroom practice
- **Science:** geology, botany, computer science, evolutionary biology, ecology, engineering, mathematics, animal behavior

- **The arts:** literature, painting, dance, theater, sculpture, music, film, poetry
- **Social science/humanities:** economics, anthropology, history, urban planning, linguistics, archaeology, philosophy, psychology

The Reading Comprehension section is an open-book test; the correct answer to every question must be directly supported by the text of the passage. This chapter lays out a strategy that is designed to take advantage of that fact. That strategy requires you to take a particular approach both to reading the passage and to answering the questions. The first two cases in this chapter concentrate on reading. They introduce annotative reading, a technique that has been designed especially for the Reading Comprehension section of the LSAT. You'll learn how to annotate the passage as you read it in a way that positions you to answer the questions quickly and with a high rate of accuracy.

Cases 3 through 8 introduce the six major types of questions you'll encounter, while Case 9 discusses question types that are unique to the Comparative Reading passage.

You'll use a three-step method in the Reading Comprehension section:

1. Read the question and identify your task.
2. Go back to the passage to find the answer.
3. Read every word of every answer choice.

The cases will demonstrate how this method should be applied to each major question type. As in the previous two chapters, the last case discusses section-wide strategy.

Three final notes before turning to the first case. First, you'll be learning a particular, specialized way of reading that you probably haven't employed before.

You may start off reading slowly. That's OK. With practice, you'll get faster at employing the annotative-reading techniques, and eventually you'll be able to work at a pace that is compatible with the Reading Comprehension section's 35-minute time constraint. In the early stages of your study, take the time to apply the techniques correctly, even if it takes you a long time to do so. Practice only helps if you're building good habits.

Second, as you work the practice Reading Comprehension passages and sections in this book, keep a log of the questions you miss and relevant details about each question. We all have different strengths and weaknesses as readers. You won't be able to identify the areas in which you need improvement unless you've been tracking your performance. A sample performance log might look like this:

PASSAGE	TOPIC	Q NO.	Q TYPE	REASON FOR ERROR

After you've worked through a few passages, look for trends among the questions you're missing. This will help you focus your studying efforts. It may also be helpful to you as you're developing your strategy for tackling the section as a whole; Case 10 will explore this possibility in greater detail.

Finally, much of the Reading Comprehension section's difficulty stems from the fact that you're probably unaccustomed to reading texts with the particular combination of length, density, and subject matter that you encounter on the LSAT. The more comfortable you can become reading this kind of material, the better you'll fare on test day. Working practice questions is not the only way you can increase your comfort level. The articles in the weekly newsmagazine *The Economist* tend to be somewhat similar to the passages on the LSAT in their length, tone, purpose, and content. Reading a few such articles each day is a good way to improve your reading skills.

Case 1

Retrieval, Not Recall: How to Read on the LSAT

This case introduces the annotative-reading method you will use to read the passages in the Reading Comprehension section. This case focuses on the "why" and "what" of annotative reading (the rationale for using this technique and the tasks it will help you accomplish), while Case 2 explains the "how" (the tools and techniques you will use to implement it).

You will read each passage with two aims in mind: (1) attaining an understanding of the passage's main idea; and (2) mapping the location of the various details, evidence, and examples so that you can quickly locate and review them as you're working the questions.

The Reading Comprehension Section as an Open-Book Test

If one of your professors gave you an open-book exam, would you bring your book and class notes into the exam room only to leave them facedown on your desk as you attempted to answer all the questions from memory? Of course not. You would double-check your answers to the exam's questions against the information in the textbook and your notes.

The Reading Comprehension section gives you the same opportunity to verify the correctness of your responses. It is effectively an open-book test. And every right answer must be objectively, demonstrably correct based solely on the information in the text. Outside information, subjective judgments, and debatable inferences can play no role in determining the correctness of an answer. Imagine a person who takes the LSAT and, upon receiving a disappointing score, decides to sue the LSAC (with a test that's administered to would-be future lawyers, the possibility is not as far-fetched as it sounds). "I'm absolutely certain," the test taker argues, "that the answers I selected to the Reading Comprehension questions were right and that the answers you identified as correct were wrong." If the judge were to ask one of the test writers, "Why is B the correct answer to question 5?" the test writer would have to be able to point to a specific portion of the passage and say, "This is the portion of the passage that makes B the correct answer." There can't be room for debate; it can't be a matter of interpretation.

This is the mind-set with which the LSAC writes Reading Comprehension questions. As a test taker, your job is to exploit that mind-set. Getting a good score on the Reading Comprehension section doesn't require you to undertake a sophisticated analysis of the passage. You don't have to come up with insightful, original things to say about it. You don't have to contemplate its broader significance or implications. All the right answers are right there on the page, in the passage.

How to Read the Passage with an Eye Toward Answering the Questions

Typically when you read, it's either for pleasure or to learn—that is, to be able to retain and recall the information in the text. Obviously you're not reading for pleasure on the LSAT. Nor are you reading for long-term recall; odds are you'll happily forget everything about the passages roughly 30 seconds after you finish the section. What may be less obvious is that you're also not reading for short-term recall either.

That's the key point: you're not reading for *recall* at all. You're reading the passages on the Reading Comprehension section for one purpose: to correctly answer as many questions as possible in 35 minutes. And the best way to correctly answer as many questions as possible is to not rely on recall, but to go back to the passage and find the answer to every question you work.

And yet the most common mistake that test takers make on this section is trying to answer the questions from memory instead of going back to the passage to retrieve the answer. Not only is it a common mistake, but it's also the mistake the test is most designed to exploit. The test writers know you're working under time pressure and will be tempted to rely on your recall. The wrong answers are carefully worded to look like right answers to test takers who are working from memory.

**The answers are in the passage.
You just have to find them.**

After you read each question, don't try to remember the answer. Go find it. All of the techniques in the later cases are derived from this single idea. By far the single most important element of an effective Reading Comprehension strategy is being able to quickly find the answer to each question. And in order to do that, you need to develop a new style of reading, an LSAT-specific reading style.

You will read each passage from start to finish just once before working any questions, annotating the passage using "upfront reading" techniques. Your annotations will allow you to quickly find the answers to the questions when you go back to the passage for your question-specific reading.

Upfront Reading

If the Reading Comprehension section were untimed, it wouldn't especially matter how you read the passage. You could pore over every word, taking as long as you needed to understand its content, purpose, and structure. In reality, you only have 35 minutes to work all four passages. This time constraint requires you to be productive, but also efficient.

Your upfront reading of the passage will be narrowly focused on accomplishing two tasks: articulating the main point of the passage as a whole and mapping the location of details, evidence, and examples.

Articulating the Main Point of the Passage as a Whole. The upfront reading is the only time you'll read the passage straight through, from start to finish. It is your chance to step back and see the whole forest. With each question, you'll study a particular tree. Almost all Reading Comprehension passages have at least one question that asks you to identify the passage's main point, and having a clear handle on the main point is a helpful tool in answering many small-picture questions, too.

You should use your upfront reading to identify the passage's main point and map the location of the various details.

Mapping the Location of Details, Evidence, and Examples. During your upfront reading your goal is *not* to carefully study and absorb all of the facts, examples, evidence, and other details that the passage discusses. Instead, you should use a system of annotations to simply map their locations, which will streamline your question-specific reading. Once marked for easy reference, you'll be able to return to them quickly.

If you pore over the details during your upfront reading, you will inevitably have to rush or even abandon some of your question-specific readings and instead rely on your recall. Doing that plays right into the traps that the test writers have laid for you.

Plus, closely studying all the details upfront will surely cause you to waste valuable time. Suppose a passage supported its main point by offering four examples. If none of the questions asked you about example number two, any time you spent memorizing it would be for naught. Why read a portion of the passage closely if doing so won't help you get a better score? The guideline is this: know exactly *where* the details are, not exactly *what* they say. You'll spend your time wisely by letting the questions guide you.

Case 2 will introduce you to the customized annotation system to mark up the passage as you read it—the nuts and bolts of annotative reading.

Case 2

The Mechanics of Annotative Reading

During annotative reading, you'll mark up the passage and make notes about its key points as you read. The primary benefit of annotative reading is that it enhances your focus and concentration. The passages on the Reading Comprehension section aren't exactly page-turners. Annotating them as you read forces you to pay attention and remain an active, engaged reader. If you're reading passively, it's all too easy to come to the end of a paragraph only to realize that you spaced out and didn't absorb anything you read. Time is of the essence; you can't afford to read the same paragraph two or three times. Annotative reading gives you a series of tasks to perform, and you can't perform them if you're not paying attention.

The system of annotative reading described in this case is tailor-made for the Reading Comprehension section. While there is room for some flexibility in how it is implemented, two aspects of it are indispensible. Whatever system of annotation you ultimately adopt must incorporate both of these aspects.

First, you are looking for three specific kinds of information in the passage:

1. The main point of each paragraph
2. Words that indicate connections between the paragraphs and the big ideas of the passage
3. Key components of factual details

Those first two bits of information will help you zero in on the passage's main point as a whole. Annotating the factual details will pay dividends when it comes time to answer the questions. Mark up the passage for this information and nothing else.

Second, you must use the same system of symbols, marks, or notations for everything. Otherwise, it's too easy to zone out and start mindlessly underlining or circling. Plus, having different annotations for different types of information will make it easier for you to locate each type quickly as you're working the questions.

This case recommends that you put brackets around each paragraph's main point, draw circles around words that indicate connections between the paragraphs, and underline the key snippets of factual detail. It also recommends making notes in the margins using the same letters or symbols. If you have a different system that works for you, feel free to use it, but do so consistently.

Understanding the Main Idea

Arriving at an understanding of the passage's main point is a three-step process. First, as you read you'll identify the main point of each paragraph. Second, you'll identify the logical relationships between the main points of each paragraph. Third, when you're done reading, you'll summarize the passage by stringing together the main points of each paragraph. Summarizing the passage will help you home in on its main point.

Identify the Main Point of Each Paragraph. To identify the main point of each paragraph, you'll draw on the skills you learned in Case 1 of Chapter 4, the discussion of Conclusion questions in the Arguments section. Each Argument contains background information, premises, and conclusions. The same is true of the Reading Comprehension passages; they're basically just longer versions of that. This is also true of each paragraph within the passage. Zeroing in on each paragraph's core idea is the first step toward identifying the main point of the passage as a whole.

To identify the main point of a paragraph, use the same two techniques you learned in Chapter 4 for identifying the conclusion of an argument. First, keep an eye out for conclusion indicators, words whose function it is to introduce a conclusion. If you see one of the words listed below, circle it.

CONCLUSION INDICATORS	
Therefore	Hence
Thus	Consequently
As a result	Clearly
Accordingly	In view of these facts
It follows that	

Second, the main point of the paragraph will typically use normative language (language that says something is "good" or "bad") to express an opinion, evaluation, solution, proposal, explanation, assessment, or prediction. However, this is not always the case. Sometimes the purpose of an individual paragraph is to simply provide factual context, offer background information, or summarize a recent development. The main point of such a paragraph will simply be the fact that all of the other details fit under.

Once you've identified the main point of the paragraph, put brackets around the sentence, and make a note next to it in the margin. You can note "MP" for "main point," "T" for "thesis," or simply use an asterisk (*) to indicate importance. If you determine that the main point isn't contained in any one sentence, you can either bracket the two sentences that it's drawn from or jot a very brief summary of it in the margin. If you take this later tack, keep it short (three to five words); making extensive notes consumes a lot of time. You'll repeat this process for every paragraph in the passage.

Circle the Connections Between Ideas. You'll also look for words that indicate the connections between the ideas contained in each paragraph. For example, authors use certain words to indicate that what they are about to say will stand in contrast to what they just said. The following list offers some of the most common contrast indicators.

CONTRAST INDICATORS

But	On the other hand
However	In contrast
Yet	In spite of
While	Despite
Nonetheless	Whereas
Nevertheless	Although
Even so	Be that as it may
Surprisingly	

If you see these words or words like them, circle them. They indicate that the passage's reasoning is changing direction.

Conversely, certain words indicate that an upcoming thought is consistent with and builds on the thought that preceded it. Circle these as well.

CONTINUITY INDICATORS

And	For example
Also	Since
In addition	Because
Plus	Indeed
What is more	For . . . and
Further	Similarly

These words indicate that the passage's argument is continuing along the same course.

Finally, circle any words of emphasis that communicate to the reader that a given portion of the passage is particularly significant to its overall argument.

EMPHASIS INDICATORS

Ultimately	Critically
Essentially	Importantly
Fundamentally	Primarily
Chiefly	Necessarily
Especially	

Circling these words will remind you later that this was a point at which the passage built to one of its big ideas.

As noted above, understanding the passage's main point requires you to be able to answer two questions: what does each paragraph say, and how do the paragraphs relate to each other? Bracketing the big-picture statements in each paragraph will help you answer the former question. Circling all of the indicator words will help you answer the latter.

Summarize the Passage. Once you've finished reading, your focus shifts from the paragraph level to the passage level. The passage is nothing more than the sum of its parts. To understand the main point of the passage, you'll figure out how the main points of its paragraphs fit together.

Start with the main points of the first two paragraphs. Is the second paragraph more of the same, or is it something different? Connect the two main points of each paragraph using a simple indicator word that captures their logical relationship, such as "and," "because," or "but."

Once you've connected the main ideas of the first two paragraphs, repeat the process for each remaining paragraph. By doing so you'll create a synopsis of the whole passage that encapsulates all of its key ideas and how they fit together.

Also keep a lookout for normative statements that are framed in sweeping, big-picture terms. Every so often, an author will come right out and state the main point of the passage in a single sentence. When you see language that looks like it's trying to synthesize, reconcile, or explain a big idea, make sure you mark it. That language is likely one of the most important portions of the passage.

In the early stages of your Reading Comprehension practice, write out this summary using complete sentences. Doing so will help you build your reading and annotating skills, and it's a good way to double-check your understanding of the passage. As you become more comfortable with the technique, use shorter summaries. Write down a few key words or phrases that capture each paragraph's main idea. Given the 35-minute time limit, you won't be able to write out full-sentence summaries of each paragraph on the day of the test. Instead, jot these shorter summaries in the margins beside each paragraph. Add an "and," "but," "because," or other appropriate connector in the margin where the next paragraph begins. These shorthand summaries will help ensure that you don't lose track of the passage's big picture as you're working through the questions.

Mapping the Location of the Details

When it comes to the details, your goal is to know exactly where they are, not exactly what they say. If one of the questions asks you about the work of a particular scholar, for example, you need to be able to scan the passage, find that scholar's name, and review what the passage says about her work. By marking the location of key factual details, your annotation system will expedite this scan-and-retrieve process.

Underline the Key Facts. Specifically, you should underline the key portion of each discrete factual topic within the passage. As you read, mark:

- The names of people (scholars, researchers, authors, critics, etc.) whose work is discussed
- The subject or findings of any experiments, studies, reports, illustrative examples, or other data
- The names of key concepts, theories, techniques, or terms of art
- Pluses and minuses, pros and cons, or strengths and weaknesses attributed to a proposal, theory, or explanation (these frequently appear in numbered lists)

Underline judiciously. Limit yourself to only the essential portion of each topic. Being disciplined about what you underline will force you to think critically about the text. Visually, you want to create a user-friendly map so that when you read a question and think, "Where did I read about that?" you can quickly glance back to the passage and find it. You won't be able to do that if you've cluttered up the page by underlining half of the words in the passage.

In short, you want to use a "Goldilocks" amount of underlining. Mark just enough of the key terms, names, words, and phrases to jog your memory about each topic. But don't mark so much that you can't easily find what you're looking for. It's rarely helpful to underline an entire sentence. It's never helpful to underline two entire sentences consecutively.

Putting Annotative Reading into Practice

Here's a summary of your annotative-reading strategy:

1. Identify the main point of each paragraph.
   - Be on the lookout for normative language.
   - Circle any conclusion indicators.
   - Once you've identified the main point, put brackets around it and make a note in the margin.
2. Determine the connections between paragraphs. Draw circles around contrast indicators, continuity indicators, and emphasis indicators.
3. Underline key factual details. Use a "Goldilocks" approach.
4. Summarize the passage's contents by stating each paragraph's main point and, where possible, connecting them with a conjunction that captures their logical relationship.

Practice

A sample passage follows. Read it and annotate it using the tools and techniques you've just learned. Don't worry about how long it takes you to finish; take the time to do it right.

An emerging school of thought in economic theory characterizes the creation of consumer preferences in rapidly emerging markets as a positive externality. A positive externality is a benefit created by
(5) a transaction that is conferred on a third party who did not participate in the transaction. In rapidly emerging markets, consumers do not yet have a known set of preferences that a new product must satisfy. The release of new, innovative products by
(10) early participants in these markets causes consumers to articulate, refine, and stabilize their preferences. These newly created consumer preferences are an externality because they benefit later participants in the market, whose products are more commercially
(15) successful because they are responsive to these preferences.

For instance, the first portable digital music players were introduced into the American market in 1998. They included some features that proved to
(20) be desirable to consumers. They also included some features that consumers did not want and lacked some features that consumers did want. However, it was only after purchasing and using these first-generation players that consumers were able to
(25) describe the features they most wanted in a portable digital music player. By successfully integrating these newly developed consumer preferences into the functionality and design of the iPod, which it released in 2001, Apple was able to win the lion's
(30) share of the lucrative digital-music-player market. Apple's success was inextricably linked to the development of consumer preferences, and the costs of that development were borne by the manufacturers of the first generation of players.
(35) Externalities are market inefficiencies; an efficient market allocates benefits to the party who bore the cost of creating them. Some economists thus contend that the creation of consumer preferences should be regulated such that the companies
(40) whose vanguard products create these preferences receive an economic benefit for doing so. A handful argue for a command-and-control regulatory scheme. Others propose a *post hoc* system of taxation and/or subsidies. While well-intentioned, these
(45) proposals are ultimately misguided. To begin with, they wrongly assume that the economic value of creating consumer preferences can be quantified and measured on a company-by-company basis. It is beyond dispute that an early-stage emerging
(50) market as a whole creates consumer preferences. But the amount that any particular early-stage market participant contributes to the formation of those preferences defies quantification. A regulation that fixed compensation for individual market partici-
(55) pants would replace one inefficiency with another.

Nor is there any demonstrated need for regulation. The central rationale for regulating a positive externality is that the failure to do so will deter investment. In theory, a company is less likely to
(60) enter a new market if it knows that it will not be

able to harness the full value of its investment. In practice, market data reveal a high level of participation in early-stage emerging markets. The incredible financial rewards that redound to the creator of a
(65) lucrative new technology have proven to be a strong enough incentive to attract numerous investors. Regulations aimed at internalizing the benefits associated with the creation of consumer preferences are unnecessary.

Before you continue reading, write down the main points of each of the passage's four paragraphs in the space below. Connect them using a simple conjunction that captures the logical relationship between the ideas.

A sample annotation of this passage follows. Before you compare your annotation to that sample, review your work and ask yourself the following questions:

1. Have I used conclusion indicators and normative language to identify each paragraph's main point?
2. Have I used contrast indicators, continuity indicators, and emphasis indicators to identify the logical relationship between each paragraph?
3. Have I created a summary of the passage that uses appropriate conjunctions to connect the main points of each paragraph?
4. Have I used a "Goldilocks" amount of underlining to highlight the key words and phrases that signal the location of the various factual details discussed in the passage?

MP [An emerging school of thought in economic theory characterizes the creation of consumer preferences in rapidly emerging markets as a positive externality.] A positive externality is a benefit created by
(5) a transaction that is conferred on a third party who did not participate in the transaction. In rapidly emerging markets, consumers do not yet have a known set of preferences that a new product must satisfy. The release of new, innovative products by
(10) early participants in these markets causes consumers to articulate, refine, and stabilize their preferences. These newly created consumer preferences are an externality because they benefit later participants in the market, whose products are more commercially
(15) successful because they are responsive to these preferences.

For instance, the first portable digital music players were introduced into the American market in 1998. They included some features that proved to
(20) be desirable to consumers. They also included some features that consumers did not want and lacked some features that consumers did want. However, it was only after purchasing and using these first-generation players that consumers were able to
(25) describe the features they most wanted in a portable digital music player. [By successfully integrating
MP these newly developed consumer preferences into the functionality and design of the iPod, which it released in 2001, Apple was able to win the lion's
(30) share of the lucrative digital-music-player market.] Apple's success was inextricably linked to the development of consumer preferences, and the costs of that development were borne by the manufacturers of the first generation of players.

(35) Externalities are market inefficiencies; an efficient market allocates benefits to the party who bore the cost of creating them. Some economists thus contend that the creation of consumer preferences should be regulated such that the companies
(40) whose vanguard products create these preferences receive an economic benefit for doing so. A handful argue for a command-and-control regulatory scheme. Others propose a *post hoc* system of taxa-
MP tion and/or subsidies. While well-intentioned, these
(45) proposals are ultimately misguided. To begin with, they wrongly assume that the economic value of creating consumer preferences can be quantified and measured on a company-by-company basis. It is beyond dispute that an early-stage emerging
(50) market as a whole creates consumer preferences. But the amount that any particular early-stage market participant contributes to the formation of those preferences defies quantification. A regulation that fixed compensation for individual market partici-
(55) pants would replace one inefficiency with another.
MP [Nor is there any demonstrated need for regulation.] The central rationale for regulating a positive externality is that the failure to do so will deter investment. In theory, a company is less likely to
(60) enter a new market if it knows that it will not be

able to harness the full value of its investment. In practice, market data reveal a high level of participation in early-stage emerging markets. The incredible financial rewards that redound to the creator of a
(65) lucrative new technology have proven to be a strong enough incentive to attract numerous investors. [Regulations aimed at internalizing the benefits asso- MP ciated with the creation of consumer preferences are unnecessary.]

Your summary of the passage should look something like this:

(1) *An emerging school of thought in economic theory characterizes the creation of consumer preferences in rapidly emerging markets as a positive externality.*

(2) *Apple's development of the iPod illustrates this phenomenon.*

_____

_____

(3) *But calls for regulation are misguided because the value of these preferences cannot be quantified or allocated.*

_____

(4) *And there is no evidence that regulation is necessary to encourage investment.*

_____

_____

CHAPTER 5 ■ LSAT READING COMPREHENSION 181

The amount of text that is circled, bracketed, and underlined in this passage is a good indicator of about how much of the passage you should be marking up as you read. This passage also demonstrates the need to be flexible as you read. Notice there is more text underlined and circled in the last two paragraphs than there is in the first two paragraphs. That's because the first two paragraphs are there to provide context and background information. The argument doesn't really gain steam until paragraphs three and four.

If you had a hard time identifying each paragraph's main point or deciding what to underline, don't despair. Annotative reading takes practice. Each of the next eight cases includes a practice passage as well as sample annotations and summaries. Take the time to fully annotate and summarize each of these passages. Everything you do in the Reading Comprehension section begins with annotative reading.

Finally, it's worth pointing out that this was not an easy passage to read. It was conceptually dense, featured a number of long sentences, and used a lot of technical terms. If it appeared on an LSAT, it would be one of the two more difficult passages in the section. In Case 10, we'll discuss how to quickly rank the passages based on difficulty so that you'll work the easier passages first. As you read and annotate the passages in the next eight cases, make notes to yourself about how difficult you find each passage and why. Those notes will help you put your section-wide strategy into practice.

A key component of that section-wide strategy is pacing. Case 10 will discuss in greater detail how you should pace yourself as you work the Reading Comprehension section. For now, all you need to know is that your goal is to eventually be able to complete your upfront reading of the passage—including making annotations and creating a summary—in somewhere between three and four minutes. In the early stages of your practice, don't worry too much about timing. But as you become more comfortable with the techniques, keep track of how long it takes you to read and annotate each passage. Gradually accelerate the process so that you are moving toward a reading pace that you can employ on test day.

Case 3

Main Idea Questions

Main Idea questions, as the name suggests, require you to pick the answer choice that most accurately states the main point of the passage as a whole. Almost every passage in the Reading Comprehension section includes a Main Idea question. The annotative-reading strategy you learned in the previous case will help you answer these questions quickly and with a high rate of accuracy.

STEP 1: Read the Question and Identify Your Task
A Main Idea question will be worded in one of the following ways:

- Which of the following most accurately expresses the main point of the passage?
- Which of the following most accurately summarizes the main idea of the passage?
- The passage most helps to answer which one of the following questions?

STEP 2: Go Back to the Passage and Find the Answer
By creating a summary of the passage as part of your annotative-reading process, you've done the hard work of finding the answer to a Main Idea question. That said, it's important to recognize that a summary is not the same thing as the main point. The main point of the passage is the core idea that it's trying to persuade you of. The summary contains the main point, but it also contains background information and evidence or arguments offered in support of the main point.

STEP 3: Read Every Word of Every Answer Choice
The right answer to a Main Idea question will be the portion of your summary of the passage that embodies the key takeaway from the passage. The right answer will usually borrow or quote some language directly from the passage itself. Since Main Idea questions ask you about a big-picture concept, it can be tempting to go beyond what you've read and speculate about the passage's significance or implications. As you work through the answer choices, keep in mind that the correct answer must be objectively, demonstrably correct based solely on the material in the passage.

COMMON TYPES OF WRONG ANSWERS

1. **Too broad in scope.** This is the most common type of wrong answer on Main Idea questions. Several of the incorrect answer choices are likely to go beyond the scope of the passage. They might discuss new information about a related topic. They might make a comparison between the topic of the passage and an outside topic that was not discussed in the passage. In particular, keep an eye out for the word *only*, which subtly makes the strongest possible comparative claim about the content of the passage.

2. **Too narrow in scope.** At least one of the wrong answers to a Main idea question is usually the main point of one paragraph. Such answer choices are designed to trick you, since they are focused on too small a portion of the passage.

3. **In the right direction, but too strong.** Finally, some wrong answers to Main Idea questions will express an idea that is similar to the one expressed in the passage but that is stated in overblown, amplified terms. The passages are excerpted from academic writing; they are cautious and precise. Watch out for answers that take the basic point of the passage and state it a little too categorically or forcefully.

Practice

Read and annotate the passage that appears on the following page. Write down the summary you create in the blanks that appear at the end of the passage. Once you're finished, compare your annotations and summary to the example on the following page.

To contain oil that has spilled into the ocean out of a tanker ship or a drilling platform, petroleum engineers have traditionally utilized a two-pronged strategy of containment and dispersal. Dispersal is

(5) accomplished by some combination of chemical and biological agents, while containment has primarily been accomplished by deploying mechanical booms. Booms are temporary physical barriers that float on the water's surface. A portion of the barrier

(10) extends above the surface of the water. Most booms are made of a highly absorbent polypropylene material so that they will absorb some of the oil that is floating on the surface. The booms are also fitted with underwater skirts that extend anywhere from

(15) 18 inches to 4 feet below the surface. The skirts contain and capture oil that has become submerged.

Industrial engineers Fjeld Nygård and Grom Eidnes have recently developed a new technology that creates a curtain of air bubbles to contain an

(20) oceanic oil spill. The technology starts with large, perforated rubber hoses (approximately 40 feet long by 5 feet wide) being attached to powerful air compressors and mounted on pieces of stainless-steel or fiberglass grating. The hoses and grating are

(25) then submerged about 7 feet below the surface of the water. Air circulated by the compressors escapes into the water through the hoses' perforations. The escaped air creates a dense curtain of bubbles, which immediately rises toward the surface. The bubbles

(30) carry the surrounding water with them as they rise. When that water reaches the surface, it creates a horizontal current. Since floating oil cannot cross the current, the current serves to contain the spill. As the pressure of the air released by the compressor

(35) increases, the strength of the current created by the bubbles increases concomitantly. The stronger the horizontal current, the better it is able to contain the oil.

The use of air-bubble curtains to contain spills

(40) has distinct advantages over the use of mechanical booms. Mechanical booms can effectively contain spilled oil in ambient currents only up to 19.7 inches per second. Stronger currents cause oil drainage to seep under the bottom of the booms'

(45) skirts, and the increased surface choppiness associated with stronger currents can cause oil to wash over the tops of the booms. Air-bubble curtains, Nygård and Eidnes claim, are presently able to contain oil spills in ambient currents as high as

(50) 27.5 inches per second, in part because the bubbles help to reduce the wave action on the surface. In theory, a denser curtain of bubbles could be effective in even stronger currents, but creating a denser curtain would require an amount of air to

(55) be forced out of the perforated hoses that exceeds the present capabilities of commercially available compressor technology. Another advantage of air-bubble curtains is that boats can travel across them on the surface of the water, while the deployment of

(60) mechanical booms renders the water nonnavigable.

SUMMARY

(1) _____

(2) _____

(3) _____

To contain oil that has spilled into the ocean out
of a tanker ship or a drilling platform, petroleum
engineers have traditionally utilized a two-pronged
strategy of containment and dispersal. Dispersal is
(5)   accomplished by some combination of chemical and
biological agents, while containment has primarily
MP   been accomplished by deploying mechanical
booms. Booms are temporary physical barriers that
float on the water's surface. A portion of the barrier
(10)   extends above the surface of the water. Most booms
are made of a highly absorbent polypropylene material so that they will absorb some of the oil that is
floating on the surface. The booms are also fitted
with underwater skirts that extend anywhere from
(15)   18 inches to 4 feet below the surface. The skirts
contain and capture oil that has become submerged.
MP   Industrial engineers Fjeld Nygård and Grom
Eidnes have recently developed a new technology
that creates a curtain of air bubbles to contain an
(20)   oceanic oil spill. The technology starts with large,
perforated rubber hoses (approximately 40 feet
long by 5 feet wide) being attached to powerful air
compressors and mounted on pieces of stainless-
steel or fiberglass grating. The hoses and grating are
(25)   then submerged about 7 feet below the surface of
the water. Air circulated by the compressors escapes
into the water through the hoses' perforations. The
escaped air creates a dense curtain of bubbles, which
immediately rises toward the surface. The bubbles
(30)   carry the surrounding water with them as they rise.
When that water reaches the surface, it creates a
horizontal current. Since floating oil cannot cross
the current, the current serves to contain the spill.
As the pressure of the air released by the compressor
(35)   increases, the strength of the current created by the
bubbles increases concomitantly. The stronger the
horizontal current, the better it is able to contain
the oil.
MP   The use of air-bubble curtains to contain spills
(40)   has distinct advantages over the use of mechanical
booms. Mechanical booms can effectively contain
spilled oil in ambient currents only up to 19.7
inches per second. Stronger currents cause oil
drainage to seep under the bottom of the booms'
(45)   skirts, and the increased surface choppiness associated with stronger currents can cause oil to wash
over the tops of the booms. Air-bubble curtains,
Nygård and Eidnes claim, are presently able to
contain oil spills in ambient currents as high as
(50)   27.5 inches per second, in part because the bubbles
help to reduce the wave action on the surface.
In theory, a denser curtain of bubbles could be
effective in even stronger currents, but creating a
denser curtain would require an amount of air to
(55)   be forced out of the perforated hoses that exceeds
the present capabilities of commercially available
compressor technology. Another advantage of air-
bubble curtains is that boats can travel across them
on the surface of water, while the deployment of
(60)   mechanical booms renders the water nonnavigable.

SUMMARY

(1) *Oil spills have historically been contained with mechanical booms.*

(2) *But there is a new method that uses curtains of air bubbles to contain spills.*

(3) *And this new method has advantages over the use of booms.*

Practice Question

Which of the following most accurately expresses the main point of the passage?

(A) Despite its limitations, the use of air-bubble curtains has proven to be more effective than any other method of containing oil spills.

(B) Two industrial chemists have made a valuable contribution to the field of petroleum engineering with their development of air-bubble curtains, a compressor-based technology for containing oceanic oil spills.

(C) The use of air-bubble curtains is a new method for containing oil spills that has distinct advantages over the use of mechanical booms.

(D) Mechanical booms, an unreliable method used to contain past oil spills, can finally be abandoned now that air-bubble-curtain technology has been developed.

(E) Most petroleum engineers today have rejected the use of mechanical booms and are embracing the use of air-bubble curtains as the most effective method for containing oil spills.

Answer and Analysis. The correct answer is choice C. Note how choice C tracks sentences two and three of the summary of the passage and quotes language from the topic sentence of the third paragraph. Even on Main Idea questions, the answer is in the passage; you just have to find it. Choice C doesn't say much about paragraph one, but that's OK; the purpose of paragraph one was to provide background information, so its content can be omitted from a statement of the passage's main point. That's the difference between a main point and a summary.

Choices A and E are wrong for the same reason: they go beyond the scope of the passage to compare air-bubble curtains to all other spill-containment technologies; the only other technology to which the passage compares air-bubble curtains is mechanical booms. Choice B accurately states the main point of paragraph two, but it omits any discussion of the opinion expressed in paragraph three. Finally, choice D takes the basic idea of the passage—which is that air-bubble curtains have some advantages over mechanical booms—and states it too strongly. Nowhere does the passage say that booms are "unreliable" or should "finally be abandoned."

Variation: Primary Purpose Questions. Consider the following question:

The author's main purpose in the passage is to

(A) defend a new technology against criticism

(B) identify the major shortcomings of the field of petroleum engineering and suggest how they should be remedied

(C) support the view that a new technology will actually be worse than the technology it was intended to replace

(D) show that the effectiveness of a new oil-spill-containment technology cannot be accurately gauged without further study

(E) explain the benefits of a new technology as compared to an existing technology

A question like this might also be worded to read, "Which one of the following most accurately states the primary function of the passage?"

These questions are just Main Idea questions that have been restated at one higher level of generality. Answering these questions requires you to (1) summarize the content of the passage; (2) *describe* that content in slightly more general terms; and (3) find the answer choice that matches your description. In comparing each answer choice to your description, you may find it helpful to draw on the technique you learned for answering Principle questions in Case 3 of Chapter 4: break each answer choice down into its constituent parts, and compare the parts to your description one at a time.

Here, we've already summarized the passage as part of the annotative-reading strategy. To restate that summary at one higher level of generality, you might say, "The passage describes an old technology, then it describes a new technology, and finally it explains two advantages that the new technology has over the old technology." Now you can compare the answer choices to that description. You can eliminate choice A because the passage does not criticize the air-bubble-curtain technology. Choice B is too broad in scope; the passage is about two specific technologies, not the entire field of petroleum engineering. Choice C is wrong for the same reason choice A is wrong; the passage argues that air-bubble curtains may be superior to booms, not inferior. And choice D falls short because the passage does not call for further study. Choice E is the correct answer; it is a slightly less-thorough version of the description just articulated.

Case 4

Line ID Questions

This case addresses Line ID questions, which are questions that direct your attention to a particular line or lines in the passage. Over the past five years, there has been an average of about one Line ID question per passage. The skills you build in learning how to work these questions will also come in handy as you work the single most common type of question in the Reading Comprehension section, Information Retrieval questions, which are discussed in the next case.

STEP 1:   Read the Question and Identify Your Task
Line ID questions require you either to determine the meaning of a word or phrase in context or to describe the purpose or function served by a particular portion of the text. The hallmark of these questions is that they include a parenthetical notation that tells you exactly what portion of the passage the question pertains to. Below are some examples of the more common wordings of Line ID questions (the blanks would be filled in with content from the passage, and the *X*s and *Y*s would be replaced by numbers):

- In saying _____ (lines X–Y), the author most likely means which one of the following?
- Which one of the following terms most accurately conveys the sense of the word "_____" as it is used in line X?
- The phrase "_____" (lines X–Y) is most likely intended by the author to mean:
- The author of the passage uses the term "_____" (line X) primarily in order to:

STEP 2:   Go Back to the Passage and Find the Answer
Line ID questions make the process of going back to the passage easy. The question tells you where the relevant material appears; you don't have to rely on your annotations to know where to go. But the portion of the passage that you reread should be broader than just the single line to which the question refers. Once you've located the word or phrase that's the subject of the question, you should also read the sentence that immediately precedes it and the sentence that's immediately after it. By reading these three sentences, you'll get a fuller sense of the context in which the word is used.

Pay especially careful attention to the sentence that follows the word or phrase under review. Line ID questions frequently ask about terms of art or technical phrases about which the passage offers some explanation. That explanation is usually not offered until after the word has been introduced.

Some Line ID questions ask the author's reason for using a particular term. Here, your annotations and your summary of the passage can help you get a handle on the function of a particular word or phrase. What is the main point of the paragraph in which the word or phrase appears? Did you circle any indicator words in the vicinity? The purpose for which a word or phrase is used depends heavily on the broader argumentative context.

STEP 3:   Read Every Word of Every Answer Choice
Right answers to Line ID questions are wholly context-dependent. To make it easier to identify the right answer, you should come up with your own answer to the question before you leave the passage to start reviewing the answer choices. Generate a synonym or a definition to which you can compare each answer choice. This will help prevent you from losing your train of thought as you're reviewing all five answer choices.

COMMON TYPES OF WRONG ANSWERS

1. **A second meaning of the word.** Many of the words and terms that appear in Line ID questions carry multiple meanings. Thus, it's common for one of the wrong answer choices to list a meaning that can be correct but is inappropriate in context. For example, if the question asked about the word *reflective* and the passage used that word to mean "capable of reflecting light," one of the answer choices would probably read "thoughtful or contemplative." You can avoid these choices by reading the sentences immediately before and after the word or phrase in question so that you have a full sense of context.

2. **An idea from a different portion of the passage.** Many wrong answers to Line ID questions recite a phrase or concept that is drawn directly from a different portion of the passage. To a test taker who is relying solely on her recall of what she read, such choices can be tempting because they accurately restate something that the test taker remembers reading. Going back to the relevant portion of the passage will help you avoid falling for this type of wrong answer.

Practice

Read and annotate the passage that appears on the following page. Write down the summary you create in the blanks that appear at the end of the passage. Once you're finished, compare your annotations and summary to the example that follows. Then work the two Line ID questions that appear on the page after the example annotation.

A trademark is a symbol or designation that is used in commerce to identify and distinguish a particular person's goods from the goods manufactured or sold by other persons. The most common
(5) type of trademark is a brand name. Companies can also trademark logos, slogans, signs, and other physical manifestations of their brands. Trademark law also protects a company's "trade dress," which is the overall appearance and image of the company's
(10) products. Trademarks provide an economically valuable function by making it easier for consumers to differentiate between brands of goods, quickly identify a preferred brand, and develop brand loyalty.

A trademark's ability to perform this function
(15) can be eroded by the conduct of a holdover trademark licensee. A holdover licensee is a person who was previously licensed to use another person's trademarks and continues to use those marks without authorization after the expiration of his
(20) license. Large companies, especially in the restaurant industry, often sign franchise agreements under which the company licenses a franchise owner to use the company's trademarks and trade dress, including its name, logo, menu, floor plan,
(25) and decorative scheme. If the franchise agreement expires, the franchisee is no longer licensed to use the company's trademarks. But in this circumstance, many former franchisees continue to use some or all of the company's trademarks. A holdover licensee's
(30) continued use of the company's trademarks can cause substantial diminution in the value of the marks by associating them with different, sometimes inferior goods. A holdover licensee also profits from the goodwill associated with the trademark
(35) despite having neither helped create that goodwill nor paid for the right to capitalize on it.

Unauthorized use of trademarks can violate federal law in either of two ways. The first is by committing trademark infringement, which occurs
(40) when the defendant uses a spurious trademark that is confusingly similar to a genuine trademark. Trademark infringement, such as attaching a deliberately misspelled "Louis Vuttion" label to a cheap handbag, creates a risk that consumers will mistak-
(45) enly believe that the defendant's products were manufactured by the trademark owner. Trademark counterfeiting is a more serious form of trademark infringement. Counterfeiting occurs when the defendant makes unauthorized use of the owner's
(50) genuine trademark, such as by attaching a forged "Louis Vuitton" label to a cheap handbag. While trademark infringement can be accidental, trademark counterfeiting is almost always intentional. Trademark counterfeiting carries more severe penal-
(55) ties, such as higher amounts of monetary damages and awards of attorneys fees.

It is apparent that holdover licensees are guilty of trademark counterfeiting, not merely of trademark infringement. The more serious penalty is
(60) appropriate because preventing consumer confusion is the primary policy goal of trademark law. The risk of consumer confusion is at an apex when a former licensee sells his or her own goods under the banner of a physically genuine, originally legitimate
(65) trademark. A trademark's value emanates from the connection it represents to a particular good. The holdover licensee's use of someone else's trademark to market a different good diminishes that value, thereby diluting the integrity of the brand repre-
(70) sented by the mark.

SUMMARY

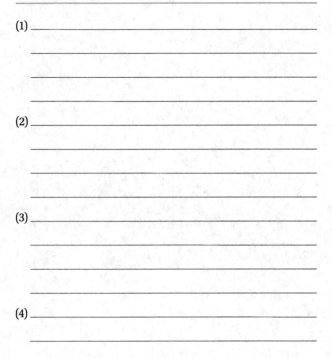

(1) _____
_____
_____
_____

(2) _____
_____
_____
_____

(3) _____
_____
_____
_____

(4) _____
_____
_____
_____

MP A trademark is a symbol or designation that is used in commerce to identify and distinguish a particular person's goods from the goods manufactured or sold by other persons. The most common
(5) type of trademark is a brand name. Companies can also trademark logos, slogans, signs, and other physical manifestations of their brands. Trademark law also protects a company's "trade dress," which is the overall appearance and image of the company's
(10) products. Trademarks provide an economically valuable function by making it easier for consumers to differentiate between brands of goods, quickly identify a preferred brand, and develop brand loyalty.

MP A trademark's ability to perform this function
(15) can be eroded by the conduct of a holdover trademark licensee. A holdover licensee is a person who was previously licensed to use another person's trademarks and continues to use those marks without authorization after the expiration of his
(20) license. Large companies, especially in the restaurant industry, often sign franchise agreements under which the company licenses a franchise owner to use the company's trademarks and trade dress, including its name, logo, menu, floor plan,
(25) and decorative scheme. If the franchise agreement expires, the franchisee is no longer licensed to use the company's trademarks. But in this circumstance, many former franchisees continue to use some or all of the company's trademarks. A holdover licensee's
(30) continued use of the company's trademarks can cause substantial diminution in the value of the marks by associating them with different, sometimes inferior goods. A holdover licensee also profits from the goodwill associated with the trademark
(35) despite having neither helped create that goodwill nor paid for the right to capitalize on it.

MP Unauthorized use of trademarks can violate federal law in either of two ways. The first is by committing trademark infringement, which occurs
(40) when the defendant uses a spurious trademark that is confusingly similar to a genuine trademark. Trademark infringement, such as attaching a deliberately misspelled "Louis Vuttion" label to a cheap handbag, creates a risk that consumers will mistak-
(45) enly believe that the defendant's products were manufactured by the trademark owner. Trademark counterfeiting is a more serious form of trademark infringement. Counterfeiting occurs when the defendant makes unauthorized use of the owner's
(50) genuine trademark, such as by attaching a forged "Louis Vuitton" label to a cheap handbag. While trademark infringement can be accidental, trademark counterfeiting is almost always intentional. Trademark counterfeiting carries more severe penal-
(55) ties, such as higher amounts of monetary damages and awards of attorneys fees.

MP It is apparent that holdover licensees are guilty of trademark counterfeiting, not merely of trademark infringement. The more serious penalty is
(60) appropriate because preventing consumer confusion is the primary policy goal of trademark law. The risk of consumer confusion is at an apex when a former licensee sells his or her own goods under the banner of a physically genuine, originally legitimate
(65) trademark. A trademark's value emanates from the connection it represents to a particular good. The holdover licensee's use of someone else's trademark to market a different good diminishes that value, thereby diluting the integrity of the brand repre-
(70) sented by the mark.

SUMMARY

(1) *Trademarks → identify and distinguish particular brands of goods.*

(2) *But holdover licensees' unauthorized use of trademarks interferes with that function.*

(3) *Unauthorized use → infringement or counterfeiting.*

(4) *And holdover licensees are guilty of trademark counterfeiting.*

Practice Question 1

Which one of the following is closest to the meaning of the word "spurious" as used in line 40?

    (A) inauthentic
    (B) accidental
    (C) alternative
    (D) clandestine
    (E) debatable

Answer and Analysis. Returning to the passage and reviewing the three sentences surrounding the word *spurious* in line 40 reveals that, in context, the passage is contrasting "spurious" trademarks with "genuine" trademarks. As the example of the deliberately misspelled "Louis Vuttion" label illustrates, you're looking for an answer choice that captures the idea that a spurious trademark is a knockoff or an imposter. Therefore, the correct answer is choice A.

Practice Question 2

The passage discusses consumer confusion (lines 59–65) most likely in order to:

    (A) explain the purpose for which trademark protection extends to a company's trade dress

    (B) support the claim that holdover trademark licensees are guilty of trademark counterfeiting

    (C) call into question the assumption that a holdover licensee will profit from the goodwill associated with a trademark

    (D) criticize large companies in the restaurant industry for failing to require franchisees to sign more restrictive franchise agreements

    (E) provide an example of the ways in which trademarks make it easier for consumers to distinguish between different brands of goods

Answer and Analysis. The correct answer is choice B. This question illustrates the value of identifying the main point of each paragraph during your upfront reading of the passage. The summary identified the notion that holdover licensees are guilty of trademark counterfeiting as the main point of paragraph four , which is the paragraph in which lines 59–65 appear. Choice B directly connects the discussion of consumer confusion to paragraph four's main point. Choices A and E each refer to topics that were discussed in the first paragraph, and they also add embellishments that go beyond the content of the passage. Choices C and D both misstate a topic that was discussed in paragraph two.

Case 5

Information Retrieval Questions

This case discusses Information Retrieval questions. Information Retrieval questions require you to select an answer choice that correctly restates one of the factual details presented in the passage. Over the past five years, this has been the single most common type of Reading Comprehension question; each passage has featured an average of between two and three Information Retrieval questions. That means that about 30 percent of the questions you answer will be Information Retrieval questions. Learning how to approach these questions is critical to your success on the Reading Comprehension section.

STEP 1: **Read the Question and Identify Your Task**
The test writers use a wide variety of wordings to ask Information Retrieval questions. The basic idea that the question will get across is, "What did the passage say about _____?" Some of the more common phrasings include:

■ According to the passage, _____?
■ The passage states (or "asserts," "indicates," "claims," "mentions") which one of the following about _____?
■ In the passage, the author makes which one of the following claims about _____?
■ Based on the passage, which one of the following is the author most likely to believe about _____?
■ Given the information in the passage, _____?

A few variations of this question type tend to be particularly time-consuming. For instance:

■ The passage provides information sufficient to answer which one of the following questions?

- The information in the passage most strongly supports which one of the following statements?
- According to the passage, each one of the following _____ EXCEPT:

The reason these variations are more time-consuming is that the question does not limit itself to a single topic. The topic varies from answer choice to answer choice, and typically the answer choices address five different topics, each of which was discussed at a different place in the passage.

STEP 2: Go Back to the Passage and Find the Answer
Your approach to Information Retrieval questions is substantively identical to the approach you took to answering Line ID questions: you'll go back to the relevant portion of the passage, review what it says about the topic of the question, and then compare each answer choice to the passage. The primary difference between the two question types is that on Information Retrieval questions, it's up to you to find the line or lines in the passage where the relevant information is located.

It's on this front that annotative reading really pays dividends. By underlining key words as you read, you mapped the location of all of the facts, details, and examples discussed in the passage. Instead of having to reread the whole passage, you can scan through your annotations until you find an underlined word or phrase that is connected to the topic of the question. Your annotations will enable you to quickly locate the discussion of any given topic.

Once you've found the relevant portion of the passage, review what it says about the topic of the question. You'll undertake this initial review at different times depending on the nature of the question. If the question limits itself to a particular topic, you should quickly review the relevant portion of the passage before you turn to the answer choices. But if you're working one of the more time-consuming types of Information Retrieval question, where the topic at issue is determined solely by the content of the answer choices, your first rereading of the passage will not take place until after you've read the first answer choice.

Your rereading process will be iterative. In other words, you won't just go back to the passage once. Instead, you'll review the relevant portion of the passage multiple times as you work your way through the answer choices. After you read each answer choice, you'll go back to the passage to see if the answer choice matches what was said in the passage. You'll go back and forth between the passage and the answer choices multiple times.

Expediting the process of finding the relevant portion of the passage on Information Retrieval questions is the primary reason you underline the facts and details during your upfront reading. As you work the practice Reading Comprehension passages in this section, as well as the practice sections at the back of this book, make sure that your annotation system is serving the purpose of expediting your scan-and-retrieve process on Information Retrieval questions. It may take you some time before you can consistently recognize when a passage has moved onto a new topic, or determine how much of each topic you need to underline. Adjust your annotating process as you practice so that it serves its most important function: streamlining the process of going back to the passage on Information Retrieval questions.

STEP 3: Read Every Word of Every Answer Choice
The right answer to an Information Retrieval question will be drawn directly from the passage with no substantive modifications. But the answer is unlikely to be a direct quote from the passage. Instead, the test writers use synonyms and paraphrasing to make the right answer harder to recognize. For example, if the passage states that a technical breakthrough "will help overcome previous limitations on computing speed," the answer might offer the paraphrase that the breakthrough "promises faster computing."

COMMON TYPES OF WRONG ANSWERS

1. **Introduces outside information on a related topic.** Some wrong answers will introduce topics that are related to the topic of the passage but were not discussed in the passage. These answers are designed to take advantage of the fact that when you read, ordinarily you're supposed to think about the broader implications of what you've read. Not so here. Anything from outside the passage is off-limits. For example, if the passage focused on a painting's aesthetic value, an answer choice might ask you about its financial value. It doesn't matter if an answer choice is true to the best of your knowledge. If it's not explicitly stated in the passage, it can't be the answer to an Information Retrieval question.

2. **Directly contradicts information in the passage.** There is usually at least one answer choice on each Information Retrieval question that states the exact opposite of something that was stated in the passage. Typically such a choice will include language that is quoted directly from the passage. These choices are designed to "sound right" to test takers who are relying on their recall of the passage. Going back to the passage to compare each answer

choice to the content of the passage will enable you to easily recognize that these choices are incorrect.

3. **In the right direction, but too strong.** You've seen this category of wrong answer before, on Main Idea questions. Answer choices that take an idea from the passage and state a more extreme version of it are commonplace on Information Retrieval questions, too. If the passage points out two short-comings of a proposal, a wrong answer might say that the proposal has no value. If the passage says that a solution is unlikely, a wrong answer might say that a solution is impossible. The right answer to an Information Retrieval question will mirror the passage's content, tone, and precision.

4. **Attributes an idea to the wrong person.** In most Reading Comprehension passages, the author will not only state her own views but also recount and summarize the views of third parties. For instance: "Behavioral economists believe X. Classical economists believe Y. In my view, Z." Wrong answers to Information Retrieval questions frequently attribute a view stated in the passage to the wrong person.

Practice

Read and annotate the passage that appears on the following page. Write down the summary you create in the blanks that appear at the end of the passage. Once you're finished, compare your annotations and summary to the example that follows. Then work the two practice questions that appear on the following page.

General circulation models are large-scale computer models used to simulate the earth's climate so that climatologists can make predictions about how the climate will change in the future. The climate
(5) scientists who design these models have struggled with the problem of predicting the effects of climate feedbacks, changes to the natural environment that are triggered by climate change and, in turn, cause additional climate change. Permafrost carbon
(10) stores could be a significant climate feedback; examining the potential positive feedback effect of these stores provides some insight into climate feedbacks generally. Climatologists now estimate that high-latitude permafrost (soil that consistently
(15) remains at or below 32 degrees Fahrenheit) contains approximately 1.5 trillion tons of frozen carbon. If the warming of the global climate were to cause the permafrost to thaw, that frozen carbon could be released into the atmosphere as carbon dioxide
(20) or as methane. This large-scale release of potent greenhouse gases could significantly accelerate the rate of global temperature rise, which in turn could cause faster melting of the permafrost, which in turn could cause the release of even more heat-trapping
(25) gases.

Many climate scientists believe that the net effect of all global climate feedbacks, including those not yet discovered, is likely to be positive. However, Richard Lindzen's research team has concluded that
(30) most general circulation models actually overesti-mate the significance of positive feedbacks. Lindzen has identified several potential negative feedback effects that he predicts will dramatically slow, if not entirely prevent, an increase in average global
(35) temperatures. A warmer climate could produce a greater number of thick, low-altitude rain clouds, the tops of which would deflect a higher percentage of the sun's radiation out of the lower atmosphere. Warmer temperatures near the equator could cause
(40) the rate at which the oceans absorb atmospheric carbon dioxide to accelerate. Trees also absorb carbon dioxide. A rise in global temperatures could cause trees to grow bigger, faster, and more densely, thereby increasing their carbon uptake.
(45) It is likely that an increase in global mean temperatures will produce some negative feedbacks that tend to mitigate the effects of that temperature increase. But it is also the case that Lindzen has likely overestimated the magnitude of these nega-
(50) tive feedback effects. For example, while it is true that clouds reflect heat back into space, they also trap heat that has been emitted from the surface. The complex balance between these two processes is unlikely to tilt heavily toward reflection; additional
(55) heat trapping is all but inevitable. Temperature increases will also cause an increase in the intensity of equatorial winds, and oceans absorb less carbon dioxide in a windy environment. In addition, posi-tive feedbacks are likely to undermine the operation
(60) of some of the negative feedbacks that Lindzen

has identified. Warmer temperatures are associated with an increase in the frequency and severity of wildfires. Any carbon dioxide that was removed from the atmosphere by the faster growth of larger
(65) trees would be rereleased into the air by a large-scale forest fire.

SUMMARY

(1) _____

_____

_____

_____

(2) _____

_____

_____

_____

(3) _____

_____

_____

_____

General circulation models are large-scale computer models used to simulate the earth's climate so that climatologists can make predictions about how the climate will change in the future. The climate
(5) scientists who design these models have struggled
MP with the problem of predicting the effects of climate feedbacks, changes to the natural environment that are triggered by climate change and, in turn, cause additional climate change. Permafrost carbon
(10) stores could be a significant climate feedback; examining the potential positive feedback effect of these stores provides some insight into climate feedbacks generally. Climatologists now estimate that high-latitude permafrost (soil that consistently
(15) remains at or below 32 degrees Fahrenheit) contains approximately 1.5 trillion tons of frozen carbon. If the warming of the global climate were to cause the permafrost to thaw, that frozen carbon could be released into the atmosphere as carbon dioxide
(20) or as methane. This large-scale release of potent greenhouse gases could significantly accelerate the rate of global temperature rise, which in turn could cause faster melting of the permafrost, which in turn could cause the release of even more heat-trapping
(25) gases.

Many climate scientists believe that the net effect of all global climate feedbacks, including those not yet discovered, is likely to be positive. However, Richard Lindzen's research team has concluded that
(30) most general circulation models actually overesti-
MP mate the significance of positive feedbacks. Lindzen has identified several potential negative feedback effects that he predicts will dramatically slow, if not entirely prevent, an increase in average global
(35) temperatures. A warmer climate could produce a greater number of thick, low-altitude rain clouds, the tops of which would deflect a higher percentage of the sun's radiation out of the lower atmosphere. Warmer temperatures near the equator could cause
(40) the rate at which the oceans absorb atmospheric carbon dioxide to accelerate. Trees also absorb carbon dioxide. A rise in global temperatures could cause trees to grow bigger, faster, and more densely, thereby increasing their carbon uptake.

(45) It is likely that an increase in global mean temperatures will produce some negative feedbacks that tend to mitigate the effects of that temperature increase. But it is also the case that Lindzen has
MP likely overestimated the magnitude of these nega-
(50) tive feedback effects. For example, while it is true that clouds reflect heat back into space, they also trap heat that has been emitted from the surface. The complex balance between these two processes is unlikely to tilt heavily toward reflection; additional
(55) heat trapping is all but inevitable. Temperature increases will also cause an increase in the intensity of equatorial winds, and oceans absorb less carbon dioxide in a windy environment. In addition, posi-tive feedbacks are likely to undermine the operation
(60) of some of the negative feedbacks that Lindzen

has identified. Warmer temperatures are associated with an increase in the frequency and severity of wildfires. Any carbon dioxide that was removed from the atmosphere by the faster growth of larger
(65) trees would be rereleased into the air by a large-scale forest fire.

SUMMARY

(1) *The climate scientists who design GCMs struggled with how to predict the effects of climate feedbacks.*

(2) *Lindzen's research team → most GCMs overestimate the significance of positive feedbacks.*

(3) *But Lindzen's research likely overestimated the magnitude of negative feedback effects.*

Practice Question 1

According to the passage, greenhouse gases released by the thawing of the permafrost

 (A) both reflect heat back into space and also trap heat that has been emitted from the surface
 (B) could cause global temperatures to increase at a substantially faster rate
 (C) is one of the potentially significant negative climate feedbacks identified by Richard Lindzen's research team
 (D) would probably be in the form of methane rather than carbon dioxide
 (E) could cause an increase in the frequency and severity of wildfires

Answer and Analysis. The question asks about the thawing of the permafrost. The annotations show that this topic was discussed in the first paragraph. After quickly reviewing the discussion at lines 10–25, you turn to the answer choices. As for choice A, nothing in the first paragraph talks about the reflecting and trapping of heat; this choice is taken from the discussion of clouds at lines 51–55. Choice B looks good; it paraphrases the content contained in lines 17–23 of the passage. Choice C contradicts lines 11–12, which state that permafrost carbon stores are a potential *positive* feedback. Plus, the permafrost is not mentioned in paragraph two's discussion of the findings made by Lindzen's research team. Choice D is a distortion of the statement at lines 19–20 that carbon released by the thawing of the permafrost would be either in the form of carbon dioxide or methane. The passage does not take a position on which of those gases would be more prevalent. Choice E references the discussion of wildfires that appears at lines 63–66. The passage states that warmer temperatures could cause more frequent and severe wildfires, and the passage also states that the thawing of the permafrost could cause warmer temperatures. It might seem reasonable to connect those two ideas. But the passage itself never makes that connection. Choice B is closely and directly tethered to the passage's content, so it is the correct answer.

Practice Question 2

The passage states that climate scientists:

 (A) have concluded that most large-scale climate models overestimate the significance of positive feedbacks
 (B) share the view that regulation is needed to slow the rate at which greenhouse gases are emitted into the atmosphere
 (C) use the results of climate models to predict future changes to the earth's climate
 (D) have made no progress in their efforts to predict the effects of climate feedbacks
 (E) generally believe that the net effect of all global climate feedbacks will be negative

Answer and Analysis. The correct answer is choice C, which restates the opening sentence of the passage (lines 1–4); its substitution of "climate scientists" for "climatologists" is supported by the sentence that begins on line 4. Choice A attributes an idea from the passage to the wrong person. This is an accurate statement of Richard Lindzen's view (lines 28–31), but that view is in direct contrast to the view of "many climate scientists" expressed in lines 26–28. Choice B introduces new, outside information that is related to the topic of the passage. Choice B may well be a true statement, but since it's not discussed anywhere in the passage it can't be the correct answer. Choice D goes in the right direction, but it is too strong. Lines 5–6 say only that climate scientists have "struggled with" how to predict the effects of climate feedbacks; to say they "have made no progress" is an overstatement. Choice E directly contradicts the information in the passage. Lines 26–28 state that many climate scientists believe that the net effect of all global climate feedbacks is likely to be positive, not negative.

These two practice questions illustrate two fundamental points about Information Retrieval questions. First, it would be difficult to overstate the extent to which the correct answer must be drawn directly from the text of the passage. Before you select an answer, you should be able to point to the particular portion of the passage that makes the answer you're picking the right answer. Second, the more thorough you are in comparing each answer choice to the passage, the better you will do on Information Retrieval questions. It's the best way to ensure that you're evaluating each answer with the necessary specificity and precision.

Case 6

Inference Questions

The focus of this case is Inference questions. On average, each passage in the Reading Comprehension section includes one Inference question. Don't let the name mislead you; even on an Inference question, the right answer will be drawn directly from the passage. For that reason, Inference questions are very similar to Information Retrieval questions. You'll utilize many of the same techniques you learned in the previous case to tackle Inference questions.

<u>STEP 1:</u>   **Read the Question and Identify Your Task**
Below are some examples of typical Inference questions:

- Which one of the following inferences is most strongly supported by the passage?
- It can be inferred from the passage that which one of the following _____?
- It can be inferred from the passage that the author would be most likely to agree with which one of the following statements?
- The passage most strongly suggests which one of the following about _____?

<u>STEP 2:</u>   **Go Back to the Passage and Find the Answer**
The term *inference* carries a very particular meaning on the Reading Comprehension section. Ordinarily you think of inferences as conclusions that, while not definitively true, are very probably true based on a particular set of facts. For example, suppose that you walked into a room and saw that a fish tank had been overturned, there was water on the floor, no fish were anywhere in sight, and a cat was sitting next to the fish tank with water on its face licking its lips. You might infer that the cat knocked over the tank and then ate the fish. That conclusion is an example of what is normally meant by calling something an inference: a reasonable but probabilistic conclusion.

That meaning goes out the window on the Reading Comprehension section. Even though the question uses the term *inference*, the correct answer to the question will still be a statement that *must be true* based solely on the information in the passage. On the LSAT, if you were presented with the above set of facts, you could "infer" that any fish that were once in the tank are no longer in the tank, or that there is at least one animal in the room. Don't read the term *inference* as an invitation to draw on outside knowledge of the topic or speculate about the significance of the content of the passage. Even on an Inference question, the answer is already there on the page; you just have to find it.

There are two main types of "inferences" you'll be asked to draw in the Reading Comprehension section. The first one is a necessary-implication inference. For example, suppose that a passage argued that a poem written in 1820 was a particularly impressive artistic accomplishment because its originality of expression inaugurated a new rhyming technique that was previously unknown to nineteenth-century writers. Based on that argument, you could infer that the author of the passage believes that the historical circumstances surrounding the creation of a work of art are important in assessing its artistic value. The passage doesn't come right out and say it, but based on what was said in the passage it necessarily must be true.

The second main type of inference you'll be able to make is a detail-combination inference. For example, suppose that line 15 of the passage characterized a certain mathematician's work as providing an exhaustive and comprehensive account of chaos theory. Suppose that line 37 of the same passage stated that the mathematician's work did not include a discussion of Feigenbaum constants. You could combine these two statements to infer that Feigenbaum constants are not part of chaos theory. Where Information Retrieval questions required you to find the line on which one topic was discussed, detail-combination Inference questions require you to combine the lines on which two topics are discussed.

In the end, your approach to working Inference questions is virtually identical to your approach to working Information Retrieval questions. After reading each answer choice, you'll reread the relevant portion (or portions) of the passage to see if the answer choice is either a combination of two statements from the passage or a necessary implication of something said in the passage. And you'll go back to the passage multiple times, once for each answer choice.

<u>STEP 3:</u>   **Read Every Word of Every Answer Choice**
As discussed above, the right answer will either be a combination of two details from the passage or a statement that is necessarily true based on a particular piece of information in the passage. With Inference questions, just as with Information Retrieval questions, the test writers are likely to disguise the correct answer by using synonyms and paraphrasing.

Common Types of Wrong Answers. The test writers use the same kinds of wrong answers on Inference questions that they use on Information Retrieval questions. So be on the lookout for answers that introduce outside information on a related topic, directly contradict information from the passage, are in the right direction but too strong, or attribute an idea to the wrong person.

Practice

Read and annotate the passage that appears on the following page. Write down the summary you create in the blanks that appear at the end of the passage. Once you're finished, compare your annotations and summary to the example that follows. Then work the practice question that appears on the following page.

Ann Cvetkovich's *An Archive of Feeling* is grounded in psychoanalytic and cultural trauma theory; the book cites and draws from the field's most well-established critics. However, *Feeling* constitutes an
(5) important departure from prior scholarship in the area. Cvetkovich advances the radical claim that trauma is a productive force that fosters creativity and engenders political activity. This central claim is premised on a critique of the core principles of
(10) traditional trauma theory. That the book is structured as an "archive of feelings" means that it treats a wide and disparate range of cultural texts as repositories of affect and public feeling. This "archive of feelings" is broad in scope—it includes the novels
(15) of Dorothy Allison and Michelle Tea, the investigative work of Margaret Randall, performances by the punk band Tribe 8, and two self-help books. Cvetkovich unifies these works by reading them for responses to trauma that do not revert to patholo-
(20) gizing approaches. Cvetkovich's way of reading is a process of excavation. She mines the "archive of feelings" for approaches to trauma that are creative rather than therapeutic, and the approaches she unearths in these texts form the foundation of her
(25) claim for the productiveness of trauma.

Once she defines her archive and her critical terms, Cvetkovich advances her central argument that trauma is a productive force. This claim critiques two traditional ideas about trauma:
(30) that trauma is a "condition" best described and considered in the realm of medical discourse; and that trauma can be understood through a series of dichotomies like public/private, therapeutic/creative, and victim/perpetrator. Cvetkovich forth-
(35) rightly states that her focus on cultural responses to trauma is part of an effort to resist the near-total authority given to medical discourses and especially the diagnosis of post-traumatic stress disorder (PTSD). She criticizes the medicalized approach for
(40) cultivating helplessness and failing to articulate any meaningful conception of subjective agency. Cvetkovich further contends that trauma is better conceived not as a disorder but as a name for politically rooted violence that destabilizes traditional
(45) binary categories. She argues that each of the texts in her "archive of feelings" simultaneously resists the impulse toward medicalized trauma discourse and creates a cultural response to trauma that holds the promise of personal empowerment and political
(50) efficacy.

Cvetkovich does not quibble with the finer points of other theorists; rather, she suggests an entirely new way of thinking about trauma by deconstructing several widely held assumptions of
(55) trauma discourse. Her book might have benefited from a more thorough and detailed engagement with the works of other theorists. Difficult questions of class and geography are left regrettably unexplored. Nonetheless, by challenging the deeply
(60) entrenched assumption that trauma is a problem or a condition to be cured or moved past, *An Archive of Feeling* successfully advances a provocative and groundbreaking claim: that affective responses to trauma can serve as the foundation for the forma-
(65) tion of public cultures.

SUMMARY

(1) _____

_____

_____

_____

(2) _____

_____

_____

_____

(3) _____

_____

_____

_____

Ann Cvetkovich's *An Archive of Feeling* is grounded in psychoanalytic and cultural trauma theory; the book cites and draws from the field's most well-established critics. However, *Feeling* constitutes an
(5) important departure from prior scholarship in the area. Cvetkovich advances the radical claim that

MP trauma is a productive force that fosters creativity and engenders political activity. This central claim is premised on a critique of the core principles of
(10) traditional trauma theory. That the book is structured as an "archive of feelings" means that it treats a wide and disparate range of cultural texts as repositories of affect and public feeling. This "archive of feelings" is broad in scope—it includes the novels
(15) of Dorothy Allison and Michelle Tea, the investigative work of Margaret Randall, performances by the punk band Tribe 8, and two self-help books. Cvetkovich unifies these works by reading them for responses to trauma that do not revert to patholo-
(20) gizing approaches. Cvetkovich's way of reading is a process of excavation. She mines the "archive of feelings" for approaches to trauma that are creative rather than therapeutic, and the approaches she unearths in these texts form the foundation of her
(25) claim for the productiveness of trauma.

Once she defines her archive and her critical terms, Cvetkovich advances her central argument that trauma is a productive force. This claim

MP critiques two traditional ideas about trauma:
(30) that trauma is a "condition" best described and considered in the realm of medical discourse; and that trauma can be understood through a series of dichotomies like public/private, therapeutic/creative, and victim/perpetrator. Cvetkovich forth-
(35) rightly states that her focus on cultural responses to trauma is part of an effort to resist the near-total authority given to medical discourses and especially the diagnosis of post-traumatic stress disorder (PTSD). She criticizes the medicalized approach for
(40) cultivating helplessness and failing to articulate any meaningful conception of subjective agency. Cvetkovich further contends that trauma is better conceived not as a disorder but as a name for politically rooted violence that destabilizes traditional
(45) binary categories. She argues that each of the texts in her "archive of feelings" simultaneously resists the impulse toward medicalized trauma discourse and creates a cultural response to trauma that holds the promise of personal empowerment and political
(50) efficacy.

Cvetkovich does not quibble with the finer points of other theorists; rather, she suggests an entirely new way of thinking about trauma by deconstructing several widely held assumptions of
(55) trauma discourse. Her book might have benefited from a more thorough and detailed engagement with the works of other theorists. Difficult questions of class and geography are left regrettably unexplored. Nonetheless, by challenging the deeply
(60) entrenched assumption that trauma is a problem or

a condition to be cured or moved past, *An Archive of Feeling* successfully advances a provocative and **MP** groundbreaking claim: that affective responses to trauma can serve as the foundation for the forma-
(65) tion of public cultures.

SUMMARY

(1) **An Archive of Feeling** *advances the radical claim that trauma is a productive force that fosters creativity and spurs political activity.*

(2) *Cvetkovich critiques the ideas that trauma is best described using medical discourse and that trauma is best understood through a series of dichotomies.*

(3) *Despite some shortcomings,* **An Archive of Feeling** *successfully advances the provocative and groundbreaking claim that affective responses to trauma can serve as the foundation for the formation of public cultures.*

Practice Question

It can be inferred from the passage that Cvetkovich would be most likely to agree with which one of the following statements?

    (A) The core principles of traditional trauma theory include the notion that trauma engenders public culture.

    (B) The diagnosis of post-traumatic stress disorder has no role to play in trauma discourse.

    (C) The idea that trauma is a productive force has been accepted by a majority of the field's most well-established critics.

    (D) Michelle Tea's novels create a cultural response to trauma that has the potential to engender political efficacy.

    (E) The investigative work of Margaret Randall exemplifies the dichotomous public–private approach to understanding trauma.

Answer and Analysis. The correct answer is choice D. This is a detail-combination inference. Lines 13–17

state that Tea's novels are part of Cvetkovich's "archive of feelings," and lines 45–50 state that Cvetkovich believes that each of the texts in her "archive of feelings" holds the promise of political efficacy.

Choice A directly contradicts information from the passage: lines 4–10 and 59–65 establish that the notion that trauma engenders public culture is a radical departure from traditional trauma theory. Choice B is in the right direction, but it goes too far: lines 34–39 establish that Cvetkovich wants to "resist the near-total authority" given to the diagnosis of PTSD, but the passage does not go so far as to say that medical diagnosis should play no role whatsoever in trauma theory. Choice C goes beyond the scope of the passage. The passage discusses the content of Cvetkovich's new theory, but it does not discuss that theory's critical reception. Finally, choice E misstates the content of the passage. The passage draws no connection between its discussions of Randall's investigative work (line 16) and the public–private dichotomy (line 33). If anything, the statement at lines 45–50 suggests that Cvetkovich's view of the relationship between the two would be the opposite of what's stated in choice E.

Case 7

Tone Questions

This case addresses Tone questions. Tone questions ask you to describe the author's attitude toward a particular topic that is discussed in the passage. They will not ask you to describe the tone of the passage as a whole. Tone questions are not especially commonplace; there is an average of about one Tone question per Reading Comprehension section (that's per section, not per passage).

<u>STEP 1:</u> **Read the Question and Identify Your Task**
You'll know you're dealing with a Tone question when you see any of the following question stems:

▪ The author's attitude toward _____ is most accurately described as:
▪ Which one of the following best characterizes the author's attitude toward _____?
▪ The author's stance toward _____ can best be described as:
▪ Which one of the following best describes the author's opinion of _____?

<u>STEP 2:</u> **Go Back to the Passage and Find the Answer**
Per usual, your first step in working a Tone question is to return to the portion of the passage that discusses the topic identified in the question. Use your underlining and annotation to quickly locate the topic. Reread the entirety of the pertinent portion of the passage. If the topic is discussed in more than one place in the passage, reread each of the discussions. As you read, try to come up with a rough formulation of the tone or attitude with which the author treats the topic.

On the LSAT, you can think about tone as having three component parts: valence, intensity, and content. *Valence* refers to the general direction or tenor of the author's attitude. There are three basic tonal valences: positive, neutral, and negative. *Intensity* is a more specific description of the valence of the author's attitude. If the tone is generally positive, how positive is it? A positive tone could be cautious, qualified, measured, enthusiastic, or unbridled, to name a few. Finally, *content* refers to the object or target of the author's tone. This will be a specific, discrete aspect of the topic heading identified by the question.

STEP 3: **Read Every Word of Every Answer Choice**
The right answer to a Tone question will apply the same combination of valence and intensity that the passage did to the relevant content. Tone is similar to purpose in that it is a restatement or description of the passage's content at a higher level of generality. As a result, you should treat Tone answer choices the same way you treat the answer choices to the Purpose questions discussed at the end of Case 3. Break them down into pieces. Each piece of the right answer will correspond to a specific piece of the passage.

COMMON TYPES OF WRONG ANSWERS

1. **Wrong valence.** Eliminating choices based on valence is the easiest way to narrow the field of answer choices. If the author's attitude toward the topic in question is generally negative, any choice that is neutral or positive can be eliminated. Sometimes this technique will be enough to eliminate most of the wrong answers. But on more difficult Tone questions, four or even all five of the answer choices will correctly capture the tone's valence.

2. **Wrong intensity.** Tone questions won't require you to parse the fine-grained distinctions between, for example, a tone that is "persuasive" versus "satisfied" versus "assured." The difference will be substantial, something like "unbridled" versus "qualified." You can select between those answers based on whether the relevant text of the passage contains any caveats or notes of caution.

Practice

Read and annotate the passage that appears on the following page, summarizing the passage in the blanks at the end of the passage. Sample annotations and a sample summary follow, and a practice Tone question appears on the page following the annotated passage.

The procedures that govern the taking of depositions, the exchange of documents, and other aspects of pretrial discovery in American courts are ordinarily supplied by the Federal Rules of Civil
(5) Procedure. However, special difficulties arise when evidence that must be turned over during pretrial discovery is located in a foreign country because one party to the lawsuit is a foreign national or a foreign corporation. To deal with these prob-
(10) lems, the United States entered into the Hague Convention on the Taking of Evidence Abroad. The Convention prescribes certain procedures by which litigants in American courts can obtain evidence that is located in a foreign country. For the next
(15) 17 years, American litigants routinely utilized the Convention's procedures, and discovery disputes in international litigation were minimized.

A landmark Supreme Court case dramatically undercut the Hague Convention's effectiveness.
(20) Several persons who had survived a plane crash in Iowa sued the manufacturer of the plane, a French corporation. The survivors wanted documents, such as copies of the plane's design schematics, that were located in France. Instead of using the procedures
(25) provided by the Hague Convention, the survivors requested these documents using the procedures provided by the Federal Rules. Up until that time, most judges, lawyers, and scholars had assumed that the Hague Convention was mandatory and
(30) that discovery materials located abroad could only be obtained by complying with the Convention's procedures. But in 1987 the Supreme Court ruled that use of the Convention's procedures was optional, such that American litigants could instead
(35) choose to use the procedures provided in the Federal Rules of Civil Procedure.

The Supreme Court's decision was contrary to the basic purpose for which the Hague Convention was enacted. American law, as codified in the
(40) Federal Rules, allows for much more extensive and intrusive pretrial discovery than is typical in most foreign nations. The United States' system of pretrial discovery allows a litigant to obtain from his or her opponent any document that has even the smallest
(45) relevant connection to the lawsuit. By contrast, the French civil law system allows for virtually no pretrial discovery at all, and what little discovery takes place is conducted by a judge, not the parties. These differences had been the source of consider-
(50) able conflict prior to the Convention's ratification. By allowing American litigants to bypass the Hague Convention's procedures, the Supreme Court thwarted the Convention's carefully crafted effort to balance the competing interests of these dispa-
(55) rate systems.

Reaction to the Supreme Court's decision among the Convention's 21 other signatories was unanimously negative. Germany and Great Britain, among others, expressed the view that the decision
(60) had effectively caused the United States to withdraw from the Convention. While such claims are unnecessarily overblown, a perception among American allies that the United States is unable or unwilling to honor its treaty commitments will be detrimental
(65) to American interests in the long run. France responded to the decision by enacting a blocking statute that prohibits French persons and companies from complying with any foreign discovery request that does not satisfy the Hague Convention's
(70) requirements. The blocking statute is a rigid, one-size-fits-all solution to a problem that demands case-by-case solutions, and it has caused Americans to suffer delays and cost overruns anytime they must bring suit against a French defendant in a US
(75) court.

SUMMARY

(1) _____

_____

_____

_____

(2) _____

_____

_____

_____

(3) _____

_____

_____

(4) _____

_____

_____

_____

The procedures that govern the taking of depositions, the exchange of documents, and other aspects of pretrial discovery in American courts are ordinarily supplied by the Federal Rules of Civil

(5) Procedure. However, special difficulties arise when evidence that must be turned over during pretrial discovery is located in a foreign country because one party to the lawsuit is a foreign national or

MP a foreign corporation. To deal with these prob-

(10) lems, the United States entered into the Hague Convention on the Taking of Evidence Abroad. The Convention prescribes certain procedures by which litigants in American courts can obtain evidence that is located in a foreign country. For the next

(15) 17 years, American litigants routinely utilized the Convention's procedures, and discovery disputes in international litigation were minimized.

MP A landmark Supreme Court case dramatically undercut the Hague Convention's effectiveness.

(20) Several persons who had survived a plane crash in Iowa sued the manufacturer of the plane, a French corporation. The survivors wanted documents, such as copies of the plane's design schematics, that were located in France. Instead of using the procedures

(25) provided by the Hague Convention, the survivors requested these documents using the procedures provided by the Federal Rules. Up until that time, most judges, lawyers, and scholars had assumed that the Hague Convention was mandatory and

(30) that discovery materials located abroad could only be obtained by complying with the Convention's procedures. But in 1987 the Supreme Court ruled that use of the Convention's procedures was optional, such that American litigants could instead

(35) choose to use the procedures provided in the Federal Rules of Civil Procedure.

MP The Supreme Court's decision was contrary to the basic purpose for which the Hague Convention was enacted. American law, as codified in the

(40) Federal Rules, allows for much more extensive and intrusive pretrial discovery than is typical in most foreign nations. The United States' system of pretrial discovery allows a litigant to obtain from his or her opponent any document that has even the smallest

(45) relevant connection to the lawsuit. By contrast, the French civil law system allows for virtually no pretrial discovery at all, and what little discovery takes place is conducted by a judge, not the parties. These differences had been the source of consider-

(50) able conflict prior to the Convention's ratification. By allowing American litigants to bypass the Hague Convention's procedures, the Supreme Court thwarted the Convention's carefully crafted effort to balance the competing interests of these disparate

(55) systems.

MP Reaction to the Supreme Court's decision among the Convention's 21 other signatories was unanimously negative. Germany and Great Britain, among others, expressed the view that the decision

(60) had effectively caused the United States to withdraw from the Convention. While such claims are unnecessarily overblown, a perception among American allies that the United States is unable or unwilling to honor its treaty commitments will be detrimental

(65) to American interests in the long run. France responded to the decision by enacting a blocking statute that prohibits French persons and companies from complying with any foreign discovery request that does not satisfy the Hague Convention's

(70) requirements. The blocking statute is a rigid, one-size-fits-all solution to a problem that demands case-by-case solutions, and it has caused Americans to suffer delays and cost overruns anytime they must bring suit against a French defendant in a US

(75) court.

SUMMARY

(1) *The Hague Convention solved special problems of international pretrial discovery.*

(2) *But its effectiveness was undermined by a 1987 Supreme Court decision.*

(3) *That decision was contrary to the basic purpose for which the Convention was enacted.*

(4) *And it has been sharply criticized by other signatories to the Convention.*

Practice Question

The author's attitude toward the international reaction to the Supreme Court's 1987 decision is most accurately described as

(A) disdain for the parochial interests that drove that reaction coupled with a dismissal of its significance

(B) acceptance of the policy reasons necessitating that reaction mitigated by a concern with the dangerous precedent it set

(C) anger over the unlawful nature of that reaction tempered by a grudging respect for the interests it advanced

(D) criticism of the force and nature of that reaction accompanied by an acknowledgment of its detrimental consequences to the United States

(E) approval of the decisive and forceful nature of that reaction tempered by a pessimistic outlook about the resolution of similar future disputes

Answer and Analysis. The correct answer is choice D. The best way to identify it as such is to break it into parts. The first portion of the answer, "criticism of the force and nature of that reaction," corresponds to the "unnecessarily overblown" characterization in lines 62–63 and the "rigid, one-size-fits-all solution to a problem that demands case-by-case solutions" language in line 72. And the second portion of the answer, "acknowledgment of [the international reaction's] detrimental consequences to the United States," corresponds to the discussion of American interests at lines 61–65 and to the discussion of costs and delays at lines 72–75.

Each of the remaining choices has a valence problem. Choices B and E are both incorrect to say that the passage characterizes the international reaction in a generally positive manner. And choices A and C each misstate the passage's attitude toward the consequences of this international reaction. The passage's attitude is one of concern or dismay. That attitude is generally negative, not unconcerned or approving.

Case 8

Arguments-Style Questions

This case discusses a group of three different question types that give you new information and ask you to apply it to the passage in a specified manner.

The question might ask you to pick an answer choice that strengthens a portion of the passage, that weakens a portion of the passage, or that is most similar or closely analogous to a portion of the passage. The common thread between these question types is that you've seen them before in the Arguments section. You'll use the same techniques you learned in Chapter 4 when you encounter Strengthen and Weaken questions in the Reading Comprehension section. This case briefly reviews those techniques. Parallel questions, on the other hand, require a slightly different approach in the Reading Comprehension section than in the Arguments section. This case introduces you to that approach.

STEP 1: **Read the Question and Identify Your Task**
Each passage will contain, on average, one Arguments-style question; the most common variation is a Parallel question. Following are some representative examples of how these questions will

be worded. The language in these questions closely tracks the language used to ask the same kinds of questions in the Arguments section.

WEAKEN

■ Which one of the following, if true, would most weaken the author's argument as expressed in the passage?

■ Which one of the following, if true, would most weaken the position that the passage attributes to _____?

■ Which one of the following, if true, most seriously undermines the author's claim that _____?

STRENGTHEN

■ Which one of the following, if true, would most strengthen the contention in the passage that _____?

■ Which one of the following, if true, would provide the most support for the _____ mentioned in lines X–Y?

PARALLEL

- As described in the passage, _____ is most closely analogous to which one of the following?
- Suppose that _____ [a new factual scenario of some kind]. Which one of the following responses to that situation would be most consistent with the views expressed at lines X–Y of the passage?
- As it is described in the passage, _____ would be best exemplified by which one of the following?
- Which one of the following is most analogous to _____?

STEP 2:   Go Back to the Passage and Find the Answer
By definition, these questions will give you new information to work with. So your task here is to find the pertinent information in the passage and then compare to it to the information in the question and answer choices. The nature of that comparison and how you'll go about making it will depend on what type of question you're working.

No matter what kind of comparison you're asked to make, you should start by reviewing the portion of the passage from which the claim is taken. The question itself usually doesn't recount all the relevant information from the passage. Use the same techniques you learned in Cases 4 and 5. Read the surrounding portions of the passage to get a sense of context, and use your summary of the passage to remind yourself of how the content of the question fits into the overall argument of the passage.

STEP 3:   Read Every Word of Every Answer Choice
Your approach to Strengthen questions will mirror the approach you learned in Case 5 of the Arguments chapter. The question will present a claim (some kind of a statement of opinion) that's taken from the passage. The claim will be phrased in general terms. The correct answer will provide a specific, concrete example that is consistent with that general claim. Common types of wrong answers include choices that weaken the claim, provide irrelevant information, make a general statement about a related topic, or offer support for a different but related claim.

Weaken questions, too, closely track their Arguments counterparts, which were discussed in Case 7 of Chapter 4. The question will present a broad-sweeping claim from the passage. The correct answer will either introduce new facts that are inconsistent with that claim or undermine the connection between the claim and any evidence offered in the passage to support it. Common types of wrong answers include choices that strengthen the claim, weaken a straw man, offer a generic background statement, or invite you to make an inference.

It's only when you encounter a Parallel question that you'll need to take a different approach. In the Arguments section, Parallel questions revolved around working with conditional statements. In the Reading Comprehension section, Parallel questions require you to take a general principle from the passage and apply it to a new situation. Sometimes the general principle will be explicitly stated in the passage. Other times you will have to extract or derive it by describing the relevant portion of the passage in general terms. Parallel questions typically involve (1) a particular person or type of person (or other actor) (2) taking an action, making a decision, or arriving at a judgment (3) for a specific reason or based on specific evidence.

Among the questions you worked in the Arguments section, it is Principle questions that are most similar to Parallel-style questions in the Reading Comprehension section. Finding the right answer to a Parallel question is a step-by-step process of breaking each answer choice down into pieces and matching each piece to the relevant portion of the passage. Work with the pieces of each answer choice one at a time. The actor, action, and reason all need to match. Here, as on Information Retrieval questions, you'll go back and forth between the passage and the answer choices multiple times.

Practice

Read and annotate the passage that appears on the following page, summarizing the passage in the blanks at the end of the passage. Sample annotations and a sample summary follow. Two practice questions appear on the page following the annotated passage.

Philosophers of science have traditionally held that science is unique as a form of inquiry because it is free from the social, moral, economic, and political values that play such an important role in
(5) structuring other knowledge-seeking enterprises. Science, on this view, is concerned only with discovering objectively verifiable factual knowledge of the world. Thus, the veracity of scientific knowledge does not depend on allegiance to a particular world-
(10) view or orthodoxy. It is this apolitical, empirical verifiability that underwrites the traditional notion that science produces a form of knowledge with a unique claim to objectivity.

Recently, this picture of science as a value-free
(15) enterprise has come under fire, with numerous critics plausibly suggesting that non-epistemic values play a constitutive role in scientific inquiry, just as in any other human undertaking. This recently emergent line of argument is distinct from the less ground-
(20) breaking claim that science is governed by epistemic values. Epistemic values are values that promote the acquisition and development of knowledge. "Medical drug experiments should be double-blind" is an epistemic value. Epistemic values are embraced
(25) because they enhance the efficacy of scientific experimentation; double-blind experiments get more accurate results. It does not seriously threaten science's claim to objectivity to admit that epistemic values such as accuracy, simplicity, breadth of scope,
(30) consistency, predictive power, and fruitfulness are constitutive of scientific practice.

Non-epistemic values are moral, social, political, cultural, and economic values. These values form the basis of any claim that a particular idea
(35) or act is "good" or "bad" for some reason other than that the idea or act will or will not facilitate scientific inquiry. The idea that non-epistemic values are constitutive of scientific practice has been a central focus of recent scholarship. Helen
(40) Longino has demonstrated that science chooses its areas of inquiry based on non-epistemic values. Government and corporate sources provide most of the funding that makes scientific research possible, and these sources choose the types of studies and
(45) experiments to which they will funnel money on the basis of economic and political values. Mark Risjord notes that moral and cultural values prohibit the use of certain research methodologies, such as experiments on nonconsenting human subjects,
(50) notwithstanding the possibility that using these methodologies would generate useful scientific knowledge.

Non-epistemic values even play a role in determining the content of some scientific theories.
(55) Anthropologists generally agree that humans evolved into the most sophisticated species of primate because they developed the ability to use tools. In the late 1970s, two competing theories sought to explain how and why humans had devel-
(60) oped this ability. One posited that men developed

the first tools to use while hunting. The other held that women developed tools to aid in meeting the greater nutritional burden that accompanies bearing children. The theories had equal scientific
(65) merit. Each could explain the contents of the fossil record and was consistent with basic principles of evolutionary theory. As a result, the fact that anthropologists uniformly chose to disregard the "woman the gatherer" theory and adopt the "man
(70) the hunter" theory as the dominant paradigm must have been driven by non-epistemic values—specifically, background assumptions about the proper roles and relative aptitudes of each gender.

SUMMARY

(1) _____
_____
_____
_____
_____

(2) _____
_____
_____
_____

(3) _____
_____
_____
_____

(4) _____
_____
_____
_____

MP Philosophers of science have traditionally held that science is unique as a form of inquiry because it is free from the social, moral, economic, and political values that play such an important role in
(5) structuring other knowledge-seeking enterprises. Science, on this view, is concerned only with discovering objectively verifiable factual knowledge of the world. Thus the veracity of scientific knowledge does not depend on allegiance to a particular world-
(10) view or orthodoxy. It is this apolitical empirical verifiability that underwrites the traditional notion that science produces a form of knowledge with a unique claim to objectivity.

Recently this picture of science as a value-free
(15) enterprise has come under fire, with numerous critics plausibly suggesting that non-epistemic values play a constitutive role in scientific inquiry, just as in any other human undertaking. This recently emergent
MP line of argument is distinct from the less ground-
(20) breaking claim that science is governed by epistemic values. Epistemic values are values that promote the acquisition and development of knowledge. "Medical drug experiments should be double-blind" is an epistemic value. Epistemic values are embraced
(25) because they enhance the efficacy of scientific experimentation; double blind experiments get more accurate results. It does not seriously threaten science's claim to objectivity to admit that epistemic values such as accuracy, simplicity, breadth of scope,
(30) consistency, predictive power, and fruitfulness are constitutive of scientific practice.

Non-epistemic values are moral, social, political, cultural, and economic values. These values form the basis of any claim that a particular idea
(35) or act is "good" or "bad" for some reason other than that the idea or act will or will not facilitate
MP scientific inquiry. The idea that non-epistemic values are constitutive of scientific practice has been a central focus of recent scholarship. Helen
(40) Longino has demonstrated that science chooses its areas of inquiry based on non-epistemic values. Government and corporate sources provide most of the funding that makes scientific research possible, and these sources choose the types of studies and
(45) experiments to which they will funnel money on the basis of economic and political values. Mark Risjord notes that moral and cultural values prohibit the use of certain research methodologies, such as experiments on nonconsenting human subjects,
(50) notwithstanding the possibility that using these methodologies would generate useful scientific knowledge.

MP Non-epistemic values even play a role in determining the content of some scientific theories.
(55) Anthropologists generally agree that humans evolved into the most sophisticated species of primate because they developed the ability to use tools. In the late 1970s, two competing theories sought to explain how and why humans had devel-
(60) oped this ability. One posited that men developed

the first tools to use while hunting. The other held that women developed tools to aid in meeting the greater nutritional burden that accompanies bearing children. The theories had equal scientific
(65) merit. Each could explain the contents of the fossil record and was consistent with basic principles of evolutionary theory. As a result, the fact that anthropologists uniformly chose to disregard the "woman the gatherer" theory and adopt the "man
(70) the hunter" theory as the dominant paradigm must have been driven by non-epistemic values—specifically, background assumptions about the proper roles and relative aptitudes of each gender.

SUMMARY

(1) *The traditional view is that science is objective because it is not influenced by social, moral, economic, and political values.*

(2) *The argument that non-epistemic values play a constitutive role in scientific inquiry is distinct from the argument that science is governed by epistemic values.*

(3) *The idea that non-epistemic values are constitutive of scientific practice has been a central focus of recent scholarship.*

(4) *Non-epistemic values even play a role in determining the content of some scientific theories.*

Practice Question 1

Which one of the following, if true, would most strengthen Longino's contention that science chooses its areas of inquiry based on non-epistemic values?

(A) A public university issues a grant to an engineer's proposed study of liquid coolants because the university believes the study has the potential to be quite lucrative.

(B) A biologist refuses to credit the results of a new experiment within her field until the results have been published in a peer-reviewed journal.

(C) An agrochemical company tests a new pesticide in the laboratory instead of in the field because the controlled environment of the lab produces more accurate results.

(D) A physicist executes a particular experiment because the experiment is simple and likely to produce fruitful results.

(E) A pharmaceutical company waits to test a new medication on human subjects until each subject has signed disclosure forms and legal releases.

Answer and Analysis. The correct answer is choice A. In lines 39–46, the passage discusses Helen Longino's contention that science chooses its areas of inquiry based on non-epistemic values. According to Longino, government and corporate entities decide which studies and experiments to fund based on economic and political values. Since this is a Strengthen question, we're looking for a concrete, fact-specific example of that general phenomenon. In choice A, a government entity (a public university) decides which study to fund (it issues a grant) based on economic values (high profit potential). Choice B is incorrect because the facts don't match; the biologist is not making a decision about what to study or which experiments to fund. Choices C and D are incorrect because the passage lists simplicity, fruitfulness, and accuracy as examples of epistemic values (lines 27–31), while Longino focuses on non-epistemic values. Choice E is an example of the argument attributed to Mark Risjord, that moral and cultural values prohibit the use of certain research methodologies (lines 46–52).

Practice Question 2

As it is presented in the passage, the approach to choosing between the two competing theories of evolution taken by 1970s anthropologists is most similar to the approach exemplified in which one of the following?

(A) A legislator refuses to participate in the debate over a bill because she is not sure which position her constituents would want her to support.

(B) A basketball coach decides which of two players will be in the starting lineup based on who has played better over the last five games.

(C) A hiring manager chooses between two equally well-qualified job candidates by hiring the candidate who grew up in the same hometown as the manager.

(D) A diner goes to a restaurant whose food is not as good as its competitors because he is friends with the chef.

(E) A reporter presents three story ideas to her editor so her editor can decide which one she should pursue.

Answer and Analysis. The passage states that in the late 1970s, anthropologists were confronted with two theories of evolution that "had equal scientific merit" (lines 64–65) and chose between them based on non-epistemic values (lines 67–73). So, the correct answer should feature a person who is confronted with two options that are equally good based on one criterion and chooses between these two options based on an unrelated criterion. Therefore, the correct answer is choice C: the hiring manager chooses between two equally well-qualified candidates by relying on a criterion (where they grew up) that is unrelated to the candidate's qualifications for the job.

Choice A is incorrect because the legislator does not actually make a choice between the two options she is confronted with. In choice B, the coach makes his selection based on relevant, intrinsic criteria. In choice D, the diner is not choosing between two equally good options; the restaurant's food is stated to be inferior to its competitors'. And in choice E, the reporter is dealing with three options, not two. She is also not the person who is making the ultimate decision about which story to write.

Case 9

The Comparative Reading Passage

This case addresses comparative reading. To refresh, of the four passages in the Reading Comprehension section, one will be a comparative reading passage. That means that instead of having to read one passage that's approximately 500 words in length, you'll have to read two passages that are approximately 250 words in length. The bulk of this case addresses the two most common question types that are unique to comparative reading passages. Before turning to that discussion, this case briefly explains how the majority of your approach to comparative reading will be largely unchanged.

You should use the same annotative-reading strategy here that you use elsewhere. The only major change you need to make to that strategy is to summarize each passage separately. The two comparative reading passages will always be about the same topic or two very closely related topics. They will have some similarities, and they will have some differences. Creating one summary for passage A and a second summary for passage B is the first step toward getting a handle on the precise nature of the relationship between the topics of the two passages.

On average, one or two of the questions following the comparative reading passage will focus exclusively on one passage. They might be Main Idea questions, Information Retrieval questions, or any of the other question types discussed in Cases 3 through 8. You should approach these single-passage questions the same way you approach them on the other three passages. The only notable difference is that you're likely to see at least one answer choice that is wrong because it is taken from the other passage. For example, if the question were to ask, "Which one of the following most accurately expresses the main point of passage A?," one of the answer choices would almost certainly present you with a picture-perfect statement of the main point of passage B. This one aspect aside, these questions are no different from the ones you work elsewhere in the section.

The four or five other questions about the comparative reading passage will require you to work with both of the passages. Although the passages will have both similarities and differences, the two-passage questions overwhelmingly focus on their similarities. That's not to say there's no chance that you'll see a question that asks you to identify a topic that was discussed in one passage but not the other. But on average, more than 80 percent of the two-passage questions will require you to identify areas where the two passages overlap and have topics in common. These questions come in two main types: two-passage Information Retrieval questions and Common Topic questions.

Two-Passage Information Retrieval Questions

As the name suggests, these questions are close cousins to the single-passage Information Retrieval questions that were covered in Case 5. Importantly, these are the most common type of two-passage question that are associated with comparative reading passages. Some typical phrasings of two-passage Information Retrieval questions include:

- Which one of the following is mentioned in both passages as _____?
- It is likely that both authors would agree with which one of the following statements about _____?
- Both passages explicitly refer to which one of the following?
- The author of passage A would be most likely to agree with which one of the following statements about _____ in passage B?
- It can be inferred from the passages that both authors would be most likely to accept which one of the followings statements about _____?

The best way to work two-passage Information Retrieval questions is to take it one passage at a time. The correct answer will be a statement, claim, or fact that appears in both passages. Start off by going back to passage A and using your annotations to locate its discussion of the relevant topic. Any answer choice that doesn't appear in passage A can be immediately eliminated. After you've limited the field to answer choices that appear in passage A, repeat this process in passage B with any choice that survived the first cut. Your basic process is unchanged from one-passage Information Retrieval questions; the only difference is that for a few choices you'll have to perform it twice.

In addition to the types of wrong answers that were detailed in Case 5, you're likely to see a couple of answer choices that are wrong because they restate a point that is discussed in one passage but not the other. The test writers often quote language from one of the passages to try to make these answer choices seem more appealing. As long as you go back to both passages on every answer choice, you should be able to avoid falling for this type of wrong answer.

Common Topic Questions

The other main variety of two-passage questions asks you to identify a big-picture topic that the two passages share in common. In essence, these are two-passage Main Idea questions. For example:

- Both passages are primarily concerned with addressing which one of the following questions?
- Which one of the following is true about the relationship between the two passages?
- The passages share which one of the following as their primary purpose?
- Both passages are primarily concerned with examining which one of the following topics?

On Common Topic questions, as on single-passage Main Idea questions, you'll lean heavily on the summaries of the two passages that you created as part of your annotative-reading process. There is a wide range of possible ways in which the two passages can relate to one another. If passage A advances a thesis, passage B might articulate a different thesis that addresses the same question, problem, or data set. Passage B might further elaborate on the thesis presented in passage A. Passage B might take a step back and advance a broader argument of which the thesis in passage A

is only one part. Or, passage B might argue that the results of an experiment call the validity of passage A's thesis into question without articulating a counter-thesis of its own. The summaries you create of the two passages will help you pinpoint the nature and scope of their relationship.

There are two main varieties of wrong answers to Common Topic questions. The first are choices that are too narrow in scope because they focus on a topic that was addressed by only one of the two passages. The second are choices that are too broad in scope. These choices will discuss material, make comparisons, or draw conclusions that are not supported by either passage. These wrong-answer types closely track the categories of wrong answers that were discussed in Case 3.

Practice

Read and annotate the comparative reading passage that appears on the following page, summarizing each short passage in the appropriate blanks at the end of the passage. Sample annotations and sample summaries follow. Two practice questions appear on the page following the annotated passage.

The following passages are adapted from critical essays on the Native American writer Samson Occom (1723–1792).

PASSAGE A

Scholars of early American literature have frequently described Occom's "Life Narrative" as giving voice to the conflicted identity and precarious subjec-
(5) tivity of a Christian Indian who found himself caught between two worlds. Most have attempted to understand the text by situating it within the Euro-American literary genre of autobiography. Elaine Elrod's 1998 essay on Occom exemplifies this common approach. Elrod places Occom's "Life
(10) Narrative" within the genre of early American "religious life writing" and claims that his "Life Narrative" is best understood with a comparativist methodology. Elrod compares Occom's writing to contemporary life writings from members of other
(15) marginalized groups, including women, African Americans, and other Native Americans. Elrod thus situates Occom's "Life Narrative" within both the generic categories of religious autobiography and early American autobiography.

(20) This widely shared understanding of "Life Narrative" as an autobiography has led scholars to explore the connections and parallels between "Life Narrative" and other autobiographical works, such as Ben Franklin's *Autobiography* or Olaudah Equiano's
(25) *An Interesting Narrative*. Reading the work as an "autobiography" (whether "religious," "spiritual," or "American") has led most scholars to conclude that "Life Narrative" is preoccupied with questions of identity and authenticity. This conclusion forms
(30) the basis of the widely accepted belief that Occom's central purpose in writing "Life Narrative" was to articulate his marginalized, hybrid identity as a Christian Indian.

PASSAGE B

It is precisely the impulse to include Occom's work within the American literary canon that allows his to be understood as a marginal voice. Many Native American scholars have rejected
(5) the notion that Occom's work can or should be fit into a Euro-American literary genre. Creek scholar Craig Womack points out that Native American literatures are first and foremost part of an older and even more foundational canon. When we read
(10) Occom's work as an autobiography, we lose the ability to read his work as arising out of the tradition of Native American literary production. Robert Allen Warrior (Osage) suggests that Occom's work is best understood not as literature but as a political
(15) document. In other words, our understanding of "Life Narrative" should be organized around Native

American intellectual traditions rather than the conventions and expectations of a Euro-American literary genre. Where most scholarship reads "Life
(20) Narrative" as primarily engaging with questions of authenticity and identity, Warrior believes that its core concern is to secure the benefits of missionary education and literacy to the Mohegan people.

Occom's work should be situated at the founda-
(25) tion of a tradition of Native American intellectual sovereignty. Occom is not "writing back" to the colonial power structure. He is working within an already centuries-old intellectual tradition. Occom was not confused cultural hybrid, caught
(30) between two worlds. "Life Narrative" is uniquely and powerfully Indian in its themes and concerns. Unfortunately, the majority of scholarship on Occom does not place him within a Native intellectual tradition. Nor does it look to Native scholars
(35) to understand his work.

SUMMARY: PASSAGE A

(1) _____
_____
_____
_____

(2) _____
_____
_____
_____

SUMMARY: PASSAGE B

(1) _____
_____
_____
_____

(2) _____
_____
_____
_____

The following passages are adapted from critical essays on the Native American writer Samson Occom (1723–1792).

PASSAGE A

Scholars of early American literature have frequently described Occom's "Life Narrative" as giving voice to the conflicted identity and precarious subjectivity of a Christian Indian who found himself
(5) caught between two worlds. Most have attempted

MP to understand the text by situating it within the Euro-American literary genre of autobiography. Elaine Elrod's 1998 essay on Occom exemplifies this common approach. Elrod places Occom's
(10) "Life Narrative" within the genre of early American "religious life writing" and claims that his "Life Narrative" is best understood with a comparativist methodology. Elrod compares Occom's writing to contemporary life writings from members of other
(15) marginalized groups, including women, African Americans, and other Native Americans. Elrod thus situates Occom's "Life Narrative" within both the generic categories of religious autobiography and early American autobiography.
(20)   This widely shared understanding of "Life Narrative" as an autobiography has led scholars to explore the connections and parallels between "Life Narrative" and other autobiographical works, such as Ben Franklin's *Autobiography* or Olaudah Equiano's
(25) *An Interesting Narrative.* Reading the work as an

MP "autobiography" (whether "religious," "spiritual," or "American") has led most scholars to conclude that "Life Narrative" is preoccupied with questions of identity and authenticity. This conclusion forms
(30) the basis of the widely accepted belief that Occom's central purpose in writing "Life Narrative" was to articulate his marginalized, hybrid identity as a Christian Indian.

PASSAGE B

It is precisely the impulse to include Occom's work within the American literary canon that allows his to be understood as a marginal voice.

MP Many Native American scholars have rejected
(5) the notion that Occom's work can or should be fit into a Euro-American literary genre. Creek scholar Craig Womack points out that Native American literatures are first and foremost part of an older and even more foundational canon. When we read
(10) Occom's work as an autobiography, we lose the ability to read his work as arising out of the tradition of Native American literary production. Robert Allen Warrior (Osage) suggests that Occom's work is best understood not as literature but as a political
(15) document. In other words, our understanding of "Life Narrative" should be organized around Native

American intellectual traditions rather than the conventions and expectations of a Euro-American literary genre. Where most scholarship reads "Life
(20) Narrative" as primarily engaging with questions of authenticity and identity, Warrior believes that its core concern is to secure the benefits of missionary education and literacy to the Mohegan people.

Occom's work should be situated at the founda-
(25) tion of a tradition of Native American intellectual *MP* sovereignty. Occom is not "writing back" to the colonial power structure. He is working within an already centuries-old intellectual tradition. Occom was not confused cultural hybrid, caught
(30) between two worlds. "Life Narrative" is uniquely and powerfully Indian in its themes and concerns. Unfortunately, the majority of scholarship on Occom does not place him within a Native intellectual tradition. Nor does it look to Native scholars
(35) to understand his work.

SUMMARY: PASSAGE A

(1) *The common approach to Occom's "Life Narrative" has been to situate it within the Euro-American literary genre of autobiography.*

(2) *This approach has led scholars to conclude that Occom was preoccupied with questions of identity and authenticity.*

SUMMARY: PASSAGE B

(1) *Many Native American scholars have rejected the notion that Occom's work can or should be fit into a Euro-American literary genre.*

(2) *Occom's work is best situated at the foundation of a tradition of Native American intellectual sovereignty.*

Practice Question 1

It is likely that both authors would agree with which one of the following statements?

(A) Occom's work should be situated at the foundation of a tradition of Native American intellectual sovereignty.

(B) Occom's "Life Narrative" is first and foremost an early American autobiography.

(C) Most religious autobiographies give voice to the conflicted identities and precarious subjectivities of their authors.

(D) Occom's work is best understood not as literature but as a political document.

(E) Most scholars believe that Occom's "Life Narrative" is primarily concerned with questions of identity and authenticity.

Answer and Analysis. The correct answer to this two-passage Information Retrieval question is choice E. Both passage A (lines 29–34) and passage B (lines 19–23) include a version of this statement about most of the scholarship on "Life Narrative." Choices A and D are incorrect because only passage B makes these claims. Nothing in passage A suggests that the author shares either of these views. Both choices B and C borrow language and terminology from passage A, but neither of these statements actually appears in passage A. Plus, neither of these statements is closely related to the topic of passage B, so there is no text-based reason to believe that the author of passage B would agree with them.

Practice Question 2

Which of the following most accurately describes a relationship between the two passages?

(A) Passage B criticizes a scholarly position that is introduced and described in passage A.

(B) Passage A anticipates and responds to the position articulated in passage B, while passage B does not comment on the position articulated in passage A.

(C) Passage B is concerned in its entirety with a scholarly problem that passage A discusses in support of a more general thesis.

(D) Passage A traces the historical origins of an intellectual movement while passage B explores its contemporary status.

(E) Passage A gives several interpretations of a piece of writing of which passage B gives only one interpretation.

Answer and Analysis. The correct answer is choice A. This is a Common Topic question. Passage A introduces and describes the common, majority approach to understanding "Life Narrative" of Samson Occom. Passage B uses the work of several Native American scholars to argue that the common interpretation of Occom's "Life Narrative" is flawed and advocate for a different way of reading the work. The sample summaries of the first paragraph of each passage highlight the nature of this relationship.

Both halves of choice B are incorrect. Passage A does not discuss or respond to the ideas presented by the Native American scholars discussed in passage B, while passage B directly criticizes the position articulated in passage A. Choice C is incorrect because both passages are concerned with the same narrow problem: how best to understand a single work by a single author. Choice D is incorrect for similar reasons. Both passage A and passage B are concerned with how to interpret a particular piece of writing, not the development of an intellectual movement. Finally, choice E is incorrect because passage A focuses exclusively on the autobiographical interpretation of Occom's "Life Narrative"; no additional interpretations are presented.

Case 10

Putting It All Together

Now that you have learned how to do annotative reading and practiced each type of reading comprehension question, try a passage with a full set of questions.

Culturally relevant science employs materials based on the culture and history of a minority or ethnic group to illustrate scientific principles and the methodology of science. Many people assume
(5) that Hispanic and American Indian cultures are either anti-scientific or, at best, a-scientific. Most of the material available on the development of science as well as the science curriculum taught in U.S. schools reflects this ethnocentric orientation.
(10) The scientific contributions of China, India, and the Islamic nations are usually minimized, and traditional native cultures are frequently depicted as permeated with superstition and magic rather than oriented toward science. Both the failure of
(15) Mexican American and American Indian children to take math and science and the small number of minority scientists can then be blamed on deficiencies in their native cultures, thus exculpating the schools and the larger society from
(20) any responsibility. The factors usually examined thus do not include failure of schools to provide a culturally relevant curriculum. To encourage Mexican American and American Indian children to develop an interest in science and to consider
(25) it as a career, a wider variety of examples from different cultures should be used in teaching science. The child can take pride in his or her culture's contribution to science and feel a greater degree of individual interest in science.
(30) There are many examples of culturally relevant materials developed from a rich, but essentially untapped resource and these can be used to enrich science education in many areas. For example, archeoastronomy has provided new information
(35) about how ancient civilizations perceived the heavens. Selected sites in the United States (the mounds of the Midwest, the medicine wheels of the Plains States, and Fajada Butte in Chaco Canyon, New Mexico) and in Mesoamerica (Teotihuacan,
(40) the Caracol at Chichen Itza, and Building J at Monte Alban) can be used for teaching astronomy, observational skills, scientific methodology, and basic mathematics.
Geology can be taught using the example of
(45) volcanic activity in Mesoamerica. This interesting phenomenon may be used to teach basic concepts in geology while studying culture and geography. The trade items of the Mesoamericans were of volcanic origin and/or of plate margin
(50) activity (obsidian, basalt, serpentine, and jade). The cenotes (sinkholes in limestone) can be used as a starting point for the study of the geological phenomenon of underground rivers and the composition of land in Yucatan.
(55) Agriculture, botany-ethnobotany, and nutrition come together to provide the basis for looking at the problem of world hunger. The different uses for and sources of many plants can be discussed with particular attention to the ways in which
(60) the Indian civilizations have contributed to food resources. Many of the practices used today in agriculture have their basis in Indian practices; in fact, we may be returning to a modified version of them today. The Aztecs developed chinampas
(65) (built-up platforms on shallow lakes, which were drought-proof and could produce several crops a year). Many of their foods show promise for relieving protein shortages and assisting in reducing the energy cost of agriculture. These
(70) new (for us) and unusual food plants can be used as a starting point to discuss the productivity and photosynthetic activity of food plants, their nutritional value, the food production policies of different countries, and what is being done about
(75) world hunger. Ethnobotany, the chemistry and uses of herbal medicines, can be used to teach students research strategies that involve literature searches, written reports, personal videotape interviews of friends and relatives, and the design
(80) of questionnaires to elicit appropriate information. At the higher grade levels, laboratory research techniques can be taught, such as chromatography of plant extracts showing students how chemical components of complicated mixtures can be
(85) isolated. These valuable research methods will be needed by the students in their future scientific studies or in their work in other disciplines. At the same time, students will be learning about the development of cultural medicine and its
(90) relevance to their own lives.
There are many ways in which science can be made culturally relevant. Archeoastronomy, agriculture, geology, botany, ethnobotany, and nutrition all can be taught from a perspective
(95) that celebrates the accomplishments of Mexican American and American Indian science and encourages exploration. Stimulated by such an approach, students who have typically not been attracted into scientific careers will perceive new
(100) possibilities.

1. The author references each of the following EXCEPT

   (A) underappreciation of Islamic scientific achievement
   (B) subterranean rivers in Yucatan
   (C) Mesoamerican manipulation of basalt
   (D) Mesoamerican sites used for the study of astronomy
   (E) the Aztecs' utilization of herbal medicine

2. The author's attitude toward Mexican American and American Indian children can best be described as

   (A) disapproval for their lack of interest in studying science
   (B) dismay at the way they have been treated by educational institutions
   (C) respectful regard for their scientific achievements
   (D) optimism that with the proper resources they can succeed in scientific careers
   (E) condemnation for their lack of knowledge about their own cultures

3. Which of the following does the author cite as a reason for Mexican American students' lack of interest in science?

   (A) their lack of resources with which to purchase materials and equipment
   (B) schools' attempts to suppress minority achievements
   (C) schools' lack of culturally relevant instruction
   (D) deficiencies in their native cultures
   (E) their lack of pride in their culture's achievements

4. The primary purpose of the passage is to

   (A) explain a recent development and propose action to remedy it
   (B) identify the reasons for a phenomenon and recommend measures to address it
   (C) persuade minority students to study science and pursue it as a career
   (D) describe the potential consequences of implementing a new policy
   (E) argue that science classes should be taught in a culturally relevant way to Mexican American students

5. The main function of the third paragraph is to

   (A) present another example of how science can be taught in a culturally relevant way
   (B) show that geology lends itself better to culturally relevant teaching methods than does biology
   (C) instruct teachers on how to teach geology without excluding minority contributions to the field
   (D) introduce an area of additional concern not mentioned earlier
   (E) argue that Mexican American and American Indian students can perform as well as other students in geology classes

6. Based on the information in the passage, which of the following methods would the author consider a culturally relevant way of teaching?

   (A) a science teacher has the class perform a lab experiment about color creation
   (B) the school principal creates a separate science class for minority students
   (C) a math teacher has students learn the Mayan mathematical system in order to study place value notation
   (D) an art teacher has students paint each other's portraits
   (E) an English teacher requires her students to read a book about Native American magic

7. Which of the following, if true, would most strengthen the author's argument in the last sentence of the passage?

   (A) In Mexico and Central America, the percentage of Hispanic students who choose a career in science is approximately the same as in the United States.
   (B) Most schools in the United States include material relevant to minority cultures in the curriculum of their art and music classes.
   (C) In the United States, the percentage of minority students studying to become laboratory technicians has been increasing for the past year.
   (D) Chinampa farming techniques are being used with great success in the arid regions of New Mexico.
   (E) After a university in Baltimore began including Native American medicinal remedies in its pharmacology courses, the percentage of Native American students who applied to graduate programs in pharmacology more than doubled.

Answers and Analysis

1. Answer: **E**. This is an Information Retrieval question. The author mentions each of the answers except for E. While herbal medicine is mentioned, the passage does not discuss Aztec use of herbal medicines. Only Aztec use of agriculture is specifically discussed. **The correct choice is answer E.**

2. Answer: **D**. This is a Tone question. The author provides ways for schools to teach science in a culturally aware fashion in order to gain minority students' interest. The last line of the passage indicates that the author hopes to attract minority student to scientific careers. **The correct choice is answer D.**

3. Answer: **C**. This is an Information Retrieval question. The author argues that students do not take science classes because the schools do not offer a "culturally relevant curriculum." **The correct choice is answer C.**

4. Answer: **E**. This is a version of a Main Idea question: primary purpose. The purpose of the passage is to argue that science classes should be taught in a culturally relevant way. There is no information to suggest that this is a recent development. Answer C is not the primary purpose, and answers B and D are too narrow. **The correct choice is answer E.**

5. Answer: **A**. This is a version of a Main Idea question on a smaller scale; this question asks only about the third paragraph. The second, third, and fourth paragraphs each describe areas of science that can be taught in a culturally relevant manner. The third paragraph suggests ways to teach geology, but does not compare it to other areas or mandate that teachers should use these particular methods.

Answer C is close, but the paragraph focuses on diversification of location rather than contributions to the field. **The correct choice is answer A.**

6. Answer: **C**. This is an Inference question. Answer C suggests a culturally relevant way to involve all students in the study of mathematics. Answers A and D would not be culturally relevant. Answer B would be against the author's purpose, as would answer E since the author criticizes the characterization of native cultures as being about superstition and magic. **The correct choice is answer C.**

7. Answer: **E**. This is an Arguments-style question as well as a Line ID question. The question refers you to the argument made in the last sentence of the passage. The author argues there that expanding culturally relevant curriculum would attract more students to scientific professions. You need an answer that strengthens that view. Answer A requires you to assume that culturally relevant curriculum is taught in Mexico and Central America and, in any case, would weaken the argument. Answer B is out of scope since the passage is about expanding science curriculum. Answer C would seem to strengthen the argument, but it does not tie the trend to culturally relevant school curriculum. Keep it, but read all the choices to find something better. Answer D is out of scope for this question, though it strengthens another argument made by the author earlier in the passage. Answer E would strengthen the argument, and the question asks for the answer that *most strengthens*. **The correct choice is answer E.**

Case 11

Section-Wide Strategy

The core of your section-wide Reading Comprehension strategy is the same as it was in the Logic Games section: work smarter, not faster. The primary purpose of this case is to give you a set of tools you can use to rank the passages in order of difficulty so that you can skip the hardest passage and go straight to work on the easier passages first. By doing so, you'll concentrate your efforts on the portion of the test where they're most likely to pay off with correct answers.

On Skipping the Hardest Passage

The key to success on Reading Comprehension is to go back to the passage and find the answer to every question. You can either correctly apply the method you've learned in this chapter to the passages and questions that will provide the biggest payoff, or you can rush your way through all four passages in the order they are presented, cutting corners, relying on your recall, and making hurried guesses. In this way, the Reading Comprehension section is similar to the Logic Games section. You're better off ranking the passages by order of difficulty so you can tailor your attack of the section as a whole. Consider: the average Reading Comprehension section has 27 questions. Suppose you annotate the three easier passages and work all 21 questions associated with those passages in 33 minutes. Because you have the time to be careful and thorough, your accuracy rate on those questions is 90 percent. With your remaining time, you work the Line ID question from the final passage. If you still have time, you can carefully read the final passage and guess on the other five questions. In that scenario, you'll answer most of the 27 questions in the section correctly.

Now let's say you read all four passages in the order in which they appear, and attempt to answer all 27 questions. If your accuracy rate on the fourth passage dips down to 50 percent, you're looking at a total of 19 questions answered correctly.

The bottom line is simple: accuracy trumps speed. Below is a five-step section-wide strategy that is designed to give you the time you need to execute a game plan that will maximize the number of questions you answer correctly:

1. **Rank the passages in order of difficulty.** The factors you can rely on to distinguish easier passages from harder passages are discussed in greater detail in the next section.

2. **Read and work the two easiest passages first.** In most Reading Comprehension sections, there is usually a pair of easier passages and a pair of more difficult passages. For ordering purposes, all that matters is for you to be able to identify the two easier passages. As long as you're working the two easiest passages first, the particular order in which you work them isn't important. Make sure you work the two easiest passages at a sustainable pace. If you're planning to work all four passages, you have about three minutes to read each passage, and you can spend about 45 seconds on each question. If you're going to work three passages, you have about four minutes to read each passage and about one minute per question. But keep in mind that those figures are just averages. You should be able to read and annotate the two easiest passages at a slightly faster clip. Similarly, certain question types will take more or less time to work. Line ID questions and Main Idea questions tend to take less time than average, while Arguments-style questions tend to take awhile. Information Retrieval questions are unpredictable. Some you'll be able to work very quickly; others can be quite time-consuming. Be sure you're taking advantage of the opportunity to pick up a little extra time on the easier passages and questions.

3. **From the two remaining passages, read and work the passage that plays to your strengths.** The criteria you should use to select which of the more difficult passages to work are also discussed in greater detail in the next section.

4. **Work the Line ID question(s) from the most difficult passage.** If you have a spare minute or two, apply the technique you learned in Case 4 to any Line ID questions about the passage you're skipping: read the sentence directly before the line reference, the sentence that contains the information cited, and the sentence directly after the line reference. This will enable you to answer Line ID questions with a pretty high rate of accuracy even without having read the rest of the passage. In this regard, Line ID questions are similar to Complete and Accurate List questions on the Games section.

5. **Work the final passage, but only if you have time.** Don't hurry through the easier passages and questions to get here. Hurrying makes you more likely to miss the questions about the easier passages, and the time you invest working the questions about the hardest passage is less likely to yield correct answers. Remember to bubble in answers to all of the questions; there's a chance you can get a point for guessing.

Ranking the Passages by Difficulty

1. Any Passage That Only Has Five Questions Is an Easier One. This simple metric is one of the most reliable ways to determine a Reading Comprehension passage's level of difficulty. There can be as many as eight and as few as five questions about any given passage. When a passage has the bare minimum of five questions, it is invariably one of the two easier passages on the section. If you come across a five-question passage on test day, it should definitely be one of the first two passages you work. The downside, of course, is that you only get to answer five questions, so you don't have quite as many opportunities to earn points. But this is still a good use of your time, as your accuracy rate is likely to be even higher than normal.

2. Look at the Amount of Ink on the Page. This might sound imprecise, but it works. Looking at how much ink is on the page is a quick and very effective way to get a rough-and-ready sense of how difficult a passage will be. Open up a sample LSAT and flip through the Reading Comprehension section. Look at the bottom portion of the right-hand page. On some of the passages, it's totally covered by text. But on others, there's a big empty block of white space. Those latter passages are likely to be easier than the former. In other words, shorter passages (less ink) are easier to work than long ones (more ink). Why? Think about the source of all that extra text. The more text there is on the page, the longer and more complicated the question stems, and the denser and more intricate the answer choices. The shorter the questions, the higher chance it's one of the easier two passages.

3. Preview the Passage. If neither of the first two indicators points you toward a workable passage, you'll have to preview the passage's content. Read the first two or three sentences of the first paragraph of the passage. Pay attention to the language that's being used. Is it clear, concrete, and straightforward, or is it jargon-laden, abstract, and dense? Do you see technical terms or terms of art that you're unfamiliar with? Also make note of the sentence structure. Short and direct sentences are easy to read. Convoluted sentences that span six lines tend to be harder to digest.

Notice that "topic" or "subject matter" is not one of the things you should be focused on as you preview the passage. It's a mistake to select or reject passages based on which of the four general topic areas they fall under. The test writers are very careful to ensure that there is no consistent correlation between topic and difficulty. The passages are designed to be background-neutral. Even if you were an English major and haven't taken a science class since high school, the science passage could be the easiest of the four. If you categorically refuse to work any passages from one of the four general topic areas, you run the risk of cutting yourself off from a prime opportunity to score points.

4. Consider the Mix of Question Types. If you're still having trouble determining which passages will be easier or harder, quickly scan the questions. Look for difficult or time-consuming question types. As a general rule, questions with long answer choices (three lines each) tend to be harder than questions with one-line answer choices. And if a passage has a lot of the Arguments-style questions discussed in Case 8 (especially Parallel questions that begin with "Suppose" and require you to analyze a lengthy factual scenario), that's a pretty good sign that it's one of the two more difficult passages in the section.

When it comes to the two harder passages, you're more likely to rely on the mix of question types to determine which of the two you want to work first. It's here that the missed-question log you've been keeping as you prep can come in handy. If there is a particular question type that you frequently miss, even after a good bit of practice, take note. If you see a passage that features two or three such questions, it makes sense to leave that passage for last.

Ranking the passages in the Reading Comprehension section in order of difficulty is admittedly an inexact science. Different test takers will have different opinions about how difficult each passage is, and the fact that you're working under time pressure means you'll have to make some snap judgments, just as you did in the Logic Games section. But if you apply these four criteria each time you work a practice section, by the time test day rolls around you should be able to come up with a reliable estimate of each passage's difficulty in relatively short order.

CHAPTER 6

The LSAT Writing Sample

The writing sample is not scored. No one from the LSAC will read your essay. The LSAC simply scans what you've written and sends a copy of it to each law school that you apply to. The law schools are free to do with it whatever they see fit.

The fact that the writing sample is not scored has two implications for you. First, studying for the writing sample will not help you get the highest score you can on the LSAT. Thus, you don't need to read this chapter any sooner than one or two weeks before you take the test. As test day draws near, read through this chapter and then work two or three practice writing samples so that you get a feel for what they look like and some experience applying the techniques in this chapter. That's all you need to do. The overwhelming majority of your preparation time should be spent on the other three sections.

Second, to succeed on this section, all you have to do is write a decent essay. It doesn't have to be perfect or even great. If an admissions officer is on the fence about your application, or if you are at the top of a short list, he or she might read your essay looking for red flags—your grammar, syntax, or spelling are atrocious, your essay is poorly organized, you didn't follow the instructions of the section (these are all warning signs that you're likely to struggle academically), or you have a bad attitude. As long as you write a competent essay that doesn't trigger any alarm bells, you've done your job. And you won't reap any additional rewards by going above and beyond that modest target.

With those two caveats in mind, the two cases in this chapter will teach you how to approach the writing sample. Case 1 introduces the five-paragraph structure you should use to write your essay. Every writing sample prompt follows the same basic format. As a result, no matter what the specific content of your prompt is, you'll be able to write an effective response to it using the five-paragraph structure. Case 1 also discusses the importance of prewriting and lays out a systematic process you can use to plan and organize the content of your essay. Case 2 discusses eight general principles of good writing that are particularly pertinent to the writing sample. Learning and adhering to these principles will help you produce a polished, reader-friendly essay.

Case 1

The Five-Paragraph Model

This case introduces the five-paragraph structure you should use to write your writing sample. It also introduces a two-stage prewriting process that you should use to plan and organize your five-paragraph essay. The prewriting process and five-paragraph essay structure you'll learn in this case will help ensure that your writing sample demonstrates clarity and good organization—two qualities that are very important to the law school admissions officers who might read your essay. Admittedly, the five-paragraph structure is a little bit mechanical and formulaic. But remember, your goal is to write an essay that is free of red flags. If you follow the advice in this case, you can rest assured that your writing sample will be good enough to keep you in the running for admission to any law school you apply to.

The Format of the Writing Sample

The writing sample is an exercise in priority setting and comparative decision making. The prompt will present you with two options and ask you to select whichever one of them better accomplishes two stated goals (we'll call them goal A and goal B). You'll then be presented with a set of facts that explain how well each option accomplishes each goal. Generally speaking, the facts will demonstrate that one option will successfully accomplish goal A but fail to accomplish goal B, and vice versa. Unlike the material in the other sections, which is dense and academic, the writing sample prompts are simple and straightforward. They involve regular people making everyday decisions: parents deciding where to send their child to preschool, a small business deciding how to expand, a vacationer deciding how to plan a trip, and so forth.

Your task is to write a persuasive essay that argues in favor of one option over the other option. There is no right answer. One option is not inherently superior to the other. In fact, the prompts are designed so that either option is a defensible choice. The quality of your answer depends not on which option you select, but rather on how well you defend the option you've selected and criticize the option you've rejected—essential skills that all future lawyers need.

The persuasive quality of any piece of writing is a function of its thoroughness and its organization. Using the following five-paragraph structure will enable you to write an essay that discusses all of the factual material from the prompt in a well-organized and logical manner:

Paragraph 1: Introduction
Paragraph 2: Discuss the goal that your option satisfies.
Paragraph 3: Discuss the goal that your option does not satisfy.
Paragraph 4: Explain why the goal that your option satisfies is the more important of the two.
Paragraph 5: Conclusion

This five-paragraph structure reflects the distinctive style of writing that is favored by the legal profession. Legal writing is relentlessly functional. Lawyers expect any piece of writing they read—be it a brief, a memo, or a letter—to (1) tell them what it's going to say; (2) say it; and (3) tell them what it just said. It might feel repetitive at first, but using it will make your writing focused, easy to follow, and persuasive. This is what good writing looks like to a lawyer. This is the style of writing that law school admissions officers and the professors on law school admissions committees are accustomed to seeing. Therefore, it's the style of writing you should adopt in your writing sample. The five-paragraph structure embodies this style.

The Two Stages of Prewriting

Think before you write. It's impossible to write a clear and organized essay unless you begin writing with an idea of what you want to say and how you want to say it. That requires upfront planning. You're given 35 minutes to work on the writing sample. You should spend roughly the first 10 minutes of your time doing prewriting. About two-thirds of the page on which the writing sample prompt appears will be blank and designated as scratch paper. Use that space to plan your essay.

The prewriting process has two separate stages: organizing and brainstorming. You already know the five-paragraph structure you'll use to write your essay, so a formal outline isn't necessary. We'll discuss organizing and brainstorming in turn, using the following sample prompt to illustrate the process:

Ron Bryant is about to move into a new apartment. He will either move into a high-rise building or a gated community. He is equally satisfied with the rent price, the amount of space, and the floor plan at both apartments. Using the facts below, write an essay in which you argue for one apartment over the other based on the following two criteria:

- Ron wants an apartment that is a short, convenient drive to his job.
- Ron wants an apartment in a neighborhood where he can maximize the amount of leisure time he spends outdoors.

The high-rise apartment is located close to a highway on which Ron can drive to his job. With no traffic, the drive takes 10 minutes, but the highway suffers from heavy traffic congestion an average of two days a week. There is an entrance to a bike trail five blocks from the high-rise building. Ron does not own a bicycle. The high-rise building is less than a block away from a public pool, which is open from May through September. The neighborhood is home to many cafés, bars, and coffee shops, most of which have outdoor patios.

The apartment in the gated community is located along a major thoroughfare that runs directly to Ron's job. With no traffic, the drive takes 20 minutes, but there is moderate traffic congestion along the route every day of the week. An outdoor walking/jogging trail runs around the perimeter of the property on which the gated community is located. The city's largest park is two blocks from the apartment. There is a farmer's market in the parking lot of a nearby shopping mall that is open for business once a week.

The first stage of prewriting is organizing. You'll take the facts from the prompt and organize them into lists according to the option they apply to and the goal they pertain to. The headings at the top of the lists will be the two options. Then, under each heading, you'll make a separate list for each of the goals:

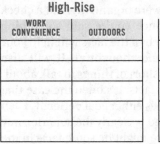

High-Rise

WORK CONVENIENCE	OUTDOORS

Gated Community

WORK CONVENIENCE	OUTDOORS

Next, you'll take each fact from the prompt and put it into the appropriate column. This is an initial determination of relevancy. Each fact that the test writers include in the prompt will pertain to one of the two goals. Sorting out the facts will help you determine how they pertain to those goals. There's no need to rewrite the facts verbatim; doing so would consume too much time and space. Instead, just jot down summaries or shorthand that convey the gist of what's in the prompt. Continuing with the sample prompt, your list now looks like this:

High-Rise

WORK CONVENIENCE	OUTDOORS
close to highway	bike trail 5 blocks
10 min. no traffic	doesn't own bike
heavy traffic 2x/week	1 block from pool
	pool open May–Sept.
	outdoor patios

Gated Community

WORK CONVENIENCE	OUTDOORS
close to major road	walking trail at apt.
20 min. no traffic	big park 2 blocks away
some traffic 7x/week	weekly farmers market

Finally, determine whether each fact is positive or negative when viewed in light of the goal that it's relevant to. Make a note of your determination by drawing a plus sign or a minus sign in the margin next to each item on your lists. This should help you start to get a sense of which option you think is stronger. Once you've made these notations, you've completed the organizing stage of your prewriting process. You should be able to complete this stage in less than five minutes.

High-Rise

WORK CONVENIENCE	OUTDOORS
+ close to highway	+ bike trail 5 blocks
+ 10 min. no traffic	– doesn't own bike
– heavy traffic 2x/week	+ 1 block from pool
	– pool open May–Sept.
	+ outdoor patios

Gated Community

WORK CONVENIENCE	OUTDOORS
+ close to major road	+ walking trail at apt.
– 20 min. no traffic	+ big park 2 blocks away
– some traffic 7x/week	+ weekly farmers market

Next up is the brainstorming stage. Start out by figuring out how the two options relate to each other. As noted above, it's typically the case that one option does a better job of accomplishing goal A, and the other option does a better job of accomplishing goal B. In our sample prompt, the high-rise apartment probably does a better job of being convenient to work; the commute time is half as long, and on most days there is no traffic. But the gated-community apartment has more options for outdoor activities.

Once you know which goal each option accomplishes, your task is to decide which option you're going to advocate in your essay. The fourth paragraph in your five-paragraph essay will be dedicated to explaining why one goal is more important than the other. It's a sensible, straightforward way to break the tie between the two options. As you're brainstorming, come up with two or three reasons why one goal is more important than the other goal.

It doesn't matter which goal you pick; all that matters is that you come up with compelling arguments defending your choice. And you're not limited by the content of the prompt. You can be creative in coming up with reasons to prioritize one goal over the other. Continuing with the sample prompt, you might argue that convenience to work is more important because a longer commute would cut into the time that Ron could spend outdoors or because he can only spend time outdoors during certain times of the year. Conversely, you might argue that it's more important that he have lots of options for being outdoors because being outside is what makes him the happiest or because he won't mind the longer commute if he's able to regularly exercise outdoors. You're free to make whatever arguments you want as long as they are sensible and plausible.

Once you've decided which option you're going to defend, you'll turn to thinking of ways to play up its strengths and downplay its weaknesses. Review the list you made of the facts that are relevant to your chosen option's ability to satisfy each of the goals. Try to think of reasons why any positive fact is especially important and why any negative fact is insignificant or unimportant. When you're done, repeat the process with the other option, only this time try to amplify the importance of the negative facts and minimize the importance of the positive facts. The ideas you come up with here will be incorporated into the second and third paragraphs of your essay. Once you've completed this process, you're ready to begin writing.

Writing the Five-Paragraph Essay

You'll recall from the introduction to this case that the five-paragraph structure you'll use to write your essay looks like this:

> Paragraph 1: Introduction
> Paragraph 2: Discuss the goal your option satisfies.
> Paragraph 3: Discuss the goal your option does not satisfy.
> Paragraph 4: Explain why the goal that your option satisfies is the more important of the two.
> Paragraph 5: Conclusion

As you begin writing, be cognizant of the fact that you have a limited amount of space to write in. There are 55 lines on the two pages that make up the writing area. Most people write between 8 and 10 words per line. That gives you about 450 to 550 words to work with. You can't afford to be verbose. You need to write five full paragraphs, so budget your space accordingly. The introduction and the conclusion should be a little bit shorter: 3 to 4 sentences each for a total of about 8 lines. The three body paragraphs should be a little longer: 4 to 5 sentences each for a total of about 13 lines. It's especially important to pay attention to the space constraints in the early stages of your essay. You'll dig yourself a hole that's very difficult to climb out of if your first paragraph is 20 lines long.

Your introductory paragraph should tell the reader everything you're about to say. The first sentence of the introductory paragraph should state your ultimate conclusion. Don't begin with a restatement of the problem or issue; take a stance right out of the gate. The second sentence should state that your option accomplishes goal A, for example, while the other option does not. The third sentence should minimize both the extent to which your option does not accomplish goal B and also the extent to which the other option does. The final sentence should briefly explain why goal A is more important. If the reader were to stop reading after that first paragraph, he or she should have a handle on the core arguments of your essay.

The second paragraph will focus on the goal that your option successfully accomplishes. You need to make two separate kinds of arguments here. First, you want to emphasize the strengths of your option vis-à-vis this goal. Second, you want to emphasize the weaknesses of the other option vis-à-vis this goal. As you do so, don't merely recite the facts as they're listed in the prompt. Interpret those facts. Explain why they are significant. Extrapolate from them to draw your own conclusions.

Try to say something about all of the facts in the prompt. As you write, refer to the list of relevant facts that you made while you were organizing. Put a check mark next to each fact once you've said something about it. Talking about each of the facts will help your essay appear thorough and thoughtful. It will also ensure that you don't run short of things to talk about.

Deal honestly with bad facts. It's often the case that neither option accomplishes either goal perfectly. Even if the option you've selected is clearly the superior way to accomplish goal A, there might be some facts in the prompt that suggest that your option will only partially accomplish goal A. If that's the case, don't ignore these bad facts. Acknowledge them, then explain them away by offering reasons to downplay their significance. A good way to accomplish this is by writing sentences that begin, "Even if" or "Even though."

The third paragraph will focus on the goal that your option does not accomplish as effectively as the option that you've rejected. Your task here is the mirror image of what it was in the second paragraph. You want to minimize the weaknesses of your option as it relates to this goal, and you want to minimize the strengths of the other option. To be clear: do not minimize the importance of the other, less-important goal in the third paragraph. Save that for paragraph four. In paragraph three, focus on why your option might be better at accomplishing this goal than it first seems and why the other option is actually not as great as it's made out to be.

The purpose of the fourth paragraph is to explain why the goal that your option satisfies is the more important of the two goals. You should offer two or three reasons to support this determination. You might simply argue that goal A is more important than goal B, period. You might make an argument about comparative effectiveness, that is, that your option will do a better job of accomplishing goal A than the other option will do of accomplishing goal B. Or you might argue that accomplishing goal A in the short run will actually make it easier to accomplish goal B in the long run. There are other possibilities, too. You're free to use any argument you can think of that provides a plausible reason for prioritizing the goals the way you did.

The first two words of your final paragraph should be, "In conclusion." Substantively, this paragraph will be very similar to your first paragraph. Remember, good legal writing tells a reader what it's about to say, says it, and then tells the reader what it just said. The final paragraph will once again state which option you're defending, emphasize how effectively that option accomplishes one goal, downplay the extent to which it fails to accomplish the other goal, and explain why the first goal is more important than the second. Don't reproduce your introductory paragraph verbatim. Vary your word choice and your sentence structure. But content-wise, there should be nothing in the last paragraph that hasn't appeared at an earlier point in the essay.

Sample Essays

Following are two sample responses to the example writing sample prompt about Ron Bryant's new apartment that was introduced earlier in this case. The first essay selects the high-rise apartment option. The second essay selects the option of the apartment in a gated community. You can refer to these essays as you practice writing essays on different topics. As these sample essays illustrate, the option you choose to defend is less important than the manner in which you defend it.

SAMPLE ESSAY 1

Ron should move into the high-rise apartment. The high-rise apartment is substantially more convenient to his job and will minimize his commute time. Although the apartment in the gated community would probably allow him to

spend more time outdoors, there are several good outdoor-entertainment options near the high-rise. And it is more important that Ron's apartment be in a convenient location, since a long commute would drastically reduce the amount of leisure time he has to spend outdoors.

The high-rise apartment is substantially more convenient to Ron's job than the apartment in the gated community. With no traffic, his commute will take half as long as it would from the other apartment. He'll save that time twice a day: going to and coming from work. Assuming a five-day workweek, that means he saves more than an hour and a half of commute time per week. It is true that the highway that runs near the high-rise apartment has two days of heavy traffic each week. But even if the traffic were so bad that it doubled his commute time to 20 minutes, the high-rise is still more convenient. Every day there is moderate traffic congestion on the major thoroughfare outside the gated community, which would add a few minutes to Ron's commute time. It is more convenient to have six 10-minute commutes plus four 20-minute commutes than it is to have ten commutes of 25 or 30 minutes.

The high-rise apartment also would allow Ron to spend a lot of leisure time outdoors. While the public pool is only open five months a year, during those months it provides Ron with an outdoor-entertainment option that is unique among all the available alternatives. The neighborhood bars, cafés, and coffee shops would allow Ron to socialize outdoors with his friends. And the bike trail would allow Ron to broaden his horizons by taking up a new hobby. At the gated community, there is an outdoor jogging trail, but he can also walk or jog in the public park. And the farmer's market is only available one day a week. There is no guarantee Ron's schedule will allow him to regularly attend.

Finding an apartment that is convenient to work is the more important of Ron's two priorities. If he moved into the apartment at the gated community, Ron would spend at least an extra hour and a half—probably more—commuting each week. That time would directly trade off with time he might otherwise spend outdoors. Plus, he has some good outdoor-entertainment options at the high-rise, while there is nothing he can do to make the gated-community apartment more convenient to his job. The relative difference in convenience is much greater than the relative difference in his ability to spend time outdoors.

In conclusion, the high-rise apartment is the better choice for Ron. He will spend substantially less time commuting to work if he moves into the high-rise, and he will have a solid range of outdoor entertainment options. In the end, it makes sense for him to make convenience to his job the higher of his two priorities.

SAMPLE ESSAY 2

Ron should move into the apartment in the gated community. The gated-community apartment will allow Ron to spend substantially more leisure time outdoors. Although the high-rise apartment's location is slightly more convenient, his commute time will be more consistent at the gated-community apartment. And it is more important for Ron to maximize the amount of leisure time he spends outdoors, since doing so will improve his outlook and demeanor.

The apartment in the gated community gives Ron vastly superior outdoor-entertainment options. The convenience of the walking/jogging trail being located on the premises will allow Ron to make use of it every day. At the nearby park, Ron can have picnics or barbecues with his friends and attend community events. Shopping at the farmer's market will allow him to spend less time indoors at a grocery store. At the high-rise, the bike trail is of no use to Ron without a bike, and the pool is of no use to him seven months a year. Patronizing commercial patios is expensive and does not allow Ron to exercise outdoors.

Although Ron's commute time might be longer from the gated community than from the high-rise, his schedule would be more regular and predictable. The level of traffic congestion on the road outside the apartment is the same every day. Ron could quickly figure out how much time the traffic would add to his commute and budget accordingly. By contrast, the level of congestion on the highway is unpredictable. Heavy congestion on a route that normally takes 10 minutes to travel at highway speeds could cause Ron's commute time to be as high 30 minutes. But on any given day, Ron will not know in advance how long his commute will take. This unpredictability is a substantial inconvenience. It will make it difficult for him to ensure he arrives at work on time, and it will put a damper on his after-work social calendar.

Finding an apartment that will allow him to maximize the amount of leisure time he spends outdoors is the more important of Ron's two priorities. Being outside is Ron's favorite pastime. A few extra minutes in the car each day will not feel like a steep price to pay for the ability to regularly socialize and exercise outdoors. Plus, the unpredictability of Ron's commute to and from the high-rise would undermine his ability to spend time outdoors. For example, it would be more difficult for Ron to join an after-work softball league if he could not arrive to practice on time. By contrast, Ron's regular, predictable commute to and from the gated-community apartment would not limit his outdoor-entertainment options.

In conclusion, the apartment at the gated community is the better choice for Ron. He will be able to spend more leisure time outdoors doing a wider variety of activities, and his commute, even if slightly longer, will be more predictable. Given that spending leisure time outdoors is Ron's favorite activity, it makes sense for him to make his ability to do so a higher priority than convenience to his job.

Case 2

Eight Principles of Good Writing

This case discusses eight general principles of good writing that are particularly important to adhere to on the Writing Sample section. The Writing Sample section is designed to allow law schools to evaluate the organization, clarity, language usage, quality of reasoning, and mechanics of your writing. The arguments that you think up during your prewriting process will improve the quality of your reasoning. The five-paragraph structure will ensure that your essay is well organized. The principles discussed in this case focus on clarity, language usage, and mechanics. They also highlight some LSAT-specific strategies you can use to make sure that your essay does not raise any red flags when it's reviewed by a law school admissions officer.

1. Try to Fill Every Line

The most surefire way to go astray on the writing sample is to fail to respond to the prompt. Obviously that means that you'll get yourself in trouble if you write an answer that is frivolous or off-topic. But it also means that you put yourself at risk if you write a topical answer that, for whatever reason, makes it seem as though you weren't giving your full effort. The easiest way to minimize this risk is to write an answer that fills up every line in your answer booklet. An admissions officer is much less likely to think that your answer is incomplete or half-hearted if you've used up all the space that you were given to write in.

2. Write Legibly and Within the Lines

If an admissions officer is unable to read what you've written, that will count against you. If you know you have messy handwriting, make a conscious effort to slow down and write neatly. This is especially important if you're a heavy computer user who's out of practice when it comes to writing by hand. Also be sure to keep your writing within the designated area on the page (the boxed-in lines). The LSAC does not scan a copy of the margins, so anything that's written there will not be transmitted to the law schools that receive your application.

3. Be Decisive and Consistent

While it does not matter which option you choose, it matters a great deal that you clearly choose one of the options and stick to it throughout your essay. Because the quality of your reasoning is a critical component of your essay, you will hurt yourself if you flip-flop in your choice or use wishy-washy language to defend it. Since the prompts are carefully designed to allow you to write a good essay defending either option, it can be tempting to try to straddle the fence by saying something along the lines of, "Well, option 1 is really good, but option 2 has some good things going for it too." If you write an essay like that, all you're doing is demonstrating that you can't follow directions. That's not the message you want to send to the law schools you're applying to. Resist the urge to hedge your bets. Pick one option and stick to it.

4. Use Proper Mechanics

Mechanics are the formal rules of writing. Make sure that your answer abides by those rules. For example, make sure your essay has multiple paragraphs. This is implicit in Case 1's recommended five-paragraph structure, but it's important enough to merit a separate mention. If there's nothing on the page but a big, uninterrupted block of text, that will be a bright red flag to any reader. In addition, you should write in complete sentences. Avoid sentence fragments and run-on sentences. Use formal, proper punctuation. And follow the rules of capitalization. This last point can be tricky for people who have gotten into the habit of writing in all capital letters when they are printing by hand.

5. Use Formal Language

Treat the writing sample like a term paper or a piece of business correspondence. Avoid slang, contractions, abbreviations, overly casual language, and jargon. If your parents wouldn't be familiar with the word, don't use it. You should also abide by the linguistic conventions of formal writing. Stick to the neutral, third-person point of view instead of using the first person (I, me, we) or the second person (you).

6. But Keep It Simple

Formal language is not the same thing as needlessly complex or pretentious language. Simple, straightforward language is the most effective way to communicate. Don't use a big word just for the sake of using a big word. If a shorter word conveys your meaning just as well, use the shorter word. Simplicity is also a virtue when it comes to sentence structure. The best writing uses short sentences that are crisp and direct. Of course, you should vary your sentence structure and mix in the occasional compound, complex, or compound-complex sentence. But most of your sentences should be short, simple sentences.

7. Focus on Your Topic Sentences

Strong topic sentences are the hallmark of good writing. Each of the five paragraphs in your essay should begin with a clear summary of that paragraph's content. The topic sentence should serve the same function in relation to the individual paragraph that your introductory paragraph serves in relation to the essay as a whole: tell the reader what you're about to say and why it's important. You can't write a strong topic sentence unless you have a clear understanding of what it is you're trying to communicate in each paragraph. Therefore, you should start thinking about your topic sentences during the brainstorming stage of the prewriting process.

8. Proofread

A law school admissions officer who reads your essay will be paying close attention to your grammar, mechanics, and language usage. If you finish your essay with a few minutes left, go back over your essay and proofread it. Look for misspelled or repeated words, grammatical errors, missing punctuation, a lack of subject-verb agreement, and other mistakes that are easy to make when you're writing under time pressure. This is not to say that you should hurry through your writing to make sure that you have time at the end to proofread. You're better off taking the time to write clearly and persuasively. But if you do wind up with some extra time, use it to clean up any mistakes in what you've written.

These eight principles are not intended to be an exhaustive list of what goes into good writing. But they do cover some of the most important basics. Remember: you don't need to write a perfect essay. All you need to do is write an essay that will not raise any red flags about your application. If you write a five-paragraph essay that is consistent with the eight principles discussed in this case, you can rest assured that your performance on the writing sample will not derail your law school application.

CHAPTER 7

Law School

In this chapter, you will learn:

- The economic climate for lawyers
- Factors to consider when choosing a school
- How location affects your school choice
- What to keep in mind when applying

"It was the best of times, it was worst of times" fairly well sums up the current state of law school in the United States. It may be the worst of times for recent grads, but perhaps it is the best of times for prospective students.

While the bulk of this book is devoted to helping you improve your score on the LSAT, in this chapter we'll step away from the nuts and bolts of test preparation to discuss the application process, the experience of attending law school, and the postgraduate realities for future law students.

Should I Go to Law School?

First of all, let's state the obvious: law school is not for everyone. The hours are long, the workload is difficult, and competition at the best schools is fierce.

But if you prepare yourself adequately for the experience, it's also likely to be one of the most invigorating, challenging, thrilling, demanding, edifying, exasperating, and satisfying experiences of your life. You will be equally exhausted and exhilarated.

The most brilliant people you'll ever meet in your life, you'll meet in law school. Your intellect and physical stamina will be pushed to the utmost limits of your endurance, and you'll know both success and frustration. You'll be given the know-how and means to effectuate real change in the lives of others, and you'll learn the (little-known) fact that lawyers are some of the most generous people in the entire world, with a profound devotion to their friends, their community, and their loved ones. Yes, there will be many sleepless nights (some of them because you were studying), but you'll arrive at the end of those three years of law school with your intellect sharpened and your critical reasoning skills honed to surgical precision.

Recently, however, schools have suffered some valid criticism that there are too many law school grads with too much debt and too few career opportunities. Recent law school grads enter the profession owing a median of approximately $75,000 in student loans, and the *New York Times* reported that these grads were facing "one of the grimmest job markets in decades."

Despite this reality, however, there has never been a better time to be a prospective law student. The journal of the American Bar Association reported that law schools could be admitting as many as 80 percent of their applicants for the fall of 2013, making it easier to gain admission to the best law schools even with a lower LSAT score or GPA. Better still, this trend is likely to continue for a few more years, making this year a great time to at least think about applying to law school.

I've Heard It's a Bad Time to Apply to Law School

It's no coincidence that the fall of 2008 saw a significant uptick in the number of LSAT administrations. September of that year marked the beginnings of the subprime mortgage crisis, soon followed by the collapse and near collapse of many banks and financial institutions. Law school has long been considered a safe port in a storm, and as more and more Americans were

227

faced with rising unemployment, recent college grads and those who had been laid off turned to law school as a safe place to ride out the economic typhoon.

In the academic year 2007–2008, the period before the global economic crisis, approximately 142,000 LSATs were administered. But in 2008–2009, the first year of the crisis, that number climbed past 151,000, the highest number since 1990–1991 (not surprisingly, a period that also saw record unemployment rates). And in 2009–2010, the number of LSAT administrations reached an all-time high of 171,514, before the numbers started to dip again.

ACADEMIC YEAR	NUMBER OF LSAT ADMINISTRATIONS	PERCENT CHANGE
2007–2008	142,331	
2008–2009	151,398	+6.4%
2009–2010	171,514	+13.3%
2010–2011	155,050	−9.6%
2011–2012	129,958	−16.2%
2012–2013	112,515	−13.4%

Source: Law School Admission Council, "LSATs Administered—Counts and Percent Increases by Admin and Year," http://www.lsac.org/lsacresources/data/lsats-administered.

The discouraging employment numbers for new lawyers in 2012 were largely echoes of the 2008 financial crisis. But how, you might ask, can the previous financial turmoil possibly be affecting employment prospects today, when unemployment rates have actually been declining for the rest of the population? That's mostly due to the legal profession's unique hiring process.

For most nonlawyers, a job search involves checking the classifieds in our local newspaper, networking with family and friends, or going online to sites like CareerBuilder or Monster.com. Hiring in the legal profession works very differently. Most law students will get that first job out of law school through a process known as on-campus interviews (OCI). Almost all law schools have some variation of OCI.

Basically, the OCI process involves various law firms, government agencies, and nonprofit organizations sending representatives to a central location to conduct mass interviews with current law students. Afterward, some students will receive callback interviews. The initial interviews are relatively short, while the callback interviews can last all day and may require the student to meet with dozens of partners and associates. The callbacks are usually held on-site (at the firm's offices), which may require the student to fly or drive extensively from city to city during the callback period.

Strangely enough, this initial OCI period usually takes place the month before a student begins his or her second year of law school (2L), even though the jobs won't start until the summer *after* the second year of law school. Most students participating will only have two semesters' worth of grades, with another two years of law school still to follow.

The career services office (CSO) at your law school will prepare you for this rather grueling period with mock interviews and résumé reviews. Suffice to say that once you've secured your job as a summer associate, you'll usually start in late May or June following your 2L year, working for a period of about 10 weeks. For many students working at larger firms, the summer associate job can be fairly lucrative, though savvy students will resist the urge to indulge in luxuries and use the paycheck to pay down debt. After the summer internship is over, firms will then decide which summer associates will receive offers of full-time employment.

Keep in mind, however, that even those successful candidates who receive offers of full-time employment still have to finish one more year of law school and pass the bar exam before they can be admitted to practice. For most students, this means graduating in May, taking the bar exam at the end of July, and receiving bar results around the beginning of November.

But think about the oddity of this time line: it basically means that law students are interviewing for full-time employment nearly two and a half years before they actually start the job.

It's this strangely protracted hiring process coupled with the financial crisis that has led to the current stark employment numbers for new attorneys. The first batch of students affected by the financial collapse took the LSAT in the fall of 2008 and started law school in the fall of 2009. This also means that the first of these students affected by the financial collapse would have been going through OCI in the fall of 2010, with a graduation date of May 2012.

Unfortunately, in the fall of 2010, the unemployment rate for all Americans was still near record high levels, and many law firms canceled or seriously curtailed recruiting during OCI. Since OCI is traditionally where most students find their full-time jobs after law school, it meant that in May 2012, law schools began graduating many prospective attorneys who had not yet secured full-time employment. Those dire employment numbers were reported widely in the media, further depressing the number of LSAT test takers. At the same time, the economy began a gradual recovery, meaning graduate school was no longer the only viable option for young people coming out of undergrad.

All of this has led to the current dip in the number of LSAT administrations, which for 2012–2013 were the lowest since 2000–2001. Fewer prospective law students means fewer attorneys in four years' time. The unemployment rate, meanwhile, has dipped to its lowest levels since 2008. With the economy currently experiencing a recovery in terms of employment numbers, this should provide a self-correction to the employment prospects of future law students. So while it might be tough out there for recent grads, it's a great time for those who are considering applying to law school.

Where Should I Apply?

Oddly, despite the stark realities faced by recent law school graduates, most of those very same graduates loved their law school experience. As reported in the *Wall Street Journal*, a survey of the class of 2012 at law schools across the country found that 90 percent of graduates gave their legal education a grade of A or B. Only 9 percent gave their law school a C grade, and 1 percent gave it a D. Even more revealing: no students in the survey gave their school a failing grade.

The critical reasoning skills you'll acquire in law school translate well to any profession. But choosing which law schools to apply to can be daunting. There are currently 202 ABA-accredited law schools in the United States (in most states, attendance at an ABA-accredited school is a prerequisite to taking the bar). And although many of the programs, like Harvard and Yale, have obvious name-brand recognition, many excellent programs fly under the radar.

Realistically, there are only a few reasons most of us have heard of any law schools. First, some schools may be universally well known for academic excellence, as in the case of the Ivy League schools. Second, you might know of a law school at an institution you attended as an undergrad or that friends or family attended. Third, if a school is nearby, you're probably familiar with it. And fourth, many people recognize law schools at institutions that are also home to an undergraduate program with a well-regarded football or basketball program. But none of these reasons for recognizing a name provides a reasonable basis for choosing a law school!

Many students begin their search for a law school by examining law school rankings. In a 2012 survey that asked prospective law students the most important factor in choosing a law school, 32 percent responded that law school rankings were their primary consideration. The best-known rankings are provided by *U.S. News & World Report* and are available online; you can find them by searching for "U.S. News law school rankings."

But despite the primacy of the rankings for prospective students, the same survey found that after three years of law school, only 17 percent of law school grads would tell prospective students to use the rankings as the most important factor in choosing a law school. Instead, recent grads prioritized job placement, affordability/tuition, geographic location, and academic programming. The *U.S. News & World Report* website also does a great job of collecting these types of data for you so you can make an informed decision.

I Know I Want to Go to Law School, But I Don't Know if I Want to Be a Lawyer

Many prospective law students know they want to go to law school but have doubts about actually being a lawyer. They may be attracted to the prospect of the intellectual rigors of law school. The prospect of spending long days in a corporate law office is less appealing.

Thankfully, the law is not a monolithic profession, and a Juris Doctor is the Swiss Army knife of graduate degrees. The day in the life of a federal prosecutor is going to be radically different from that of a solo practitioner who specializes in family law. From public-interest or government work to law enforcement to corporate megafirms, the law offers a wide spectrum of experiences. Some lawyers may specialize in litigation; others may spend their entire career in the legal profession without ever setting foot in front of a jury.

Big firms tend to offer big paychecks, with starting salaries around $160,000 a year. But Big Law, as it is affectionately known, also requires associates to work long hours. Some associates thrive in the pressure cooker of Big Law and relish the experience, but others may prefer more leisure time and choose to work for a small firm or government agency. For students considering public-interest or government work, this does usually mean a smaller salary, but many schools now offer loan repayment assistance programs (LRAPs), which provide debt forgiveness of government-backed student loans after a predetermined period. A complete list of schools offering LRAPs can be found through the American Bar Association website at http://apps .americanbar.org/legalservices/probono/lawschools/ pi_lrap.html.

Also consider creating your own specialization in law school. Although there isn't really such a thing as a "major" in law schools, students can certainly create their own concentrations. The first-year curriculum is largely prescribed, but students have great latitude in choosing their course work in the second and third years of school. Promising practice areas with growth potential include alternative-energy law, health care, copyright and intellectual property, and financial regulation. Lisa L. Abrams's *The Official Guide to Legal*

Specialties is a great place to begin when considering different practice areas, and Federal Reports Inc.'s "600+ Things You Can Do with a Law Degree (Other than Practice Law)" provides a thorough survey of alternative career prospects for law school grads and attorneys.

Do I Need to Attend Law School in the State Where I Plan to Practice?

One of the strangest things you'll learn in law school is that law school doesn't really prepare you for the bar exam. Certainly, law school teaches you to "think like a lawyer" (a phrase you'll hear over and over), but that doesn't mean you'll have all the applicable statutes memorized by the time you graduate.

For most students, this means taking a six-week bar prep class immediately following graduation. Although many companies offer competing courses, the landscape is basically dominated by two firms: BarBri and Kaplan PMBR. The courses are offered for all 50 states and Washington, DC, meaning you can go to law school anywhere in the country and still return to the state in which you intend to practice in order to take that particular bar exam.

It's also important to remember that most law schools offer an identical first-year curriculum, with courses in civil procedure, constitutional law, contracts, criminal law, property, torts, and legal research/writing. And the fact of the matter is, the laws in most states are fairly uniform. The U.S. Constitution in Rhode Island, after all, is the same U.S. Constitution used in Alaska. The Federal Rules of Civil Procedure are identical in all states because they're federal rules. Contracts are governed by the Uniform Commercial Code, which has been enacted in one form or another in all 50 states. And property law finds its roots in the common-law practices of medieval England (explaining why a landlord is called a "land lord" in the first place).

That being said, there are some advantages to going to a law school in the place where you ultimately plan to practice. A primary consideration for many in choosing a law school is the *portability* of the degree. Portability in a law degree basically means what the name implies: the ability to take your law degree, travel anywhere in the country, and still get a job. The more prestigious the program, the more portable the degree.

Students looking at lower-ranked programs may benefit from considering their postgraduate career plans. A degree from Northeastern University and a degree from Harvard both give graduates access to the Boston legal market, but the Harvard degree is ultimately more portable. However, if the student intends to stay in the Boston area, a Northeastern degree could be a great (and more affordable) choice.

Also remember that the law is very much a relationship-driven profession. Your law school classmates are also future judges, hiring partners, and opposing counsel. Alumni of the same school tend to look out for each other in the hiring process or when offering referrals, and established law schools with extensive alumni networks may offer a competitive advantage over law schools of more recent provenance. Thus, while *U.S. News & World Report* may rank UCLA as a better law school than Emory (number 15 versus number 24), for students practicing in Atlanta, Emory may be the better choice.

Finally, wherever you choose to go to school, make sure you're going to be happy. You're going to be spending at least three long, stressful years in that place, and quality of life is an important consideration. The University of Minnesota School of Law offers a great program, but if you don't like cold weather, you're likely to be unhappy for about six months of the year. Love the sunshine? Maybe the University of Washington–Seattle isn't a good fit. If it's important to be home for Thanksgiving, a law school on the opposite side of the country may not be right for you.

Best Law Schools for Standard of Living

SCHOOL	LOCATION
1. University of Texas	Austin, TX
2. University of Georgia	Athens, GA
3. Vanderbilt University	Nashville, TN
4. University of Virginia	Charlottesville, VA
5. Northwestern University	Chicago, IL
6. University of Chicago	Chicago, IL
7. University of North Carolina	Chapel Hill, NC
8. University of Michigan	Ann Arbor, MI
9. Washington University in St. Louis	St. Louis, MO
10. Duke University	Durham, NC
11. Southern Methodist University	Dallas, TX
12. Emory University	Atlanta, GA
13. University of Notre Dame	Notre Dame, IN
14. Stanford University	Stanford, CA
15. Washington and Lee University	Lexington, VA
16. Yale University	New Haven, CT
17. Harvard University	Cambridge, MA
18. University of California–Berkeley	Berkeley, CA
19. Boston University	Boston, MA
20. University of Pennsylvania	Philadelphia, PA

Source: "Best Law Schools for Standard of Living," *National Jurist*, June 30, 2011, http://www.nationaljurist.com/content/best-law-schools-standard-living.

Best Cities for Young Attorneys

CITY	% OF PEOPLE AGES 24–34	NUMBER OF FIRMS	AREA LAW SCHOOLS
1. Washington, DC	20.7	2,966	American, Catholic, George Mason, George Washington, Georgetown, Howard, University of DC
2. Atlanta, GA	19.8	2,689	Emory, Georgia State, John Marshall, Mercer, University of Georgia
3. Boston, MA	20.7	2,102	Boston College, Boston University, Fletcher, Harvard, Massachusetts Law, New England, Northeastern, Southern New England, Suffolk, University of Massachusetts, Western New England
4. Denver, CO	20.5	1,997	University of Colorado, University of Denver
5. Dallas, TX	18.4	3,075	Baylor, University of Houston, South Texas, Southern Methodist, St. Mary's, University of Texas, Texas Southern, Texas Tech, Texas Wesleyan
6. Seattle, WA	20.8	1,815	Gonzaga, Seattle University, University of Washington, Lewis & Clark, University of Oregon, Willamette
7. Chicago, IL	19.1	4,819	Chicago-Kent, DePaul, John Marshall, Loyola, Northern Illinois, Northwestern, Southern Illinois, University of Illinois, University of Chicago
8. San Francisco, CA	20.9	2,960	UC–Berkeley, Empire College, Concord, Golden Gate, Lincoln, San Francisco Law, San Joaquin, Stanford, Santa Clara, UC–Davis, UC–Hastings, University of the Pacific, University of San Francisco
9. Minneapolis, MN	21.0	1,266	Hamline, University of Minnesota, William Mitchell
10. Houston, TX	17.8	4,741	Baylor, University of Houston, South Texas, Southern Methodist, St. Mary's, University of Texas, Texas Southern, Texas Tech, Texas Wesleyan
11. Salt Lake City, UT	20.9	771	Brigham Young, University of Utah
12. Los Angeles, CA	16.8	4,637	Abraham Lincoln, American College, California Western, California Southern, Chapman, Concord, Loyola, Pacific Coast, People's College, Pepperdine, San Joaquin, Southwestern, UC–Los Angeles, University of Southern California, University of San Diego, Taft, University of La Verne
13. Alexandria, VA	24.4	542	William & Mary, George Mason, Liberty, University of Richmond, Regent, University of Virginia, Washington & Lee
14. St. Louis, MO	18.1	1,318	St. Louis, University of Missouri, Washington University
15. Mountain View, CA	21.1	171	See San Francisco–area law schools
16. Irvine, CA	15.8	1,102	See Los Angeles–area law schools
17. Philadelphia, PA	16.1	1,899	Penn State, Drexel, University of Pennsylvania, Temple, Rutgers, Seton Hall, Villanova. See also New York–area law schools
18. Oakland, CA	17.4	973	See San Francisco–area law schools
19. Newport Beach, CA	13.7	766	See Los Angeles–area law schools
20. New York, NY	17.0	8,906	Brooklyn, Cardozo, Columbia, CUNY, Fordham, Hofstra, New York Law, NYU, Pace, St. John's, Touro, Rutgers, Seton Hall, University of Connecticut, Quinnipiac, Yale

Source: "Best Cities for Young Attorneys." *National Jurist*, October 2012, Volume 22, Number 2, pp. 22–26, http://www.nxtbook.com/nxtbooks/cypress/nationaljurist1012 /index.php#/22.

What Else Do I Need to Do to Complete My Law School Applications?

The LSAT and GPA are the primary components used in making admissions decisions, weighed in about a two-to-one ratio in favor of the LSAT. Law schools believe that these numbers are the most reliable predictors of your success in law school. Your undergraduate GPA is viewed as a rough measure of your ability to work hard and apply yourself, and your LSAT score is believed to be a good measure of your native intellectual ability.

Thus, you can use those two numbers to make a reasonably accurate prediction about whether you're likely to gain admission to a particular law school. The Law School Admissions Council, which creates and administers the LSAT along with processing your law school applications through its Credential Assembly Service, hosts an LSAT/GPA calculator on its website at http://officialguide.lsac.org.

You can use the calculator not only to gauge your chances of admission, but also to help determine your goal LSAT score. If it has always been your dream to attend the University of Pittsburgh School of Law, Pitt's website will tell you that for the most recent class, the median LSAT score was 158, and the median GPA was 3.34. But what if you have a 3.0 GPA? You can plug your GPA into the GPA/LSAT calculator and play around with different LSAT scores to find the score with which you have roughly a 50% chance of being admitted (in this case, an LSAT score of 162). This gives you a more personalized target score when prepping for your LSAT.

That's not to say you should limit your applications solely to those schools that offer you the best chance of admission. Everyone should reach a little bit beyond what his or her numbers would indicate are "safe" prospects. You are more than two numbers on a grid, after all, and every school admits a few students who don't line up numerically with the rest of the class, on the basis of the strength of the qualitative portions of their applications.

What do these "qualitative" components consist of? For most schools, your application checklist will include the following:

- Personal statement (two to three pages)
- Recommendations or evaluations (two to three)
- Résumé or work history
- List of honors and extracurricular activities

Don't overlook the importance of these more subjective portions of your application! Remember, applicants at most schools are a self-selecting group. That is to say, the applicants tend to resemble each other, numerically at least. If you have a 3.2 GPA and a 158 on your LSAT, you're probably not likely to apply to Yale. You're more likely to apply to schools where you have a better chance of acceptance. And since most people operate in a similarly rational fashion, most other applicants are going to look just like you on paper.

Ultimately, the rest of your application is there to create points of difference between yourself and the competition. Why do you deserve to take a spot at this particular law school over someone who is your numerical twin? And in that regard, your personal statement is likely to prove the third most important part of your application after LSAT and GPA.

That isn't to diminish the importance of well-written, detailed recommendation letters or a résumé highlighting significant accomplishments. But ask yourself: Do they really create points of difference between myself and my peers? After all, ideally, most people will ask for letters from college professors. And ideally, those professors will have nice things to say about you and your class work. But if every letter says great things, then how does that create a point of difference?

The same goes for résumés. The bulk of law school applicants are relatively young. In 2011, just over 80 percent of law school applicants were younger than 30, and 62 percent of applicants were younger than 25. For most young people, this means fairly thin résumés at this juncture of their professional careers. For those coming directly out of undergrad into law school, this may even mean no professional experience. Again, this isn't to diminish the importance of a great résumé; your professional experience, internships, leadership roles, and community involvement can only help your candidacy. But they may not make you as different as you imagine, especially when so many law students come from such similar backgrounds.

So it comes down to the personal statement. Don't overlook this very important document, and don't try to write the entire thing in an evening. Devote substantial time to brainstorming, writing, editing, and revising. And don't merely recycle the personal statement you used to get into your undergraduate university! The person you were at age 17 is very different from the person you are now.

All law schools require you to submit a personal essay as a part of your application, and for the most part, you should be able to use the same personal statement for all of your applications. Typically, the personal statement is a short (two to three pages) piece of writing designed to give the admissions committee insight into your character, personality, and motivations for attending law school. It should be a *personal* statement, containing information not found elsewhere on your application, not merely a narrative version of your résumé. And unless you plan to practice public-interest law, it shouldn't necessarily be about why you are a good person. Too many law students craft personal statements containing vague promises to "change the world" if they have a law degree. But if your résumé doesn't demonstrate that you've ever engaged in significant community involvement, volunteerism, or charitable work, then why should the admissions officer believe that's all going to change once you've completed law school?

Instead, think of your personal statement as your interview on paper. Most law schools don't require or even offer an interview, so this is the chance to share who you are. What stories do you tell people when you meet them for the first time? How do you spend your time when you're not in school? What have been the formative events in your life? What are your hobbies or passions? What makes you different from absolutely everyone else?

You'll also want to devote significant time to proofreading. Your personal statement also functions as a technical writing sample that the admissions committee will scrutinize for grammar, mechanics, style, organization, and clarity. Admissions officers are far more likely to read your personal statement for this purpose than they are to read your response to the Writing Sample section of the LSAT. For that reason, it's a good idea to take a draft of your personal statement to your college writing center or your prelaw adviser. If you enlist proofreaders, make sure they understand that you want critical feedback, not merely validation of a job well done.

You are about to embark on a truly remarkable journey, one you will look back upon as being the most exciting, most transformative, and most exhausting few years of your life. On behalf of everyone at McGraw-Hill Education, we wish you all the best and hold nothing but the highest hopes for your future success in law school and beyond!

PART II

LSAT Practice Tests

LSAT Practice Test 1

You can also take this practice test on your tablet or smartphone as well as your laptop or home computer. See page 7A of the Welcome insert for more information.

Answer Sheet

Directions: Before beginning the test, photocopy this answer sheet or remove it from the book. Mark your answer to each question by filling in the corresponding answer oval in the columns below. If a section has fewer questions than answer spaces, leave the extra spaces blank.

Section I	Section II	Section III	Section IV
1. (A) (B) (C) (D) (E)	1. (A) (B) (C) (D) (E)	1. (A) (B) (C) (D) (E)	1. (A) (B) (C) (D) (E)
2. (A) (B) (C) (D) (E)	2. (A) (B) (C) (D) (E)	2. (A) (B) (C) (D) (E)	2. (A) (B) (C) (D) (E)
3. (A) (B) (C) (D) (E)	3. (A) (B) (C) (D) (E)	3. (A) (B) (C) (D) (E)	3. (A) (B) (C) (D) (E)
4. (A) (B) (C) (D) (E)	4. (A) (B) (C) (D) (E)	4. (A) (B) (C) (D) (E)	4. (A) (B) (C) (D) (E)
5. (A) (B) (C) (D) (E)	5. (A) (B) (C) (D) (E)	5. (A) (B) (C) (D) (E)	5. (A) (B) (C) (D) (E)
6. (A) (B) (C) (D) (E)	6. (A) (B) (C) (D) (E)	6. (A) (B) (C) (D) (E)	6. (A) (B) (C) (D) (E)
7. (A) (B) (C) (D) (E)	7. (A) (B) (C) (D) (E)	7. (A) (B) (C) (D) (E)	7. (A) (B) (C) (D) (E)
8. (A) (B) (C) (D) (E)	8. (A) (B) (C) (D) (E)	8. (A) (B) (C) (D) (E)	8. (A) (B) (C) (D) (E)
9. (A) (B) (C) (D) (E)	9. (A) (B) (C) (D) (E)	9. (A) (B) (C) (D) (E)	9. (A) (B) (C) (D) (E)
10. (A) (B) (C) (D) (E)	10. (A) (B) (C) (D) (E)	10. (A) (B) (C) (D) (E)	10. (A) (B) (C) (D) (E)
11. (A) (B) (C) (D) (E)	11. (A) (B) (C) (D) (E)	11. (A) (B) (C) (D) (E)	11. (A) (B) (C) (D) (E)
12. (A) (B) (C) (D) (E)	12. (A) (B) (C) (D) (E)	12. (A) (B) (C) (D) (E)	12. (A) (B) (C) (D) (E)
13. (A) (B) (C) (D) (E)	13. (A) (B) (C) (D) (E)	13. (A) (B) (C) (D) (E)	13. (A) (B) (C) (D) (E)
14. (A) (B) (C) (D) (E)	14. (A) (B) (C) (D) (E)	14. (A) (B) (C) (D) (E)	14. (A) (B) (C) (D) (E)
15. (A) (B) (C) (D) (E)	15. (A) (B) (C) (D) (E)	15. (A) (B) (C) (D) (E)	15. (A) (B) (C) (D) (E)
16. (A) (B) (C) (D) (E)	16. (A) (B) (C) (D) (E)	16. (A) (B) (C) (D) (E)	16. (A) (B) (C) (D) (E)
17. (A) (B) (C) (D) (E)	17. (A) (B) (C) (D) (E)	17. (A) (B) (C) (D) (E)	17. (A) (B) (C) (D) (E)
18. (A) (B) (C) (D) (E)	18. (A) (B) (C) (D) (E)	18. (A) (B) (C) (D) (E)	18. (A) (B) (C) (D) (E)
19. (A) (B) (C) (D) (E)	19. (A) (B) (C) (D) (E)	19. (A) (B) (C) (D) (E)	19. (A) (B) (C) (D) (E)
20. (A) (B) (C) (D) (E)	20. (A) (B) (C) (D) (E)	20. (A) (B) (C) (D) (E)	20. (A) (B) (C) (D) (E)
21. (A) (B) (C) (D) (E)	21. (A) (B) (C) (D) (E)	21. (A) (B) (C) (D) (E)	21. (A) (B) (C) (D) (E)
22. (A) (B) (C) (D) (E)	22. (A) (B) (C) (D) (E)	22. (A) (B) (C) (D) (E)	22. (A) (B) (C) (D) (E)
23. (A) (B) (C) (D) (E)	23. (A) (B) (C) (D) (E)	23. (A) (B) (C) (D) (E)	23. (A) (B) (C) (D) (E)
24. (A) (B) (C) (D) (E)	24. (A) (B) (C) (D) (E)	24. (A) (B) (C) (D) (E)	24. (A) (B) (C) (D) (E)
25. (A) (B) (C) (D) (E)	25. (A) (B) (C) (D) (E)	25. (A) (B) (C) (D) (E)	25. (A) (B) (C) (D) (E)
26. (A) (B) (C) (D) (E)	26. (A) (B) (C) (D) (E)	26. (A) (B) (C) (D) (E)	26. (A) (B) (C) (D) (E)
27. (A) (B) (C) (D) (E)	27. (A) (B) (C) (D) (E)	27. (A) (B) (C) (D) (E)	27. (A) (B) (C) (D) (E)
28. (A) (B) (C) (D) (E)	28. (A) (B) (C) (D) (E)	28. (A) (B) (C) (D) (E)	28. (A) (B) (C) (D) (E)
29. (A) (B) (C) (D) (E)	29. (A) (B) (C) (D) (E)	29. (A) (B) (C) (D) (E)	29. (A) (B) (C) (D) (E)
30. (A) (B) (C) (D) (E)	30. (A) (B) (C) (D) (E)	30. (A) (B) (C) (D) (E)	30. (A) (B) (C) (D) (E)

SECTION I

Time—35 minutes
25 Questions

Directions: The questions in this section are based on the reasoning contained in brief statements or passages. For some questions, more than one of the choices could conceivably answer the question. However, you are to choose the *best* answer; that is, the response that most accurately and completely answers the question. You should not make assumptions that are by commonsense standards implausible, superfluous, or incompatible with the passage. After you have chosen the best answer, blacken the corresponding space on your answer sheet.

Questions 1–2

Jamey: Scientists recently trained a bacterium to survive and grow on a diet of arsenic rather than phosphorus, which is one of the six required elements to sustain life in our universe. Based on their results, there may be life in the universe that does not require the same elements that we've assumed were necessary for life. This proves that we need to expand our search parameters for life on other planets.

Lorne: No, the bacterium survived on arsenic, but it grew much faster when fed phosphorus. Thus, your conclusion seems unwarranted and to invest significant effort in expanding our search parameters for alien life forms would be a waste of scientific resources.

1.   Which one of the following, if true, provides the strongest defense of Jamey's argument against Lorne's criticism?

(A)   The bacterium, while on a diet of arsenic, had a life span only half that of a bacterium on a diet of phosphorus.

(B)   The bacterium, while on a diet of arsenic, showed signs that other elements necessary for life's existence, like carbon, were toxic to it.

(C)   Infrared satellite images of planets rich in phosphorus exhibit only four of the five other elements necessary to sustain life.

(D)   Scientists have proven that due to exposure to arsenic over long periods of time other organisms can develop a tolerance to small amounts of the poison.

(E)   Infrared satellite images of planets rich in arsenic and devoid of phosphorus have shown no signs of conditions that could foster life.

2.   Which one of the following most accurately describes Lorne's criticism of Jamey's argument?

(A)   It argues that while Jamey's facts are correct her conclusion does not follow from those facts.

(B)   It provides an alternative set of facts that, while it does not completely invalidate Jamey's set of facts, may undermine her conclusion.

(C)   It presents new information that disproves Jamey's conclusion.

(D)   It offers facts irrelevant to Jamey's argument in an attempt to challenge her credibility.

(E)   It points out Jamey's conclusion is too far of a leap in logic to be supported by her facts.

GO ON TO THE NEXT PAGE

3. Educator: Scholars are concerned that the increasing popularity of online universities and low-residency degree programs will render the classroom experience obscure. They object to this trend, saying that online courses do not offer the level of collaboration and support that the traditional classroom does. At Plymouth Online, however, we offer a fully interactive experience with web video, web-based collaboration software, online chat, and video conferencing sessions. It is therefore possible to join our online university and experience a very close approximation of the in-classroom experience, and in some situations, the experience is a richer and more satisfying one.

The educator's argument proceeds by

(A) referring to a scholarly authority to challenge a widely held belief
(B) questioning the accuracy of evidence given in support of an opposing position
(C) offering a counterexample to a prevalent belief among experts in the field
(D) proposing an alternative sociological explanation for a pedagogical practice
(E) making a distinction between instructional approaches

4. The eyes of the female cichlid fish feature five photoreceptor cones, the most of any vertebrate and two more than the three that human eyes have. The dull-colored female cichlid fish uses its highly discriminating color vision to locate the more colorful male cichlids so that it may successfully choose a mate. If the color of the male's scales is altered the female can unknowingly bypass the male altogether. Increased water turbidity due to deforestation and economic development has altered the visual environment of fish. Thus, it will be difficult for the female cichlids to find mates and the survival of the cichlid population will be seriously threatened.

Which one of the following, if true, LEAST strengthens the argument above?

(A) An experiment showed that the eyes in some varieties of cichlids adapted when the fish were switched between blue to green waters.
(B) The female cichlid is incapable of distinguishing certain shades of red in its mates when the light permeating the water diminishes in the evening.
(C) The tilapia, a type of cichlid, has shown a marked decrease in population in a lake near an industrial park near Chicago.
(D) Turbidity in the waters has caused various non-cichlid species to move to other bodies of water, leaving the cichlids a more open mating environment.
(E) The discriminating vision of the female cichlid has been found to make it more susceptible to eye-borne diseases that threaten the cichlid population.

GO ON TO THE NEXT PAGE

5. Coffee houses in City A have experienced a decrease in coffee revenues due to a downturn in the economy of City A, so much so that some of the most popular coffee houses may have to close. At the same time, however, more people are visiting coffee houses in City A than ever before and the number of successful coffee houses in City A is greater than ever.

Which one of the following, if true, most helps to resolve the apparent discrepancy in the information above?

(A) More coffee houses opened in City A during the last year have survived than in any previous year.

(B) Because of the economic downturn, people of City A are brewing their own coffee at home rather than buying it at coffee houses.

(C) The patronage for a popular bakery far exceeds the patronage of even the most popular coffee house.

(D) Coffee is the main source of revenue only for the most popular coffee houses; other coffee houses rely on pastries and other food items for revenue.

(E) Most coffee houses lower their prices for coffee during an economic downturn.

Questions 6–7

Manager: Last year the total number of dropped cell phone calls on our network of cell towers decreased, so our effort to increase cell tower effectiveness worked.

Technician: If you look at the statistics for individual cell towers, however, you find that the number of dropped calls actually increased substantially for every tower that was in operation both last year and the year before. The number of dropped calls has clearly increased, given that the set of towers, the only ones for which we have dropped-call figures that allow a comparison between last year and the year before, demonstrate a trend toward more dropped calls.

6. If the dropped-call figures cited by both the manager and the technician are accurate, which one of the following must be true?

(A) The market share of the company's cell phone service fell last year.

(B) The company erected at least one new cell tower in the last two years.

(C) The volume of the company's cell phone calls has changed over the last two years.

(D) The quality of the company's cell tower system has not improved over the last two years.

(E) The company's cell phone calls are of lower quality than they once were.

7. Which one of the following, if true, most seriously calls into question the technician's argument?

(A) Most of the company's cell towers that were in operation throughout last year and the year before are located in areas where cell phone usage overall skyrocketed last year.

(B) Discounts to the heavier cell phone users did not increase cell phone usage.

(C) Prior to last year there was an overall downward trend in cell tower traffic.

(D) Those cell towers that experienced a decrease in dropped calls were not positioned in high-traffic areas.

(E) The company's cell towers last year handled less traffic from the company's other wireless services.

GO ON TO THE NEXT PAGE

8. Professor: To define what is considered literature is futile. Any definition of what constitutes literature would either exclude some works that are, in fact, literature or include others that might not be worthy of the designation. The notion of music and art are equally problematic. This is why the viability of a humanities department at our university should be seriously questioned.

The reasoning in the argument is questionable because the argument

(A) is advanced by someone who has a vested interest in eliminating a humanities department

(B) makes the unsupported claim that defining literature is futile

(C) fails to show any specific link between the indefinability of the arts such as literature and the maintenance of a humanities department

(D) ignores the fact that some people view literature as definable

(E) generalizes from an unrepresentative sample to all literature

9. New research studies showed that there is a higher rate of stroke in the southern states than the rest of the country. The studies also found that people in these states eat more fried fish and less non-fried fish than the rest of the country. We can conclude from this that eating fried fish increases one's chances of suffering a stroke. Therefore, people who want to reduce their risk of suffering a stroke should not eat fried fish.

The argument above has an error in reasoning because it

(A) presumes that a real or perceived relationship between two events means that one is the cause of the other

(B) assumes what is true in one area is not also true in another

(C) relies on too small a sample size to be representative of the population in question

(D) plays on people's fears in order to convince them to change a behavior

(E) uses stereotypes to reach an unfounded conclusion

10. Mr. Thomas: Ms. Garcia said that she gave up her sales responsibilities and was focusing only on her administrative duties. But I overheard a colleague of hers say that Ms. Garcia is working harder than ever before and will be gone for much of the next year visiting customers; that does not sound like she has given up her sales responsibilities to me. At least one of them is not telling the truth.

Mr. Thomas's reasoning is flawed because it

(A) fails to consider that Ms. Garcia's colleague may have been deceived by her

(B) draws a conclusion on equivocal language

(C) is based partly on hearsay

(D) fails to infer that Ms. Garcia may be a person of poor character, given her lack of ambition

(E) criticizes Ms. Garcia rather than the claims she made

11. David: The quality of Company A's management is declining in its ability to provide effective leadership to its employees and to generate high growth. There must be a return to the company's traditional values of risk and innovation.

Talia: There is no need to switch gears. Revenue growth might not be what it used to be, but most managers consider the current growth rate acceptable. Expectations for growth are unrealistic for this stage of the company's history.

David and Talia disagree over whether corporate growth

(A) can be changed

(B) is decreasing or increasing

(C) is perceived by management the same as employees

(D) is adequate as it is

(E) is changing over time

GO ON TO THE NEXT PAGE

12. In defending the new toy-manufacturing regulations aimed at protecting children from harmful defects in toys, the government regulator in charge of enforcing the rules pointed to recent success in catching defects: inspections discovered 60 percent more defects among toys produced under the new regulations than under the previous rules.

   The argument assumes that

   (A) the defects were caught mostly in toys aimed at children aged one to four years
   (B) the rules cause manufacturing companies to incur additional costs that hurt profitability
   (C) the quality of toys manufactured domestically is higher than that of toys produced by foreign manufacturers
   (D) the increase in discovered defects will decrease the number of incidents in which children are hurt by defective toys
   (E) the regulations are more stringent than those enforced by similarly industrialized nations

13. There are few things worse for a new parent than listening to a baby scream in hunger while a bottle of formula slowly warms up in a bowl of hot water. So why not just pop the bottle in the microwave and zap it for 20 seconds? Because microwaves heat fluids unevenly, and a hot pocket in the formula could seriously injure the baby.

   Which of the following is presupposed in the argument against heating formula in the microwave?

   (A) Babies generally refuse to eat formula that has been heated in a microwave, no matter the temperature.
   (B) Microwave radiation might break down some of the proteins in formula that are vital to a baby's health.
   (C) Parents cannot be expected to consistently even out the temperature of a microwaved bottle by shaking it vigorously and then checking the temperature before giving it to the baby.
   (D) Different microwaves use different amounts of power, and consequently some models could heat a bottle to scalding temperature faster than others.
   (E) Most pediatricians agree that microwaving a bottle can be dangerous and warn parents against using that method of heating.

14. Studies indicate that the rate at which soil erosion is increasing is leveling off: the amount of soil lost to erosion this year is almost identical to the amount of soil lost to erosion last year. If this trend continues, soil erosion will no longer be getting more serious.

   The reasoning is questionable because it ignores the possibility that

   (A) the effects of soil erosion are cumulative
   (B) crop-destroying insects and climate change are becoming more serious
   (C) the leveling-off trend of soil erosion will not continue
   (D) some soil erosion has no noticeable effect on farm productivity
   (E) the areas of soil erosion this year were less critical than those that occurred last year

15. Marisa always picked out an outfit for her daughter Lori to wear to school the next day and would lay it out on the dresser for her. Once Lori entered middle school, however, Marisa told her to choose her own outfits and never criticized her fashion choices.

   Which of the following principles is exemplified by the situation above?

   (A) We must not interfere with the decisions of competent adults.
   (B) We have an obligation to bring about good in all our actions.
   (C) We have an obligation to provide others with whatever they are owed or deserve.
   (D) We have an obligation to respect the autonomy of other persons and to respect the decisions made by other people concerning their own lives.
   (E) We must not harm others, or if harm is unavoidable, we must seek to minimize the harm we cause others.

GO ON TO THE NEXT PAGE

16. After purchasing a trailer for his truck from a car dealer in Abilene, Jason was informed by an Abilene city official that he would not be allowed to keep his trailer, since the city codes consider a trailer an industrial vehicle, and individuals cannot park industrial vehicles within the city of Abilene.

The city official's argument depends on assuming which one of the following?

(A) Trailers are not classified as residential vehicles in Abilene.
(B) It is legal for car dealers to sell trailers in Abilene.
(C) Vans and flatbed trucks are not classified as industrial vehicles.
(D) Any vehicle not classified as an industrial vehicle may be parked in Abilene.
(E) Jason lives in Abilene.

17. Energy expert: It is true that over the past 10 years there has been a fivefold increase in government funding for the development of alternative energy technologies, while the practical applications in use from this research have increased alternative energy usage by a meager 10 percent. Even when inflation is taken into account, the amount of funding now is at least two times what it was 10 years ago. Nevertheless, current government funding for developing alternative energy technologies is inadequate and should be increased.

Which one of the following, if true, most helps to reconcile the energy expert's conclusion with the evidence cited above?

(A) More people today, engineers and non-engineers, are working to develop alternative energy technologies.
(B) The idea that the government should develop alternative energy technologies was more popular 20 years ago than it is today.
(C) Research over the past 10 years has enabled engineers today to identify new alternative energy technologies faster than was thought possible 10 years ago.
(D) Over the past 10 years, the salaries of engineers employed by the government to work on alternative energy technologies have increased at a rate higher than the inflation rate.
(E) The government agency responsible for administering alternative energy funds has been consistently mismanaged and run inefficiently over the past 10 years.

GO ON TO THE NEXT PAGE

18. Mayor Espinol governed his city with one utilitarian tenet in mind: Always try to achieve the greatest good for the greatest number of people.

    Which of the following is an example of the principle set forth by the mayor?

    (A) After a forest fire, the forest floor was cleaned of debris and opened up to sunlight. The soil was nourished and local residents were able to use the land to grow food.
    (B) There are two movies scheduled tonight that Sergio wants to watch, but he can only watch one because they will air at the same time. He likes one more than the other, so that is the one he decides to watch.
    (C) The Eichenberg family took a vote on their summer vacation. Both parents voted for a trip to the beach. The three children voted for a trip to an amusement park. After much heated discussion, Mrs. Eichenberg announced that they would go to the beach.
    (D) There is a 1 in 13,983,816 chance of winning the state lottery. Many residents of the state spend more money on lottery tickets than they can afford, even though they know the odds.
    (E) Fifteen out of twenty people at a meeting prefer wheat bread to white bread. The company providing lunch for the meeting will serve only one type of bread. The leader of the meeting ordered wheat bread, even though she herself prefers white bread.

The sudden boom in business startups in a certain region's economy is said to be causing people not even employed by these businesses to spend more freely, as if they too were gaining economic power. Clearly, however, actual spending by such people is remaining unchanged, because there has been no unusual decrease in the amount of money held by those people in savings accounts.

19. The argument in the passage proceeds by doing which of the following?

    (A) arguing that because two alternative developments exhaust all the plausible possibilities, one of those developments happened and the other did not
    (B) arguing that because people's economic behavior is guided by economic self-interest, only misinformation or error will cause people to engage in economic actions that harm them economically
    (C) concluding that because only one of the two predictable consequences of a certain sort of behavior is observed to happen, this observed phenomenon cannot, in the current situation, be a consequence of such behavior
    (D) concluding that because a probable consequence of a supposed development failed to occur, that development itself did not occur
    (E) concluding that because the evidence concerning a supposed change is ambiguous, it is most likely that no change is actually occurring

20. Which one of the following is an assumption on which the argument relies?

    (A) There exist no statistics for sales of goods in the region.
    (B) People in the region who are not employed by business startups and who have relatives employed by startups commonly borrow money from those relatives to make large purchases.
    (C) If people in the region who are not employed by business startups are making large purchases, they are not paying for them by taking on debt.
    (D) People in the region not employed by startups are optimistic about their prospects for increasing their incomes.
    (E) If people in the region who are employed by startups change jobs, the new jobs generally pay more than the ones they lost.

GO ON TO THE NEXT PAGE

21. Criminal actions, like all actions, are ultimately products of a natural predisposition. It is not the criminals or their environment but the inherent flaws in human nature that create and maintain the criminal element in society—it is simply human nature. Therefore, the prison system should be abolished immediately.

What is the assumption upon which the argument depends?

(A) It is the nature of humanity and nothing else that should be held responsible for crime.

(B) There is an ambiguity inherent in the term *nature*.

(C) The statistical evidence is drawn from only a small segment of the population.

(D) Someone becomes a criminal solely by virtue of having committed a crime.

(E) Some actions are socially acceptable and some are not.

22. Each December 31 in Country B, a tally is made of the country's total available natural gas inventory—that is, the total amount of natural gas that has been produced throughout the country but not consumed. In 2010 that amount was considerably lower than it had been in 2009. Furthermore, Country B has not imported or exported natural gas since 1990.

If the statements above are true, which one of the following must also be true on the basis of them?

(A) In Country B, the amount of natural gas consumed in 2009 was greater than the amount of natural gas consumed in 2010.

(B) In Country B, more natural gas was mined in 2009 than was mined in 2010.

(C) In Country B, more natural gas was consumed during the first half of 2010 than was consumed during the first half of 2009.

(D) In Country B, the amount of natural gas consumed in 2010 was greater than the amount of natural gas mined in 2010.

(E) In Country B, the amount of natural gas consumed in 2010 was greater than the amount of natural gas consumed in 2009.

23. People are often told to eat a substantial breakfast because it reduces the amount of food consumed during the rest of the day. Yet, a recent study reported that for both obese and normal weight adults, eating a large, small, or no breakfast made no difference at all with regard to their non-breakfast calorie intake during the rest of the day.

Which of the following is most reasonably supported by the information above?

(A) Dieters who eat small breakfasts benefit from the same reduction of calories as those who eat no breakfast at all.

(B) Dieters who eat a large breakfast eat less food for the rest of the day but because they eat higher-calorie non-breakfast foods the calorie intake remains the same.

(C) Dieters who eat a small or no breakfast may actually reduce their calorie intake while those who eat a large breakfast probably increase their calorie intake.

(D) Whether dieters eat a large, small, or no breakfast makes no difference to their overall calorie intake.

(E) Dieters who eat no breakfast at all eat more during the rest of the day, but because they eat lower-calorie non-breakfast foods the calorie intake remains the same.

GO ON TO THE NEXT PAGE

24. Joanie: Property losses due to natural disasters have increased significantly. Also, fatalities due to natural disasters over the last two years have skyrocketed. It is obvious that the rate of natural disasters is on the increase.

Lonnie: I agree with your facts but not with your inference. Increased development has given natural disasters more to destroy. Also, over the last two years, the world has experienced some unusually large-scale natural disasters.

Lonnie criticizes Joanie's argument by pointing out

(A) that the rate of natural disasters is a difficult statistic to quantify

(B) that statistics, when it comes to natural disasters, are notoriously untrustworthy

(C) that the trends portrayed by the statistics on natural disasters do not represent the underlying causes that lead to her conclusion

(D) her lack of qualifications to make such a judgment regarding the rate of natural disasters

(E) other statistics that support the opposite conclusion

25. A political leader is considered great by assessing the decisions and actions that the political leader performed while in office. An inventory of the leaders' decisions and actions is the only indicator of greatness. Therefore, to say that a political leader is great is just to summarize the quality of his or her known decisions and actions, and the leader's greatness can provide no basis for predicting the quality of the leader's future decisions or actions.

Which one of the following arguments contains reasoning that is most similar to that used in the argument above?

(A) The bacteria that cause ear infections are not all the same, and they differ in their effects. Therefore, although it may be certain that a child has an ear infection, it is impossible to predict how the infection will progress.

(B) Although ear infections are very common among children, there are some children who never or only very rarely develop an ear infection. Clearly these children must be in some way physiologically different from other children who develop ear infections frequently.

(C) The only way of knowing whether a child has an ear infection is to observe symptoms. Thus, when a child is said to have an ear infection, this means only that the child has displayed the symptoms of having an ear infection, and no prediction about the patient's future symptoms is warranted.

(D) Unless a child displays ear infection symptoms, it cannot properly be said that the child has an ear infection. But each of the symptoms of an ear infection is also the symptom of another disease. Therefore, one can never be certain that a child has an ear infection.

(E) A child's ear infection is caused by bacteria trapped by a blocked eustachian tube in the ear. Each type of bacteria is different and the aperture of a child's eustachian tube changes constantly depending on the weather. Therefore, it is not possible to predict from a child's history of infection how susceptible he or she will be in the future.

STOP

IF YOU FINISH BEFORE TIME RUNS OUT, CHECK YOUR WORK ON THIS SECTION ONLY. DO NOT GO ON TO ANY OTHER TEST SECTION.

SECTION II

Time—35 minutes
25 Questions

Directions: The questions in this section are based on the reasoning contained in brief statements or passages. For some questions, more than one of the choices could conceivably answer the question. However, you are to choose the *best* answer; that is, the response that most accurately and completely answers the question. You should not make assumptions that are by commonsense standards implausible, superfluous, or incompatible with the passage. After you have chosen the best answer, blacken the corresponding space on your answer sheet.

1. Reynolds Dairy is attempting to dominate the organic yogurt market by promoting its nonfat "Slim-gurt," its most popular line of yogurt, with a costly new sweepstakes giveaway. But market research shows that, in the opinion of 76 percent of all consumers, "Slim-gurt" already dominates the market. Since any product with more than 55 percent of the sales in a market is, by definition, dominant in that market, Reynolds Dairy dominates the market now and need only maintain its current market share in order to continue to do so.

   Which one of the following is an assumption on which the argument above depends?

   (A) Market research studies describing the current situation are able to predict the future as well.
   (B) What the consumer believes to be true about a product is in fact the true conditions in the marketplace.
   (C) Consumers' belief in market dominance is required for a company's product to actually achieve market dominance.
   (D) Market research studies are thorough and accurate and it is foolish for a company to ignore the results of a study that counters its strategy in the marketplace.
   (E) Consumers' perception of market dominance actually results in popular demand for a product.

2. Not surprisingly, there are no astronauts under the age of twenty-one. And, as is well known, no one under the age of twenty-one can purchase alcohol. Finally, some scientists are astronauts, some purchase alcohol, and some are under twenty-one.

   If the statements above are true, then on the basis of them which one of the following must also be true?

   (A) Some astronauts neither purchase alcohol nor are scientists.
   (B) Some scientists are neither astronauts nor purchase alcohol.
   (C) Some people who purchase alcohol are not astronauts.
   (D) All scientists either are astronauts, purchase alcohol, or are under twenty-one.
   (E) No astronauts are twenty-one years old.

GO ON TO THE NEXT PAGE

Questions 3–4

Aligorian Wildlife Defense League: Uncontrolled logging in industrialized nations has endangered many species. To protect wildlife we must regulate the logging industry and its activities in Aligorian; future forest development must be offset by the development of replacement forest habitats. Thus, development would cause no net reduction of forests and pose no threat to the species that inhabit them.

Aligorian Logging Commission: Other nations have flagrantly developed forest areas at the expense of wildlife. We have conserved. Since Aligorian logging might not affect wildlife and is necessary for economic growth, we should allow logging to proceed unfettered. We have as much right to govern our own resources as countries that have already put their natural resources to commercial use.

3.   Which one of the following is an assumption on which the argument advanced by the Aligorian Logging Commission depends?

(A)   The species that inhabit Aligorian forests are among the most severely threatened of the designated endangered species.

(B)   Aligorian regulation of logging has in the past protected and preserved wildlife.

(C)   In nations that are primarily agricultural, logging does not need to be regulated.

(D)   The species indigenous to natural forests will survive in specially constructed replacement forest habitats.

(E)   More species have been endangered by the uncontrolled logging of forests than have been endangered by any other type of development.

4.   Which one of the following principles, if accepted, would most strongly support the Aligorian Logging Commission's position against the Aligorian Wildlife Defense League's position?

(A)   Regulation should be implemented to prevent further damage only when a reduction of populations of endangered species by logging has been found.

(B)   The economic needs of individual nations are not as important as the right of future generations to have wildlife preserved.

(C)   It is careless to allow further depletion of natural resources.

(D)   Environmental regulation must aim at preventing further environmental damage and cannot consider the different degrees to which different nations have already harmed the environment.

(E)   When wildlife is endangered, national resources should be regulated by international agreement.

GO ON TO THE NEXT PAGE

5. Goni: You cannot blame me for the tax penalty we incurred. Even though the penalty was assessed due to my error, you know full well that the error was due to my poor handwriting, and I certainly cannot be held responsible for the fact that my handwriting has deteriorated with age.

   Avi: But I can hold you responsible for your poor bookkeeping, because you know how poor your handwriting is. People are responsible for the consequences of actions that they voluntarily undertake, if they know that those actions risk such consequences.

   The principle that Avi invokes, if established, would justify which of the following judgments?

   (A) Jack was not responsible for losing his board position, because, knowing that his position was vulnerable in the election, he did everything possible to preserve it.
   (B) Jack was responsible for missing his daughter's dance recital, because he decided to hold a meeting with his staff late in the workday even though he knew the meeting might go long and he might miss the recital.
   (C) Jack was responsible for his dog being frightened, because, even though it was his brother who set off the firecracker, he knew that dogs are often frightened by loud noises.
   (D) Jack was responsible for having offended his friend when he made an offensive comment about her colleague, although he did not know his friend would mistakenly understand the comment to be about herself.
   (E) Jack was responsible for his bicycle being stolen last month, because he did not take any of the precautions that the city police recommended in the antitheft pamphlet they published this week.

6. Editorial: The governor's chief prosecutor assures the governor that with a thorough investigation and ample time to assemble the evidence he can root out political corruption at all levels of the state government. But the governor should not listen to the prosecutor, who in his youth was convicted of fraud. Surely his legal advice is as untrustworthy as he is himself, and so the governor should discard any hope of rooting out corruption and simply do the best he can to execute the state's business despite such hindrances.

   Which one of the following is a questionable argumentative strategy employed in the editorial?

   (A) trying to win support for a plan by playing on people's fears of what could happen if not implemented
   (B) rejecting a plan on the grounds that a particular aspect of the plan is likely to fail
   (C) presupposing what the plan sets out to prove
   (D) criticizing the source of a plan rather than examining the plan itself
   (E) taking lack of evidence for that a plan has worked in the past as proof that the plan will fail

7. Lawyer: Consider any situation where a moral injustice is committed. There are always situations in which it is right to protest the nature of that injustice. So, there are always situations in which it is right to protest taxation without representation.

   The conclusion of the argument follows logically if which one of the following is assumed?

   (A) Taxation without representation can always be protested.
   (B) Some kinds of injustices are dangerous to protest.
   (C) An injustice is of a moral nature only if it can be protested.
   (D) All injustices that can be protested are of a moral nature.
   (E) Taxation without representation is a moral injustice.

GO ON TO THE NEXT PAGE

8. A recent survey reveals that 83 percent of Americans support recycling; however, only 23 percent of households do any recycling at all, and most of those recycle only glass and paper.

Which of the following, if true, would best resolve the apparent contradiction in the statement above?

(A) Most people really do not want to reduce garbage and increase recycling.
(B) Most recycling campaigns are ineffective.
(C) Recycling is too difficult because it requires cleaning of the items to be recycled.
(D) Some people plan to do something, but do not always follow through with completing the task.
(E) Recycling uses more energy than is saved, so it really is not helping the environment.

9. Most people who use their cell phone more than 10 times a day do not have a landline phone installed in their home. In Ronde County most people used their cell phone more than 10 times a day. Therefore, in Ronde County most people do not have a landline phone installed in their home.

Which one of the following arguments has a flawed pattern of reasoning most like the flawed reasoning in the argument above?

(A) It is clear that most citizens in Eastland are law abiding since there is a very low crime rate in Eastland and most crimes are not very serious.
(B) It is clear that Halley cannot cook, since she does not own a pot or pan and no one in her family who does not own a pot or pan can cook.
(C) It is clear that Alvarez's friends usually carpool to work, since all of his friends can drive and all of his friends go to work.
(D) It is clear that most people in Daytown vote in early voting, since most people who live in retirement communities vote in early voting and most people in Daytown live in retirement communities.
(E) It is clear that most of Richard's friends love jazz, since he only goes to concerts with people who love jazz and he goes to concerts with most of his friends.

10. Current sales maps showing the areas of the United States where our products are most likely to secure loyal customers are based on sales data gathered 10 years ago from a small number of regional salespeople. New maps are being compiled using sales data from hundreds of retail centers and input from a network of loyal customers. These sales maps will be much more useful.

Each of the following, if true, helps to support the claim that the new maps will be more useful EXCEPT:

(A) Market information has changed in the past 10 years.
(B) Sales information is the most important factor in determining whether customers will become loyal.
(C) Some of the retail centers have been open more than 10 years.
(D) Customers can provide information on the market that retail centers cannot.
(E) Sales information can be described more accurately when more information is available.

11. Editorialist: TV dramas are contributing to an increase of violence in our society. By constantly being shown violent crimes such as murder and assault, viewers begin to think such actions are the norm and that there is something wrong with acting in a more civil manner.

TV drama producer: Well, if there is such an increase, it's not because of TV dramas: we simply give people what they want to see. What can be wrong with letting the viewers decide? Furthermore, if restrictions were put on my show, that would amount to censorship, which is wrong.

The editorialist and the TV drama producer's statements provide the most support for holding that they disagree about whether

(A) TV dramas influence people's conception of what is the norm
(B) it is wrong not to let the viewers decide what they want to see on TV
(C) TV dramas, by depicting violent crimes, are causing an increase of violence in society
(D) TV dramas should be censored
(E) the level of violence in society has changed

GO ON TO THE NEXT PAGE

12. A billboard company executive recently announced an increase in its billboard rental rates by 5 to 10 percent next year over rates this year and expects other billboard companies to follow suit. The executive argued that despite this increase, advertisers will continue to profit from billboard advertising, and so billboard rentals will be no harder to secure than this year.

Which one of the following, if true, would most support the billboard company executive's argument?

(A) The number of billboards leased by providers of services is increasing, while the number of billboards leased by products is decreasing.

(B) Most costs of production and distribution of services typically advertised on billboards are expected to rise 2 to 5 percent in the next year.

(C) Next year billboard leases will no longer be available for periods shorter than nine months.

(D) A recent survey has shown that the average number of people commuting in their own cars along routes with billboards is increasing at the rate of 2 percent every three months.

(E) The method of estimating the traffic passing a particular billboard will change next year.

13. Announcement for a television program: Are female politicians more effective than male politicians at applying policies that help the homeless and indigent citizens among their constituency? To get the answer we'll ask politicians of both sexes this question. Tune in tomorrow.

Which one of the following, if true, identifies a flaw in the plan for the program?

(A) Those who are best able to provide answers to the question are the homeless and indigent constituents of the respective politicians.

(B) The homeless and indigent need more advocacy groups arguing for their rights.

(C) Politicians are in general unwilling to disparage other politicians with whom they have to develop policy with.

(D) Homeless and indigent citizens among their constituents generally do not vote.

(E) Female politicians make up only 15 percent of the US Congress, and this number is even smaller in state legislatures.

14. Business consultant: The practice of streamlining this business process to reduce costs cannot be adequately supported by the claim that any simplification of a business process is more effective than doing nothing at all to reduce costs. What must also be taken into account is that such streamlining may hurt quality of service and reduce customer satisfaction.

Which one of the following most accurately expresses the main point of the business consultant's argument?

(A) Streamlining a business process is more effective than other forms of solutions for reducing costs.

(B) Streamlining a business process's effectiveness at reducing costs is not sufficient justification for using it.

(C) Streamlining a business process is more effective than not streamlining a business process at all for reducing costs.

(D) Streamlining a business process hurts quality of service and reduces customer satisfaction more than other solutions for reducing costs.

(E) Streamlining a business process should not be used to reduce costs unless it improves quality of service and increases customer satisfaction.

GO ON TO THE NEXT PAGE

15. Jason: The solar cooker provides free energy for cooking, baking, and cleaning water. People who use it avoid indoor smoke inhalation, fire hazards, and injuries from gathering firewood. They also have environmental benefits such as reducing deforestation, lowering energy costs, and reducing CO_2 emissions. The solar cooker is a simple solution to a host of problems in the developing world.

Zola: While I agree with your arguments, I disagree with your conclusion. Solar cookers have all of those benefits. Unfortunately, it takes a long time for them to bring water to a boil—usually between two and three hours—and they require ample sunlight, which is not always available in the rainy season. In practice, they are not a perfect solution by far.

Zola responds to Jason's argument using which one of the following argumentative techniques?

(A) She argues that Jason's conclusion is just a restatement of his fallacious arguments.

(B) She argues that Jason's conception of the ills of developing nations is too limited in scope and thus his conclusion is insufficient.

(C) She questions the integrity of Jason's research and whether his conclusion is based on a faulty foundation.

(D) She gives an alternate interpretation of the assumptions that results in a different conclusion altogether.

(E) She introduces caveats that weaken several of Jason's assumptions.

Questions 16–17

Park ranger: The only reason for us to restrict climbing in the park is to protect those inexperienced climbers from hurting themselves. Climbing on Mount Brunda is undoubtedly dangerous, but we should not restrict climbing. If inexperienced climbers cannot climb in our park they will most certainly travel to the next county over to climb in their parks, which have much more dangerous terrain than ours.

16. The pattern of reasoning in which one of the following is most similar to that in the park ranger's argument?

(A) The reason for the ordinance restricting loud music in residential areas after 10 p.m. was to protect those who were being disturbed by parties in their neighborhood as well as to maintain property values. Loud music had become a serious problem, but it has now been eliminated from our neighborhoods. So, we can probably remove the restriction now.

(B) The reason for requiring financial audits is to ensure that our business plans are operating within the budget constraints set by our accountants. Currently, financial concerns are less compelling than product development concerns, but in the long run, our financial viability must be ensured. Therefore, the requirement of financial audits should not be discontinued.

(C) Detention is used to separate a poorly behaving child from the well-behaving children. A poorly behaving child hinders the education of the other children, but detention also stigmatizes that child. Since the disruption to the other students is less a problem than the stigmatization of a poorly behaving child the practice of detention should be discontinued.

(D) Speed bumps on streets are meant to slow down traffic and reduce the danger to pedestrians. However, it would be detrimental to the Riverside Street area to have traffic move slower. So, speed bumps should not be implemented there.

(E) The function of an antivirus software is to prevent harmful programs from infecting a computer. However, Bulwark computers are built to be resistant to harmful programs and thus do not need an antivirus program. Antivirus programs, therefore, should not be installed on Bulwark computers.

GO ON TO THE NEXT PAGE

17. Which one of the following principles, if established, would provide the strongest support for the park ranger's argument?

(A) Since safety in a recreational activity depends on the level of skill of the participant in that activity, the climbing restrictions should be left to the discretion of the professional climbing instructors operating in the area.

(B) If recreational activities constitute a danger to the participants in those activities, then the park administrators should enact restrictions prohibiting those activities.

(C) Since the park could be held legally liable for accidents that occur within the park's borders, restrictions apply to any unnecessarily dangerous activities within the park.

(D) Restrictions that seek to eliminate dangers should not be enacted if their enactment would lead to dangers that are greater than those they seek to eliminate.

(E) Restrictions of recreational activities of the park visitors should not be put into effect unless those activities pose a danger to participants.

18. I have read her paper arguing for a new, more rigorous approach to analyzing literature and M frequently ascribes bad faith to scholars who disagree with her. It is troubling that M asserts that these scholars' opinions are colored by laziness and loyalty to outdated schools of thought. Add to this that M has often shown herself to be arrogant, overly ambitious, and sometimes plain nasty, and it becomes clear that M's paper does not merit attention from serious scholars.

The author of the above scholarly review commits which one of the following reasoning errors?

(A) dismissing an approach to literary criticism by giving a biased account of it

(B) failing to distinguish between the criteria of being true and of being sufficiently interesting to merit attention

(C) using an attack on the moral qualities of the author of the paper as evidence that the paper is not worthy of scholarly discussion of its truth

(D) presenting as facts several assertions about the paper under review that are based only on strong conviction and would be impossible for others to verify

(E) taking it for granted that a scholar is unlikely to do the work necessary and question an established school of thought

GO ON TO THE NEXT PAGE

Questions 19–20

Because excessive income taxes can make business activity difficult if not impossible, their use by governments is never justified. Purists, however, claim that all business taxes, such as sales tax, transportation fees, and export tariffs, should be prohibited because government should never be a burden to business activity. This is ridiculous; almost every interaction between government and business is some sort of burden, from work safety to food safety rules to labor regulations to payroll requirements. Yet, none of these is prohibited on the basis of being a burden. Furthermore, we should be attending to far more serious infrastructure problems that cause unnecessary restrictions to growth and business failures. Therefore, the use of some taxes, fees, and tariffs is acceptable and should not be prohibited.

19. Which of the following statements, if true, would be the strongest challenge to the conclusion?

    (A) Unnecessary restrictions to growth and business failures happen to nonprofits and individual citizens as well.
    (B) There would be more unnecessary restrictions to growth and business failures if it were not for sales tax, transportation fees, and export tariffs.
    (C) Income taxes are just as burdensome to businesses as other taxes such as sales taxes and transportation fees.
    (D) Sales tax, transportations fees, and export tariffs together can make business activity difficult if not impossible.
    (E) Some taxes, fees, and tariffs help businesses by making them avoid socially unproductive activities.

20. Which one of the following can be inferred from the passage above?

    (A) Some of the unnecessary restrictions to growth and business failures are caused by excessive income taxes.
    (B) The fact that something is a burden to business is not sufficient reason for prohibiting it.
    (C) The use of excessive income taxes by governments should be prohibited because excessive taxes are burdensome to business.
    (D) Excessive income taxes by governments on business are a less serious problem than are unnecessary business failures.
    (E) There is nothing burdensome about the use of nonexcessive taxes by governments.

21. Jack said he was not going to include members of the marketing department in the project-planning meeting. However, among the items each attendee left the meeting with was a sales report that Jack felt was important. Since members of the marketing department had promised to produce just such a sales report and intended to give it to Jack at the meeting, at least some members of the marketing department must have been at the project-planning meeting.

A reasoning error in the argument is that the argument

    (A) fails to establish that something true of some people is true of only those people
    (B) uses a term that is innately evaluative as though that term was purely descriptive
    (C) treats the evidence of someone's presence at a given event as an assurance that that person had a legitimate reason to be at that event
    (D) overlooks the possibility that a person's interest in one kind of thing is compatible with that person's interest in another kind of thing
    (E) disregards the possibility that a change of mind might be warranted by a change in circumstances

GO ON TO THE NEXT PAGE

22. Most people make major purchases such as cars and appliances without doing any research of their own. Some of these people rely solely on advice from friends or a salesperson, whereas some others make decisions merely on an emotional response. Only a few always do their own research before making such a purchase. Nonetheless, a majority of buyers say that they are happy with their purchase.

If the statements in the passages are true, which one of the following must also be true?

(A) Some people who research large purchases on their own, while just as often relying on advice from their friends and a salesperson or on emotions, are happy with their purchases.

(B) Most people who make large purchases either rely solely on advice from their friends or a salesperson or make decisions based merely on emotion.

(C) Some people are happy with their purchase even though they do not do any research on their own.

(D) Most people who rely solely on advice from their friends or a salesperson rather than emotions are happy with their purchases.

(E) Most people who make large purchases without doing any research on their own are happy with their purchases.

23. Many people believe that the remedy for our education problems is to reduce the size of the classes, but recent statistics from New York City show that while class sizes in the city varied widely, city-wide standardized test scores were similar.

The statistics cited function in the argument to

(A) illustrate the need for reducing class size in schools across the nation

(B) demonstrate that there is no relation between class size and the quality of education

(C) suggest that the size of classes is not the only influence on the quality of education

(D) establish that the size of classes does not need to be reduced

(E) prove that standardized testing is a poor way to gauge the success of an educational system

24. While most people normally believe that well-watered plants grow best on a bright sunny day, studies show that, in fact, the reverse is true. Plants actually benefit from the haze caused by carbon dioxide in the atmosphere, enabling them to absorb 25 percent more carbon than normally possible. The burning of fossil fuels and other human industrial activities are the main cause of increased carbon dioxide. Therefore, such industrial activities are obviously beneficial to agriculture and those who depend on it.

The flawed reasoning in the argument above is most similar to that in which one of the following?

(A) Vigorous exercise has been proven to help prevent a number of diseases, ailments, and injuries, so obviously no harm, and a great deal of good, can come from vigorous exercise.

(B) Excessive use of certain antibiotics increases one's susceptibility to certain antibiotic-resistant infections. Therefore, the best policy is to avoid using such antibiotics, thereby strengthening the body's ability to resist disease.

(C) Because a low-carbohydrate diet has been shown to be more healthful than a diet high in carbohydrates, a diet in which foods with low carbohydrate content have been entirely replaced by foods with high amounts of carbohydrates is bound to be even more healthful.

(D) Fresh fruits and vegetables contain more vitamins and minerals than processed fruits and vegetables. Therefore, one ought to completely abandon processed for fresh fruits and vegetables.

(E) Excessive stress can lead to sleep disorders and physical and mental illnesses, so if one wishes to avoid health problems associated with stress, one ought to take a day off from work every week.

GO ON TO THE NEXT PAGE

25. Columnist: A democratic society cannot function unless strong bonds of mutual trust have formed among its citizens. Only by participation in civic organizations, political parties, and other groups outside the family can such bonds be formed and strengthened. Thus, it is obvious that the widespread reliance on e-mail and Internet social networking for interaction has an inherently corrosive effect on democracy.

Which one of the following is an assumption on which the columnist's argument depends?

(A) Civic organizations cannot usefully advance their goals by using social networking.

(B) Anyone who relies on e-mail and social networking for interaction is unable to form a strong bond of mutual trust with another citizen.

(C) Relying on e-mail and social networking for interaction generally makes people less likely to participate in groups outside their families.

(D) People who rely on e-mail and social networking for interaction are generally closer to their families than are those who do not.

(E) Meetings and other forms of personal interaction strengthen, rather than weaken, democratic institutions.

STOP

IF YOU FINISH BEFORE TIME RUNS OUT, CHECK YOUR WORK ON THIS SECTION ONLY. DO NOT GO ON TO ANY OTHER TEST SECTION.

SECTION III

Time—35 minutes

25 Questions

Directions: Each passage in this section is followed by a group of questions to be answered on the basis of what is *stated* or *implied* in the passage. For some of the questions, more than one of the choices could conceivably answer the question. However, you are to choose the *best* answer; that is, the response that most accurately and completely answers the question, and blacken the corresponding space on your answer sheet.

PASSAGE A

In recent years, there has been an increasing interest among justices and legal scholars in the use of foreign law as a prism through which to interpret the Constitution. Nowhere has this garnered more
(5) attention than when references to foreign law and precedent appear in opinions emanating from the Supreme Court. Given the name "comparativism" by one of its strongest advocates and practitioners, Justice Stephen Breyer, the practice dates back to the
(10) late nineteenth century, but increasing globaliza- tion has given comparativism an increased stature and prominence. With this widening perspective on the law, Justice Breyer and others have cited foreign law in opinions in several high-profile cases
(15) covering issues like the death penalty for minors and the mentally handicapped, anti-sodomy laws, and affirmative action.

Supporters of comparativism rightly contend that the United States has been required to take on an
(20) increasingly important role as part of a more inte- grated world order. And as the United States adjusts to its role as the planet's sole remaining superpower, the impact of its judicial decisions are likely to have implications far beyond its borders. This "globaliza-
(25) tion" of law and the resulting developments force justices to address issues in a larger context and with a less insular vision. Increasingly, justices find them- selves acting as international arbitrators of issues that go beyond simple domestic concerns, and as
(30) globalization continues, their ability to remain isolationist will become increasingly difficult.

PASSAGE B

There is a growing concern among some legal authorities over the practice of judicial "comparativism"—a doctrine that allows the intro- duction of foreign precedent into American courts.
(5) Several judges have gone on the record to state that foreign precedent is completely irrelevant to US law. Some of these opponents, usually conservatives who oppose federal intervention in certain legal matters, describe comparativism as un-American.
(10) When Supreme Court Justice Anthony Kennedy

used foreign precedent as a basis for striking down anti-sodomy laws, these same opponents of comparativism called for his impeachment and even proposed legislation to outlaw justices from
(15) using foreign precedent, except English common law, when interpreting the Constitution.

Opponents of comparativism have offered several legitimate arguments against the practice. One is that justices may use foreign precedents to
(20) their advantage, choosing only those precedents that justify their positions. Also, since they are not as versed in the nuances of a foreign court system, they may misapply a decision by ignoring other aspects of that country's legal system. Another
(25) significant concern is that comparativism breaks with the American democratic system as it was established in the Constitution. The Constitution entrusts American jurists with the power to review and shape the law of the land, and thus, justices
(30) should not be looking to foreign law for guidance in purely American concerns. A corollary of this is that since a foreign country's law did not develop along with American society it is irrelevant and should not even be considered in a decision that involves
(35) only members of that American society.

GO ON TO THE NEXT PAGE

1. Which of the following, if true, would most strengthen the position held by opponents of comparativism?

    (A) Great Britain allows comparativist precedent in its courts because it can provide new solutions to shared problems.
    (B) Evidence comes to light that comparativism was used with success in ancient Greek and Roman courts.
    (C) Comparativism works best when legal perspectives are shared between nations with similar legal systems.
    (D) A federal appellate court rules that foreign precedent may not be used as the only support for a case.
    (E) A conservative judge who opposes abortion cites international precedents that restrict abortion in Germany and Ireland when overturning a law allowing teens to have abortions without parental consent.

2. It can be inferred that the author of passage A would most likely hold which one of the following attitudes towards the opponents of comparativism discussed in passage B?

    (A) Derisive because the basis of their arguments is close-minded and rooted in bigotry.
    (B) Appreciative of the role they are taking in the public discourse while ultimately feeling their arguments are wrongheaded.
    (C) Critical because their arguments ignore the reality of the current legal and political situation.
    (D) Scornful because their arguments are irrelevant to the current scholarly discourse.
    (E) Dismissive of their political response but respectful of the basis for their opposition.

3. Which one of the following statements about those who oppose comparativism can be inferred from lines 5–16 of passage B?

    (A) They support the execution of minors and the mentally handicapped, support anti-sodomy laws, and oppose affirmative action.
    (B) They consider the fact that the United States is unique in the world in some of its legal practices as a relevant consideration when interpreting the Constitution.
    (C) They are not as well versed in foreign court systems as those who support comparativism.
    (D) They believe that globalization is a short-term economic trend and that legal scholars should not allow constitutional interpretation to be influenced by such fleeting shifts in the economy.
    (E) They believe that the trust that Americans have given their justices is misplaced and should be reinstituted in a smaller body of justices that will not be so easily swayed by foreign adjudications.

4. According to information contained in passages A and B, Supreme Court Justices Kennedy and Breyer would be most likely to agree about which of the following?

    (A) English law is more applicable to US law than that of other nations.
    (B) Foreign law can validly be used as precedent in US courts.
    (C) Foreign law should be the central consideration with regard to constitutional issues.
    (D) Comparativism has had more influence in other nations than in the United States.
    (E) The use of comparativism is only applicable in the Supreme Court.

GO ON TO THE NEXT PAGE

5. The opponents of comparativism, as discussed in passage B, would most likely analogize the use of comparativism in domestic cases as

   (A) a doctor who is unsure what the correct medicine is for a treatment and consults with other doctors for their opinion before making a recommendation

   (B) a teacher who is unsure what method to use for teaching a difficult subject in grammar, so she consults several teaching guides, some of which are for foreign students learning English

   (C) a board member of a long-standing organization who must determine a new policy and uses the policies of another, younger but similar organization to determine the language of that policy

   (D) a candidate for public office who argues during a debate that a national policy currently in effect is wrongheaded because France and Germany do not have such a policy in effect

   (E) an international corporation that recalls a product in Germany because it fails to meet German health standards and then recalls it in France and England as well even though the product meets their health standards

6. It can be inferred that the opposition in the case in which Justice Kennedy used comparativism

   (A) held that Justice Kennedy made the right decision but that using foreign law as a justification was wrong

   (B) thought that Justice Kennedy's decision would have been correct if he had based it on English common law instead of current foreign precedents

   (C) saw comparativism as unacceptable in cases involving laws governing moral issues but acceptable in all others

   (D) used comparativism as a cover for a deeper disagreement to Kennedy's decision

   (E) alleged that comparativism was equivalent to committing treason

7. The issues that are central to both passages A and B can best be described as

   (A) offering an a priori justification for a new approach to interpreting the Constitution

   (B) criticizing a trend in constitutional interpretation by Supreme Court justices

   (C) proposing an alternative method of interpreting the Constitution that will resolve high profile cases being argued before the Supreme Court

   (D) explaining the origins of some new techniques of constitutional interpretation being used by current Supreme Court justices

   (E) describing the nature of a legal controversy and the polarization of those on both sides of the argument

GO ON TO THE NEXT PAGE

The long-dominant school of neoclassical economics, with its focus on supply-and-demand curves and the efficient allocation of resources, has come under fire by economists, scholars, and policy (5) makers arguing for a new approach with better predictive models. Recent failings in predicting economic downturns have only heightened the intensity of their voices. These critics say that the neoclassical model is untenable considering the (10) current strain on raw materials and energy sources. One particular approach that has emerged from an unusual assembly of ecologists, evolutionary biologists, and ecological economists is the oddly termed "biophysical economics." Their model (15) is not too dissimilar from established ecological economics, except that it ventures beyond traditional economics to incorporate the laws of physics, more specifically the law of thermodynamics, into the analysis of the economic process. Ever since (20) the environmental movement of the 1970s there has been a growing interest in economics that incorporates environmental factors into its models. Even so, biophysical economics is a departure even from traditional environmental economics, which (25) is simply an application of neoclassical economics to environmental problems.

Based on a steady state model, biophysical economics like ecological economics challenges the neoclassical notion of constant growth. While (30) ecological economics orients around natural resources and how it fuels or limits the economic system to a steady state, the focus of biophysical economics centers on one particular measure that is both an input and an output—energy. The (35) central equation for this nascent field of economics is a physics concept called the energy return on investment, or EROI, which is the ratio of the energy delivered by a process to the energy used directly and indirectly in that process. Biophysical (40) economics states that an economic system requires a positive EROI in order to survive. Unlike neoclassical economics, the use of EROI enables biophysical economists to take into account technological change affecting production and factors out (45) the changes in consumer preferences and market forms that mask the underlying physical realities of the economy.

In line with its focus on only the physical realities of an economy, biophysical economists believe (50) the production of certain natural resources such as oil and coal will eventually reach their maximum. Even before that happens the EROI for that resource will already have begun its slide as it becomes increasingly more expensive to derive that resource. (55) As EROI diminishes, energy from these resources will become increasingly unsustainable. Biophysical economists argue that the EROI for oil has already begun its descent, starting its slide at the beginning of the new century.

(60) Of course, this new field is subject to the same internal conflicts that have plagued economists since the beginnings of their field of study. Not all proponents focus so entirely on energy, particularly the ecologists. Also, attributing numbers to energy (65) used or derived has proven difficult in some cases. Lastly, the school has already split into factions, one arguing that serious collapse of the world economy is imminent and the other that there is time to correct the ship's trajectory and avoid a dismal end.

8. The economists mentioned in lines 56–59 are assuming that

(A) oil has a lower energy return on investment than does natural gas
(B) the supply of oil in almost every part of the world is nearly depleted
(C) the energy required to extract oil and make it usable is becoming closer to the amount of energy provided by the oil
→ (D) the energy return on investment for oil is shrinking exponentially and is no longer positive
(E) there are no undiscovered oil resources that could restore the EROI of oil to its previous value

9. It can be inferred that which one of the following is true of the theories put forward by the biophysics economists?

(A) An economy can sustain positive growth as long as it has a stable or increasing EROI.
(B) An economy can sustain positive growth as long as it has the supply of natural resources to support its energy needs.
(C) An economy can grow despite any technological advances or physical changes when there are market forces that overcome such deficiencies.
(D) Biophysical economists and ecological economists agree about the physical limitations to the world economy but disagree about the solutions.
(E) Of the proponents of biophysical economics, the ecologists are the majority of those who believe that the collapse of the world economy is imminent.

GO ON TO THE NEXT PAGE

10. According to the passage, which of the following, if true, would most directly affect the biophysical economic models?

    (A) Consumers switch their preference from gasoline-powered to electric-powered automobiles.
    (B) The government increases taxes on gasoline, coal, and natural gas.
    (C) In order to maintain current supply levels, the largest mining companies must use a more costly and dangerous method to source coal.
    (D) In order to maintain current supply levels, oil companies must take on more debt to explore new areas and drill new wells.
    (E) An energy company derives a new technology for drilling a new deep-sea oil well that avoids an increase in cost the company had expected.

11. According to the passage, which one of the following best describes the biophysical economist view of oil supplies for energy?

    (A) scarce supply and expensive to source
    (B) stable or slightly decreasing supply, yet increasingly cheaper to source
    (C) unknown supply, yet increasingly cheaper to source
    (D) decreasing supply, yet inexpensive to source
    (E) abundant or stable supply, yet increasingly expensive to source

12. Which one of the following best describes the function of the final paragraph?

    (A) gives supporting facts for why biophysical economics has better predictive models than neoclassical economics
    (B) shows that while biophysical economics may offer stronger theories, certain practicalities will hinder its progress in overturning the dominance of classical economics
    (C) exhibits the conflict between biophysical economists and ecological economists
    (D) explains that while biophysical economics is new it is not immune to the problems that have led to the distrust of neoclassical economics
    (E) demonstrates how a disagreement between the factions within the biophysical economics community will only serve to make their arguments against neoclassical economics stronger

13. The author's attitude toward the use of EROI can best be described as

    (A) optimistic that this model has the flexibility to better depict the actual economy
    (B) critical of its inability to predict economic downturns
    (C) skeptical of its application to the energy market
    (D) ambivalent about the use of biophysical economics versus neoclassical economics
    (E) excited about the potential it provides to the growth of alternative sources of energy

GO ON TO THE NEXT PAGE

While it is commonly believed that the conflicts in the life of Galileo Galilei (1564–1642) are between science and religion, between a heliocentric and a geocentric view of the universe, and between (5) Galileo and Pope Urban VIII, some questions have arisen recently to put doubt on the story and even question the very foundation of these conflicts.

One area of focus has been the injunction brought against Galileo by the Inquisition. As early (10) as 1955, historian Giorgio de Santillana claimed in his work *The Crime of Galileo* that the document was a forgery. Heavily influenced by the political environment in the United States at the time, Santillana argued that Galileo was mostly betrayed by his (15) compatriot scholars and intellectuals who wanted to protect their way of life and turned to a higher authority to quiet the dissident. Later, other scholars argued that even if the injunction was not a forgery it was not notarized as required by law and thus (20) lacked authority. The injunction ordered Galileo not to teach Copernicanism in any form, but Galileo more likely abided the letter he received from the Catholic theologian Robert Bellarmine warning him against supporting the Copernican view of the (25) universe. The injunction, notarized or not, probably bore little influence on his actions.

More recently, Pietro Redondi, in his book *Galileo Heretic*, questioned whether Copernicanism was even the basis for the conflict in the first place, (30) suggesting that the conflict that has come down through history was a cover-up for a more serious infraction of religious doctrine. Redondi based his argument on a document he found in the Vatican archives. The document indicated that Galileo's (35) observations about the earth's motion was not condemnable and that another complaint had been filed. Redondi found the other complaint at issue was an attack by an anonymous accuser thought to be Jesuit astronomer Orazio Grassi, (40) S.J. Grassi attacked Galileo's support of atomism, which directly contradicts the church's long-held belief in the Eucharist, specifically that the wine and wafer through transubstantiation become the blood and body of Christ. If atomism was the true (45) offense of Galileo, then the question arises, why was the pretense of Copernicanism used to cover it up, and why would Pope Urban VIII allow such a cover story? One theory is that Galileo enjoyed the support of the Medici family, a stalwart supporter (50) of the church, and monetary influence bought favor with the Vatican. This may also explain why even when Copernicanism became the issue Galileo was not burned at the stake as his contemporary Giordano Bruno was in 1600. Also, the reset of the (55) conflict means that the trial's origin moves from the publication of the *Dialogue Concerning the Two Chief World Systems* in 1632 to the earlier publication of *The Assayer* in 1623, yet one may wonder why the Vatican never added *The Assayer* to the index of (60) proscribed books during that period.

Even though more than four hundred years of scholarship have not resolved some issues, there are some indisputable facts: the Vatican did bring Galileo up on charges of heresy and he (65) was sentenced to house arrest for disobeying the church's orders.

14. Which one of the following best states the main idea of the passage?

(A) Recent theories and discoveries put forward by scholars have raised some doubt about the authenticity of Galileo Galilei's work and argue that the conflict with the Catholic Church may have been unjust.

(B) Recent theories and discoveries put forward by scholars have put doubt on the church's motives for trying Galileo Galilei, and a conspiracy may surround his fall from grace. Nevertheless, the facts of his trial and house arrest are undeniable.

(C) Scholars questioning the story of Galileo Galilei's conflict with the church have been heavily influenced by current political events and should be discounted, especially since the facts of his trial and house arrest are indisputable.

(D) The recent discovery of authentic and unambiguous documents have put the story of Galileo Galilei's fall from grace into serious question, and scholars are currently pursuing explanations regarding the truth of his crime and his house arrest.

(E) The two areas in question today with scholars are whether Galileo Galilei was ever put on trial by the Catholic Church and for what reason. His house arrest was never in doubt, but why he was not burned at the stake like his compatriots still confounds some scholars.

15. Which of the following political events of his time was most likely to have influenced Giorgio de Santillana while writing his book *The Crime of Galileo*?

(A) the dropping of the atomic bomb on Japan
(B) the end of Nazism and the rise of communism
(C) the House Un-American Activities Committee hearings
(D) the cold war and the resulting Korean War
(E) the rise of television as a source of entertainment and news

GO ON TO THE NEXT PAGE

16. The passages suggests that Pietro Redondi would most likely agree with which of the following statements about Galileo Galilei?

(A) The forgery of the injunction issued for the arrest of Galileo Galilei was one more piece of evidence that there was a conspiracy within the Catholic Church to cover up a more serious crime committed by the scientist.

(B) Galileo's contemporaries were jealous of his achievements and betrayed him to the church, so the church invented the crime of Copernicanism to cover up its culpability in this betrayal.

(C) The Medici family financed Galileo Galilei and urged him to challenge church doctrine, but they failed to protect him when he came to trial, which is why he was ultimately put under house arrest.

(D) The theory that the earth and other planets revolved around the sun was less offensive to the Catholic Church than the natural philosophy theorizing that atoms were indestructible and immutable.

(E) The Jesuit astronomer Orazio Grassi, S.J., disliked Galileo Galilei and his theories, regardless of their truth, and it was Grassi's determination to destroy the scientist that resulted in his trial and house arrest.

17. Which of the following, if true, would most weaken the author's argument about the difference in punishment between Giordano Bruno and Galileo Galilei?

(A) Both scientists supported Copernicanism, but they differed on the theory of atomism.

(B) Both scientists offended the church, but Galilei enjoyed the protection of a wealthy benefactor.

(C) Both scientists supported atomism, but they differed on the theory of Copernicanism.

(D) Both scientists offended the church, but the crimes committed by Bruno were much more serious than those of Galilei.

(E) Both scientists supported Copernicanism, but they differed on God's relationship to the order of the universe.

18. The passage implies which of the following with regard to the church and publications in the time of Galileo Galilei?

(A) Publications were registered with the church regardless of whether they offended church doctrine.

(B) The church probably would not have put an author on trial for a theory published in a book that had not been put on the list of proscribed books.

(C) The church put every author who had a book on the proscribed list on trial and all except Galileo Galilei were burned at the stake.

(D) Books on the church's proscribed list were not necessarily considered offensive to the church and not every book that was offensive to the church was on the proscribed list.

(E) Even though the church considered Galileo Galilei's *The Assayer* offensive, it did not add it to the list due to the patronage of the Medici family.

19. The author's primary purpose in the passage is to

(A) summarize recent discoveries that give further insight into the story of Galileo Galilei's conflict with the Catholic Church

(B) describe a dispute between two scholars who disagree regarding the basis for Galileo Galilei's trial and punishment by the Catholic Church

(C) present and assess two theories from scholars that have called into question aspects of the story of Galileo Galilei's conflict with the Catholic Church

(D) explain the complicated aspects of the Catholic Church's considerations when it put Galileo Galilei on trial and decided his punishment

(E) criticize the theories of two scholars that have questioned the validity of aspects of the story of Galileo Galilei's conflict with the Catholic Church

GO ON TO THE NEXT PAGE

A growing number of educators in the United States are advocating single-sex schools or classrooms to improve academic achievement in the public schools. Private and parochial schools have been
(5) maintaining single-sex classrooms for at least a century, but the unanswered question is whether it can work in the much more diverse laboratory of the American public school system. There are, however, two approaches to single-sex education, the more
(10) dominant genetic differences approach and the older sociological approach. Neither agrees with the other and there are critics of both with regard to evidence and efficacy. More than 40 studies have been accepted as viable, but as with most educa-
(15) tional institution studies, each study involves too many complicating factors that make it difficult to draw a conclusion, and in some cases the study found single-sex education to actually be harmful. Nevertheless, both approaches forge ahead despite
(20) the critics and lack of evidence, and an increasing number of public schools offer at least single-sex classrooms as an option to parents.

The most prominent advocate for the genetic approach is psychologist Leonard Sax, MD, PhD,
(25) who argues that single-sex education is necessary due to inherent differences between the sexes. The idea that girls and boys learn differently has been around for decades. The modern move toward single-sex public schools began in the 1980s, when
(30) some schools experimented with the format to deal with at-risk African American boys, but this effort originated from a distinct social problem and incorporated race factors as well. It was in the 1990s that Sax's ideas gained more general attention and
(35) became the central motivating factor. Sax argues that the physical and psychological differences between how the sexes learn supports separation into different learning environments. He points to studies that supported the argument that girls and
(40) boys have hormonal, physiological, and neurological differences that require different learning environ- ments. Sax uses the example that girls from a very early age have more sensitive hearing than boys and thus require a quieter and more orderly classroom
(45) while boys are better able to work within a noisy and disorderly environment. The American Civil Liberties Union and others fear this approach fuels dangerous stereotypes that undermine any progress achieved by improved educational performance.
(50) The second approach, advanced by several school administrators, argues that separation is necessary as a solution to the modern social pressures that put students' education at risk. These social pressures between the sexes vary from those that diminish
(55) a child's sense of self-worth to those that drive the child out of school altogether. In some cases it leads the student to devalue education and, in the worst case, unplanned pregnancies.

Beyond the proposed evidence by either side,
(60) other critics contend that single-sex education ultimately moves public education away from one of its traditional goals, to encourage and integrate American values into its students, and separating the sexes seems to them inconsistent with the
(65) American value of social integration.

20. The passage is primarily concerned with discussing which of the following?

(A) two interpretations of roles played by gender in the classroom and how it effects the learning process
(B) two unsubstantiated theories of an educational strategy, neither of which agrees with the other or has quelled recent criticism
(C) two studies on single-sex education that are controversial and have been criticized by the academic community
(D) two revolutionary discoveries of how children learn in the classroom that are just beginning to be incorporated into public schools
(E) how a practice long successful in private and parochial schools is being applied to public education but not without controversy over application and efficacy

21. The reference to studies on single-sex education in lines 13–18 serves primarily to

(A) give credibility to the arguments in favor of single-sex education
(B) exhibit the academic environment and research that currently surrounds the development of contemporary single-sex education
(C) offer a caveat that might give the reader pause when accepting the arguments for single-sex education
(D) create doubt in readers' minds so that they will favor Dr. Sax's approach over the other approach
(E) describe the historical background that led education to develop the modern concept of single-sex education

GO ON TO THE NEXT PAGE

22. The passage suggests that Dr. Sax would probably agree with which one of the following statements about the children in the classroom?

    (A) Because girls are more susceptible to pressures to keep quiet in social situations, they should be separated from boys to allow them to express themselves more freely.
    (B) Because boys would rather look strong than smart in front of the opposite sex, they should be separated from them so that they can express themselves more honestly.
    (C) Because there is a stark difference between how boys and girls perform on standardized tests, different tests should be given to each based on their learning differences.
    (D) Because boys are inherently more adept with visual stimuli, boys should be separated from girls so that they may benefit from a more visual educational environment.
    (E) Because there is no difference between how boys and girls perform on manual dexterity tests, any nonacademic courses should be coed.

23. Which of the following statements best exemplifies the American Civil Liberties Union's concern mentioned in lines 46–49?

    (A) Boys are separated from girls because they can handle a more disorderly environment than girls. Therefore, only boys are taught how to organize their belongings more effectively.
    (B) Girls are separated from boys because their listening is better. Therefore, girls never learn to listen to the opposite sex effectively.
    (C) Boys are separated from girls because they have better visual acuity. Therefore, boys take only jobs that involve their visual abilities.
    (D) Girls are separated from boys because boys pester them in class. Therefore, girls never learn to negotiate the cross-gender dynamic.
    (E) Boys are separated from girls because they can handle a more disorderly environment than girls. Therefore, the school reinforces the misconception that boys are better than girls for jobs with chaotic environments.

24. The passage suggests that critics of both the genetic and social approaches to single-sex education would agree with which of the following statements?

    (A) Single-sex education makes sense as long as each class teaches the fundamentals of American values.
    (B) Single-sex education is warranted only to protect children from instilling in them un-American values.
    (C) Single-sex education is an excellent method of ensuring that American values are taught in a way that is appropriate for the particular gender.
    (D) Single-sex education is an inherently flawed model of educating children because it authorizes a particularly un-American separation rather than integration of the sexes.
    (E) Teachers of single-sex education classes are unable to instill truly good values in their students since the opposite sex is not present to give their unique perspective.

25. Which of the following best expresses the author's conclusion about single-sex education?

    (A) Single-sex education is only a minor force in American public education, and its popularity will fade.
    (B) As long as single-sex education controverts American values of integration, people will oppose its growth in the American public school system.
    (C) Research has failed to prove the efficacy of single-sex education.
    (D) Anecdotal evidence and high-profile advocates will propel single-sex education into the mainstream of American public education.
    (E) The social malaise of the American public school system will quell the genetic approach and advance the sociological approach.

STOP

IF YOU FINISH BEFORE TIME RUNS OUT, CHECK YOUR WORK ON THIS
SECTION ONLY. DO NOT GO ON TO ANY OTHER TEST SECTION.

SECTION IV

Time—35 minutes
26 Questions

Directions: Each group of questions in this section is based on a set of conditions. In answering some of the questions, it may be useful to draw a rough diagram. Choose the response that most accurately and completely answers each question and blacken the corresponding space on your answer sheet.

Questions 1–5

A conference planner must schedule six keynote speakers—Chapman, Dabu, Forest, Gant, Hart, and Jonas—over six days of a conference—days 1 through 6. The speakers are assigned to the days, one speaker per day, according to the following conditions:

> Chapman and Dabu must speak on days that are separated from each other by exactly one day.
> Chapman and Gant cannot speak on consecutive days.
> Gant must speak on a later day than Forest.
> Jonas must speak on day 3.

1. Which one of the following lists an acceptable schedule of the speakers for days 1 through 6, respectively?

    (A) Hart, Forest, Jonas, Dabu, Gant, Chapman
    (B) Forest, Gant, Chapman, Jonas, Dabu, Hart
    (C) Gant, Hart, Jonas, Chapman, Forest, Dabu
    (D) Forest, Chapman, Jonas, Dabu, Gant, Hart
    (E) Chapman, Dabu, Jonas, Forest, Gant, Hart

2. Which one of the following is a complete and accurate list of the days to which Chapman could be assigned?

    (A) 2, 4, 5
    (B) 2, 4, 6
    (C) 2, 3
    (D) 2, 4
    (E) 1, 2

3. Which one of the following CANNOT be true?

    (A) Hart is scheduled to speak on day 2.
    (B) Dabu is scheduled to speak on day 2.
    (C) Chapman is scheduled to speak on day 2.
    (D) Forest is scheduled to speak on day 1.
    (E) Forest is scheduled to speak on day 5.

4. Which one of the following must be true?

    (A) Either Forest or else Gant is scheduled to speak on day 2.
    (B) Either Forest or else Gant is scheduled to speak on day 5.
    (C) Either Chapman or else Dabu is scheduled to speak on day 2.
    (D) Either Chapman or else Dabu is scheduled to speak on day 4.
    (E) Either Forest or else Hart is scheduled to speak on day 6.

5. Which one of the following CANNOT be true?

    (A) Dabu and Gant are scheduled to speak on consecutive days.
    (B) Forest and Chapman are scheduled to speak on consecutive days.
    (C) Forest and Hart are scheduled to speak on consecutive days.
    (D) Dabu and Gant are scheduled to speak on days that are separated from each other by exactly one day.
    (E) Forest and Jonas are scheduled to speak on days that are separated from each other by exactly one day.

GO ON TO THE NEXT PAGE

Questions 6–12

Exactly six students—Bjorn, Chaim, Dottie, Fran, Gertie, and Heste—need to be assigned to four tutors: Sosa, Upton, Willie, and Zane. Each student is assigned to exactly one tutor, with at least one student assigned to each tutor. Sosa tutors only in math. Upton tutors only in physics and chemistry. Willie tutors only in math and physics. Zane tutors only in chemistry and English. Each student needs tutoring in only one of the subjects offered by the tutors and needs tutoring in no other subject.

The following rules govern the assignment of the students to the tutors:

> At least Bjorn and Chaim are assigned to Willie.
> At least Fran is assigned to Zane.
> If Dottie is assigned to Upton, then Gertie needs tutoring in math

6. Each of the following could be true of the assignment of students to tutors EXCEPT:

   (A) It assigns Gertie to Upton and Dottie to Zane.
   (B) It assigns Gertie to Sosa and Dottie to Zane.
   (C) It assigns Fran to Zane and Gertie to Zane.
   (D) It assigns Dottie to Willie and Heste to Zane.
   (E) It assigns Dottie to Sosa and Gertie to Upton.

7. Which one of the following must be true?

   (A) Sosa is assigned exactly one of the students.
   (B) Zane is assigned fewer than three of the students.
   (C) Upton is assigned fewer than two of the students.
   (D) Zane is assigned exactly one of the students.
   (E) Willie is assigned exactly two of the students.

8. Each of the following could be true EXCEPT:

   (A) Both Dottie and Gertie need tutoring in English.
   (B) Both Dottie and Heste need tutoring in chemistry.
   (C) Both Dottie and Heste need tutoring in math.
   (D) Both Dottie and Gertie need tutoring in math.
   (E) Both Dottie and Bjorn need tutoring in physics.

9. If Fran and Heste need tutoring in the same subject as each other, then the maximum number of students who need tutoring in physics is

   (A) two
   (B) three
   (C) four
   (D) five
   (E) six

10. If Dottie and Fran need tutoring in the same subject as each other, then which one of the following must be true?

    (A) Dottie and Fran need tutoring in English.
    (B) At least two students need tutoring in math.
    (C) At least two students need tutoring in English.
    (D) At least one of Gertie and Heste needs tutoring in math.
    (E) At least one of Gertie and Heste needs tutoring in chemistry.

11. If exactly two students are assigned to Upton, then which one of the following could be true?

    (A) Gertie needs tutoring in chemistry and Dottie needs tutoring in chemistry.
    (B) Gertie needs tutoring in math and Dottie needs tutoring in chemistry.
    (C) Heste needs tutoring in math and Dottie needs tutoring in physics.
    (D) Heste needs tutoring in English and Fran needs tutoring in English.
    (E) Heste needs tutoring in math and Gertie needs tutoring in math.

12. If Bjorn, Chaim, Gertie, and Heste all need tutoring in the same subject as each other, then which one of the following could be true?

    (A) Exactly two of the students need tutoring in physics.
    (B) Dottie needs tutoring in English.
    (C) Dottie needs tutoring in math.
    (D) Exactly two students need tutoring in English.
    (E) Exactly three of the students need tutoring in chemistry.

GO ON TO THE NEXT PAGE

Questions 13–19
In a small town, there are six buildings that need to be certified by two inspectors as earthquake-safe, three government buildings—I, J, and K—and three commercial buildings—M, N, and O—each evaluated once by inspector Harris and once by inspector Limon, during six consecutive weeks—week 1 through week 6. Each inspector inspects one building per week. No building will be inspected by Harris and Limon during the same week. The following additional constraints apply:

> Limon cannot inspect any government building until Harris has evaluated that building.
> Harris cannot evaluate any commercial building until Limon has evaluated that building.
> Limon cannot inspect any two government buildings consecutively.
> Harris must inspect building M during week 4.

13. Which one of the following is an acceptable inspection schedule, with the buildings listed in order of inspection from week 1 through week 6?

    (A) Harris: I, N, J, M, K, O
        Limon: N, I, M, J, O, K
    (B) Harris: K, N, I, M, J, O
        Limon: M, K, O, I, N, J
    (C) Harris: I, J, M, O, K, N
        Limon: M, I, O, J, N, K
    (D) Harris: J, O, I, M, K, N
        Limon: O, I, M, J, N, K
    (E) Harris: J, K, I, M, N, O
        Limon: M, J, K, N, O, I

14. If Harris inspects building K during week 3 and Limon inspects building J during week 6, which one of the following must be true?

    (A) Limon inspects N during week 5.
    (B) Limon inspects M during week 1.
    (C) Harris inspects J during week 2.
    (D) Harris inspects I during week 1.
    (E) Harris inspects O during week 6.

15. If Harris inspects building O during week 2, then Limon must evaluate which one of the following buildings during week 5?

    (A) O
    (B) K
    (C) N
    (D) M
    (E) I

16. Which one of the following must be true?

    (A) Harris does not inspect any two government buildings consecutively.
    (B) Harris inspects N before inspecting J.
    (C) Harris inspects a commercial building during week 2.
    (D) Limon inspects a commercial building during week 3.
    (E) Limon inspects K during week 6.

17. If Limon inspects M during week 1 and I during week 2, which one of the following could be true?

    (A) Harris does not inspect any two government buildings in a row.
    (B) Harris inspects O during week 6.
    (C) Harris inspects J during week 5.
    (D) N is the first of the commercial buildings to be inspected by Harris.
    (E) M is the third of the commercial buildings to be inspected by Harris.

18. Which one of the following is a complete and accurate list of the weeks during which Harris must inspect a government building?

    (A) week 1, week 3, week 5
    (B) week 1, week 2, week 3
    (C) week 1, week 5
    (D) week 1
    (E) week 6

19. Which one of the following could be true?

    (A) Limon inspects K during week 2.
    (B) Limon inspects I during week 3.
    (C) Limon inspects M during week 5.
    (D) Harris inspects O during week 1.
    (E) Harris inspects I during week 6.

GO ON TO THE NEXT PAGE

Questions 20–26

A lumberyard offers exactly 10 types of lumber—both domestic and exotic varieties of cherry, maple, oak, pine, and walnut. The lumberyard is having a sale on some of these types of lumber. The following conditions must apply:

> Exotic oak is on sale; domestic maple is not.
> If both types of oak are on sale, then all walnut is.
> If both types of cherry are on sale, then no pine is.
> If neither type of cherry is on sale, then domestic oak is.
> If either type of pine is on sale, then no walnut is.

20. Which one of the following could be a complete and accurate list of the types of lumber that are on sale?

    (A) exotic maple, exotic oak, domestic pine, exotic pine
    (B) exotic cherry, exotic oak, domestic walnut, exotic walnut
    (C) exotic maple, domestic oak, exotic oak, domestic walnut
    (D) domestic cherry, exotic oak, exotic pine, domestic walnut
    (E) domestic cherry, exotic cherry, exotic maple, exotic oak, domestic pine

21. If domestic walnut is not on sale, then which one of the following must be true?

    (A) At least one type of oak is not on sale.
    (B) At least one type of cherry is not on sale.
    (C) Exotic maple is not on sale.
    (D) Domestic pine is not on sale.
    (E) Domestic pine is on sale.

22. If both types of cherry are on sale, then which one of the following is the minimum number of types of domestic lumber that could be included in the sale?

    (A) one
    (B) two
    (C) three
    (D) four
    (E) five

23. Which one of the following CANNOT be true?

    (A) Neither type of cherry and neither type of maple is on sale.
    (B) Neither type of maple and neither type of pine is on sale.
    (C) Neither type of cherry and neither type of pine is on sale.
    (D) Neither type of maple and neither type of walnut is on sale.
    (E) Neither type of cherry and neither type of walnut is on sale.

24. If neither type of cherry is on sale, then each of the following must be true EXCEPT:

    (A) Exotic pine is not on sale.
    (B) Domestic walnut is on sale.
    (C) Exotic walnut is on sale.
    (D) Domestic pine is not on sale.
    (E) Exotic maple is on sale.

25. If domestic walnut is the only type of domestic lumber on sale, then which one of the following CANNOT be true?

    (A) Exotic walnut is not on sale.
    (B) Exotic cherry is not on sale.
    (C) Exotic pine is not on sale.
    (D) Exotic maple is not on sale.
    (E) Exotic walnut is on sale.

26. If exactly four of the five types of exotic lumber are the only lumber on sale, then which one of the following could be true?

    (A) Neither type of cherry is on sale.
    (B) Neither type of pine and neither type of walnut is on sale.
    (C) Exotic cherry is not on sale.
    (D) Exotic pine is not on sale.
    (E) Exotic maple is not on sale.

STOP

IF YOU FINISH BEFORE TIME RUNS OUT, CHECK YOUR WORK ON THIS SECTION ONLY. DO NOT WORK ON ANY OTHER TEST SECTION.

LSAT Practice Test 1 Answer Key

Section I	Section II	Section III	Section IV
1. C	1. B	1. E	1. D
2. B	2. B	2. C	2. B
3. C	3. D	3. B	3. A
4. A	4. A	4. B	4. D
5. D	5. B	5. C	5. C
6. B	6. D	6. D	6. D
7. A	7. E	7. E	7. B
8. C	8. D	8. C	8. A
9. A	9. D	9. A	9. B
10. B	10. C	10. C	10. D
11. D	11. C	11. E	11. B
12. D	12. D	12. D	12. C
13. C	13. A	13. A	13. A
14. A	14. B	14. B	14. D
15. D	15. E	15. C	15. C
16. E	16. C	16. D	16. D
17. B	17. D	17. D	17. B
18. E	18. C	18. B	18. D
19. D	19. D	19. C	19. A
20. C	20. B	20. B	20. B
21. A	21. A	21. C	21. A
22. D	22. C	22. D	22. A
23. C	23. C	23. E	23. E
24. C	24. A	24. D	24. E
25. C	25. C	25. C	25. B
			26. D

Calculate Your Score

Complete the following table.

Your Raw Score

SECTION	TYPE	NUMBER OF QUESTIONS	NUMBER CORRECT
1	Arguments	25	_____
2	Arguments	25	_____
3	Reading Comprehension	25	_____
4	Logic Games	26	_____

Total Raw Score _____

Your Approximate Scaled Score

It is impossible to say with complete precision what raw score will translate to what scaled score on future LSATs, but here is a rough estimation.

NUMBER OF QUESTIONS MISSED	APPROXIMATE SCALED SCORE
3	~180
8	~175
15	~170
20	~165
25	~160
25–35	between 155–160
35–45	between 150–155
45–55	between 145–150
55–60	between 140–145
60–70	between 135–140
70–80	between 125–135
More than 80	120–125

LSAT Practice Test 1 Answers and Explanations

SECTION I

1. Answer: **C**

STEP 1: **Read the question and identify your task.**

This is a Strengthen question. The question asks that you find among the answers the strongest defense against Lorne's criticism of Jamey's argument.

STEP 2: **Read the argument with your task in mind.**

You read through Jamey's and Lorne's statements, paying particular attention to the basis for Lorne's criticism. In this case, Lorne believes that the results of the test that bacteria can survive on arsenic is not enough support to justify further research into life on other planets.

STEP 3: **Know what you're looking for.**

You look through the answers to assess their potential to undermine this belief.

STEP 4: **Read every word of every answer choice.**

Answer A actually supports Lorne's criticism by saying that bacteria survive better on phosphorus. Answer B brings up the toxicity of carbon while the bacteria were surviving on arsenic, which might also be seen as support for Lorne's position since it gives further evidence that life based on an arsenic diet is unsustainable. Answer C provides evidence in favor of Jamey's claim. It also shows that there is less chance of finding life on phosphorus-rich planets than on arsenic-rich planets, which implies the denial of Lorne's implicit claim, that because of the higher likelihood of finding life on phosphorus-rich planets we should search there for life. Answer D gives some additional support to Jamey's argument that life can survive on arsenic, but it does not necessarily undermine Lorne's criticism that life on phosphorus is more sustainable. Finally, answer E says that they have not found proof of life on planets rich in arsenic and devoid of phosphorus. Although this doesn't mean they do not exist, it does not strengthen Jamey's argument against Lorne. Therefore, **the correct choice is answer C.**

2. Answer: **B**

STEP 1: **Read the question and identify your task.**

This is a Describe question. It asks that you describe Lorne's approach to criticizing Jamey's argument.

STEP 2: **Read the argument with your task in mind.**

You reread Lorne's argument and see that he brings forth a new fact, that the bacterium survived longer on phosphorus than on arsenic, which may undermine Jamey's conclusion.

STEP 3: **Know what you're looking for.**

The correct answer will describe Lorne's attempt to undermine Jamey's conclusion by bringing up that new fact.

STEP 4: **Read every word of every answer choice.**

Answer A is fairly accurate. Lorne does agree with Jamey's facts and says they do not support the conclusion. This may be your answer, but you should evaluate the rest of the options to see whether there is a better one. Answer B says that Jamey presents new facts that undermine her conclusion, which matches your own evaluation. This is much better than answer A and is very likely your answer. You should continue to evaluate the rest of the options. Answer C cannot be correct because Lorne definitely does not support Jamey's conclusion. Regarding answer D, Lorne's facts are not irrelevant and he attacks Jamey's conclusion, not her credibility. Answer E says that Lorne attacks Jamey's logic, but Lorne's criticism is centered on the results of the study. He makes no criticism of Jamey's logic. Thus, you cannot choose answer E. **Answer B is the correct choice.**

3. Answer: **C**

STEP 1: **Read the question and identify your task.**

This is a variation of a Describe question—a Describe How the Argument Proceeds question. The question is in complete-the-sentence form, and thus the answer will be a description of how the argument is formed and not necessarily anything specific within the argument.

STEP 2: __Read the argument with your task in mind.__

The educator describes what the critics say about online universities and low-residency degree programs and then discusses how Plymouth Online is the exception to those objections.

STEP 3: __Know what you're looking for.__

You will look for something similar in your answer options.

STEP 4: __Read every word of every answer choice.__

Answer A is incorrect because the educator makes no reference to any scholarly authority during the challenge. Answer B is incorrect because the educator does not, in fact, question the validity of the objections the critics make. The educator merely states how Plymouth Online overcomes those issues. Answer C may be your answer because the educator does use Plymouth Online as a counter-example to what the scholars say are the prevalent beliefs about the distance programs. You must review the rest of the answers to be sure whether you are finished. Answer D is off the mark because the term *sociological* is an inaccurate description of the educator's discussion. The educator makes no sociological observations as to why distance programs are used. Also, this answer fails to mention the educator's use of his or her own program as an example. Finally, answer E is not accurate because the educator does not compare two approaches. Also, this answer ignores the dynamic between the critical scholars and the educator's discussion of Plymouth Online. **The correct choice is answer C.**

4. Answer: **A**

STEP 1: __Read the question and identify your task.__

This is a Weaken question. The question asks that you find among the options the statement that least strengthens the argument. This means that four out of the five statements will strengthen the argument while one will actually weaken the argument.

STEP 2: __Read the argument with your task in mind.__

In essence, the argument states that environmental damage will hinder the survival of the cichlid fish population.

STEP 3: __Know what you're looking for.__

You will look for a statement that says this is not true, that in fact the cichlid fish will survive despite environmental damage to the waters in which they swim.

STEP 4: __Read every word of every answer choice.__

Answer A is very promising. It says that the eyes of the cichlids can adapt to a change in water conditions, which would suggest that the cichlid population would manage to survive despite the environmental damage described in the argument. This may be your answer, but you should evaluate the remaining options to be sure. Answer B gives a fact that further supports the argument's notion that the cichlid's enhanced vision requires clearer water for the species to survive. Answer C suggests that a particular population of cichlids may have been adversely affected by its proximity to an industrial plant, supporting the idea that pollution affects their survival and supporting the argument. Answer D says cichlids, in order to survive, have fled to clearer waters, also supporting the argument. Finally, answer E offers another phenomenon that hindered the cichlid vision and adversely affected the survival of the cichlid population, again linking the success of vision to survival and supporting the argument. **The correct choice is answer A.**

5. Answer: **D**

STEP 1: __Read the question and identify your task.__

This is a Paradox question. The question asks that you choose the answer that helps resolve a discrepancy, or in other words, a seeming contradiction in the statements.

STEP 2: __Read the argument with your task in mind.__

The statements discuss two economic conditions. The first says that coffee revenues are down and popular coffee houses may have to close. The second says that more people are visiting coffee houses and the number of successful coffee houses is higher. The first focuses on coffee and popular coffee houses, the second on coffee houses in general.

STEP 3: __Know what you're looking for.__

The correct answer will find a way to resolve this difference between these groups.

STEP 4: __Read every word of every answer choice.__

Answer A focuses on coffee houses but does nothing to address the fact that coffee sales are down; thus, this answer does not resolve the discrepancy.

Answer B may explain the downturn in coffee sales, but it does not address the growth of coffee houses in the second economic scenario. Answer C enters into another area altogether, comparing a bakery to coffee houses, and this is far afield of what you are looking for. Answer D says that the most popular coffee houses rely on coffee while other coffee houses rely on food for revenue. This would seem to explain the discrepancy, for if coffee revenues are down this would only affect those coffee houses that rely on coffee for most of their revenues, while the other coffee houses might grow and grow in number because they do not rely on coffee for most of their revenues. This seems to be your most likely candidate. Finally, answer E focuses on coffee and its price but not on the growth in coffee houses, so it cannot be the answer. **The correct choice is answer D**.

6. Answer: B

STEP 1: Read the question and identify your task.
This is a Deduction question. This question asks you to derive a conclusion from the seemingly contradictory statements made by the manager and the technician.

STEP 2: Read the argument with your task in mind.
You analyze their statements and discover that the manager says that the total number of dropped cell phone calls on the network is down. The technician says that for the cell towers in operation last year and the year before the trend is toward a higher number of dropped cell phone calls.

STEP 3: Know what you're looking for.
You can assume the answer will have to do with the fact that the manager is looking at the total number of dropped calls and the technician is looking at a specific group of cell towers (those that were in operation last year and the year before).

STEP 4: Read every word of every answer choice.
Answer A discusses a drop in market share for the cell phone service. While this might be the result of a large drop in cell phone calls, there is no definitive connection between the two, so this cannot be your selection. Answer B says that at least one new cell tower was erected in the last two years. This would mean that there is at least one tower included in the manager's statistics that is

excluded in the technician's and may explain why the manager's number shows an increase and the technician's a decrease. This could very likely be your answer, but you must review the rest of your options to make sure. Answer C focuses on cell phone calls, but the manager and technician are discussing the number of *dropped* cell phone calls. Also, this answer does not say what kind of change, so it is too inexact to be your choice. Regarding answer D, a lack of quality improvement would seem to indicate that the number of dropped calls would remain basically the same, so it does not reconcile the difference between the manager's and technician's statements regarding an increase or decrease in dropped calls. Finally, answer E discusses the quality of the calls that are not dropped, which is another topic altogether. **The correct choice is answer B**.

7. Answer: A

STEP 1: Read the question and identify your task.
This is a Weaken question. This question asks you to choose the answer that most undermines the technician's argument against the manager.

STEP 2: Read the argument with your task in mind.
You can reread the technician's argument and see that there has not been an increase in efficiency based on dropped cell phone calls for cell towers that existed last year and the year before. Also, the technician says there is a trend toward more dropped calls, so the second year's number must be higher than the number for the previous year.

STEP 3: Know what you're looking for.
The correct answer will probably undermine one aspect of these bases.

STEP 4: Read every word of every answer choice.
Answer A says that the cell towers that existed last year and the year before experienced an abnormally high number of calls last year. This might explain why there was a trend toward more dropped calls for those towers and seems to undermine the technician's claim that the company has not achieved better efficiency. This may be your answer, but you must review the remaining options to be sure. Answer B in essence says the opposite of answer A, indicating that cell phone usage has not increased, which might be seen as support for the technician's argument. Answer C says before last year

there was a downward trend in usage, but it says nothing about what happened last year. While it implies that the trend might have changed, you cannot be sure and, thus, you cannot know this answer's implications for the technician's argument. Answer D somewhat undermines the manager's argument, but it only addresses the decrease in dropped calls, not the increase, and is not as strong as answer A. Answer E compares the company's results with those of another company, which is irrelevant. You only care about the internal results at issue with the manager and technician. **The correct choice is answer A.**

8. Answer: **C**

   <u>STEP 1:</u> **Read the question and identify your task.**
   This is a Flaw question. The question asks that you identify why the argument is questionable.

   <u>STEP 2:</u> **Read the argument with your task in mind.**
   The professor is arguing that the need for a humanities department should be questioned because literature and other areas of the humanities cannot be clearly defined.

   <u>STEP 3:</u> **Know what you're looking for.**
   The correct answer will most likely point out the unjustified leap the professor makes from the difficulty of defining literature to questioning the need for a humanities department.

   <u>STEP 4:</u> **Read every word of every answer choice.**
   Considering answer A, you do not know what kind of professor is making the statements, so you do not know whether he or she has a vested interest in eliminating a humanities department. Answer B cannot be correct because the professor does give some support for literature's lack of definability. Answer C says that the professor has failed to link the indefinability to the maintenance of a humanities department, which is exactly what you formulated as the expected answer. This is most likely your answer, but you must review the remaining options to see if one of them is better. Answer D may be true, but this is outside the argument the professor is making and does not deal with the logic of the statements. Answer E makes an observation that is not in evidence. The professor does not mention any sample at all. His statements are entirely general, so this answer is off the mark. **The correct choice is answer C.**

9. Answer: **A**

   <u>STEP 1:</u> **Read the question and identify your task.**
   This is a Flaw question. You are asked to find the error in the argument's reasoning.

   <u>STEP 2:</u> **Read the argument with your task in mind.**
   This argument concludes that people can reduce their risk of stroke by not eating fried fish. It relies on the premises that Southern states have a higher risk of stroke and people in those states eat more fried fish. The author assumes that eating fried fish causes strokes.

   <u>STEP 3:</u> **Know what you're looking for.**
   You need an answer that describes the flaw of assuming that correlation equals causation.

   <u>STEP 4:</u> **Read every word of every answer choice.**
   Answer A is exactly what you are looking for, but read all the answers to be sure. Answer B is not an assumption that is made, but rather premises. You must accept the facts from the study. Answer C cannot be a flaw, because no sample size is given. Answer D may seem true, but it is not the flaw in the logic. Answer E is not correct, because the argument does not really exploit a stereotype. **The correct choice is answer A.**

10. Answer: **B**

    <u>STEP 1:</u> **Read the question and identify your task.**
    This is a Flaw question. The question asks that you identify the flaw in Mr. Thomas's logic.

    <u>STEP 2:</u> **Read the argument with your task in mind.**
    You read the argument and see that Mr. Thomas believes that the fact that Ms. Garcia said that she was giving up her sales responsibilities is in contradiction to the pattern of visiting customers.

    <u>STEP 3:</u> **Know what you're looking for.**
    The correct answer will most likely highlight a misunderstanding of Ms. Garcia's words versus her perceived actions.

    <u>STEP 4:</u> **Read every word of every answer choice.**
    Answer A says that Mr. Thomas failed to consider that the colleague misled him. This may be true, but you are only concerned with the reasoning Mr. Thomas uses with the given facts, not whether the foundation of that reasoning is flawed. Answer B says the flaw is making a conclusion

based on equivocal language. This is very possibly the flaw because just working harder and visiting customers do not mean that Ms. Garcia is necessarily continuing her sales responsibilities. Such activities are ambiguous and could be interpreted in many ways. This may be your answer, but you must review the remaining options to be sure. Similar to A, answer C may be true, but again you are concerned only with Mr. Thomas's logic using the facts he has and not the origin of them. Answer D also does not discuss the flaw in logic, but rather says Mr. Thomas failed to make a judgment regarding Ms. Garcia's lack of character. Regarding answer E, Mr. Thomas does not really criticize Ms. Garcia. Instead, he says that either she or the colleague is lying, leaving open the option that Ms. Garcia is telling the truth. Therefore, **the correct choice is answer B.**

11. Answer: **D**

STEP 1:   Read the question and identify your task.

This is a Deduction question. The question asks that you qualify Talia and David's disagreement with regard to growth.

STEP 2:   Read the argument with your task in mind.

In this case, David believes the company needs to change in order to return to earlier levels of growth. Talia believes that the company has reached an acceptable level considering the age of the company.

STEP 3:   Know what you're looking for.

The correct answer will qualify the disagreement with regard to current versus past growth.

STEP 4:   Read every word of every answer choice.

Answer A says the disagreement is over whether growth can be changed, but this cannot be correct. Talia never says that the company cannot change, only that change is unnecessary. Answer B cannot be correct because both Talia and David acknowledge that growth has slowed. Answer C adds an irrelevant element not even mentioned in the discussion. Neither Talia nor David discusses a difference in perception among managers and employees, so this answer cannot be correct. Answer D says the disagreement is over whether growth is currently adequate, and this does seem to accurately qualify the disagreement because David believes that current growth is inadequate and the company needs to do something about it. Talia believes current growth is adequate and that

the company should stay the course. This would seem to be your answer, but you must review the last option to be sure. Answer E says the disagreement is over whether growth is changing over time, but both agree that growth has changed from the early days. It is only the current status of growth that is under discussion. Thus, **answer D is the correct choice**.

12. Answer: **D**

STEP 1:   Read the question and identify your task.

This is an Assumption question. You are asked to find an assumption made by the regulator.

STEP 2:   Read the argument with your task in mind.

The regulator argues that the new rules are more effective because they have enabled the discovery of 60 percent more defects in toys than before. Since the argument is narrow—it only applies to injuries from defective toys—you may think the reasoning is fairly sound. However, there is a gap in the logic. The regulator assumes that catching more defects will result in fewer injuries. What if the company caught more defects but did nothing to fix them?

STEP 3:   Know what you're looking for.

Find an answer that says something about the assumption that catching more defects will result in fewer injuries.

STEP 4:   Read every word of every answer choice.

Answer A is too narrow in scope. The argument was not restricted to a particular age group. Answers B and C are both irrelevant. Answer D looks good. Answer E might be true, but the regulator's defense has nothing to do with the regulations of other nations. **The correct choice is answer D.**

13. Answer: **C**

STEP 1:   Read the question and identify your task.

This is an Assumption question. You are asked to find the assumption made in the argument.

STEP 2:   Read the argument with your task in mind.

The author argues that people should not use a microwave to heat a bottle of formula, because microwaves heat unevenly and there could be hot pockets within the bottle. This assumes that the parent has no way to counter the uneven heating.

STEP 3:   Know what you're looking for.

You need an answer that describes the assumption that a parent cannot or will not even out the temperature of the bottle before giving it to the baby.

STEP 4:   Read every word of every answer choice.

Answer A is not relevant to the topic. Answer B, if true, is a different argument against using microwaves to heat formula, but it has no relation to this argument. Answer C is close to what you are looking for, so keep it. Answer D is certainly true, but the argument is not about overall heating, but uneven heating. Answer E is irrelevant to this argument. **The correct choice is answer C.**

14.   Answer: **A**

STEP 1:   Read the question and identify your task.

This is a Flaw question. The question asks that you find among the possible answers a statement that identifies the failure in the argument. In this case, the question asks that you finish the sentence with the element that is ignored by the argument.

STEP 2:   Read the argument with your task in mind.

The argument makes a judgment that soil erosion will no longer be getting more serious based on two years of data, during which the amount of soil lost remained the same.

STEP 3:   Know what you're looking for.

You expect the correct answer to point out the fact that the data only cover two years or that the level of erosion, regardless of the growth factor, is still a threat.

STEP 4:   Read every word of every answer choice.

Answer A seems a likely candidate since it says that the effects of soil erosion are cumulative, meaning that damage done previous to these two years as well as the loss over the two years has mounted and there needs to be significant movement in reverse to indicate that the problem is abating. Answer B may be true but these other problems (insects, climate change) are not relevant to the reasoning at hand. Regarding answer C, the statements do take into account the future and explicitly say "if this trend continues"; the argument does not ignore this possibility. Answer D links erosion to farm productivity, another factor that is irrelevant to the reasoning in the statements. The only reasoning you are concerned

with is that which leads to the conclusion that soil erosion will no longer become more serious. The effects of soil erosion are not at issue. Finally, answer E also adds an irrelevant factor, geographic location of the erosion, in an attempt to confuse you. You are concerned with overall erosion only, not how it is distributed among areas. Therefore, **the correct choice is answer A.**

15.   Answer: **D**

STEP 1:   Read the question and identify your task.

This is a Principle question. You are asked to find the general principle being applied in this situation.

STEP 2:   Read the argument with your task in mind.

Marisa used to pick out her daughter's clothes, but she now allows her daughter to choose her own outfits.

STEP 3:   Know what you're looking for.

You need an answer that describes the process of letting someone make her own decisions, or something about transferring responsibility to children once they reach an age at which they can handle it.

STEP 4:   Read every word of every answer choice.

Answer A is close, but Lori is not an adult yet. So keep this answer for now, but look for a better choice. Answer B cannot be correct, because you do not know if this is "good." Answer C is not correct, because we do not know if this is something that Lori deserves. Answer D describes exactly what is happening and is a better answer than answer A. Answer E is irrelevant because there does not seem to be any harm in this situation. **The correct choice is answer D.**

16.   Answer: **E**

STEP 1:   Read the question and identify your task.

This is a Strengthen question. The question asks that you choose which among the possible answers supports the argument made by the city official that Jason would not be able to keep his trailer due to an Abilene city ordinance denying parking rights for industrial vehicles.

STEP 2:   Read the argument with your task in mind.

Jason bought his trailer in Abilene, only to be told that he cannot keep it because trailers and other industrial vehicles cannot be parked within the city.

STEP 3: **Know what you're looking for.**
The correct answer will match Jason's situation with the stipulations of the city ordinance.

STEP 4: **Read every word of every answer choice.**
Answer A says that trailers are not classified as residential vehicles, but this does not mean that they are necessarily classified as industrial vehicles either, which is the stipulation under the code. Answer B is about whether car dealers can sell trailers in Abilene, which is obviously true since Jason bought his trailer in that city. The code stipulates where people can park a trailer, not where they can sell it. Answer C says that vans and flatbed trucks are not classified as industrial vehicles, but the argument is concerning Jason's trailer, not his van or flatbed truck, so this cannot be the right choice. Answer D is in essence a restatement of the code as it relates to nonindustrial vehicles, but Jason's trailer is considered an industrial vehicle, so this cannot be what the official's argument depends on. Finally, answer E says Jason lives in Abilene. By process of elimination this is your answer, but it also makes sense. For the official to argue that the code applies to Jason and his trailer, Jason must live in Abilene. Thus, **the correct choice is answer E.**

17. Answer: **C**

STEP 1: **Read the question and identify your task.**
This is a Paradox question. It wants you to reconcile the energy expert's conclusion with the contradictory evidence the expert presents.

STEP 2: **Read the argument with your task in mind.**
Even though funding for alternative energy technologies has increased significantly, there has been little impact on the use of these technologies. Yet the expert concludes that the government should increase funding for alternative technologies.

STEP 3: **Know what you're looking for.**
The correct answer will give a rationale for why an increase in funding is justified today in spite of the slow adoption rate of alternative energy.

STEP 4: **Read every word of every answer choice.**
Answer A discusses the number of professionals involved in developing alternative energy technologies, but it mentions nothing about the funding, which is the central focus of the energy expert's conclusion, so this cannot be your answer. Answer B, regarding the popularity of the idea that government should fund the development of alternative energy technologies, doesn't explain why an increase in funding is justified today. Answer C suggests technological change has made it possible for funding to be converted into success at a better rate. This would be a clear justification for increasing funding, despite the slow adoption rate. Answer D gives some explanation as to why the government may have to increase funding, mainly to fund higher salaries, but it does not reconcile why that increase should happen considering the meager adoption of practical applications of the new technologies. Answer E does not reconcile the expert's conclusion; rather, it undermines it by saying that the money that has been spent so far has been wasted. Thus, **the correct choice is answer C.**

18. Answer: **E**

STEP 1: **Read the question and identify your task.**
This is a Principle question. You are asked to find a situation that matches the general principle described.

STEP 2: **Read the argument with your task in mind.**
The mayor's policy is to do the most good for the most people.

STEP 3: **Know what you're looking for.**
You need an answer that describes a situation in which the maximum benefit is achieved for the most people.

STEP 4: **Read every word of every answer choice.**
Answer A seems to have a good outcome, but it does not involve a principle at all since the event was beyond human control. Answer B is an example of utilitarianism, but there is only one person involved. Keep this choice for now. Answer C violates the principle of utilitarianism because the decision did not favor the majority. Answer D presents a situation in which people presumably are following their wishes, but are not achieving the maximum good for the maximum number of people. Answer E is a good example of this principle since the majority prefer wheat bread. Answer E is more parallel to the situations faced by the mayor in governing a city than is answer B, so it is a better choice. **The correct choice is answer E.**

19. Answer: **D**

STEP 1: Read the question and identify your task.

This is a Describe question. The question asks you to identify the most accurate description of how the argument proceeds.

STEP 2: Read the argument with your task in mind.

The argument states that a phenomenon is expected to occur, namely that people not employed by the startups will be encouraged by the boom to spend more money, and then argues that because people's savings accounts are not decreasing, in actuality this cannot be the case.

STEP 3: Know what you're looking for.

The correct answer will most likely describe the argument as assuming that because one phenomenon is not occurring (savings not decreasing), the cause is not occurring (people not spending more).

STEP 4: Read every word of every answer choice.

Answer A cannot be your answer because the argument does not give two alternative developments. One development, the boom, causes the other, the spending, but they are not alternatives to each other. Answer B goes off on a tangent. The argument says nothing about economic self-interest, misinformation or error, or economic harm. Answer C cannot be correct because the argument discusses only one consequence of their behavior, a decrease in savings, not two, and there is no indication that the consequence is predictable. Answer D is right on the mark. It says that the argument concludes that the development (increased spending) did not occur because a supposed consequence (lower savings) did not occur. This would seem to be your answer, but you should evaluate your last option. Answer E indicates the evidence of the change is ambiguous; however, the argument clearly states savings accounts have not decreased, so there is no ambiguity and this cannot be your answer. **The correct choice is answer D**.

20. Answer: **C**

STEP 1: Read the question and identify your task.

This is an Assumption question. The question asks you to find the assumption upon which the argument relies.

STEP 2: Read the argument with your task in mind.

The argument assumes that increased spending by those not employed by the new businesses would result in an unusual decrease in their savings.

STEP 3: Know what you're looking for.

You review your options with that understanding in mind.

STEP 4: Read every word of every answer choice.

Whether answer A is true or not is irrelevant to the argument since it does not focus on sales. Rather, it focuses on spending by a certain subgroup of the population. Answer B actually contradicts the argument by saying that the people not employed by startups are in fact spending more by borrowing money from relatives. Answer C states the opposite from answer B, saying that people not employed by the business startups are not borrowing to make large purchases, which would support the notion that if they were making large purchases their savings would decrease. This is very likely your answer, but you must review the remaining options to be certain. Answer D also contradicts the argument by merely restating in other words the reason that people are expected to spend more. The argument says this is not the case because savings have not decreased. Finally, answer E discusses people who are employed by startups, but the argument is only concerned with people not employed by the startups and their spending habits. This cannot be your answer. **The correct choice is answer C**.

21. Answer: **A**

STEP 1: Read the question and identify your task.

This is an Assumption question. It is asking you to find among the options the one answer that identifies the assumption that makes the argument work.

STEP 2: Read the argument with your task in mind.

The argument says that criminal actions are simply human nature and concludes that the prison system should be abolished immediately. Therefore, the assumption is that criminals should not be punished for their crimes because they are naturally predisposed to commit those crimes.

STEP 3: **Know what you're looking for.**
The correct answer will state that criminals cannot be held accountable for the crimes they commit.

STEP 4: **Read every word of every answer choice.**
Answer A fits your requirement perfectly because it states that only human nature can be held responsible for crime. This may very well be your answer, but you must review the remainder of the options to be certain. Answer B is not only inaccurate—there is no ambiguity inherent in the term *nature* in this argument—but it also does not address the issue of accountability, and therefore is not your answer. Answer C seems way off the mark because the argument is not based on any statistical evidence, and it is not trying to extract observations of criminals to make a generalization on the entire population. And again, it does not address the issue of responsibility, so this cannot be correct. Answer D cannot be the correct choice because the argument does not distinguish criminals from crimes. It directly links them in the first sentence. Answer E seems to be discussing another argument altogether, since the argument you are concerned with does not discuss socially acceptable or socially unacceptable actions. These are vague terms when your discussion deals with the more specific actions of crime. Thus, **the correct choice is answer A.**

22. Answer: **D**

STEP 1: **Read the question and identify your task.**
This is a Deduction question. The question asks that you select from among the possible answers the one statement that must be true after taking into account the given statements regarding a country's natural gas inventory.

STEP 2: **Read the argument with your task in mind.**
The discussion says that the country's supply is down from the year before and that the country has not imported or exported natural gas in 10 years.

STEP 3: **Know what you're looking for.**
The correct answer will have to be consistent with a scenario in which what is used decreases the inventory and what is not used remains in inventory. There is no external use or source of inventory.

STEP 4: **Read every word of every answer choice.**
Answer A is impossible to know because you do not know anything about the inventory that carried over from 2008. The inventory was higher in 2009, but the carryover from 2008 could have been very little or none, so it is possible that consumption was much lower than 2010. There is simply no way to know for sure. Without the 2008 data or consumption numbers, answer B is difficult to conclude. You cannot know which year had more mining. Answer C muddles things by breaking the years into halves, but the statements only discuss full years and there is nothing in the statements that enables you to conclude anything with regard to parts of the year. This cannot be your answer. Answer D says more natural gas was consumed than mined in 2010. You know that some inventory carried over from 2009, so for the inventory in 2010 to be lower than that in 2009, the country must have consumed more natural gas in 2010 than was produced. This must be your answer. Answer E requires that you know the inventory that carried over from 2008. Otherwise, you cannot know how consumption in 2010 compared to 2009. **The correct choice is answer D**.

23. Answer: **C**

STEP 1: **Read the question and identify your task.**
This is a Conclusion question. The question asks you to identify the statement supported by the argument.

STEP 2: **Read the argument with your task in mind.**
The argument is about a misconception that a large breakfast decreases calorie intake for the rest of the day when it actually makes no difference whatsoever.

STEP 3: **Know what you're looking for.**
The correct answer might support a statement that says eating a large breakfast either makes no difference or counteracts efforts to reduce calories.

STEP 4: **Read every word of every answer choice.**
Answer A is not supported by the information. The argument implies that the size of breakfast has no effect on calorie intake outside of breakfast. This means the calorie intake outside of breakfast is fixed or unchanged. On the other hand, this also implies that the size of the breakfast may have beneficial or detrimental effects,

and a small breakfast versus no breakfast may in fact have different dieting benefits. This cannot be your answer. Answer B may give an explanation for why the non-breakfast food calorie intake remains unchanged, but nothing in the argument supports that notion. It is equally possible that they eat lower-calorie food for the rest of the day but more of it, thus overall calorie intake remains the same. There is nothing in the argument that allows you to choose one theory over the other. Answer C says that a small or no breakfast can reduce calorie intake while a large breakfast increases it. The argument supports this statement because it says that the size of the breakfast has no effect on calorie intake for the remainder of the day, but this means that the size of the breakfast may very well increase or decrease overall calorie intake. This is most likely your answer, but you should review the remaining answers to confirm the wisdom of your choice. Answer D says the size of the breakfast makes no difference, but the argument specifies that it will make no difference to calorie intake for the rest of the day. It does not indicate that the size of the breakfast will have no overall effect. In fact, it implies the opposite (answer C). Answer E has the same fault as answer B. It may give an explanation for why the non–breakfast food calorie intake remains unchanged, but nothing in the argument supports that notion. It is equally possible that they eat less of higher-calorie foods. **The correct choice is answer C.**

24. Answer: **C**

STEP 1:   **Read the question and identify your task.**

This is a Describe question. The question asks that you qualify what exactly Lonnie is pointing out in his criticism of Joanie's statement.

STEP 2:   **Read the argument with your task in mind.**

Joanie observes an increase in property losses and fatalities due to natural disasters and concludes that there has been an increase in natural disasters. Lonnie agrees about the increased property losses and fatalities but says there are other reasons for the increase, including increased development and more "large-scale" disasters, and these other reasons undermine Joanie's conclusion.

STEP 3:   **Know what you're looking for.**

The correct answer will most likely say that Lonnie agrees with the result but not necessarily with the underlying causes.

STEP 4:   **Read every word of every answer choice.**

For answers A and B, Lonnie never questions the statistics and actually uses them in his criticism, so you can eliminate both these options. Answer C is fairly close to what you want. Lonnie accepts the statistics but states that they do not represent the underlying causes that lead to her conclusion. This is most likely your answer, but you must review the remaining options. Answer D cannot be your choice because Lonnie never questions Joanie's qualifications. Lastly, regarding answer E, Lonnie never brings up other statistics. He accepts the same statistics that Joanie uses, but he interprets them differently. Thus, **the correct choice is answer C.**

25. Answer: **C**

STEP 1:   **Read the question and identify your task.**

This is a Parallel question. The question asks you to read the argument and find another argument that uses a similar form of reasoning, questionable though it may be.

STEP 2:   **Read the argument with your task in mind.**

In this case, the argument states that a political leader is considered great based on past decisions or actions and only on this basis, and that being considered great now is no basis for predicting future performance by the leader. In essence, this is saying that an assessment can be made based on past conditions, but given that assessment you cannot predict whether that assessment will remain valid in the future.

STEP 3:   **Know what you're looking for.**

Scanning through the answers, you notice they all are oriented around the same subject, ear infections in children. The correct answer will also make a statement about past or present situations not allowing you to predict the future of that condition.

STEP 4:   **Read every word of every answer choice.**

Answer A gives you a fact about the unpredictability of the various bacteria that cause ear infections and says that if the child has an ear infection, it is impossible to predict how it will progress. This answer switches from the unpredictability of bacteria to the unpredictability of the infection, but your sample remains focused on one subject, a leader, so this answer does not follow the same pattern. Answer B discusses children who do not contract ear infections, but it never discusses whether their special nature allows you to predict or not predict whether they will contract one in the future, so this does not follow the pattern. Answer C essentially argues that children are only considered to have an ear infection if they show the symptoms, but having such symptoms does not allow you to predict whether such symptoms will continue in the future. This would seem to approximate the logic of the argument and is likely your answer, but you must review the remaining options to be sure. Answer D starts out well, saying that only with the proper symptoms can a child be considered to have an ear infection, but then it says that the child may not have an ear infection because the symptoms are shared by other diseases. Nothing about predicting future ear infections is mentioned. Answer E never says that a child has an ear infection. Instead it speaks generally about the disease itself. Although the last sentence approximates the conclusion of your statements, this cannot be your answer. **The correct choice is answer C.**

SECTION II

1. Answer: B

STEP 1: **Read the question and identify your task.**

This is an Assumption question. It is asking you to identify among the answers the assumption upon which the argument bases its statement that "Slim-gurt" already dominates the market.

STEP 2: **Read the argument with your task in mind.**

The argument bases its claim on an opinion poll in which 76 percent of the respondents consider "Slim-gurt" the dominant yogurt on the market. Then, you learn that a company that enjoys more than 55 percent of sales in the marketplace is considered dominant.

STEP 3: **Know what you're looking for.**

The correct answer will justify the leap from the poll to the dominance qualification in the marketplace.

STEP 4: **Read every word of every answer choice.**

The argument does not make any claim about future dominance. It is only concerned about the current situation, so answer A cannot be correct. Answer B states that what the consumer believes is true is in fact true in the marketplace. This would justify the argument's link between the consumer opinion poll and the conclusion that the company is in fact dominant in the marketplace. This is most likely your answer, but you should review the remaining options to make sure. Answer C says that the consumer belief in dominance is a requirement or precondition for dominance, but there is nothing in the statements that implies such a causal relationship. Most of the argument revolves around the current situation, not a causal one. Answer D focuses on the market research but says nothing about market dominance, which is the main idea of the argument. Also, nothing in the argument implies that the company is ignoring the market research. Answer E may be true, but it is speculative about a future dominance while the argument is concerned with current dominance. **The correct choice is answer B.**

2. Answer: B

STEP 1: **Read the question and identify your task.**

This is a Conclusion question. The question asks you to identify the statement that must be true given the statements in the argument.

STEP 2: **Read the argument with your task in mind.**

The argument makes several assertions regarding astronauts, age, and purchasing alcohol, and you must determine whether they support one of the possible answers. The statements can be simplified as follows: astronauts > 21; purchase alcohol > 21; some scientists are astronauts; some scientists purchase alcohol; and some scientists < 21.

STEP 3: **Know what you're looking for.**

The correct answer will be consistent with the logical statements stated in step 2.

STEP 4: **Read every word of every answer choice.**

Answer A cannot be supported by the statements because you know only that some scientists are astronauts. None of the statements says how many astronauts are scientists. Answer B is supported by the statements. If only some of the scientists are astronauts and only some of the scientists purchase alcohol, then it logically follows that some scientists are not astronauts and some astronauts do not purchase alcohol. This is most likely your answer, but you must review the remaining options. Answer C cannot be correct because none of the statements reveals a relationship between those who purchase alcohol and astronauts. Without such a statement, you cannot come to this conclusion. Answer D cannot be true because the statements tell you that some scientists are not astronauts, some do not purchase alcohol, and some are over the age of twenty-one. Therefore, it is possible that there is at least one scientist who is not an astronaut, does not purchase alcohol, and is over twenty-one. Finally, answer E cannot be correct because the first statement says that there are no astronauts under the age of twenty-one, but this does not negate the possibility that there is an astronaut who is exactly twenty-one years old. The statement would have to say that there are no astronauts aged twenty-one or younger, but this is not the case. **The correct choice is answer B.**

3. Answer: **D**

STEP 1:   Read the question and identify your task.

This is an Assumption question. It asks that you identify an assumption upon which the Commission bases its argument.

STEP 2:   Read the argument with your task in mind.

Reading through the League's and the Commission's arguments you learn that the Commission believes that due to conservation efforts, unfettered logging will have no effect on the country's wildlife.

STEP 3:   Know what you're looking for.

The correct answer will support the notion that the nation's conservation efforts are adequate or that unfettered logging will not cause harm to those efforts.

STEP 4:   Read every word of every answer choice.

Answer A says that the Aligorian wildlife includes some of the most threatened species, but this would seem to be the basis of the League's argument, not the Commission's. The Commission's argument is that its conservation efforts are adequate regardless of what wildlife lives in the forest. Answer B also seems to be supporting the League's argument and not the Commission's, since the League is arguing that there should be a continuance or increase of such regulation, while the Commission is arguing against further regulation. Answer C says that agricultural nations need not have logging regulated, but neither the League nor the Commission tells you that Aligoria is a primarily agricultural nation, so this cannot be the correct choice. Answer D says that the indigenous species will survive in specially constructed habitats. The assumption is that such conservation efforts are adequate to protect the nation's threatened species. Even though it seems rather general, this would fit your expectations for a valid assumption upon which the Commission bases its argument. Though not perfect, it might be your best option. Answer E is again an assumption supporting the League's argument and not the Commission's, since the Commission believes that uncontrolled logging will not affect its wildlife. **The correct choice is answer D**.

4. Answer: **A**

STEP 1:   Read the question and identify your task.

This is a Strengthen question. It asks that you identify a principle among the possible answers that supports the Commission's position.

STEP 2:   Read the argument with your task in mind.

Since the Commission believes that the nation's conservation efforts have done well enough to allow unfettered logging, you would expect the principle to justify allowing an unregulated logging industry to thrive.

STEP 3:   Know what you're looking for.

The correct answer will most likely support the notion that regulations should be slowed or not instituted at all.

STEP 4:   Read every word of every answer choice.

Answer A says that regulations should not be implemented until logging has actually caused a reduction in population of an endangered species. This is a fairly supportive statement for the Commission's argument, since it supports holding off on any regulations until something bad actually happens. This is a good contender, but you must review the remainder of the answers to see whether a better one can replace it. Answer B puts wildlife preservation for future generations above the current economic needs of the nation, which does not support the Commission's argument. Answers C and D are actually supported by the League's statement, which argues for more control over logging and thus against further depletion of natural resources. The League's argument also supports the notion that Aligoria must handle its own environmental problems without regard to other nations' experiences. Thus, these answers are unsupportive of the Commission's argument, which is what your question is asking for. Finally, answer E is supported by neither argument since both argue under the assumption that it is Aligoria's responsibility to deal with the issue, not an international governing body. Thus, **the correct choice is answer A.**

5. Answer: **B**

STEP 1:   Read the question and identify your task.

This is a Principle question. It is asking that you apply Avi's reasoning to a judgment in a different situation.

STEP 2: **Read the argument with your task in mind.**

Goni argues that the tax penalty is not her fault because her advanced age has resulted in her having poor handwriting, which led to the bookkeeping error. Avi argues that regardless of such a physical limitation, Goni was aware of the problem and its effect on her bookkeeping and thus was taking a risk in her job, and thus she can be held responsible for her mistake.

STEP 3: **Know what you're looking for.**

The correct answer will be a situation where a person knowingly takes a risky action and must be held accountable for the resulting negative effect.

STEP 4: **Read every word of every answer choice.**

Answer A says that Jack was not responsible for losing his board position. You know immediately this cannot be right because your answer must hold the person responsible. Answer B says that Jack was responsible for missing the recital because he held a meeting that he knew would go on for too long. Here, a person did something knowing it was risky and he must be held responsible for the consequences. This would seem to be your answer, but you must review the remaining options to be sure. Answer C says that Jack is responsible for something his brother did and had no control over just because he knew his dog would be scared by that action. This does not follow your pattern since Jack was not taking the risky action himself. Answer D says Jack is responsible for offending a friend by telling her something that he had no idea she would take personally. This does not follow your pattern because he did not know that his action would result in such an offense, so he did not willingly take such a risk. Finally, answer E says that Jack is responsible for something that happened to him because he did not take recommended precautions. The key with this one is that the consequence happened to him rather than being something that he in fact caused. **The correct choice is answer B.**

6. Answer: **D**

STEP 1: **Read the question and identify your task.**

This is a Flaw question. The question asks that you identify among the answers the faulty strategy used by the editorial.

STEP 2: **Read the argument with your task in mind.**

The editorial argues that the governor should ignore the statements made by the chief prosecutor due to the prosecutor's own criminal conviction in the past.

STEP 3: **Know what you're looking for.**

The correct answer will most likely focus on the editorial's strategy of using the prosecutor's past behavior to justify its recommendation.

STEP 4: **Read every word of every answer choice.**

Answer A cannot be the correct choice because the editorial does not support the plan recommended by the prosecutor. It actually argues against implementing the plan. Answer B is out of scope. The editorial speculates as to the success or failure of the prosecutor's plan based on the prosecutor's character, not a particular aspect of the plan. Answer C is a bit vague, but while the editorial does presuppose that the prosecutor is untrustworthy, this is not what the editorial is setting out to prove. The editorial is not really trying to prove anything. It is merely making a recommendation. Answer D says the editorial is criticizing the prosecutor rather than addressing the prosecutor's plan itself, and this is exactly what the editorial is doing. This is most likely your answer, but you have one more option to consider. Answer E states that without proof that the prosecutor's plan has worked before, then it is destined to fail. Again, the editorial focus is on the character of the prosecutor, not the viability of the plan. **The correct choice is answer D.**

7. Answer: **E**

STEP 1: **Read the question and identify your task.**

This is an Assumption question. The question asks you to determine which answer is an assumption upon which the lawyer's argument is based.

STEP 2: **Read the argument with your task in mind.**

The lawyer argues that it is always justified to protest a moral injustice and then argues that it is always justified to protest taxation without representation. You see quickly that the argument equates taxation without representation with moral injustice.

STEP 3: **Know what you're looking for.**

The correct answer will most likely state something similar.

STEP 4: **Read every word of every answer choice.**

Answer A is just a restatement of the last sentence in the argument and is not really an assumption upon which the argument is based. Answer B speaks of danger, but the argument says nothing about the danger of protesting. It does not even imply such danger. Answer C offers a qualification for an injustice to be considered moral, but the argument assumes the injustice is already considered moral regardless of whether it is protested or not, so this qualification does not function in this case. Answer D tries to reverse an "if . . . then" statement given by the lawyer. The lawyer says if it is a moral injustice, then it should be protested. This answer is saying that if an injustice can be protested, it must be of a moral nature. You cannot reverse an "if . . . then" statement and expect it to be true, and the lawyer's statements do not support such a reversal. Answer E says that taxation without representation is a moral injustice. This fits your expected answer and is, in fact, the correct answer since it connects logically the lawyer's second statement concerning injustice and the statement regarding taxation without representation. **The correct choice is answer E.**

8. Answer: **D**

STEP 1:   **Read the question and identify your task.**
This is a Paradox question. You are asked to find an answer that explains a contradiction in the argument.

STEP 2:   **Read the argument with your task in mind.**
According to the argument, people say they support recycling, but most don't actually do it.

STEP 3:   **Know what you're looking for.**
You need an answer that explains why people might not do what they say they want to do.

STEP 4:   **Read every word of every answer choice.**
Answer A may seem plausible, but that would mean a large number of people are just liars. Keep this answer for now, but look for a better choice. Choice B is irrelevant to the paradox. Choice C may explain why people don't recycle, but it doesn't explain why they say that they want to. Choice D is a logical solution to the paradox and is a better answer than choice A. Choice E is out of scope. **The correct choice is answer D.**

9. Answer: **D**

STEP 1:   **Read the question and identify your task.**
This is a Parallel question. The question asks that you find among the possible answers the one that

has reasoning that matches the reasoning in the argument.

STEP 2:   **Read the argument with your task in mind.**
In essence, the argument says that most people who depend on their cell phone have no landline. In Ronde County, most people depend on their cell phone. Therefore, in Ronde County most people don't have a landline. The logic goes from general to the specific without taking into consideration that the specific group, in this case Ronde County, might have its own distinguishing characteristics.

STEP 3:   **Know what you're looking for.**
You look at the answers for a similarly flawed logic.

STEP 4:   **Read every word of every answer choice.**
Answer A bases a conclusion about the citizens of Eastland on crime facts about Eastland. There is no generalization applied to a specific group, so this does not follow your expected pattern. Answer B is problematic from the start because its conclusion is regarding one person, not a group. Answer C has the same problem as answer A; it judges a group based on facts about that group. There is no generalization being applied to them. Answer D says that most people who live in retirement communities take part in early voting, and since most people in Daytown live in retirement communities, then most of them must take part in early voting. This is exactly the reasoning used in your argument. A generalization regarding retirement communities and early voting is applied to the people of Daytown who mostly live in retirement communities. This is most likely your answer, but you must review the last option to make sure you have found your correct answer. Answer E has the same problem as answers A and C in that it judges a group by facts about that group. No generalization is applied to them. **The correct choice is answer D.**

10. Answer: **C**

STEP 1:   **Read the question and identify your task.**
This is a Weaken question. The question asks that you identify the one statement among the answers that fails to support the argument that the new sales maps will be more useful.

STEP 2: **Read the argument with your task in mind.**

The argument rests on the idea that the maps are based on newer data sourced from more locations around the country.

STEP 3: **Know what you're looking for**

The correct answer will most likely fail to support that expectation or will simply have nothing to do with it.

STEP 4: **Read every word of every answer choice.**

Answer A supports the claim because obviously if the data have changed over the last 10 years, newer data will be more useful. Answer B supports the claim because it justifies the need for the data in the first place: the data provide information about the company's customers. Answer C says retail centers have been open more than 10 years, but it is unclear how this supports the claim that the new report will be useful. This seems only to indicate that the older report excluded these centers for some reason, but you do not know why. This may be your answer, but you must review the remaining options to be sure. Answer D supports the claim because it justifies the inclusion of input from the network of loyal customers. Lastly, answer E supports the claim because it justifies the use of more data in the new report. You are left with answer C, which does not seem to support any particular claim at all. **The correct choice is answer C.**

11. Answer: **C**

STEP 1: **Read the question and identify your task.**

This is a Deduction question. The question asks that you choose from among the answers the statement that describes what exactly the editorialist and the producer disagree on.

STEP 2: **Read the argument with your task in mind.**

The editorialist believes that TV dramas contain enough violence to actually increase violence in society. The producer believes TV dramas just reflect what people want to see and that limiting content would be censorship.

STEP 3: **Know what you're looking for.**

You would expect the correct answer to center on the role TV dramas play in fostering violence in society.

STEP 4: **Read every word of every answer choice.**

Answer A is promising because the editorialist does believe dramas influence people's conception of the norm while the producer believes dramas are just answering people's demand, but it is also true that the producer does not directly address the influence issue, which makes this answer somewhat inadequate. You must review the remainder of the answers to see if this is the best answer. Regarding answer B, the editorialist does not argue that viewers should not be able to decide what they want to see on TV. The editorialist only describes the influence of dramas, so this cannot be your answer. Answer C says they disagree whether TV dramas are causing violence in society by depicting violent crimes, and this is exactly what they disagree on. The editorialist surely believes this is true, and the TV drama producer says in the first statement that such an increase is not because of TV shows. This is a better answer than A and is probably your best choice. Answer D would be a good choice if the editorialist actually argued for censorship, but he or she does not. Only the producer brings up censorship. Answer E cannot be your choice because the editorialist and the producer both accept that violence has increased in society. **The correct choice is answer C.**

12. Answer: **D**

STEP 1: **Read the question and identify your task.**

This is a Strengthen question. The question asks that you identify the statement among the possible answers that most supports the billboard company executive's argument.

STEP 2: **Read the argument with your task in mind.**

You read the executive's statements and learn that the executive defends an increase in rates by arguing that there will be no ill consequences as a result, namely that advertisers will still profit from this form of advertising and they will still be able to find billboards to rent.

STEP 3: **Know what you're looking for.**

You can assume the correct answer will support this logic by giving credence to the claim that billboard advertising will continue to be successful for advertisers.

STEP 4: Read every word of every answer
choice.

Answer A differentiates billboards leased by service providers from those rented by product makers. The executive makes no such distinction, so this cannot be your answer. Also, without knowing the amount of increase and decrease for these groups, you cannot know whether the net change supports or weakens the executive's argument. Answer B discusses the cost of production or delivery of services, but the executive's reference to profitability is intended to refer to the benefit derived from advertising expenditures, not the traditional accounting profit as this answer suggests. Answer C says short leases will no longer be available to advertisers, but the length of the lease is irrelevant to the executive's argument, since it only concerns pricing, not length of leases. Answer D suggests that billboards will enjoy more exposure going forward. This does support the executive's claim that despite the price increase, billboards will continue to be a good investment for advertisers. This could very well be your answer, but you must review the last option to be sure. Answer E says a measurement factor will change for billboards, but it does not say what effect that change will have on the metrics for billboard advertisers. This option is too tangential to be your answer. **The correct choice is answer D.**

13. Answer: **A**

STEP 1: Read the question and identify your
task.

This is a Flaw question. It asks you to identify among the possible answers the one that describes accurately a flaw in how the program will achieve its goal.

STEP 2: Read the argument with your task in
mind.

By reading the description of the program you learn that the moderators will attempt to find out which politicians are more effective, males or females, by asking the politicians themselves.

STEP 3: Know what you're looking for.

The correct answer will probably point out that the program is going to foolishly ask politicians to assess their own effectiveness, something even a nonpolitician would have difficulty doing well.

STEP 4: Read every word of every answer
choice.

Answer A says that the target of the politicians' treatment would be a better source for evaluation, and this is another way of saying that the

politicians are not the right people to be asking to evaluate their own effectiveness. This is probably your answer, but you should evaluate the remaining options to make sure you have selected the right one. Answer B may be true, but it does not seem to have anything to do with the television show's topic, which focuses on the politicians, not advocacy programs that hold them accountable on this matter. Answer C might be a flaw if the politicians on the program work together on policy. There is nothing to suggest such a relationship. They could be politicians in completely different governing bodies, so this cannot be your answer. Answer D describes a situation beyond the scope of the show. It does not matter whether or not homeless and indigent citizens vote. Finally, answer E may be true, but the program is not focused on how many male or female politicians there are in the country. Thus, **the correct choice is answer A.**

14. Answer: **B**

STEP 1: Read the question and identify your
task.

This is a Conclusion question. The question asks that you identify the statement that gives the essence of the business consultant's point.

STEP 2: Read the argument with your task in
mind.

The consultant is arguing that streamlining for the sake of doing anything to reduce costs is not worth it if it hurts the quality of service and reduces customer satisfaction.

STEP 3: Know what you're looking for.

The correct answer will simplify that very sentiment that streamlining for streamlining's sake is insufficient reason to do it.

STEP 4: Read every word of every answer
choice.

Answer A cannot be your answer because the consultant does not express any preference for a particular solution and actually makes an argument against streamlining as a means to just reduce costs. Answer B says that the effectiveness of streamlining at reducing costs is not justification enough to do it, which is exactly what the consultant is saying and it matches what you formulated as your expected answer. This is very likely your answer, but you must review the remaining options. Answer C restates what the consultant is arguing against, that streamlining to reduce costs is better than not doing it, so this cannot be your answer. Answer D cannot be correct because the consultant says only that streamlining *may* hurt quality of service and reduce customer satisfaction, and the consultant does not make an evaluation that streamlining is more or less harmful in this way. Answer E cannot be your choice either because the consultant does not discuss the possibility that streamlining might improve these aspects of the business. The consultant only mentions the risk that the opposite will happen. **The correct choice is answer B.**

15. Answer: **E**

STEP 1: **Read the question and identify your task.**

This is a Describe question. The question asks that you describe what argumentative method Zola uses to respond to Jason.

STEP 2: **Read the argument with your task in mind.**

Reading their arguments, you discover that Zola argues that the long cooking time and the ample sunlight necessary to operate the solar cooker are problems, meaning that the solar cooker is not such a perfect answer to "a host of problems in developing nations." She sees the arguments on which the conclusion is based as sound and logical, but she feels the conclusion doesn't take other factors into account.

STEP 3: **Know what you're looking for.**

You will look for something similar in your answer options.

STEP 4: **Read every word of every answer choice.**

Zola actually agrees with Jason's arguments and does not believe them to be "fallacious," so answer A cannot be correct. While Zola disagrees with Jason's conclusion, her problem is specific to the cooker, not his insufficient definition of the problems in developing nations, so answer B cannot be correct. Answer C has the same problem as answer A. She does not disagree with his arguments or their basis. With answer D, Zola is not reinterpreting anything, so this answer cannot be correct. Zola gives caveats that weaken several of Jason's assumptions, and this is what you find in answer E. Thus, **the correct choice is answer E.**

16. Answer: **C**

STEP 1: **Read the question and identify your task.**

This is a Parallel question. The question asks that you find among the answers the one that uses the same logic as the park ranger's argument.

STEP 2: **Read the argument with your task in mind.**

You read the ranger's argument, paying close attention to the ranger's logic. The ranger argues that restrictions are to protect less-experienced climbers and enacting such restrictions would only force them to go to other, more dangerous parks to climb. The logic is that rules are meant to protect someone, but if by enacting those rules you are actually causing more harm to those people, you should not enact those rules.

STEP 3: **Know what you're looking for.**

The correct answer will follow a similar pattern.

STEP 4: **Read every word of every answer choice.**

Answer A argues that the rule was to protect someone, but now that the problem is gone, the rule no longer should be enforced. This does not match your pattern. Answer B argues that a rule is in effect for a good reason, but priorities have changed, making the rule less important, but in the long run, problems may arise so the rule should remain in effect. This is obviously not your pattern either. Answer C says that a rule is used to protect someone but this rule actually causes harm to that person, and since that harm is greater than it would be without the rule, that rule should not be in effect. This is very close to your pattern and is most likely your answer. You must review the remaining options to be sure. Answer D says a rule will protect people, but that rule will have an unintended negative consequence to other people and thus the rule should not be instituted. This is close, but this answer has the rule having an ill effect on people other than those who must abide by the rule. In your pattern the ill effect is experienced by those directly affected by the rule. Answer E says that a program can protect something but that something is already protected against the danger, so the program should not be instituted. This is not your pattern because it is saying that no harm will come to the protected something because it already has enough defenses against the danger. Thus, **the correct choice is answer C.**

17. Answer: **D**

STEP 1: **Read the question and identify your task.**

This is a Strengthen question. This question asks you to identify among the possible answers the axiom that gives support to the ranger's argument.

STEP 2: **Read the argument with your task in mind.**

You read the ranger's argument, paying close attention to the justifications for his argument. The ranger argues that restrictions are to protect less-experienced climbers and enacting such restrictions would only force them to go to other, more dangerous parks to climb. The logic is that rules are meant to protect someone, but if by enacting those rules you are actually causing more harm to those people, you should not enact those rules.

STEP 3: **Know what you're looking for.**
The correct answer will say that rules should not be put into effect if they cause more harm than if they were not in effect.

STEP 4: **Read every word of every answer choice.**
Answer A may or may not support the ranger's argument depending on the instructors in the ranger's area. The ranger does not give you this information and thus, this cannot be your answer. Answers B and C both are principles supporting the opposition to the ranger's argument. They both support the idea that restrictions should be instituted, either to avoid harm or for legal reasons, so these cannot be correct. Answer D says the rules should not be instituted if those rules will cause more harm than the harm they are supposed to eliminate. This is very much in support of the ranger's argument and is likely your answer. Answer E is a principle that supports the ranger's opposition, although more weakly than B and C. **The correct choice is answer D.**

18. Answer: **C**

STEP 1: **Read the question and identify your task.**
This is a Flaw question. The question asks you to identify a logical error in the scholarly review.

STEP 2: **Read the argument with your task in mind.**
The author takes issue with M's paper and its claims based on M's tendency to ascribe bad faith to scholars who disagree with her and the distasteful nature of M's personality. Based on those observations, the author recommends that M's paper should be ignored by scholars.

STEP 3: **Know what you're looking for.**
You expect that the correct answer will point out the problem with basing criticism of the paper on M's past behavior and M's personality.

STEP 4: **Read every word of every answer choice.**

Answer A cannot be correct because there is no indication that the author's account of M's criticism is biased in any way. It is very possible that the author's recounting of M's criticism is accurate, so this cannot be the error. Answer B cannot be the error because the author does not question the veracity of M's criticism. The author merely comments on the significance of M's criticism given the nature of the source. Regardless of whether the criticism is true or not, it seems that the author would still argue that the paper does not merit attention. Answer C is exactly what you expected to be the correct answer. The author uses an attack on M's character as evidence that M is not competent as a scholar and that M's criticism does not merit attention from "serious scholars." This is likely your answer, but you must review the remaining options to be certain of your choice. Answer D cannot be the error because the author makes no assertions concerning the paper. The author merely mentions the substance of M's criticism. Answer E cannot be your answer because it is more likely an error that M would commit if M argued a point based on the paper. **The correct choice is answer C.**

19. Answer: **D**

STEP 1: **Read the question and identify your task.**
This is a Weaken question. The question asks you to identify the one statement among the possible answers that most challenges the argument.

STEP 2: **Read the argument with your task in mind.**
You read the argument and discover that it claims, put simply, that some business taxes are acceptable even if burdensome because business is able to function with other burdens that nobody objects to.

STEP 3: **Know what you're looking for.**
You expect the correct answer to challenge this notion by saying that the taxes are in fact a worse burden than suggested in the argument and should be opposed.

STEP 4: **Read every word of every answer choice.**
Answer A cannot be your choice because it is outside the scope of the argument. What happens to nonprofits and individual citizens has no bearing on the argument, which is only concerned with businesses. Also, the argument says

nothing about failures. Answer B might be used to support the argument, saying that further restrictions would occur if it were not for the imposition of such taxes. Answer C is a restatement of the argument but using income taxes instead of the regulatory burdens as the comparison, and since this supports the argument, this cannot be your choice. Answer D says that taxes mentioned in the argument are in fact so burdensome that business activity is almost impossible. This would be a strong challenge to the notion that such taxes are no more burdensome than regulation and thus tolerable. This may be your answer, but you have one more option to consider. Answer E offers support to the argument by saying that such taxes are actually helpful to businesses. **The correct choice is answer D.**

20. Answer: **B**

    STEP 1: **Read the question and identify your task.**
    This is a Deduction question. This question asks that you choose a statement among the possible answers that can be inferred from the argument.

    STEP 2: **Read the argument with your task in mind.**
    The argument states that some business taxes are acceptable even if burdensome because business is able to function with other burdens that nobody objects to.

    STEP 3: **Know what you're looking for.**
    The correct answer will have something to do with the level of burden that taxes, regulations, and so on, have on businesses and whether businesses can viably function under that burden.

    STEP 4: **Read every word of every answer choice.**
    Answer A contradicts the argument by saying the taxes are too burdensome, and thus, this statement cannot be inferred. Answer B says that being burdensome to business is not reason enough for a prohibition, and this is exactly what the argument is saying about the business taxes. This statement can be inferred from the argument and is most likely your choice, but you must review the remaining options to be sure. Regarding answer C, the argument says that excessive income taxes are not justified, but it never says that they should be prohibited. It is conceivable that the person making the argument might say this, but given the argument you cannot know this. Answer D says that business failures are a bigger problem than excessive taxes, but the argument says that

business failures are just a symptom of what is really the more important issue, infrastructure problems. This inference is mixing up issues to confuse you and cannot be your answer. Answer E says that the nonexcessive taxes are not burdensome at all, but this is not what the argument implies. Actually, the argument says that they do create a burden but a burden no different from that created by regulations that are considered acceptable. Therefore, **the correct choice is answer B.**

21. Answer: **A**

    STEP 1: **Read the question and identify your task.**
    This is a Flaw question. The question asks you to identify the error in reasoning in the argument.

    STEP 2: **Read the argument with your task in mind.**
    The argument states that Jack said he was not going to include the marketing department in a meeting, but people left the meeting with a report that the marketing department had promised to produce and deliver at the meeting, so at least some members of the marketing department must have been at the meeting.

    STEP 3: **Know what you're looking for.**
    You might guess that the answer will identify the flaw as the assumption that the marketing department is the only department that could produce that particular sales report.

    STEP 4: **Read every word of every answer choice.**
    Answer A is a close approximation of that exact flaw. It says that the argument fails to establish that something which is true for some people is true for only those people. Just because the marketing department promised to produce and deliver the report does not mean they are the only people who could produce and deliver the report. Someone else at the meeting could have fulfilled Jack's need. This is most likely your answer, but you must review the remaining options. Answer B cannot be correct because the only such term used in the argument is the importance Jack put on the report, but this is not a flaw and is irrelevant to the logic of the argument. Answer C ignores the basis for the conclusion, that the report was delivered, and focuses on whether someone has a right to be at the meeting, which is an irrelevant factor, since you do not know whether or not the marketing department was at the meeting in the first place. Answer D is about Jack's interest in the

report, but whether or not he wanted the report is unimportant since the reasoning is based on the fact that the report was produced and delivered at the meeting, so this cannot be your answer. Finally, answer E says that the flaw is that Jack could have changed his mind based on changing circumstances, but you have no evidence of that change. **The correct choice is answer A.**

22. Answer: **C**

STEP 1: **Read the question and identify your task.**

This is a Deduction question. The question asks that you identify among the answers the one statement that must also be true, when taking into consideration the statements in the argument.

STEP 2: **Read the argument with your task in mind.**

The argument describes how people make decisions on major purchases. It speaks about them in terms of groups, using words like *most*, *some*, and *majority*. These terms are important to help you identify your answer.

STEP 3: **Know what you're looking for.**

Since the "majority" is the most exact number and the largest, the correct answer will most likely be about that group.

STEP 4: **Read every word of every answer choice.**

Answer A may be true but does not necessarily have to be so. Since so few do research on their own (according to the argument) and rely on other advice, then it is only slightly less likely that this group is in the minority that are not happy with their purchases than it is that they are in the majority that are happy with their purchases. Answer B is trying to trick you: it seems to be saying exactly what the argument is saying, but it is not. The argument says that most people make the purchases without doing any research, but only *some* of those are relying on advice from friends or a salesperson and only *some* make the decision based on emotions. You have no idea what share each of those groups composes within the larger group, so answer B may or may not be true and thus cannot be your answer. Answer C is your best option so far. You know that a majority of buyers are happy with their purchases, and you know that most buyers make these purchases without doing any research. Logically, *majority* and *most* are interchangeable, and there must be some overlap of these groups. Therefore, you know that at least some of the buyers who do not do any

research must be happy with their purchases. This is most likely your answer, but you must review the remaining options. Answer D is impossible to know. You know only that some of the people who purchase without research use advice from their friends or salespeople, and this group could easily be in the minority that is unhappy with their purchases. Nothing gives you an indication that this group overlaps with the majority that is happy with their purchases. Answer E is possible, but there is no way to know. There is no indication as to the level of overlap with these groups. As indicated with answer C, you know that at least some of those who buy without research are happy with their purchases, but any more than that is impossible to know. **The correct choice is answer C.**

23. Answer: **C**

STEP 1: **Read the question and identify your task.**

This is a Describe question. The question asks that you identify the reason that the argument cites the statistics.

STEP 2: **Read the argument with your task in mind.**

The argument discusses a particular view, that smaller class size improves education. The statistics seem to contradict this notion, or at least they indicate that class size is an insufficient solution.

STEP 3: **Know what you're looking for.**

The correct answer will most likely describe how the statistics counter the view that class size is the answer to the problem.

STEP 4: **Read every word of every answer choice.**

Answer A cannot be the correct choice because it indicates that the statistics support the idea of smaller class size. Answer B is a bit too extreme. The argument definitely uses the statistics to create doubt about reduced class size as a solution, but it does not use the statistics to eliminate it outright. Answer C is a viable option. The argument does indeed use the statistics toward establishing that the size of classes is not the only influence. For now, this is your best choice, but you need to review the remaining options in case there is a better one. Answer D, like answer B, is too extreme. The argument does not seek to completely eliminate the idea of reducing class size, especially since the statistical sample is described as a mix of class sizes. If the argument wanted to eliminate the notion, it would compare small classes with large classes. This cannot be your answer. And the viability of standardized testing as a measurement of an effective school system is outside of the scope of the argument, so answer E is incorrect. **The correct choice is answer C.**

24. Answer: **A**

    STEP 1:   **Read the question and identify your task.**
    This is a Parallel question. It asks that you identify the argument among the possible answers that uses the same reasoning as in the main argument.

    STEP 2:   **Read the argument with your task in mind.**
    You read the main argument paying close attention to how the logic functions. In essence, it tells you that an activity (industrial activity) has a positive effect (haze for plants) and that such activity is beneficial to everyone involved without reservation.

    STEP 3:   **Know what you're looking for.**
    The correct answer will describe an activity that has a positive effect, and it will say that everyone who engages in that activity derives such benefit without reservation.

    STEP 4:   **Read every word of every answer choice.**
    Answer A says that vigorous exercise is good for people and that no harm can come from it. While this does not follow the same pattern as your argument, it is very similar. It says that an activity (vigorous exercise) has a positive effect (prevents ailments) and that activity is beneficial to everyone involved without reservation. This would seem to be your answer, but you have to review the remaining options to be sure. Answer B is easy to eliminate right off because it describes an action's negative effect and simply makes a judgment that the effect justifies avoiding that action. This is not your pattern at all. Answer C is close to using the same reasoning, but it makes an extreme recommendation, beyond that suggested by the possible benefit, and the argument does not make a recommendation that people increase or transform all activity to industrial activity. Answer D does the same as answer C; it makes a drastic recommendation based on an observed benefit. The argument does not recommend that people increase their industrial activities based on the observed benefit. Answer E gives a negative effect and then recommends against the causal behavior. This is not your pattern. Also, the answer gets a bit too specific with its recommendation (take a day off). Your argument remains

very general with its statements. **The correct choice is answer A.**

25. Answer: **C**

    STEP 1:   **Read the question and identify your task.**
    This is an Assumption question. The question asks that you identify among the possible answers the assumption upon which the columnist's argument is based.

    STEP 2:   **Read the argument with your task in mind.**
    You read the argument seeking the basis for the columnist's conclusion. The columnist argues that the reliance on e-mail and Internet social networking threatens the strong bonds of mutual trust necessary for a democratic society.

    STEP 3:   **Know what you're looking for.**
    The correct answer will link e-mail and Internet social networking to this negative effect.

    STEP 4:   **Read every word of every answer choice.**
    Answer A cannot be your choice because the argument makes no claim with regard to effectiveness of social networking as a tool for civic organizations. This may be an implication of the argument but not an assumption upon which it depends. Regarding answer B, the argument may suggest that these people are not forming the necessary strong bonds, but it is not saying that they are incapable of it, so this cannot be the correct choice. Answer C is very promising. The argument that e-mail and social networking are corroding democracy is based on the judgment that these activities keep people from forming strong social bonds outside their families. This would seem to be your answer, but you should review the remaining options to be sure. Also, while the argument mentions family, it makes no judgment regarding the closeness of citizens to their families. It only judges their ability to form bonds outside the family. Thus, answer D cannot be correct. Finally, answer E is an implication or restatement of the second statement and is certainly a partial basis for the argument, but it is not comprehensive enough to consider as an assumption upon which the argument depends. **The correct choice is answer C.**

SECTION III

Passage 1

1. Answer: E

STEP 1: **Read the question and identify your task.**

This is an Arguments-style question. You are asked to find an answer that supports opponents of comparativism. In other words, it must weaken the position of comparativists.

STEP 2: **Go back to the passage to find the answer.**

Since the first passage focuses more on support for comparativism and the second focuses on opposition, refer to your summaries of both positions.

STEP 3: **Read every word of every answer choice.**

Answer A would perhaps strengthen the support for comparativism because America and Great Britain are similar. Answer B also might strengthen the supporting position because it shows that this isn't a new idea and other societies have done it. Answer C is probably true, but it is unclear how this would weaken or strengthen either position. Answer D sounds like it weakens the position of comparativists, but it actually affirms the use of foreign precedent: it says foreign precedent may not be the *only* support used, which means it can be used. Answer E presents a situation that the opponents of comparativism warn against: a judge using foreign law to support his or her own position on an issue. **The correct choice is answer E.**

2. Answer: C

STEP 1: **Read the question and identify your task.**

This is an Inference question. It asks that you find among the possible answers the one that expresses the author of passage A's attitude toward the opposition to comparativism.

STEP 2: **Go back to the passage to find the answer.**

Scan for key words in the second paragraph that clue you into the author's perspective. The author states that comparativism's supporters "rightly" contend that the United States is taking on an increased role in world events.

STEP 3: **Read every word of every answer choice.**

Answer A is too one-sided and we can quickly eliminate it as an option. Answer B has the basic disagreement between the two authors correct, but there is no evidence to support either the "appreciative" or "wrongheaded" claim. Answer C is most likely your answer. Since the author of passage A suggests that the increasingly role of the United States in world affairs is inevitable and that it is right to be involved in that legal framework, then the author must also believe that those who ignore this inevitability must be wrong and are ignoring the reality of the global legal and political situation. You must review the remaining options to see whether any one of them is better. Answer D is too strong a condemnation of the opponents to comparativism. The author is certainly not that antagonistic to their opposition. While the author of A is not "scornful," neither is that author "dismissive" of the claims made by the opponents of comparativism, making answer E unlikely. Therefore, **the correct choice is answer C.**

3. Answer: B

STEP 1: **Read the question and identify your task.**

This is a Line ID question. The question asks that you identify among the possible answers a statement about the opposition to comparativism that can be inferred from the passage.

STEP 2: **Go back to the passage to find the answer.**

Look for the correct answer in paragraph four, which is where the author explores opponents' views.

STEP 3: **Read every word of every answer choice.**

Answer A is too extreme. The anti-comparativists did not object to the Supreme Court decisions regarding executions, anti-sodomy laws, and affirmative actions. Rather, they objected to the court using comparativism to make those decisions. Answer B might very well be inferred from the passage. The opponents definitely believe that the United States should develop its own unique legal precedents based on its own legal system as set forward by the nation's forefathers. This is one of the bases for opposing comparativism. This is most likely our answer but we must review the remaining options. Answer C cannot be inferred from the passage because the author never discuses the qualifications of those involved in the public discourse. As far as we know it is possible the opposition is more versed in foreign court systems. Regarding answer D, nothing in the passage indicates one way or the other the opposition's views on globalization. Also, none of their objections are based on globalization. Finally, while the opposition took measures to restrain comparitivism in the courts they never suggested that the structure of the justice system be changed. **The correct choice is answer B.**

4. Answer: **B**

STEP 1:   **Read the question and identify your task.**
This is a Line ID question. Go back to the statements concerning Kennedy and Breyer made in passages A and B and find the point of overlap.

STEP 2:   **Go back to the passage to find the answer.**
Passages A and B only mention that both Kennedy and Breyer have used comparativism in making judicial decisions. Look for any answer that suggests this commonality in the use and acceptance of foreign law.

STEP 3:   **Read every word of every answer choice.**
Answer choice A discusses a point of view held by the opponents of comparativism, not Kennedy and Breyer. Answer choice B, however, tells you that foreign law can be used in foreign courts, something you know that the two justices believe. This must be your correct answer. Answer choice C is too extreme. While you know that Kennedy and Breyer have used foreign law in making their decisions, there is nothing to suggest that this is the central concern. Answer choice D compares the use of comparativism in the United States to other nations, something that is never discussed. And answer choice E is too extreme. While Breyer and Kennedy are both identified as Supreme Court justices, you don't know that they believe comparative law to be only applicable in the Supreme Court. **The correct choice is answer B.**

5. Answer: **C**

STEP 1:   **Read the question and identify your task.**
This is an Information Retrieval question. The question asks that you find an analogy that the opponents of comparativism might use for those who use comparativism in domestic cases.

STEP 2:   **Go back to the passage to find the answer.**
You refer to passage B and look for comparisons.

STEP 3:   **Read every word of every answer choice.**
Answer A says doctors will consult other doctors, but the opposition would support judges consulting other judges to make a decision, so this does not fit. Answer B says teachers use guides, some of which are for teaching foreign students, but the opposition would not oppose judges referring to law books or even law books used by foreign judges to understand American law, so this analogy does not work. Answer C says a board member uses the policies of another, very different organization to write its own policies. The opposition would very well oppose judges using the law of another nation to write law in the United States. This analogy seems close enough to be your answer, but you should review the remaining options. Answer D says the candidate argues that a rule is bad because other countries do not have that same rule. The opposition would not object to a judge voicing his or her opinion regarding US law versus foreign law. This might lead to politicians changing the law, so this analogy is not right. Answer E is a company applying the rules in a stricter nation universally to its product. This analogy does not fit because the judge is not judging a law solely on the standards of a foreign country and then discarding it altogether. Therefore, **the correct choice is answer C.**

6. Answer: **D**

STEP 1:   **Read the question and identify your task.**
This is an Inference question. The question asks that you identify an inference that can be derived from the passage's discussion of Justice Kennedy's use of comparativism.

STEP 2:   **Go back to the passage to find the answer.**
You refer to the passage and see that opposition members suggested impeaching Kennedy, which is a harsh reaction. The correct answer will reflect this.

STEP 3: **Read every word of every answer choice.**

Answer A says that the opposition supported the decision but not Kennedy's use of comparativism. Again, the vehemence of their reaction to his decision does not support this as a possible correct answer. Answer B also suggests that the opposition supported the decision and does not seem to be implied by the passage. Answer C says the opposition was of two minds with regard to comparativism, but the passage does not indicate any such doubt. The passage implies the opposite, that opponents were fairly strict in wanting no foreign involvement at all in determining law in the United States. Answer D, that the opposition perhaps utilized the comparativism argument as a cover, could very well be inferred from the passage and is exactly what you expected to see as your correct answer. Answer E is too extreme. While opposition members wanted to impeach Kennedy, they did not suggest that he had committed treason, nor did they demand a trial to determine if he had done so. **The correct choice is answer D.**

7. Answer: **E**

STEP 1: **Read the question and identify your task.**

This is a variation of a Main Idea question—a Primary Purpose question. The question asks you to identify among the answers the one that expresses the primary purpose of the passage.

STEP 2: **Go back to the passage to find the answer.**

Refer to your passage summary.

STEP 3: **Read every word of every answer choice.**

Answer A cannot be the correct choice because the passage is not justifying comparativism. Answer B attributes too strong a position to the author. The author is not so biased as to be considered a critic of either side of the comparativism argument. Regarding answer C, the author cannot be considered to be proposing the use of comparativism. It is already in use and the author does not seem to be promoting it. In fact, at the end of the passage the author indicates that adopting it is more a matter of giving in to certain globalization pressures than anything the author has to say about the practice. Answer D cannot be correct because it ignores the fact that the author uses much of the passage to discuss the opposition to comparativism. Finally, answer E must

be your answer. The passage is intended to discuss the nature of a legal controversy, in this case comparativism, and it does describe the opposing sides of the issue. **The correct choice is answer E.**

Passage 2

8. Answer: **C**

STEP 1: **Read the question and identify your task.**

This is an Arguments-style question. You are asked to find an assumption made by the economists in lines 56–59.

STEP 2: **Go back to the passage to find the answer.**

Refer to the lines given. The economists argue that the EROI of oil has already begun to decline. That means that the energy required to get the oil is becoming greater. When it gets too close to the amount of energy the oil provides, oil as a fuel source will no longer be sustainable.

STEP 3: **Read every word of every answer choice.**

Answer A makes a comparison that the passage does not. Answer B is not a necessary assumption. It may be that there is plenty of oil, but the effort required to get it or refine it is growing. Answer C must be true for the EROI to be declining. Keep this choice. Answer D heads in the right direction, but it is too extreme. Answer E is not a necessary assumption. The economists did not predict that the decline cannot stop. **The correct choice is answer C.**

9. Answer: **A**

STEP 1: **Read the question and identify your task.**

This is an Inference question. The question asks that you determine which of the possible answers can be inferred from the theories put forward by biophysical economists.

STEP 2: **Go back to the passage to find the answer.**

You refer to the passage.

STEP 3: **Read every word of every answer choice.**

Answer A says that an economy can survive as long as it has a stable or increasing EROI. This is exactly how the passage describes the function of the EROI. It says that an economic system requires a positive EROI in order to survive. This is probably your answer, but you must review the remaining options to be certain. Answer B tries to trick you by linking natural resources to energy, but the focus of this statement is still natural resources, which is the central focus of ecological economics, not biophysical economics. Answer C is an argument that would be made by neo-classical economics, which believes that market forces can solve most major economic problems. Answer D seems viable as a choice, but the passage really does not indicate what solutions these two groups offer for solving the world's economic problems, so you do not know whether they agree or not about solutions. You know only that these two groups have different ways of approaching and defining the problems. Answer E cannot be concluded from the information you have. You know only that the ecologists tend to focus less on energy than other proponents of biophysical economics. Thus, **the correct choice is answer A.**

10. Answer: **C**

    STEP 1: **Read the question and identify your task.**
    This is an Information Retrieval question. The question asks that you choose which event among the possible answers would most directly affect a biophysical economic analysis.

    STEP 2: **Go back to the passage to find the answer.**
    Since their approach is based on the EROI, you are looking for an event that directly affects the energy delivered by a process or used in that process.

    STEP 3: **Read every word of every answer choice.**
    Answer A seems like a good potential answer. A consumer switch from gasoline-powered to electric-powered automobiles may indirectly affect energy consumption, but this is still a consumer preference and a market-based influence and it could be masking an underlying process that is using more energy (like the production of electric cars). Answer B involves government intervention in the economy, and taxes will only affect consumer behavior and not the underlying energy delivery or consumption. Answer C definitely affects the EROI economic model. If the cost to maintain current energy supply levels goes up significantly, it could affect the long-term viability of that energy source and thus the survival of the economic system. This is most likely your answer, but you must review the remaining options. Answer D involves debt in the equation

and debt may or may not be related to increased costs. It could also be due to poor management. Because you do not know the reason for taking on more debt, you cannot know whether or not this affects the biophysical economic model. Answer E says the new technology helps the company avoid an increase, which means the cost remains the same and thus has no impact on the economic model at all. **The correct choice is answer C.**

11. Answer: **E**

    STEP 1: **Read the question and identify your task.**
    This is an Information Retrieval question. The question asks you to identify among the possible answers the view that the biophysical economist has of oil supplies for energy.

    STEP 2: **Go back to the passage to find the answer.**
    Look back at paragraph three and read the last sentence, which states that biophysical economists believe the EROI for oil has already begun its descent, which means that the cost of producing oil is becoming increasingly expensive while supplies have not risen equally.

    STEP 3: **Read every word of every answer choice.**
    Answer A says oil is scarce and expensive, but the passage implies that oil has not reached its peak in supply, so the first part is wrong even if the second part is right. Answer B says oil is stable or slightly decreasing and cheaper to source. The first part might be right, but the second part is incorrect: the passage makes it clear that oil is becoming more expensive to source. Answer C says the supply is unknown and it is cheaper to source. Again, the second part cannot be right according to the passage. Answer D is completely wrong. Oil is not decreasing in supply and it is not inexpensive to source, according to the passage. Answer E is your last available option, and it is right on target. The economists view oil as abundant or stable in supply and it is increasingly expensive to source, which is why the EROI has already begun its descent. **The correct choice is answer E.**

12. Answer: **D**

    STEP 1: **Read the question and identify your task.**
    This is a Main Idea question. The question asks that you identify the answer that best describes the function of the final paragraph within the passage.

STEP 2:   Go back to the passage to find the
           answer.

The final paragraph is essentially saying that
biophysical economics is not immune to the
problems that other economic schools experience, so the paragraph is attempting to equalize
things a bit between the new type of economics
and the old.

STEP 3:   Read every word of every answer
           choice.

Answer A is in many ways the antithesis of what
the final paragraph is saying, establishing the
superiority of biophysical economics over neoclassical. This does not match what you know
and cannot be your answer. Answer B says that
certain practicalities will hinder the ability of
biophysical economics to surpass classical economics, but the last paragraph says only that
biophysical economics experiences the same
problems as classical economics, not that it will
not overcome those problems and even surpass
the other schools of thought. Answer C feeds off
the second sentence, which indicates a small dis-
sonance between the ecologists and the rest of
biophysical economics supporters, but to say that
the entire paragraph functions to show the "conflict" between them is extreme and inaccurate.
Answer D matches your understanding of how
the last paragraph functions. The last paragraph
does indeed explain that the new economics is
not immune to the problems that have plagued
classical economics and made it problematic for
noneconomists. This is probably your answer,
but you must review your last option. Answer E
says the last paragraph makes the disagreement
within the biophysical economics community
into an advantage over classical economics, but
you know that the paragraph implies that the flaw
makes the new economics more similar to classical economics, at least as an economic discipline
if not in substance. Thus, **the correct choice is
answer D.**

13. Answer: **A**

STEP 1:   Read the question and identify your
           task.

This is a Tone question. You are asked to describe
the author's attitude towards the use of EROI.

STEP 2:   Go back to the passage to find the
           answer.

Refer to the second paragraph where the author
discusses EROI. In lines 42–47, the author says
EROI enables economists to account for certain

factors and see past others to better see the actual
economy.

STEP 3:   Read every word of every answer
           choice.

Answer A is good paraphrase of lines 42–47. Keep
this choice, but check them all. Answers B and C
are not correct, because the author's attitude is
positive. Answer D is too passive. The author does
seem to like the use of EROI, which was developed by biophysical economists. Answer E is too
extreme and goes too far. "Excited" is too extreme
for this author's tone, and the author does not
conclude that the decline of oil's EROI means the
rise of EROI for alternative sources of energy. **The
correct choice is answer A.**

Passage 3

14. Answer: **B**

STEP 1:   Read the question and identify your
           task.

This is a Main Idea question.

STEP 2:   Go back to the passage to find the
           answer.

Refer to your passage summary.

STEP 3:   Read every word of every answer
           choice.

Answer A says that the passage puts doubt on
Galileo's work, but you know from the passage
that the doubt is not with his work but with the
story behind the church's persecution of Galileo,
so this answer cannot be correct. Answer B
encapsulates the idea of the passage perfectly.
The passage does in fact purport that there are
new theories as to why Galileo was targeted by
the church and it does say that his trial and house
arrest are fact. This may be your answer, but you
must review the remaining options. Answer C
focuses on a part of the passage that mentions
that Santillana was influenced by the political
environment in the United States, but while this
observation may show the author's own doubts
regarding his theories, the author does not suggest that Santillana's theories be discounted
on the basis of the factual elements in the case.
Answer D is a promising candidate, but it falls
just short of answer B by not mentioning the last
paragraph and its factual claims. Also, it says that
scholars are "currently pursuing explanations,"
but the passage indicates that much of the pursuit has already occurred. Either way, answer B is
still a better option. Answer E makes the error of
saying that the existence of a trial is in question,

when this is one of the elements that is considered fact by the passage. **The correct choice is answer B.**

15. Answer: **C**

STEP 1: Read the question and identify your task.

This is an Inference question. The question asks you which historical political event influenced Santillana while writing his book.

STEP 2: Go back to the passage to find the answer.

Reread the section about his book, *The Crime of Galileo.* Santillana wrote about how Galileo's contemporaries turned on him and denounced him to the church to protect their own way of life. You look through the events and assess their similarity to Santillana's description of Galileo's situation.

STEP 3: Read every word of every answer choice.

Answer A cannot be correct because Galileo's contemporaries obviously did not bomb Galileo's home. Answer B cannot be right because the fall of Galileo was not the fall of a homicidal dictator, nor was it the rise of a new type of government. Answer C is promising. The House Un-American Activities Committee demanded that people suspected of being un-American come before the committee and name their associates who were Communists or consorting with Communists. Scientists and artists denounced their friends in order to save their own careers. This is probably your answer due to its striking similarity to Galileo's situation, but you should review the remaining options. Answer D cannot be correct because Galileo and his peers were not in a standoff that resulted in two sides building up armaments, which led to an indirect conflict. Answer E cannot be your choice because Galileo's peers were not supporting an industry that would supplant Galileo's outdated form of industry. *Note: If you were unfamiliar with the House Un-American Committee hearings you could easily eliminate the incorrect answers, which would leave answer C as your only option.* **The correct choice is answer C.**

16. Answer: **D**

STEP 1: Read the question and identify your task.

This is an Information Retrieval question. The question asks you to identify the statement that

Pietro Redondi would agree with regarding Galileo Galilei.

STEP 2: Go back to the passage to find the answer.

Refer to the part of the passage that explains Redondi's views. Redondi believed that Galileo's persecution by the church had nothing to do with his theory that the earth revolved around the sun (i.e., Copernicanism) and not the other way around. Redondi believed it had more to do with Galileo's belief in atomism, which contradicted the church's belief in transubstantiation.

STEP 3: Read every word of every answer choice.

Answer A focuses on the forged injunction, but Redondi regards the Copernicanism argument irrelevant to his theory, and there is no evidence in the passage for his views on the injunction. Answer B says that Galileo's contemporaries betrayed him out of jealousy, but the passage says that they did so to protect themselves. Also, Redondi believes the church invented the Copernicanism justification not to protect Galileo's contemporaries but to abide by the wishes of wealthy benefactors who liked Galileo. Answer C cannot be your choice because nothing in the passage indicates that Galileo's face-off with the church was at the urging of the Medici family. Also, the passage says Redondi believed his house arrest rather than the death penalty was probably the result of the intervention of the Medici family, not the result of their inaction. Answer D would probably be supported by Redondi. He believed that Galileo's real crime of believing in atomism was covered up with the Copernicanism justification to gratify the Medici family. That indicates Copernicanism was less offensive than atomism, and this is probably your answer, but you have one last option. Answer E puts Orazio Grassi, S.J., at the center of the entire story, and while Redondi might entertain such a notion, it is doubtful he would agree with this since Pope Urban VIII must have been involved as the leader of the church. Therefore, **the correct choice is answer D.**

17. Answer: **D**

STEP 1: Read the question and identify your task.

This is an Arguments-style question. You are asked to find an answer that will weaken the author's argument about the difference in punishment between Bruno and Galilei.

Your only connection between the two in the passage is that one was executed (Bruno) while the other (Galileo) was spared. The passage suggests that Galileo was spared because he had the favor of the Medici family while Bruno did not have such a supporter. You can expect the answer will revolve around these connections in some way.

Answer A says that Bruno and Galileo agreed on Copernicanism but differed on atomism, but the passage suggests no such thing. Actually, the passage gives no insight as to whether they agreed or disagreed on Copernicanism, and there is a slight suggestion that they agreed on atomism since the author uses their punishment differences as part of his argument. Answer B is the argument that the author is making. Answer C presents a possible alternative reason for the difference in punishment. This would weaken the author's view that Galilei's wealthy patrons were the reason. Answers D and E have the same problem as Answer A. None are related to the author's argument, and there is no basis for assuming that if those views differed the punishments would have differed. **The correct choice is answer D.**

18. Answer: **B**

This is an Inference question. The question asks that you choose a statement from among the possible answers that describes the relationship between the church and publications during the time of Galileo.

This question deals with the last part of paragraph three, which discusses how the church's list of proscribed publications figured into Redondi's analysis.

Answer A cannot be your choice because the passage questions why *The Assayer* was not added to the proscribed list if the ideas in it were offensive to the church, suggesting that offensive books were denied registration with the church. Answer B says that an author probably would not have been put on trial for a book that had not been proscribed, and this is exactly the question posed by the passage. The author questions why *The Assayer* was not on the proscribed list if, according to Redondi, Galileo was really persecuted for the ideas put forward in this book. This answer is very much implied by this section of the passage and is probably your answer, but you must review the remaining options. Answer C is a bit extreme. Nothing in the passage indicates that every author of a book that was proscribed was put on trial and (except for Galileo) burned at the stake. Answer D may be an answer to the question posed by the author of the passage, but it is not the implication of the question. Answer E is an interesting theory and might connect the dots for the author of the passage, much like answer D, but it is a bit too far a reach for an answer to this question. **The correct choice is answer B.**

19. Answer: **C**

This is a variation of a Main Idea question—the Primary Purpose question.

Refer to your passage summary.

Answer A is a viable option. The passage does discuss recent discoveries and give insight into the Galileo story, but the answer is a bit too general and words like *summarize* and *discoveries* seem rather inexact when applied to what is presented in the passage. The author is doing more than summarizing, and the passage presents scholarly theories in addition to discoveries. Therefore, this answer is somewhat unsatisfactory. Still, you should keep it in mind as you review the remaining options. Answer B cannot be the correct choice because the passage does not mention a conflict between two scholars. For all you know, Santillana and Redondi agree completely on each other's theories. Answer C is a more specific and more accurate description of the passage's purpose. The passage does present and assess Santillana's and Redondi's theories that call into question aspects of the Galileo story, so this is probably your answer, but you should review the remaining options to be certain. Answer D focuses on the church's considerations when putting Galileo on trial, and this is certainly not the primary purpose of the passage since it ignores Santillana's and Redondi's theories altogether.

Finally, answer E uses the word *criticize* to characterize the author's purpose, and the passage does not exactly criticize Santillana's and Redondi's theories; rather, the author poses some questions that might cast some doubt on them. Still, the author seems to acknowledge that they do have some valid ideas. Therefore, **the correct choice is answer C.**

Passage 4

20. Answer: **B**

STEP 1: **Read the question and identify your task.**
This is a Main Idea question.

STEP 2: **Go back to the passage to find the answer.**
If needed, you can review the first sentence of each paragraph to remind yourself of the progression of thought through the passage.

STEP 3: **Read every word of every answer choice.**
Answer A would be more likely a study performed by the psychologist Leonard Sax, but it does not encompass the full scope of the passage and cannot be the answer. Answer B seems like a good description of the passage. The passage does put forward two theories, both of which have questionable evidence to support them and have drawn criticism. This might be your answer, but you should review the remaining options to be certain. With answer C, language is important. The passage is not discussing two studies. Rather, it is discussing two approaches to single-sex education, each of which is under study. The difference is subtle but important and disqualifies this option. Answer D makes the mistake of saying that the practice is just beginning to be incorporated into public schools. The passage makes it clear that this is not a new practice. Finally, answer E is tempting because the passage does discuss single-sex education generally in this manner, but this answer ignores the two schools of thought with regard to single-sex education and thus cannot be your answer. **The correct choice is answer B.**

21. Answer: **C**

STEP 1: **Read the question and identify your task.**
This is a Line ID question. The question asks you to find the answer that best describes the purpose of the specified lines.

STEP 2: **Go back to the passage to find the answer.**
The lines in question discuss how the studies that have been done are not reliable as evidence to support single-sex education and that in some cases they actually undermine such support. The correct answer will be some variation on this summary.

STEP 3: **Read every word of every answer choice.**
Answer A says the opposite of what the lines say. The content of the lines definitely does not favor single-sex education. Answer B is too innocuous. The lines do not simply exhibit or discuss the research. There is an obvious point being made by the lines discussing such uncertain studies. Answer C is an accurate description of the lines. The discussion of the questionable studies offers a caveat to any support offered by Sax or other supporters of single-sex education. This is probably your answer, but you must review the remaining options to be certain. Answer D says the lines give favor to Dr. Sax's approach to single-sex education, but the lines speak of studies on single-sex education in general. They do not specify whether the studies diminish one approach in relation to another. Answer E cannot be your answer because these particular lines give no historical perspective. In fact, the lines that come before these are intended for that purpose. **The correct choice is answer C.**

22. Answer: **D**

STEP 1: **Read the question and identify your task.**
This is an Inference question. The question asks that you identify the statement among the possible answers with which Dr. Sax would agree.

STEP 2: **Go back to the passage to find the answer.**
You know from the passage that Dr. Sax believes that using genetic differences is how single-sex education should be formulated. So the answer will most likely be consistent with that perspective.

STEP 3: **Read every word of every answer choice.**
Answer A says that social pressures should be involved in determining single-sex education, and this is consistent with the other school of thought, not Sax's, so this cannot be your answer. Answer B says boys fear looking smart in front of girls, but this is not a genetic factor. Rather, it seems to be

a social factor, something the opposing school of thought would use to justify single-sex education. Answer C says that because boys and girls test differently, they should be given different tests based on learning differences. This cannot be the correct choice because it is basing its conclusion on performance on academic tests rather than on genetic factors. Answer D says that because of an inherent difference between boys and girls, they should be separated into different environments that take this difference into account. This is much stronger than answer C, because the term *inherent* suggests that the difference is genetically determined, and using such a determinant in single-sex education is right in line with Sax's views. This is most likely your answer, but you have one last option to review. Answer E argues for coed education based on testing, and Sax does not support coed education, so this cannot be your answer. **The correct choice is answer D.**

23. Answer: **E**

STEP 1: **Read the question and identify your task.**

This is an Information Retrieval question. The question asks you to identify a statement that is consistent with the ACLU's concerns discussed in the specified lines.

STEP 2: **Go back to the passage to find the answer.**

The lines discuss the point that the ACLU is concerned that Sax's approach will encourage dangerous stereotypes and ruin any gender progress that has been made in education. The correct answer will be consistent with this fear of stereotypes.

STEP 3: **Read every word of every answer choice.**

Answer A is Sax's approach in action, and while an imbalance is described, there is no indication that a dangerous stereotype is being encouraged. Answer B may be the negative effect of Sax's theory in practice, but this is a result, not a stereotype being propagated. Answer C may be an effect of Sax's approach, but this could be a positive result and the ACLU is not concerned that students might find jobs more appropriate to their genetic disposition. Answer D is another possible negative effect of Sax's theory in practice, but this is not a stereotype being fostered. Finally, answer E says the perception that boys are better

than girls for jobs with chaotic environments is a stereotype created or fostered by Sax's ideas, and this is exactly what the ACLU is concerned about. **The correct choice is answer E.**

24. Answer: **D**

STEP 1: **Read the question and identify your task.**

This is an Information Retrieval question. The question asks you to determine which of the statements is consistent with the views of single-sex education critics.

STEP 2: **Go back to the passage to find the answer.**

Review the final paragraph, which deals mainly with the critics.

STEP 3: **Read every word of every answer choice.**

Answer A says single-sex education is OK as long as the fundamentals of American education are taught, but this is not what the critics are saying. The passage says nothing about the critics taking issue with the content of the education. Rather, they object to the structure itself. Answer B has the same problem as answer A. It is not the content of education or some threat of learning un-American values that is the danger. Answer C is in support of single-sex education as a method of instilling American values, and this is definitely in conflict with your understanding of the critics' point of view in the final paragraph. They believe quite the opposite. Answer D is very much in line with the critics' point of view. They view the model of single-sex education as inherently flawed; the structure itself is an un-America idea of segregation. This is probably your answer, but you must review your last option to be sure. Answer E focuses on pedagogy, saying that single-sex education teachers are incapable of instilling good values because of the structure. This seems off the mark and is not as good an answer as D. **The correct choice is answer D.**

25. Answer: **C**

STEP 1: **Read the question and identify your task.**

This is an Arguments-style question. You are asked to find an answer that states the conclusion of the author's argument about single-sex education.

STEP 2: Go back to the passage to find the answer.

Refer to your passage summary. The author is not in favor of single-sex education and criticizes the lack of evidence to support its use.

STEP 3: Read every word of every answer choice.

Answer A is not true based on the passage. The author says that the trend is growing. Answer B is not the main point the author is trying to make. Answer C is consistent with the answer developed in Step 2. Keep this choice. Answer D speculates on the reason for the growth in single-sex education, but the author does not do so. Answer E makes a comparison that the author does not. **The correct choice is answer C.**

SECTION IV

Questions 1–5

As with all logic games you follow the six-step process.

STEP 1:   Identify the game type.

You are asked to arrange the elements in sequential order, one speaker per day and according to certain conditions, so you recognize this as a one-tier ordering game.

STEP 2:   Begin your diagram.

Since there are six days in the conference, you can build a grid with six columns, each representing a day of the conference, and a placeholder for each. You shorten the names of the speakers to their initials (C, D, F, G, H, and J) and write them in the upper right corner above the grid.

STEP 3:   Symbolize the clues.

In the game description, the first rule you notice is that there can be only one speaker per day and that each speaker cannot repeat. To symbolize your clues you go through them one by one.

Clue 1: Chapman and Dabu must speak on days that are separated from each other by exactly one day.

Using the box form for symbolization, you can symbolize this clue as follows:

Since C and D could speak before or after each other, you alter it slightly as follows:

Clue 2: Chapman and Gant cannot speak on consecutive days.

You can use the box form for symbolizing this clue as well, as follows:

Notice that you use the same double arrow to indicate that C cannot be before G and G cannot be before C.

Clue 3: Gant must speak on a later day than Forest.

This can be symbolized simply by using a line to indicate the order in which they have to be placed:

F — G

Clue 4: Jonas must speak on day 3.

This requires no symbolization. You can insert J into your diagram where he belongs, on day 3.

STEP 4:   Double-check your symbolizations.

To double-check your symbolizations you translate your symbolized clues back into normal English and see whether they match the original language of each clue. Once you are certain that your symbolizations are correct, you can insert them beside your diagram for easy reference. Below is what your diagram should look like after you have created and confirmed the validity of all your symbolizations.

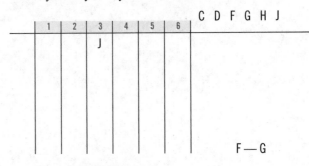

STEP 5:   Make deductions.

1. Can't-be-first-or-last deductions

   From your third clue you know that F can never be last because G must come after F. You can put ~F above the sixth column on your diagram to represent that F can never be in that column.

2. Repeated-element deductions

   You see that speaker C is repeated in the first two clues and G is repeated in the second and third clues. No hard and fast deductions can be derived from these repetitions. You can see that there might be situations where G is forced to be before or after D because C and D must have one day between them and G cannot occupy that gap, but depending on where C is located, this will not always be the case.

3. Down-to-two deductions

There are no down-to-two deductions that can be derived from the clues.

4. Block-splitting deductions

Even though there must be a day between them, C and D form a block. In essence, they form a block of three days if you include the unassigned day between them. Looking at your diagram, you notice that there are only two days before J, so you know that C or D cannot be on day 1, because that would force the other to be assigned to day 3, which is unavailable. You also know that neither can be assigned to day 5. This would also force the other to be assigned to day 3, and there is no day beyond day 6. To represent these, you can put ~C/D over days 1 and 5.

Adding your deductions you now have this diagram:

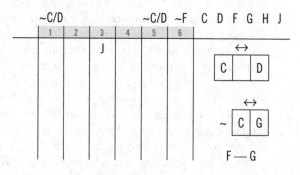

STEP 6: Answer the questions in the smartest order. On test day, answer the questions in this order:

1. Answer the Complete and Accurate List question.

2. Answer questions that give you more information to work with.

3. Answer the remaining questions.

Questions 1 and 2 are Complete and Accurate List questions, although the second is not the typical variety of this kind of question.

None of the questions gives further information.

That leaves questions 3, 4, and 5, and these can be answered in that order.

THE ANSWERS

1. Answer: **D**

The question asks you to identify the one answer with an acceptable schedule for all six days. Using your diagram, you can quickly work through each answer and eliminate those that break with your clues. For example, you can quickly eliminate answer A because C and G are scheduled consecutively, which is inconsistent with your second clue. You can also eliminate answer B because it does not have J scheduled on day 3. You eliminate answer C because G is scheduled before F, which is inconsistent with your third clue. You can also eliminate answer E because C and D are scheduled consecutively, which is inconsistent with your first clue. You are left with answer D and this schedule is consistent with your clues. You can represent this schedule on the diagram as follows:

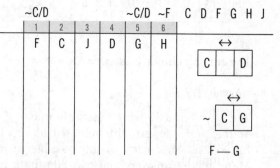

The correct choice is answer D.

2. Answer: **B**

The question asks you to identify a complete list of the days that C can be assigned to. You know from your deductions that C cannot be scheduled on day 1 or day 5, so you can eliminate answers A and E. You also know that nobody but J can be scheduled for day 3, so you can eliminate answer C. You are left with answers B and D. The only difference between these answers is that B includes day 6 as a possibility, and you know from your rules that C can easily be scheduled for day 6 as long as D is scheduled for day 4 and G is scheduled on any day that is not consecutive with day 6. Both are possible, so answer B offers you a complete and accurate list for C. **The correct choice is answer B**.

3. Answer: **A**

The question asks you to identify the scheduling option among the possible answers that *cannot* be true. This means all but one of the options is possible. You can evaluate each answer at a time. For answer A, you use your diagram to test the scheduling of H on day 2. You see that C and D must occupy day 4 and day 6 (or vice versa) to have a day between them. According to your second clue, G cannot be scheduled consecutively before or after C. This forces you to schedule G on day 1, but this means that G is scheduled before F, which is inconsistent with clue three. Thus, it cannot be true that H is scheduled on day 2, and this is the correct answer to the question. For learning purposes, the remaining scenarios have been diagrammed to demonstrate that they all work.

	~C/D				~C/D	~F
	1	2	3	4	5	6
(A)	G	H	J	C	F	D
(B)	F	D	J	C	G	H
(C)	F	C	J	D	G	H
(D)	F	G	J	C	H	D
(E)	H	C	J	D	F	G

C D F G H J

↔
C ☐ D

~ C G

F — G

The correct choice is answer A.

4. Answer: **D**

The question asks which scenario must be true. Your experience up to this point will be very helpful in assessing each of the possible answers. Many of the answers you can eliminate based on the scenarios of question 3, but in case you skipped that question we will work through each answer here. The easiest way to test the answers is to create a schedule that does not abide by the scenario given in each answer, and if it is possible to create such a schedule, then the answer is not necessarily true. The one answer or schedule that is impossible to create must be your answer. For example, answer A says that either F or G is scheduled to speak on day 2. You test this answer by creating a schedule in which neither F nor G is scheduled on day 2. If such a schedule is consistent with the rules of the game, then the answer is not necessarily true and cannot be your answer. What follows are the scenarios you created to test each answer. As you can see, for answer D, it was impossible to create a schedule in which C or D was not scheduled on day 4.

	~C/D				~C/D	~F
	1	2	3	4	5	6
(A)	H	C	J	D	F	G
(B)	F	G	J	C	H	D
(C)	F	G	J	C	H	D
(D)	—	—	—	—	—	—
(E)	F	C	J	D	H	G

C D F G H J

↔
C ☐ D

↔
~ C G

F — G

The correct choice is answer D.

5. Answer: **C**

The question asks you to identify which scenario among the possible answers cannot be true. Similar to question 4, you test each answer by attempting to create a schedule that is consistent with the answer and the rules of the game. If you can create such a scenario, then the answer can be true and it cannot be your answer. For example, answer A says that D and G are scheduled to speak consecutively. As you can see in the diagram that follows, you can create a schedule in which D and G are scheduled to speak on consecutive days and the schedule is consistent with the rules of your game, so this cannot be the correct choice. For answer C, it is impossible to create a schedule in which F and H are scheduled on consecutive days, because if you put them before day 3, then it forces G and C to be on consecutive days, which is inconsistent with clue 2. If you schedule them on days 4 and 5, then G must be scheduled on day 6 to be consistent with clue 3, and C and D must be scheduled on days 1 and 2, which is impossible because they must have one day between them according to clue 1. If you schedule them on days 5 and 6, then G will have to be scheduled before F and this is inconsistent with clue 3. Answer C cannot be true and must be your answer.

	~C/D				~C/D	~F
	1	2	3	4	5	6
(A)	F	C	J	D	G	H
(B)	F	C	J	D	G	H
(C)	—	—	—	—	—	—
(D)	H	C	J	D	F	G
(E)	F	C	J	D	H	G

C D F G H J

↔
C ☐ D

↔
~ C G

F — G

The correct choice is answer C.

Questions 6–12
As with all logic games you follow the six-step process.

STEP 1: **Identify the game type.**
This is a grouping game. You can tell that it is a grouping game because it is asking you to assign each student to a particular tutor and each tutor is assigned at least one student. The tutors in their respective disciplines serve as the groups (or group leaders, if that helps). There are six students to assign to four tutors (groups). There is a twist to this grouping because each student needs to be tutored in only one subject matter and all but one of the tutors can teach more than one subject.

STEP 2: **Begin your diagram.**
Your diagram will be a grid with four columns, one for each group. You shorten the group names to their initials: S, U, W, and Z. You can do the same thing with the students—B, C, D, F, G, and H—and list them in the upper right corner above your diagram for reference. Since each group specializes in a particular subject matter, it might help to show each tutor's specialties in the diagram. You can shorten those as well, to Ch, E, M, and P. Your initial diagram might look like this:

	S (M)	U (P & CH)	W (M & P)	Z (CH & E)	B C D F G H

STEP 3: **Symbolize the clues.**
You go one by one through the clues and symbolize them.

Clue 1: At least Bjorn and Chaim are assigned to Willie.

This clue need not be symbolized. The clue says that B and C are assigned to W. It also says they might not be the only ones assigned to W. You can put B and C into the W column and they will remain there through each question.

Clue 2: At least Fran is assigned to Zane.

This is another clue that need not be symbolized. Similar to the previous clue, it says that F is assigned to Z and there may be more students assigned to Z. You can put F into the Z column and it will remain there through each question.

Clue 3: If Dottie is assigned to Upton, then Gertie needs tutoring in Math.

This clue can be symbolized, but you must first recognize that only two teachers tutor in math, S and W.

You can reduce this clue to an "if . . . then" statement as follows:

$$D = U \rightarrow G = S/W$$

STEP 4: **Double-check your symbolizations.**
To double-check your symbolizations, you translate your symbols back into normal English and see whether they match the original language of each clue. In this case only one clue has been symbolized, but once you have verified that it works, then you can add your symbolizations to your diagram. Your diagram should look as follows:

	S (M)	U (P & CH)	W (M & P)	Z (CH & E)	B̶ C̶ D F G H
			B	F	D = U → G = S/W
			C		

STEP 5: **Make deductions.**
Finally, before you tackle the questions, you see if you can make any deductions based on the setup of the game and the clues. You go through each type of deduction.

1. Can't-be-first-or-last deductions

   This is not an ordering game, so this deduction does not apply to this particular game.

2. Repeated-element deductions

   There are no repeated elements among the rules in this game.

3. Down-to-two deductions

   There are no down-to-two deductions in this game.

4. Block-splitting deductions

   There are no instances of block splitting in this game.

STEP 6: **Answer the questions in the smartest order.**
Approach the questions in this order:

1. Answer the Complete and Accurate List question.

2. Answer questions that give you more information to work with.

3. Answer the remaining questions.

   This group of questions does not have a Complete and Accurate List question. Questions that provide more information are:

Question 9 ("Fran and Heste need tutoring in the same subject . . .")

Question 10 ("Dottie and Fran need tutoring in the same subject . . .")

Question 11 ("Exactly two students are assigned to Upton . . .")

Question 12 ("Bjorn, Chaim, Gertie, and Heste all need tutoring in the same subject . . .")

That leaves questions 6, 7 and 8, which you can answer in that order.

THE ANSWERS

6. Answer: **D**

The question asks which one of the possible answers cannot be true. You evaluate each answer, one by one. You assume your diagram remains as drawn, with B and C in W and F in Z. You also notice that the subject matter (math, physics, etc.) does not come into play for this question. Placement is the only factor. For answer A, if G = U and D = Z, then you can put H with S and you have a valid grouping. For answer B, if G = S and D = Z, then you can put H with U and you have a valid grouping. For answer C, if F = Z and G = Z, then you can put D with S and H with U and you have a valid grouping. For answer D, if D = W and H = Z, you know from clue 3 that G must be with W or S. Regardless of which tutor G is assigned to, you are still left with no student to assign to U. Each tutor must have at least one student, so this scenario cannot work and it must be your correct answer. For answer E, if D = S and G = U, then you can assign H to any of the tutors and still have a valid grouping. **The correct choice is answer D.**

7. Answer: **B**

The question asks which scenario among the possible answers must be true. This means all but one of the answers has the possibility of being not true, but only one must be true no matter what the grouping. Again, you review each answer, one at a time. To determine whether the answer has the possibility of being not true, you attempt to create a scenario in which the stipulation in the answer is not true, and if you can create such a grouping and it is consistent with the rules of your game, then it cannot be your choice. You assume that your diagram remains as drawn, with B and C in W and F in Z. Also, you notice that the subject matter (math, physics, etc.) does not come into play in this question. Placement is the only factor. Answer

A says that S tutors exactly one student, so you test whether more than one student can be assigned to S. You assign two students, H and D, to S and then G to U. This is a valid grouping, so answer A cannot be your choice. Answer B says that Z is assigned fewer than three students, so you can test whether Z can be assigned three or more students, but such a test is unnecessary. If Z is assigned three student and you already know that W is assigned two students, then you are left with only one student to assign to S or U. One of the tutors will be left with nobody to teach, and your game requires that each tutor be assigned at least one student. It must be true that Z is assigned fewer than three students and B must be your answer for this question. Let's review the remainder of the possible answers for learning purposes. Answer C says U is assigned fewer than two students, so you test whether U can be assigned two or more students. You assign G and H to U, which leaves D to be assigned to S. This is a valid grouping and thus cannot be your answer. Answer D says exactly one student is assigned to Z, so you test whether more than one student can be assigned to Z. You assign D to Z, along with F, making it two students. You assign G to S, and H to U. This is a valid grouping, and this cannot be your answer. Finally, answer E says that W is assigned exactly two students. You already know that W must be assigned at least two students, B and C, so you test whether W can be assigned three. You assign G to W (along with B and C), D to U, and H to S. This is a valid grouping and cannot be your answer. Therefore, **the correct choice is answer B.**

8. Answer: **A**

The question asks that you find the one statement that cannot be true, no matter the grouping. That means all but one of the answers has the possibility of being true. You review each answer and test whether it can be true or not. To test the answer, you create a grouping that is consistent with the answer and the rules of the game, and if such a grouping is possible, then it cannot be the correct choice. If such a grouping is impossible, then it must be your choice. Your diagram remains as drawn, with B and C in W and F in Z. Also, this is the first question that uses the subject matter as a determinant for the grouping. It will change the dynamic of your scheduling. Answer A says D and G need tutoring in English, which means they must be with Z, since Z is the only tutor that can teach English. This would mean Z would teach three students (F included), and you know from question 7 that this cannot be true. If Z has three students and W already has two students, there is only one student left to assign to either S or U. The game requires that each tutor have at least one student, so the correct answer to this question is A. Let's review the remaining options for learning purposes. Answer B says that D and H need to learn chemistry, which means they could be assigned to U or Z. There are numerous groupings possible here, but one could be that you assign D to Z and H to U, which leaves H to be assigned to S, and you have a valid grouping. Answer C says that D and H need tutoring in math. Only S and W teach math. You can assign both D and H to S and G to U and you have a valid grouping. Answer D says that D and G need tutoring in math. Only S and W teach math. You can assign D and G to S and assign H to U and you have a valid grouping. Finally, answer E says both D and B need tutoring in physics. Only U and W tutor physics. If both D and B are assigned to U, then clue 3 says you must assign G to S or W. You choose to assign G to S, and you have a valid grouping. **The correct choice is answer A.**

9. Answer: **B**

The question tells you that F and H need tutoring in the same subject and then asks what is the maximum number of students who need physics. Essentially, the question is asking you to create a situation that maximizes the number of students U and W are teaching under the given scenario. You use your diagram to illustrate this grouping. You know from your clues that F must be assigned to Z, but you do not know whether F is being tutored in chemistry or English. In the interest of maximizing the number available to assign to W, you will assume F is being tutored in chemistry. Therefore, you can assign H to U (if you assumed English, they would both have to be assigned to Z). This allows you to assign D to S and G to W. There is no way to assign more to U or W without depriving another tutor of a student. For the sake of this question you can assume all of W's students are studying physics, and you know that H is studying chemistry. Therefore, the maximum number of students studying physics is three.

S (M)	U (P & CH)	W (M & P)	Z (CH & E)	B̶ C̶ D̶ F̶ G̶ H̶
D	H	B	F	D = U → G = S/W
		C		
		W		

The correct choice is answer B.

10. Answer: **D**

The question tells you that D and F need tutoring in the same subject and then asks you to determine which of the possible answers must be true. This means all but one of the answers may not true, but only one must be true no matter what the grouping. You know that F is assigned to Z, but you do not know in which subject, chemistry or English, F is being tutored, so D also may be tutored in either chemistry or English. Therefore, while F can be assigned only to Z, D can be assigned to either U or Z. You will test both scenarios. First, you will assign D to U. According to clue 3, if D is assigned to U, then G must be with either S or W. If you assign G to S, then H can be assigned to any tutor. If you assign G to W, then H must be assigned to S.

	S (M)	U (P & CH)	W (M & P)	Z (CH & E)	B̶ C̶ D̶ F̶ G̶ H̶
	G	D	B	F	D = U → G = S/W
		H	C		
OR	H		G		

In the second scenario you assign D to Z. In this case, G and H must be distributed between S and U.

	S (M)	U (P & CH)	W (M & P)	Z (CH & E)	B̶ C̶ D̶ F̶ G̶ H̶
	G	H	B	F	D = U → G = S/W
			C	D	
OR	H	G			

Now, you look at your answers and evaluate each one. Answer A says D and F are tutored in English, but you have already shown that it is possible for D to be tutored in chemistry, since Z and U both tutor chemistry. Answer B says at least two students need tutoring in math. If you assume all of W's students are being tutored in physics, then it is possible that only one student (G or H) is tutored in math. Therefore, it is possible that this answer is not true. Answer C says at least two students are tutored in English. In the first scenario above, there are no students tutored in English (F and D are tutored in chemistry), so this answer has the possibility of being untrue. Answer D says that at least one of G and H is tutored in math. In both scenarios above, no matter the configuration, you see that either or both of G and H are being tutored in math. This answer must be true, so this is your choice. The final option, answer E, says that at least one of G and H must be tutored in chemistry. In the first scenario you see a grouping where neither G nor H is being tutored in chemistry, so this answer may be untrue. **The correct choice is answer D.**

11. Answer: **B**

The question tells you that U is assigned exactly two students and asks you to determine which of the answers gives facts that *could* be true. You must determine which is possible, which means that all but one of the answers are impossible. For the remaining unassigned students, D, G, and H, there are three scenarios for assigning exactly two students to U: DG, DH, GH. You can quickly eliminate the DG scenario because it is inconsistent with your clues. When D is assigned to U, G must be assigned to S or W, so G cannot be assigned to U. You are left with DH and GH. You create both of these scenarios in your diagram. Your initial diagram remains as drawn previously, with B and C in W and F in Z. Answer A cannot be correct because if G needs tutoring in chemistry, then D must need math. Answer B could be true, because when G needs Math, D could be learning chemistry. This is your answer, because it could be true. Answer C cannot be true because if H is learning math, D and G must be together with U, and this is impossible under the rules of the game. Answer D cannot be correct because under the provisions of the question, H must be with either S or U. Answer E cannot be correct because if H and G are both learning math, then there is only one student with U, and that breaks the rules set by the question.

GH

	S (M)	U (P & CH)	W (M & P)	Z (CH & E)	B C D F G H
	D	G	B	F	D = U → G = S/W
		H	C		

DH

	S (M)	U (P & CH)	W (M & P)	Z (CH & E)	B C D F G H
	G	D	B	F	D = U → G = S/W
		H	C		

The correct choice is answer B.

12. Answer: **C**

The last question tells you that B, C, G, and H all need tutoring in the same subject and then asks you to identify the one statement among the possible answers that could be true. This means that all but one of the statements must be impossible. You know from your clues that B and C are assigned to W, and W tutors only math and physics. Therefore,

S, W, and U are the only tutors who can receive G and H. If B and C are learning math, then at least one of G and H must go to S. Also, if B and C are learning physics, at least one of G and H must go to U. You evaluate each answer and eliminate those that are impossible. Answer A says that exactly two students learn physics. This is impossible. If the two physics students are B and C, then G and H must also learn physics and that adds up to more than two. If you try to put two physics students with U, then one of them must be G or H, which would mean B, C, G, and H are learning physics and again you have more than two. This answer cannot be true and cannot be the correct choice. Answer B says D is learning English. This is also impossible. Since G and H must be assigned to the same subject, either S or U will be left without a student. D must be assigned to either S or U. Answer C says D learns math. This is very possible if B, C, G, and H all learn physics. They will be distributed among U and W, leaving S to teach D. This is your answer, but let's review the remaining options for learning purposes. Answer D says exactly two students learn English. This is impossible because you have already proven that G, H, and D must be assigned to S or U depending on the dominant subject. Thus, Z must have only one student and Z is the only tutor teaching English. This cannot be your answer. Answer E says that exactly three students learn chemistry. This is impossible because you know that B, C, G, and H learn the same subject and chemistry cannot be one of them. That leaves only two possible students to learn chemistry. **The correct choice is answer C.**

Questions 13–19
As with all logic games you follow the six-step process.

STEP 1: **Identify the game type.**
This game is a two-tiered ordering game. It has all three of the telltale signs of this type of game. First, it has the language of both ordering and grouping games. For each inspector, all the buildings must be scheduled over six weeks, and within each week, the schedule of one inspector affects the schedule of the other inspector. Some buildings cannot be inspected before another building and certain buildings cannot be inspected by one inspector until the other inspector has inspected it. This is typical language for an ordering game. At the same time, each building must be assigned to a particular week with another building, and no building can be inspected by both inspectors in the same week, and they can only be inspected once by each inspector. This is typical grouping language.

STEP 2: Begin your diagram.

Your diagram will take the form of a grid with the inspectors listed on the left and the weeks going from left to right. You can abbreviate government to G and commercial to C. The building letters appear above and to the right of the diagram and they are grouped into their respective sets (G and C). Since there are only two inspectors, you will not abbreviate their names.

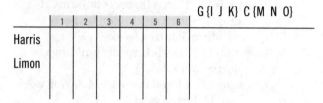

STEP 3: Symbolize the clues.

Once you have your diagram, you can proceed to symbolize your clues. You symbolize them one at a time below.

Clue 1: Limon cannot inspect any government building until Harris has evaluated that building.

This can be reworded to say that if it is a government building, then Harris must inspect it before Limon. This can be symbolized as follows:

$$G \rightarrow H - L$$

Clue 2: Harris cannot evaluate any commercial building until Limon has evaluated that building.

This is similar to the first clue and can be reworded to say that if it is a commercial building, then Limon must inspect it before Harris. This can be symbolized as follows:

$$C \rightarrow L - H$$

Clue 3: Limon cannot inspect any two government buildings consecutively.

You can use box notation to symbolize this clue. There are several ways to symbolize this, but the simplest is as follows:

~ | G | G (box notation)

You put G in the bottom boxes because in your diagram Limon's schedule appears below Harris's schedule. Another way to represent the same clue is to show each configuration of consecutively scheduled government buildings. You use the double arrow to

show that regardless of order, these buildings cannot be inspected consecutively. For example:

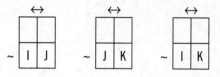

For the purposes of the exercise here, we will use the simpler one.

Clue 4: Harris must inspect building M during week 4.

This clue need not be symbolized. You can simply put M on Harris's schedule during week 4.

STEP 4: Double-check your symbolizations.

To double-check your symbolizations, you translate your symbolized clues back into normal English and see whether they match the original language of each clue. Once you have confirmed that your symbolizations represent the clues correctly, you can insert them to the right of your diagram for easy reference. Your page should look as follows:

	1	2	3	4	5	6	G {I J K} C {M N O}
Harris				M			$G \rightarrow H - L$
Limon							$C \rightarrow L - H$

~ | G | G

STEP 5: Make deductions.

Before you tackle the questions, you see if you can make any deductions based on the setup of the game and the clues. You go through each type of deduction.

1. Can't-be-first-or-last deductions

Because Harris must inspect each government building before Limon can inspect it, you can deduce that Harris cannot schedule a government building during week 6, because this would not give Limon a chance to inspect it. Nor can Limon schedule a government building in week 1, because Harris would not have had a chance to inspect it. Similarly, because Limon must inspect a commercial building before Harris can inspect it, you can deduce that Limon cannot schedule a commercial building in week 6, because this would not give Harris time to inspect it. Nor can Harris schedule a commercial building in week 1 because Limon would not have had a chance to inspect it. These deductions can be symbolized as follows:

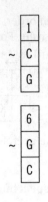

2. Repeated-element deductions

There are no repeated element deductions you can make for this game.

3. Down-to-two deductions

There are no down-to-two deductions you can make for this game.

4. Block-splitting deductions

In effect, the government buildings form a block on Limon's schedule. They cannot be consecutive and none of them can be scheduled for week 1. Therefore, they must be scheduled for weeks 2, 4, and 6, and Limon's commercial buildings must be scheduled for weeks 1, 3, and 5. Instead of symbolizing this deduction you will note it at the bottom of the diagram, keeping in mind this is a deduction for Limon's schedule and not Harris's.

You add your deductions to the diagram so that it now looks as follows:

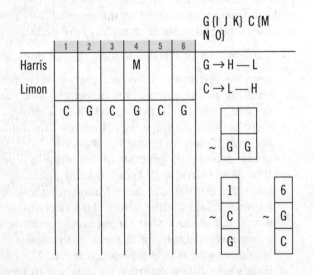

STEP 6: **Answer the questions in the smartest order.**
Answer the questions in the following order:

1. Answer the Complete and Accurate List question.

2. Answer questions that give you more information to work with.

3. Answer the remaining questions.

Questions 13 and 18 are both Complete and Accurate List questions and should be answered first. Questions that give more information include the following:

> Question 14 ("Harris inspects building H during week 3 and Limon inspects building G during week 6 . . .")
> Question 15 ("Harris inspects building O during week 2 . . .")
> Question 17 ("Limon inspects M during week 1 and I during week 2 . . .")

That leaves questions 16 and 19, and they can be answered in that order.

THE ANSWERS

13. Answer: **A**

The question asks which of the schedules is acceptable. You must analyze each schedule to see whether it is inconsistent with your clues. For answer A, you notice that Harris inspects every government building a week before Limon, and Limon inspects every commercial building a week before Harris. Also, Limon does not inspect two government buildings consecutively. Therefore, this is the correct answer, but for learning purposes let's evaluate the remaining answers. Answer B is an unacceptable schedule because Harris inspects commercial building N before Limon, and this is inconsistent with clue 2. Answer C is an unacceptable schedule because it does not have Harris inspecting building M in week 4 and this is inconsistent with clue 4. Answer D is unacceptable because Limon inspects government building I before Harris and this is inconsistent with clue 2. Lastly, answer E is unacceptable because Limon inspects government buildings J and K consecutively, and this is inconsistent with clue 3. **The correct choice is answer A.**

14. Answer: **D**

The question gives you new information, that Harris inspects building K in week 3 and Limon inspects building J in week 6. You add this new information to your diagram, and you deduce certain requirements that this scenario creates.

If Harris inspects K in week 3, then Limon must schedule K for week 4, because he must inspect K after Harris inspects it. Also, Limon cannot schedule K for week 5 because Limon cannot have two government buildings scheduled consecutively. Therefore, Limon must schedule I for week 2. He cannot schedule I for week 3 or 5 because I and K or I and J would be consecutive, and he cannot schedule I for week 1 because Harris must have at least a week before to inspect a government building. You now evaluate your answers. Answer A cannot be correct because Limon can easily schedule N in week 1 or 3, which still gives Harris enough time to inspect it after him. Answer B is completely inconsistent with clue 4. Answer C cannot be the answer because Harris does not have to schedule J during week 2. He can also schedule it during week 5 because that is still before the week that Limon has scheduled it. Answer D, as you know from your deductions, must be true. Harris must inspect I during week 1. This is your answer. Answer E cannot be correct because Harris can also schedule O during week 2 and 5, both of which give Limon advance time to inspect it before him.

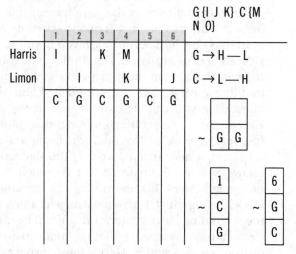

The correct choice is answer D.

15. Answer: **C**

The question tells you that Harris inspects O in week 2 and asks which of the buildings Limon must inspect in week 5. You add this new information to your diagram and see what deductions you can make with regard to which building Limon must inspect in week 5. You can deduce that if Harris inspects O in week 2, then Limon must have inspected O in week 1, because Limon must inspect each commercial building before Harris and week 1 is the only week available for Limon to

inspect building O. Your deduction tells you that the government buildings are in weeks 2, 4, and 6. This means that Limon will have to inspect M in week 3 in order to inspect it before Harris and remain consistent with clue 2. That leaves N as the one remaining building Limon must schedule, and it must be in week 5. This is your answer. You do not have to evaluate the other answers.

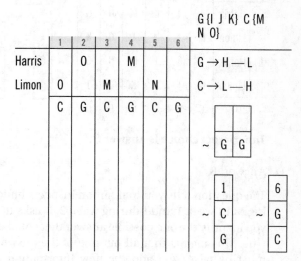

The correct choice is answer C.

16. Answer: **D**

The question asks you to identify among the possible answers the one statement that must be true. This means that all but one of the answers may not be true. If you give the answers a quick read, you can quickly see that answer D must be true because you already deduced that Limon must inspect a commercial building in week 3, but for learning purposes let's review the remaining answers. The following diagram shows a scenario for each answer that proves it does not have to be true. Answer A shows that Harris can inspect two government buildings consecutively and the scheduling can still be consistent with the rules of the game. Answer B shows that Harris can inspect J before N. Answer C shows that Harris can inspect a government building during week 2. Lastly, answer E shows that Limon can inspect a government building other than K during week 6.

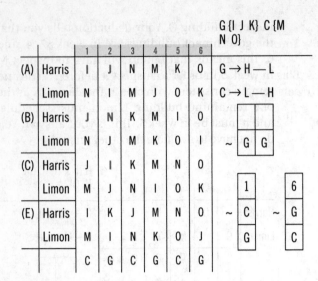

The correct choice is answer D.

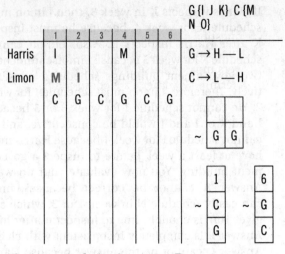

The correct choice is answer B.

17. **Answer: B**

The question tells you that Limon inspects building M in week 1 and I during week 2. It asks that you identify the one possible answer that could be true. This means that all but one of the answers must be false. You add the new information to your diagram. You can use clue 1 to deduce that Harris inspects I during week 1. Now you evaluate your possible answers. For answer A, Limon does not inspect his two remaining commercial buildings until week 3. Therefore, Harris cannot do his two remaining commercial buildings (N and O) until weeks 5 and 6. Harris must inspect his two remaining government buildings (J and K) during weeks 2 and 3, which means he must inspect two consecutive government buildings and answer A must be false. Using the same logic, answer B could be true. One of the commercial buildings Harris inspects during week 5 or 6 can be O, so answer B could be true and this is your answer. We'll analyze the remaining answers for learning purposes. Answer C cannot be true because, based on your initial deductions, Harris cannot inspect a government building in week 5. Answer D cannot be true because you have already deduced that Harris's first inspection must be I so that Limon can inspect I during week 2. Finally, answer E cannot be true because clue 4 tells you that Harris must schedule M for week 4.

18. **Answer: D**

The question asks you to identify from among the possible answers the complete and accurate list of the weeks during which Harris must inspect government buildings. This means that all but one of the answers include weeks that may or may not be scheduled for a government building for Harris. The only clue that affects when Harris inspects a government building is the requirement that he inspect it before Limon, so Limon's schedule will most likely be the determining factor in your consideration of each answer. Your initial deductions tell you that Limon must inspect a government building during weeks 2, 4, and 6. From this knowledge you can determine that in week 3 Harris must inspect the building that Limon inspects in week 1. Therefore, whichever answer is correct, it must include week 1. This deduction allows you to eliminate answer E, which does not include week 1. Determining the remaining weeks during which Harris must inspect a government building means determining when he must inspect the government buildings Limon inspects during weeks 4 and 6. Harris must inspect the week 4 building during either week 2 or week 3, but it does not really matter which. Regarding the week 6 building, Harris can inspect this in week 2, 3, or 5. All of these weeks come before the week Limon inspects the building and do not cause conflicts with the scheduling of commercial buildings after Limon inspects them. Because the other two buildings have such flexibility, week 1 is the only week that he *must* inspect a government building. **The correct choice is answer D.**

19. Answer: **A**

The question asks which among the answers could be true. This means all but one of the possible answers must be false. You analyze each answer to determine whether a schedule could exist with the stated fact. Luckily, the first answer turns out to be your answer. Answer A could indeed be true because K is a government building and your initial deductions tell you that Limon can schedule only government buildings in weeks 2, 4, and 6. Answer B cannot be true because I is a government building and Limon cannot schedule a government building in week 3. Answer C cannot be true because Harris cannot inspect a commercial building until Limon has inspected it. Harris must schedule M for week 4 according to clue 4. Therefore, Limon cannot inspect M after week 4. Answer D cannot be true because O is a commercial building and your deductions tell you that Harris cannot schedule a commercial building during the first week. Such scheduling does not allow Limon to inspect the commercial building before Limon. Answer E cannot be true because I is a government building and your deductions tell you that Harris cannot schedule a government building in week 6 because it does not allow time for Limon to inspect it after Harris. **The correct choice is answer A.**

Question 20–26
As with all logic games you follow the six-step process.

STEP 1: Identify the game type.
This is a grouping game, but the terse nature of the descriptions somewhat obscures the game's nature. Put simply, there are two categories of lumber, domestic and exotic, and they are being allocated to the "On Sale" and "Not on Sale" groups. Within each category there are five different types of wood: cherry, maple, oak, pine, and walnut.

STEP 2: Begin your diagram.
The diagram will be a simple four-box grid with Domestic and Exotic on one side and On Sale and Not on Sale across the top (you could do it the other way as well). You abbreviate the types of wood as C, M, O, P, and W. Each type of wood will appear in the grid twice, because both domestic and exotic are offered.

C M O P W

	ON SALE	NOT ON SALE
Domestic		
Exotic		

STEP 3: Symbolize the clues.
You symbolize the clues one at a time.

Clue 1: Exotic oak is on sale; domestic maple is not on sale.

These do not need to be symbolized. You will simply put an "O" in the exotic and on sale box, and you will put an "M" in the domestic and not on sale box.

Clue 2: If both types of oak are on sale, then all walnut is on sale.

This can be symbolized using your block format, as follows:

O	
O	

→

W	
W	

Clue 3: If both types of cherry are on sale, then no pine is on sale.

This can be symbolized using your block format, as follows:

C	
C	

→

	P
	P

Clue 4: If neither type of cherry is on sale, then domestic oak is on sale.

This can be symbolized using your block format, as follows:

	C
	C

→

O	

Clue 5: If either type of pine is on sale, then no walnut is.

This can be symbolized using your block format, as follows:

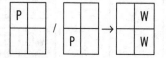

It might be useful to convert this to a contrapositive. You must keep in mind that the right side could be interpreted as meaning that both domestic walnut *and* exotic walnut are on sale and could be rewritten as follows:

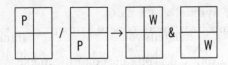

You form the contrapositive as follows:

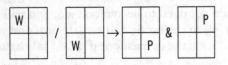

Notice that terms have switched sides of the arrow and the negation has switched the letters to the opposite boxes. The "or" has become an "and" and vice versa. You can compact the right side into one box as follows:

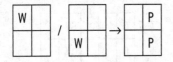

This says that if either type of walnut is on sale, then both types of pine must not be on sale.

STEP 4: **Double-check your symbolizations.**
To double-check your symbolizations, you translate your symbolized clues back into normal English and see whether they match the original language of each clue. Once you confirm that you have the correct symbolizations, you proceed to write them next to your diagram, including the contrapositive for the last clue. Your page should look something like this:

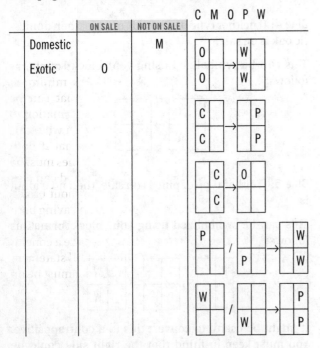

STEP 5: **Make deductions.**

1. Can't-be-first-or-last deductions

   This is not an ordering game, so there are none of these types of deductions to be made.

2. Repeated-element deductions

   There is a repeated element implied by the clues that is a bit tricky. Clue 1 says that exotic oak is on sale. Clue 4 says that if no type of cherry wood is on sale, then domestic oak is on sale. In essence, this says that if no type of cherry wood is on sale, then all oak is on sale. Clue 2 says that if all oak is on sale, then all walnut is on sale. You can deduce that if both types of cherry wood are not on sale, then both types of walnut are on sale. This deduction could be written as follows:

   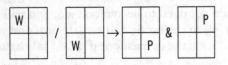

3. Down-to-two deductions

   There are none of these types of deductions to be made.

4. Block-splitting deductions

   There are none of these types of deductions to be made.

STEP 6: **Answer the questions in the smartest order.**
On test day, answer the questions in this order:

1. Answer the Complete and Accurate List question.

2. Answer questions that give you more information to work with.

3. Answer the remaining questions.

   Question 20 is a Complete and Accurate List question and should be answered first. Questions that offer more information are as follows:

   > Question 21 ("domestic walnut is not on sale . . .")
   > Question 22 ("both types of cherry are on sale . . .")
   > Question 24 ("neither type of cherry is on sale . . .")
   > Question 25 ("domestic walnut is the only type of domestic lumber on sale . . .")
   > Question 26 ("exactly four of the types of exotic lumber are the only lumber types on sale . . .")

The only remaining question is 23.

THE ANSWERS

20. Answer: B

The question asks you to identify a complete and accurate list of the types of lumber that are on sale. You must review each answer and test them against your clues. You apply each one to your diagram. You place the letters in the On Sale column and the remaining in the Not on Sale column. With answer A, both types of cherry wood are not on sale and according to clue 4, domestic oak must be on sale, so this grouping is not consistent with the game and cannot be the answer. Answer B is completely consistent with your rules, and it can be a complete and accurate list of the lumber on sale. This is your answer, but let's review the remaining answers for learning purposes. Answer C cannot be your answer because it is inconsistent with clue 2. Both oaks are on sale so both types of walnut must be on sale, but in this grouping exotic walnut is not on sale. Answer D is inconsistent with clue 5. Exotic pine is on sale and therefore neither walnut can be on sale, but in this grouping domestic walnut is on sale, so this answer cannot be a complete and accurate sale list. Answer E cannot be your answer because both domestic and exotic cherry wood are on sale, which means neither pine type can be on sale, but in this grouping domestic pine is on sale.

		ON SALE	NOT ON SALE
(A)	Domestic	P	M O C W
	Exotic	O M P	C W
(B)	Domestic	W	M C O P
	Exotic	O C W	P M
(C)	Domestic	O W	M P C
	Exotic	O M	W C
(D)	Domestic	C W	M O P
	Exotic	O P	M W C
(E)	Domestic	C P	M O W
	Exotic	O C M	P W

The correct choice is answer B.

21. Answer: A

The question tells you that domestic walnut is not on sale and asks which of the possible answers must be true based on this fact. You look first for the clues that affect walnut, which brings you to the second clue. It says that if both types of oak are on sale, then both types of walnut must be on sale as well, but this question says that domestic walnut is not on sale so you know that both oaks cannot be on sale. Clue 1 says that exotic oak must be on sale. Taking both of these clues together, you can deduce that in order for domestic walnut not to be on sale, domestic oak cannot be on sale. Answer A says that at least one type of oak is not on sale, and based on your deductions this must be true, so this is your answer. Neither answer B nor answer C can be correct because according to the clues, whether or not walnut is on sale has no effect on the sale status of the types of cherry wood or maple. Neither answer D nor answer E can be your choice because your clues do not help you understand the sale status of pine if domestic walnut is not on sale. Clue 5 works in only one direction (from pine to walnut). Knowing that one of the walnuts is not on sale tells you nothing about the types of pine. Your contrapositive would help only if the domestic walnut was on sale, but that is not the fact given to you. **The correct choice is answer A.**

22. Answer: A

The question tells you that both types of cherry wood are on sale, then asks you the minimum number of *domestic* lumber types that can be included in the sale. You add this information to your diagram and attempt to ascertain what this number might be. Clue 3 tells you that if both cherry woods are on sale, then both pines must be not on sale. The rest of the types of wood can also be put in the Not on Sale column without breaking any of your rules. Remember that having both types of walnut not on sale tells you nothing. This question once again tempts you to make a conclusion based on reversing the "if . . . then" statement in clue 5. The only domestic wood that must be on sale is cherry wood.

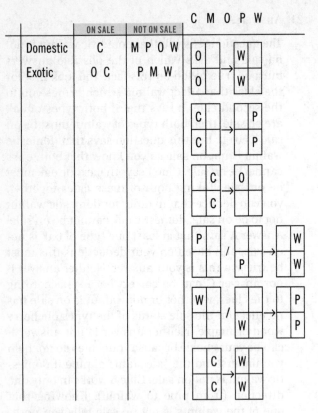

	ON SALE	NOT ON SALE	C M O P W
Domestic	C	M P O W	
Exotic	O C	P M W	

The correct choice is answer A.

23. Answer: **E**

The question asks which of the possible answers cannot be true. Answer A could be true. The clues tell you nothing about the relationship between cherry and maple. Regardless of whether both types of cherry are on sale, you can put exotic maple on sale or not. Answer B has the same problem. Your clues tell you nothing about a relationship between maple and pine, and therefore it could be true that neither type of maple and neither type of pine is on sale. If both types of cherry are on sale, clue 4 tells you that domestic oak must be on sale, but it says nothing about pine. Clue 3 tells you only what happens if both cherry woods are on sale, not when they are not on sale, so answer C cannot be correct. Answer D has the same problem as answers A and B. There is no relationship between maple and any of the other woods, so this scenario could be true. Finally, consider answer E. This answer conflicts with your deduction that if neither type of cherry is on sale, then both walnut types must be on sale. This answer cannot be true and must be your answer. **The correct choice is answer E.**

24. Answer: **E**

The question tells you that neither cherry type is on sale and asks you to determine which statement among the possible answers is not necessarily true. You create the scenario using your diagram. Because both cherry types are not on sale, clue 4 tells you that domestic oak is on sale. Because both oak types are now on sale, clue 2 tells you that both walnuts are on sale. Your contrapositive tells you that because either the domestic walnut or the exotic walnut is on sale, both pines are not on sale. This leaves only one type undetermined, exotic maple. Based on the preceding logic, answers A, B, C, and D all must be true. Only answer E may or may not be true. Exotic maple can be either on sale or not on sale. Nothing in this scenario tells you one way or the other.

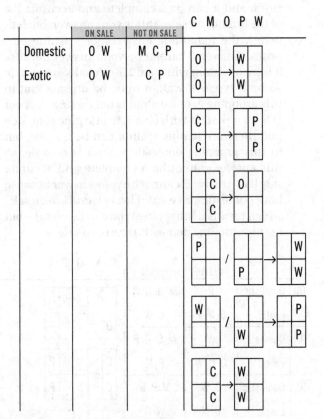

	ON SALE	NOT ON SALE	C M O P W
Domestic	O W	M C P	
Exotic	O W	C P	

The correct choice is answer E.

25. Answer: **B**

The question tells you that domestic walnut is the only type of domestic lumber on sale and then asks you to determine which among the possible answers cannot be true. This means that all but one of the options are possible. You use your diagram to visualize the scenario. Answer A could be true. If exotic walnut is not on sale, you can still maintain domestic walnut as the only domestic wood on sale. No clue changes this requirement. Regarding answer B, if exotic cherry is not on sale, then both cherries are not on sale and clue 4 requires that domestic oak be on sale. This would mean that walnut would not be the only domestic wood on sale, and that goes against the information given by the question. This is your answer. Answer C is true because the very fact that domestic walnut is on sale triggers the contrapositive of clue 5. Exotic maple is one wood that is not restricted by the clues of this game, so it can be on sale or not on sale. It does not matter. In this particular question, exotic walnut is not restricted by the clues either and can be on sale or not on sale. Therefore, neither answer D nor answer E can be correct.

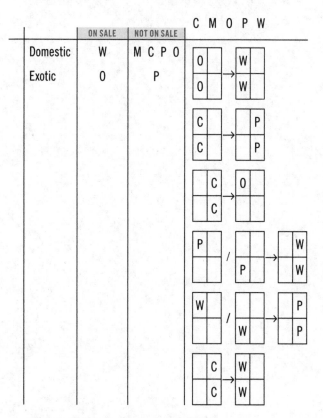

The correct choice is answer B.

26. Answer: **D**

The question tells you that four of the five types of exotic lumber are the only lumber types on sale. It then asks you to determine which of the possible answers could be true. This means that all but one of the possible answers is impossible given the clues in the game. Because the exotic woods are the only ones on sale, there can be no

domestic woods on sale. Everything else is not on sale. You test each one on your diagram. Answer A cannot be the correct choice because clue 4 tells you that when both cherry woods are not on sale, then domestic oak must be on sale. Answer B cannot be correct because you have only five types of exotic woods. If neither exotic pine nor exotic walnut is on sale, that leaves only three exotic woods on sale. Answer C has the same problem as answer A. If exotic cherry is not on sale, then both types of cherry wood are not on sale, and clue 4 tells you that if this is the case, then domestic oak is on sale. Answer D could be true. This grouping is consistent with all of the clues, including clue 5, which is triggered by this configuration. This is your answer. Answer E cannot be true because it is inconsistent with clue 5. If exotic maple is not on sale, then exotic pine must be. However, because pine is on sale, then both types of walnut must not be on sale, and that means you would have only three exotic woods on sale, not the four required.

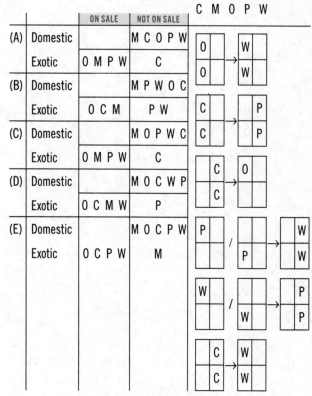

The correct choice is answer D.

LSAT Practice Test 2

You can also take this practice test on your tablet or smartphone as well as your laptop or home computer. See page 7A of the Welcome insert for more information.

Answer Sheet

Directions: Before beginning the test, photocopy this answer sheet or remove it from the book. Mark your answer to each question by filling in the corresponding answer oval in the columns below. If a section has fewer questions than answer spaces, leave the extra spaces blank.

Section I	Section II	Section III	Section IV
1. Ⓐ Ⓑ Ⓒ Ⓓ Ⓔ	1. Ⓐ Ⓑ Ⓒ Ⓓ Ⓔ	1. Ⓐ Ⓑ Ⓒ Ⓓ Ⓔ	1. Ⓐ Ⓑ Ⓒ Ⓓ Ⓔ
2. Ⓐ Ⓑ Ⓒ Ⓓ Ⓔ	2. Ⓐ Ⓑ Ⓒ Ⓓ Ⓔ	2. Ⓐ Ⓑ Ⓒ Ⓓ Ⓔ	2. Ⓐ Ⓑ Ⓒ Ⓓ Ⓔ
3. Ⓐ Ⓑ Ⓒ Ⓓ Ⓔ	3. Ⓐ Ⓑ Ⓒ Ⓓ Ⓔ	3. Ⓐ Ⓑ Ⓒ Ⓓ Ⓔ	3. Ⓐ Ⓑ Ⓒ Ⓓ Ⓔ
4. Ⓐ Ⓑ Ⓒ Ⓓ Ⓔ	4. Ⓐ Ⓑ Ⓒ Ⓓ Ⓔ	4. Ⓐ Ⓑ Ⓒ Ⓓ Ⓔ	4. Ⓐ Ⓑ Ⓒ Ⓓ Ⓔ
5. Ⓐ Ⓑ Ⓒ Ⓓ Ⓔ	5. Ⓐ Ⓑ Ⓒ Ⓓ Ⓔ	5. Ⓐ Ⓑ Ⓒ Ⓓ Ⓔ	5. Ⓐ Ⓑ Ⓒ Ⓓ Ⓔ
6. Ⓐ Ⓑ Ⓒ Ⓓ Ⓔ	6. Ⓐ Ⓑ Ⓒ Ⓓ Ⓔ	6. Ⓐ Ⓑ Ⓒ Ⓓ Ⓔ	6. Ⓐ Ⓑ Ⓒ Ⓓ Ⓔ
7. Ⓐ Ⓑ Ⓒ Ⓓ Ⓔ	7. Ⓐ Ⓑ Ⓒ Ⓓ Ⓔ	7. Ⓐ Ⓑ Ⓒ Ⓓ Ⓔ	7. Ⓐ Ⓑ Ⓒ Ⓓ Ⓔ
8. Ⓐ Ⓑ Ⓒ Ⓓ Ⓔ	8. Ⓐ Ⓑ Ⓒ Ⓓ Ⓔ	8. Ⓐ Ⓑ Ⓒ Ⓓ Ⓔ	8. Ⓐ Ⓑ Ⓒ Ⓓ Ⓔ
9. Ⓐ Ⓑ Ⓒ Ⓓ Ⓔ	9. Ⓐ Ⓑ Ⓒ Ⓓ Ⓔ	9. Ⓐ Ⓑ Ⓒ Ⓓ Ⓔ	9. Ⓐ Ⓑ Ⓒ Ⓓ Ⓔ
10. Ⓐ Ⓑ Ⓒ Ⓓ Ⓔ	10. Ⓐ Ⓑ Ⓒ Ⓓ Ⓔ	10. Ⓐ Ⓑ Ⓒ Ⓓ Ⓔ	10. Ⓐ Ⓑ Ⓒ Ⓓ Ⓔ
11. Ⓐ Ⓑ Ⓒ Ⓓ Ⓔ	11. Ⓐ Ⓑ Ⓒ Ⓓ Ⓔ	11. Ⓐ Ⓑ Ⓒ Ⓓ Ⓔ	11. Ⓐ Ⓑ Ⓒ Ⓓ Ⓔ
12. Ⓐ Ⓑ Ⓒ Ⓓ Ⓔ	12. Ⓐ Ⓑ Ⓒ Ⓓ Ⓔ	12. Ⓐ Ⓑ Ⓒ Ⓓ Ⓔ	12. Ⓐ Ⓑ Ⓒ Ⓓ Ⓔ
13. Ⓐ Ⓑ Ⓒ Ⓓ Ⓔ	13. Ⓐ Ⓑ Ⓒ Ⓓ Ⓔ	13. Ⓐ Ⓑ Ⓒ Ⓓ Ⓔ	13. Ⓐ Ⓑ Ⓒ Ⓓ Ⓔ
14. Ⓐ Ⓑ Ⓒ Ⓓ Ⓔ	14. Ⓐ Ⓑ Ⓒ Ⓓ Ⓔ	14. Ⓐ Ⓑ Ⓒ Ⓓ Ⓔ	14. Ⓐ Ⓑ Ⓒ Ⓓ Ⓔ
15. Ⓐ Ⓑ Ⓒ Ⓓ Ⓔ	15. Ⓐ Ⓑ Ⓒ Ⓓ Ⓔ	15. Ⓐ Ⓑ Ⓒ Ⓓ Ⓔ	15. Ⓐ Ⓑ Ⓒ Ⓓ Ⓔ
16. Ⓐ Ⓑ Ⓒ Ⓓ Ⓔ	16. Ⓐ Ⓑ Ⓒ Ⓓ Ⓔ	16. Ⓐ Ⓑ Ⓒ Ⓓ Ⓔ	16. Ⓐ Ⓑ Ⓒ Ⓓ Ⓔ
17. Ⓐ Ⓑ Ⓒ Ⓓ Ⓔ	17. Ⓐ Ⓑ Ⓒ Ⓓ Ⓔ	17. Ⓐ Ⓑ Ⓒ Ⓓ Ⓔ	17. Ⓐ Ⓑ Ⓒ Ⓓ Ⓔ
18. Ⓐ Ⓑ Ⓒ Ⓓ Ⓔ	18. Ⓐ Ⓑ Ⓒ Ⓓ Ⓔ	18. Ⓐ Ⓑ Ⓒ Ⓓ Ⓔ	18. Ⓐ Ⓑ Ⓒ Ⓓ Ⓔ
19. Ⓐ Ⓑ Ⓒ Ⓓ Ⓔ	19. Ⓐ Ⓑ Ⓒ Ⓓ Ⓔ	19. Ⓐ Ⓑ Ⓒ Ⓓ Ⓔ	19. Ⓐ Ⓑ Ⓒ Ⓓ Ⓔ
20. Ⓐ Ⓑ Ⓒ Ⓓ Ⓔ	20. Ⓐ Ⓑ Ⓒ Ⓓ Ⓔ	20. Ⓐ Ⓑ Ⓒ Ⓓ Ⓔ	20. Ⓐ Ⓑ Ⓒ Ⓓ Ⓔ
21. Ⓐ Ⓑ Ⓒ Ⓓ Ⓔ	21. Ⓐ Ⓑ Ⓒ Ⓓ Ⓔ	21. Ⓐ Ⓑ Ⓒ Ⓓ Ⓔ	21. Ⓐ Ⓑ Ⓒ Ⓓ Ⓔ
22. Ⓐ Ⓑ Ⓒ Ⓓ Ⓔ	22. Ⓐ Ⓑ Ⓒ Ⓓ Ⓔ	22. Ⓐ Ⓑ Ⓒ Ⓓ Ⓔ	22. Ⓐ Ⓑ Ⓒ Ⓓ Ⓔ
23. Ⓐ Ⓑ Ⓒ Ⓓ Ⓔ	23. Ⓐ Ⓑ Ⓒ Ⓓ Ⓔ	23. Ⓐ Ⓑ Ⓒ Ⓓ Ⓔ	23. Ⓐ Ⓑ Ⓒ Ⓓ Ⓔ
24. Ⓐ Ⓑ Ⓒ Ⓓ Ⓔ	24. Ⓐ Ⓑ Ⓒ Ⓓ Ⓔ	24. Ⓐ Ⓑ Ⓒ Ⓓ Ⓔ	24. Ⓐ Ⓑ Ⓒ Ⓓ Ⓔ
25. Ⓐ Ⓑ Ⓒ Ⓓ Ⓔ	25. Ⓐ Ⓑ Ⓒ Ⓓ Ⓔ	25. Ⓐ Ⓑ Ⓒ Ⓓ Ⓔ	25. Ⓐ Ⓑ Ⓒ Ⓓ Ⓔ
26. Ⓐ Ⓑ Ⓒ Ⓓ Ⓔ	26. Ⓐ Ⓑ Ⓒ Ⓓ Ⓔ	26. Ⓐ Ⓑ Ⓒ Ⓓ Ⓔ	26. Ⓐ Ⓑ Ⓒ Ⓓ Ⓔ
27. Ⓐ Ⓑ Ⓒ Ⓓ Ⓔ	27. Ⓐ Ⓑ Ⓒ Ⓓ Ⓔ	27. Ⓐ Ⓑ Ⓒ Ⓓ Ⓔ	27. Ⓐ Ⓑ Ⓒ Ⓓ Ⓔ
28. Ⓐ Ⓑ Ⓒ Ⓓ Ⓔ	28. Ⓐ Ⓑ Ⓒ Ⓓ Ⓔ	28. Ⓐ Ⓑ Ⓒ Ⓓ Ⓔ	28. Ⓐ Ⓑ Ⓒ Ⓓ Ⓔ
29. Ⓐ Ⓑ Ⓒ Ⓓ Ⓔ	29. Ⓐ Ⓑ Ⓒ Ⓓ Ⓔ	29. Ⓐ Ⓑ Ⓒ Ⓓ Ⓔ	29. Ⓐ Ⓑ Ⓒ Ⓓ Ⓔ
30. Ⓐ Ⓑ Ⓒ Ⓓ Ⓔ	30. Ⓐ Ⓑ Ⓒ Ⓓ Ⓔ	30. Ⓐ Ⓑ Ⓒ Ⓓ Ⓔ	30. Ⓐ Ⓑ Ⓒ Ⓓ Ⓔ

SECTION I

Time—35 minutes
25 Questions

Directions: Each group of questions in this section is based on a set of conditions. In answering some of the questions, it may be useful to draw a rough diagram. Choose the response that most accurately and completely answers each question and blacken the corresponding space on your answer sheet.

Questions 1–5

From among eight candidates, an epidemiological think tank must choose four medical scientists for a special research project. Four of the candidates—Bosch, Cristof, Eber, and Gross—are published scientists, and four—Hoff, Jackson, Klipp, and Mann—are unpublished scientists. Bosch, Hoff, Klipp, and Mann are microbiologists whereas Cristof, Eber, Gross, and Jackson are immunologists. The scientists must be selected according to the following conditions:

Exactly two published scientists and two unpublished scientists are selected.
Exactly two microbiologists and two immunologists are selected.
Either Klipp or Gross or both are selected.

1. Which one of the following is an acceptable selection of the scientists for the research project?

   (A) Cristof, Gross, Hoff, and Mann
   (B) Eber, Gross, Jackson, and Mann
   (C) Bosch, Cristof, Jackson, and Mann
   (D) Bosch, Gross, Hoff, and Klipp
   (E) Bosch, Hoff, Jackson, and Klipp

2. If Bosch and Klipp are selected for the research project, the other two scientists selected must be

   (A) two immunologists, both of whom are published scientists
   (B) two immunologists, both of whom are unpublished scientists
   (C) an immunologist who is a published scientist and an immunologist who is an unpublished scientist
   (D) an immunologist who is a published scientist and a microbiologist who is an unpublished scientist
   (E) an immunologist and a microbiologist, both of whom are published scientists

3. If Bosch and Cristof are selected for the research project, which one of the following must also be selected?

   (A) Hoff
   (B) Eber
   (C) Gross
   (D) Mann
   (E) Jackson

4. If Hoff and Mann are selected for the research project, which one of the following could be, but need not be, selected for the research project?

   (A) Klipp
   (B) Bosch
   (C) Jackson
   (D) Cristof
   (E) Gross

5. If Jackson is selected for the research project, which one of the following must also be selected?

   (A) Gross
   (B) Bosch
   (C) Mann
   (D) Cristof
   (E) Hoff

GO ON TO THE NEXT PAGE

Questions 6–12

A tour operator has chosen six stops along the route of the tour—J, K, L, M, N, and P—each with at least one of the following features: scenic views, a historic landmark, and restroom facilities. No stop has any other features. The following conditions must apply:

> K has scenic views and restroom facilities.
> L has scenic views and a historic landmark.
> L and N have no features in common.
> M has more features than L.
> K and P have exactly one feature in common.
> J has fewer features than P.

6. For exactly how many of the stops is it possible to determine exactly which features each one has?

   (A) six
   (B) five
   (C) four
   (D) three
   (E) two

7. Which one of the following must be false?

   (A) Exactly four of the six stops have restroom facilities.
   (B) Exactly four of the six stops have scenic views.
   (C) Exactly four of the six stops have historic landmarks.
   (D) Exactly five of the six stops have restroom facilities.
   (E) Exactly five of the six stops have historic landmarks.

8. If all the stops that have historic landmarks also have scenic views, which one of the following must be false?

   (A) P has scenic views.
   (B) P has restroom facilities.
   (C) K has scenic views.
   (D) J has scenic views.
   (E) J has restroom facilities.

9. If P has no features in common with J but has at least one feature in common with every other stop, then which of the following must be false?

   (A) Exactly four of six stops have scenic views.
   (B) Exactly four of six stops have restroom facilities.
   (C) Exactly four of six stops have historic landmarks.
   (D) J has scenic views.
   (E) P has restroom facilities.

10. Suppose that no two stops have exactly the same features as one another. In that case, each of the following could be true EXCEPT:

    (A) Exactly four of the six stops have restroom facilities.
    (B) Exactly three of the six stops have restroom facilities.
    (C) Exactly four of the six stops have historic landmarks.
    (D) Exactly three of the six stops have scenic views.
    (E) Exactly four of the six stops have scenic views.

11. If exactly four of the six stops have historic landmarks, and exactly four of the six locations have scenic views, then each of the following must be true EXCEPT:

    (A) N and P have no features in common.
    (B) J and K have no features in common.
    (C) J and N have no features in common.
    (D) J and P have exactly one feature in common.
    (E) L and P have exactly one feature in common.

12. Suppose that the condition requiring that M has more features than L is replaced by a new condition requiring that M and L have exactly two features in common. If all of the other original conditions remain in effect, which one of the following must be false?

    (A) J and M have no features in common.
    (B) M and P have exactly two features in common.
    (C) M and P have no features in common.
    (D) K and M have exactly one feature in common.
    (E) K and M have exactly two features in common.

GO ON TO THE NEXT PAGE

Questions 13–18

Exactly seven different buses are arriving at Bellevert Station from Delbert, Evans, Fortman, Hampton, Janistown, Koenig, and Lynnville. The following conditions govern their arrivals:

> The buses arrive one at a time.
> Either the Lynnville or the Koenig arrives fourth.
> The Fortman arrives at some time after the Koenig but at some time before the Lynnville.
> Both the Hampton and the Janistown arrive at some time after the Evans.
> The Hampton does not arrive next after the Janistown; nor does the Janistown arrive next after the Hampton.

13. Which one of the following could be the order in which the buses arrive, from first to last?

    (A) Delbert, Evans, Koenig, Fortman, Janistown, Lynnville, Hampton
    (B) Hampton, Evans, Delbert, Koenig, Fortman, Lynnville, Janistown
    (C) Evans, Hampton, Janistown, Koenig, Fortman, Lynnville, Delbert
    (D) Evans, Hampton, Delbert, Koenig, Fortman, Lynnville, Janistown
    (E) Evans, Koenig, Delbert, Lynnville, Hampton, Fortman, Janistown

14. If the Koenig arrives at some time before the Evans, then exactly how many different orders are there in which the seven buses could arrive?

    (A) four
    (B) five
    (C) six
    (D) seven
    (E) eight

15. Which one of the following must be true?

    (A) The first bus to arrive is from Evans.
    (B) The Koenig arrives at some time before the Lynnville.
    (C) The Delbert arrives at some time before the Fortman.
    (D) The Janistown arrives at some time before the Lynnville.
    (E) The Evans arrives at some time before the Koenig.

16. Which one of the following could be true?

    (A) The Delbert is the next bus after the Koenig.
    (B) The Delbert is the next bus after the Fortman.
    (C) The Fortman is the next bus after the Delbert.
    (D) The Evans is the next bus after the Hampton.
    (E) The Evans is the next bus after the Fortman.

17. If exactly one of the buses arrives after the Koenig but before the Lynnville, then which one of the following could be true?

    (A) The first bus to arrive is the Evans.
    (B) The second bus to arrive is the Fortman.
    (C) The third bus to arrive is the Evans.
    (D) The sixth bus to arrive is the Fortman.
    (E) The sixth bus to arrive is the Hampton.

18. If the Delbert arrives at some time before the Evans, then the Koenig must arrive

    (A) sixth
    (B) fifth
    (C) fourth
    (D) third
    (E) second

GO ON TO THE NEXT PAGE

Questions 19–25

A scientist must create two test groups—group 1 and group 2—from six of seven lab rats—three brown rats named Abby, Carl, and Dennis; and four white rats named Elle, Fern, Horn, and Iris. Each group will have three rats. No rat can be in more than one group. Each group must have a least one brown rat and one white rat. The composition of the groups must conform to the following conditions:

 Neither group includes both Abby and Iris.
 Neither group includes both Elle and Horn.
 If a group includes Dennis, it includes neither Horn nor Iris.
 If group 1 includes Carl, group 2 includes Horn.

19. Which of the following could be the makeup of the two groups?

   (A) Group 1: Abby, Fern, Horn
       Group 2: Carl, Elle, Iris
   (B) Group 1: Carl, Dennis, Iris
       Group 2: Abby, Elle, Fern
   (C) Group 1: Carl, Dennis, Elle
       Group 2: Fern, Horn, Iris
   (D) Group 1: Abby, Elle, Iris
       Group 2: Carl, Fern, Horn
   (E) Group 1: Abby, Dennis, Fern
       Group 2: Carl, Elle, Horn

20. If Carl is in group 1, which one of the following pairs must be in group 2 together?

   (A) Fern and Iris
   (B) Abby and Horn
   (C) Horn and Iris
   (D) Elle and Fern
   (E) Dennis and Fern

21. If Elle is in group 1, which one of the following pair of rats could be in group 1 together with Elle?

   (A) Fern and Iris
   (B) Carl and Fern
   (C) Carl and Horn
   (D) Abby and Carl
   (E) Carl and Iris

22. If Abby is in the same group as Dennis, which one of the following could be true?

   (A) Both Elle and Fern are in group 2.
   (B) Horn is in group 1.
   (C) Carl is in group 1.
   (D) Both Elle and Fern are in group 1.
   (E) Iris is in group 2.

23. Each of the following pairs of rats could be in group 2 together EXCEPT:

   (A) Carl and Horn
   (B) Abby and Horn
   (C) Abby and Carl
   (D) Abby and Dennis
   (E) Carl and Dennis

24. Which one of the following could be true?

   (A) Carl is in group 1 and Elle is in group 2.
   (B) Abby is not in any group and Carl is in group 1.
   (C) Abby is in group 1 and Elle is in group 2.
   (D) Abby is in group 2 and Dennis is in group 2.
   (E) Abby is in group 2 and Carl is not in any group.

25. If Dennis is in group 2, which one of the following must also be in group 2?

   (A) Horn
   (B) Fern
   (C) Iris
   (D) Carl
   (E) Abby

STOP

IF YOU FINISH BEFORE TIME RUNS OUT, CHECK YOUR WORK ON THIS SECTION ONLY. DO NOT GO ON TO ANY OTHER TEST SECTION.

SECTION II

Time—35 minutes
25 Questions

Directions: The questions in this section are based on the reasoning contained in brief statements or passages. For some questions, more than one of the choices could conceivably answer the question. However, you are to choose the *best* answer; that is, the response that most accurately and completely answers the question. You should not make assumptions that are by commonsense standards implausible, superfluous, or incompatible with the passage. After you have chosen the best answer, blacken the corresponding space on your answer sheet.

1. David: The only way for a professional athlete to be successful after having suffered a serious injury is to relearn how he originally played the game before the injury. It is futile for an athlete to learn a whole new way to play the game.

    Kathy: Wrong. Sam Daughton was a professional quarterback who suffered a serious leg injury and had to go through significant physical therapy and training. When he returned to the game he had left his older, more physical style of play behind and embraced a more successful style of finesse.

    Kathy uses which one of the following argumentative techniques in countering David's argument?

    (A) She establishes a solution by excluding the only plausible alternative to that solution.
    (B) She offers a developed and relevant analogy that supports his claim.
    (C) She undermines his claim by showing that it rests on an equivocation.
    (D) She presents an example that counters his claim.
    (E) She offers a different explanation for a phenomenon.

Questions 2–3

Digital camera manufacturers typically advertise their products by citing the resolutions of their cameras, usually measured in pixels and indicating the degree of detail at which the camera's sensor is capable of recording the image in memory. Differences between cameras in this respect are irrelevant, however, since all modern sensors record far more detail into memory than can be represented on electronic screens or printed on photographic paper.

2. Which one of the following most accurately states the main point of the argument?

    (A) Advertised differences among cameras in the resolution of their sensors have no practical bearing on the cameras' relative quality as photographic tools.
    (B) Digital camera manufacturers should concentrate on incorporating other desirable qualities into their cameras, rather than concentrating only on the sensors' resolution.
    (C) By concentrating their advertising on the issue of resolution, manufacturers are making a mistake about the interests of potential purchasers of cameras.
    (D) Differences among electronic screens and photographic paper have a more significant effect on the quality of the image than do differences in the resolution of digital camera sensors.
    (E) Apart from differences in resolution, there is no practical difference among modern digital cameras in the quality of images they produce.

GO ON TO THE NEXT PAGE

3. The argument depends on assuming which one of the following?

(A) In determining the amount of detail reproduced in the photographic image, differences in the resolutions of available cameras neither compound nor decrease the deficiencies of available electronic screens and photographic paper.

(B) Flawless photographic technique is necessary to achieve the maximum image resolution possible with the equipment and materials being used.

(C) Software used to represent and print images produced by digital cameras do not have any significant effect on the image quality.

(D) The only factors important in determining the degree of detail reproduced in the final photographic image are the resolution of the camera's sensor and the resolution of the electronic screen.

(E) The definition of the term "resolution" does not represent a significant determinant of the quality of photographic instruments and their results.

4. Richard: Literary tools such as "prefaces" and "prologues," unlike the novel itself, serve no purpose.

    Jeri: I agree; and since such literary tools are meaningless they should be eliminated from literature.

    Jeri's remarks indicated that she interpreted Richard's statement to imply that

(A) literary tools that are not useful are meaningless

(B) only literary tools that serve a purpose have meaning

(C) literary tools that serve a purpose are meaningful

(D) all literary tools that serve a purpose are useful

(E) if a literary tool does not serve a purpose, it should be eliminated from literature

5. A group of 1,000 homeowners was randomly selected from three cities in the Midwest and asked the question "Do you plan to pay off your mortgage in full through regular payments or the sale of your home?" More than 92 percent answered, "Yes." This shows that the overwhelming majority of homeowners want to pay off their mortgage, and that if the national mortgage default rate among homeowners is high, it cannot be due to a lack of desire on the part of homeowners.

The reasoning of the argument above is questionable because the argument

(A) attempts to make two conflicting conclusions using the results of one survey

(B) fails to justify its assumption that 92 percent is an overwhelming majority

(C) contradicts itself by admitting that there may be a high default rate among homeowners while claiming that most homeowners want to pay off their mortgages

(D) treats homeowners from three cities in the Midwest as if they are representative of homeowners nationwide

(E) overlooks the possibility that there may in fact not be a high default rate among homeowners

GO ON TO THE NEXT PAGE

Questions 6–7

Professor Allyn: The literature department's undergraduate courses should cover only true literary works, and not such questionable material as political speeches.

Professor Raleigh: Political speeches might or might not be true literary works, but they have a powerful and sometimes dangerous effect on society—largely because people cannot discern the actions implied by the words. The literature department's courses give students the critical skills to analyze and understand texts. Therefore, it is the literature department's responsibility to include the study of political speeches in its undergraduate courses.

6. Which one of the following principles most strongly supports Professor Raleigh's argument?

   (A) All undergraduate students should take at least one course that helps them develop critical skills.
   (B) Political speeches should be discussed in a way that makes the implied actions clear.
   (C) The literature department's courses should enable students to analyze and understand all kinds of texts that can have a powerful and sometimes dangerous effect on society.
   (D) Any professor teaching an undergraduate course in the literature department should be free to choose whatever materials are necessary to teach that course.
   (E) All texts that are subtly constructed and capable of influencing people's thoughts and actions should be considered a form of literature.

7. Which one of the following is an assumption on which Professor Raleigh's argument depends?

   (A) The literature department's academic responsibility is not limited to teaching students how to analyze true literary works.
   (B) Political speeches given at legitimate political rallies are not dangerous to society.
   (C) The literature department does not teach students in their courses any other skills besides those needed to analyze and understand texts.
   (D) Texts that are true literary works never are detrimental to society.
   (E) Courses offered by the literature department cannot include both true literary works and material such as political speeches.

8. If a teacher gives a child only a few options for how he or she can spend time in class, the child is more likely to adhere to the teacher's instructions than if the teacher gives the child many options.

Which one of the following most accurately expresses the principle illustrated above?

   (A) Children dislike calculating the best of a variety of options unless they can see a clear difference among the benefits that would result from each option.
   (B) The tendency children have to alter their behavior varies inversely with the number of alternative activities made available to them by an adult.
   (C) Children are likely to ignore instructions from their teachers if they are confused about those instructions.
   (D) To get good results, the clarity with which a teacher can instruct the children is of equal importance to the quality of the proscription for not following the teacher's instructions.
   (E) Most children are unlikely to follow their teacher's instructions unless they can vividly imagine the consequences of not following the teacher's instructions.

GO ON TO THE NEXT PAGE

9. A fungus caused by spores called late blight can destroy whole crops of tomatoes and can reach epidemic levels in areas where tomatoes are grown. The spores that cause the fungus can be controlled with a synthetic fungicide, but the fungicide can pose health hazards to people living nearby. The fungicides are thus unsuitable for small farms, garden stores, and backyard gardens near populated areas. Fortunately, commercial tomato fields are in isolated locations where fungicides can be used safely. Therefore, most of the nation's tomato crops are not seriously threatened by late blight.

Which one of the following is an assumption on which the argument depends?

(A) The fungus caused by late blight spores is the only disease that threatens tomatoes nationwide.

(B) It will eventually be possible to breed tomatoes that are resistant to late blight spores.

(C) The fungus caused by late blight spores spreads more slowly on commercial tomato fields than in small tomato farms, garden stores, and backyard gardens.

(D) Most of the tomato plants that have not been exposed to the late blight spores grow in small tomato farms, garden stores, and backyard gardens.

(E) Commercial fields produce most or all of the nation's tomatoes.

10. Lawyer: Our next objection will probably be overruled, because normally about half of all objections that the judge considers are overruled, and our last five objections have all been sustained.

The lawyer's reasoning is flawed because it presumes, without giving warrant, that

(A) the judge is required to overrule at least half of all objections raised

(B) the likelihood that an objection will be overruled is influenced by the potential influence it may have over the expected verdict

(C) the last five objections having been sustained guarantees that the next five objections will be overruled

(D) having the last five objections sustained affects the likelihood that the next objection will be sustained

(E) the majority of the last five objections deserved to be sustained

11. Economist: The automobile industry seems to be on the way to recovery from an earlier slump. Recent figures show that the auto companies are purchasing more equipment and spending more on R&D than ever before, indicating that they expect sales to increase in the near future.

That the auto companies are purchasing more equipment and spending more on R&D than ever before figures in the economist's argument in which one of the following ways?

(A) It is an inference drawn from the premise that the auto companies expect sales to increase in the near future.

(B) It is an inference drawn from the premise that the automotive industry is recovering.

(C) It is the primary evidence from which the argument's conclusion is drawn.

(D) Its truth is required in order for the argument's conclusion to be true.

(E) It is the phenomenon that the argument seeks to explain.

GO ON TO THE NEXT PAGE

Questions 12–13

City mayor: An independent group has released a new study that shows that more than 63 percent of our students graduate from high school. That is an increase of 15 percent from what the graduation rate was when I entered office. This proves that my education policies are a success and that we should continue implementing them.

Critic: While I applaud your success at increasing the graduation rate I must point out that of those who graduated only 29 percent tested as being prepared for college and well-paying careers. That is less than half and that proves that your policies are a complete failure.

12.   The critic counters the mayor's argument by

(A)   questioning the mayor's motives for reaching a certain conclusion
(B)   asserting that measuring progress toward educational goals is difficult and therefore the statistics lack credibility
(C)   attempting to show that the mayor's description of the facts is misleading
(D)   discrediting the mayor's methods while applauding the goal
(E)   disputing the accuracy of the figures cited by the mayor

13.   Which one of the following could the mayor properly cite as indicating a flaw in the critic's reasoning concerning the education study?

(A)   The high school students that tested as being unprepared for college and well-paying careers are isolated to a particular region of the city.
(B)   The high school students that tested as being prepared for college and well-paying careers did not, in fact, continue on to enter college or begin well-paying careers.
(C)   The increase in graduation rate was due to the annexation of a school district with a high graduation rate among its high schools.
(D)   The test for preparedness is a new test and does not have any previous results with which to compare the current results.
(E)   Other cities in the same state have a lower rate of preparedness for college and well-paying jobs.

14.   The retail price of bleached flour is considerably higher than that of unbleached flour. However, the process by which flour is bleached is fairly simple and not very costly. Therefore, the price difference cannot be accounted for by the greater cost of providing bleached flour to the consumer.

The argument relies on assuming which one of the following?

(A)   Grocery stores do not expect that consumers are willing to pay more for bleached flour than for unbleached flour.
(B)   There is little competition among companies that process bleached four.
(C)   Price differences can generally be accounted for by such factors as supply and demand for the products, not by differences in production costs.
(D)   The only factor relevant to the cost of providing bleached flour to the consumer is the cost of the bleaching process.
(E)   Processing unbleached flour costs more than processing bleached flour.

GO ON TO THE NEXT PAGE

Question 15–16

A newspaper article on lawsuits in the United States argued that they are on the decline as a method of resolving disputes. The article's evidence was the decreasing number of court verdicts in civil cases, as if the only method of resolving civil cases is through a lengthy and expensive court hearing. Surely, in a modern legal system, the fact that a case reached a court verdict is a sign that the legal system failed to resolve the dispute by other means. The parties to a lawsuit have ways other than through the courts to resolve their differences, such as settlement through arbitration and mediation.

15. The argument criticizing the newspaper article is directed toward establishing which one of the following as its main conclusion?

    (A) There is no reason to believe, on the basis of what the newspaper article said, that lawsuits as a method of resolving disputes are on the decline.
    (B) Without the possibility of lengthy and expensive court hearings, professionals involved in arbitration and mediation would not be thriving.
    (C) Because court hearings are lengthy and costly, other methods of resolving disputes such as arbitration and mediation are necessary.
    (D) Lawsuits are unsuccessful if the only way of resolving the dispute is through a court hearing.
    (E) Although lawsuits are a popular and effective method for citizens to gain remuneration for being wronged, that does not preclude them from using other methods to resolve their disputes.

16. The argument criticizing the newspaper article employs which one of the following strategies?

    (A) arguing that the article's conclusion is motivated by a desire to promote the reduction in number of lawsuits
    (B) detailing historical changes that make the article's analysis outdated
    (C) pointing to the common interests between the lawyers and judges who manage court hearings, which the article ignores
    (D) reinterpreting evidence that the article uses as indicating the negation of what the newspaper concludes
    (E) questioning the accuracy of the statistical evidence that the article uses

17. President of company X: Did the manager hire the best engineer to design the new product?

    Vice president: Yes.

    President: And the best production team?

    Vice president: Yes.

    President: In fact everyone he assigned to designing and manufacturing the product was the very best he could find?

    Vice president: That's correct.

    President: So, your report deliberately misrepresented the manager's performance when you claimed he never really wanted the new product to succeed.

    Each of the following accurately describes a flaw in the president's reasoning displayed above EXCEPT:

    (A) It takes for granted that the product could fail only if the manager wanted it to fail.
    (B) It ignores the possibility that the vice president failed to make the correct inferences from the facts known and therefore his report's negative assessment was unintentional.
    (C) It takes for granted that the manager was not forced to assign the people he did to design and manufacture the product.
    (D) It ignores the possibility that the manager failed to allot enough time or resources to the production team.
    (E) It ignores the possibility that the manager knew that the people assigned to the product would not work well together.

GO ON TO THE NEXT PAGE

18. My brother likes spinach, but not cabbage, which he says is too bitter. So it is not true that whoever likes cabbage likes spinach.

The flawed reasoning in the argument above most closely resembles that in which one of the following?

(A) Sophia enjoys managing computer networks, but not computer programming, which she says is tedious. So it is not true that whoever enjoys managing computer networks enjoys computer programming.

(B) Although a man is more than seven feet tall, he is not considered a giant. Thus, it is not the case that all giants are more than seven feet tall.

(C) All minimalist music compositions were written after the year 1960. This music composition is minimalist, so it must be true that it was written after the year 1960.

(D) People who repair their own plumbing are do-it-yourself fanatics. My next-door neighbors are do-it-yourself fanatics, so it follows that they repair their own plumbing.

(E) This photographic print is not in color, but it is expensive. So it is not true that some color photographic prints are expensive.

19. Expert witness: We have tested the explosive used in the bank robbery 10 times under controlled circumstances. Each time we detonated 5 square inches of the explosive substance coated with a dye to measure the distance of the explosion. In all 10 cases, the dye covered an area much less than 20.7 square feet. In fact, the dye-covered area was always between 9.2 and 12.5 square feet. I conclude that 5 square inches of the explosive substance destroys an area much less than 20.7 square feet.

Which one of the following, if true, most undermines the value of the expert's evidence as basis for the conclusion?

(A) Another explosive substance was substituted, and in otherwise identical circumstances, the dye covered between 21.1 and 23.1 square feet.

(B) Not all expert witnesses are the authorities in their fields that they claim to be.

(C) Expert witnesses are notoriously unreliable because they tend to adjust their evidence to support the prosecution's case.

(D) On the eleventh detonation of the explosive substance the area covered was also less than 20.7 square feet—this time covering 20.1 feet.

(E) If similar results had been found after 100 test detonations of the explosive substance, the evidence would be stronger.

GO ON TO THE NEXT PAGE

20. Historian: The spread of access to the Internet allows more people to learn about injustices and, in the right circumstances, leads to an increased capacity to distinguish true reformers from mere opportunists. However, widespread access to the Internet invariably comes faster than the development of a generally enlightened education system. In the interim, the populace is vulnerable to clever charlatans calling for change. Consequently, some relatively reasonable regimes may be toppled by their own progressive policies to bring new technologies to the masses.

Which one of the following is an assumption on which the historian's argument depends?

(A) A lack of enlightened education affects the ability to differentiate between legitimate and illegitimate calls for reform.

(B) Any reasonable regime that fails to provide a generally enlightened education system will be toppled by a clever charlatan.

(C) A charlatan can never enlist the public support necessary to topple an existing regime unless a generally enlightened education system is in place.

(D) Without access to the Internet there can be no general awareness of injustice in a society.

(E) Any generally enlightened education system will tend to preserve the authority of reasonable regimes.

21. Many sleep aid drugs increase appetite. While dieting can help counterbalance the increased weight gained from taking such sleep aids, some weight gain is unlikely to be preventable.

The information above most strongly supports which one of the following?

(A) At least some patients taking sleep aid drugs gain weight as a result of taking them.

(B) All patients taking sleep aid drugs should diet to maintain their weight.

(C) The weight gain experienced by patients taking sleep aid drugs should be attributed to lack of dieting.

(D) A physician should not prescribe any sleep aid drugs for a patient if that patient is overweight.

(E) People who are trying to lose weight should not ask their doctors for sleep aid drugs.

22. Economist: The vast majority of nations that have a low corporate tax rate tend to run high budget deficits, but some nations with a high corporate tax rate also run a high budget deficit. What all nations that run high budget deficits have in common, however, is that they are saddled with large entitlement programs.

If all of the economist's statements are true, which one of the following must also be true?

(A) Some nations with large entitlement programs do not have a high budget deficit.

(B) The majority of nations with large entitlement programs have a low corporate tax rate.

(C) Some nations with large entitlement programs have a high corporate tax rate.

(D) Every nation with large entitlement programs has a low corporate tax rate.

(E) Fewer high corporate tax rate nations than low corporate tax rate nations have large entitlement programs.

23. Attacks on your opponent's character should be avoided before a football game. Such attacks have nothing to do with the opponent's competitiveness; instead they attempt to question the opponent's moral right to compete in the game at all.

Which one of the following principles, if valid, most helps to justify the reasoning above?

(A) Attacking the character of one's opponent does nothing to preserve one's moral right to play in further football games.

(B) Questions of character should be raised before a football game if they are relevant to the opponent's ability to compete on the field.

(C) Attacks on the opponent's character should not impress the spectators at the game.

(D) Attacks on an opponent's character result from an inability to compete effectively with the opponent on the field.

(E) Behaviors that have nothing to do with the aspects of playing the game on the field should be avoided.

GO ON TO THE NEXT PAGE

24. Reporter: A recent report presented evidence that cooking meat at the high temperatures used in grilling creates heterocyclic amines (HCAs) and polycyclic aromatic hydrocarbons (PAHs), compounds linked with some cancers. This report, however, has had a negligible effect on consumer behavior. Our station conducted an extensive survey about this report, and few consumers said that they planned to reduce their consumption of grilled meats because of the report. Yet sales of grills declined sharply in the months after the report was issued.

Which of the following best explains the apparent contradiction described above?

(A) The report caused people who had previously purchased a grill to stop utilizing it.

(B) Sales of meat also declined during the months after the report was issued.

(C) Sales of nonessential household appliances declined overall during the same time period.

(D) People are not concerned about their health when it comes to making decisions about how to prepare food.

(E) Consumers surveyed reported their intended future behavior truthfully.

25. French film director Claude Morrel was accused by Russian film director Slovan Stipich of plagiarizing a movie he made that had been released 15 years before Morrel's. The two movies are set in different periods and regions, but they contain enough plot similarities to make the resemblance unlikely to be coincidental. Morrel's defense rests on his argument that plagiarism was impossible because Stipich's movie was made in Russian, a language Morrel does not understand, and because the movie was never subtitled or reviewed in any other language.

The argument in Morrel's defense depends on the assumption that

(A) there is a common myth between both cultures to which both directors referred to subconsciously in the movies in question

(B) Morrel is familiar with an old Cyrillic language that is extinct but related to the modern Russian language

(C) Morrel has never met Stipich

(D) Stipich's movie did not become popular in Russian

(E) nobody related the plot of Stipich's movie in detail to Morrel before Morrel produced his movie

STOP

IF YOU FINISH BEFORE TIME RUNS OUT, CHECK YOUR WORK ON THIS SECTION ONLY. DO NOT GO ON TO ANY OTHER TEST SECTION.

SECTION III

Time—35 minutes
24 Questions

Directions: Each passage in this section is followed by a group of questions to be answered on the basis of what is stated or implied in the passage. For some of the questions, more than one of the choices could conceivably answer the question. However, you are to choose the *best* answer; that is, the response that most accurately and completely answers the question, and blacken the corresponding space on your answer sheet.

PASSAGE A

Even as the world trends toward globalization there still exists tensions within some nations between the movement toward Western-style social struc- tures and older, long-repressed traditional cultures.
(5) No better example of this tension exists than that between the governments trying to establish Western-style legal systems that will bring them in line with the larger modern world and their indigenous communities striving to maintain tradi-
(10) tional customs and legal structures. Many of these governments attempt to maintain a difficult "legal pluralism" that requires judges and government officials to balance the "rule of law" with the more politically sensitive aspects of cultural identity. This
(15) balance is most difficult for nations just emerging from the grip of colonial rule, since they have a stronger desire for acceptance beyond their borders, but they also feel internal pressures to respect the restoration of traditional law and institutions long
(20) repressed by their previous rulers.

Examples of this judicial tension are especially easy to find in Africa. Many modern African states that have recently achieved independence set up governments with Western-style branches and
(25) balances of power, but they wrote into their consti- tutions an acknowledgement of traditional law and institutions. Despite such fundamental consider- ations they still face the practical difficulties of managing the contradictions between the contem-
(30) porary legal system established under a constitution and the traditional laws that operate in the districts and townships. Under this system of legal pluralism, conflicts inevitably arise as these competing legal systems coexist in the same geographical area and
(35) attempt to resolve civil and criminal cases under systems that may produce starkly different results.

PASSAGE B

After Zimbabwe achieved independence from Great Britain in 1980, the new government stripped its tribal chiefs of all legal powers. A new legal system was implemented, one based upon Western ideals,
(5) but after 14 years of ineffective and frequently

corrupt administration, partial legal authority was restored to the tribes. The government placed tribal chiefs on the payroll of the national government, but despite this reform, conflicts arose between
(10) traditional leaders and the modern national govern- ment. One rather public dispute occurred when the president appointed a female chief to an Ndebele tribe.

Under national law, discrimination based on
(15) gender is illegal in Zimbabwe yet the larger Ndebele community objected to a woman being appointed to such a position. The tribal leaders eventually acqui- esced but not before a great deal of public discord. Another conflict developed over the nation's
(20) attempt to reform its water management system. In practice, informal systems and traditional institu- tions maintained control over water use, frustrating the government's attempts to implement a more modern natural resource management system.
(25) As the government of Zimbabwe strove to manage a legally pluralistic society, an argument against this sort of plurality took hold among some human rights organizations. These organizations argued that Western interests had exacted a new
(30) kind of imperialism by imposing Western legal systems on tribal societies. Ironically, this claim has gained most traction among the nations that have felt pressure from international organizations to enact human rights reforms. Some of these
(35) governments have used their indigenous culture and institutions as a defense of unsavory behavior toward their own peoples.

GO ON TO THE NEXT PAGE

1. Which of the following issues is central to both passages A and B?

    (A) As globalization takes hold of nations across the world they are leaving behind their local and traditional legal systems to build more Western-style institutions.
    (B) As globalization takes hold of nations across the world many newly independent nations are designing constitutions to better integrate with both the world at large and their own people's interests.
    (C) Some nations, as they transition to Western-style legal systems, have found that these systems occasionally conflict with traditional customs and legal structures.
    (D) As nations transition to more Western-style legal systems the adjudication of legal cases has been taken over by the rule of law from traditional, more informal institutions.
    (E) Nations, as they transition to more Western-style legal systems, have suffered a new type of imperialism that is more harmful than what they suffered over the last 100 years.

2. What is the main purpose of the second paragraph of passage A?

    (A) exhibit how legal pluralistic arrangements have been highly successful in one particular area of the world
    (B) describe the forms of legal pluralism that have existed through the years
    (C) argue that legal pluralism is an unworkable solution for governments trying to transition to modernity
    (D) describe the manner in which an abstract problem described elsewhere has actually arisen
    (E) explain how legal pluralism has only led to disastrous results throughout history and into modernity

3. According to information in passage A, which of the following would best describe the attitude of newly independent governments towards traditional leaders?

    (A) respectful tolerance
    (B) disdainful accommodation
    (C) angry resentment
    (D) suspicious unease
    (E) uncertain anxiousness

4. The author of passage B uses the example of Zimbabwe's attempts to reform its water management system in order to

    (A) describe the extent to which Zimbabwe has gone to bring its country into the family of modern nations
    (B) contrast the local traditional method of dealing with administrative issues with that of the national government
    (C) illustrate the range of difficulties experienced by Zimbabwe in its legally pluralistic society
    (D) exemplify the conflict between foreign interests and the traditional institutions on a particular health-related issue
    (E) introduce a circumstance when the government failed to work with the local tribal chiefs to modernize the nation's infrastructure

5. Which of the following best describes the relationship between passage A and passage B?

    (A) Passage A presents an alternative perspective on legal pluralism that passage B rejects.
    (B) Passage A offers a resolution to the conflict inherent to legal pluralism and passage B questions the validity of that solution.
    (C) Passage A discusses the origins of legal pluralism and passage B suggests that a global human rights conflict is attributable to the practice of legal pluralism
    (D) Passage A discusses a tension inherent to legal pluralism and passage B presents a specific example that illustrates that tension.
    (E) Passage A discusses the issue of globalization and human rights and passage B places this issue in its proper context.

GO ON TO THE NEXT PAGE

Published in 1936, the novel *Absalom, Absalom!* has come to be regarded as William Faulkner's quintessential exploration of a decaying southern paternalism in the early twentieth century. Many
(5) critics focus their attention on the story of Thomas Sutpen, which is seemingly at the center of the novel. While the fascinating story of Sutpen's rise and fall appears central to the novel, some modern critics believe the reader could ignore the details
(10) of the story altogether and see it as just a vehicle by which Faulkner challenges the reader's understanding of the novel as a construct in and of itself. He does this by structuring the novel around questions such as who is telling Sutpen's story, how he
(15) is telling it, and why he is concerned with the story in the first place. In this sense, these critics believe *Absalom, Absalom!* is one of Faulkner's greatest contributions to modernism, a novel that by its very telling plants a seed of doubt concerning its effec-
(20) tiveness as a storytelling medium.

The nature of *Absalom, Absalom!* may have to do with Faulkner's own circumstances at the time. He wrote much of the novel during his time as a frustrated screenwriter in Hollywood dealing with
(25) the realities and unrealities surrounding him. In the novel, Quentin Compson, Faulkner's frequent proxy, interviews several people who knew Sutpen, including his own grandfather. Then, he collaborates with his roommate at Harvard on developing
(30) Sutpen's story. Central to their collaboration is solving several mysteries, including the murder of Charles Bon by Sutpen's son and Sutpen's own murder at the hands of Wash Jones. Faulkner's two collaborators pursue the truth in a not too dissimilar
(35) manner as that of two detectives. Faulkner had a great appreciation for Raymond Chandler and other detective novelists, and he would later write the screenplay for the adaptation of Chandler's *The Big Sleep*. Faulkner gives Compson and his roommate's
(40) collaboration the quality of two detectives sorting through clues, of which they have very few, to figure out what happened. In this case, it's a "why-done-it" mystery rather than a "who-done-it," since they already know who committed the crimes.
(45) Seen from this perspective, the details of Sutpen's story are less central to the novel since there is so little hard evidence for Faulkner's "detectives" to work from. Quentin and his roommate weave their own versions of the story from secondhand
(50) accounts and vague scraps of evidence. Of course, the two do not always agree. Both are biased by their very different life experiences, Quentin by his struggle with his own southern heritage and his roommate, a Northerner, by his outsider's view
(55) of the South. If a critic looks at it from this point of view the novel is less about story than about the storytellers themselves.

The modernist view of the novel may solve the mystery of the last chapter, when the roommate asks
(60) Quentin why he hates the South and Quentin denies

that he does so, repeatedly, an interchange that to many critics seems completely unrelated to the rest of the novel. The interchange may be the strongest support for the modern critic's approach. Quentin's
(65) repeated denials reveal a deep ambivalence toward his own heritage that calls into question all that came before, thus revealing that the nature and intent of the novel may itself be up for question.

6. Which of the following best states the conclusion of the argument made by the author?

(A) The idea that Faulkner's novel is an allegory of the breakdown of the social fabric of Southern society in the early twentieth century is a misinterpretation.

(B) Faulkner's novel is a reinterpretation of the Southern gothic novel and a new representation of its complexities.

(C) While Faulkner's novel explores aspects of Southern social structures, it also explores the limitations of the novel, as a storytelling device.

(D) There can be no definitive interpretation of Faulkner's novel because the very nature of the novel is one that questions whether interpretation is even possible.

(E) Faulkner's authorship of the novel is in question because of his collaboration with fellow Hollywood screenwriters.

GO ON TO THE NEXT PAGE

7. The passage suggests that the author would be most likely to agree with which one of the following statements about the contemporary critics of Faulkner's *Absalom, Absalom!*?

    (A) The critics fail to take into account the central story of Henry Sutpen and his rise to power, which aligns with Faulkner's main concern, the breakdown of southern culture.

    (B) The critics' theories may not take into account the influences on Faulkner's style, but the novel's structure and its conclusion give some credence to them.

    (C) The critics have become too focused on structuralist concepts that have led them on a tangent when it comes to addressing the dominant themes of Faulkner's novel.

    (D) The critics allowed the influence of Hollywood and detective novels on Faulkner's writing to color this perspective and depart from accepted critical notions.

    (E) The critics have done an excellent job of overthrowing all previously accepted theories concerning the novel and narrative theory.

8. The primary purpose of the second paragraph is to

    (A) give evidence that casts some doubt on a critical theory

    (B) offer biographical information that supports a critical theory

    (C) describe the circumstances under which critics came to their conclusion

    (D) detail the historical background that surrounded the creation of the novel

    (E) clarify the underlying foundations of a particular critical theory

9. The passage implies which one of the following with regard to Faulkner's character Quentin Compson in the novel?

    (A) He was not in fact from the South even though he identifies himself as a Southerner.

    (B) His character was inspired by Hollywood scriptwriters whom Faulkner encountered.

    (C) He hates his Southern heritage and his account of Sutpen's history indicates as much.

    (D) He appears in other novels and serves to express Faulkner's own perspective.

    (E) His character was derived through reading detective novels by Raymond Chandler.

10. The modern critics of Faulkner discussed in the passage would be most likely to agree with which of the following statements?

    (A) Faulkner intended the Sutpen murder mysteries to represent the decay of the southern paternal system.

    (B) It is the reader who must supply the evidence that is sorely lacking in the novel so that the mysteries at the heart of the Sutpen story can be solved.

    (C) All novels are a collaboration between the novelist and the reader and only together can they unlock the mysteries put forward by the text.

    (D) Despite Faulkner's efforts to the contrary there are specifics revealed within the story that give incontrovertible proof of what really occurred during Sutpen's life.

    (E) The novel is an inherently misleading medium, given that the author's voice is by its nature untrustworthy, demanding that the reader figure out which, if any, information in the novel is accurate.

11. According to the passage Faulkner's writing of the novel was heavily influenced by all of the following EXCEPT:

    (A) scriptwriting
    (B) noir detective novels
    (C) Southern culture
    (D) gothic story structure
    (E) the author's own struggles with a southern heritage

12. The author of the passage primarily presents which type of evidence in making his or her argument?

    (A) historical background that may have affected the content of a novel

    (B) an exploration of a critical theory as to why an author structured a novel as he did

    (C) description of several conflicting literary critical approaches

    (D) an explanation of why an author included a mysterious chapter at the end of a novel

    (E) a discussion of the influences that resulted in an author's unique approach to writing a novel

GO ON TO THE NEXT PAGE

The success of two measures to reform legislative reapportionment in November's election may presage a shift to less partisan influence on the drawing of electoral maps. In November, a coali-
(5) tion of California election-reform groups, civil rights nonprofits, and former officials succeeded in putting Proposition 20 on the ballot, and 61 percent of voters approved the measure. The proposition directed the state to take control of legislative reap-
(10) portionment or redistricting for congressional seats from the state legislature and turn it over to the Citizens Redistricting Commission. In Florida, voters approved restrictions on the redistricting process, requiring that districts meet strict demo-
(15) graphic and geographic requirements.

Since the early years of the nation, political parties have actively participated in redistricting, or the more technical term, "border delimitation." In 1964, the Supreme Court ruled in the landmark case
(20) *Wesberry v. Sanders* that all congressional districts must contain an equal number of persons. This decision established the "one person, one vote" requirement. Despite the Supreme Court's efforts, political parties continued to influence the process
(25) mainly through control of the state legislatures and governorships. The California and Florida measures intend to reduce partisan influence, specifically to stop the practice of gerrymandering. Gerrymandering strategies involve one of two
(30) tactics. One is to put all voters of a particular type into a single district and limit their influence on other districts. Another is to divide these voters among several districts to dilute their influence.

With California in particular, the coalition
(35) behind Proposition 20 argued that under the old system representatives are sent to Washington with a rather narrow mandate because their district is gerry-mandered to secure incumbency. Thus, entrenched politicians faced little incentive to make compro-
(40) mises on public policy. The resulting polarization makes it difficult for Congress to achieve progress on some very important issues. The opposition to Proposition 20 argued that the measure would create a whole new bureaucracy that would cost the
(45) taxpayers millions. The law offered no guidelines for how the commission would create fair and competi-tive districts. Also, it created a very complicated system for choosing the members of the commission. Lastly, Proposition 20 was undemocratic because it
(50) took the process out of the voters' hands and voters had to accept the commission's map even if they did not like it. Nevertheless, the voters approved both measures with a convincing majority. Even more convincing was that in California a competing
(55) measure, Proposition 27, which was to eliminate the Citizens Redistricting Commission altogether, failed on the ballot. This would have kept all redistricting, both state and congressional, in the hands of the political parties.

(60) In both California and Florida, the intent was to take politics out of the redistricting process. Now that the voters in these states have approved these measures, reform-minded groups in other states will be watching to see how successful they are at
(65) keeping the political parties from influencing the legislative apportionment process.

13. The primary purpose of the passage is to provide an answer to which one of the following questions?

(A) How has the Supreme Court failed to protect the "one person, one vote" precedent and how have voters taken action to correct its failure?

(B) What mistakes are states making by trying to solve a national problem on a state level and how will their solutions hinder democracy and create unfairness in congressional elections?

(C) What are California and Florida's unique electoral redistricting problems and what efforts have voters taken to solve them?

(D) What legislation have voters in two states approved as solutions to a perceived political problem and what major opposing arguments might be used in future such efforts as exemplified by a particular case?

(E) How have reform-minded citizens misinterpreted the legislative apportionment problem and enacted costly and unwise solutions?

GO ON TO THE NEXT PAGE

14. Which of the following would have been true prior to the 1964 Supreme Court ruling?

    (A) Political parties had no say or control in legislative apportionment.
    (B) Some citizens' votes counted for less than a full vote.
    (C) A district could be designed to contain more constituents than another.
    (D) Gerrymandering was allowed for some states and not others.
    (E) The Supreme Court could overrule any redistricting based on the "one person, one vote" requirement.

15. The discussion of the Supreme Court *Wesberry v. Sanders* case in lines 18–26 is intended primarily to

    (A) show that the Supreme Court failed to solve the "one person, one vote" problem that has plagued the electoral system since the early beginnings of the nation
    (B) explain the legal underpinnings of the proposed solutions to the legislative apportionment issue
    (C) explain that while one branch of the nation's government was trying to solve the problem another branch was undermining that effort
    (D) give a historical perspective to a problem with democratic representation that has yet to be resolved through legislative reapportionment
    (E) establish that the Supreme Court is in fact the original cause of gerrymandering and other interference by political parties in the electoral mapping process

16. The discussion of Proposition 27 in lines 53–59 implies that which of the following was true before the passage of Proposition 20?

    (A) The Citizens Redistricting Commission, though a good idea, was an impracticable institution and needed to be eliminated for redistricting to work properly.
    (B) The politicians wanted to create confusion by having both propositions on the same ballot, hoping that voters would favor Proposition 27 over Proposition 20.
    (C) The Citizens Redistricting Commission existed before the election to redistrict the state legislative map but lacked the authority on the congressional map.
    (D) Voters rejected Proposition 27 because it conflicted with Proposition 20 but would have approved it if a compromise had been struck.
    (E) The Citizens Redistricting Commission was unconstitutional and if the voters did not eliminate it the courts would have to do it.

17. Which of the following, if true, would most undermine the arguments for California's Proposition 20 discussed in the third paragraph?

    (A) It is proven that a significant majority of voters reelect their representatives because they are happy with their performance.
    (B) Several bills were passed recently because both Republican and Democratic congressmen were able to come together and achieve compromises on the legislation.
    (C) The proposition would deny the commission the right to use income, race, or gender as factors in determining the shape and size of the district.
    (D) It is discovered that one of the members under consideration for the commission is actually a member of a political party.
    (E) Population movements among districts are so fluid from year to year that it is almost impossible to predict voting patterns for a particular district in any election.

18. Which of the following accurately expresses the meaning of the word "entrenched" as it is used in line 38 of the passage?

    (A) Unelectable
    (B) Deep-seated
    (C) Unshakeable
    (D) Stubborn
    (E) Inexorable

Louis D. Brandeis and Samuel Warren wrote their article *The Right to Privacy* in 1890. The article greatly influenced the American judicial system, and the citizenry's understanding of its basic rights has (5) never been the same. While this article's influence rose to the level of a landmark in legal history, the origins were not quite so high-minded. Evidently, Warren enlisted Brandeis to write the article mainly because he was peeved about the amount of gossip (10) in the New England papers concerning the lives of higher society, a segment which included Warren himself.

Of course, the article took a more serious form and was heavily influenced by the times in which (15) these two scholars lived. They wrote their article when the rise of yellow journalism and the advent of the portable camera were changing the nation's sense of what is private and what is public. Brandeis and Warren seemed mainly concerned with the (20) spread of individuals' "portraiture" beyond their control, but the article also focused on copyright common law with regard to the artist or writer and his or her creative product. At the time, the country was at the very beginning of the Museum Period in (25) America, when museums had begun to sprout up around the nation and art was becoming a form of public entertainment rather than a private one. So, Brandeis and Warren oriented their discussion around aspects of a person's personal expression and (30) how it was used or exposed by others. This is why they devoted so much of *The Right to Privacy* not to the right to property, as many scholars framed the issue, but right to maintain one's "personality."

Among other legal scholars the portraiture issue (35) took the form of the physical portrait itself as a source of exposure and profit, but Brandeis and Warren oriented the right to privacy around an "inviolate personality" that can be published or exposed to public scrutiny. This is a more ambig- (40) uous concept and one that forces one to define the concept of personality and draw a line between the private and public aspects of personality. It was unclear how the press or other intrusive groups could violate a person's personality, but Warren (45) and Brandeis did make it clear that to violate it was to cause "mental pain and distress," much like a physical assault causes the body such injury. According to Brandeis and Warren, privacy gave the individual the right to prevent public portraiture or, (50) as it has become known today, the right to prevent appropriation of one's name or likeness. The central element is a privacy that encompasses personal writings and other productions, but the protection goes beyond the form of the exposure and ventures into (55) protecting the exposure in and of itself, whatever the nature of the publication.

An extension of their approach is that protection extends beyond publication and protects the works before they are published, since they are an (60) extension of a person's personality. They go as far as to argue that the right to privacy extends to the "thoughts, sentiments, and emotions" as they might be expressed to others. This is by far the greatest venture beyond the property view of the protection, (65) and it advanced their intent to orient the right to privacy around protecting personality.

19. Brandeis and Warren argued that individuals have the right to prevent public portraiture. Which of the following situations is most analogous to a violation of that right?

(A) A photographer waits outside a clothing store and takes photographs of a celebrity's children as they emerge from the store.
(B) A hacker releases several embarrassing texts between a company CEO and his biggest competitor.
(C) A song from a new album is leaked on the Internet prior to the album's release, thus depriving the artist of potential income.
(D) A magazine uses a photo posted on an individual's social media site for an advertisement without obtaining the individual's permission.
(E) A graphic artist holds a gallery show exhibiting her "selfies," photos of the artist taken by the artist with a handheld camera.

20. It can most reasonably be inferred from the passage that Brandeis and Warren's approach to the right to privacy was

(A) based on their observations of serious deficiencies in the current law
(B) intended to protect their own property interests, specifically some portraits each of them owned
(C) revenge upon those who had slandered their acquaintances
(D) intended to neutralize actions directed at Warren and his acquaintances as objects of public gossip
(E) intended to protect some very talented and creative people among their relatives

GO ON TO THE NEXT PAGE

21. The passage suggests that the other scholars referred to in the passage would be most likely to believe which one of the following statements?

    (A) If person B steals a short story written by person A and publishes it word for word in a local pamphlet, A's privacy has been infringed upon.
    (B) If person B steals person A's photograph from A's home and publishes the photograph, A's privacy has not been infringed upon.
    (C) If person A writes a story that has not yet been published and person B reads it and later publishes his or her own version of the story, A's privacy has been infringed upon.
    (D) If person A tells person B a personal anecdote and person B publishes that anecdote in the local newspaper, person A's privacy has been infringed upon.
    (E) If person A gives a photograph to person B and person B, in turn, publishes that photograph in a local newspaper, person A's privacy has been infringed upon.

22. According to the passage, Brandeis and Warren's approach to personality was

    (A) an evolution of earlier ideas
    (B) a tweak to existing law that had larger ramifications
    (C) a discounted side step from their central argument
    (D) a revolutionary expansion of the existing law
    (E) a redefinition, which was poorly understood by existing scholars, of an existing concept

23. The function of the second paragraph is to

    (A) clarify elements within the essay that led to their conclusions
    (B) explicate the structure of the essay
    (C) explore the underlying cultural phenomena that influenced the writers
    (D) give the reasons that they wrote the essay
    (E) portray the writers and their personal reasons for writing the essay

24. The attitude of the author can best be described as

    (A) amused at the origins of a historic legal argument
    (B) skeptical of the validity of an archaic legal argument
    (C) curious about the modern applications of a significant legal doctrine
    (D) puzzled about two different conceptions of the right to privacy
    (E) persuasive about the importance of a landmark legal essay

STOP

IF YOU FINISH BEFORE TIME RUNS OUT, CHECK YOUR WORK ON THIS SECTION ONLY. DO NOT GO ON TO ANY OTHER TEST SECTION.

SECTION IV

Time—35 minutes
27 Questions

Directions: The questions in this section are based on the reasoning contained in brief statements or passages. For some questions, more than one of the choices could conceivably answer the question. However, you are to choose the *best* answer; that is, the response that most accurately and completely answers the question. You should not make assumptions that are by commonsense standards implausible, superfluous, or incompatible with the passage. After you have chosen the best answer, blacken the corresponding space on your answer sheet.

1. Arbus: It has been argued that adding a 3-D effect to a movie degrades the integrity of the original 2-D version, and that nobody should be required to wear special glasses to experience a work of art. But nobody argues that we should not transform a theatrical movie into a home video that people can view at home because it erodes the value of the theatrical version, nor do they argue that people should not be required to use a video player to watch it. The home video version is a technologically different production that stands on it own. Judgments of it do not reflect on the original theatrical version. Similarly, a 3-D version of a movie is a distinct version from the original and should be judged on its own merit. It does not degrade the integrity of the original 2-D version.

   Arbus's argument uses which one of the following techniques of argumentation?

   (A) It appeals to an inference from a general principle and a set of facts.
   (B) It draws on popular opinion on the matter at issue.
   (C) It proffers an example counter to a general principle.
   (D) It invokes an analogy between similar cases.
   (E) It distinguishes facts from value judgments.

2. During the meeting of the G-20 summit of major economic countries the member nations authorized a rescue package to aid one of its members in handling a debt crisis that threatened its economic future. Afterward, the parliament of one of the G-20 members passed a resolution condemning its own prime minister for promising to contribute funds to the rescue package. A parliamentary leader insisted that the overwhelming vote for the resolution did not imply the parliament's opposition to the financial intervention; on the contrary, most members of parliament supported the G-20 action.

   Which one of the following, if true, most helps to resolve the apparent discrepancy presented above?

   (A) In the parliamentary leader's nation, it is the constitutional prerogative of the parliament, not of the prime minister, to initiate financial aid to foreign entities.
   (B) Members of the parliament traditionally are more closely attuned to public sentiment, especially with regard to the use of public money, than are prime ministers.
   (C) The public would not support the financial rescue unless it was known that the parliament approved of the action.
   (D) The G-20 nations cannot legally commit funds of a member nation to a financial intervention.
   (E) The treasury would be responsible for providing the funding vouchers necessary to move the money across borders for such rescue packages.

GO ON TO THE NEXT PAGE

3. The game Complicus requires a great deal of manual dexterity. Laurie is a highly capable auto mechanic. Therefore, Laurie would make an excellent Complicus player.

    The flawed pattern of reasoning in the argument above is most similar to that in which one of the following?

    (A) Any good cyclist can learn to in-line skate eventually. Katherine is a champion cyclist. Therefore, Katherine could learn to in-line skate in a day or two.
    (B) The role of Ebenezer Scrooge in community productions is often played by an experienced actor. Irving has played Ebenezer Scrooge in the community production for several years. Therefore, Irving must be an experienced actor.
    (C) People who work with their hands for a living invariably enjoy do-it-yourself projects. Larry has been a successful construction manager for many years. Therefore, Larry enjoys do-it-yourself projects.
    (D) People with long arms make good volleyball players. Everyone in Jackie's family has long arms. Therefore, Jackie would make a good volleyball player.
    (E) All horseracing jockeys have excellent balance. Ricardo is a champion cyclist. Therefore, Ricardo would make a good horseracing jockey.

4. Psychologist: Doctors should stop refusing to prescribe drugs to help people with depression. Most cases of depression that psychiatrists treat are known to be caused by chemical imbalances. This suggests that people suffering from depression do not need months or even years of therapy, but rather need the right drugs to alter their biochemistry and alleviate what is causing their depression.

    Each of the following describes a flaw in the psychologist's reasoning EXCEPT:

    (A) It neglects the possibility that for some people the available drugs are completely ineffective at treating their types of chemical imbalances.
    (B) It presumes, without providing any evidence, that depression contributes to a chemical imbalance.
    (C) It fails to consider the possibility that for some people therapy is the only treatment known to be effective for cases of depression not caused by a chemical imbalance.
    (D) It presumes, without providing justification, that the cases of chemical imbalance psychiatrists treat are representative of all cases of chemical imbalance.
    (E) It overlooks the possibility that therapy could help depressed people cope with their chemical imbalance.

GO ON TO THE NEXT PAGE

5. An antidote for whooping cough has been developed, but researchers warn that its widespread use could be dangerous, despite the fact that this drug has no serious side effects and is currently very effective at limiting the duration and severity of whooping cough.

Which one of the following, if true, helps most to reconcile the apparent discrepancy indicated above?

(A) The drug can be fatal when misused, such as taking larger-than-prescribed doses.
(B) The drug does not prevent the spread of whooping cough from one person to another, even when the drug eventually cures the disease in the first person.
(C) The drug must be administered several times a day, so patient compliance is likely to be low.
(D) Use of the drug contributes to the development of deadlier strains of whooping cough that are resistant to the drug.
(E) The drug is very expensive and making it widely available would be infeasible.

6. Juan: It is wrong to think that the same managerial style should be used with all employees. For many employees their work experience has been more team oriented than others and they would therefore function better on group, rather than solo, projects. An employee's accustomed style of work environment should always dictate how they are managed.

Dorothy: No, not always. Flexibility in the workplace, being able to work either on one's own or on a team, is invaluable to a company and its ability to function in the marketplace.

The conversation lends the most support to the claim that Juan and Dorothy disagree on which one of the following?

(A) It is sometimes desirable to tailor managerial styles to the way the employee functions best.
(B) The main purpose of management is to train employees to be flexible within the work environment of the company.
(C) All employees should learn to adapt to various managerial styles.
(D) Many employees would work better on a team rather than solo projects.
(E) All employees work better when assigned solo projects.

7. Human resources manager: Information privacy, or data privacy, is the relationship between collection and dissemination of data, technology, the public expectation of privacy, and the legal and political issues surrounding them. Privacy concerns exist wherever personally identifiable information or otherwise sensitive information is collected, stored, and used. An organization is responsible for personal information under its control.

Which of the following would be a violation of the principle of personal privacy described above?

(A) A person leaves a personal letter on the table in the company break room, and it is read by another employee.
(B) A commercial claims that a certain athlete uses a product, but that athlete did not agree to endorse the product.
(C) A dental clinic disposes of old files of former patients by putting boxes filled with the files in the dumpster.
(D) A person uses binoculars to observe people walking on the street below his apartment.
(E) Video surveillance of a celebrity attacking his girlfriend in a hotel elevator is shown on the national news.

8. Media consultant: Electronic media are bound to bring an end to the traditional news organizations in our society. This is because the emergence of the traditional news organization, characterized by a group of journalists managed by an erstwhile news editor, was facilitated by the low cost and ease of publishing and distributing a newspaper. Currently, however, newspapers are being overtaken by electronic media. So, it is inevitable that the traditional news organization will not survive in our society.

The reasoning in the consultant's argument is flawed because it

(A) relies inappropriately on an expert's opinion
(B) confuses the value of an institution with the method by which it operates
(C) presupposes as a premise what it is trying to prove
(D) presupposes that just because something might happen it will happen
(E) mistakes something that enables an institution to arise for something necessary for the survival of the institution

GO ON TO THE NEXT PAGE

Questions 9–10

David: The effort of advanced nations to create new biofuels has increased demand for the world's crops and diverted them from being used as food. As a result, prices for food have risen, increasing world hunger and political instability across numerous developing world nations. Advanced nations should scale back their efforts to produce more environmentally friendly fuels.

Lucie: There are many other factors that could be responsible for driving up the prices of food. Last year severe weather destroyed crops of wheat in Russia and China. Also, a mealy bug infestation decreased Thailand's output of cassava.

9. Which one of the following most accurately describes Lucie's criticism of David's explanation?

    (A) It points out that David's explanation is based on two hypotheses that contradict each other.
    (B) It cites an analogous case in which David's explanation clearly cannot hold.
    (C) It offers an alternative explanation that is equally supported by the evidence that David cites.
    (D) It refers to sources of additional data that cannot easily be reconciled with the facts David cites.
    (E) It cites facts that suggest David's argument overlooks alternative explanations.

10. Which one of the following, if true, could be used by David to counter Lucie's rejection of his argument?

    (A) Russia, China, and Thailand are not the only countries supplying crops for use in developing biofuels.
    (B) Wheat and cassava are minor crops in the development of biofuels.
    (C) The amount of crops affected by severe weather and pest infestation has remained unchanged for the last five years.
    (D) Infestations by the mealy bug can be easily managed by introducing farmers to new pesticide technologies.
    (E) Political instability is directly attributable to food riots over price increases.

11. A safety report indicates that, on average, automobile accidents decline by about 9 percent in those areas in which the city has reduced the number of traffic signs posted. In a certain city, the city reduced its number of traffic signs by 50 percent and over a three-year period the number of automobile accidents remained the same.

Which one of the following, if true, does NOT help resolve the apparent discrepancy between the safety report and the city's public safety records?

    (A) In the last three years, most of the automobile accidents occurred due to a lack of attention to traffic signs.
    (B) Bureaucratic errors left many of the more accident-prone areas of the city still with the same number of traffic signs as before the reduction.
    (C) The city now includes accidents involving pedestrians in its yearly total of automobile accidents, whereas three years ago it did not.
    (D) Three years ago speed limits in the city were increased by as much as 10 kph (6 mph).
    (E) In the time since the city reduced its number of traffic signs the city has experienced a higher than average increase in automobile traffic.

GO ON TO THE NEXT PAGE

12. Fred achieved the highest revenues in the fourth-quarter sales challenge by beating Gigi, the winner of each of the three previous quarters. We can conclude from this that Fred took sales training during the last year.

The conclusion follows logically if which one of the following is assumed?

(A) If Gigi took sales training, she would win the sales challenge.
(B) Gigi did not take as much sales training as Fred did.
(C) Gigi is usually a better salesperson than Fred.
(D) If Fred took sales training, he would win the sales challenge.
(E) Fred could beat a three-time winner only if he took sales training.

13. Historian: Anyone who thinks that the extreme military tactics of the ancient empire of T were the product of a warmongering political class is overlooking the basic truth: the political class was made up primarily of intellectuals with a vision of a more civilized world. Empire T conquered and slaughtered many tribes in pursuit of its goals; but it later became clear that the new world, as the empire defined it, was unachievable. So at least some of the ordinary people of T were in fact murderers.

Which one of the following principles, if valid, provides the most support for the historian's argument?

(A) Aggressiveness in pursuit of what is eventually found to be unachievable constitutes warmongering.
(B) The pursuit of a civilized world justifies warmongering.
(C) The pursuit of a civilized world does not justify warmongering.
(D) Warmongering in pursuit of a civilized world constitutes inhumanity.
(E) Conquest in pursuit of what is later found to be an unachievable vision constitutes murder.

14. Art critic: The meaning of a work of art is ever shifting, not fixed, and therefore it may attract many equally valid interpretations. Interpretations essentially involve imposing meaning on a work of art, rather than discovering meaning in it, so interpretations need not consider the intentions of the artist. Thus, any interpretation of a work of art reveals more about the critic than about the artist.

Which one of the following is an assumption required by the art critic's argument?

(A) In order to truly understand a work of art one must know the artist's history.
(B) A critic of a particular work of art can never know the true intentions of the creator of that work of art.
(C) An artist's intentions are relevant to a valid interpretation of the artist's work.
(D) A meaning imposed on a work of art reflects facts about the interpreter.
(E) There are no criteria by which to distinguish the validity of different interpretations of works of art.

GO ON TO THE NEXT PAGE

15. The studies showing that the replacement of an older power plant with a modern one decreases the incidence of major illnesses do not distinguish between a conventional or nuclear power plant; their survey included at least some areas powered by a nuclear power plant. The studies may also be taken as showing, therefore, that there is no increased health risk associated with living next to a nuclear power plant.

The pattern of flawed reasoning in which one of the following is most similar to the pattern of flawed reasoning in the argument above?

(A) Research has shown that it takes more energy to produce a paper bag than a plastic bag, but after each is used and deposited as waste in a landfill a plastic bag lasts longer and takes up more space than a paper bag. There is, therefore, no more environmental harm from a plastic bag than from a paper bag.

(B) Research shows that there is no greater long-term health benefit connected to taking vitamin supplements than with a moderate increase in the intake of fruits and vegetables. Clearly, then, there is no long-term health risk connected to the failure to take vitamin supplements, so long as enough fruits and vegetables are consumed.

(C) Research has shown that young people who drive a car with an accompanying adult and receive one full year of intensive driving instruction are less likely to become involved in accidents than those who simply pass a driving test and start driving on their own. This shows that adults are inherently more responsible drivers than young people.

(D) Research shows that the incidence of cancer is decreased by eating fruits and vegetables. The fact that this benefit exists regardless of whether they are grown conventionally or organically shows that there is no increased cancer risk to eating fruits and vegetables containing pesticide residues.

(E) Research has shown that there is no long-term health risk connected to a diet consisting largely of foods high in saturated fat and cholesterol if such a diet is consumed by someone who is genetically predisposed to process such a diet. Therefore, the health of a person's parents is more important than diet.

Questions 16–17

Mr. Anderson: I am upset that my daughter's entire soccer team has been suspended for two games because some of her team members were taunting members of the opposing team. She was not taunting them, and it was clear to everyone who the culprits were.

League director: I'm sorry you are upset, Mr. Anderson, but your daughter's situation is like being stuck at the airport because of a delayed flight. People who aren't involved in causing the delay nevertheless have to suffer by waiting there.

16. If the league director is speaking sincerely, then it can be inferred from what the league director says that the league director believes that

(A) Mr. Anderson's daughter might not have taunted members of the opposing team

(B) a flight delay is generally caused by weather or inefficiencies in the air traffic control system

(C) Mr. Anderson's daughter knows who it was that taunted members of the opposing team

(D) being suspended from two games will deter future unsportsmanlike behavior

(E) many team members were taunting members of the opposing team

17. The league director's response to Mr. Anderson's complaint is most vulnerable to criticism on which one of the following grounds?

(A) It attempts to confuse the point at issue by introducing irrelevant facts about the incident.

(B) It makes a generalization about all the members of the team, which is not justified by the facts.

(C) It assumes that Mr. Anderson's daughter is guilty when there is evidence to the contrary that the director has disregarded.

(D) It suggests that taunting members of the opposing team produces as much inconvenience as does being caught at the airport due to a flight delay.

(E) It does not acknowledge the fact that waiting at the airport due to a flight delay is unavoidable while the mass punishment was avoidable.

GO ON TO THE NEXT PAGE

18. Larry: The federal government audited our books and assessed our company with a significant fine for a minor tax law infraction. Other companies in our industry were not audited even though we know for certain that they have committed the same infraction. This is unfair treatment by the federal government.

    Elizabeth: You were not treated unfairly, since the federal government cannot afford to audit every company that it thinks is breaking the law. Each company in your industry that broke the law had an equal chance of being audited.

    Which one of the following principles, if established, would most help to justify Elizabeth's position?

    (A) It is fairer not to enforce a tax law at all than to enforce it in some, but not all, of the cases to which it applies.

    (B) Fairness in the application of a tax law is ensured not by all violators' having an equal chance of being fined for their violation of the law, but rather by fining all known violators to the same extent.

    (C) The fines attached to tax laws should be imposed on all people who violate those laws, and only those people.

    (D) If all companies that broke a tax law in a given year are equally likely of being audited and fined for breaking it, then the law is fairly applied to whomever among them is then fined.

    (E) The fines attached to breaking the tax code should be assessed not as punishments for breaking the law but rather as deterrents for unethical bookkeeping.

19. Due to wider commercial availability of electronic books, sales of printed books have dropped significantly.

    Which one of the following conforms most closely to the principle illustrated above?

    (A) Because of the wide variety of high-quality home video recorders, sales of high-quality televisions have improved.

    (B) Because a new brand of chewing gum entered the market, consumers reduced their consumption of an established brand of chewing gum.

    (C) Because neither of the two most popular spreadsheet programs has all of the features consumers want, neither has been able to dominate the market.

    (D) Because a child was forbidden to watch television until the child completed homework, that child avoided dawdling and focused on homework.

    (E) Because of the rising cost of union labor, manufacturers began to make more extensive use of robots in the manufacturing process.

GO ON TO THE NEXT PAGE

Questions 20–21

George: It was wrong of Kristen to tell our boss that the reason the project will not succeed is that our company does not have the talent or resources to successfully execute all the steps necessary to make the project come to fruition. Saying such falsehoods can never be other than morally wrong and we do have the talent and the resources—Kristen just does not believe in the project and did not want to do the work.

20.   The main conclusion drawn in George's argument is that

(A)   it is always wrong not to tell the truth
(B)   the real reason Kristen did not support the project is that she does not believe in it and does not want to do the work
(C)   it was wrong of Kristen to tell her boss that the project would not succeed because she believes the organization cannot execute all the steps necessary to make the project a success
(D)   it is wrong to avoid expressing one's own opinion by blaming the failure on deficiencies within the organization
(E)   Kristen did not tell her boss the truth

21.   The justification George offers for his judgment of Kristen's behavior is most vulnerable to criticism on the grounds that the justification

(A)   relies on an illegitimate appeal to pity to obscure the fact that the conclusion does not logically follow from the premises advanced
(B)   attempts to justify a judgment about a particular case by citing a general principle that stands in far greater need of support than does the particular judgment
(C)   judges behavior that is outside an individual's control according to moral standards that can properly be applied only to behavior that is within such control
(D)   ignores an important moral distinction between saying something that is false and failing to say something that one knows is true
(E)   confuses having identified the cause of a given effect with having eliminated the possibility of there being any other causes of that effect

22.   Research indicates that members of the police force generally were raised in economically disadvantaged households. For it was discovered that, overall, police officers grew up in communities with average household incomes that were lower than the average household income for the nation as a whole.

The reasoning in the argument is flawed because the argument

(A)   does not take into account the fact that members of the police force generally have lower salaries than their counterparts in the private sector
(B)   fails to take into account the fact that many police officers live in high-density urban communities, which generally have low average household incomes
(C)   fails to note there are some communities with low average household incomes in which no members of the police force grew up
(D)   presumes without justification that members of the police force generally were raised in households with incomes that are average or below average for their communities
(E)   inappropriately assumes a correlation between household income and economic advantage

23.   Every school of psychology has a theory as to how we can achieve happiness. However, most people would judge someone who follows every prescription for happiness given by one of these theories to not be truly happy—not the life they would want for themselves or their children.

The statements above, if true, most strongly support which one of the following?

(A)   It is impossible to develop a psychological theory that accurately describes happiness.
(B)   A person who achieves what is necessary under one theory of happiness does not necessarily achieve happiness under another theory.
(C)   Happiness as defined by psychology is unachievable in practice.
(D)   Most people do not know what is truly necessary to achieve happiness.
(E)   Most people do not have a conception of happiness that matches that defined by any school of psychology.

GO ON TO THE NEXT PAGE

24. For years, invasive plant species like kudzu have smothered broad swaths of the local forests, taken over our wetlands, and clogged our waterways. Invasive plants have proven to be a potent threat to biodiversity. However, scientific studies show that invasive plant species are rarely the cause of native species' extinctions.

Which of the following, if true, most helps to resolve the apparent discrepancy in the information above?

(A) Invasive plants are not considered a threat to human health and therefore biodiversity has less importance.

(B) Kudzu's growth crowds out other invasive plants that could be harmful to biodiversity.

(C) While kudzu and other invasive plants can adversely affect biodiversity in a particular locality, they have less affect on a larger geographic scale, and most species range over such large geographic scales.

(D) The biodiversity of forests, wetlands, and waterways was decreasing even before being threatened by kudzu and other invasive plant species.

(E) Scientific studies attribute extinctions to industrial waste, pollution from automobiles, and other harmful human activities.

25. During an eight-month period, the total output of offshore oil rigs within the nation of Salveria remained constant. During this period monthly output of oil rigs owned by Cenpan Oil Company doubled, and its share of the oil market within Salveria increased correspondingly. At the end of this period, new safety standards were imposed on oil rigs owned by Salveria companies. During the four months following this imposition, Cenpan Oil Company's share of the Salveria market declined substantially even though its monthly output within Salveria remained constant at the level reached in the eighth month of the eight-month period.

If the statements above are true, which one of the following CANNOT be true?

(A) A decrease in the total monthly output of oil within Salveria will occur if the safety standards remain in effect.

(B) Over the four months before the imposition of the safety standards, the combined market share of companies other than Cenpan Oil Company with offshore oil rigs in Salveria decreased.

(C) Since the imposition of the safety standards, Cenpan Oil Company's average profit on each barrel of oil sold within Salveria has increased.

(D) If the safety standards had not been imposed, Cenpan Oil Company's share of the Salveria oil market would have decreased even more than, in fact, it did.

(E) The total monthly output within Salveria of oil from oil rigs owned by companies other than Cenpan Oil Company decreased over the four months following the imposition of safety standards.

GO ON TO THE NEXT PAGE

26. Regulatory regimens are created to institute fairness in the delivery of government services. Thus, despite growing dissatisfaction with complex regulatory systems, it is unlikely that regulations will be simplified.

The claim that regulatory regimens are created to institute fairness in the delivery of government services plays which one of the following roles in the argument?

(A) It is used to weaken the claim that regulations should be simplified.
(B) It is a conclusion for which the claim that regulations are unlikely to be simplified is offered as support.
(C) It is cited as evidence that regulatory systems are becoming more and more complex.
(D) It is a conclusion for which the only support offered is the claim that dissatisfaction with complex regulatory systems is growing.
(E) It is a premise offered in support of the claim that it is unlikely that regulations will be simplified.

27. Presidents cannot achieve greatness as long as they remain in the capital city. Their abilities to listen, analyze, and negotiate, which government functions hone, are useful to a leader, but an understanding of the citizen's everyday experiences and frustrations can be obtained only by the immersion in communities around the country that is precluded by being a government functionary.

Which one of the following is an assumption on which the argument depends?

(A) Presidents cannot achieve greatness without an intuitive grasp of a citizen's everyday experiences and frustrations.
(B) Participation in communities, interspersed with impartial observation of everyday experiences and frustrations, makes presidents great.
(C) No great president lacks the power to listen, analyze, and negotiate.
(D) Knowledge of the citizen's everyday experiences and frustrations cannot be acquired by merely listening, analyzing, and negotiating in life.
(E) Presidents require some impartiality to get an intuitive grasp of a citizen's everyday experiences and frustrations.

STOP

IF YOU FINISH BEFORE TIME RUNS OUT, CHECK YOUR WORK ON THIS
SECTION ONLY. DO NOT WORK ON ANY OTHER TEST SECTION.

LSAT Practice Test 2 Answer Key

Section I	Section II	Section III	Section IV
1. A	1. D	1. C	1. D
2. C	2. A	2. D	2. A
3. E	3. A	3. A	3. E
4. D	4. B	4. C	4. B
5. B	5. D	5. D	5. D
6. C	6. C	6. C	6. C
7. E	7. A	7. B	7. C
8. B	8. B	8. B	8. E
9. C	9. E	9. D	9. E
10. B	10. D	10. E	10. C
11. E	11. C	11. D	11. A
12. C	12. C	12. B	12. E
13. D	13. D	13. D	13. E
14. A	14. D	14. C	14. D
15. B	15. A	15. D	15. D
16. E	16. D	16. C	16. A
17. E	17. A	17. E	17. E
18. D	18. B	18. B	18. D
19. A	19. D	19. D	19. B
20. B	20. A	20. D	20. C
21. E	21. A	21. A	21. B
22. E	22. C	22. D	22. D
23. D	23. E	23. C	23. E
24. C	24. C	24. E	24. C
25. D	25. E		25. E
			26. E
			27. A

Calculate Your Score

Complete the following table.

Your Raw Score

SECTION	TYPE	NUMBER OF QUESTIONS	NUMBER CORRECT
1	Logic Games	25	_____
2	Arguments	25	_____
3	Reading Comprehension	24	_____
4	Arguments	27	_____
	Total Raw Score		_____

Your Approximate Scaled Score

It is impossible to say with complete precision what raw score will translate to what scaled score on future LSATs, but here is a rough estimation.

NUMBER OF QUESTIONS MISSED	APPROXIMATE SCALED SCORE
3	~180
8	~175
15	~170
20	~165
25	~160
25–35	between 155–160
35–45	between 150–155
45–55	between 145–150
55–60	between 140–145
60–70	between 135–140
70–80	between 125–135
More than 80	120–125

LSAT Practice Test 2 Answers and Explanations

SECTION I

Questions 1–5

As with all logic games, you follow the six-step process.

STEP 1: **Identify the game type.**

This is a grouping game. You know it is a grouping game because the description says you must "choose" four scientists for a project. It also says the scientists must be "selected" according to certain rules that limit the composition of the group. Furthermore, the game gives you two qualifications that exclude or include the candidate from the project: publication and specialization.

STEP 2: **Begin your diagram.**

You can create your diagram as a grid with four slots. You can abbreviate the scientists' names to their initials. There are two ways you can handle the placement of the variables: you can list them outside the grid and then place them into the grid as they are assigned, or you can put them into the grid and select those who qualify or eliminate those who do not qualify when handling each question. Because it simplifies things visually, let's put them in the grid as follows:

	PUBLISHED	UNPUBLISHED
Microbiologist	B	H K M
Immunologist	C E G	J

STEP 3: **Symbolize the clues.**

Clue 1: Exactly two published scientists and two unpublished scientists are selected.

You do not need to create symbolizations of this clue. You can simply put the number 2 below each column to show that the elements in each column must add up to 2.

Clue 2: Exactly two microbiologists and two immunologists are selected.

You do not need to create a symbolization of this clue either. As with the previous clue, you can put the number 2 to the right of each row to show that each row must add up to 2.

Clue 3: Either Klipp or Gross or both are selected.

Essentially, this clue is saying that there is no situation where neither K nor G is included in the group. If K is not in the group, then G must be in the group. If G is not in the group, then K must be in the group. Finally, both K and G can be in the group, but it cannot be the case that neither is in the group. You symbolize this clue as follows:

K / G / K & G

Logically, the above can be reduced to K/G. The logical disjunction "or" does not exclude that both can be in the group.

STEP 4: **Double-check your symbolizations.**

To double-check your symbolizations, you translate your symbolized clues back into normal English and see whether they match the original language of each clue. In this case you have only one clue that has been symbolized. Once you have verified that it works, you can add the symbolizations to your diagram. Your diagram should look as follows:

	PUBLISHED	UNPUBLISHED	
Microbiologist	B	H K M	2
Immunologist	C E G	J	2
	2	2	K / G

STEP 5: **Make deductions.**

1. Can't-be-first-or-last deductions

   No deductions of this type are possible in this game.

2. Repeated-element deductions

   No deductions of this type are possible in this game.

3. Down-to-two deductions

   No deductions of this type are possible in this game.

4. Block-splitting deductions

   No deductions of this type are possible in this game.

STEP 6: Answer the questions in the smartest order.
As you take the test, answer the questions in this order:

1. Answer the Complete and Accurate List question.

2. Answer questions that give you more information to work with.

3. Answer the remaining questions.

Question 1 is a Complete and Accurate List question and should be answered first. Questions that give you more information include the following:

Question 2 ("Bosch and Klipp are selected for the research project . . .")
Question 3 ("Bosch and Cristof are selected for the research project . . .")
Question 4 ("Hoff and Mann are selected for the research project . . .")
Question 5 ("N is selected for the research project . . .")

There are no remaining questions.

THE ANSWERS

1. Answer: A

The question asks you to identify the answer that gives an acceptable selection of scientists for the project. This means that all but one of the groupings is unacceptable. You can quickly eliminate answer C because it does not include K or G, which is inconsistent with clue 3. You can look at each of the remaining scenarios using your diagram to determine whether it is acceptable or not. Answer A includes G and it gives you two unpublished, two published, two microbiologist, and two immunologist scientists. This is an acceptable selection and must be your answer. Let's look at the remaining options for learning purposes. Answer B has three immunologists and only one microbiologist, so it is inconsistent with clue 2. Answer D has three microbiologists and only one immunologist, so it is inconsistent with clue 2 as well. Answer E has three microbiologists and only one immunologist, which is also inconsistent with clue 2. It also has three unpublished and only one published scientist, which is inconsistent with clue 1. **The correct choice is answer A.**

	PUBLISHED	UNPUBLISHED	
Microbiologist	B	[H] K [M]	2
(A) Immunologist	[C] E [G]	J	2
Microbiologist	B	H K [M]	2
(B) Immunologist	C [E] [G]	[J]	2
Microbiologist	[B]	[H] [K] M	2
(D) Immunologist	C E [G]	J	2
Microbiologist	[B]	[H] [K] M	2
(E) Immunologist	C E G	[J]	2
	2	2	K / G

2. Answer: C

The question tells you that both B and K are selected and then asks you to determine which answer gives you the two other scientists who must be selected with them. You use your diagram to determine the correct answer. Because B and K are both microbiologists, you determine that the other two must be immunologists in order to be consistent with clue 2. Also B is published while K is unpublished. Therefore, the other two must be split the same way, one published and one unpublished, so that the group is consistent with clue 1. The question already requires the selection of K, so you do not need to be concerned with abiding by clue 3. Restating your requirements, you need two immunologists, one who is published and one who is unpublished. This is exactly what answer C gives you, so **the correct choice is answer C.**

	PUBLISHED	UNPUBLISHED	
Microbiologist	B	[H] K [M]	2
Immunologist	C E G	J	2
	2	2	K / G

3. Answer: E

The question tells you that B and C are selected and asks you to choose from among the possible answers the one scientist who must be selected. Of the two remaining slots, G or K must be one of them, but you cannot select G because that would put three published scientists into the group, which is inconsistent with clue 1. Therefore, the third slot must be taken by K, but K is not one of your possible answers, so you must determine which scientist occupies the fourth slot. Looking at the diagram, you notice that you need an unpublished immunologist in order to satisfy both clues 1 and 2. The only scientist that satisfies that requirement is J. **The correct choice is answer E.**

	PUBLISHED	UNPUBLISHED	
Microbiologist	[B]	H [K] M	2
Immunologist	[C] E G	J	2
	2	2	K / G

4. Answer: **D**

The question tells you that H and M are selected for the group and asks you to select from among the possible answers the one scientist who could be, but need not be, selected. This means that all but one of the options either must be selected or cannot possibly be selected. The answer will be the one scientist whom you have the flexibility to include or not include. You use your diagram to evaluate the scenario. Clue 3 requires that you select either K or G for the group, but you cannot select K, because this would give you three microbiologists and three unpublished scientists, which is inconsistent with clues 1 and 2. Therefore, you can eliminate answer A as a possible answer. Because you cannot select K, you must select G for the group. Therefore, you can eliminate answer E as a possible answer. Answer B is impossible because selecting B would give you three microbiologists. Answer C is impossible because selecting J would give you three unpublished scientists. You are left with answer D. Selecting scientist C is consistent with the clues and gives you an acceptable group, but you do not necessarily have to select C. You could select E as well and it is this flexibility that leads you to select answer D. **The correct choice is answer D.**

	PUBLISHED	UNPUBLISHED	
Microbiologist	B	[H] [K] [M]	2
Immunologist	C E [G]	J	2
	2	2	K / G

5. Answer: **B**

The question tells you that J is selected for the group and asks you to determine which of the answers gives you the scientist that must be selected as well. You use your diagram to analyze the scenario. J is the only unpublished immunologist, which means that in order for there to be two unpublished scientists, you must select only one from the unpublished microbiologist group. Also, in order for the group to have two

immunologists, you must select only one from the published immunologist group. This leaves only one slot, and it must come from the published microbiologist group. Since B is the only published microbiologist, you must select B to the group. **The correct choice is answer B.**

	PUBLISHED	UNPUBLISHED	
Microbiologist	B	H K M	2
Immunologist	C E G	[J]	2
	2	2	K / G

Questions 6–12

As with all logic games, you follow the six-step process.

<u>STEP 1:</u> **Identify the game type.**

Though it is worded in a manner to suggest there is an ordering process (a tour usually follows along a particular path), this is a grouping game. The stops along the route are being assigned to "feature" groups—scenic views, historic landmarks, and restroom facilities. The tour operator has already chosen the six stops along the tour, so you are not scheduling the tour, but you are told that each stop has at least one of the features, so you know that you are assigning features to stops.

<u>STEP 2:</u> **Begin your diagram.**

The game is to assign stops to features. You could work this game the other way around, assigning features to stops, but working with three pools rather than six will make your task simpler. You can diagram this game using a grid with the features abbreviated along the left side as SV, HL, and RF. The stops are along the top, and you will mark off the features with an X as you attempt to solve the problems given by the questions.

	J	K	L	M	N	P	
SV							
HL							
RF							

<u>STEP 3:</u> **Symbolize the clues.**

Clue 1: K has scenic views and restroom facilities.

This clue does not require symbolization. You can mark off the SV and RF boxes for K.

Clue 2: L has scenic views and a historic landmark.

Same as clue 1, this clue does not require symbolization. You can simply mark off the SV and HL boxes for L.

Clue 3: L and N have no features in common.

This says that L and N cannot have the same features. Therefore, it can be symbolized as follows:

$$L \neq N$$

Clue 4: M has more features than L.

For your purposes, this is saying that M will have more feature boxes marked off than L. In the simplest terms possible you can symbolize this as follows:

$$M > L$$

Clue 5: K and P have exactly one feature in common.

You can use your box notations to symbolize this one as follows:

Clue 6: J has fewer features than P.

This is similar to clue 4 and can be symbolized as follows:

$$J < P$$

<u>STEP 4</u>: **Double-check your symbolizations.**
To double-check your symbolizations, you translate your symbolized clues back into normal English and see whether they match the original language of each clue. Once you have verified that your symbolizations work, you can add them to your diagram. Your diagram should look as follows:

	J	K	L	M	N	P
SV		X	X			
HL			X			
RF		X				

L ≠ N

M > L

K P / X X = 1

J < P

<u>STEP 5</u>: **Make deductions.**
Finally, before you tackle the questions, you see if you can make any deductions based on the setup of the game and the clues. You go through your types of deductions.

1. Can't-be-first-or-last deductions

   No deductions of this type are possible in this game.

2. Repeated-element deductions

   Stop K appears in clues 1 and 5. Clue 1 says that K has SV and RF. Clue 5 says that K and P have exactly one feature in common. Therefore, at least one of P's features is either SV or RF, but it cannot have both. The next repeated-element deduction allows you to go further toward determining the feature set for P.

   Stop P appears in clues 5 and 6. Clue 5 says that K and P have exactly one feature in common. You have already determined that P must have either SV or RF but not both in its feature set. Therefore, P cannot have all three features. At most, it can have two. Clue 6 says that J has fewer features than P. Since every stop must have at least one feature, then J must have one and P must have two, which means that P has HL as a feature. You write a number 2 below P's column to indicate that it can have only one more feature (either SV or RF, of course). You write a number 1 below J's column to show that it can have only one feature.

   Stop L appears in clues 2, 3, and 4. According to clue 2, L has SV and HL. According to clue 3, L and N cannot have the same features. Therefore, N cannot have SV or HL. Since it must have at least one feature, it must have RF, the only remaining feature, so you will mark off N as having RF and only that feature on your grid; you can black out SV and HL. Clue 4 says that M has more features than L. Clue 2 tells you that L has two features. Therefore M must have all three features in order to have more features than L. You can mark off all three features for M in your grid.

3. Down-to-two deductions

   No deductions of this type are possible in this game.

4. Block-splitting deductions

   No deductions of this type are possible in this game.

Here is your new diagram with all your clues and deductions added to it:

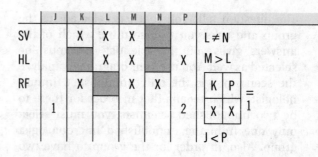

STEP 6: **Answer the questions in the smartest order.**
As you take the test, answer the questions in the following order:

1. Answer the Complete and Accurate List question.

2. Answer questions that give you more information to work with.

3. Answer the remaining questions.

    There are no Complete and Accurate List questions, so you must move on to questions that give more information. Those include:

    Question 8 ("all the stops that have historic landmarks also have scenic views ...")
    Question 9 ("P has no features in common with J but has at least one feature in common with every other stop ...")
    Question 10 ("no two stops have exactly the same features as one another ...")
    Question 11 ("exactly four of the six stops have historic landmarks, and exactly four of the six locations have scenic views ...")
    Question 12 ("the condition requiring that M has more features than L is replaced by a new condition requiring that M and L have exactly two features in common ...")

    The remaining questions are 6 and 7 and can be answered in that order.

THE ANSWERS

6. Answer: **C**

    The question asks how many stops you can determine the features for without any further information. Through your deductions, you determined four of the stops, leaving J and P as uncertain. Therefore, **the correct choice is answer C.**

7. Answer: **E**

    The question asks which of the answers must be false. This means that all but one of the answers could possibly be true. If J has RF and P has SV, then it is possible that four of the six stops have RF, so answer A cannot be your answer. If J has SV as its only feature and P has RF, then answer B could be true. If J has HL as its only feature, then answer C could be true. If J and P have RF, then answer D could be true. Answer E is impossible

because the only stops that can have HL are J, L, M, and P. Your deductions determined that K and N could not have HL. Therefore, **the correct choice is answer E.**

8. Answer: **B**

The question tells you that all the stops that have HL also have SV and asks you to determine which among the possible answers must be false. This means that all but one of the answers could possibly be true. The new information tells you that the second feature of P must be SV since it also has HL. Since P cannot have more than two features, it cannot have RF. Therefore, you can quickly determine that answer B must be false and it must be your choice. Answer A is your deduction from the new information and must be true. Answer C is the result of your original deductions and must be true. Answers D and E may or may not be true. J does not have HL, but that does not mean that it cannot also have SV. Likewise, you cannot determine whether it has RF or not. Since these statements cannot be determined as false or true, neither can be your answer. **The correct choice is answer B.**

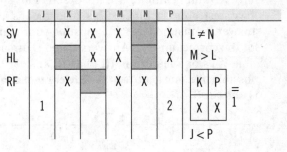

9. Answer: **C**

The question tells you that P and J have no features in common but that P has one feature in common with every other stop. Then, it asks you to determine which answer must be false. This means that all but one of the answers either must be true or could possibly be true. You apply the new information to your diagram. In order for P to have one feature in common with every stop other than J, it must have RF. If you assigned SV to P, then P would still not have a feature in common with stop N. Therefore, J must have SV, because it is the only remaining feature that P does not have. With the feature set determined for all the stops, it should be easy to find your answer. Answers A, B, D, and E are all reflected in the following diagram. Only answer C is impossible because J can only have one feature (SV) and K and N cannot have HL. **The correct choice is answer C.**

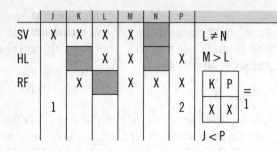

10. Answer: **B**

The question tells you that no two stops have exactly the same features as one another and asks you to identify which of the answers cannot be true. All but one of the answers could be true. You apply the new information to your diagram. You need only worry about J and P, since they are the only stops whose features remain variable. For stop J, you can determine only that it does not have RF, because the only other stop with one feature is N. Therefore, J must have SV or HL. For stop P, the only other stop with two features is L, which has SV and HL. P already has HL, so it must have RF as its second feature. According to your diagram, answer A must be true. Because P must have RF and J cannot have RF, exactly four stops have restroom facilities. This also means that answer B must be false and must be your choice for the correct answer. Answers C and D are possible if J's one feature is HL. Lastly, answer E is possible if J's one feature is SV. **The correct choice is answer B.**

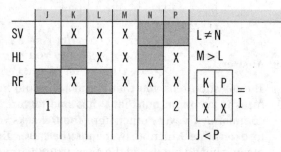

11. Answer: **E**

The question tells you that exactly four stops have HL and exactly four have SV, then asks you to determine which answer could be false. That means all but one of the possible answers must be true. You apply the new information to your diagram. For four stops to have historic landmarks, J must have HL, because your deductions determined that K and N could not have HL. Because J must have HL, P must have SV in order to satisfy the second requirement that four stops have SV. With all the features set, it is just a matter of

looking through the answers for the one that conflicts with your diagram. You can quickly see that answer E cannot be true. Since P must have SV, stops P and L have two features in common and cannot have exactly one in common. All the remaining answers match your diagram perfectly and must be true. **The correct choice is answer E.**

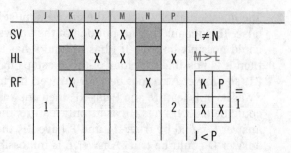

12. Answer: **C**

This question changes the clues and gives you a different starting point for solving the game. It removes the requirement that M have more features than L and sets a new requirement, that M and L have the same two features. This change does not alter your other deductions, and it also does not change the possibility that M has all three features, but it does remove RF as a required feature for stop M. You remove the mark from RF for M, but you do not black that box out. The question asks you to determine which among the answers must be false. Answer A may or may not be true. Even under the new conditions, J may have any one of the three features, so it is possible that J and M have a feature in common. Since there is a possibility it can be true, this cannot be your choice. Answer B also could be true. The new conditions do not prohibit stop P from having SV and HL, which are the same features as M. By the same token, it is impossible that M and P have no features in common. Stop M must have SV and HL. Stop P must have HL, so even under the new conditions, M and P will share at least one feature. This must be your choice for the correct answer. Answer D must be true because K and M both must have SV. Answer E could be true if M also has RF. **The correct choice is answer C.**

Question 13–18

As with all logic games, you follow the six-step process.

STEP 1: **Identify the game type.**

This is an ordering game. You know this because you are being asked to determine the order of arrival of the seven buses.

STEP 2: **Begin your diagram.**

There are seven buses that will arrive in order from first to seventh. You can create a grid with seven columns, and to make your job easier, you can abbreviate the names of the buses to their first initials. The arrivals go in order from left to right. For reference, write the list of buses in the upper right corner above your grid.

D E F H J K L

1	2	3	4	5	6	7

STEP 3: **Symbolize the clues.**

Symbolize the clues to make them easy to refer to as you work through the questions.

Clue 1: The buses arrive one at a time.

This sort of requirement is usually incorporated into the description of the game and is not listed among the clues. It does not require symbolization, but it tells you that no more than one bus can arrive at a time. If desired, you could put a number 1 below each column, indicating that each slot can only add up to one bus.

Clue 2: Either the Lynnville or the Koenig arrives fourth.

To indicate that either L or K but no other bus will arrive fourth, you put L/K above the fourth column.

Clue 3: The Fortman arrives at some time after the Koenig but at some time before the Lynnville.

This clue tells you that the F bus arrives between the K and the L buses. You can use the following notation to show this relationship:

K — F — L

Clue 4: Both the Hampton and the Janistown arrive at some time after the Evans.

You can use the following notation to symbolize this relationship:

E — H & J

Clue 5: The Hampton does not arrive next after the Janistown; nor does the Janistown arrive next after the Hampton.

Essentially, this clue is saying that the J bus and the H bus cannot arrive consecutively. You can represent this relationship using your box notation and the double arrow, as follows:

STEP 4: **Double-check your symbolizations.**

To double-check your symbolizations, you translate your symbolized clues back into normal English and see whether they match the original language of each clue. Once you have verified that they work, you can add your symbolizations to your diagram. Your diagram should look as follows:

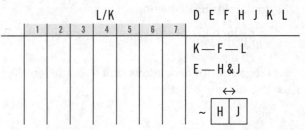

STEP 5: **Make deductions.**

Before you tackle the questions, you attempt to make deductions based on the setup of the game and the clues. You go through each type of deduction.

1. Can't-be-first-or-last deductions

   Clue 3 tells us that L must come after F, so F cannot be last in the order. It also tells you that K cannot be last or even second to last because both F and L have to come after it. The opposite is true as well: bus F cannot be first and bus L cannot be earlier than third. You can represent these deductions in your diagram by placing the negation above the columns in which they cannot appear (see the diagram that follows).

   Clue 4 tells you not only that E cannot be last but also that the latest it can be is fifth, because both H and J must come after it (this will change again later, but for now, you are focusing only on this particular deduction). This clue also tells you that neither H nor J can arrive first because E must arrive before both of them. You represent these deductions by placing the negation above the columns in which they cannot appear.

2. Repeated-element deductions

Buses H and J are repeated in clues 4 and 5. Clue 4, as we have seen, tells you that H and J must come after E. Clue 5 tells you that H and J cannot be consecutive in whatever order they arrive. There must be at least one bus between H and J. Therefore, the latest E can arrive is not fifth, as previously determined, but fourth, because there has to be another bus between H and J (for example, if J arrives fifth, then H must arrive seventh with another bus arriving sixth). You must put a ~E above the fifth column. Now you notice that E is restricted to arriving first, second, or third.

3. Down-to-two deductions

No deductions of this type are possible in this game.

4. Block-splitting deductions

No deductions of this type are possible in this game.

Your diagram with deductions added should look like this:

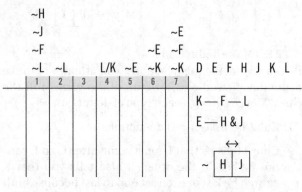

STEP 6: Answer the questions in the smartest order. As you take the test, answer the questions in this order:

1. Answer the Complete and Accurate List question.

2. Answer questions that give you more information to work with.

3. Answer the remaining questions.

Question 13 is a Complete and Accurate List question and should be answered first. The questions that give more information are as follows:

Question 14 ("Koenig arrives at some time before the Evans . . .")
Question 17 ("exactly one of the buses arrives after the Koenig but before the Lynnville . . .")

Question 18 ("Delbert arrives at some time before the Evans . . .")

Remaining are questions 15 and 16, and they can be answered in that order.

THE ANSWERS

13. Answer: **D**

The question asks you to identify the answer that gives an acceptable order for the buses to arrive. You can look at each answer in your diagram and evaluate whether it is consistent with your clues and deductions. You quickly eliminate answer A because neither L nor K arrives fourth. In answer B, bus H arrives first and that is inconsistent with clue 4 and your deductions. Answer C has buses H and J arriving consecutively, which is inconsistent with clue 5. Answer D is completely consistent with the clues of the game and is your choice for the correct answer. Answer E has bus L arriving before bus F, which is inconsistent with clue 3. **The correct choice is answer D.**

	~H				~E			
	~J					~E	~F	
	~F					~E	~F	
	~L	~L		L/K	~E	~K	~K	D E F H J K L
	1	2	3	4	5	6	7	
(A)	D	E	K	F	J	L	H	K — F — L
(B)	H	E	D	K	F	L	J	E — H & J
(C)	E	H	J	K	F	L	D	
(D)	E	H	D	K	F	L	J	~ [H↔J]
(E)	E	K	D	L	H	F	J	

14. Answer: **A**

The question tells you that bus K arrives before bus E and asks how many different orders are possible given this condition. You can create the various orders in your diagram. You know right off that L and not K must arrive fourth because the latest E can arrive is fourth, and if K must be earlier than E, then K must arrive earlier than fourth. Clue 3 tells you that not only K and E but also F must arrive before L. Therefore, K, F, and E must be the first three buses to arrive. K must be first because it must arrive before F (clue 3) and E (the question's requirement). The only two of these buses that can change in the order are F and E, alternating between the second and third arrival. After the fourth arrival (bus L), clue 5 tells you that H and J must arrive fifth and seventh with D arriving between them. The only two of these that can change in order are H and J. As you see in the diagram that follows, there are only four orders with F and E alternating positions and H and J alternating positions. Since there are only four possible orders, **the correct choice is answer A.**

```
~H
~J                    ~E
~F              ~E   ~F
~L  ~L    L/K  ~E  ~K  ~K   D E F H J K L
```

1	2	3	4	5	6	7
K	F	E	L	H	D	J
K	F	E	L	J	D	H
K	E	F	L	H	D	J
K	E	F	L	J	D	H

K—F—L

E—H & J

↔
~ [H | J]

15. Answer: **B**

The question asks that you choose the answer that must be true. This means that all but one of the answers could be false. Answer A could be true. Bus E could be first—nothing in the clues tells you otherwise—but it could just as easily be false, so this cannot be your answer. Answer B must be true. Clue 3 tells you that bus K must arrive before bus F and before bus L, so your choice must be answer B. You could stop there, but let's look at the other choices for learning purposes. Answer C could be true or false since D is the one bus that can arrive pretty much at any time except fourth (K/L). Answer D could be true or false since there is no clue governing the relationship between the J and L buses. Also, the L bus has the freedom to arrive last, so the J or any other bus could easily arrive before it. Answer E could be true or false. This answer tries to confuse you by using the reverse order stipulated by the previous question. You must be sure to forget the information given by the previous question and return to the original game each time you assess a question. In this case, the E bus is restricted to arriving in the first three places, but the K bus has the freedom to arrive anytime between the first and fifth places. Bus E could arrive first and K second, or vice versa without contradicting your clues. Therefore, this answer cannot be your answer. **The correct choice is answer B.**

16. Answer: **E**

The question asks that you choose the answer that could be true, which means that all but one of the answers must be false. You can test each answer in your diagram. Answer A cannot possibly be true. If L arrives fourth, then clue 3 tells you that K and F must arrive before L in an order consistent with the clue (K-F-L). Buses E, H, and J are forced to arrive together in the fifth, sixth, and seventh slots. On the other hand, if K is the fourth arrival, clue 3 tells you that D, F, and L have to occupy the fifth, sixth, and seventh arrivals in a manner consistent with the clue and E, H, and J are forced to arrive together in the first, second, and third slots. Unfortunately, neither leaves the possibility for an order that is consistent with clues 4 and 5. In either situation, E, H, and J are forced to arrive consecutively, and clues 4 and 5 say this is not possible. Bus E must arrive before H and J, and H and J cannot arrive consecutively. Answer A cannot be the correct choice. Answers B and C have the same problem as answer A. The arrival of D after or before F in any configuration forces E, H, and J to arrive consecutively, so these cannot be your answer. Answer D could not possibly be true. Clue 4 says that E must arrive before H and J. The E bus cannot arrive after either of those buses or the order will be inconsistent with this clue. Finally, answer E could be true. You have already seen in question 14 that E can be the next bus to arrive after F. It was one of the four possible orders that were acceptable. **The correct choice is answer E.**

17. Answer: **A**

The question tells you that one of the buses arrives after K but before L and then asks you which of the possible answers could be true. That means all but one of the answers are false. If exactly one bus arrives between K and L, then clue 3 tells you it must be F. Buses K, F, and L must arrive consecutively. This creates a block and you can look at two different orders, one with K arriving fourth and the other with L arriving fourth. You can plot both of these possibilities in your diagram (marked 1 and 2). When K arrives fourth, answer A could be true because E can be scheduled first or second without causing an inconsistency with the clues. When L arrives fourth, E must arrive first. Therefore, this must be your choice for the correct answer. For learning purposes let's assess the remaining answers. Answer B is not possible. Because K, F, and L form a block and clue 2 locks K or L into the fourth arrival, F must arrive either fifth or third. Answer C cannot be true either.

When K arrives fourth, E can only arrive first or second. When L arrives fourth, E can only arrive first. Answer D cannot be true for the same reason as answer B: bus F can only arrive fifth or third. Finally, answer E cannot be true because H and J cannot be consecutive. When K is fourth, the K, F, and L block takes over the sixth arrival. When L is fourth, bus E is forced to be first, which means H and J must arrive fifth and seventh so that another bus may arrive between them. **The correct choice is answer A.**

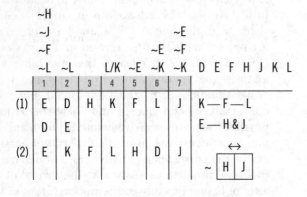

18. Answer: **C**

The question gives you a situation in which the D bus arrives before the E bus and asks you to determine when K arrives. For D to arrive before E, they must both arrive earlier than fourth, which leaves only one spot available for another bus to arrive before the fourth bus. If L arrives fourth, there are not enough slots available for both K and F, so K must arrive fourth. **The correct choice is answer C.**

Questions 19–25
As with all logic games you follow the six-step process.

STEP 1:   Identify the game type.
Several clues tell you that this is a grouping game. The most obvious is that the game tells you that there are two test "groups." Also, it tells you that no rat can be in more than one group, and it tells you a condition under which the rats should be divided ("at least one brown rat and one white rat") into the two groups.

STEP 2:   Begin your diagram.
Create a diagram that represents the two test groups. In this case, a grid with two columns suits your purposes perfectly. Leave space to the right of your diagram for the symbolization of your clues. Also, abbreviate your rats' names and group them according to color (B for brown and W for white).

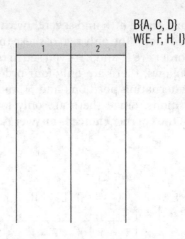

STEP 3:   Symbolize the clues.
Before you go through the clues, you must recognize what is said in the setup for the game, that each group must have at least one brown rat and one white rat. This cannot be easily symbolized, but you can represent it in your diagram by creating slots for the required rats in each group. Now, you go clue by clue and simplify them into easy-to-read equations.

Clue 1: Neither group includes both Abby and Iris.

This clue is worded in a way to confuse you, but it is basically saying that A and I cannot be together in the same group. You can symbolize it as follows:

$$A \rightarrow \sim I$$
$$I \rightarrow \sim A$$

Clue 2: Neither group includes both Elle and Horn.

This is worded the same way as clue 1, so you can symbolize it in the same way:

$$E \rightarrow \sim H$$
$$H \rightarrow \sim E$$

Clue 3: If a group includes Dennis, it includes neither Horn nor Iris.

Again, the wording is meant to make it more difficult to understand what the clue is really saying. In this case, it says that if a group includes D, then H and I cannot be in that group. This can be symbolized as follows:

$$D \rightarrow \sim H \& \sim I$$

Due to the complexity of this one it might be useful to create the contrapositive of this clue as well. That is symbolized as follows:

$$H/I \rightarrow \sim D$$

Clue 4: If group 1 includes Carl, group 2 includes Horn.

This is a simple "if ... then" statement. If Carl is in group 1, then Horn is in group 2. It can be symbolized as follows:

$$C = 1 \rightarrow H = 2$$

STEP 4: **Double-check your symbolizations.**
To double-check your symbolizations, translate your symbolized clues back into normal English and see whether they match the original language of each clue. When you are through, your page should look like this:

B{A, C, D}
W{E, F, H, I}

1	2
B	B –
W	W –

$A \rightarrow \sim I$

$I \rightarrow \sim A$

$E \rightarrow \sim H$

$H \rightarrow \sim E$

$D \rightarrow \sim H \ \& \ \sim I$

$H/I \rightarrow \sim D$

$C = 1 \rightarrow H = 2$

STEP 5: **Make deductions.**
Before you tackle the questions, see if you can make any deductions based on the setup of the game and the clues. Go through each type of deduction.

1. Can't-be-first-or-last deductions

Because this is not an ordering game this deduction does not apply.

2. Repeated-element deductions

You see that H is repeated in several clues. Of particular interest is the repetition between clue 4 and the contrapositive of clue 3. You can deduce that if C is in group 1, then because H is in group 2, D cannot be in group 2. This could be symbolized as follows:

$$C = 1 \rightarrow D \neq 2$$

3. Down-to-two deductions

There is a minimum of two rats to each group (one brown, one white). You notice that D is a brown rat. Because of clue 3, if D is in a group, then the only white rats it can be grouped with are E and F. You also notice that F is the only rat that is a free agent. It has no limitations on where it can be grouped and who it can be grouped with.

4. Block-splitting deductions

There are no deductions of this kind to be made.

STEP 6: **Answer the questions in the smartest order.**
Answer the questions in this order:

1. Answer the Complete and Accurate List question.

2. Answer questions that give you more information to work with.

3. Answer the remaining questions

Though it is not worded as such, question 19 is a Complete and Accurate List question and should be answered first. Questions that give more information include the following:

Question 20 ("Carl is in group 1 ... ")
Question 21 ("Elle is in group 1 ... ")
Question 22 ("Abby is in the same group as Dennis ... ")
Question 25 ("Dennis is in group 2 ... ")

That leaves questions 23 and 24, which can be answered in that order.

THE ANSWERS

19. Answer: **A**

This question is asking for which answer gives a possible grouping of the rats. The key word in the question is *could*, which means that four out of the five answers are not possible. You must go through each answer and test it against your diagram and the clues listed to the right.

(A) Group 1: Abby, Fern, Horn
    Group 2: Carl, Elle, Iris

As you can see by the diagram, no clues are violated and each group has one brown rat and one white rat. This is your answer and you could move on to the next question, but let's evaluate the other answers for learning purposes.

B{A, C, D}
W{E, F, H, I}

	1	2
	B – A	B – C
	W – F	W – E
	H	I

A → ~I

I → ~A

E → ~H

H → ~E

D → ~H & ~I

H/I → ~D

C = 1 → H = 2

C = 1 → D ≠ 2

(B) Group 1: Carl, Fern, Horn
      Group 2: Abby, Dennis, Elle

You can see the problem here without looking at your diagram. According to the fourth clue, if C is in group 1, then H must be in group 2. Since H is in group 1, this cannot be your answer.

(C) Group 1: Carl, Dennis, Elle
      Group 2: Fern, Horn, Iris

This cannot be your answer because group 2 does not include a brown rat and each group must have at least one brown rat and one white rat.

(D) Group 1: Abby, Elle, Iris
      Group 2: Carl, Fern, Horn

Abby and Iris cannot be in the same group according to the first clue, so this cannot be your answer.

(E) Group 1: Abby, Dennis, Fern
      Group 2: Carl, Elle, Horn

Elle and Horn cannot be in group 2 together according to the second clue. This cannot be your answer.

The correct choice is answer A.

20. Answer: **B**

This question gives you a fact, that C is in group 1. Based on that fact, you must figure out which of the pairs listed in the answers *must* be in group 2 together. One deduction you can make before looking at the answers is that since C is in group 1, then H must be in group 2 (clue 4). From your contrapositive of clue 3, you know that D cannot be in the same group as H, so it cannot be in group 2. This leaves rat A as the only available brown rat for group 2. You look at your answers and see

that B says A and H must be in group 2 together. This is your answer. There is no need to review the remaining options. **The correct choice is answer B.**

B{A, C, D}
W{E, F, H, I}

	1	2
	B – C	B – A
	W –	W – H
	H	

A → ~I

I → ~A

E → ~H

H → ~E

D → ~H & ~I

H/I → ~D

C = 1 → H = 2

C = 1 → D ≠ 2

21. Answer: **E**

This question tells you that E is in group 1 and asks you to find the pair that *could* be in group 1 along with E. This means that four out of the five pairs cannot be in Elle's group. You can see immediately that E is a white rat and that one of the two rats must be brown or the conditions of the game will not be met. You look through your answers and evaluate them one by one.

B{A, C, D}
W{E, F, H, I}

	1	2
	B –	B –
	W – E	W –

A → ~I

I → ~A

E → ~H

H → ~E

D → ~H & ~I

H/I → ~D

C = 1 → H = 2

C = 1 → D ≠ 2

(A) Fern and Iris

Both are white rats, so this cannot be your answer.

(B) Carl and Fern

If Carl is in group 1, then H is in group 2. Because H is in group 2, rat D cannot also be in group 2, so the brown rat for group 2 will be A. This leaves H and I to fill out the rest of group 2, but clue 1 says that A and I cannot be in the same group, so this does not work. This cannot be your answer.

B{A, C̶, D}
W{E̶, F̶, H, I}

1	2	
B – C	B – A	A → ~I
W – E	W–	I → ~A
F		E → ~H
		H → ~E
		D → ~H & ~I
		H/I → ~D
		C = 1 → H = 2
		C = 1 → D ≠ 2

(C) Carl and Horn

You know this cannot be your answer because clue 4 tells you if C is in group 1, H must be in group 2.

(D) Abby and Carl

Since this scenario takes two brown rats, it leaves only D to be the brown rat in group 2. Thanks to your deduction that if C is in group 1 then D cannot be in group 2, you know that this cannot be true and this option cannot be your answer.

(E) Carl and Iris

This scenario leaves A and D available to be the brown rat in group 2, but you know that D cannot be in group 2 since C is in group 1. Therefore, A automatically becomes the brown rat in group 2. You can easily put E and F in group 2 and remain consistent with the game and clues. This is your answer.

B{A, C̶, D}
W{E̶, F̶, H, I̶}

1	2	
B – C	B – A	A → ~I
W – E	W– E	I → ~A
I	F	E → ~H
		H → ~E
		D → ~H & ~I
		H/I → ~D
		C = 1 → H = 2
		C = 1 → D ≠ 2

The correct choice is answer E.

22. Answer: **E**

The question tells you that Abby is in the same group as Dennis and then asks you to find the true statement among the options. This means that four out of the five options are impossible given the game setup and clues. For the purposes of this question, you now have the clue A → D and D → A. This also tells you that C will be the brown rat for the group that A and D are not in. This creates the following clues:

C → ~D & ~A and D/A → ~C

You must test each answer to see which could be true.

(A) Both Elle and Fern are in group 2

Elle and Fern are both white rats, so you need one brown rat to round out the group. Since D and A must be together, it must be C. This scenario leaves H or I to fill the last remaining slot in group 1, but D cannot be in the same group with H, and A cannot be in the same group with I. Therefore, this cannot work and this is not your choice.

B{A, C̶, D̶}
W{E, F, H, I}

1	2	
B – D	B – C	A → ~I
W –	W– E	I → ~A
A	F	E → ~H
		H → ~E
		D → ~H & ~I
		H/I → ~D
		C = 1 → H = 2
		C = 1 → D ≠ 2

(B) Horn is in group 1

According to the contrapositive of clue 3, if Horn is in group 1, then D and A must be in group 2. This forces C to be the brown rat in group 1 and this is impossible. According to clue 4, if C is in group 1, then H must be in group 2. This cannot be your answer.

B{A, C, ~~D~~}
W{E, F, H, I}

1	2	
B –	B – D	A → ~I
W – H	W –	I → ~A
	A	E → ~H
		H → ~E
		D → ~H & ~I
		H/I → ~D
		C = 1 → H = 2
		C = 1 → D ≠ 2

(C) Carl is in group 1

If C is in group 1, then H is in group 2 according to clue 4. D and A must be in group 2 as well, but this conflicts with your contrapositive—D and H cannot be in the same group—so this cannot be your answer.

B{A, ~~C~~, ~~D~~}
W{E, F, H, I}

1	2	
B –	B – D	A → ~I
W –	W– H	I → ~A
	A	E → ~H
		H → ~E
		D → ~H & ~I
		H/I → ~D
		C = 1 → H = 2
		C = 1 → D ≠ 2

(D) Both Elle and Fern are in group 1

Because each group must have three rats and this arrangement leaves only one place in group 1, you can determine that D and A must be in group 2. C must fill that spot in group 1 so that there is a brown rat. This scenario leaves H or I to fill the last remaining spot in group 2, but clue 3 says that neither H nor I can be in the same group as D, so this cannot be your answer.

B{~~A~~, ~~C~~, ~~D~~}
W{E, F, H, I}

1	2	
B – C	B – D	A → ~I
W – E	W –	I → ~A
F	A	E → ~H
		H → ~E
		D → ~H & ~I
		H/I → ~D
		C = 1 → H = 2
		C = 1 → D ≠ 2

(E) Iris is in group 2

This is your last remaining option and must be the correct answer, but let's analyze it to make sure. With I in group 2, you know that D and A must be in group 1 and C must be in group 2. This scenario leaves E, F, and H to assign to the remaining three open spots, and there are a number of configurations that work. Below is one of them. This is your answer.

B{~~A~~, ~~C~~, ~~D~~}
W{E, F, H, I}

1	2	
B – D	B – C	A → ~I
W – H	W – I	I → ~A
A	E	E → ~H
		H → ~E
		D → ~H & ~I
		H/I → ~D
		C = 1 → H = 2
		C = 1 → D ≠ 2

The correct choice is answer E.

23. Answer: **D**

The question asks you to find among the answers the one pair that could *not* be in group 2 together. You can use your experience from question 17 and quickly choose D as your answer. Why? You discovered when working on that question that when A and D are both in group 2, it forces C to be in group 1, since it is your one last remaining brown rat. According to clue 4, when C is in group 1, H must be in group 2 and D and H cannot be in group 2 together. There is no reason to check any other answers. **The correct choice is answer D.**

24. Answer: **C**

The question asks that you find which of the answers *could* be true, so four out of the five answers are impossible. Answering this question is a matter of eliminating answers that are impossible to find the one that is possible.

(A) Carl is in group 1 and Elle is in group 2

This cannot be true because clue 4 tells you that if C is in group 1, then H is in group 2. Clue 2 tells you that E and H cannot be in group 2 together, so you can eliminate this choice.

(B) Abby is not in any group and Carl is in group 1.

If A is taken out altogether and C is in group 1, then D must be the brown rat for group 2. Clue 4 tells you that if C is in group 1, then H is in group 2. Clue 3 tells you that D and H cannot be in group 2 together, so this cannot be your answer.

(C) Abby is in group 1 and Elle is in group 2.

You can see in the sample diagram that you can create every possible scenario under this option's conditions. Therefore, this is your answer. Let's review the rest of the options for learning purposes.

B{A, C̶, D}
W{E, F, H, I̶}

1	2	
B – A	B – C	A → ~I
W – H	W– E	I → ~A
F	I	E → ~H
		H → ~E
		D → ~H & ~I
		H/I → ~D
		C = 1 → H = 2
		C = 1 → D ≠ 2

(D) Abby is in group 2 and Dennis is in group 2.

This option has the same problem that question 18 posed. If both A and D are in group 2, then C must be the brown rat for group 1. If C is in group 1, rat H must be in group 2. Rats D and H cannot be in group 2 together, so this cannot be your answer.

(E) Abby is in group 2 and Carl is not in any group.

This option forces an untenable situation. With A in group 2 and thus D in group 1, you must divide the remaining white rats among the two groups. Unfortunately, clue 1 tells you that A and I cannot be in the same group together and clue 3 tells you that D and I cannot be in the same group together, so you are stuck with nowhere to put I. This cannot be your answer choice.

The correct choice is answer C.

25. Answer: **D**

The question tells you that D is in group 2 and asks you to find among the answers the one rat that, if assigned to a group, must also be in group 2. You already know from your previous work that if Carl is in group 1 and D is in group 2, the scenario cannot work. Carl in group 1 forces H to be in group 2, and D and H cannot be in the same group. So, answer D must be correct. All the other options can be easily assigned to group 1 and do not necessarily have to be in group 2, and answers A and C are impossible because D cannot be in the same group as H or I. **The correct choice is answer D.**

SECTION II

1. Answer: **D**

> STEP 1:   **Read the question and identify your task.**
> This is a Describe question. It asks you to assess Kathy's argumentative tactic in countering David's argument.
>
> STEP 2:   **Read the argument with your task in mind.**
> Read both David's and Kathy's arguments. David argues that after an injury an athlete must relearn how to play the game in the manner that the athlete did before the injury. Kathy disagrees and tells a story about a professional quarterback who suffered an injury and afterward adjusted his game to a new style.
>
> STEP 3:   **Know what you're looking for.**
> The correct answer will describe Kathy's technique as one using a counterexample that undermines David's argument.
>
> STEP 4:   **Read every word of every answer choice.**
> Answer A is incorrect because Kathy is not really establishing any solution. She is merely giving an example of a particular quarterback's solution to his problem. Also, the term *solution* seems wrong. Neither David nor Kathy is offering a solution. Rather, they are offering or suggesting a prescription. The difference is subtle but enough of a reason to exclude this as a possible answer. Answer B cannot be correct because at the outset it is obvious Kathy disagrees with David. She does not support his claim. Regarding answer C, there is no equivocation in David's argument. He makes a fairly straightforward statement that the only way an athlete can be successful after an injury is to relearn the athlete's original method of play. Kathy is equally unequivocal and uses stark language to disagree. Answer D is exactly what you formulated as the correct answer. Kathy does in fact use an example to counter David's claim, so this is most likely your answer. Answer E cannot be your answer. David and Kathy are not trying to explain the same phenomenon. On the contrary, they are offering a different path to success. **The correct choice is answer D.**

2. Answer: **A**

> STEP 1:   **Read the question and identify your task.**
> This is a Conclusion question. The question asks that you identify the answer that most accurately states the main point of the argument.
>
> STEP 2:   **Read the argument with your task in mind.**
> You read the argument, which states that digital camera manufacturers advertise a particular feature for their cameras but evidently this feature is irrelevant because it is incompatible with other technologies and thus can be considered impractical.
>
> STEP 3:   **Know what you're looking for.**
> The central assumption of the argument maintains that the memory capacity of digital cameras typically is far in excess of electronic screen capabilities, so differences in memory are not really significant.
>
> STEP 4:   **Read every word of every answer choice.**
> Answer A seems to be giving exactly the meaning of the argument, that the resolution of the cameras' sensors has no bearing on their relative quality as tools. This would seem to be your answer, but you must review the remaining options to be sure. Answer B says the argument is making a recommendation that manufacturers add more features to their cameras, but the argument never makes such a recommendation. The argument focuses entirely on resolution as an advertised feature and its inherent problems. This cannot be your answer. Answer C says the argument is making an assessment of the manufacturers' decision to focus on resolution, but the argument is only describing the flaw in that decision. Such an assessment may be implied or the next step, but what you have before you makes no judgment regarding their decision. This cannot be the correct choice. Answer D is incorrect because it focuses on the last part of the argument and ignores the manufacturers and their choice of what to emphasize in advertising. Finally, answer E cannot be the answer because it suggests that resolution is the only practical difference between the cameras. Also, the argument does not make a claim concerning the difference in quality between cameras. It only claims that the emphasis on resolution is misplaced as a quality measure. **The correct choice is answer A.**

3. Answer: **A**

STEP 1:   **Read the question and identify your task.**
This is an Assumption question. It asks which answer gives the assumption upon which the argument depends.

STEP 2:   **Read the argument with your task in mind.**
The assumption is that the memory capacity of the camera is not a critical concern because modern electronic screens and photographic paper transfer methods cannot convey a majority of the data captured.

STEP 3:   **Know what you're looking for.**
The answer should contain wording that makes a connection between the very high data memory capacity of digital cameras and the much lower resolution abilities of electronic screens and other methods related to image display.

STEP 4:   **Read every word of every answer choice.**
Essentially, answer A states that differences in resolution do not affect the deficiencies in screens and paper. The argument does in fact argue that resolution is irrelevant because the deficiencies in screens and paper limit the level of detail. Thus, the argument depends on resolution having no effect on those deficiencies, which is what this answer states. This is most likely your answer, but you must review the remaining options to be sure. Answer B cannot be correct because the argument bases its claim on technology, in particular the resolution and its interaction with screens and photographic paper, not on the skill of the photographer. Answer C may be true but your argument does not even mention the software involved in displaying digital photographs on screens. It is uncertain that software is even part of the equation, so you cannot choose this as your answer. Answer D actually contradicts part of the argument by stating that resolution determines the degree of detail reproduced. The argument makes the opposite argument. Answer E makes a strange connection between the definition of the term *resolution* and its effect on judging the quality of photographic instruments. The argument does not necessarily depend on the definition of the term *resolution*. Rather, it depends on how the measure of resolution is used by manufacturers and their claims' relationship to practical uses. This cannot be your answer. **The correct choice is answer A.**

4. Answer: **B**

STEP 1:   **Read the question and identify your task.**
This is a Deduction question. The question asks that you assess Jeri's interpretation of Richard's statement.

STEP 2:   **Read the argument with your task in mind.**
Jeri says that all prefaces and prologues are meaningless and recommends that all prefaces and prologues be eliminated from literature. This recommendation is based on Richard's assessment that they are extraneous and serve no purpose.

STEP 3:   **Know what you're looking for.**
The correct answer will likely have something do with Jeri's equating "extraneous and serve no purpose" with being "meaningless," since this is the justification for her recommendation that prefaces and prologues be eliminated from literature. It will behoove you to pay close attention to the language of each answer.

STEP 4:   **Read every word of every answer choice.**
Answer A uses the word *useful*, which is not a term used by either Richard or Jeri. While "not useful" can be seen as an equivalent of "extraneous and serve no purpose," you must be careful not to make such a leap, even if it seems warranted. Answer B is a viable option because this is how Jeri perceives Richard's meaning, but in the positive. Jeri does think that Richard is saying that only literary tools that serve a purpose (Richard's exact words) have meaning, which could be flipped to say all literary tools that serve no purpose are meaningless. This is most likely your answer, but you must review the remaining options to make sure there is not a better one. Answer C is very similar to answer B, but in the interest of choosing the best answer you might consider answer C a lesser choice. It changes the word *meaning* to *meaningful*, which has a different connotation and it lacks the absolute meaning that the word *only* offers in answer B. Answer B is still your best choice so far. Answer D does not link Jeri's remarks to Richard's. It also uses the word *useful*, which is not the same terminology as that used by Richard. Answer E takes the logical leap that Jeri makes in her statement, but it does not explain her interpretation and how it might lead to the conclusion to eliminate prefaces and prologues from literature. **The correct choice is answer B.**

5. Answer: **D**

STEP 1: **Read the question and identify your task.**

This is a Flaw question. The question asks that you determine why the argument is questionable.

STEP 2: **Read the argument with your task in mind.**

The argument describes a survey covering three cities in the Midwest and from the results argues that the national mortgage default rate cannot be attributed to homeowners' lack of desire to pay off their mortgages.

STEP 3: **Know what you're looking for.**

You can expect the correct answer to point out some flaw in the survey or the conclusion that the survey of the Midwest justifies a conclusion regarding the entire nation.

STEP 4: **Read every word of every answer choice.**

Answer A cannot be your choice because the argument does not include two conclusions, conflicting or not. The argument makes only one conclusion, which is that the high mortgage default rate is not due to a lack of desire on the part of the homeowners to pay off their mortgages. Answer B cannot be your choice because 92 percent is an overwhelming majority by any expert or nonexpert's standards. Answer C cannot be your choice because the high default rate does not contradict what could be considered a desire on behalf of those homeowners to pay off their mortgages. They are two very different statistics, one based on actual behavior, the other based on what people want for the future. Answer D fits into your expectations for the correct answer. It points out that the argument is using a survey of the Midwest as a basis for a statement regarding the entire nation. This seems to be your answer, but you must review the final option. Answer E cannot be your answer because the argument does not overlook this possibility. The argument says *if* the default rate is high, and it is only concerned with this possibility. The implication is that the opposite is possible but not of concern in this particular argument. **The correct choice is answer D.**

6. Answer: **C**

STEP 1: **Read the question and identify your task.**

This is a Strengthen question. The first question asks you to identify the principle or axiom that supports Professor Raleigh's side of the argument.

STEP 2: **Read the argument with your task in mind.**

Professor Allyn argues that political speeches are not true literary works and should be excluded from the literature department's curriculum. Professor Raleigh believes that regardless of whether they are considered true literary works, political speeches should be included because the department can give their students the skills to help them be better citizens in the larger society.

STEP 3: **Know what you're looking for.**

You expect the correct answer to be a principle supporting the department's responsibility to make their students better citizens through teaching them to better analyze political speeches.

STEP 4: **Read every word of every answer choice.**

Answer A cannot be correct because it is too general and does not even address the specifics of their argument. Also, both professors would probably agree with this principle, and you are being asked which answer supports only Raleigh's argument. Professor Raleigh might agree with answer B, but it is a principle that assumes speeches are already taught in the department. Essentially, it puts the cart before the horse. Answer C says pretty much what you formulated as your expected correct answer. It says that the literature department should enable students to handle all texts that have an effect, dangerous or otherwise, on society. This is most likely your answer, but you should review the remaining answers. Answer D is supportive of Raleigh's position and contradicts Allyn's position, but it is a bit too general and does not address the subject of political speeches. Answer E supports a claim that Raleigh does not make. Raleigh says that whether political speeches are a literary form or not they should still be taught. Therefore, this principle does not fit Raleigh's argument. **The correct choice is answer C.**

7. Answer: **A**

STEP 1: **Read the question and identify your task.**

This is a Assumption question. It asks that you identify the assumption upon which Raleigh bases his argument.

STEP 2: **Read the argument with your task in mind.**

Raleigh's argument seems to be based on the idea that the literature department should be teaching students something beyond just true literary works, so you expect your answer to be a similar idea.

STEP 3: **Know what you're looking for.**

The correct answer will state that the literature department's responsibility includes more than teaching true literary works.

STEP 4: **Read every word of every answer choice.**

Answer A says that a literature department's academics should not be limited to analyzing true literary works. Raleigh's argument depends on the idea that the literature department should be doing more than just teaching true literary works since he is advocating that they teach about political speeches whether they are considered literature or not. This option is most likely your answer, but you should continue to review the remaining answers. Answer B is incorrect because Raleigh talks about all political speeches and does not make a distinction regarding the circumstances surrounding the political speech. Answer C focuses on Raleigh's statement concerning the goal of the department's courses, but this is a rather limited assumption and Raleigh's argument does not exactly depend on it. If this assumption proved false and courses taught other skills, it would not diminish his argument concerning political speeches. In fact, it might strengthen it. Answer D cannot be correct because Raleigh's argument considers political speeches important regardless of whether they are considered true literary works. Therefore, since the literary status of political speeches is irrelevant to his argument, then whether true literary works are detrimental or not to society is irrelevant as well. Finally, answer E cannot be the answer because it actually states the opposite of what Raleigh is arguing. **The correct choice is answer A.**

8. Answer: **B**

STEP 1: **Read the question and identify your task.**

This is a Principle question. The question asks you to identify which answer most accurately illustrates the principle expressed in the argument.

STEP 2: **Read the argument with your task in mind.**

The argument states that a child follows a teacher's instructions better if given a few options rather than many.

STEP 3: **Know what you're looking for.**

The correct answer will most likely restate this principle in a different manner while remaining consistent with the intent of the argument.

STEP 4: **Read every word of every answer choice.**

Answer A cannot be your answer because it ignores the many-versus-few options aspect of the argument and states that success is a matter of defining the benefits of each option. This is certainly not in the same spirit of the argument. Answer B states that there is an inverse relationship between children's change of behavior and the number of alternatives given them, so children will alter their behavior (abide by instructions) more if they have fewer choices and alter their behavior less (refuse to abide by instructions) if they have more choices. This is exactly what your argument is saying and is most likely your answer, but you must review the remaining options. Answers C, D, and E focus on the delivery of instructions and not the content of them. Your argument is more concerned with the content, mainly how many options, so none of these answers can be correct. **The correct choice is answer B.**

9. Answer: **E**

STEP 1: **Read the question and identify your task.**

This is an Assumption question. The question asks you to identify the assumption upon which the argument depends.

STEP 2: **Read the argument with your task in mind.**

The argument tells you about a fungus threatening crops of tomatoes and a synthetic fungicide that can control it. The fungicide is harmful to humans, so it cannot be used in populated areas. Then the argument makes the conclusion that the nation's tomato crops are not threatened by the fungus because commercial tomato fields are not located near populated areas and the fungicide can be used on them.

STEP 3: **Know what you're looking for.**

You can guess that the correct answer will have something to do with equating the nation's tomato crops with commercial tomato fields, since its final statement is based on that assumption.

STEP 4: **Read every word of every answer choice.**

Regarding answer A, the argument is concerned only with the threat of late blight on tomato crops, but it does not depend on it being the only threat. The existence of other threats would not diminish the argument in any way. Answer B is concerned with a possible future, but the argument is concerned only with the current threat. This cannot be the correct choice. Answer C discusses the speed with which the fungus spreads through particular crops, but the argument is not based on the speed of the attack. Instead, it is based on the fungicide used to stop it and its side effects. This cannot be correct. Answer D is irrelevant because the argument is about the commercial farms and the nation's tomato crops. It is not about these smaller sources of tomatoes. Finally, answer E states that commercial fields produce most or all of the nation's tomatoes. This is what you formulated as your possible answer. The argument's main assumption is that the commercial fields are equal to the nation's tomato crops. Without that assumption, the conclusion that the nation's tomato crops are not seriously threatened is not possible. **The correct choice is answer E.**

10. Answer: **D**

   STEP 1:   **Read the question and identify your task.**
   This is a Flaw question. The question asks that you identify the false presumption at the heart of the argument.

   STEP 2:   **Read the argument with your task in mind.**
   The lawyer predicts that the next objection will be overruled by the judge based on a statistic.

   STEP 3:   **Know what you're looking for.**
   You can guess that the probable answer will identify the false presumption as that of using a statistic to solidly predict the next result.

   STEP 4:   **Read every word of every answer choice.**
   Answer A cannot be the presumption because no such requirement guiding the judge's ruling is mentioned in the argument and such a presumption would eliminate the word *probably* from the lawyer's argument. It would make the overruling a certainty. Answer B cannot be the presumption because the lawyer's prediction is based on past behavior, plain and simple, not a more complicated expectation based on the influence past decisions had on the verdicts in those cases. Answer C cannot be the presumption because the lawyer says the next objection will "probably" be overruled, which implies likelihood, not a guarantee. A presumption of a guarantee would lead

the lawyer to state that the objection *will* be overruled. Also, the lawyer only states that the next object will likely be overruled, not the next five as the answer presumes. Answer D could very well be your presumption. It is very similar to answer C, but the lawyer does presume the likelihood of the next objection when he or she says it will "probably" happen. Also, this presumption only concerns itself with the next objection, which is exactly the lawyer's prediction. This is most likely your answer, but you have one last option to consider. Answer E cannot be the presumption because the lawyer's prediction is based on the judge's decisions and not on the quality of those decisions. **The correct choice is answer D.**

11. Answer: **C**

   STEP 1:   **Read the question and identify your task.**
   This is a Describe question. It asks you to describe how a certain fact is being used within the argument.

   STEP 2:   **Read the argument with your task in mind.**
   When you read through the argument, you pay close attention to this fact and how it functions. In this case, that the auto companies are purchasing more equipment and spending more on R&D seems to be a justification or evidence supporting the conclusion of the argument. This argument actually has the conclusion in the first sentence.

   STEP 3:   **Know what you're looking for.**
   The correct answer discusses the fact as a justification or evidence.

   STEP 4:   **Read every word of every answer choice.**
   Answer A states that the fact is an inference from a premise when, in fact, it is the exact opposite. That companies expect sales to increase is the inference from the fact under consideration. Answer B is incorrect for the same reason; your fact is not an inference but a premise or basis for inference. Answer C states that the fact is the primary evidence for the conclusion, and this seems like your answer because the economist concludes that industry is on the way to recovery based on the fact under consideration, as you formulated from reading the question and the argument. Answer D states that the fact is required for the conclusion to be true, but the conclusion may be true based on other facts that you do not have on hand, so this is not the function of the facts under consideration. Finally, the argument does not explain

why the companies are spending more. It merely makes a judgment based on that fact, so answer E cannot be correct. **The correct choice is answer C.**

12. Answer: **C**

STEP 1:   **Read the question and identify your task.**

This is a Describe question. The question asks you to choose the answer that describes the argument that the critic makes in response to the mayor's argument.

STEP 2:   **Read the argument with your task in mind.**

The city mayor argues that an increase in percentage of students graduating from high school is proof that the mayor's education policies are a success. The critic argues that another metric concerning preparedness for college and jobs proves the opposite.

STEP 3:   **Know what you're looking for.**

You expect the correct answer to state that the critic uses new data to show that the mayor's data leads to the wrong conclusion.

STEP 4:   **Read every word of every answer choice.**

Answer A is incorrect because the critic sticks to the numbers and says nothing about the mayor personally or the mayor's motives. Answer B cannot be your answer because the critic uses a statistic to support his or her conclusion, so the critic obviously believes that statistics have credibility and that measuring progress toward education goals is not difficult. Answer C says the critic attempts to show that the mayor's use of facts is misleading. This is indeed what you expected the answer to say. The critic uses a statistic to show that the mayor's facts lead to the wrong conclusion. This is most likely your answer, but you must review the remaining options. Answer D is tempting and the critic's attack might be read that way, but the critic does not exactly discredit the mayor's methods so much as undermine the mayor's argument in support of his methods. Also, this description ignores the use of statistics within the argument. Answer E cannot be your choice because the critic does not dispute the mayor's statistics. The critic points out only that the mayor's facts do not lead to the right conclusion. **The correct choice is answer C.**

13. Answer: **D**

STEP 1:   **Read the question and identify your task.**

This is a Flaw question. The question asks you to identify a fact that the mayor could use to counter the critic's claim.

STEP 2:   **Read the argument with your task in mind.**

You expect the correct answer will undermine the basis for the critic's argument, which is that the test indicates the students' lack of preparedness.

STEP 3:   **Know what you're looking for.**

The correct answer will make the case that the test is inadequate in some manner.

STEP 4:   **Read every word of every answer choice.**

Answer A points out that the students who tested poorly were located in a particular region, but this does not invalidate the test or its use as support for the critic's argument. Answer B is irrelevant since the critic is not using the students' eventual career in college or in the work world as a basis for the argument. Answer C is a statement the critic might use to undermine the mayor's argument, not the other way around, so this cannot be your answer. Answer D undermines the test by saying that it is new and the results this year cannot be compared to anything, which, if true, undermines the use of this test in the argument since the mayor makes his argument based on statistics over the several years he has been in office. This is probably your answer, but you have one more option to consider. Answer E is irrelevant since both the mayor and the critic are concerned only with their own city and no other city. **The correct choice is answer D.**

14. Answer: **D**

STEP 1:   **Read the question and identify your task.**

This is an Assumption question. The question asks that you identify the assumption upon which the argument relies.

STEP 2:   **Read the argument with your task in mind.**

The argument says that bleached flour is priced much higher than unbleached flour even though the process to bleach the flour is not very costly. It concludes that the price difference must have to do with something other than the cost of "providing" bleached flour to the consumer.

<u>STEP 3:</u>   **Know what you're looking for.**
You can expect the assumption to be that the cost of bleaching is the only cost that should be considered when attributing causes for the price difference.

<u>STEP 4:</u>   **Read every word of every answer choice.**
Answer A is somewhat outside the scope of the argument because it focuses on consumer demand. The argument suggests that something other than cost may be responsible but does not indicate what that may be. The argument bases its conclusion on cost. Also, this assumption indicates that consumer demand should force bleached and unbleached to be priced the same. Answer B is also outside the scope of the argument. It might be a conclusion you draw from the argument, but it is not an assumption upon which the argument is based. Answer C is a clarification or furthering of the conclusion, and it is not an assumption upon which the argument is based. Answer D states that the cost of the bleaching process is the only factor relevant to the cost of providing bleached flour to the consumer. This is probably your answer, but you have one more option to consider. Answer E seems to actually contradict the argument and thus cannot be an assumption upon which it is based. **The correct choice is answer D.**

15. Answer: **A**

<u>STEP 1:</u>   **Read the question and identify your task.**
This is a Conclusion question. It asks you to identify the main conclusion that can be drawn from the argument.

<u>STEP 2:</u>   **Read the argument with your task in mind.**
The argument states that a newspaper article's claim that lawsuits are on the decline is based on a misleading statistic, court verdicts, and that one should consider alternative methods of resolving lawsuits.

<u>STEP 3:</u>   **Know what you're looking for.**
You can expect the correct answer to be that by considering these other methods it becomes clear the article's claim is not true, lawsuits are not on the decline.

<u>STEP 4:</u>   **Read every word of every answer choice.**
Answer A states this conclusion exactly. This is very likely your answer, but you must review the

remaining options to be sure. Answers B and C may be true, but nothing in the argument gives you a cause-and-effect relationship between the length and expense of court hearings and the growth of arbitration and mediation. The argument tells you only that the hearings are a result of the failure of these other means. The success or failure of lawsuits through court hearings is not even discussed in the argument. The argument is concerned only with the length and expense of the process, so answer D cannot be your choice. Answer E has to be true for the argument to work, but it is not the conclusion. Rather it is a precondition. **The correct choice is answer A.**

16. Answer: **D**

<u>STEP 1:</u>   **Read the question and identify your task.**
This is a Describe question. It asks that you identify the strategy used by the argument.

<u>STEP 2:</u>   **Read the argument with your task in mind.**
The argument looks at the basis for the claim in the article, the decreasing number of court verdicts, and says that this statistic can be understood differently by looking at it in a wider context and taking into consideration alternative methods of resolving disputes, thus leading to a very different conclusion.

<u>STEP 3:</u>   **Know what you're looking for.**
You expect the correct answer to give a succinct description of this approach.

<u>STEP 4:</u>   **Read every word of every answer choice.**
Answer A is incorrect because the argument makes no claim regarding the motivation of the journalists. The argument sticks to attacking the journalist's argument itself. Answer B obviously cannot be your answer because the argument does not explore the history of lawsuits and alternative dispute resolution. Like the newspaper article, the argument concentrates on the current situation. Answer C also cannot be correct because the argument says nothing about the relationship between lawyers and judges. Answer D says exactly what the argument does and fits your expectations of the correct answer perfectly. The argument does in fact look at the evidence used by the article and reinterprets it to reach the opposite conclusion. This is most likely your answer, but you have one last option to consider. Answer E cannot be your answer because the argument does not question the statistic or

its accuracy. Instead, the argument accepts the statistic as true but questions how the statistic is interpreted. **The correct choice is answer D.**

17. Answer: **A**

STEP 1: **Read the question and identify your task.**

This is a Flaw question. The question asks that you identify the one answer that fails to point out a flaw in the president's reasoning. This means that all the options but one are valid flaws in the president's reasoning.

STEP 2: **Read the argument with your task in mind.**

The president is questioning the vice president about a manager's decisions. Based on the manager's hiring the best engineer and the best production team and the best staff, the president questions the vice president's assessment that the manager did not want the new product to succeed.

STEP 3: **Know what you're looking for.**

The correct answer will either have nothing to do with the president's logic or it will actually support his criticism of the vice president.

STEP 4: **Read every word of every answer choice.**

Answer A does not seem to describe the president's logic at all, nor does it describe a flaw in the president's logic. The relationship between the manager's desires and the success of the product is not at issue. What's at issue is the judgment of the vice president regarding the manager. This is most likely your answer, but you must review the remaining options to be sure. Answer B essentially says the president fails to acknowledge that the vice president misinterpreted the facts and made a poor assessment of the manager. Therefore, the vice president did not willfully misrepresent the manager's performance. With regard to the president's accusation against the vice president, this is definitely a flaw in the logic and cannot be your choice. Answer C is also a flaw. The president does assume the manager hired the engineer, team, and staff upon his own will, so this could be considered a flaw because if the manager had no choice, then the manager could very well have wanted the new product to fail despite the nature of the hires. Answers D and E are also valid flaws. They both point out factors outside the hires. Despite the quality of those hires, if the manager failed to allot enough time

and resources or if the manager knew the hires would not work well together, these facts would indicate that the manager wanted the new product to fail. **The correct choice is answer A.**

18. Answer: **B**

STEP 1: **Read the question and identify your task.**

This is a Parallel question. The question asks you to match the flawed reasoning in the argument with the answer that exhibits similarly flawed logic.

STEP 2: **Read the argument with your task in mind.**

Essentially, the argument says a person likes X, but not Y. Therefore, it is not true that any person who likes Y likes X. You also notice that the statements go from the specific (my brother) to the general (whoever). You are looking for the same pattern among your options.

STEP 3: **Know what you're looking for.**

The correct answer will follow the pattern described in step 2.

STEP 4: **Read every word of every answer choice.**

Answer A says that a person likes X but not Y. Therefore, it is not true that any person who likes X likes Y. Notice that the second half of the pattern has been reversed (XY instead of YX). This answer does not match your pattern. Answer B says a person is X (7+) but not Y (a giant). Therefore it is not true that any person who is Y (a giant) is X (7+). Even though the wording is somewhat different, the flawed logic follows the same pattern and this is most likely your answer. You should review the remaining options to be sure. Answer C says all compositions that are X (minimalist) are Y. Therefore if a composition is X, then it is Y. Again, the pattern is not the same, plus the order is reversed, moving from the general to the specific while the argument goes from the specific to the general. Answer D says people who do X are Y. Therefore, the neighbors who are Y are X. The order of terms is correct but this option, like answer C, also goes from the general to the specific, which is the wrong direction of logic. Finally, answer E says a photo that is not X is Y. Therefore, it is not true that some photos that are X are Y. The order is wrong and the logical terms are wrong. The first term is in the negative. Also, the general statement is not categorical (all, every, etc.) but "some." **The correct choice is answer B.**

19. Answer: **D**

STEP 1:   **Read the question and identify your task.**

This is a Weaken question. The question asks that you determine which fact most undermines the basis for the expert's conclusion.

STEP 2:   **Read the argument with your task in mind.**

The expert says that they tested 5 square inches of an explosive substance 10 times, and every time it failed to explode an area beyond 20.7 square feet. The expert's evidence is that the tests exploded areas between 9.2 and 12.5 square feet. The expert concludes that 5 square inches of the substance explodes an area much less than 20.7 square feet.

STEP 3:   **Know what you're looking for.**

You expect the correct answer to be some fact that counters the evidence presented by the tests and offers proof that the explosive may explode an area close to or beyond 20.7 square feet.

STEP 4:   **Read every word of every answer choice.**

Answer A is about testing another type of explosive in identical circumstances, but this does not undermine the expert's evidence since another explosive tells you nothing about the explosive used in the bank robbery. Answer B has nothing to do with the evidence and attempts to undermine the expert's qualifications. This is not what the question is asking. Answer C also tries to undermine the expert's qualifications by describing a common malpractice, but it is still not relevant to the evidence at hand and it is too general a statement to be of use. Answer D says that another test was done that still did not cover 20.7 square feet, but it came close at 20.1 feet. This seems close enough to lay some doubt about the expert's use of only the 10 previous tests and the conclusion that the substance destroys an area "much less" than 20.7 square feet. This may be your answer, but you have one more option to consider. Answer E is a hypothetical and may be true, but it is not as strong as answer D at undermining the expert's evidence and conclusion. **The correct choice is answer D.**

20. Answer: **A**

STEP 1:   **Read the question and identify your task.**

This is an Assumption question. The question asks that you identify an assumption upon which the argument depends.

STEP 2:   **Read the argument with your task in mind.**

The argument claims that the Internet increases the awareness of injustices for those attempting to solve injustices. Then it says that Internet access comes faster than an enlightened education system, and that people are vulnerable to questionable reformers promising solutions. Thus, countries with enlightened technology policies may cause their own downfall.

STEP 3:   **Know what you're looking for.**

The correct answer will most likely connect poor education to a lack of ability to recognize fake reformers.

STEP 4:   **Read every word of every answer choice.**

Answer A says that a lack of enlightened education affects the ability of people to recognize between legitimate and illegitimate reformers. This matches your expectations for the correct answer exactly and is most likely your answer, but you must review the remaining options to be sure. Answer B offers a direct causal relationship between the education level and the toppling of the nation, but the argument says that only *some* countries, not all, *may* experience such a connection, and it definitely does not make its claims with such certainty. Answer C supports the opposite of what the argument is saying. Answer C says that a charlatan can topple a government only if there is an enlightened education system in place, but the argument says that it is the lack of an enlightened educational system that enables charlatans to achieve such a result. The argument says that Internet allows more people to be aware of injustices, but it does not say that the Internet is the only source, so answer D cannot be your answer. Finally, answer E makes a connection between enlightened education and the sustaining of reasonable regimes. The argument connects a lack of enlightened education with the toppling of reasonable regimes. It makes no claim regarding the opposite condition, so this cannot be correct. **The correct choice is answer A.**

21. Answer: **A**

STEP 1:   **Read the question and identify your task.**

This is a Deduction question. The question asks you to identify the statement that is most strongly supported by the argument.

STEP 2: **Read the argument with your task in mind.**

The argument states that sleep aids increase appetite and that some of the resulting weight gain can be counterbalanced by dieting.

STEP 3: **Know what you're looking for.**

You can expect the correct answer to be related to the connection between sleep aids and gaining weight.

STEP 4: **Read every word of every answer choice.**

Answer A says that some patients who take sleep aids gain weight as a result. This matches your expected answer. Nothing in the statement is unsupportable by the argument, and this most likely is your answer, but you must review the remaining options to see if there isn't a better one. Answer B states a recommendation in categorical terms, but the argument does not say that all people who take sleep aids gain weight, nor does it say that dieting helps all people gain weight. This cannot be your answer. Answer C is unsupportable by the argument because the argument links the weight gain to taking the drugs, not to dieting or lack of dieting. Answers D and E are incorrect because the argument does not go into the decision of whether or not to prescribe. Nor does it go into a patient's decision to request the drug. These elements are beyond the scope of the argument, which is concerned only with those who have already taken the drugs and how they deal with the resulting weight gain. **The correct choice is answer A.**

22. Answer: **C**

STEP 1: **Read the question and identify your task.**

This is a Deduction question. The question asks that you take all the statements into account and determine which among the answers must also be true.

STEP 2: **Read the argument with your task in mind.**

You must pay close attention to the logical terms—"vast majority," "some," and "all"—found in the statements.

STEP 3: **Know what you're looking for.**

The correct answer will be based on these qualifications for the particular groups: low corporate tax rate, high budget deficit, and large entitlement programs.

STEP 4: **Read every word of every answer choice.**

Answer A cannot be the correct choice because the last statement says that all countries with a high budget deficit have large entitlement programs and the equation works in reverse as well. Answer B tries to draw a conclusion based on the last two statements, but those statements say that only some of the countries with a low corporate tax rate have a high budget deficit. The term *some* does not necessarily mean a majority. It could mean as few as one or two countries. Answer C tries also to draw a conclusion from the last two statements, and it succeeds where answer B failed. You know that all countries with high budget deficits have large entitlement programs. You also know that some of the countries that have high budget deficits have a high corporate tax rate. Therefore, it must be true that some of the countries with large entitlement programs also have a high corporate tax rate. This is most likely your answer. You can be sure that Answer D is not true. You know that all countries with a high budget deficit have large entitlement programs. The second statement says that some of the countries with a high budget deficit have a high corporate tax rate. Therefore, it cannot be the case that all countries with large entitlement programs have a low corporate tax rate. Finally, answer E may be true, but for the purposes of this exercise it leaves out an important link between the corporate tax rate and entitlement programs, that the countries have a high budget deficit. This answer wants to make a statement regarding all nations that have high and low corporate tax rates whether they have a high budget deficit or not, and that is not relevant to your discussion. Therefore, **the correct choice is answer C.**

23. Answer: **E**

STEP 1: **Read the question and identify your task.**

This is a Principle question. The question asks you to identify the principle or axiom that most justifies the claim made in the argument.

STEP 2: **Read the argument with your task in mind.**

The argument says that you should avoid attacking an opponent's character before a football game and that such attacks have nothing to do with competitiveness; rather, they question the team's moral right to compete.

<u>STEP 3:</u> **Know what you're looking for.**
You expect the principle to state that attacks that are not related to competitiveness are irrelevant or something to that effect.

<u>STEP 4:</u> **Read every word of every answer choice.**
Answer A attempts to say that attacks on character fail to achieve a moral result, but the argument is saying that such attacks should not be used in the first place, so this cannot be your answer. Answer B says that attacks on character are warranted in certain cases, but the argument makes it clear that such attacks are never warranted. Answer C may be true, but the perception of the attacks by the spectators is not the concern of the argument, so this cannot be correct. Answer D offers a theory as to why teams attack the character of the opposing team, but this is an explanation, not a justification for the argument. Finally, answer E states your expected answer perfectly. If such behaviors should be avoided, then definitely attacks on character, which the argument says have nothing to do with competing on the field, should be avoided. **The correct choice is answer E.**

24. Answer: **C**

<u>STEP 1:</u> **Read the question and identify your task.**
This is a Paradox question. You are asked to find an answer that explains an apparent contradiction.

<u>STEP 2:</u> **Read the argument with your task in mind.**
A report stated that cooking meat at the high temperatures used in grilling creates chemical compounds linked with some cancers. A survey said that people did not plan to reduce their consumption of grilled meats. However, in the months after the report, grill sales fell dramatically.

<u>STEP 3:</u> **Know what you're looking for.**
You are asked to find an answer that explains why grill sales fell even though people said they would not change their habits.

<u>STEP 4:</u> **Read every word of every answer choice.**
The discrepancy is that grill sales fell even though consumers said they would not stop eating grilled

meats. Answer A is irrelevant since the evidence presented is regarding sales of grills, not previously purchased grills. Answer B continues the contradiction. Answer C explains how that could be possible: if all sales of nonessential appliances fell, then the report may not be the reason for the decline in grill sales. Answer D does not explain why grill sales declined. Answer E does not resolve the paradox. **The correct choice is answer C.**

25. Answer: **E**

<u>STEP 1:</u> **Read the question and identify your task.**
This is an Assumption question. The question asks you to identify the assumption upon which Morrel's defense depends.

<u>STEP 2:</u> **Read the argument with your task in mind.**
Morrel argues that he is not guilty of plagiarism because Stipich made his movie in Russian and it was never subtitled.

<u>STEP 3:</u> **Know what you're looking for.**
You can expect the correct answer to be something to the effect that Morrel had no other way than viewing the original film, subtitled or not, to learn the plot.

<u>STEP 4:</u> **Read every word of every answer choice.**
Answer A cannot be your choice because Morrel does not defend himself by saying he knew of the plot from some other source. Answer B might indicate that Morrel might be able to figure out the language in the movie, so this would actually make him look more guilty and would certainly not be an assumption underlying Morrel's claim of innocence. Answer C cannot be correct. Morrel does not base his defense on being unable to understand Stipich if and when they ever met. Answer D cannot be correct because the popularity of Stipich's movie is irrelevant to whether Morrel plagiarized the movie. Answer E fits your expected answer well. Morrel is assuming that there was no other way for him to learn plot elements of Stipich's movie than by viewing the film, so he is also assuming that nobody told him the plot of Stipich's movie before he made his movie. This is your answer. **The correct choice is answer E.**

SECTION III

Passage 1

1. Answer: **C**

STEP 1: **Read the question and identify your task.**

This is a Main Idea question. The question asks that you identify the answer that gives you the main idea of the passage.

STEP 2: **Go back to the passage to find the answer.**

Refer to your passage summary.

STEP 3: **Read every word of every answer choice.**

Answer A offers the opposite of what the passages are saying. The passage discusses nations attempting to maintain both Western and traditional legal systems, not attempting to supplant traditional with a Western-style system. Answer B is tempting because it discusses the efforts of the countries to create constitutions that satisfy the competing interests, but it does not mention the difficulties the countries have faced in attempting to integrate Western and traditional legal systems, and this is a central aspect of the passages. Answer C is better. It talks about how nations are working toward Western-style legal systems, but their efforts to balance competing interests have encountered conflicts with traditional legal structures. You must review the remaining options to see if there is a better one. Answer D is too focused on legal cases while the passage is more general. Also, the passage discusses how the rule of law moved legal cases back to traditional, more informal institutions after the court system proved inadequate to the task. Finally, answer E is too limited to the last paragraph and the accusation by human rights groups. It leaves out the rest of the passage. **The correct choice is answer C.**

2. Answer: **D**

STEP 1: **Read the question and identify your task.**

This is a Main Idea question. This question asks for the main idea of just the second paragraph of passage A.

STEP 2: **Go back to the passage to find the answer.**

Look back to that particular paragraph and read the first and last sentences to recall that paragraph's purpose.

STEP 3: **Read every word of every answer choice.**

Answer A cannot be your answer because the paragraph does not suggest that these legally pluralistic nations have been highly successful; if anything, it suggests that they have been problematic. Answer B cannot be correct because the paragraph does not discuss the history of legal pluralism or different forms it has taken over time. Answer C cannot be correct. While the paragraph does discuss the difficulties of achieving legal pluralism, it does not make a prognosis that it is unworkable. Answer D describes paragraph 2 very well. The first paragraph discusses the issue of legal pluralism in general, while paragraph 2 presents Africa as a place where the abstract problem has actually arisen. This is probably your answer, but you have one last option. Answer E is a bit extreme. It does not say that the results have been "disastrous" throughout history. In the reading-comprehension section you should always be suspect of answers that use such extreme words or descriptions of any passage. **The correct choice is answer D.**

3. Answer: **A**

STEP 1: **Read the question and identify your task.**

This is an Inference question. The question asks you to identify the attitude newly independent governments have toward traditional leaders as implied by the passage.

STEP 2: **Go back to the passage to find the answer.**

There is little specific information in the passage regarding their attitude, but the passage does give the impression of governments earnestly trying to integrate the two, so there is a willingness on their part to create a system of legal pluralism that works.

STEP 3: **Read every word of every answer choice.**

Answer A seems like a good description of a government trying to integrate traditional values into a wider world value system even though it is difficult to do so and the attempt does not always work very well. To be sure that this is your answer, however, you must review the other options. Answer B could be our choice. The word "accommodation" looks right, but the "disdain" is a bit harsh. Disdain requires evidence that the traditional leaders are coercing or pressuring the governments to create legal pluralism and that is not evident in this passage. Answer C is also too extreme and has the same problem as answer B. There is no evidence that the governments are being forced to create legal pluralism. They are just trying to work out a compromise. If the governments felt anger and resentment they would probably be much less willing to attempt legal pluralism in the first place. Answer D would require that the traditional leaders gave the governments reasons to be suspicious or uneasy, and none of those elements are explored here. Lastly, answer E is wrong because if there was anything to be uncertain or anxious about it would be Western legal systems, not their own traditional leaders. They might be uncertain or anxious about integrating the two systems, but not the traditional leaders. **The correct choice is answer A.**

4. Answer: **C**

STEP 1: **Read the question and identify your task.**
This is a Line ID question. The question asks that you identify the reason the passage uses the example of Zimbabwe's attempts to reform its water management system.

STEP 2: **Go back to the passage to find the answer.**
Find the discussion of this subject, which is in the second paragraph of passage B. This example seems to be used to further exhibit the difficulties governments face at creating legal pluralism when they must accommodate traditional interests. You expect the correct answer to say something along those lines.

STEP 3: **Read every word of every answer choice.**
Answer A might be correct if the example described a success, specifically the creation of a new water management system, but the example does not do this. Instead, it shows how such an effort did not succeed, at least not at first. Answer B cannot be correct because the example does not explore the different approaches to water management. You are given no specifics. It says only that the conflict existed because informal systems and traditional institutions controlled water systems. Answer C is most likely your answer because the example does come after another example of the difficulties with legal pluralism, and it is far from similar to the first example. Thus, it offers insight

into the range of difficulties. You must review the remaining options to be sure this answer is correct. Answer D mentions "foreign interests," and nothing in the example indicates that foreign interests were involved in the attempt to achieve reform of the water management system. Answer E is tempting, but the example says only that a conflict ensued. It says nothing about the end result, so you do not know whether there was a failure or not. **The correct choice is answer C.**

5. Answer: **D**

STEP 1: **Read the question and identify your task.**
This is a Main Idea question. In the case of paired passages, look for the points of comparison between the main ideas of passages A and B.

STEP 2: **Go back to the passage to find the answer.**
Refer to your passage summaries. Note that passage A discusses legal pluralism in general, whereas passage B discusses problems specific to Zimbabwe.

STEP 3: **Read every word of every answer choice.**
Passage B does not reject any contention made by passage A, it only elaborates upon passage A, so you can reject answer choice A. Similarly, passage B never questions the validity of any statements made in passage A, so you can reject answer choice B as well. Answer choice C is tempting but too extreme. Passage B does not suggest that legal pluralism is the cause of a "global human rights conflict." We know that pluralism has caused some problems, but not on the scale suggested by answer choice C. Answer choice D, however, correctly identifies our relationship. Passage A discusses legal pluralism in general, and passage B discusses the specific example of Zimbabwe. Passage A never discusses human rights, so you can eliminate answer choice E. **The correct choice is answer D.**

Passage 2

6. Answer: **C**

STEP 1: **Read the question and identify your task.**
This is an Arguments-style question that asks you for the author's conclusion. This is similar to a Main Idea question in that you need to find the author's central point.

STEP 2: **Go back to the passage to find the answer.**

Refer to your passage summary.

STEP 3: **Read every word of every answer choice.**

Answer A uses the first few sentences of the first paragraph as a basis for its idea, but the passage does not say those critics are misinterpreting the novel. It just says that the reader could read the novel from a very different perspective than the one offered by those critics. Answer B seems to contradict what the passage is saying by centering its idea on the southern novel. The passage discusses critics who view *Absalom, Absalom!* as exploring the nature of the novel in general, not just the southern novel, so this cannot be your answer. Answer C is very promising. The passage does discuss the novel's interpretation as an exploration of southern social structures and some critics' view that it is also an exploration of the novel form and whether it can hold any truths. This is most likely your answer, but you should review the remaining options to be sure. Answer D may be tempting since the passage says that the novel might be calling into question the novel as a form of storytelling, but the passage does not suggest that the novel's nature makes it impossible to interpret, nor does it suggest that critics have failed to do so. In fact, the passage is giving validity to just such an interpretation. Finally, answer E cannot be correct because the passage mentions the Hollywood circumstance only incidentally, and it is not a central element of the passage's discussion. **The correct choice is answer C.**

7. Answer: **B**

STEP 1: **Read the question and identify your task.**

This is an Information Retrieval question. The question asks that you identify the statement with which the author would agree concerning the contemporary critics.

STEP 2: **Go back to the passage to find the answer.**

Look back at the discussion of the contemporary critics.

STEP 3: **Read every word of every answer choice.**

The author would most likely not agree with answer A because the author states that the new critics recognize the central story but they argue that the reader can ignore it. It would be inaccurate to say that they fail to take it into account.

Answer B looks promising. The author points out the influences that led to the novel's structure but does not attribute these to the critics, implying they might not have taken these into account, but the author does believe the structure and end of the novel give validity to their theories. This may be your answer, but you should review the remaining options to be sure. Answer C says the opposite of what the author might say. The author seems to acknowledge that the critics have a valid perspective, so the author would surely not be so critical. Also, this is one of those answers that sounds too extreme to be the right answer. Answer D tries to confuse you by attributing the author's observations to the critics. The author makes the connections to Hollywood and detective novels but does not attribute these influences to the critics' analysis. Finally, regarding answer E, the author does not state that the new critics have overthrown previously accepted theories. Instead, the author merely suggests that the new critics are offering a different theory, one that fits into the modernist way of thinking. Never does the author suggest that previous theories have been supplanted. **The correct choice is answer B.**

8. Answer: **B**

STEP 1: **Read the question and identify your task.**

This is a Main Idea question. The question asks you to identify the purpose of the second paragraph.

STEP 2: **Go back to the passage to find the answer.**

Review the second paragraph. It gives some biographical information on Faulkner at the time that he wrote the novel as well as some outside circumstances that might have influenced the structure of the novel.

STEP 3: **Read every word of every answer choice.**

Answer A cannot be correct because the paragraph does not attempt to cast doubt on the new critical theory or any theory for that matter. If anything, the paragraph seems to be supporting the new theory by discussing how the influences affected the structure of the novel. Answer B seems right. As we have already discussed, the second paragraph gives biographical information that could be seen as supportive of the new structuralist critical theory. This is probably your answer, but you must review the remaining options to be sure. Answer C cannot be correct because the paragraph is about Faulkner, not the critics or their process. Answer D is tempting and would finish a strong second to answer B, but the paragraph is not really focused on providing a historical background. Lastly, answer E is also a tempting answer because the paragraph could be viewed as discussing the foundations of the theory, but the language is a bit too general when compared to answer B or even answer D. The word "foundations" could be interpreted too many ways, while "biographical information" is more specific and more accurate. **The correct choice is answer B.**

9. Answer: **D**

STEP 1: **Read the question and identify your task.**
This is an Inference question. The question asks what the passage implies with regard to Faulkner's main character in the novel, Quentin Compson.

STEP 2: **Go back to the passage to find the answer.**
Find within the passage the section that discusses this character and reread it.

STEP 3: **Read every word of every answer choice.**
Answer A cannot be correct because the passage never implies that Quentin is not from the South. It does the opposite, in fact, by noting Quentin's "own southern heritage." Answer B cannot be correct because the second paragraph (as we've already explored) implies that it was the structure of the novel that was influenced by Faulkner's time in Hollywood, not the characters of the novel. Answer C may or may not be true. The passage does imply that Quentin's account of what happened to the Sutpens indicated such a hatred—otherwise his roommate would not have asked the question—but the passage never indicates his true feelings, so this cannot be the correct choice. Answer D is indeed implied by the passage when the author writes that Quentin is Faulkner's "frequent proxy," which implies that the character appears in other novels and that he represents Faulkner's perspective. This is most likely your answer, but you have one more option to consider. Answer E has the same problem as answer B: the detective novels influenced the structure, not the characters. **The correct choice is answer D.**

10. Answer: **E**

STEP 1: **Read the question and identify your task.**
This is an Information Retrieval question. The question asks you to identify a statement that the modern critics would agree with.

STEP 2: **Go back to the passage to find the answer.**
If you read the entire passage, you should be able to answer this question, but returning to the first and last paragraphs may help as well, since those paragraphs address specifically how the modern critics view the novel.

STEP 3: **Read every word of every answer choice.**
Answer A is a statement that the older, more traditional critics would make, because they emphasize the story central to the novel, specifically the Sutpen family and how they represent the decay of the southern paternal system. Answer B suggests that the reader is a participant along with Quentin and his roommate in solving the mystery, but the passage does not discuss the reader's role in the mysteries in the novel. Readers are discussed only with regard to being challenged about how they perceive the novel or novels in general. Answer C may or may not be true, but this answer goes beyond anything in the passage. The critics propose that the writer challenges readers concerning the nature of the novel, but they do not go as far as to suggest that there is a collaboration going on. The only collaboration mentioned in the passage is between Quentin and his roommate. Answer D cannot be your answer because it is the lack of such details that give the critics fuel for their theory. Finally, the critics would very likely agree with answer E because it states exactly (as discussed in the passage) what the critics think Faulkner was trying to achieve, a structure that allows readers to question whether what they are reading is important or true and to wonder what is the nature of the novel as a medium. **The correct choice is answer E.**

11. Answer: **D**

STEP 1: **Read the question and identify your task.**
This is an Information Retrieval question. The question asks that you identify the one element that according to the passage did *not* influence Faulkner's novel.

STEP 2: **Go back to the passage to find the answer.**

You refer to the passage and scan for all the influences mentioned. You should be able to eliminate from the answer choices all those that are specifically included in the passage.

STEP 3: **Read every word of every answer choice.**

Answer A is mentioned in the first part of paragraph two. Answer B is mentioned in the latter part of paragraph two. Paragraph one discusses the southern aspects of the novel, giving support to answer C. Answer D may be true, but the passage does not discuss gothic story structure, so this may be your answer. You need to consider your last option. Answer E is not as clear as the others, but the passage says that Quentin is Faulkner's proxy, so it is implied that Faulkner also has such struggles. **The correct choice is answer D.**

12. Answer: **B**

STEP 1: **Read the question and identify your task.**

This is an Arguments-style question that asks you to categorize the type of premise information used as evidence.

STEP 2: **Go back to the passage to find the answer.**

Refer to your passage summary. If necessary, scan the passage to see what type of evidence is cited.

STEP 3: **Read every word of every answer choice.**

Answer A concentrates only on paragraph two and thus cannot be the correct choice, because it ignores the rest of the passage. Answer B looks promising because the author is definitely exploring a critical theory and how Faulkner's novel is structured to lead to that theory. Answer C is not correct, because multiple approaches are only discussed in the first paragraph and they are not necessarily conflicting. Answer D focuses only on the last paragraph and excludes everything that came before it, so it is too narrow. Answer E has the same problem since it concentrates on paragraph two. **The correct choice is answer B.**

Passage 3
13. Answer: **D**

STEP 1: **Read the question and identify your task.**

This is a variation of a Main Idea question—a Primary Purpose question. You are required to

select from among the choices the answer that best describes what the passage is attempting to achieve.

STEP 2: **Go back to the passage to find the answer.**

Since this is a Main Idea question type, refer to your summary of the passage. Then describe that content in slightly more general terms, and find the answer choice that matches this description.

STEP 3: **Read every word of every answer choice.**

Answer A concentrates too much on the Supreme Court's role. While the passage discusses a Supreme Court decision, *Wesberry v. Sanders*, the passage focuses much more on the propositions approved by the state referendums. Answer B talks about mistakes, but the passage does not make any judgments as to whether the states have made a mistake or not. LSAT passages almost always avoid making such extreme judgments on any person or subject. Answer C speaks of "unique" problems, but the passage makes it clear that these states are addressing problems that exist across the nation and are not unique at all. Answer D says that the passage is about the legislation approved by voters to solve a problem, which is exactly what the passage does in the first two paragraphs. The passage uses those paragraphs to discuss the propositions to solve the problem of political gerrymandering. The answer then says the passage discusses arguments brought by the opposition that might be used in future such propositions raised in other states, which is exactly what the second and third paragraphs discuss. This must be your answer, but you must review the remaining choices to be sure. Answer E has the same problem as answer B. It attributes a very biased intent to the passage, saying that it judges the reform efforts to be "costly and unwise." **The correct choice is answer D.**

14. Answer: **C**

STEP 1: **Read the question and identify your task.**

This is an Information Retrieval question. The question asks that you assess each answer to see whether it is true based on what you read.

STEP 2: **Go back to the passage to find the answer.**

In this case, the key word or term is the year "1964." You must look back at the passage and reread the sentences that discuss that year. You discover that 1964 was the year of the Supreme

Court decision in *Wesberry v. Sanders*, which said that all congressional districts must contain an equal number of persons and established the "one person, one vote" requirement in designating congressional districts. Your question asks what would have been the situation before this case was decided by the Supreme Court.

STEP 3: **Read every word of every answer choice.**

Answer A says it is implied that political parties had no influence before 1964, but the opposite is actually implied by the passage. Political parties had even more control before 1964, which is why the decision was necessary in the first place. Answer B says that some citizens' votes counted for less than a full vote. The passage says nothing about the value of a vote being less than full. Instead, it discusses districting and its effect on elections. Answer C seems promising since it talks about the design of a district and how it could create an imbalance in favor of a particular group. This could be your answer, but you should assess the remaining choices. For answer D, there is no indication that the Supreme Court case dealt with an incongruity between states or that one state had an advantage over another in this regard. Answer E has things reversed. It was after 1964 that the Supreme Court gained the ability to overrule redistricting planes, not the other way around. **The correct choice is answer C.**

15. Answer: **D**

STEP 1: **Read the question and identify your task.**

This is a Line ID question. The question is asking you to put a particular section of the passage in context and find among the answers the best description of how it fits into that context.

STEP 2: **Go back to the passage to find the answer.**

In this case, the section concerns one you investigated already in question 2, the *Wesberry v. Sanders* decision. You can use your knowledge from question 2 to answer this question. Go through each answer and assess its potential.

STEP 3: **Read every word of every answer choice.**

Answer A cannot be correct because "one person, one vote" was created by the decision. It was not a problem that the decision intended to solve. Answer B is tempting because the Supreme Court decision was an early legal action that led to the recent propositions, but the direct connection is

tenuous. Still, you will keep this answer in mind as you review the remaining options, and if a better answer does not come up then this may be your selection. Answer C cannot be correct because there is no mention of the Supreme Court decision in relation to any effort by the executive or legislative branches of the United States government. Answer D is fairly accurate. The section of the passage does give some historical perspective. There are several key phrases that make this choice optimal, such as "Since the early years," "In 1964," and "continued to influence." These are historical-sounding phrases. Answer E cannot be correct because the Supreme Court was trying to solve gerrymandering, not create it. While answer B seemed promising, answer D is much better, so **the correct answer is D.**

16. Answer: **C**

STEP 1: **Read the question and identify your task.**

This is a Line ID question. This question tells you to refer to specific lines (53–59) in the passage and asks you to find among the answers an inference you can derive from those lines in relation to Proposition 20.

STEP 2: **Go back to the passage to find the answer.**

You find the lines in the passage and discover that they discuss Proposition 27 and its attempt to eliminate the Citizens Redistricting Commission. With this in mind you look at your choices.

STEP 3: **Read every word of every answer choice.**

Answer A gives what might have been the opinion of those supporters of Proposition 27, but it has nothing to do with Proposition 20. Answer B attributes a motive to the supporters of Proposition 27 that is not in evidence in the lines. Answer C first says that the commission existed before the election. Since Proposition 27, if approved, was to eliminate the commission then it must have existed before the election. Also, Proposition 20 was intended to make the commission able to draw districts for the congressional map, so you can definitely infer that they did not have this authority before the election. Since both elements of answer C are implied by the lines, this is most likely your answer, but you should review the rest of the options to be sure. Nothing in the lines implies in any way what the voters might have done in any other scenario, so D cannot be correct. Finally, in answer E, nothing in the lines implies the unconstitutionality of the commission or how the courts would react if Proposition 27 was not approved. Also, this answer has nothing to do with Proposition 20, which is what the question is asking for. **The correct choice is answer C.**

17. Answer: **E**

STEP 1: **Read the question and identify your task.**

This is a Weaken question. You must find among the answers the statement that most undermines support for Proposition 20.

STEP 2: **Go back to the passage to find the answer.**

Refer to the passage and skim over the third paragraph and its arguments in favor of Proposition 20. In this case, the paragraph discusses the fact that without Proposition 20, politicians have secure incumbency due to gerrymandering. The population of their district is narrowly defined, and thus they have to satisfy only that specific constituency to be reelected. The correct answer will state a fact proving that even with such gerrymandering the politicians are still not secure in their incumbency.

STEP 3: **Read every word of every answer choice.**

Answer A is tempting. Why would people want to change the system if most voters are happy with their representatives? But Proposition 20 is meant to help the minority and underrepresented, not the majority. While this option might be tempting, it is not the strongest. Regarding answer B, compromise and cross-party-line success in a few cases does not make much of a case against the proposition. Answer C actually seems to make a stronger case for the proposition by saying that it will be income, race, and gender blind. For answer D, this is a technical issue and even if every member of the commission is a member of a political party, this does not mean that it cannot be balanced to avoid one party having more influence over the other. Finally, answer E indicates that population movements may make the proposition impossible to execute. This would definitely undermine the arguments for Proposition 20 because, if answer E is true, even if approved it would not be effective. **The correct choice is answer E.**

18. Answer: **B**

STEP 1: **Read the question and identify your task.**

This is a Line ID question. The question is asking you to find among the options a synonym for the word *entrenched* that gives the meaning as it is used in the passage.

STEP 2: **Go back to the passage to find the answer.**

Refer to the passage and read the sentence that includes the word *entrenched* to determine how it is being used. In this case, you notice that entrenched politicians do not have to compromise on policy since they are assured of keeping their job. The correct answer will probably be a word similar to having such a secure position.

STEP 3: **Read every word of every answer choice.**

Answer A could be seen as the opposite of what the word means since the politicians are elected over and over to the same office. Answer B is promising since the politicians are able to keep their position despite any failures on their part. They are "deep-seated" in their position. You review the rest of the answers to see if there is a better option. Answer C seems more like an adjective for a person in a pressure situation. If the politicians were more vulnerable but principled in their stances on issues, they might be described as unshakeable, but this is not the case here. Answer D is similar to answer C, but the politicians are not stubborn, nor do they face any opposition. Answer E would mean that the politicians are taking action and are unable to be persuaded to change their minds. This is also an inexact match to your definition. **The correct choice is answer B.**

Passage 4

19. Answer: **D**

STEP 1: **Read the question and identify your task.**

This is an Arguments-style question that asks you to identify a situation parallel to a violation of the right to prevent public portraiture.

STEP 2: **Go back to the passage to find the answer.**

Refer to your passage summary and to lines 48–51 where this right is specifically discussed.

STEP 3: **Read every word of every answer choice.**

Answer A sounds promising, but it does not say that the photographer published the photos. If the photos are not seen in a public forum, this does not correspond with Brandeis and Warren's description of this right. Answers B and C may seem like privacy violations, but they are not public viewings of photos or likenesses of a person. Answer B in particular might be considered under the expansion of the right as discussed in the last paragraph, but it does not violate the right as originally stated. Answer D would violate the right because a person's image is used without that person's permission. Answer E does not violate the right, because the subject of the portraiture is the person who published the portraiture. **The correct choice is answer D.**

20. Answer: **D**

STEP 1:   Read the question and identify your task.

This is an Inference question. The question asks that you identify a statement regarding Brandeis and Warren's approach to the privacy issue that can be inferred from the passage.

STEP 2:   Go back to the passage to find the answer.

You refer to the passage and read through the first paragraph, which discusses the origin and basis of their work.

STEP 3:   Read every word of every answer choice.

Answer A may be true and is a viable choice, but the passage actually says that the legal profession had defined privacy according to property and was satisfied with that definition. The implication is that Brandeis and Warren decided to redefine the law, not correct deficiencies. While this could be your answer, you cannot be certain and need to review the remaining options. Answer B cannot be your answer because it says that the concern was property, not personality, which was their basis for changing the law. Answer C is one of those extreme answers that you can reject altogether. Nothing in the passage implies such hostility or desire for revenge. Regarding answer D, the passage says that Warren enlisted Brandeis because he was "peeved" about gossip about higher society, and since Warren was very likely a member of high society, it is likely he was seeking a way to neutralize efforts to slander or blacken his and his friends' reputation. This could very well be your answer, but you have one last option to consider. Answer E cannot be your choice because no such relation is even hinted at in the passage. **The correct choice is answer D.**

21. Answer: **A**

STEP 1:   Read the question and identify your task.

This is an Inference question. The question asks that you identify a statement that scholars other than Warren and Brandeis would agree with.

STEP 2:   Go back to the passage to find the answer.

Since Warren and Brandeis believed privacy extended to personality and not just property, you can expect the correct answer to favor defining privacy protection as a matter of protecting only property.

STEP 3:   Read every word of every answer choice.

Answer A discusses the stealing of a short story (written by person A) and the subsequent publishing of that story. The short story could be considered private property, and publishing it could be seen by the other scholars as an infringement of person A's privacy because the property has been stolen word for word. This is most likely your answer, but you must review the remaining options to be certain of your choice. Answer B says the opposite of answer A. The photograph could be considered property, and stealing it and publishing it would be the same as the story in answer A, but this answer says the scholars would *not* consider it an infringement of privacy, which they actually would. This cannot be your answer. Answer C describes a person who steals the essence of someone else's story and publishes his or her own version of the story. Since the exact story was not published, it is not the property of the original writer, so this would not be a breach of privacy according to the other scholars. Of course, Warren and Brandeis would very much consider this a breach under their more open definition of privacy that considers an unpublished work as an extension of a person's personality, but that is not what the question asks. Answer D is a situation that covers gossip, which is the problem Warren was trying to solve in the first place. Obviously, other scholars thought this was acceptable behavior. Regarding answer E, the first person willingly gave the photograph to the second person, and it is unlikely that any scholar, Warren, Brandeis, or otherwise, would consider this an infringement of privacy. **The correct choice is answer A.**

22. Answer: **D**

STEP 1: Read the question and identify your task.

This is an Information Retrieval question. The question asks you to identify how the passage portrays Brandeis and Warren's approach to personality.

STEP 2: Go back to the passage to find the answer.

Look back at paragraphs three and four, which discuss their approach to personality.

STEP 3: Read every word of every answer choice.

Answer A cannot be correct because the passage says that Brandeis and Warren were influenced by trends in society, not by earlier ideas, which were focused on property. The passage actually implies that their ideas were a stark departure from earlier ideas. Answer B suggests that their approach was a tweak, but the passage really implies that the definition of privacy as protecting personality was a bigger change than just a tweak. Answer C seems completely off the mark. Their approach to personality *was* central to their argument and was definitely not a side step. Answer D seems like a good description of their approach as portrayed in the passage. The passage treats their approach to personality as a significant event that changed the legal definition of privacy going forward. This is most likely your answer, but you have one more option to consider. Answer E suggests that existing scholars poorly understood their approach, but nothing in the passage suggests such a problem. The passage does not really discuss the reception by existing scholars, so this cannot be your answer. **The correct choice is answer D.**

23. Answer: **C**

STEP 1: Read the question and identify your task.

This is a Main Idea question. The question is asking you to identify how the second paragraph functions within the passage.

STEP 2: Go back to the passage to find the answer.

You refer to the passage and review the second paragraph to assess its purpose. Reading just the first sentence, you get the sense that the second paragraph gives some historical context to Warren and Brandeis's approach to privacy.

STEP 3: Read every word of every answer choice.

Answer A might be correct if you focused on just one or two sentences in the paragraph, but there is much more to the paragraph than just the essay, and while the paragraph does mention some elements within the essay, there is not much clarification of those elements in that paragraph. Answer B cannot be correct because the paragraph does not even address the structure of the essay other than to say that much of it is devoted to the right to personality. Answer C is an appropriate description of the paragraph's function. The paragraph discusses the rise of yellow journalism and the beginning of the Museum Period. These could be considered cultural phenomena that influenced Brandeis and Warren. This is most likely your answer, but you have two more options to consider. Answer D is actually a description of the first paragraph, not the second. Answer E cannot be your answer because part of the first paragraph functions this way and there are no personal details about the writers in the second paragraph. **The correct choice is answer C.**

24. Answer: **E**

STEP 1: Read the question and identify your task.

This is a Tone question that asks you to find an answer that describes the author's attitude towards the subject.

STEP 2: Go back to the passage to find the answer.

Refer to your passage summary.

STEP 3: Read every word of every answer choice.

Answer A may seem like a good choice because the author does sound a bit amused that the essay was the result of Warren being upset about newspaper gossip, but amusement is not really the main attitude of the passage. Look for a better choice. Answer B is incorrect because the author is not skeptical. Answer C is not correct, because the author does not really delve into modern applications. Answer D does not describe the author's attitude either, because the author does not seem puzzled about anything. Answer E is accurate. The author's main point is that this essay has become a landmark in legal thought and that the right described has been expanded over time. **The correct choice is answer E.**

SECTION IV

1. Answer: D

STEP 1: **Read the question and identify your task.**

This is a Describe question. It asks you to identify the technique used in the argument.

STEP 2: **Read the argument with your task in mind.**

Arbus argues that to make a 3-D version of a movie does not degrade the original version because a home video version of a movie is not considered a degradation of the original theatrical version; it is considered a different production altogether and is treated as such.

STEP 3: **Know what you're looking for.**

The correct answer will point out that Arbus makes his argument by likening one case to an analogous case that supports a different conclusion.

STEP 4: **Read every word of every answer choice.**

Answer A cannot be correct because Arbus does not cite some general artistic or critical principle that guides the situation. Answer B cannot be correct because Arbus does not even discuss the popularity of 3-D movies. He addresses only the criticism itself. Answer C has the same problem as answer A. There is no general principle at work within the argument. Answer D says exactly what you expected the correct answer to say. The argument works by using an analogous situation to show the flaw in the criticism. This is most likely your answer, but you have one more option to consider. Answer E cannot be correct because the argument makes no such distinction between facts and value judgments. Also, the argument discards the value judgment in the criticism of 3-D movies but accepts it in the analogous situation with home video, so this cannot be your answer. **The correct choice is answer D.**

2. Answer: A

STEP 1: **Read the question and identify your task.**

This is a Paradox question. The question asks you to identify the answer that helps resolve the discrepancy in the argument.

STEP 2: **Read the argument with your task in mind.**

The argument discusses an international economic body deciding to help bail out a country.

The prime minister of a member nation commits his nation to help out with the bailout. The parliament of his country condemns its prime minister for that commitment but supports the bailout.

STEP 3: **Know what you're looking for.**

You can expect the correct answer to resolve the discrepancy by saying that the parliament had a problem with its prime minister making the commitment without some sort of approval from the people of the country or the parliament itself.

STEP 4: **Read every word of every answer choice.**

Answer A gives you a close approximation of what you need. It says the parliament is the only official body of that nation that can make such a commitment. This is probably your answer, but you should review the remaining options to be certain this is the right choice. Answer B may be true, but as a logical argument it is weakly constructed and does not resolve the discrepancy anywhere near as strongly as answer A, which is constitutionally enforceable. Answer C has the same problem as answer B in that it is a weaker resolution than the constitutionally enforced answer A. Answer D would be a good choice if the discrepancy existed between the G-20 and the member nation, but the discrepancy is between the parliament's support for the bailout and lack of support for the prime minister, so this cannot be your answer. Finally, answer E is a logistical issue and is irrelevant to the discrepancy between support for the effort and lack of support for the prime minister. **The correct choice is answer A.**

3. Answer: E

STEP 1: **Read the question and identify your task.**

This is a Parallel question. The question asks you to choose the answer that most resembles the flawed reasoning in the argument.

STEP 2: **Read the argument with your task in mind.**

Essentially, the argument says that a game requires a particular skill. Because a woman is skilled in a profession (which you are meant to assume requires the same skill), she would make an excellent participant in that game.

STEP 3: **Know what you're looking for.**

The correct answer will follow the same pattern.

STEP 4: Read every word of every answer
choice.

Answer A says a person who performs one activity will be good at another, so a woman who is good at the one activity could learn to be good at the other. This is not the same pattern at all, especially since the logic orients between activities and not skills. Also, saying that someone can learn an activity is not saying the person will be good at it. This cannot be your answer. Answer B says that a particular activity is performed by a person with a particular skill. Because a man has been engaged in that activity for several years, he must have that skill. This is not your pattern either because it is saying the person will have the skill as evidenced by participating in the activity rather than saying he will be good at the activity as evidenced by having the skill or participating in a similar activity that requires that skill. Answer C says that people who have a certain skill invariably enjoy an activity. Because a man has a certain profession, he must enjoy that activity. This does not follow your pattern either. The activity does not require the skill and there is no claim that because the man is in a particular profession he would be very good at the activity. Answer D says that people with a physical attribute are good at an activity and that everyone in a woman's family has that physical attribute so she must be good at that activity. The use of a physical attribute instead of a skill is problematic, and just because the woman's family has the attribute does not necessarily mean that she has the attribute, so this cannot be your answer. Finally, answer E says a profession requires a skill. Then it says that a man participates in another profession (which you are to assume requires the same skill). Finally, it says that he will be good in the first profession. This is very close to the logic pattern in the argument and must be your answer. **The correct choice is answer E.**

4. Answer: **B**

STEP 1: Read the question and identify your
task.

This is a Flaw question. The question asks you to find the one answer that is *not* a flaw in the psychologist's reasoning. This means that four out of the five possible answers are flaws in the psychologist's reasoning.

STEP 2: Read the argument with your task in
mind.

The psychologist argues that psychiatrists should not resist prescribing antidepressant drugs to patients suffering from depression because most cases of depression are caused by a chemical imbalance and the drugs help eliminate such imbalances.

STEP 3: Know what you're looking for.

The only way to identify the one that is not a flaw is to review the answers one by one.

STEP 4: Read every word of every answer
choice.

Answer A is a flaw and cannot be your answer because the psychologist makes a categorical statement that doctors should stop refusing to prescribe the drugs altogether, which means that the psychologist makes no allowance for the fact that the drugs might be ineffective for some patients. Answer B is not a flaw because the psychologist does not say depression causes a chemical imbalance. The psychologist actually argues the opposite, so this must be your choice, but you should review the remaining options to be sure. Answer C can be considered a flaw for the same reason as answer A. The psychologist makes an unsupportable categorical statement that drugs should be prescribed for all. Answer D can be considered a flaw as well because the psychologist does assume that the chemical imbalances addressed by the drugs are a complete and known factor, and if this is not the case the psychologist has made an error in supporting the unrestrained prescription of such drugs. Finally, answer E can be considered a flaw. The psychologist assumes that drugs are the only way to treat the chemical imbalances, but if therapy can deal with them, then the psychologist's argument that drugs are a complete solution falls apart. **The correct choice is answer B.**

5. Answer: **D**

STEP 1: Read the question and identify your
task.

This is a Paradox question. The question asks you to find among the answers the statement that resolves the discrepancy described in the argument.

STEP 2: Read the argument with your task in
mind.

The argument describes a situation in which an antidote to whooping cough has a good success rate but scientists warn that widespread use of the drug could be dangerous.

STEP 3: Know what you're looking for.

You expect that the correct answer will identify that widespread use versus limited use affects the safety of the drug in some way.

<u>STEP 4</u>: **Read every word of every answer choice.**

Answer A cannot be the correct choice because the researchers warn about widespread use, not overuse. Nothing in the argument indicates a risk of incorrect dosages. Answer B assumes that the drug is supposed to be something more than an antidote and actually prevent the spread of the disease, which it is not. The discrepancy cannot be a result that is not expected of the drug in the first place. This cannot be your answer. Answer C may explain why the drug might be difficult to administer, but it does not indicate why it is dangerous even when effective as an antidote. Answer D offers a valid explanation for the discrepancy. Even if the drug is effective, if its use eventually results in the development of deadlier strains of the disease, then the drug could very well be too dangerous. This is most likely your answer, but you have one more option to consider. Answer E is an administrative concern but not one that would indicate why the drug is dangerous even if effective. **The correct choice is answer D.**

6. Answer: **C**

<u>STEP 1</u>: **Read the question and identify your task.**

This is a Deduction question. The question asks that you identify the basis for the disagreement between Juan and Dorothy.

<u>STEP 2</u>: **Read the argument with your task in mind.**

Juan argues that managers should adjust their managerial style to the employees, and Dorothy believes that employees should be flexible enough to adjust to the company's needs. It could be said that the disagreement is over whether management should adjust to employees or employees should adjust to management.

<u>STEP 3</u>: **Know what you're looking for.**

You expect the correct answer to be similar to one of those two options.

<u>STEP 4</u>: **Read every word of every answer choice.**

Answer A is problematic because it uses the word *sometimes*. Neither Juan nor Dorothy speaks in such half-terms. Answer B cannot be correct because their argument is not about training. Answer C says all employees should learn to adapt to managerial styles. This is similar to the answer you formulated and is most likely your choice. You should review the remaining options to be sure. Answers D and E cannot be correct

because their argument is not over the nature of employees' projects. Rather it is over the interaction between employees and managers. **The correct choice is answer C.**

7. Answer: **C**

<u>STEP 1</u>: **Read the question and identify your task.**

This is a Principle question. You are asked to find an answer that gives an example of the general principle described.

<u>STEP 2</u>: **Read the argument with your task in mind.**

The argument is about information privacy and a company's duty to protect personal data it collects, uses, or stores.

<u>STEP 3</u>: **Know what you're looking for.**

You need an answer that shows a company not properly protecting personal information.

<u>STEP 4</u>: **Read every word of every answer choice.**

Answer A does not apply, because it is not about the actions of a company, but of individuals. Answer B may be a violation of privacy, but it is not a violation of *information* privacy. Answer C describes a violation of information privacy since personal information in patients' files was not shredded or otherwise properly disposed of. Answer D is not a violation of anyone's privacy. Answer E is also not a violation of information privacy. **The correct choice is answer C.**

8. Answer: **E**

<u>STEP 1</u>: **Read the question and identify your task.**

This is a Flaw question. The question asks you to identify the flaw in the media consultant's argument.

<u>STEP 2</u>: **Read the argument with your task in mind.**

The media consultant argues that electronic media is bringing an end to traditional news organizations. The consultant implies that the low cost and ease of publishing and distributing a newspaper no longer exist, and thus electronic media will make traditional news organizations obsolete.

<u>STEP 3</u>: **Know what you're looking for.**

You expect the correct answer to point out that just because the low cost and ease of publishing and distribution do not exist, that does not necessarily mean that traditional news organizations will cease to exist.

<u>STEP 4:</u> **Read every word of every answer choice.**

Answer A cannot be correct because the consultant never makes use of an expert opinion in supporting the argument. Answer B cannot be correct because the consultant does not make an assessment regarding the value of a traditional news organization. At issue is whether another industry will put it out of business, not whether the value of that new industry will surpass the value of the traditional news organization. Answer C cannot be correct because the consultant is not presupposing that traditional news organizations will die out. The consultant is attempting to prove it by pointing out conditions that exist in the industry (more costly and difficult to publish, takeover by electronic media, etc.). Answer D is incorrect because the consultant is consistent in logical terms. The words "are bound to" are almost exactly the same as "inevitable," and there is no inconsistency that is similar to saying that something will happen based on what might happen. Finally, answer E states that the consultant mistakes something that enables an institution to arise for something necessary for that institution's survival. This is the flaw you expected. The consultant assumes that just because circumstances such as low cost and ease of publishing and distributing the newspaper no longer exist, traditional news organizations will die out. But it is possible that these organizations can find another way to survive, such as adopting the tools of electronic media, for example. **The correct choice is answer E.**

9. Answer: **E**

<u>STEP 1:</u> **Read the question and identify your task.**

This is a Describe question. The question asks that you identify the statement that most accurately describes Lucie's criticism of David's statement.

<u>STEP 2:</u> **Read the argument with your task in mind.**

David states that the effort to create new biofuels has caused an increase in demand for crops usually used for food. The resulting price increase for food is causing hunger and instability throughout the developing world, so he argues that advanced nations should scale back their efforts. Lucie criticizes his argument by citing factors other than biofuels that could be causing the increased prices that produced the problems.

<u>STEP 3:</u> **Know what you're looking for.**

The correct answer will describe Lucie's logic as citing other factors that undermine David's assumptions.

<u>STEP 4:</u> **Read every word of every answer choice.**

Answer A cannot be correct because Lucie does not point out any contradictions in David's statements. In fact, she does not exactly question his underlying facts, only the connection he draws between them. Answer B cannot be correct because Lucie brings up no such analogy. The crops in Russia and China and the meal bug infestation are not analogous to the demand for biofuels putting price pressure on food crops since the former are disasters and the latter is a market demand occurrence. Answer C cannot be your answer because Lucie's argument is not supportable by any of David's facts. Again, the difference between a market occurrence and a disaster prohibits this sort of logical flexibility. Answer D is incorrect because Lucie's facts are not in conflict with David's facts, so they can be easily reconciled since they are concerning different phenomena. Finally, answer E is your correct answer because Lucie does not question David's facts. She only points out that his conclusion does not follow so easily from them. She thinks that his assumption that the development of biofuels is responsible for the increase in food prices is questionable. **The correct choice is answer E.**

10. Answer: **C**

<u>STEP 1:</u> **Read the question and identify your task.**

This is a Weaken question. The question asks that you choose the statement that David might use to counter Lucie's objection.

<u>STEP 2:</u> **Read the argument with your task in mind.**

David states that the effort to create new biofuels has caused an increase in demand for crops usually used for food. The resulting price increase for food is causing hunger and instability throughout the developing world, so he argues that advanced nations should scale back their efforts. Lucie criticizes his argument by citing factors other than biofuels that could be causing the increased prices that resulted in the problems.

<u>STEP 3:</u> **Know what you're looking for.**

You expect that David would somehow prove that the disasters that affected the crops were inconsequential to the price increases that caused all the problems in the developing world.

STEP 4: Read every word of every answer choice.

Answer A might be true, but the concern was the worldwide price increase, not just that affecting biofuels. This statement does not change the fact that the disasters in those countries could have affected the overall world crop supplies. Answer B has the same problem as answer A. The issue is food supplies, not just supplies for biofuels. Answer C is exactly what you are looking for. It says that the disasters are nothing new and could therefore be considered an inconsequential factor in the rise of world food prices. This is most likely your answer, but you must review your last two options. Answer D is an irrelevant statement since it is future-oriented and has nothing to do with the current increase in prices. Answer E is actually helpful to Lucie's argument by giving another statement that undercuts David's dependence on the development of biofuels as the reason for the price increases. You are looking for a statement to undercut Lucie, not help her, so **the correct choice is answer C.**

11. Answer: **A**

STEP 1: Read the question and identify your task.

This is a Paradox question. The question asks that you identify the answer that does *not* help resolve a discrepancy between a report and some safety records. This means that four out of the five possible answers resolve the discrepancy.

STEP 2: Read the argument with your task in mind.

The argument discusses a safety report indicating that a reduction in traffic signs leads to a decline in automobile accidents, but a certain city reduced its traffic signs by 50 percent and saw no decline in automobile accidents over a three-year period.

STEP 3: Know what you're looking for.

You must go answer by answer and test whether each one resolves the discrepancy.

STEP 4: Read every word of every answer choice.

Answer A explains the accidents that occurred but does not explain why the decrease in signs did not have the desired effect of lowering the number of accidents. This is most likely your answer, but you should review the remaining options to be certain. Answer B indicates that bureaucratic errors resulted in the same number of traffic

signs as before. Therefore, the reduction of 50 percent was misleading and you should not have expected the reduction in accidents to occur. This explains the discrepancy. Answer C indicates that the number of automobile accidents actually did decrease but due to the addition of a new category of accidents the total number of accidents is hiding a result that is actually consistent with the safety report. This explains the discrepancy. Answer D says there was an increase in the speed limit, which is another change in traffic conditions that could alter or change the results. You do not know, but it definitely makes the city's results suspect and gives at least a partial explanation of the discrepancy. Answer E is another change in traffic conditions that could explain the increase in accidents. This also gives at least a partial explanation for the discrepancy. **The correct choice is answer A.**

12. Answer: **E**

STEP 1: Read the question and identify your task.

This is a Strengthen question. The question asks that you identify the statement among the possible answers that helps the argument reach its conclusion.

STEP 2: Read the argument with your task in mind.

After reading the argument you determine that the statement must link sales training to Fred's success at winning the sales challenge over Gigi.

STEP 3: Know what you're looking for.

The correct answer will link sales training to winning the challenge.

STEP 4: Read every word of every answer choice.

Answer A would be correct if the conclusion involved Gigi, but it doesn't. The conclusion is regarding Fred, so this cannot be your answer. Answer B would be useful if the conclusion was a matter of who had more sales training than the other, but your conclusion is concerned only with Fred's sales training. Answer C restates something already established or implied by the first statement in the argument. Gigi has obviously been a better salesperson in the past, but you are only concerned with supporting the conclusion, which explains why Fred beat Gigi in the challenge in the fourth quarter, not with what is usual or in the past. Answer D is a viable option for your choice. It says that if Fred took training, he would win the sales challenge. You might choose this as your answer if you stopped here, but you must review the final option. Answer E is your strongest contender. It says that the only way Fred could win over Gigi is if he took sales training. The certainty of its term *only* makes it a much stronger choice. **The correct choice is answer E.**

13. Answer: **E**

STEP 1: **Read the question and identify your task.**
This is a Strengthen question. The question asks that you identify the axiom or principle that gives support for the historian's judgment of the ordinary people of empire T.

STEP 2: **Read the argument with your task in mind.**
The historian tells of an empire that conquered other nations in the name of its vision of a more civilized world. In the process, the people of the empire slaughtered people, and the historian says that because their vision was unachievable, the people of empire T were murderers.

STEP 3: **Know what you're looking for.**
The correct answer will explain how conquering other nations can be equated to murder.

STEP 4: **Read every word of every answer choice.**
Answer A actually contradicts the historian's statements by saying that empire T's actions were warmongering; at the very beginning the historian argues that the leaders of the empire were *not* warmongering and were pursuing a vision of a more civilized world. Regarding answers B and C, the historian speaks of warmongering as the alternative view to their pursuit of a civilized world. One does not justify the other or vice versa. Also, the historian says they are not warmongering and both these principles state that they are warmongering. Answer D uses a term not even mentioned in the argument—the historian never discusses inhumanity—and it says empire T was warmongering, something the historian is actually arguing against. Finally, answer E is the only answer that actually discusses the historian's accusation of murder. It also says that conquest in pursuit of what is later found to be an unachievable vision is murder, and this supports the historian's accusation against the people of empire T perfectly (to a "T"). **The correct choice is answer E.**

14. Answer: **D**

STEP 1: **Read the question and identify your task.**
This is an Assumption question. The question asks that you choose from among the answers the assumption the artist requires to make the argument.

STEP 2: **Read the argument with your task in mind.**
The artist argues essentially that the meaning of a work of art is variable and that the intentions of the artist are irrelevant. Therefore, the interpretation reveals more about the critic than the artist.

STEP 3: **Know what you're looking for.**
You expect the correct answer will link the meaning of a work of art directly to the critic or interpreter.

STEP 4: **Read every word of every answer choice.**
Answer A cannot be correct because it links understanding of the art to the artist's history, which is in direct conflict with the statements saying that the artist's intentions are irrelevant to an interpretation. Answer B cannot be correct because it states that the interpreter can never know the real intentions of the artist, but the art critic does not base the argument on not being able to know the artist's intentions. Rather, the critic feels that those intentions are irrelevant to any interpretation. Answer C is similar to answer A in that it expresses the opposite of what the critic is arguing. Answer D makes a direct connection between the meaning of the work of art and the interpreter. This is the assumption as you formulated it and is likely the right answer, but you have one more option to consider. Answer E might be something the critic would say at the end of the argument, but nothing in the statements before you show that the critic is seeking to establish the validity of interpretations. Rather, the critic is making an observation about the nature of interpretations of works of art. This cannot be your answer. **The correct choice is answer D.**

15. Answer: **D**

STEP 1: **Read the question and identify your task.**
This is a Parallel question. The question asks you to identify which of the answers follows the same pattern of reasoning as the argument.

STEP 2: **Read the argument with your task in mind.**

The argument says that a study proves that replacing an older power plant with a newer one reduces the incidence of major illnesses but does not distinguish between conventional and nuclear power plants. Therefore, the argument claims, there is no increased health risk from living next to a nuclear power plant. The logic works off the fact that the study fails to distinguish between two types of subjects, and then makes a dubious conclusion based on that failure.

STEP 3: **Know what you're looking for.**

The correct answer will follow the same pattern.

STEP 4: **Read every word of every answer choice.**

Answer A is straightforward concerning the two types of bags, but it does not base its conclusion on a failure to distinguish between two types of bags. It merely states its facts and derives a conclusion based on those facts. This does not follow the same pattern of reasoning and cannot be your answer. Answer B also features a study with no failure to distinguish between types. The study gives a choice between supplements and eating fruits and vegetables, and the statement says you can choose the latter over the former without health risk. This does not follow your pattern. Answer C makes a dubious claim based on questionable evidence but not on any failure to distinguish between two types of drivers. This cannot be your answer. Answer D features a study claiming that fruits and vegetables help reduce the incidence of cancer and says this benefit exists regardless of whether they are grown conventionally or organically. It then makes a dubious claim that there is no risk of increased cancer from eating fruits and vegetables containing pesticide residues. The claim is based on the fact that the study does not distinguish between the types of fruits and vegetables. This follows your pattern and is most likely your answer, but you have one more option to consider. Answer E does not base its claim on a failure to distinguish between genetic types. The dubious claim or leap in logic is based on a simple link between health and a genetic predisposition to eat an unhealthy diet. Therefore, this does not follow your pattern. **The correct choice is answer D.**

16. Answer: **A**

STEP 1: **Read the question and identify your task.**

This is an Deduction question. The question asks you to choose the statement that expresses a probable belief held by the league director based on his statements.

STEP 2: **Read the argument with your task in mind.**

Mr. Anderson presents the situation, saying that his daughter's entire soccer team was suspended because some members of the team were taunting members of the opposing team. He is angry because his daughter was not one of those doing the taunting, and everyone knows the culprits. The league director defends the decision to suspend the entire team by using an analogy to passengers forced to endure a delayed flight even though they had nothing to do with the reason the plane is delayed. It is obvious that the league director believes that Mr. Anderson's daughter is innocent but should be punished along with the others anyway.

STEP 3: **Know what you're looking for.**

The correct answer will indicate the league director's belief in the innocence of Mr. Anderson's daughter.

STEP 4: **Read every word of every answer choice.**

Answer A says the league director believes Mr. Anderson's daughter might be innocent, and this is exactly what is implied by his statements since he compares her to an airline passenger who is delayed even though he or she had nothing to do with the delay. This is most likely your answer, but you must review the remaining options to be certain. Answer B focuses on an irrelevant aspect of the director's argument, the causes of flight delays. While he might believe in this statement, there is nothing in the argument that leads us to infer that he understands why a flight is delayed. He only knows that the passengers are not responsible. Answer C cannot be correct because it is Mr. Anderson who says "everyone" knows who taunted them, which you can assume includes his daughter, but the league director does not suggest such knowledge, and the question asks what can be inferred only from the league director's statements, not from Mr. Anderson's. Answer D cannot be correct because the league director does not indicate what result he hopes to achieve from the punishment. He only attempts to justify the nature of the punishment. Finally, answer

E cannot be correct because the league director's statements suggest only that he believes that many team members did not taunt. His statements imply this by saying that some passengers on the plane were blameless for the delay. He gives no hint regarding his idea of the number of those who actually taunted the opposing team, or in accordance with the analogy, those people responsible for the delay. **The correct choice is answer A.**

17. Answer: **E**

STEP 1: **Read the question and identify your task.**

This is a Weaken question. The question asks that you identify a vulnerability in the league director's statements.

STEP 2: **Read the argument with your task in mind.**

Mr. Anderson presents the situation, saying that his daughter's entire soccer team was suspended because some members of the team taunted members of the opposing team. He is angry because his daughter was not one of those doing the taunting, and everyone knows the culprits. The league director defends the decision to suspend the entire team by using an analogy to passengers forced to endure a delayed flight even though they had nothing to do with the reason the plane is delayed.

STEP 3: **Know what you're looking for.**

The correct answer will be based on the flaw in comparing the punishment, which the league director may choose to impose or not, to the flight delay, which is unavoidable.

STEP 4: **Read every word of every answer choice.**

Answer A cannot be your answer because the director does not discuss any facts about the incident. Answer B cannot be correct because he makes no such generalization regarding the entire team. He does not discuss the team at all. Answer C cannot be correct because the director compares Mr. Anderson's daughter to airline customers who are blameless for the delay, so he must consider her blameless as well. Answer D cannot be your answer because it is not the taunting that is being compared to the inconvenience. It is the punishment that is being compared to the inconvenience. Finally, answer E says that the complaint does not acknowledge that the inconvenience of a flight delay is unavoidable, but the director could have chosen not to impose the punishment. This is a strong criticism of the director's argument, so **the correct choice is answer E.**

18. Answer: **D**

STEP 1: **Read the question and identify your task.**

This is a Strengthen question. The question asks you to selected the axiom among the options that most justifies Elizabeth's argument.

STEP 2: **Read the argument with your task in mind.**

Elizabeth believes Larry's complaint of unfairness is wrong because as long as each company in Larry's industry has an equal chance of being audited by the government, then his company was treated fairly.

STEP 3: **Know what you're looking for.**

The correct answer will equate the equal probability of being audited to fairness.

STEP 4: **Read every word of every answer choice.**

Answer A says it would be fairer not to enforce the rule at all than enforce it sometimes. Elizabeth might agree with this principle, but it is not supporting what she says regarding the fairness with which Larry's company has been treated. Answer B discusses the fairness of fines, or punishment, and even though Larry mentions that his company was fined as a result of the audit, Elizabeth addresses only the fairness of audits. She makes no statement regarding the fairness of the fine, so this principle is beyond the scope of Elizabeth's argument. Answer C is also about the fairness of fines and for the same reason as answer B is disqualified. Answer D expresses almost exactly what you formulated before reviewing the options. It equates equal likeness of being audited with fairness, regardless of who is eventually fined. This is very likely your answer, but you must review the last option to make sure. Answer E discusses the aspects of assessing fines and does not relate to the nature of auditing. Thus, **the best choice is answer D.**

19. Answer: **B**

STEP 1: **Read the question and identify your task.**

This is a Parallel question. The question asks you to identify which statement most closely resembles the argument.

STEP 2: **Read the argument with your task in mind.**

The argument states that the increased availability of electronic books has caused a decrease in sales of printed books. The logic is that an increased availability of a related product is causing the decrease in demand for another product.

STEP 3: **Know what you're looking for.**
The correct answer will follow the same pattern.

STEP 4: **Read every word of every answer choice.**

Answer A does not conform to your model because it says the increase of one related product causes the increase of another product (increase-increase). Answer B says that the introduction of a new product has caused the decrease of an older related product. This does conform to your model since the increase of one causes the decrease of the other. This is likely your choice, but you must review the remaining options. Answer C does not conform because it says that two products are both insufficient to dominate the market. You have no idea whether the increase of one is causing the decrease or increase of the other. Answer D does not conform because it says that when a child cannot do one activity, the child does more of another activity. A decrease leads to an increase, which is not the same as your model argument. Finally, answer E does not conform because it says that a decrease in the use of union labor leads to an increase in the use of robots. A decrease leads to an increase, which is similar to answer D and cannot be your choice. **The correct choice is answer B.**

20. Answer: **C**

STEP 1: **Read the question and identify your task.**

This is a Conclusion question. The question asks that you identify George's main conclusion.

STEP 2: **Read the argument with your task in mind.**

George argues that Kristen was wrong to tell their boss that they do not have the talent and resources to complete the project because they do have the talent and resources. George believes that Kristen told this to the boss because she did not want the project to succeed.

STEP 3: **Know what you're looking for.**
The correct answer will state something to the effect that Kristen should not have said what she did for the reasons she gave.

STEP 4: **Read every word of every answer choice.**

Answer A cannot be George's conclusion. George says that Kristen's lie in this situation was wrong, but you cannot be sure he does not believe that lying in other cases is not warranted. Answer B focuses on the last sentence, expecting you to assume that the last sentence is the conclusion, but it is not. The last sentence is what George believes is the reason for Kristen's lie and is meant to support his conclusion. George's argument is intended to influence you regarding Kristen's lie, not to inform you why she lied. Answer C states the conclusion George wants you to come to. He wants you to believe that it was wrong for Kristen to tell their boss that the project would fail due to a lack of talent and resources. This is likely your answer, but you should review the remaining options to be certain. Answer D cannot be correct because Kristen is not blaming the failure on the deficiencies. She is actually predicting the failure. Finally, answer E cannot be your choice because it leaves out the ethical judgment George is making. **The correct choice is answer C.**

21. Answer: **B**

STEP 1: **Read the question and identify your task.**

This is a Flaw question. The question asks you to identify the statement that reveals a vulnerability in the justification George uses to make his judgment.

STEP 2: **Read the argument with your task in mind.**

George argues that Kristen was wrong to tell their boss that they do not have the talent and resources to complete the project because they do have the talent and resources. George believes that Kristen told this to the boss because she did not want the project to succeed.

STEP 3: **Know what you're looking for.**
The correct answer will attack the general statement regarding morality that George uses to justify his argument.

STEP 4: **Read every word of every answer choice.**

Answer A cannot be correct because George does not invoke pity upon Kristen. If anything, George is morally indignant toward Kristen. Answer B refers to the statement "saying such falsehoods can never be other than morally wrong . . . ," which is indeed a general principle that needs further justification than the judgment regarding

Kristen's actions. This is most likely your answer, but you must review the remaining options. Answer C cannot be correct because surely what Kristen says concerning the project is within her control and can be judged by such a moral standard. Answer D cannot be correct because you do not know (and George does not say) what Kristen knows or does not know with regard to the talent and resources of the company, so George's justification cannot be judged vulnerable on this basis. Answer E cannot be correct because no cause and effect is being addressed in the argument. The entire argument concerns a prediction of what might happen, not what did happen. **The correct choice is answer B.**

22. Answer: **D**

STEP 1:   **Read the question and identify your task.**
This is a Flaw question. The question asks you to identify the flaw in the argument.

STEP 2:   **Read the argument with your task in mind.**
The argument says that members of the police force were raised in economically disadvantaged households and bases this conclusion on the fact that the communities in which they grew up had household incomes lower than the average household income for the nation as a whole.

STEP 3:   **Know what you're looking for.**
You would expect the correct answer to note that just because the communities in which the police officers grew up had a lower average household income than the nation as a whole, this does not necessarily mean that the individual families of the police officers had a lower household income than the nation as a whole.

STEP 4:   **Read every word of every answer choice.**
Answer A cannot be correct because the argument concerns the incomes of the households in which the officers grew up, not their current household income. Answer B cannot be correct because it simply clarifies the basis for the argument by describing the type of neighborhood without pointing out a flaw in that description. Answer C cannot be your answer because the argument concerns the police officers and where they grew up, but it is not concerned with how many communities facilitated the rearing of future police officers. Answer D points out that the argument assumes that within their communities the officers lived in households with

average or below-average income. This is exactly the problem with the argument. If the police officers grew up in households with above-average (or even the highest) incomes for their communities, then the fact that the community has below-average household income compared to the country is no longer relevant and it is possible they grew up in economically advantaged households. This is most likely your answer, but you have one more option to consider. Answer E cannot be correct because it raises a broader issue than the argument at hand. It is true that other factors like debt and assets might affect a household's economic situation, but household income is the logical basis the argument uses for economic advantage or disadvantage. Either way, answer E is not as strong as answer D. **The correct choice is answer D.**

23. Answer: **E**

STEP 1:   **Read the question and identify your task.**
This is a Strengthen question. The question asks that you identify among the answers the one that is justified by the statements in the argument.

STEP 2:   **Read the argument with your task in mind.**
The argument says that there are many schools of thought as to how to achieve happiness, but most people would not consider someone who follows every tenet of one of these schools to be happy. This seems to imply that either happiness is unachievable or that there is some other solution to achieving happiness.

STEP 3:   **Know what you're looking for.**
The correct answer will support the notion that people have their own definition of happiness that may not be addressed by the schools of thought.

STEP 4:   **Read every word of every answer choice.**
Answer A cannot necessarily be concluded from the argument because the argument does not say that psychology has failed to accurately describe happiness. It says only that abiding by every prescription of the theories may not lead to happiness as people define it. Answer B discusses the difference in results between following competing theories. Nothing in the argument suggests that some psychological theories regarding happiness are mutually exclusive, so this cannot be the correct choice. Regarding answer C, the argument does not say that happiness as defined by the theories is not achievable in practice. Rather

it says that achieving it might not be perceived as happiness by most people. Answer D may be true, but the argument is only concerned with their definition of happiness with regard to those who abide by psychological theories. Answer E says that most people's conception of happiness does not match that defined by psychology and this is definitely supported by the argument, because in essence it is saying that most people who look at those who abide by the psychological theories do not see their definition of happiness. **The correct choice is answer E.**

24. Answer: **C**

STEP 1: **Read the question and identify your task.**

This is a Paradox question. The question asks you to identify the answer that resolves a discrepancy in the argument.

STEP 2: **Read the argument with your task in mind.**

The argument discusses how the spread of kudzu and other invasive plant species has posed a threat to biodiversity, but then the argument says that scientific studies show that invasive plant species are rarely the cause of native species' extinctions.

STEP 3: **Know what you're looking for.**

You expect the correct answer to point out that while kudzu and other such invasive species threaten the biodiversity in local areas, they do not threaten the overall extinction of species.

STEP 4: **Read every word of every answer choice.**

Answer A may affect how you value the importance of the discussion by devaluing the threat to biodiversity, but it does nothing to resolve the discrepancy. Answer B might be seen as a benefit of kudzu when compared to other invasive plants, but this statement does not resolve the question of why kudzu affects local biodiversity but does not cause species' extinctions. Answer C resolves the discrepancy by saying that kudzu can affect local biodiversity while not threatening the existence of species on a wider scale. This is most likely your answer, but you must review the remaining options to be sure there is not a better one. Answer D may be true, but it does not negate the existing damage caused by invasive species, nor does it resolve the discrepancy in the facts at hand now. Answer E explains the extinctions, but it does not address why kudzu is not included in their list of causes even though it does so much

damage to local biodiversity. **The correct choice is answer C.**

25. Answer: **E**

STEP 1: **Read the question and identify your task.**

This is a Deduction question. The question asks you to identify the statement that *cannot* be true based on the statements in the argument. Four out of the five options are true.

STEP 2: **Read the argument with your task in mind.**

The argument might seem complicated, but you can simplify it quickly. It says that for the first eight months, Cenpan increased its output and market share while the output of the entire industry (including Cenpan) remained constant. After the regulations, Cenpan's share decreased but its output remained the same, while the output of the entire industry (including Cenpan) remained constant. You can deduce that in the first eight months the companies other than Cenpan lost market share and decreased output. Also, you can deduce that after the regulations, because Cenpan's output did not change and its market share decreased, the total output of companies other than Cenpan must have increased. Most likely more companies came into the market.

STEP 3: **Know what you're looking for.**

You judge the answers based on these deductions. If an answer is possible, then it cannot be the correct answer.

STEP 4: **Read every word of every answer choice.**

Answer A is possible. Even though nothing in the argument indicates that this will definitely happen, there is no reason to say it would not happen. Answer B is not only possible, it is certain, for if Cenpan gained market share, then the other companies as a whole must have lost market share. Answer C is possible. You know nothing about Cenpan's costs or pricing, and it is hard to believe that the increased cost of abiding by the new safety standards did not adversely affect the company's profit margin. Nevertheless, there is nothing in the argument to indicate that the company's average profit did not improve after the imposition of the new safety standards. Answer D also is possible because nothing in the argument would cause us to deny that the company might have been worse off if the safety standards had not been imposed. Finally, answer E cannot be true, because you know that after the imposition of the safety standards, Cenpan's market share decreased while its output remained the same. For that to happen, the other companies as a whole must have produced more. Thus, their output could not have decreased. **The correct choice is answer E.**

26. Answer: **E**

    STEP 1: Read the question and identify your task.
    This is a Describe question. It asks you to choose the statement that describes the role of the first sentence in the argument.

    STEP 2: Read the argument with your task in mind.
    The argument states that regulatory regimens are created to make sure government services are delivered fairly. Thus, despite qualms with the system, it is unlikely the government will simplify regulations. The first sentence seems to be a supporting fact that justifies the conclusion.

    STEP 3: Know what you're looking for.
    The correct answer will offer a supporting fact or premise that justifies the conclusion that regulations are unlikely to be simplified.

    STEP 4: Read every word of every answer choice.
    Answer A cannot be correct because the conclusion that regulations will not be simplified is based on the fact that they are created as they are in order to ensure fairness. The statement does not weaken the conclusion. Answer B cannot be true because the word *thus* tells you that it is the first sentence that leads the author to conclude the second sentence, not the other way around. Answer C cannot be correct because instituting fairness does not justify the complexity of the regulations. It justifies why they will remain complex and not be simplified. Answer D cannot be correct because the phrase "growing dissatisfaction with complex regulatory systems" does not support the fairness in regulatory systems. If anything, it is the one statement that controverts that effort. Finally, answer E is the one premise that supports the claim that it is unlikely things will change. The effort for fairness supports the conclusion that regulations will not be simplified. **The correct choice is answer E.**

27. Answer: **A**

    STEP 1: Read the question and identify your task.
    This is an Assumption question. The question asks you to choose the answer that gives an assumption upon which the argument depends.

    STEP 2: Read the argument with your task in mind.
    The argument claims that presidents cannot achieve greatness by remaining in the capital city and that they must go out and immerse themselves in communities around the country in order to gain an understanding of the citizens' everyday experiences.

    STEP 3: Know what you're looking for.
    You can guess that the correct answer will link a president's greatness to gaining an understanding of a citizen's everyday experiences.

    STEP 4: Read every word of every answer choice.
    Luckily, answer A is right on the mark. It says that presidents cannot achieve greatness without an intuitive grasp of a citizen's everyday experiences and frustrations. This is exactly the assumption that supports the argument and it is likely your answer, but you must review the remaining options to be certain. Answer B adds details to the interaction a president may participate in while immersed in outside communities, but it is not the participation that will make the president great but the understanding the president obtains through that participation, so this cannot be your answer. Answer C says the skills the president hones while in the capital city are necessary for greatness, but the argument says these are useful but not enough for greatness, so this cannot be your answer. Answer D cannot be correct because the argument says nothing about life experience. Its statements revolve around activities while in office. Finally, answer E cannot be the correct choice because the argument does not say what approach or methodology the president must take when immersed in communities, so the president could remain impartial or get actively involved in issues. **The correct choice is answer A.**